1991
Yearbook
of Science
and the
Future

1991

Yearbook
of Science
and the
Future

Encyclopædia

Britannica, Inc.

Chicago
Auckland
Geneva
London
Madrid
Manila
Paris
Rome
Seoul
Sydney
Tokyo
Toronto

1991
Yearbook of Science and the Future

Encyclopædia Britannica, Inc.

Chairman of the Board
Robert P. Gwinn

President
Peter B. Norton

Contents

Encyclopædia Britannica Science Update

The Science Year in Review

A Science Classic

Institutions of Science

HOW THE 20TH CENTURY FOUND THE FUTURE

For the past century the makers of popular culture have helped shape a "history of the future" through entertainment and mass communication. A look at these past visions offers insights into society's often passionate, occasionally icy affair with science and technology.

by BRIAN HORRIGAN

"I just take everything one day at a time." The expression is a commonplace heard thousands of times, and each time it sounds like good, common sense. No one really does, though; it just is not part of human nature. Every day people dream and think about—and act on—the next day, the next year, and far into the hoped-for future. They buy life insurance and save their money to buy a house or to send their children to college. They read horoscopes, make New Year's resolutions, speculate on the stock market, or invest in hog and corn futures. They consult tea leaves, palm readers, ouija boards, Tarot cards, and crystal balls. Part of everyone, even the most rational, finds the notion of a knowable, predictable future attractive and seductive. Beliefs in the hereafter, together with words and images bodying forth those beliefs, are part of what sets humans apart from other beings.

Of course, for centuries the future was identified with spiritual reward or punishment after death. The modern world, especially since the Industrial Revolution, added a material dimension to this apparently innate impulse to believe in the knowability of the future. Since at least the late 19th century, a portrait of the future as a secular utopia erected on scientific and technological progress has loomed large in popular culture. Gathered together, the images of that world of tomorrow make up a modern eschatology, a collective belief of the postindustrial age in the earthly hereafter.

Lately there has been a fairly steady outpouring of interest in—to put it simply, if ironically—the history of the future. The rhetorical question that serves as the title of a recent compilation of images from old popular science magazines, *Wasn't the Future Wonderful?* (1979), typifies the sense of nostalgia and delight that has motivated so many of these popular histories. People have been attracted by the buoyant, giddy optimism of 1930s world's fairs, by the dashing escapades of early science fiction heroes, by the dazzling automotive fancies of the 1950s. Part of the appeal comes undoubtedly from the pleasures of hindsight, of looking backward from today's vantage point of technological advancement to see how often predictions were simply and amusingly wrong. However, the escape into the "tale of the future," as British historian I.F. Clarke has called it, has a darker impulse as well. The failures of technology in modern times—for example, the disasters of Chernobyl and *Challenger* and environmental degradation—have all but shattered the once axiomatic equation between technological innovation and human progress. People are suspicious of science and technology now and wonder if their blissful faith in its beneficence was not tragically misplaced.

This essay looks backward to a simpler era, primarily from about 1890 through the 1950s, when confidence in progress was firm. The main focus is admittedly on the United States, though much of what is concluded can be extrapolated to include other modern capitalist societies. The focus has a corollary, for the subject of the essay is popular culture, and it has been America's popular culture that has had the widest global reach. The future, as an idea and an act of the imagination, does not exist apart from the expressive medium. Put another way, it is through the

BRIAN HORRIGAN is a Writer and Editor with the U.S. Information Agency, Washington, D.C. He served as cocurator of the Smithsonian Institution's exhibition "Yesterday's Tomorrows: Past Visions of the American Future" and is coauthor of a book of the same title.

(Overleaf) Illustration by Ron Villani

10

agency of the forms of popular expression that the future is displayed. This essay takes up both the media and the messages, apparent and concealed, that they contain.

From the late 19th century on through the present, the future has been made available for mass consumption by the makers of popular culture in the widest possible spectrum of forms—in fiction and mass-market magazines; in advertising; in Broadway's burlesque houses and at Coney Island; at world's fairs, amusement parks, and department stores; in children's games and toys; in comic strips; on radio and television; and in movies and video arcades. In fact, the development of forms of mass communication and entertainment helped to shape the modern vision of a future erected on the twin towers of technology and consumerism.

A ticket to the Moon, please . . . and a hot dog

The first wave of the future in popular culture came in the latter half of the 19th century with the widely, even fanatically read works of the French fantast Jules Verne, the British novelist and critic H.G. Wells, and the American novelist Edward Bellamy. Verne's thrilling *Voyages extraordinaires,* serialized in English translations beginning in the early 1870s, inspired generations of readers with their blends of exoticism and adventure. Wells brought a different sensibility to bear on his journeys to the future, that of a social critic, profoundly influenced by Darwinian theory.

The slightly overlapping careers of Verne and Wells bracket the extraordinary outpouring of interest in the future that flowed from the publication in 1888 of Bellamy's *Looking Backward, 2000–1887.* One of the most widely read books in history, *Looking Backward* is a "sleeper awakes" story, transporting a young Bostonian from 1887 into a future 113 years hence. The chaos, disorder, and inequality of the late 19th century have been supplanted by a new, utopian, and clearly socialist order. America in the year 2000 is a "universal reign of comfort."

The popularity of *Looking Backward* generated a veritable industry in popular literature. In the U.S. alone perhaps as many as 200 different works of fiction and nonfiction with utopian and anti-utopian themes were published before about 1910. These writings became standard fare in the new mass-market magazines, aimed at the burgeoning literate middle classes. A fabulous future of dizzying skyscrapers, airships, and machinery of domestic comfort was set forth in the magazines. A story by Verne, "In the Year 2889," appeared in *The Forum* in 1889 at the zenith of the Bellamy craze. Verne's 29th-century denizens were "surfeited" by such refinements of civilization as houses as tall as modern high rises and travel by pneumatic tube and airship. In a story published in *McClure's Magazine* in 1905, English writer Rudyard Kipling foresaw dirigibles and other future wonders in the year 2000. Some writers attempted to ascend to Bellamy's high moral and political plane, but many others aimed lower, toward pure entertainment.

New York City, already bristling with beehive-like towers and humming with subways and elevated trains by 1910, was the here-and-now

"I do not believe I go too far when I say that in the future we will have trains of projectiles in which people will be able to travel comfortably from the Earth to the Moon." So states Jules Verne in the novel whose cover illustration, from an 1872 U.S. edition, appears above. Combining adventure and exoticism, Verne's Voyages extraordinaires gave many Victorian readers their first taste of a dazzling future erected on science and technology.

Photograph by Christine Haycock from the collection of Sam Moskowitz

inspiration for much of this imagery of the city of the future (and, not coincidentally, the publishing capital of the country as well). New York would be the hub of the future for decades to come.

In 1902, across the East River from the sky-reaching towers of Manhattan, thousands of visitors to Coney Island took A Trip to the Moon, a ride aboard a fanciful airship. Disembarking passengers were greeted by giants and midgets in Moon-man costumes and by dancing Moon maidens passing out bits of green cheese. A few years later New Yorkers frolicked at the Hippodrome, a colossal pleasure palace featuring a Ziegfield-type show set in a fantastic Martian future. The *gaîeté parisienne* flavor of these burlesques recalls Georges Méliès' pioneering film, *Le Voyage dans la lune,* which had some sporadic distribution in the U.S. soon after its release in 1902.

Rides like A Trip to the Moon or the extraterrestrial attractions at Coney Island's next-door rival, Luna Park, transformed fantasies that were heretofore strictly literary or private into events that were public and, for all their silliness, real. Paradoxically these imaginative flights into the future left little to imagination. The event was carefully controlled, the experience essentially one of passive consumption. In popular literature as well as in these public entertainments, the future became another destination, like the historical past or exotic foreign lands, to which paying customers could escape for leisure and amusement.

2026? Across from luggage

The "discovery" that one could sell tickets to the future, as it were, was soon applied in other arenas. One institution that has received little attention for its contributions to the tale of the future is the department store. At its beginnings, in the Bellamy years of the late 19th century, the large urban department store was hailed by its champions in utopian and vaguely socialist terms. (This was the premise, for example, of Bradford Peck's tract *The World a Department Store,* published in 1900.) A serene, orderly environment, centrally controlled, animated by pneumatic tubes for communication and elevators for transportation, where

To stimulate sales of its line of modern furniture, the Marshall Field department store in Chicago arranged for R. Buckminster Fuller to exhibit a model of his futuristic, mass-produced Dymaxion House (below). For two weeks in 1929 Fuller delivered lectures describing his design—a central aluminum mast from which walls of glass and casein and floors of inflatable rubber were suspended by cable. The mast doubled as a household service center, providing such features as an automatic laundry, a power generator, an appliance-studded kitchen, and automatic climate control that would make bed blankets and even indoor clothing unnecessary. A "get on with life" room—equipped with radio, television, phonograph, telephone, typewriter, and other office machines integrated into one unit—anticipated both today's home entertainment center and the still largely futuristic concept of the "electronic cottage," in which people work at home on computers linked to their employers' remote central offices.

consumer desires could be encyclopedically satisfied—this surely was the embodiment of the turn-of-the-century American ideal of the City Beautiful movement.

Department stores of the 1920s used futuristic attractions to stimulate sales. American engineer and architect R. Buckminster Fuller's stunning public debut came at Marshall Field's store in Chicago in 1929. A large model of his Dymaxion house was the sensational bait to attract crowds to a display of "modernistic" furniture. Having floors and walls literally suspended by wires from a central "mast" that contained all household services, and projected to be built on assembly lines, Fuller's house imparted a distinct glow of glamour and futurism to the strange new furniture from European designers. In 1925, for the opening of a new building for the John Wanamaker store in New York City, the great architectural delineator Hugh Ferriss designed Titan City, a "pictorial prophecy of New York's growth, 1926–2026," a spectacular evocation of towering skyscraper canyons, pedestrian bridges, and airships. All of these events signaled an appreciation on the part of retailers that futurism and consumerism were compatible, even mutually reinforcing.

Interest in the future reached a high level in this period not simply because of commerce or fantasy. These years witnessed a bewildering, at times terrifying acceleration in technology and science. The development of the X-ray machine; the growth of communications technology, especially radio; the rapid growth in aviation and experiments in rocketry; and the mechanization of death in the air and in the fields of the Great War—all must have made the future seem thrillingly near. New chapters to the tale of the future, and new ways of telling the tale, were added during the first decades of the 20th century. Given the reactive, extrapolatory nature of the enterprise of futuristic speculation, it could hardly have been otherwise.

Build a time machine you wear on your wrist

Translating the meanings of technological and scientific developments for a mass audience, especially a youthful one, became the self-assigned

Massive skyscraper-bridge hybrids form the main element in one of a series of visionary, mural-sized paintings by Hugh Ferriss, collectively called Titan City. Rendered to publicize the opening of a new building for John Wanamaker's New York department store in 1925, Titan City envisioned New York a century hence as a centralized, monumental metropolis comprising a commercial city in its lower stories and luxurious apartments above.

Avery Architectural and Fine Arts Library, Columbia University in the City of New York

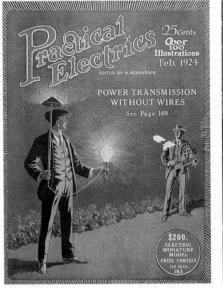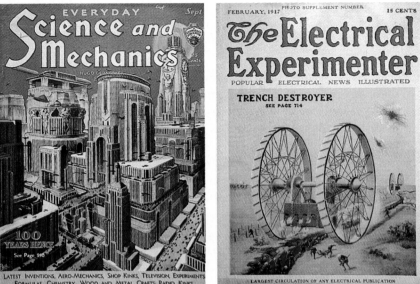

The genre of science and mechanics hobby magazines that arose in the 1910s and 1920s not only explained new scientific and technological advances to a mass audience but also served as a forum for popular speculation about the future. A 1924 issue of Practical Electrics *(left)* carried an edifying article on broadcast power, a revolutionary— and ultimately impractical—methodology for delivering electricity without wires, pioneered by Nikola Tesla. New York of the early 21st century *(center)* dwarfs the Empire State Building, in the lower foreground, in a design conceived by architectural draftsman Frank R. Paul for a 1932 Science and Mechanics cover. The horrors of World War I inspired the speculative "trench destroyer" featured in a 1917 issue of Electrical Experimenter *(right)*.

Photographs by Christine Haycock from the collection of Sam Moskowitz

task of new genres of popular literature. The popular science and mechanics magazines that arose in the 1910s and 1920s—among them *Popular Science, Science and Invention, Popular Mechanics*, and *Modern Mechanix*—provided for young people a mixture of "practical" things one could do at home and simple explanations of science and technology. Almost as a bonus these activities were linked to the future, splashed in dramatic color across the magazines' covers. Spurred by the horrors of World War I, illustrators for *Electrical Experimenter* (which became *Science and Invention* in 1920) specialized in particularly violent engines of destruction such as a "trench destroyer" or a "submarine land dreadnaught." Transportation machines, impossibly huge flying wings and "rocket trains," for example, dominated these so-called hobby magazines in the 1930s and 1940s. The very act of transportation, of moving forward through space and time, seemed a most apt and obvious metaphor for the era's hurtling progress toward the future.

Closely linked, at least at the beginning, with the hobby magazines and their stress on wholesome, educational science activities was the rise of science fiction pulps. The key figure was Hugo Gernsback, a radio pioneer and publisher of magazines for science amateurs, who began slipping fiction into his hobby magazines as early as 1911. (His own futuristic boy-meets-girl novel, *Ralph 124C 41+*, was serialized in *Modern Electrics* in 1911–12.) In 1926 Gernsback brought out *Amazing Stories*, the first magazine devoted to science fiction, or "scientifiction," as he called it. The motto of the magazine, printed beneath a picture of Jules Verne rising from the tomb, was "Extravagant Fiction Today; Cold Fact Tomorrow," a pithy iteration of science fiction writers's oft-repeated claim of oracular gifts.

Amazing Stories was soon joined by many others, including *Science Wonder Stories, Air Wonder Stories*, and *Astounding Stories of Super-Science* (which by the 1960s had mutated into *Analog*, a highly respected and influential digest). The plots and predictions were as various and

14

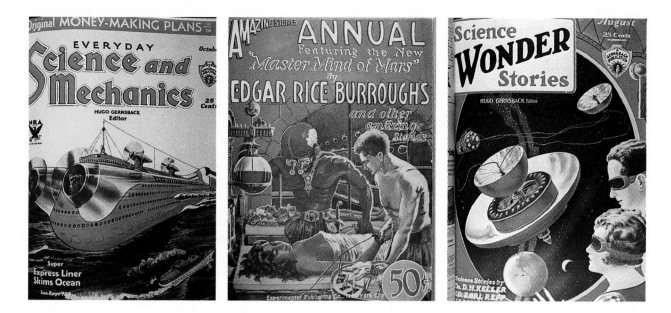

outlandish as can be imagined, but by far the favorite formula of the genre remained the "space opera," a sweeping adventure set in a future filled with brawny heroes, bizarre aliens, and mind-boggling futuristic technology. Science fiction in print declined precipitously after the waves of enthusiasm of the 1930s, with many pulps disappearing forever. After World War II, with the advent of the nuclear age and space exploration, the avalanche began again, however, and it continued unabated to the point that in the 1980s nearly one in four published books was either fantasy or science fiction.

To utopia via rocket belt

Still, the greatest impact on popular perceptions of tomorrow's world, at least since the 1930s, has come not from print but from the electronic media—first radio and movies and then television. The successive leaps that the character of Buck Rogers made in the late 1920s and 1930s neatly summarize this shift. Traveling through time (a hoary plot device beloved of the pulp masters) to a contentious 25th-century America, Buck first appeared in a "sleeper awakes" story in *Amazing Stories* in 1928. Two years later (eventually acquiring a ray gun and traveling by rocket belt, which became his trademarks) he jumped to the comic pages of the newspapers, and in 1932 he moved to radio and to his greatest notoriety. Savvy marketing contributed to the phenomenal level of his popularity. Setting a pattern for comic books and media creations to come, the creators of Buck Rogers licensed a flood of games, books, box-top premiums, and toys (such as an "atomic pistol—absolutely harmless"), more perhaps than for any single character since, with the exception of Mickey Mouse. Something about Buck Rogers clearly connected with millions of Americans, for his name has been virtually identified with the popular image of the future for more than 60 years.

In 1926, two years before Buck Rogers made his bow in popular culture, another milestone was reached in the tale of the future: German film

Conceptions of mammoth transportation machines graced many a hobby magazine cover of the 1930s and 1940s—visual expressions of a Depression era's yearnings for progress toward a better tomorrow. An issue of Science and Mechanics *for 1931 (left) features Frank R. Paul's version of an oceangoing "super express liner." Science fiction pulps of the period often pictured the future in galaxy-hopping epic adventures. Key ingredients of these "space operas"—a muscular hero, an endangered girlfriend, grotesque aliens, and superscientific trappings—are all gathered on the cover of the 1928* Amazing Stories Annual *(center), which shows a brain operation in progress. A 1929* Science Wonder Stories *issue (right) is unique in its first color depiction of artificial Earth satellites, painted for an article on "The Problems of Space Flying."*

Photographs by Christine Haycock from the collection of Sam Moskowitz

15

director Fritz Lang's frightening and powerful *Metropolis* was released. Inspired by a 1924 trip to Manhattan, Lang's city of the future (the exact date is not mentioned) is a stunning landscape of towers built over a *Nibelheim*-like underworld of oppressed workers enslaved to machines. Lang's film was not the first to journey to the future, but it was certainly the most influential. From this auspicious point filmmakers regularly employed futuristic settings, though not always with such dark portent.

Just Imagine, an American movie of 1930 set in the New York City of 1980, was, incredibly, a giddy musical comedy. Oddities abound in this future Gotham: people have numbers for names; meals are golf-ball-sized pills; and babies are ordered from automats, perhaps the first pop-culture prediction of genetic engineering. The plot and songs are forgettable, but its spectacular miniaturized set and special effects are still a delight.

Though vastly more serious in tone, the 1936 film version of H.G. Wells's *The Shape of Things to Come* (film title, *Things to Come*) is also remembered more for the art direction than for the script, written by Wells himself. Only the last 40 minutes of the film are set in the future, in AD 2036 in Everytown, a breathtaking technocratic utopia. The launching of a manned space vehicle, heretofore unattempted, forms the climax to the movie. Opposed by a band of 21st-century Luddites, it is a controversial action. If Wells was off on the date, he nevertheless got the cultural impulse exactly right: space exploration is equated with scientific progress—indeed, with human destiny. "All the universe or nothing," offers the progressive leader as the film ends. "Which shall it be? Which shall it be?"

A future in every garage

The fad for the future so evident in the 1930s was bound to have an effect on the most pervasive—indeed, the archetypal—product of consumer culture. Advertising is one of the richest lodes of images of tomorrow from the 1930s on. The future is pressed into service

16

A looming, colossal presence emanates from the Manhattan-inspired city of the future (left) presented in German filmmaker Fritz Lang's Metropolis *(1926). New York, extrapolated 50 years, is likewise the basis for the miniaturized set of brilliantly lit towers, airy bridges, and swarming vehicles (below) used in the American-made film* Just Imagine *(1930).*

in advertising not simply because of its color or glamour but because 20th-century society has become accustomed to thinking of the future in commodity terms. By focusing on the progress of technology and material well-being, the future becomes essentially a matter of material things—of their invention, improvement, and acquisition. Such connections become quite explicit during the 1930s and 1940s, when a future deferred first by economic depression and then by war was held out by advertisers to be, like prosperity or peace, "just around the corner." Commercial illustrators produced alluring futuristic backdrops for products as diverse as refrigerators, plumbing fixtures, tires, pencils, plastic, gasoline, whiskey, and, of course, automobiles ("There's a Ford in Your Future!"). "The _____ of Tomorrow Is Here Today!" became a ubiquitous catchphrase whose appeal has remained undiminished over the years. The electronics revolution of the last decade has made advertisers hardly more subtle, as in the advertisement for a personal computer that exhorts the consumer to "Buy Your Kids the Future."

The intersection of futuristic images and promises with corporate culture is perhaps most palpable at world's fairs and expositions, beginning in the 1930s and continuing through recent (and presumably future) fairs. Trade and commerce, of course, had played an important role at such antecedents to modern fairs as the 1876 Centennial Exposition in Philadelphia and the World's Columbian Exposition of 1893 in Chicago. There, however, commercial motivations were less obvious, sequestered behind a facade of loftier ideals. At the Great Depression fairs in the U.S., the effect was somewhat reversed. The inspiring themes were still present, though often difficult to detect behind the complex scrim of commercial promotion.

Though large-scale fairs were held in several American cities in the 1930s, the best remembered were those in Chicago (1933–34) and New York (1939–40). Huge corporations such as Ford, Westinghouse, and General Motors vied for attention with large, modernistic buildings filled with dazzling displays of the future. By far the most popular exhibits were those that avoided abstract or complex expositions of science or culture and instead focused on particular, immediate consumer desires and needs. This focus translated, overwhelmingly at both fairs, into houses and cars.

A giant cannon (below) is prepared for the launch of a manned space vehicle in a scene from Things to Come (1936). The last 40 minutes of the film, scripted by H.G. Wells, depict the science-wrought futuristic utopia of Everytown, whose technocratic elite (bottom) regard the conquest of space as a part of human destiny.

(Top) Culver Pictures; (bottom) The Museum of Modern Art/Film Stills Archive, New York City

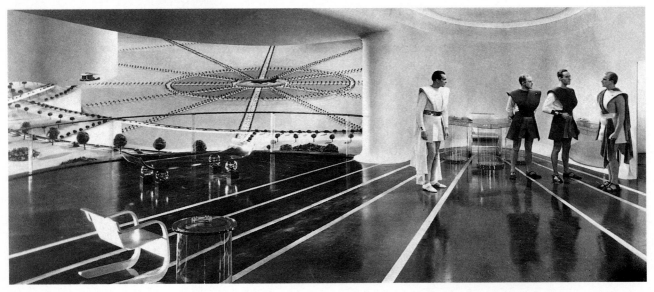

One of the more striking displays at the Century of Progress Exposition, as the fair in Chicago was formally called, was the House of Tomorrow, designed by local architect George Keck. The strict modernism of the architecture, with its steel and glass walls and flat roofs ringed with ship railings, was made more enticing by luxurious modern furnishings and conveniences inside (all carefully credited with their sources in downtown department stores) and by the most futuristic touch: a hangar for the family airplane. Keck's other entry at the fair was the Crystal House, a steel exoskeleton enclosing a severe glass cube, duly sponsored by Pittsburgh Plate Glass. Substituting for the airplane here was Fuller's teardrop-shaped, three-wheeled Dymaxion car, one of three working prototypes that were actually built.

The planners of the New York World's Fair of 1939–40 more explicitly than ever before identified the fair with a vision of the future. "Building the World of Tomorrow with the Tools of Today" was its epic theme, and everywhere one turned there was the future, arrayed in gleaming, confident form. In the large Perisphere building at the fair's core was Democracity, a huge diorama of a city of the future, having a skyscraper center and wide swaths of greenbelts.

Corporate exhibits at the New York fair strenuously sold their own versions of a future of technological progress. The Borden Co.'s Dairy World of Tomorrow featured a "rotolactor," a stainless-steel milking machine for 150 cows. Westinghouse exhibited a panoply of future household appliances, including a television and a dishwasher, as well as the family robot Elektro, who walked, talked, smoked cigarettes, and frolicked with his robot dog. General Electric had its own Magic House, equipped with gleaming appliances that "walked and talked." RCA also exhibited the new marvel of television, but most fair visitors expressed skepticism about its future in their own homes.

Amid this orgy of futurism, consumerism, and unabashed showmanship, one attraction stood out: Futurama, the centerpiece of the General Motors pavilion Highways and Horizons. Designed by Norman Bel Geddes, a member of the new profession of industrial design and already famed as an "authority on future trends," Futurama linked the future of the city with progress in transportation, explicitly highways and automobiles. Seated in plush "sound chairs" fixed to a moving conveyor belt, visitors viewed a vast panoramic model of a typical American scene of the future. It was not the unconscionably distant Buck Rogers future, however. This land of elegant cities and wholesome farms and towns, linked by a system of high-speed freeways, was the possible world of the very near future—1960, to be exact. At the end of the ride visitors found themselves outdoors in a full-scale replica of the last intersection in the city diorama, now filled, showroom-style, with currently available General Motors automobiles.

Too cheap to meter

With prosperity returning at the end of the 1930s, this effortless, streamlined future might well have been believable to fairgoers. The real 1960,

A future equated by 20th-century society with the invention, improvement, and acquisition of material things prompted commercial illustrators beginning in the 1930s to make the same explicit connections in their works. Husband-and-wife car buyers in a 1950 magazine ad (top) literally blast off into the future astride an Oldsmobile "Rocket 8." In an ad from 1945 (above) the returning war veteran and his sweetheart can see their long-deferred dreams of prosperity, domestic bliss, and, of course, a Ford automobile finally coming true.

(Top) Courtesy, Oldsmobile Division, General Motors Corporation; (bottom) Ford Motor Company

19

(Opposite page) Futuristic images and promises perhaps achieved their most corporeal form at world's fairs and expositions beginning in the 1930s as large corporations vied for attention with dazzling displays of tomorrow. An overview of the New York World's Fair of 1939–40 (top left) shows the central Perisphere and Trylon and the Transportation Zone in the foreground, with the General Motors pavilion at lower center and part of Ford's spiral Road of Tomorrow to the right. Centerpiece of the GM exhibit was Futurama, where visitors seated on moving chairs viewed a vast panoramic future landscape (bottom left) comprising a half million model buildings, a million scaled-down trees, and thousands of fingertip-sized moving vehicles (bottom center). Borden's Dairy World of Tomorrow featured a "rotolactor" milking machine for 150 cows (top right). The Democracity diorama (center right), another urban vision of the future, was displayed in the Perisphere. In addition to seeing the miracles of television and dishwashers, visitors to the Westinghouse exhibit met Elektro and Sparko, the family mechanical man and dog (bottom right).

Among the more eye-catching exhibits at the 1933–34 Century of Progress Exposition in Chicago was George Keck's House of Tomorrow (below), a steel and glass design of strict modernism that included a hangar for the family airplane. Another sensation at the Chicago fair was a working prototype of Buckminster Fuller's streamlined, three-wheeled Dymaxion car (below right).

Photos, Hedrich-Blessing

however, did not arrive so easily. The world was again to suffer through a war more hideous than ever imagined, a war that was to end with deployment of yet another "ultimate" weapon, the atomic bomb.

The power unleashed in 1945 over Japan could also, in peacetime, unroll "the greatest magic carpet of all ages," as a *Popular Mechanics* writer prophesied in the same year. "Nuclear utopianism," as one historian has called it, had arrived. Borrowing a line from the electrical utopians of the turn of the century, nuclear fission would produce "power too cheap to meter." The popular press seized on such predictions, coming almost daily from distinguished scientists and government officials. "The atom" would eventually create so much leisure time, reasoned an *Amazing Stories* scribe in 1946, that people would pass their time coasting across the landscape in a giant "pleasure bubble." Replaceable nuclear batteries would power planes, washing machines, ocean liners, watches, and rockets to the Moon. One of the hundreds of "cars of the future" modeled and promoted by American automobile companies in the 1950s was the Ford Nucleon, which was designed to have a reactor mounted in the trunk like a shiny spare tire. According to some investigations made by the U.S. Atomic Energy Commission's Project Plowshare, canals would be dug, mountains blasted, icebergs shattered, and roads paved by small, controlled nuclear explosions. Atomic energy would make deserts bloom, eliminate disease, and unlock the secrets of life itself.

One has to be grateful that much of this future was stopped before it began; the prospect of sharing the freeway with millions of little reactors is sobering. To be sure, there were many people, professionals and laypersons alike, who refused to succumb to such dreamy promises, and there are even fewer today who can look at nuclear energy with an unjaundiced eye. Nevertheless, the nuclear utopianism episode of the postwar years provides eloquent testimony to the American devotion to the "technological fix" and to the belief in a future effected by technology alone.

When you wish upon a spaceship

Along with nuclear power the dream of space exploration dominated the discourse on the future in the years after World War II. In the wake of anxiety created by Soviet acquisition and testing of nuclear weapons and the not-unrelated UFO scares of the late 1940s, attention in popular culture (not to mention in government circles) focused on

humanity's future in space. Commissioning writings from learned space scientists, the editors of *Collier's* magazine produced an influential series of articles in the early 1950s, asserting "What you will read here is not science fiction; it is serious fact." Never before could such a claim be so confidently made.

An unparalleled wave of space travel themes engulfed the media. Pulp science fiction boomed again between 1950 and 1953. Future themes returned to the radio waves in the 1950s, after an absence of some years, with such dramatic series as "Dimension X" and "X-Minus One." Hollywood churned out an incredible spate of space-oriented science fiction films, beginning with the rival productions *Destination Moon* and *Rocketship XM* (both 1950), two highly realistic manned space adventures with a contemporary feel. A true futuristic space opera burst onto the screen in 1956—*Forbidden Planet*, the still wonderful movie that introduced the benign presence of Robby the Robot. The space-opera matinee serial enjoyed renewed popularity, though today there are probably few who can recite lines from *Zombies of the Stratosphere* (1952). Two subgenres of the futuristic motion picture were the "space invaders" film, such as *The War of the Worlds* (1953), and the "nuclear-mutant monster" film, such as *Them!* (1954). Neither was set in the future but both responded to strong currents of anxiety about the evils and inadequacy of technology and the looming threat of Communist invasion. The new medium of television, itself a futuristic dream come true, competed in this 1950s market vigorously. Saturday morning and early prime time "kiddie shows" predominated with such offerings as "Captain Video and His Video Rangers," "Tom Corbett, Space Cadet," and "Space Patrol."

Documentary-style projections of a future in space also appeared on television. The most famous was Walt Disney's "Man in Space," which aired in three parts between 1955 and 1957. Prepared in consultation with German rocket scientist Wernher von Braun and other advisers, the Disney series differed from other popular treatments of manned space travel in one essential: it was consciously meant to shape public opinion and government policy. "Man in Space" was didactic, even hortatory in tone, confident in its assertion that spaceflight was inevitable and urgent

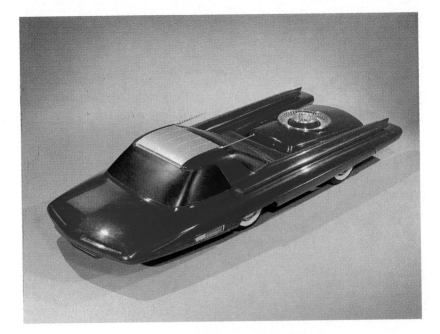

Among "cars of the future" promoted by automakers in the 1950s was the Ford Nucleon. For propulsion the vehicle's designers envisioned a small atomic reactor core, located under the circular cover at the rear, that would be recharged periodically with nuclear fuel.

Ford Motor Company

for more action to ensure that "a peaceful nation" (that is, America, not the Soviet Union) be the first in space. After the first episode ran, U.S. Pres. Dwight D. Eisenhower personally contacted Disney to borrow the film in order to run it repeatedly for top brass. Soon thereafter, Eisenhower made the historic announcement of America's plans to launch the country's first satellite.

"Man in Space" originated as the television corollary to Tomorrowland, one of three divisions planned for Disney's pioneering multitheme park, Disneyland, then under construction on farmland outside Los Angeles. While Fantasyland would spin off from fairy tales and Frontierland from western yarns, Tomorrowland would be, self-evidently, about the future. In fact, the very idea of an amusement park with a difference, with a higher purpose and a more sophisticated ride experience, not to mention the idea of commercial sponsorship, had come to Disney himself on a trip through the Futurama exhibit in 1939—hence, the rocket ride at Tomorrowland, sponsored by Trans World Airlines, and the spaceflight simulation, sponsored by McDonnell Douglas.

One other attraction (which, like the rocket, has also disappeared) at the original Disneyland had echoes of a 1930s world's fair, the Monsanto House of the Future. In this case, however, the model of futuristic efficiency was not the automotive assembly line but the scientific laboratory. The house was constructed of reinforced molded polyester, much like the soon-to-be-ubiquitous modern chairs, and was the direct product of research done at the Massachusetts Institute of Technology. Plastic was

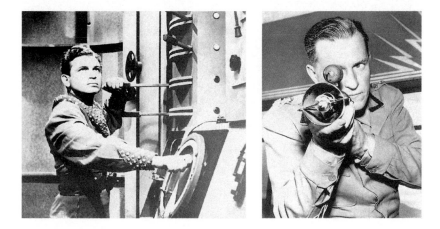

Strong popular interest in the future is reflected in Walt Disney's choice of Tomorrowland (above) as one of the three themes of his pioneering amusement park Disneyland, which opened in 1955. The idea of an amusement park with a difference, and of commercial sponsorship for it, came to Disney during a visit to the New York World's Fair Futurama exhibit in 1939. Echoes of a world's fair are evident in the Monsanto House of the Future (right), an early Disneyland attraction made of molded polyester plastic.

the material analog to nuclear power in the period—incredibly cheap and universally applicable. The ever sanguine *Popular Mechanics* had predicted in 1940 that "the American of tomorrow . . . clothed in plastics from head to foot . . . will live in a plastics house, drive a plastics auto and fly in a plastics plane"—predictions that, for better or for worse, are coming closer to fruition than any of the nuclear counterparts.

Finally, in the 1970s and early 1980s, the Disney juggernaut took the world's fair model to spectacular lengths with the building of Epcot Center in central Florida. The word *Epcot* has become a kind of brand name, like Kodak, but it began as an acronym for Experimental Prototype Community of Tomorrow. The dream originally was to build just that— an entire community, with housing, workplaces, schools, and parks, with the most advanced transportation and services available and a gentle treatment of the landscape—a utopia, in short. Along the way the ideals faded, and what emerged in 1982 was essentially a permanent world's fair complete with foreign-country pavilions and corporate-sponsored, futuristic attractions, such as General Motors' World of Motion. It is a delightfully odd, oxymoronic place, making something permanent out of something—the future—so mutable, so evanescent.

In a way Epcot Center brings the discussion nearly full circle, to Luna Park and Coney Island's A Trip to the Moon or, for that matter, to Bellamy and his minutely described Boston of the year 2000. The shapers of the image of the future in 20th-century culture recognized from the start that the future, to be meaningful, could not be merely an idea or a set of beliefs or a collection of hopes. The way to the future had to be clearly marked, with recognizable signposts hewn from past and present values. The future in the popular imagination became a place where one can still, however briefly, suspend disbelief and enter.

Disney's Epcot Center in Florida has taken the exposition-style evocation of the future to new lengths. Originally conceived as a functioning model community of tomorrow, it emerged on completion in 1982 as a kind of permanent world's fair complete with corporate-sponsored futuristic attractions.

THE JOURNEYS OF THE VOYAGERS

by Edward C. Stone

Launched in 1977, the two Voyager spacecraft exceeded all expectations in fulfilling their mission to explore the four giant planets of the outer solar system.

Since their launch in 1977 two Voyager spacecraft have explored Jupiter, Saturn, Uranus, and Neptune, the four giant planets of the outer solar system. With their deep atmospheres, many moons, multiple rings, and giant magnetospheres, these planets differ greatly from the rocky inner planets such as the Earth and Mars. Providing the first close look at many of these objects, the Voyagers revealed a diversity unexpected of bodies in the cold outer reaches of the solar system.

The spacecraft found remarkably active atmospheres on the giant planets, with high-speed jet streams that give rise to large storm systems. Flowing fluids generate magnetic fields that not only rotate with the planetary interiors but also may be offset and tilted with respect to the planets' rotational axes. Moons orbiting within the magnetospheres absorb high-energy ions trapped in the magnetic fields and supply low-energy plasma ions.

Each planet has a unique ring system, shaped by complex gravitational interactions with nearby moons that shepherd narrow rings and create waves in broader rings. Many of the 57 moons of these planets are at least half ice, with distinctive appearances caused by collisions and internal heating. With sulfur-driven volcanoes on Io, nitrogen-driven plumes on Triton, and organic photochemistry (the effect of radiant energy in producing chemical changes) in the dense nitrogen and methane atmosphere on Titan, the many worlds in the outer solar system provide new insight into the physical processes that underlie the continuing evolution of the solar system.

Planning the mission

Once every 176 years the four giant planets are arranged so that a single spacecraft can visit all of them, using the flyby of one as a means of propulsion toward the next. With this "gravity assist" technique each planetary flyby acts like a slingshot, boosting the speed of the spacecraft and aiming it toward the next planet. By so using gravity, scientists reduced the flight time to Neptune from 30 years to 12.

In 1972, when a spacecraft designed for the 12-year flight proved to be too expensive, the Jet Propulsion Laboratory (JPL) of the U.S. National Aeronautics and Space Administration (NASA) began work on a four-year mission to Jupiter and Saturn that would involve the launch of two Mariner spacecraft in 1977. Two years before launch the Jupiter-

27

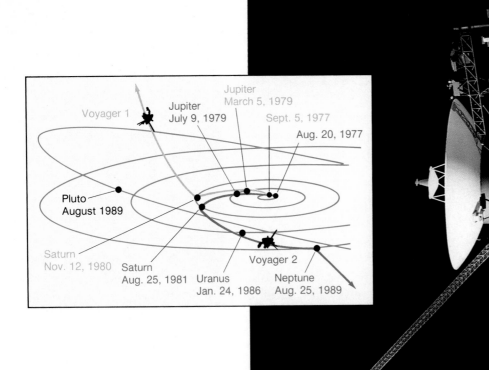

Voyager 1

Jupiter
July 9, 1979

Jupiter
March 5, 1979

Sept. 5, 1977

Aug. 20, 1977

Pluto
August 1989

Saturn
Nov. 12, 1980   Saturn
Aug. 25, 1981   Uranus
Jan. 24, 1986

Voyager 2

Neptune
Aug. 25, 1989

Saturn mission was modified to include the possibility of an extended flight to Uranus and Neptune. This new mission was soon to be renamed Voyager.

Planning for the Voyager mission greatly benefited from the Pioneer 10 and 11 encounters with Jupiter in 1973 and 1974 and the Pioneer 11 flyby of Saturn in 1979. These encounters revealed some of the unexpected complexity that Voyager would find during its subsequent journeys past these two giant planets. The merits of more than 10,000 trajectories were studied before the choice was made of the two that allowed close flybys of Jupiter and its large moon Io and Saturn and its large moon Titan while preserving the option for at least one spacecraft to continue to Uranus and Neptune.

Voyager 1's flyby of Saturn took the spacecraft behind Titan and the planet's rings. This deflected it out of the ecliptic plane in which the planets orbit, and, therefore, away from any further planetary encounters. By 1990 Voyager 1 was leaving the solar system at a speed of 520 million kilometers per year, at an angle of 35° above the ecliptic plane. (One kilometer equals 0.62 mile.)

Voyager 2's flyby of Saturn allowed it either to follow the path planned for Voyager 1 or to remain in the ecliptic plane, headed to Uranus. The

EDWARD C. STONE *is Vice President for Astronomical Facilities and Professor of Physics at the California Institute of Technology, Pasadena, and Voyager Project Scientist at the Jet Propulsion Laboratory, Pasadena.*

latter option was chosen, and the Uranus flyby allowed a close approach to Miranda, the planet's innermost moon.

At Neptune, Voyager 2 dived sharply over the north pole in order to come close to the moon Triton. In 1990 Voyager 2 was leaving the solar system at an angle of 48° below the ecliptic plane and a speed of 470 million kilometers per year.

The Voyagers were controlled and their data returned by radio communications through the Deep Space Network (DSN), a global spacecraft tracking and communications system operated by JPL for NASA. DSN antenna sites are located in California's Mojave Desert, in Spain near Madrid, and near Canberra, Australia. Each of them used one 70-meter-diameter antenna and one or two 34-meter antennas to track the Voyagers. (One meter equals 3.3 feet.) Because the radio signal of Voyager 2 was much weaker at Uranus, the antennas at the Australian DSN site were electronically combined, or arrayed, with a 64-meter antenna provided by the Australian government's Parkes Radio Observatory. Voyager 2's signal from Neptune was even fainter, and, along with the Australian combination, the California DSN complex was combined with the 27 25-meter-diameter dishes of the National Radio Astronomy Observatory's Very Large Array (VLA) near Socorro, New Mexico. Additional tracking was provided by a 64-meter-diameter antenna at Japan's Usuda Deep Space Center.

The spacecraft

The two Voyager spacecraft were built to withstand the rigors of launch and deep space. Each was equipped with a 3.7-meter-diameter dish antenna for communications with the Earth and with three programmable computer subsystems, three nuclear power generators, and instruments for 11 scientific investigations. Because their journeys would take them too far from the Sun for solar cells to be effective, each Voyager carried three plutonium-238 radioisotope thermoelectric generators (RTGs) that provided about 370 watts at Neptune.

The cameras and spectrometers were mounted on steerable platforms that could point them at the planets, moons, and rings. Six other instruments measured the particles and electromagnetic fields surrounding each planet as well as those in interplanetary space. Even the radio systems of the spacecraft were used as scientific instruments to probe atmospheres and rings.

The Voyagers were designed to operate autonomously for long periods, but should any subsystem malfunction, the spacecraft would automatically protect itself according to preprogrammed instructions and then await new commands from the Earth.

Most of the scientific data were transmitted directly to the Earth, although as many as 100 images could be stored on a digital tape recorder for later transmission. To maintain contact, the spacecraft pointed their antennas toward the Earth, using the Sun and another star for reference. Pointing control and corrections to the flight path were achieved through the firing of small thrusters fueled by hydrazine.

Voyager spacecraft (opposite page, right) weighs about 825 kilograms (1,800 pounds), uses a dish antenna 3.7 meters (12 feet) in diameter for communications with the Earth, is nuclear-powered, and carries instruments for 11 scientific investigations at the outer planets and in interplanetary and interstellar space. Diagram (opposite page, left) shows the routes of the two Voyagers from their launches on the Earth in 1977 to the time that they left the solar system.

29

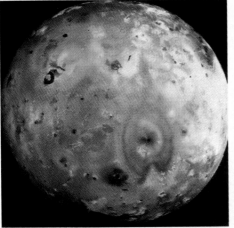

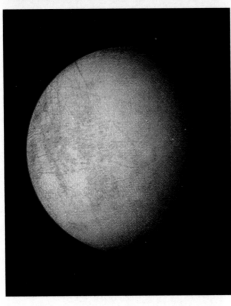

Top right, Jupiter's moons Io (left) and Europa were photographed passing in front of the planet's Great Red Spot. Io and Europa are about the size of the Earth's Moon. The Great Red Spot (bottom right) is a giant storm in Jupiter's atmosphere that has a variable diameter as large as three times that of the Earth. The white oval below the Great Red Spot is a similar storm. The surface of Io (top left) is marked by volcanoes and is coated with deposits of sulfur and sulfur dioxide. Europa (bottom left) has a remarkably smooth and flat surface; the dark markings may have been fractures in the thin ice crust along which low ridges of ice formed.

Jupiter

As the closest of the giant planets, Jupiter was the most familiar before the Voyager encounters in March and July 1979. Like the Sun, it is a giant ball of gas with no solid surface. It consists primarily of hydrogen and helium, with small amounts of methane, ammonia, and water vapor, traces of other compounds, and a core of melted rock and ice. Emitting about twice as much heat as it absorbs from the Sun, Jupiter has a dynamic weather system, as revealed by the motions of the ammonia ice clouds that form bright latitudinal bands.

Dozens of large, circular storms are apparently generated by the turbulent flow associated with jet streams of more than 300 kilometers per hour. The Great Red Spot is the largest, a high-pressure region more than three Earth diameters across and rotating counterclockwise once every six days. Its color remained unexplained but may be due to traces of sulfur or phosphorus compounds.

Io, the innermost of Jupiter's four large moons, provided the greatest surprise of the Voyager mission. Although only about the size of the Earth's Moon, Io is the most volcanically active object in the solar

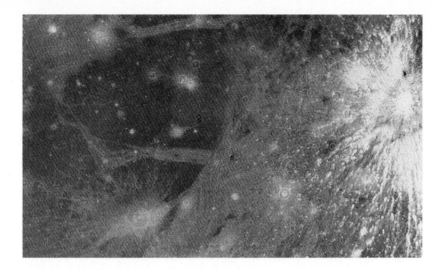

system. Nine active volcanoes were spotted, with plumes as high as 300 kilometers. More than 10 trillion kilograms of material may erupt each year, obliterating all evidence of impact craters. (One kilogram equals 2.2 pounds.) These volcanic eruptions are driven by pressurized gaseous sulfur and sulfur dioxide, heated by tidal flexing of Io's crust. Much as the Moon raises tides in the Earth's oceans, Jupiter's immense gravity creates a tidal bulge in Io's rocky surface. Because Io has a slightly noncircular orbit, the tidal bulge moves back and forth across its surface. As the rocky crust flexes, enough heat is produced to melt Io's interior.

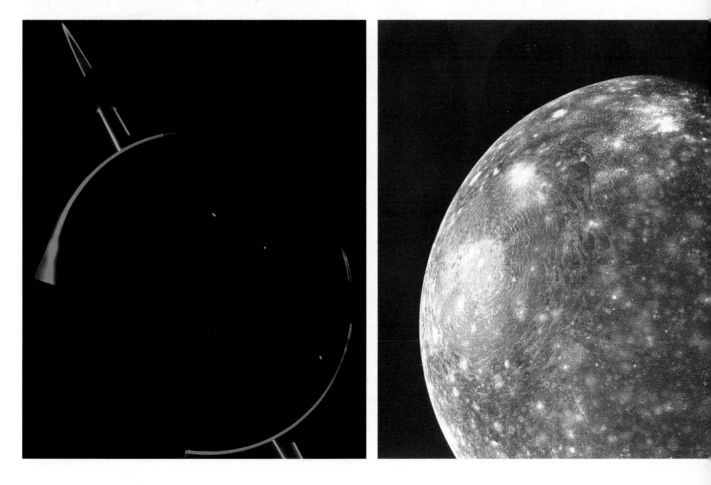

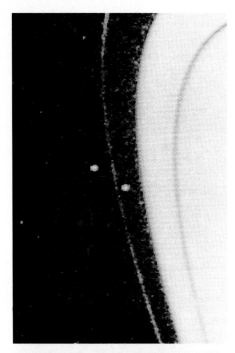

Having a similar rocky composition and size, Europa is in many ways Io's twin. However, Europa's orbit is farther away from Jupiter and, consequently, the moon is only weakly heated by tidal flexing. Even so, astronomers speculated that it may have a tidally heated ocean beneath its thin, icy crust. Europa's surface is remarkably smooth and uncratered, marked only by darker streaks with elevations of less than 100 meters that may be fractures.

The outer two of Jupiter's large moons, Ganymede and Callisto, are also twins. Both the size of Mercury, they are half ice and half rock. Surprisingly, Ganymede's icy surface has experienced significant faulting and flooding, resulting in a grooved terrain bounding patches of the original surface. In contrast, Callisto has retained all of its original surface, the most heavily cratered in the solar system and believed to be among the oldest. A huge impact basin known as Valhalla has a central bright zone about 600 kilometers across; numerous concentric rings extend outward for nearly 2,000 kilometers.

Voyager also discovered Metis, Adrastea, and Thebe, three small, rocky moons orbiting between Io and Jupiter. Metis and Adrastea appear to shed the micrometer-sized grains that form Jupiter's tenuous ring. Some particles spiral inward, forming a diffuse halo extending down to Jupiter's atmosphere, while others form a gossamer ring extending outward.

Jupiter's rings and moons are embedded in an intense radiation belt of electrons and ions trapped in the planet's magnetic field. These particles and fields comprise the Jovian magnetosphere that extends three million to five million kilometers toward the Sun and has a wind-sock-like magnetic tail reaching at least 750 million kilometers, all the way to Saturn's orbit.

Even though Jupiter has a surface magnetic field 13 times stronger than that of the Earth, its magnetic field is greatly distorted by sulfur and oxygen ions from Io. As the magnetosphere rotates with Jupiter, it sweeps past Io, stripping away from the moon about 1,000 kilograms of matter per second and forming a torus, a doughnut-shaped ring of ions, that glows in the ultraviolet. As these heavy ions migrate outward from the planet, their pressure inflates the Jovian magnetosphere to more than twice its expected size. Some of the more energetic sulfur and oxygen ions precipitate along the magnetic field into the atmosphere, causing intense ultraviolet auroral emission. As Io moves through Jupiter's magnetic field, it acts as an electrical generator, developing 400,000 volts across its diameter and generating an electrical current of three million amperes that flows along the magnetic field to Jupiter's ionosphere.

Saturn

Because Saturn is twice as far from the Sun as Jupiter, somewhat less was known about it as Voyager 1 approached in November 1980, with Voyager 2 following in August 1981. Like Jupiter, Saturn is composed primarily of hydrogen and helium and radiates about 80% more energy than it absorbs from the Sun. This indicates that an internal source heats the atmosphere as well, though the total energy available to drive the weather system is only about 25% of that at Jupiter. Saturn's atmosphere is much blander in appearance than Jupiter's, with fewer hurricane-like storm systems. A red spot in Saturn's southern hemisphere is one-third the size of Jupiter's Great Red Spot.

Because of Saturn's smaller amount of heating and fewer giant storm systems, scientists were surprised to find an equatorial jet stream approaching 1,800 kilometers per hour, six times faster than on Jupiter and nearly half the speed of sound. Voyager also found that the amount of helium in the atmosphere is less than half that on Jupiter, consistent with the suggestion that the precipitation of helium out of the mainly hydrogen atmosphere could be supplying the internal heat radiated by the planet.

Two small moons, Pandora (outer) and Prometheus (inner), flank the F-ring of Saturn (opposite page, top left), confirming the theory that such satellites play a role in maintaining rings around planets. Saturn's rings are revealed in a high-resolution photograph (opposite page, top right) taken by Voyager 2 from a distance of four million kilometers (2.5 million miles). Dust particles electrostatically levitated above the ring plane may account for the fingerlike "spokes" that appear above the B-ring. Full-disk view of Saturn (opposite page, bottom left) shows a ring system that is the brightest and most extensive in the solar system. Artist's drawing reveals the distribution of particle sizes in a small section of Saturn's A-ring (opposite page, bottom right). Particle diameters range from 2 to 70 centimeters (about 1 to 28 inches); instead of the spheres shown here the actual ring particles probably are irregularly shaped snowballs.

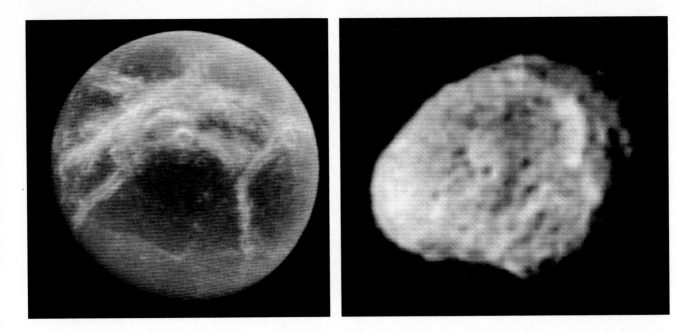

Wispy streaks on the surface of the Saturn moon Dione (above) may be ice deposits from water that filled large surface cracks early in the satellite's evolution. Hyperion (above right), one of the most battered bodies ever seen in the solar system, is probably the remains of a larger satellite that was destroyed in a collision. It tumbles chaotically in its orbit around Saturn. Saturn's largest moon, Titan (opposite page, bottom), has a dense atmosphere of nitrogen and methane and is completely swathed in a thick, orange, photochemical haze. An additional higher haze layer appears over the north polar region in this color-enhanced image.

The beautiful rings of Saturn, comprising countless icy particles, are especially complex and interesting. Transient radial markings, or "spokes," above the broad B-ring are probably small grains electrostatically levitated above the larger ring particles for several hours before dispersing. Two moons, Pandora and Prometheus, shepherd the ring particles that are between them into the narrow F-ring, and other unseen shepherding moons create waves in the edges of gaps in the main rings.

The main rings display a variety of small-scale structures, including spiral waves generated by the gravitational wake of moons orbiting outside the rings. On a still smaller scale, individual ring particles range in size from grains to occasional lumps 10 meters in diameter. The rings are not much thicker than these largest particles.

It is thought that the rings formed from larger moons that were shattered by the impact of comets or meteoroids. The irregular shapes of the 8 smallest of Saturn's 17 moons suggest that they too are fragments of larger bodies. Two of the small moons, Epimetheus and Janus, even share essentially the same orbit, while three others share orbits with either Tethys or Dione, two larger moons. Another of the larger moons, Hyperion, is also irregularly shaped, tumbling chaotically as it orbits Saturn. Although regular in shape, Mimas has an impact crater of about one-third its diameter. If the impacting object had been slightly larger, Mimas would have shattered.

These larger moons are intermediate in size, having diameters less than 30% of those of the Jovian moons Ganymede and Callisto. Though of modest size and consisting more than half of ice, several have surface features indicating early geologic activity. Bright markings on Rhea and Dione may correspond to extensive fracture systems, and a valley extending more than half the circumference of Tethys likely resulted from internal stresses. Portions of Enceladus' surface are nearly devoid of impact craters, and other regions have parallel grooves, suggesting a particularly complex geologic history.

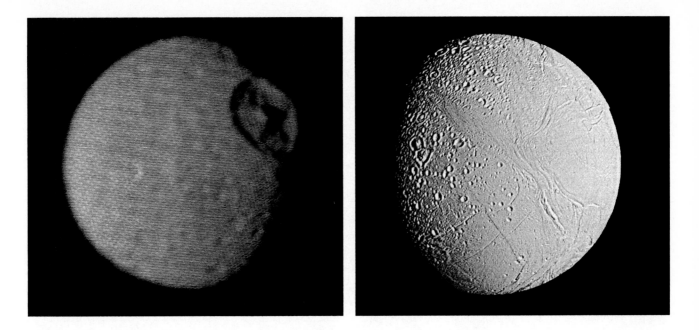

Little is known about the geologic history of the largest moon, Titan, because its surface is hidden from view by an opaque organic haze. Although this limited the use of the cameras of Voyager 2, Titan was also observed with other instruments. Similar in size to Ganymede and Callisto, Titan has a dense nitrogen atmosphere with a surface pressure 60% greater than that on Earth. Photochemistry converts some atmospheric methane to other organic molecules, such as ethane, that are thought to accumulate in lakes or oceans. Other more complex hydrocarbons form the haze particles that eventually fall to the surface, coating it with a thick layer of organic matter. The chemistry occurring in Titan's atmosphere today may strongly resemble that which occurred on Earth before life evolved.

The Saturn moon Mimas (above left) reveals a giant crater that might have split the satellite apart if it had been much larger. Enceladus (above) is the most geologically evolved of Saturn's moons, with faults, parallel ridges, and areas where icy flows have covered all evidence of impact craters.

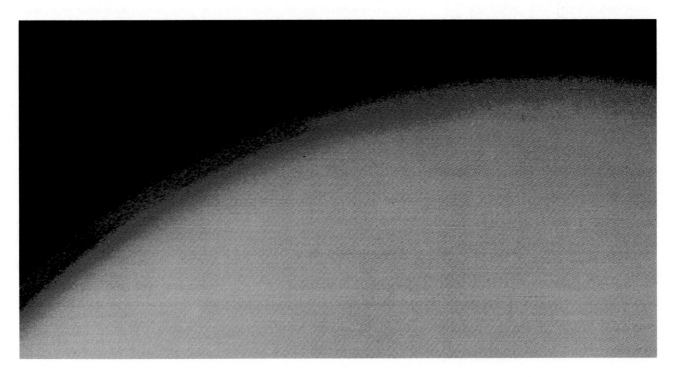

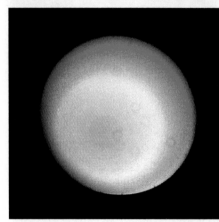

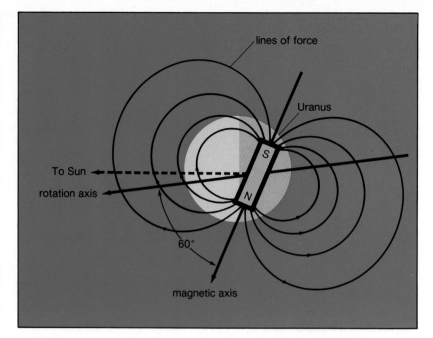

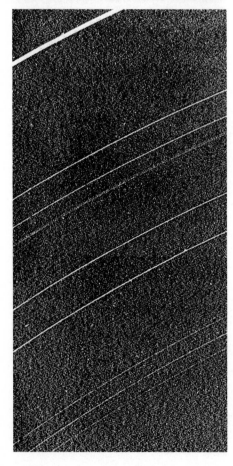

Titan is often embedded in Saturn's magnetosphere, creating a wake in the plasma ions and shedding photochemically produced hydrogen to form a torus. Deeper in the magnetosphere, sputtering (dislodging the atoms from) the surfaces of icy moons produces oxygen ions that form an equatorial plasma sheet. Additional ions come from the rings and from Saturn's ionosphere.

Because Saturn's surface magnetic field of 0.21 gauss is only 5% of Jupiter's, its magnetosphere is smaller, extending sunward only one million to two million kilometers. The axis of the magnetic field is almost perfectly aligned with the rotation axis of the planet.

Bursts of radio emission (175 kilohertz) occur with a period of 10.66 hours, corresponding to the rotation period of the planet's interior where the magnetic field originates. The radio emissions emanate from high northern latitudes, where there are also strong ultraviolet auroral emissions.

Uranus

Uranus offered the opportunity for yet more discoveries as Voyager 2 headed for an encounter on Jan. 24, 1986. Twice as far from the Sun as Saturn and tipped on its side with its south polar region facing the Sun at the time of encounter, Uranus was known to be circled by nine narrow rings and by five intermediate-sized moons.

Uranus has a much shallower hydrogen atmosphere than either Jupiter or Saturn, and its diameter is less than half that of its larger neighbors. A mixture of melted ice and rock forms Uranus' fluid interior, and atmospheric methane gives the planet its blue-green color.

Although the Sun directly heats the polar regions and there is little additional internal heat, Voyager found that the temperatures at the poles and equator are nearly the same. A few discrete methane clouds revealed the presence of mid-latitude winds of nearly 600 kilometers per

36

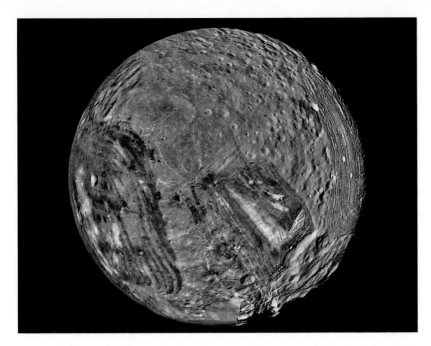

hour. The atmosphere is otherwise relatively inactive, with no visible hurricane-like storm systems.

Voyager discovered an additional ring and an extensive set of dust rings apparent only when they are backlighted by the Sun. The centimeter-sized ring particles have a charcoal-black coating of either carbonaceous grains or irradiated methane. Atmospheric drag from Uranus' extended upper atmosphere may sweep smaller dust particles out of the rings.

Miranda, the smallest of the five previously known moons, has a diverse and complex surface. Rolling, heavily cratered plains adjoin three large oval-to-trapezoidal regions patterned by parallel grooves and ridges. Other regions contain cliffs up to 20 kilometers high and fault valleys 10 to 15 kilometers deep. The surprising amount of geologic activity on such a small, cold moon suggests there may have been strong tidal heating, possibly during a period of chaotic orbital motion.

Although the surface of Ariel is younger than that of Miranda, it is much less complex. Extended fault valleys scar the surface, and there is evidence of viscous ice flows in valley floors and elsewhere. Complex valleys and fault lines also etch the surface of Titania, possibly resulting from the expansion of subsurface water as the moon's interior froze.

Oberon and Umbriel have the oldest surfaces, little changed except by impacts since their formation. On Oberon the principal signs of tectonic activity are several fault valleys that cut across its surface and the distinctive materials that apparently flooded the floors of a few of the largest impact craters. With a surface darker than those of its companions, Umbriel may have been blanketed by a layer of dark debris. Any methane in its icy crust would have been darkened from the continual bombardment by ions trapped in Uranus' magnetic field.

Voyager 2 discovered 10 Uranian moons orbiting near the rings, bringing the total number of known moons in the system to 15. Two of the

Blue-green color of Uranus (opposite page, top left) results from the absorption of red light by methane gas in the planet's cold atmosphere. False color and extreme contrast enhancement (opposite page, middle) reveal a south polar haze layer consisting of progressively lighter concentric bands. (The doughnut shapes are caused by dust in the camera's optics.) Uranus has 10 narrow rings of charcoal-black particles (opposite page, bottom); the faintest is about midway between the bright outermost ring and the next easily visible ring down. The axis of Uranus' magnetic field is tilted by about 59 degrees from its rotation axis, and the center of the magnetic field is offset from the planet's center by almost one-third of Uranus' radius (opposite page, top right). Above, much of the surface of Uranus' moon Ariel is densely pitted with craters, while older terrain is broken by a global system of fractures and faults. Uranus' moon Miranda (above left) reveals terrain so varied that scientists believe the satellite may once have been shattered and then reassembled.

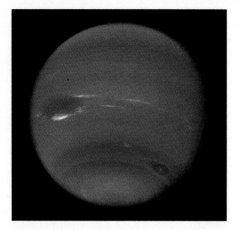

Neptune's south pole was tipped slightly toward Voyager 2 as the spacecraft approached; atmospheric banding is most apparent in the southern hemisphere (above). Also visible in the color-enhanced photograph are Neptune's Great Dark Spot and Dark Spot 2. Bright cloud bands of methane ice near Neptune's north pole (above right) appear to cast shadows on the main cloud deck 50 to 100 kilometers (30 to 60 miles) below. Neptune's two main rings are seen backlit by the Sun (below); the rings rotate in a clockwise direction.

new moons, Cordelia and Ophelia, shepherd Uranus' outermost ring, but the moons shepherding the other rings may have been too dark or too tiny for Voyager's cameras to record.

Although Uranus' surface magnetic field of 0.23 gauss is similar to Saturn's, its orientation was unexpected. On other planets, including the Earth, the axis of the magnetic field is nearly parallel to the rotation axis, placing the magnetic poles near the geographic poles. Uranus' magnetic axis, however, is tilted about 59° from the axis of rotation and is offset from the center of the planet by 30% of its radius, placing the magnetic poles nearer the equator. This peculiar orientation suggests that the magnetic field is generated at an intermediate depth in the interior where the pressure is high enough for water to become electrically conducting.

Radio emissions peaking at 400 kilohertz originate from the strong magnetic-field regions in the hemisphere facing away from the Sun. As Voyager passed by Uranus, it recorded variations in the strength of the emissions every 17.24 hours, corresponding to the rotation period of the planet's interior where the magnetic field is generated.

Neptune

Orbiting near the edge of the solar system, Neptune was a planet of mystery before the Voyager 2 encounter on Aug. 25, 1989. The spacecraft found Neptune's atmosphere surprisingly dynamic. Winds streak

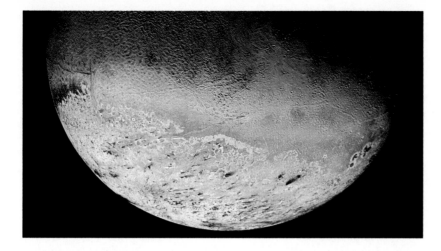

South polar region of Neptune's moon Triton is covered with a cap of nitrogen and methane ice dotted with impact craters and geyser vents. In the equatorial region long faults with parallel ridges of extruded ice cut through complex terrain, while smoother plains dominate the region to the right.

westward at nearly supersonic speeds of more than 2,000 kilometers per hour, the highest yet observed. The Great Dark Spot, an Earth-sized storm system resembling Jupiter's Great Red Spot, rolls counter-clockwise with a 16-day period and travels westward at almost 1,200 kilometers per hour. A smaller dark spot and bright clouds of methane ice also mark Neptune's atmosphere. Such an active weather system was unexpected because there is only 5% as much energy to drive winds as there is on Jupiter. Evidently the winds on Neptune are less turbulent and, therefore, less energy is needed to maintain their high speeds.

As at Uranus, Neptune's magnetic poles are much closer to the equator than expected. Not only is the magnetic axis tilted by 47° from the rotation axis but the center of the magnetic dipole is also offset from Neptune's center by more than half the planet's radius. The similarity of Neptune's and Uranus' magnetic fields suggests a similarity in the flows of electrically conducting water inside the two planets. Neptune's magnetic field is weaker, however, with a typical strength of 0.133 gauss.

Because Neptune's magnetic axis is tilted, the magnetic polar region faces almost directly into the solar wind once every 16.11 hours as the planet rotates. This unusual orientation allows the ions in the solar wind access to the magnetic axis, where they can penetrate closer to the planet than is otherwise possible.

The ring system at Neptune is also unique. Three diffuse, almost transparent rings and a broad sheet of ring particles completely encircle the planet, with a larger proportion of small grains than in the ring systems of the other planets. Three dense regions in the outer ring suggest "ring arcs." This confinement of the ring material may be due to unseen shepherding moons, because the particles otherwise should have spread uniformly around the ring in just a few years. Such moons could have escaped detection if they had diameters of less than 30 kilometers.

Six moons, with diameters ranging from 54 to 400 kilometers, orbit near Neptune. Like the rings, the smaller of these are probably fragments of larger moons broken up by the impact of comets and meteoroids. Even the larger of these are irregularly shaped, and their charcoal-black color suggests a surface coating similar to that on the rings and small moons at Uranus.

Too close to Neptune to have been sighted from the Earth, the dark, irregularly shaped, and cratered moon 1989N1 was viewed by Voyager 2 from a distance of 146,000 kilometers (91,000 miles).

Triton, the largest of Neptune's moons, is much different. Its polar ice cap of frozen nitrogen and methane is highly reflective. Because it absorbs little solar energy, Triton's surface temperature of 38 K (−245° C; −409° F) is the coldest yet observed in the solar system. Sublimation of the polar cap (changing directly from the solid to the vapor form and then condensing back to a solid) produces a seasonally varying atmosphere of nitrogen and methane.

Although Triton is very cold, several active geyser-like plumes were spewing dark material eight kilometers above the polar cap. These plumes are likely driven by the explosive release of gaseous nitrogen that carries ice-entrained darker material to high altitudes, where it is swept away by high-speed winds.

Near the equator crisscrossing fault valleys in the water ice surface are filled by ridges of ice extruded from the interior, and the floors of volcanic craters show signs of repeated flooding. Tidal flexing of Triton's crust following its capture by Neptune—and radioactive heating from its rocky core—probably provided the energy to melt the moon's interior and cause the extensive geologic activity on its surface.

Triton and the outermost planet in the solar system, Pluto, are similar in several ways. Almost the same size, both are approximately 75% rock and 25% ice and have a surface layer of frozen methane. Thus, Voyager 2 may have already provided a hint of what the only unexplored planet, Pluto, is like.

The interstellar mission

Having completed their grand tour of the outer planets, the two Voyagers are now in search of the heliopause, the boundary between the solar wind and interstellar space. In addition, they will continue to observe stellar and extragalactic sources of extreme ultraviolet emissions. If they remain healthy, both spacecraft have enough electrical power and thruster fuel to continue operating until at least the year 2015. By that time Voyagers 1 and 2 will be, respectively, 20 billion and 17 billion kilometers from the Sun.

During the long cruise the two spacecraft will join Pioneers 10 and 11 in measuring the properties of the supersonic solar wind composed of ions and electrons that blows outward from the Sun at 400 kilometers per second. This wind, which becomes more dilute with increasing distance from the Sun, forms the heliosphere, a giant magnetic bubble that blocks ions from interstellar space. The supersonic solar wind must slow down well before it reaches the bubble's boundary, or heliopause. The velocity will probably decrease abruptly in a shock wave. In this region some ions are thought to be accelerated to speeds greater than 10% that of light, becoming cosmic-ray particles.

Beyond the shock region lies the heliopause, perhaps as little as 15 billion kilometers from the Sun. Sometime in the next 10 years the Voyagers are expected to cross the shock. If so, they may become the first spacecraft to pass through the heliopause and return data from interstellar space.

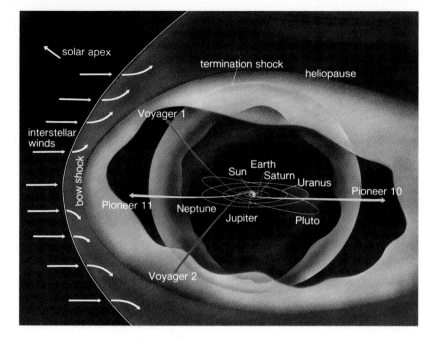

Four spacecraft—two Pioneers and two Voyagers—are traveling out of the solar system, each in a different direction. By the year 2000 the two Voyagers may have crossed the termination shock, where the 1.6 million-kilometers-per-hour (1 million-miles-per-hour) solar wind slows to about 400,000 kilometers (250,000 miles) per hour as the pressure of interstellar space impinges on the Sun's influence. Beyond the termination shock lies the heliopause, the outer limit of the solar wind and the true beginning of interstellar space. With enough electrical power and thruster fuel to last through 2015, the Voyagers may be the first spacecraft to return data from this region.

Eventually, the two Voyagers will cease sending data, thereafter destined to wander silently through the Milky Way forever. Although silent, they will not be forgotten, because they have revealed a solar system with distinctive worlds of unexpected diversity. Future generations should be challenged and enlightened by further exploration of these worlds, much as current ones have been by the Voyager journeys of discovery.

FOR ADDITIONAL READING

J. Kelly Beatty, Brian O'Leary, and Andrew Chaikin (eds.), *The New Solar System*, 2d ed. (Cambridge University Press and Sky Publishing Corp., 1982).

Robert Hamilton Brown and Dale P. Cruikshank, "The Moons of Uranus, Neptune and Pluto," *Scientific American* (July 1985, pp. 38–47).

Joseph A. Burns and Mildred Shapley Matthews (eds.), *Satellites* (University of Arizona Press, 1986).

Jeffrey N. Cuzzi and Larry W. Esposito, "The Rings of Uranus," *Scientific American* (July 1987, pp. 52–66).

Tom Gehrels and Mildred Shapley Matthews (eds.), *Saturn* (University of Arizona Press, 1984).

Richard Greenberg and André Brahic (eds.), *Planetary Rings* (University of Arizona Press, 1984).

Andrew P. Ingersoll, "Uranus," *Scientific American* (January 1987, pp. 38–45).

Richard P. Laeser, William I. McLaughlin, and Donna M. Wolff, "Engineering Voyager 2's Encounter with Uranus," *Scientific American* (November 1986, pp. 36–45).

David Morrison (ed.), *Satellites of Jupiter* (University of Arizona Press, 1982).

Laurence A. Soderblom and Torrence V. Johnson, "The Moons of Saturn," *Scientific American* (January 1982, pp. 100–116).

Press "Up" for Space

by Jerome Pearson

Twenty years from now a person wanting to travel in space may be able to ride an elevator up to a rendezvous with an orbiting space station.

Imagine yourself preparing for a flight into space 20 years from now. Instead of training for years to ride a dangerous rocket into orbit, strapped to an enormous fuel tank with millions of pounds of flammable fuel beneath you, you take the easy way—the elevator. You simply fly to the equatorial spaceport, board a capsule that looks much like the interior of a modern passenger jetliner, and enjoy a smooth ride upward. You can see the Earth fall away beneath you as your vehicle climbs a silvery tower that reaches 100 miles high. At the top your elevator stops and lets you out inside a large space station. As you acclimate yourself to the station, you notice rockets being refueled from a giant fuel tank, which floats far above the space station on a thin tether. Off to one side a vertical elevator support extends both upward and downward, lightly tethering a variable-gravity research facility. You are surrounded by tethers and space elevators. Welcome to space travel in the 21st century!

Tall towers have excited the imagination since ancient times. The Bible tells the stories of Jacob's Ladder and the Tower of Babel, and in 1989 celebrations marked the 100th anniversary of Gustave Eiffel's magnificent tower in Paris. The space elevator has much in common with these imaginative structures; it is a bold attempt to break the force of gravity that holds us firmly to the Earth.

Konstantin Tsiolkovsky was the first space researcher to study the mechanics of long structures in space. In 1895 this Russian schoolteacher dreamed of a "cosmic railway" around the Earth above the atmosphere, supported on tall towers between Earth and sky. He imagined a tower so high that the weight felt by objects higher and higher on the tower would become less and less and that eventually the pull of the Earth's gravity would be overcome by the rotational inertia, or "centrifugal force," caused by the Earth's rotation. The balance point, where gravity and the inertial forces cancel one another, is at precisely the 36,000-kilometer (22,000-mile) height of the geostationary communication satellites; if one stepped off Tsiolkovsky's tower there, one would be in orbit, keeping exact pace with the tower and the Earth.

42

JEROME PEARSON is Chief of the Structural Dynamics Branch of the Flight Dynamics Laboratory at Wright-Patterson Air Force Base, Ohio. He is one of the inventors of the space elevator.

(Overleaf) Artist's conception reveals a variable-gravity research module in orbit at one end of a space tether. At the lower end is a space shuttle. Research instruments and equipment can be moved up or down the tether. Painting by Robert T. McCall, © Bantam Books, NY/Space Art International

Tsiolkovsky dealt only with thought experiments, and it was left to another Russian, Leningrad engineer Yury Artsutanov, in an article published in 1960, to propose seriously the first space elevator. A colleague gave Artsutanov a sample of a very strong yet lightweight material, and he amused himself by imagining how high a tower one could build out of the substance. When the answer turned out to be several hundred miles, he realized, from Tsiolkovsky, that the force of gravity falls off significantly at those heights, allowing the tower to be built even higher. He eventually recognized that if the tower were tapered, it could reach all the way into geostationary orbit; if it were then extended past that point, the upper part would experience an upward force sufficient to balance the lower part, stabilizing the entire structure and creating the elevator into space.

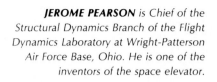

Tether fundamentals

An elongated object in orbit aligns itself vertically, whether it is a rope, a satellite, or our slightly elongated Moon; this is why we see only one side of the Moon. If the object is rotated and released, it oscillates about the vertical position like a pendulum.

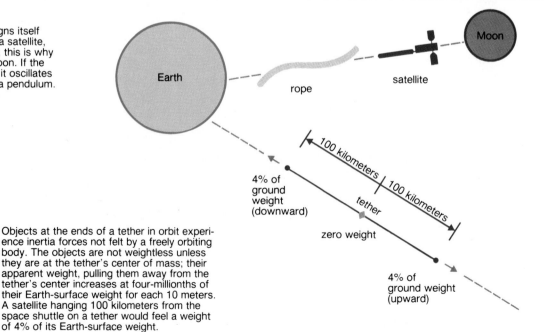

Objects at the ends of a tether in orbit experience inertia forces not felt by a freely orbiting body. The objects are not weightless unless they are at the tether's center of mass; their apparent weight, pulling them away from the tether's center increases at four-millionths of their Earth-surface weight for each 10 meters. A satellite hanging 100 kilometers from the space shuttle on a tether would feel a weight of 4% of its Earth-surface weight.

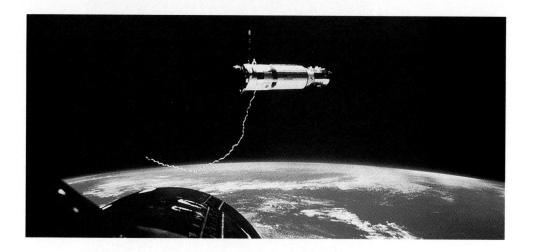

The space elevator was invented independently by John Isaacs of the Scripps Institution in La Jolla, California, and by the author at the U.S. Air Force's Flight Dynamics Laboratory near Dayton, Ohio. These later inventions received the first scientific notice, but Artsutanov is now universally recognized as the first person to conceive of the space elevator. Unfortunately, these concepts of a space elevator reaching into geostationary orbit require materials far stronger than any that are now available. The strongest materials now in existence are synthetic fibers—Kevlar from Du Pont and Spectra from Union Carbide. They are five times as strong as their weight in steel, but even so they are not strong enough for building an elevator into geostationary orbit. The other difficulty with the grand schemes for space elevators is the sheer mass of material required for building a tower longer than the distance around the Earth. However, as discussed below, there are newer space elevator concepts that solve both these problems of strength and mass.

Space tethers

Even though the space elevator to geostationary orbit is just a dream, shorter structures, called space tethers, are now being developed. Some of them have surprising capabilities that could greatly reduce the cost

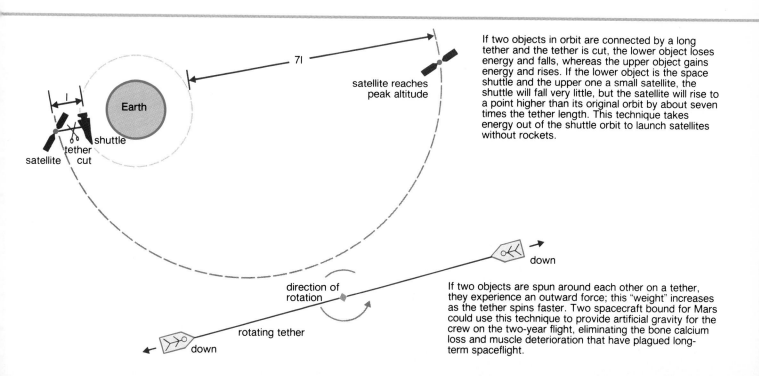

If two objects in orbit are connected by a long tether and the tether is cut, the lower object loses energy and falls, whereas the upper object gains energy and rises. If the lower object is the space shuttle and the upper one a small satellite, the shuttle will fall very little, but the satellite will rise to a point higher than its original orbit by about seven times the tether length. This technique takes energy out of the shuttle orbit to launch satellites without rockets.

If two objects are spun around each other on a tether, they experience an outward force; this "weight" increases as the tether spins faster. Two spacecraft bound for Mars could use this technique to provide artificial gravity for the crew on the two-year flight, eliminating the bone calcium loss and muscle deterioration that have plagued long-term spaceflight.

Tethered Satellite System 1 (right) was scheduled to be launched in May 1991. Artist's drawing reveals the satellite and its electrodynamic tether. Consisting of copper sheathed in nylon insulation and Kevlar, the tether (opposite page, top) would be run out from a space shuttle and, at a length of 20 kilometers (12.5 miles), would generate four to five kilowatts of power by using the motion of the shuttle through the Earth's magnetic field.

of space travel. Space tethers have already been used on a small scale. During the Gemini program of the U.S. National Aeronautics and Space Administration (NASA) in the 1960s, astronauts left their space capsules and "walked" in space, held firmly to the spacecraft on long nylon tethers. A stronger tether connected the Gemini spacecraft to its Agena upper-stage rocket while the two were spun around each other, creating the "centrifugal force" that gave the astronauts the feeling of weight.

In 1972 an Italian space scientist, Mario Grossi, working at the Smithsonian Astrophysical Observatory in Cambridge, Massachusetts, proposed the use of long tethers that would orbit in the Earth's magnetic field and generate electrical power from their orbital motions. In 1974 his colleague Giuseppe Colombo of the University of Padua, Italy, proposed a series of experiments to tether a satellite far below the space shuttle in order to make scientific measurements in the upper atmosphere. In

Tether fundamentals (continued)

Spinning tethers in orbit could fling payloads from their tips to other tethers, providing spacecraft launching without rockets. A spinning tether in higher orbit would act as a "velocity bank," taking energy from descending payloads and adding it to ascending payloads to send them on their way.

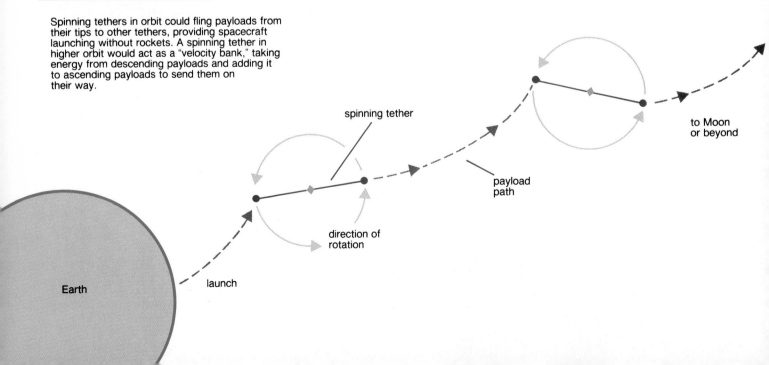

spinning tether

to Moon
or beyond

payload
path

direction of
rotation

Earth

launch

a remarkable series of papers Colombo envisioned tethers with hooks to launch satellites from the shuttle and tethers that could drop payloads onto the lunar surface or retrieve them so that the spacecraft would not have to land on the Moon and take off from it.

In 1978 NASA built upon Grossi's and Colombo's ideas by starting a series of workshops and international conferences to examine the applications of tethers in space. These meetings brought together hundreds of practical space engineers and visionary space scientists. They identified scores of exciting possibilities for tethers. These potential uses cover the gamut of space applications, from low-Earth orbit to lunar operations and interplanetary space probes.

Current tether programs

NASA in 1990 had under way two programs that would employ space tethers. The first would use Grossi's idea to deploy an electrodynamic tether 20 kilometers (12.5 miles) upward out of the cargo bay of the space shuttle. The tether would generate four to five kilowatts of power from the motion of the shuttle through the Earth's magnetic field. Only about three millimeters (⅛ inch) in diameter, the tether would consist of a slender copper wire sheathed in nylon insulation and a strengthening layer of Kevlar. If the tether extended 100 kilometers (60 miles) from the shuttle, the resulting power output would be about 20 to 25 kilowatts. A much longer tether could generate perhaps 100 kilowatts, the same as the proposed multibillion-dollar nuclear reactor program. The Tethered Satellite System (TSS) hardware for the first mission was scheduled to be delivered to the Kennedy Space Center in April or May 1990 and to be flown into space on May 10, 1991, on the shuttle orbiter *Atlantis*. If the results of TSS-1 are promising, the tether experiment will be reflown after 18 months.

The electrodynamic tether can also operate in reverse, as a motor. If a current were generated by solar panels and forced through the tether, the current would exert a force on the tether and thus on the shuttle. The force would increase the spacecraft's velocity, raising its orbit. The

A conducting tether can use the Earth's magnetic field to operate as an electric generator or as a motor. As a generator the tether is carried through the magnetic field by the attached space vehicle. The result is an induced current that provides power to the vehicle. As a motor the tether carries an electric current from solar cells in the opposite direction. The tether then produces thrust that increases the vehicle's orbital velocity.

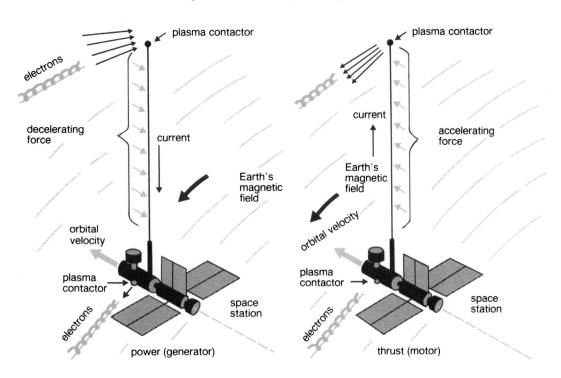

Tethered Satellite System 2 is scheduled for a 1994 launch with the satellite to be deployed in the upper atmosphere about 100 kilometers (60 miles) below the space shuttle (above right). Above, the satellite undergoes tests in Italy. It was being designed to make scientific measurements at altitudes that are too high for balloons and too low for orbiting satellites.

(Left) Aeritalia; (right) Martin Marietta

electrodynamic tether can thus transform electrical energy into orbital energy, taking the place of rocket thrust. A spacecraft with solar panels and a conducting tether could operate either way, converting energy back and forth, to adjust its orbit and to generate or store power at will. The electrodynamic spacecraft would have unprecedented maneuverability and orbit-adjusting capability compared with conventional rocket-powered vehicles.

The second NASA-planned tether flight experiment is called TSS-2; it will carry a 500-kilogram (1,100-pound) satellite, about 1.6 meters (5.3 feet) in diameter, and a tether longer than that of TSS-1. The satellite will be lowered 100 kilometers from the shuttle into the upper atmosphere to make scientific measurements. The satellite is being built by the Italian Space Agency and the tether system for both TSS-1 and TSS-2 by the Martin Marietta Corp. TSS-2 has been scheduled for a shuttle launch in 1994.

In the early 1980s Paul Siemers of the NASA Langley Research Center in Hampton, Virginia, and the author each proposed that flight models of hypersonic vehicles be suspended from the space shuttle into the upper atmosphere on long tethers. These models could be controlled remotely from the shuttle to investigate their lift, drag, and control characteristics at 25 times the speed of sound and at altitudes of 80 to 150 kilometers (50 to 95 miles). This "hypersonic tethered wind tunnel" would be a low-cost alternative to building a new generation of ground-based wind tunnels for hypersonic vehicles. It would allow easy testing of the single-stage-to-orbit British HOTOL and U.S. National Aerospace Plane and the two-stage West German Sänger.

Tethers on the space station

The largest space project under way in 1989 was the NASA space station, *Freedom.* The project was given the go-ahead by U.S. Pres. Ronald Reagan and was reaffirmed by Pres. George Bush in 1989, on the 20th anniversary of the landing of Apollo 11 on the Moon. *Freedom* was being built in cooperation with Canada, Europe, and Japan. The extensive use of space tethers on this international facility could significantly improve its economic payoff to the world.

One of the most important scientific uses of the space station will be to study the effects of microgravity (very low gravitational force) on living creatures and industrial processes. This work could be greatly enhanced by the creation of a variable-gravity research facility. Many useful processes, from electronic crystal growth to separation of biochemicals, can be done most efficiently under conditions of microgravity. Using a set of long cables tethered to the space station, a powered elevator could move along the cables to select the exact level of microgravity required. The effective gravity felt in the elevator increases by four microgravities (0.000004 of Earth-surface gravity) for every 10 meters it moves from the center of the station. Several experiments could be stationed at various levels of microgravity, all isolated from the disturbances from the space station by the flexible tether. The experimental packages containing valuable processed materials could be released from the lower end of the tether for automatic reentry and recovery.

Tethers also show great promise in replacing rockets for propelling spacecraft and solar cells for generating power. The space station will require large amounts of electrical power for operations; also, propellant must be brought up regularly by space shuttles. A long tether between the shuttle and the station could meet both these needs. After the crew and supplies have been transferred to the station, the shuttle could be lowered several kilometers on the tether and released. As the shuttle loses energy and reenters the atmosphere without rockets, the space station would recover the orbital energy that it had lost to air drag, without using precious rocket fuel. With a tether, hundreds or thousands of pounds of rocket fuel could be saved on each shuttle flight. An electrodynamic tether could also bleed off the excess orbital energy gained when one shuttle leaves Earth orbit and have enough to provide 25 kilowatts of electrical power for 29 days.

Space tethers could even improve the operation of the space shuttle itself by recovering the large external fuel tank. This tank delivers thousands of tons of liquid hydrogen and liquid oxygen to the shuttle engines. Then, just short of orbit, the tank is jettisoned and crashes into the ocean, still carrying a few thousand pounds of fuel. Each shuttle mission represents the loss of a structure with a diameter of 8.4 meters (27.5 feet), a length of 47 meters (154 feet), and a mass of 35,000 kilograms

Hypersonic test vehicles can be tethered 100 kilometers below the space shuttle and trolled through the upper atmosphere at 25 times the speed of sound to test their aerodynamics and heat shields.

(77,000 pounds). These tanks are so huge that the Wright brothers could have made their first powered flight entirely inside one. Unfortunately, the space shuttle program has already thrown away nearly 30 of them.

Some space engineers have proposed saving the external tanks and using them for a wide range of space experiments. Using tethers to recover the tanks can make the space shuttle system more efficient. One proposal is to carry the external tank all the way into orbit, still attached to the shuttle orbiter, using every drop of propellant in the tank. Once in orbit, the shuttle crew would disengage from the tank, extend the tank upward on a long tether, and keep it in orbit during the mission. When the shuttle was ready to reenter the Earth's atmosphere, the crew would simply cut the tether and allow the tank to go upward and the shuttle fall downward. This would put the tank into a higher orbit, where it would be safe from orbital decay until it could be used on later missions; it might be joined by other tanks to form an orbiting "tank bank" for a variety of purposes. An added saving is that by raising the tank into a higher orbit the shuttle is automatically lowered for atmospheric entry, without the normal need for retro-rockets. Each shuttle flight could then carry an additional payload of 35,000 kilograms into orbit, saving fuel in the process.

Private space companies envision potential profits in recovering the external tanks. The External Tank Corp. of Boulder, Colorado, signed an agreement with NASA to start using the tanks for suborbital experiments and eventually to boost them into orbit. Global Outpost, Inc., of Alexandria, Virginia, planned to use an external tank for crystal growth and pharmaceutical manufacturing in orbit.

One of the principal cargoes launched to the space station *Freedom* will be rocket fuel for orbital transfer vehicles, station keeping, and Earth-escape launches. This fuel could be safely stored some distance above the station in a space shuttle external tank attached to *Freedom* by a long tether. This would keep it easily accessible yet safely away from the station in case of fire or explosion. Because the gravity forces are so small, even a slim, lightweight tether a few millimeters in diameter could support a fully loaded external tank.

Severing a tether connecting two satellites gives the upper body additional orbital energy at the expense of the lower one. This fact can be helpful in the design of methods of launching satellites from the shuttle into higher orbits without using rocket propellants. The satellite is simply reeled upward on a long, thin tether until it is perhaps 50 or 100 kilometers above the shuttle. The force of gravity will automatically align the two bodies vertically. The tether is then cut, taking energy from the shuttle and giving it to the satellite. Because the shuttle is much more massive than the satellite, it hardly moves at all, but the satellite will reach an orbit that is seven tether lengths higher than its initial orbit. A satellite released from the end of a 100-kilometer-long tether attached to the shuttle in a 400-kilometer orbit would therefore reach a peak altitude of 1,100 kilometers. A rocket burn at that point to make the orbit circular would put the satellite into the higher orbit with less than half the fuel

An electrodynamic tether extending from a space station could be used as an auxiliary power system for the station. It could convert the excess mechanical energy gained when a shuttle leaves Earth orbit into 25 kilowatts of electrical power for 29 days.

NASA

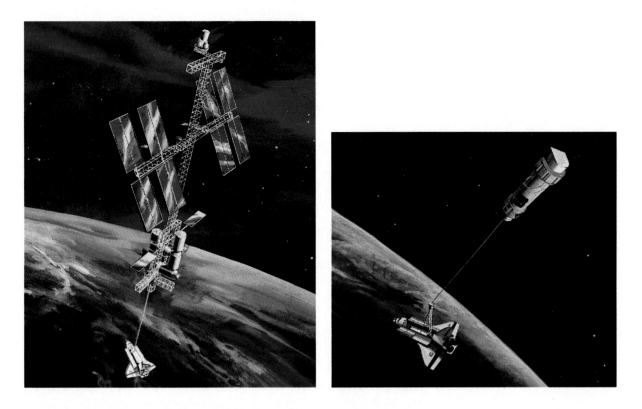

required by rockets alone. The lightweight tether could then be reeled back into the shuttle for reuse, and the energy taken from the shuttle would allow it to reenter the Earth's atmosphere without retro-rockets.

Even more ambitious schemes are possible, including spinning tethers that could fling payloads from their ends fast enough to escape the Earth and go to the Moon. These tethers could provide large launch velocities to their payloads, their rotational velocities being limited only by their material strength.

Obstacles to development

Building and deploying space tethers pose some difficulties. Joseph Carroll of the California Space Institute recognized one serious problem for space tethers—the danger of collision with space debris and the accidental severing of a long tether, with possibly catastrophic results. Tethers are very vulnerable to meteoroid damage because their great length gives them a large exposed area. Tethers longer than a few kilometers would probably be hit at least once a year by a particle as large as one millimeter in diameter. A particle this size would sever many of the tethers now planned.

The answer to this problem may be to use shorter, thicker tethers with multiple strands to guard against natural meteoroids. There is also a need to sweep up all of the man-made debris in Earth orbit. With the growing interest in flight safety since the *Challenger* explosion in 1986, an international effort to limit and to clean up space debris has become more likely.

Tethers on the international space station Freedom (*above left*) *are to be used to attach space shuttle supply vehicles to the station, to keep fuel tanks at a safe distance from it, and to extract energy from the shuttles. Satellites can be released from the ends of long tethers (*above*) instead of being released directly from the cargo bay of the shuttle. When released from a tether, a satellite gains energy at the expense of the shuttle, rising to a peak altitude that is seven times the length of the tether above the shuttle orbit.*

Photos, NASA

51

A second problem in building space tethers is that the strong synthetic fibers are susceptible to degradation by the atomic oxygen and ultraviolet radiation experienced in Earth orbit. These tethers will require protective coatings, such as Nomex. The coating, however, makes the tether heavier and less strong.

A third problem is the difficulty of ensuring safety because of the unusual dynamics of such long, thin structures. Trolling a satellite on the end of a 100-kilometer-long tether is far more difficult than throwing a perfect cast into a tree-shaded pool 15 meters (50 feet) away. When shuttle astronauts reel in a tethered satellite, it will oscillate with larger and larger amplitudes, threatening to wrap itself completely around the shuttle. Because of these problems the first missions of the tethered satellite system will allow 7 hours for unreeling the satellite and more than 10 hours for reeling it back inside. The safety of the shuttle demands that all possible mishaps, such as wrapping a tether around the shuttle so that it could not close its payload doors for reentry, be studied and eliminated before flight.

Tethers for the Moon and planets

Beyond Earth orbit the next target identified by the U.S. National Space Council in its 1989 recommendation is a return to the Moon. A goal for this mission will be to establish a base for finding and exporting lunar resources. In this effort tethers may be invaluable. Rotating tethers placed on the lunar surface could fling payloads of lunar material high above the Moon, where they could be captured by orbiting tethers that are also rotating. The payloads could then be launched by those tethers into high-Earth orbit for construction of solar power satellites and into low-Earth orbit for the development of the gigantic scientific, engineering, and tourist complexes planned for the next century. The use of such lunar resources would vastly reduce the amount of material that would have to be launched at great cost from the Earth's surface into space.

Beyond the Moon the mystery of Mars beckons. After the infrastructure has been developed in Earth-Moon space, U.S. astronauts will be prepared for an expedition to the "red planet," perhaps as part of a pro-

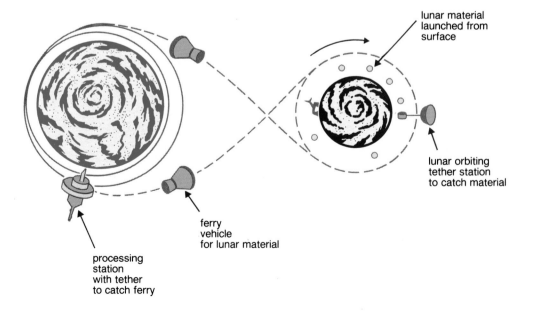

lunar material
launched from
surface

lunar orbiting
tether station
to catch material

ferry
vehicle
for lunar material

processing
station
with tether
to catch ferry

gram in cooperation with the Soviets and others. On the long voyage to Mars, tether-generated artificial gravity may be required for preventing the astronauts from suffering bone loss and heart muscle deterioration. These problems have plagued the Soviet cosmonauts on their *Mir* space station and U.S. astronauts on the Skylab missions in the 1970s.

For missions beyond Mars to the asteroids, tethers could be even more important. One of the most useful ideas in celestial dynamics is to use the gravity fields of the planets to increase the energy of space probes by means of a swing-by maneuver. The Voyager 2 spacecraft, which flew by the planets Saturn, Uranus, and Neptune, used the gravitational field of the giant planet Jupiter to perform its interplanetary "grand tour" mission to all the major planets, years sooner and with much more payload than it could have accomplished otherwise. The Magellan spacecraft, launched in 1989 to explore Venus, will use gravity swing-bys of the Earth and Venus to achieve its final Venus orbit.

Paul Penzo of NASA's Jet Propulsion Laboratory in Pasadena, California, proposed the use of tethers to perform gravity-assisted maneuvers without a planetary gravitational field. His technique requires that the spacecraft extend a long tether with an anchor on the end as it approaches an asteroid. The tether would attach itself to the surface of the asteroid, and the spacecraft would then "wind up" around the asteroid on the tether. When the spacecraft turned far enough for its new orbit, the tether would be released from the asteroid and reeled back in. Thus, one robot spacecraft using a deployable tether with an anchor on the end could carry out an extensive reconnaissance of the asteroid belt between Mars and Jupiter with just a few pounds of rocket fuel for orbit corrections.

Prospects for space elevators

Recent research shows how space engineers might move beyond even these applications of tethers in space and eventually construct the space elevator. Instead of using static strength to support such elevators, engineers can use the dynamics of bodies in motion. To understand how this can be done, one might imagine a hollow tube circling the Earth like a

When U.S. astronauts return to the Moon, tethers may be helpful in studying and utilizing lunar materials (opposite page). For example, rotating tethers placed on the Moon's surface could fling payloads of lunar material to orbiting tether stations, which in turn would send them into Earth orbit for the construction of satellites. Below, tethers could be used to help spacecraft swing around bodies too small to have appreciable gravitational fields. A spacecraft could use a tether to attach itself to an asteroid, swing partway around the asteroid, collect a sample of asteroid material, and then, on a new trajectory, proceed to its next target.

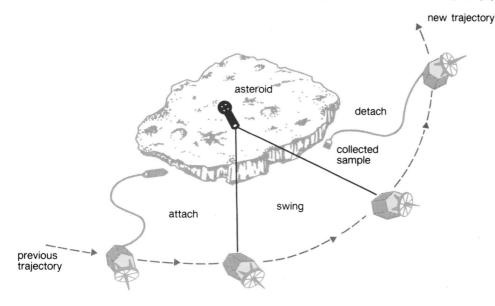

thin doughnut. If a conducting wire were threaded through the doughnut in a continuous loop around the Earth and then electromagnetically accelerated above the orbital velocity of the tube, the rotational inertia of the wire would tend to lift the tube away from the Earth. If the wire moved fast enough, it would support the tube without the need for towers. Cables suspended from the tube down to the ground could lift payloads into space without rockets. Such an "orbital ring," first proposed by Paul Birch of the Marconi Co. in Great Britain, would be one way to create the space elevator without requiring extremely strong materials. It could be built of Kevlar or Spectra.

However, placing a ring around the Earth 40,000 kilometers (25,000 miles) long would require lifting an enormous amount of material into orbit by conventional rockets. There is a better way to make such a conductor without using a million tons of tube and wire, and that is to use a stream of magnetic grains. Planetary scientists have discovered rings of small particles around every one of the major planets—Jupiter, Saturn, Uranus, and Neptune. In addition to the well-known, broad rings of Saturn, there are thin rings with few particles that surround each major planet. The stability of these rings has been explained by the presence of small "shepherding satellites" just outside the orbit of the ring particles. These satellites constantly apply small gravitational forces on the ring particles, keeping them in place and preventing their dissipation. No planetary scientist predicted this phenomenon from gravitational theory, but the theory does allow this kind of stable orbital motion.

Benoit Lebon, of the Centre National d'Études Spatiales in Toulouse, France, recently proposed launching into Earth orbit a thin stream of magnetic grains that could function as the conductor of an orbital ring. Using electromagnetic forces (which are much stronger than the gravitational forces of shepherding satellites), hollow solenoids (long, cylindrical coils of wire) could focus the grain stream as it passed through them. This stabilizing technique could allow the artificial Earth ring to support a space elevator without the enormous mass required by a solid conductor and its tube. The motion of the ring particles would support the solenoids, and the solenoids could then support vertical cables hun-

A space elevator would utilize a thin ring of magnetic grains placed in Earth orbit. Hollow solenoids (current-carrying coils of wire) in low-Earth orbit (LEO) and geostationary Earth orbit (GEO) would keep the ring from flying apart. The motion of the ring particles would support the LEO solenoid and space station and, thereby, a space elevator descending to the Earth's surface.

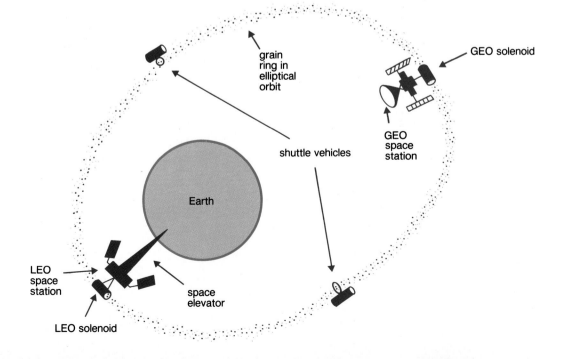

Artist's conception shows a space elevator stretching from the Earth's Equator to a rotating-wheel space station in geostationary Earth orbit, 36,000 kilometers (22,000 miles) above the surface. Once in orbit, passenger and cargo capsules would be driven electromagnetically along the particle stream.

U.S. Air Force photo; painting by John Gromosiak

dreds of kilometers long on which space elevators could be suspended. Cargo and passenger vehicles could be accelerated along the stream electromagnetically, providing a complete space-transportation system at a cost of just a few dollars per kilogram. Eventually, such a conducting ring could even be constructed in a large orbit around the Sun. Threaded along such a long, thin conductor, doughnut-shaped spacecraft could be accelerated to a few percent of the speed of light—enough to escape the solar system and to reach planets around nearby stars.

These visions of gigantic space tethers and space elevators are awe-inspiring, but they are based on simple physical principles and natural laws. They require no superscience for making them possible, just competent space engineering. Such rings, strings, and towers are the elegantly simple structures that could be created out of space tethers to truly revolutionize spaceflight in the 21st century.

FOR ADDITIONAL READING

William A. Baracat and Cyrus L. Butner, eds., *Tethers in Space Handbook* (NASA Office of Space Flight, 1986).

Arthur C. Clarke, "The Space Elevator: Thought Experiment or Key to the Universe?" pp. 183–194 of his *Ascent to Orbit* (John Wiley & Sons, 1984).

Luciano Guerriero and Ivan Bekey, eds., *Space Tethers for Science in the Space Station Era* (Societa Italiana di Fisica, Bologna, Italy, 1988).

Jerome Pearson, "Ride an Elevator into Space," *New Scientist* (Jan. 14, 1989, pp. 58–61).

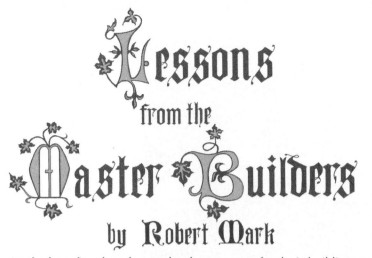

Lessons from the Master Builders

by Robert Mark

Despite the benefits of modern technology, many of today's buildings are still poorly designed. For help, structural archaeologists are looking to the edifices of ancient Rome and medieval Europe to understand how their builders incorporated sound engineering into their architecture.

The form of the roof of the Kresge Auditorium, designed by noted Finnish-born architect Eero Saarinen and constructed on the campus of the Massachusetts Institute of Technology in 1955, appears to derive from structural demands. In fact, as became painfully evident even during the roof's construction, the form was conceived for visual effect, with little regard to structure.

The roof, a concrete, lead-covered, equilateral spherical-triangular shell having a 49-meter (160-foot) span, was originally intended to be of uniform thickness and supported only at the three corners. However, because of problems with cracking that arose after removal of the temporary rigid timber centering (support work) over which the concrete had been poured, the concrete was thickened and the window mullions (vertical frame members) were strengthened to provide additional support. Even with these modifications, the combined effect of the dead weight of the shell acting over the years and the variations in environmental temperature led to further cracking. With every heavy rain the auditorium flooded. More critically, the cracks exposed steel reinforcement within the shell, and the steel became so badly corroded that the roof began to lose its inherent strength. In 1979 the building was shut down for more than a year to allow for costly, major reconstruction.

Across the Charles River in Boston the 60-story John Hancock Tower, designed by the firm of I.M. Pei and Partners, was still under construction when several of its oversize, mirrored-glass windows popped out during a severe storm in 1971. In the two years following, almost a quarter of the tower's 10,300 panes of glass—intended to reflect the downtown scene and allow the tallest structure in the city to fade into the background—were similarly lost. Because of the vast quantity of plywood used for sealing the openings of the missing windows, Boston's fire chief declared the building a fire hazard. Adding visual insult to injury, he ordered the expanse of plywood painted with a black fire-retardant substance. Occupancy had to be postponed for almost four more years while workers

ROBERT MARK is Professor of Architecture and Civil Engineering at Princeton University.

(Overleaf) Manuscript illustration by Jean Fouquet in the collection of the Bibliothèque Nationale; photograph, Giraudon/Art Resource

installed new glazing and extensive structural modifications intended to stiffen the building's frame against the action of high winds.

The experience of both the Kresge Auditorium and the Hancock Tower represents extremes of a not uncommon problem with new large-scale buildings in which technological performance falls far short of the designer's intention. Considering that scientific theory, often backed up by wind-tunnel model testing and computer-based analysis and graphics, is now used in the process of design, one would expect the level of technology in buildings from past eras, long before these aids became available, to be far inferior. From a number of model simulations recently carried out at Princeton University, however, it was found that many early large-scale building designs are surprisingly sophisticated. Perhaps even more unexpected, the studies of the ancient buildings also have pointed to possible remedies for some of the technological problems of modern design.

Analyzing the masterworks

The ability of early builders to create new forms for covering vast interior spaces without resort to scientific design methods—particularly in the great temples and baths of imperial Rome after the 1st century AD and in the light, soaring structures of Gothic cathedrals beginning around the end of the 12th century—has been a persistent puzzle to historians. Before the 18th century, structural theory was rudimentary. It was only in the middle of the 19th century, with the need to build structures to withstand far greater loads than in earlier times (such as bridges for the new steam railways) and with the introduction of new building materials such as iron, that scientific methods became regularly employed for design. Nevertheless, even these methods would not permit reliable analysis of many of the early building forms.

Fortunately, experimental and computer-modeling techniques that can be used to analyze force distributions in such complex architectural structures are now available. Originally developed to help design mechanical components in the nuclear and aerospace industries, they have added a whole new dimension to the study of historic buildings. Hitherto, architectural history had been concerned largely with style and with the ways architects solved aesthetic problems. The recently available methods of structural analysis are giving clues as to how early designers solved the fundamental problem of making their buildings stand up and how style and structure interacted. This new approach to historic architecture, which can be called structural archaeology, is illustrated by the modeling of the ancient Roman Pantheon, studies of the first flying buttresses of the cathedral of Notre-Dame de Paris of medieval France, and Sir Christopher Wren's design of 1705 for the dome of St. Paul's Cathedral in London.

The Roman Pantheon

The Pantheon, constructed in its present form between AD 118 and 128, is a cylindrical building of brick-faced concrete roofed with a great concrete dome that rises from a circular drum. Its 43.3-meter (142-foot) unsupported span is far greater than that of any known earlier domed building, and it remained unmatched for 1,300 years. Construction of the huge dome was aided by the general Roman adoption of cast structural concrete, composed of small stones and rubble held together by pozzolana cement and used previously only for utilitarian structures. Modern historians have viewed this change in ancient construction, which took place at the end of the first century, to have been part of a "Roman architectural revolution"—one characterized by a shift away from masonry structures of brick or stone to domed and vaulted buildings using cast concrete that acts as a single piece, or monolith, for the load-bearing structure. The building most generally taken to represent the culmination of this revolution is the Pantheon, whose dome has been interpreted as a concrete pot lid, merely resting on top of the wall and held together largely by the internal bonding of the concrete.

To better understand how the structure of the Pantheon really works, civil-engineering student Paul Hutchinson and I used a technique known

The Colosseum, inaugurated in AD 80, was one of the last monumental buildings to be erected in Rome with a conventional load-bearing skeleton of cut stone. Near the end of the first century, Roman architecture underwent a revolutionary shift from masonry structures of brick and stone to domed and vaulted buildings using monolithic cast concrete for the load-bearing structure.

© Robert Frerck from TSW—CLICK/Chicago

The Roman Pantheon (below), constructed between AD 118 and 128, boasts a domed roof whose diameter remained the largest of any building for the next 13 centuries. Light for the temple's interior (right) is provided by a single oculus, an unglazed overhead opening eight meters (26 feet) in diameter.

(Below) J. Allan Cash Photolibrary; (right) Robert Mark

as finite-element modeling to construct a computer model of the building. A first series of tests, which assumed that the concrete acts as a monolith without cracking into smaller pieces, revealed extensive regions of tensile (pulling) hoop stress in the supporting wall and dome as the weight of the dome pushes the wall outward. Nonetheless, the maximum levels of stress were low, about equivalent to the pressure exerted by the weight of the atmosphere on an object on the Earth's surface.

This series of tests also revealed a surprising feature of the set of prominent stepped rings that encircle the base of the dome. It generally had been assumed that the structural function of the rings was to reinforce the base of the dome. When the rings were removed from the computer model, however, tensile stresses actually decreased by about 20%, suggesting that the rings have an entirely different purpose.

A second series of model tests was then run, based on an assumption consistent with modern engineering theory: that ancient unreinforced concrete could actually withstand no tensile stress without cracking. Although Roman concrete is similar to modern concrete in having good compressive strength (strength to resist crushing), it differs from modern concrete construction in two crucial ways. First, the consistency of modern concrete mix is fluid and homogeneous, allowing it to be poured into forms. By contrast, Roman concrete was thick and was hand-layered around large chunks of aggregate. Second, integral reinforcing steel gives modern concrete structures the great tensile strength required for resistance to being pulled apart. Roman construction used no reinforcement and, with that assumption accounted for, the new model of the dome and supporting wall now indicated extensive cracking in a pattern similar to the meridians on a globe, beginning at the base of the dome and extending more than halfway to the top. Thus, the dome acted as a single piece of shell above the cracking and as a circular array of wedge-shaped arches below.

In this case the presence of the stepped rings around the base of the dome makes functional sense. When the rings were deleted from the new model, tensile stresses in the cracked, segmented dome base increased appreciably. Each segment behaved like a simple arch whose weight generates an outward thrust at the support. When the rings were added, the extra weight produced an opposing compression in the arch segments, stabilizing them. This effect is similar to that which the Romans achieved by adding extra fill, or surcharge, in the form of cut stones over the vertical supports of their arches. Faith in the model was strengthened further when its predicted extent of cracking, calculated to rise to 54° above the dome's base, agreed almost exactly with measurements of the actual cracks in the dome.

Schematic of the Pantheon (top left) shows how the stepped rings around the dome base seem to give circumferential reinforcement, keeping the base from splaying outward. When the rings were removed from a finite-element model, however, tensile stresses actually decreased. While the model assumed the dome to act as a single piece, modern engineering theory indicates that ancient unreinforced concrete would crack under tensile stress. A diagram of force distribution in a monolithic dome (bottom left) shows compressive forces (solid lines) along meridians from crown to base but compressive circumferential forces only at the crown, changing at the base to tensile forces (dashed lines), which lead to meridian cracking in the lower dome. A second model incorporating this assumption showed that the cracked lower dome acted like a circular array of arches and that the weight of the rings stabilized each arch segment in a way similar to what the Romans achieved by adding cut-stone surcharges over the vertical supports of their arches (below, part of a Roman aqueduct at Segovia, Spain). Portion of a finite-element computer model of the Pantheon (center) shows a segment of dome and wall.

(Top left) Illustration based on a drawing by Y.S. Huang; (center) computer graphic generation by L.A. Van Gulick; (right) Robert Mark

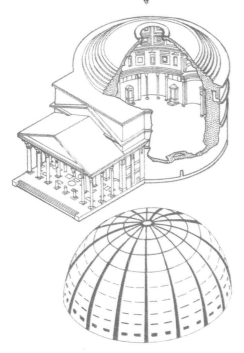

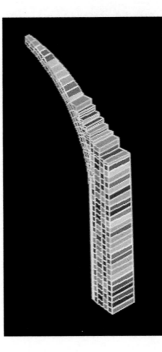

Notre-Dame de Paris (top), begun in 1163, was the first of the giant French cathedrals of the high Gothic period and the tallest Gothic church of the 12th century. Its nave walls were supported by the first flying buttresses, which were taken down and replaced early in the 13th century. The present flying buttresses date from a 19th-century restoration. During the first half of the 13th century new cathedrals soared ever higher, the peak of the movement being the cathedral of Saint-Pierre at Beauvais (right).

The agreement of predicted behavior from the second series of model tests with that of the Pantheon's actual structure indicates that for practical purposes the Roman builders could not have counted on their concrete to exhibit appreciable tensile strength. As such, Roman concrete offered no significant structural advantage over conventional masonry construction of brick or stone. The decision to employ concrete in large-scale Roman architecture seems to have been made entirely upon constructional rather than structural considerations; placement of concrete by unskilled labor was simpler and cheaper than construction in brick or cut stone by skilled masons.

This finding of another motive for the shift in construction in no way diminishes the achievements of the Roman architects. If their structures were not revolutionary in the same sense as the introduction of modern reinforced concrete, the Pantheon was, because of its giant scale, an even more daring experiment in construction than has been hitherto understood.

62

Notre-Dame de Paris

Gothic cathedrals represent, probably better than any other artifact, the resurgence of the West six centuries after the fall of Rome. Among the largest structures of the Middle Ages, the high Gothic cathedrals of France stand out for their enormous height and technological daring. Beginning in the late 12th century, French towns vied with each other to build the loftiest cathedral. Over the course of the first half of the 13th century, cathedrals became taller and taller, the peak of the movement being the cathedral of Saint-Pierre at Beauvais, whose vaults (arches that span an entire roofed area) leap 48 meters (158 feet) above the floor.

The floor plan of Notre-Dame (top left) illustrates the disposition of the nave, choir, and transepts of a typical Gothic church. Overhead view of Notre-Dame (left), taken from one of its west towers, shows the north and south transepts and the nave supported by flying buttresses. Embedded in the inner face of a wall buttress near the end of the south transept is an arch (above) that probably repeats the arc of the flyers of the original nave. Although the arch has never been open, it provides the major clue in reconstructing the cathedral's first flying buttresses.

(Top left) Adapted from *French Gothic Architecture of the 12th and 13th Centuries* by Jean Bony, University of California Press, 1983; (left) Scala/Art Resource; (above) W.W. Clark

The first of the giant cathedrals of the high Gothic period was Notre-Dame de Paris. Its masonry structure is of singular historical importance because its vaults, which rise 33 meters (108 feet) above the floor, took a leap of a full one-third over any earlier Gothic church. This was to be the largest incremental height increase of the era for a new church over an earlier building.

Prescientific structural design had to be based almost entirely on experience with earlier, similar buildings. In effect, an earlier building usually acted as a "model" to confirm the stability of a new design. With the great increment in height intended for Notre-Dame, though, this approach may have been inadequate for planning. The builders would have been concerned with more than supporting the extremely high vaults. They also would have had to contend with a new environmental realm mainly associated with tall buildings: large lateral forces caused by high winds. Wind speeds are significantly greater at higher elevations, and since wind pressures are proportional to the square of the wind speed, earlier experience with lower profiled churches (which also present smaller "sail areas" to the wind) would not have fully prepared the builders of Notre-Dame for this new design problem. Nonetheless, their concern appears to have led to the introduction of an important structural and stylistic device: the flying buttress.

Flying buttresses, or flyers, are essentially exposed stone arches, which carry forces generated in the upper parts of a Gothic building away from the building's actual wall, directing these forces to free-standing stone piers set back from the wall. By relieving the interior walls, they allowed architects to increase the amount of wall space taken up by windows. Had flying buttresses not been developed, the walls of the largest cathedrals would have been extremely thick in order to withstand the forces from the dead weight of the vaults and the wind loads on the roof, making the interiors of these buildings hopelessly dark. Unfortunately, since extensive rebuilding altered Notre-Dame's entire buttressing system as early as the 1220s, and other partial reconstructions were carried out during

Cutaway view of Notre-Dame (below right) shows the reconstructed original elevation of the nave, before the 13th-century campaign of rebuilding. The elevation comprises four "stories" consisting of (from the floor up) arcade, gallery, oculus, and clerestory. In the rebuilding the gallery roof was lowered, eliminating the oculus and allowing the clerestory to be extended downward. Photoelastic model of the original nave structure (below) reveals the distribution of internal forces induced by simulated wind loading and indicates the probable structural cause for the rebuilding. In photoelastic modeling a transparent epoxy-plastic representation is viewed with the aid of polarizing filters. The resulting interference pattern is a contour map in which colors correspond to different levels of stress. Closely spaced colored lines identify critical regions. Significant tensile stress was found where the flying buttresses abut the clerestory and the gallery. Cracking of the mortar in these regions probably elicited frequent repairs.

(Left) Robert Mark; (right) illustration based on a drawing by E. Neuman

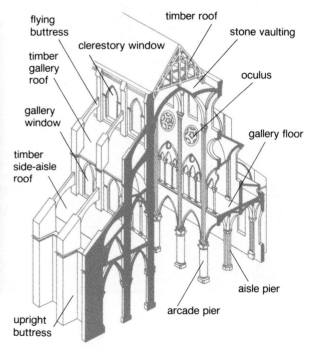

succeeding centuries, there is only indirect evidence for the specifics of the development of flying buttresses.

Because of the significance of the flying buttress for both the history of architecture and the history of technology, historian William Clark and I undertook an archaeological reconstruction of the original structure of the nave. The most important evidence for the reconstruction is an embedded arch found on the back side of the terminal wall buttress of the 12th-century transept. While it has never been open in the manner of the arch of a true flying buttress, it nonetheless reflects the disposition of the open flyers that existed in the adjacent bay of the nave.

Historians had assumed that the 13th-century rebuilding of Notre-Dame was undertaken to improve the level of the cathedral's interior light by removing solid wall and adding window space. Changes in the structural system, therefore, were interpreted as a by-product of the need to change the window design. Inherent structural problems within the original design had never been considered as a reason for the rebuilding, despite the fact that anyone visiting the cathedral today will observe that it remains a dark building. Indications of a possible structural rationale for the alteration of the buttressing did emerge, however, as a result of our model study.

Initially undertaken to confirm the validity of the archaeological reconstruction of the cathedral's original structure, photoelastic modeling revealed some unanticipated, critically stressed regions in that first configuration. In these tests we viewed a transparent epoxy-plastic model of a typical structural section of the cathedral through polarizing filters. The resulting interference pattern is read as a contour map in which colors correspond to different levels of stress. On the basis of loadings simulating the distributed dead weight and the effects of high winds on the cathedral walls and roof, the scaled-model results indicated two local regions of tension on the windward buttressing, both occurring at points of abutment where the upper ends of the flyer arches rested against the clerestory and gallery walls. After heavy storms, such as modern records

The buttressing of the cathedral at Bourges (above), whose vaults are some three meters (10 feet) higher than those of Notre-Dame, is striking in its economy. The steep uppermost flying buttresses, which seem to have been added after onset of the buttressing problems at Notre-Dame, are much lighter than those of all other high Gothic cathedrals. The upper flying buttresses of the cathedral at Chartres (above left), added as an afterthought during the last stages of construction, apparently also were a response to the problems at Notre-Dame. Although the vaults of Chartres are somewhat lower than those of Bourges, its buttressing weighs 2½ times as much.

Photos, Robert Mark

65

Portrait of Sir Christopher Wren, painted about 1700, shows him holding the plan for St. Paul's Cathedral, which he rebuilt after the earlier cathedral was destroyed by the Great Fire of 1666. The London skyline in the background includes some of Wren's parish churches and St. Paul's with an earlier dome design that was not actually built.

Thomas-Photos, Oxford

indicate could have taken place from time to time during the 40-odd years of life of the original configuration, the builders would have noticed some cracking in the joints where the stones were pulled apart. Repairs, including the repointing (remortaring) of all the affected joints, would have had to be made promptly after every great storm to prevent more general deterioration, despite inconvenience of access to the affected regions. This need for constant observation and regular maintenance suggests that it was more than coincidence that these very regions were eliminated in the 13th-century rebuilding.

Further confirmation of this explanation of the reasons for the 13th-century reconstruction is provided through an examination of the buttressing details of other buildings constructed contemporaneously or somewhat later than Notre-Dame. The evidence of, among others, the still taller French cathedrals of Bourges and Chartres, begun in 1194–95, suggests that their builders were well aware of the problem we have identified at Paris.

Archaeological analysis of the choir of Bourges revealed that its original buttressing scheme was altered during the course of construction. A steep upper tier of flyers supporting the tall clerestory was apparently an addition made around 1210. At Chartres a tier of light upper flyers was also hastily erected during the last stages of its construction around 1220. Notre-Dame was shown to be the initial model for determining the subsequent modifications in the configurations of each of their buttressing systems. And, in turn, benefiting from those experiences were the modifications incorporated into the buttressing of the nave of Notre-Dame itself in the 1220s. By that time the flying buttress, originally introduced because of structural need, had also become a stylistic hallmark of the great Gothic cathedrals. Gothic design was, therefore, an evolutionary process; master builders responded to structural exigency and modified their designs on the basis of their own and other builders' experience.

Wren's dome for St. Paul's

Sir Christopher Wren (1632–1723), the architect of St. Paul's Cathedral, London, is often portrayed as the prototypical scientist-architect. This reputation would seem to follow from his career as professor of astronomy at London and Oxford, a founder and president of the Royal Society, and his appointment as surveyor general (royal architect) of England. Yet for historians one of the most perplexing aspects of Wren's career is the elusiveness of demonstrable connections between his scientific inquiries and his architecture. Even Wren's greatest technological and visual triumph, the central dome of St. Paul's, came not from scientific analysis but rather from the experience of earlier construction. To understand this best, one needs to return again to 2nd-century Rome.

The "rediscovery" of the Pantheon as an artistic and architectural ideal during the Renaissance inspired a number of major building projects. The most important, particularly as it relates to St. Paul's, was the rebuilding of St. Peter's Basilica in Rome, begun in 1506. Under the direction of the first principal architect, Donato Bramante (1444–1514),

66

Drawing (above left) by Dutch painter
Maerten van Heemskerck about 1520
shows the massive stone piers architect
Donato Bramante called for to support
the central dome of St. Peter's Basilica in
Rome. Bramante's successors, believing
the piers not massive enough, reinforced
them with additional stone. The dome
itself (left), designed by Michelangelo,
was constructed between 1588 and 1593.
Comparative cross sections of St. Peter's
and the Pantheon (above) reveal that,
whereas the dome of the more ancient,
lower profiled building is well braced
by a massive wall, the enormous raised
dome of the newer building (which
also bears a heavy central lantern) is
supported by a comparatively thin wall.
Consequently, to prevent its spreading
outward, the dome of St. Peter's is girdled
by seven iron chains.

(Top left) Staatliche Museen Preussischer Kulturbesitz
Kupferstichkabinett, Berlin (West); photo, Jörg P.
Anders; (left) Scala/Art Resource; (above) illustration
based on a drawing after Harold Dorn and Robert Mark

construction started on the four massive stone piers that would support the central dome. Although Bramante apparently made no detailed design for the dome itself, the piers set its unsupported diameter at only a meter less than that of the Pantheon. Few large domes had been built in the West since the end of the Roman era, and Bramante was clearly using the Roman building as a prototype. It was left for Michelangelo (1475–1564) to plan and begin the construction of the dome itself, although the dome was not finally completed until 1593.

The dome of Saint Peter's was plagued with structural problems from the beginning. Their major cause becomes evident when sections of St. Peter's and the Pantheon are compared. In the ancient building the dome's outer profile is relatively flat, and buttressing against the outward thrust of the dome is well provided for by the massive cylindrical concrete wall. In order to give St. Peter's dome great visibility, Michelangelo designed it with a very high profile. While this dome exerts an outward thrust similar to that of the Pantheon, it possesses only the relatively thin cylindrical drum below the dome to provide what proved to be inadequate resistance. Thus, the dome began to crack along meridians as it spread outward. Over the years a total of seven iron chains have been placed around the dome to halt the spreading, but the problem is aggravated by the great weight of the masonry dome itself, which generates extremely large outward forces.

Although the diameter of St. Paul's dome was to be but three-quarters that of St. Peter's, Wren seems to have been alarmed by reports of the problems at the Roman basilica, which was a century old when he worked on his design. He worried over his dome for years and hesitated making the final design almost until construction of the dome was begun in 1705. As late as 1694 there are several references in Wren's notes to experimental dome models, and some dome sketches made under his direction and dated 1703 are not yet the final version.

Wren's final solution is based on a majestic, lightweight outer dome profile of lead-sheathed timber, which has relatively little structural function. The outer shell is supported by two structures: a thin, unseen, chain-girdled brick cone, which also holds the 850-ton lantern atop the dome, and a separate brick dome that is seen only from the interior. The brick cone, which provides almost all of the support for the outer dome, has a straight-line profile. Hence, under the weight of the heavy lantern, the cone experiences compression throughout rather than the pernicious tension characteristic of heavy spherical domes.

In further contrast to Saint Peter's, Wren's single iron chain, which acts to girdle the inner brick dome as well as the cone, proved sufficient to maintain the integrity of the relatively light structure against outward thrusts. Numerical model studies of the structure indicated that stresses within the supporting masonry drum below the dome are generally low under both gravity and wind forces and that the single chain is well placed to fulfill its role. In fact, Wren's structural scheme became the standard for all the large dome projects that followed St. Paul's well into the 19th century, including the dome over the U.S. Capitol. As with the

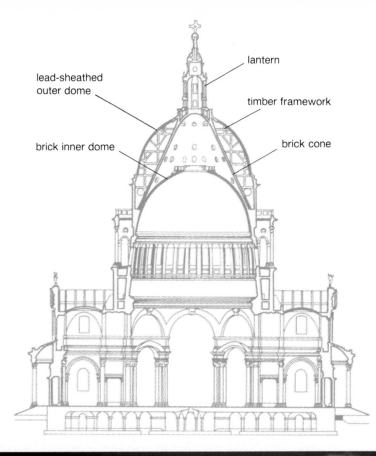

lead-sheathed
outer dome

lantern

timber framework

brick inner dome

brick cone

Although building of St. Paul's Cathedral (below) began in 1675, Wren hesitated in making a final design for the great dome almost until its construction started in 1705. Today the cathedral looks very much as it did when Wren finished it in 1710. Wren's structural solution for the dome (shown in a cross section at left) consists of three layers: an outer dome of lead-sheathed timber, a brick-cone middle layer that supports both the outer dome and the central lantern, and an inner lightweight brick dome. Under the weight of the lantern the cone experiences mainly compressive forces throughout; hence only a single iron chain is needed to prevent outward spreading.

Gothic cathedrals, a successful structure arose from careful reflection on difficulties that had been observed in earlier buildings.

Lessons for modern designers

Our technical studies, spanning almost two millennia of construction, have helped illuminate the "mystery" of the earlier builders—how they achieved remarkable success with large-scale structures. In the first place, early building design followed an evolutionary pattern; practical experience substituted for much of the information that would be available today from numerical modeling. In effect, one or more previous buildings served as models for new design.

Moreover, the elegance of so many of the early structural solutions led us to realize that the master builders used a technique that, although available to today's designers, is rarely exploited because of the usual separation of the modern design office from the building site—and often, too, because of a misplaced confidence in theoretical methods of analysis. The ancient builders could make detailed observations of undesirable behavior, particularly cracking in the fabric of the building, as their designs were being erected. The steps they took to eliminate these shortcomings then led to refinements in design. In a sense, this approach is the forerunner of modern instrumentation of full-scale structures using electronic sensors to detect strains and accelerations (which are usually employed only after major problems in a building show up). In this light one might wonder if construction workers high up in Boston's Hancock Tower were not already well aware of excessive motion in the building's frame even before installation of the glass cladding.

Perhaps most important of all for modern architectural design, the studies indicated a general interaction between structural and stylistic experimentation in early large-scale building. The stepped rings, originally added to reduce pernicious tension in Roman domes, became their stylistic hallmark. Indeed, these rings are found in many domes constructed as late as the 20th century, for example, in the Jefferson Memorial in Washington, D.C., although they are not needed in domes of steel-reinforced concrete. Likewise, the introduction of flying buttresses in Gothic cathedrals had a most profound stylistic effect.

By contrast, the form of Boston's Hancock Tower would seem entirely unrelated to the problem of designing a tall building to withstand high winds. Unlike the early master builders, many architects today feel entirely free to design almost any form of building, no matter what its scale or environment, relying on their consulting engineers to come in after the design is fairly well fixed and somehow make the building perform. This is not to imply that all great architecture must come directly from technological exigency, as shown by Wren's design for a monumental sculptural dome. Nevertheless, all the studies of historic buildings indicate that appropriate structure should always form part of the basic concept of design for large-scale buildings, a point of view that seems sadly lost in the planning of the roof of the Kresge Auditorium and in other contemporary architecture.

70

FOR ADDITIONAL READING

Jean Bony, *French Gothic Architecture of the 12th and 13th Centuries* (University of California Press, 1983).

Harold Dorn and Robert Mark, "The Architecture of Christopher Wren," *Scientific American* (July 1981, pp. 160–173).

J.E. Gordon, *Structures: or, Why Things Don't Fall Down* (Da Capo Press, 1981).

Robert Mark, *Experiments in Gothic Structure* (MIT Press, 1982).

Robert Mark, *Light, Wind, and Structure* (MIT Press/McGraw-Hill, 1990).

Robert Mark and William W. Clark, "Gothic Structural Experimentation," *Scientific American* (November 1984, pp. 176–185).

Robert Mark and Paul Hutchinson, "On the Structure of the Roman Pantheon," *Art Bulletin* (March 1986, pp. 24–34).

Frank Sear, *Roman Architecture* (Batsford, 1982).

E.F. Sekler, *Wren and His Place in European Architecture* (Macmillan, 1956).

Marvin Trachtenberg and Isabelle Hyman, *Architecture, from Prehistory to Post-modernism* (Prentice-Hall/Abrams, 1986).

The dome of the U.S. Capitol building (above), built of iron between 1856 and 1864, is of similar scale to the dome of St. Paul's and employs a similar structure. In fact, Wren's structural approach for St. Paul's became the standard for all large dome projects that followed well into the 19th century. The stepped rings on the dome of the Jefferson Memorial (above left), which was constructed between 1938 and 1943, strongly echo the style of the Pantheon. The rings have become a hallmark for modern domes designed in the classical style, even though they no longer serve the structural purpose for which the Roman master builders developed them.

THE NATIONAL AQUARIUM IN BALTIMORE:

A Window on the World of Water

by Victoria L. Aversa

Dedicated to "education through entertainment," the National Aquarium in Baltimore displays more than 7,000 fish, birds, reptiles, amphibians, marine mammals, and invertebrates in imaginatively designed exhibits.

A pretty, blonde "mermaid" arranged herself on the rocks. A lively crowd was gathering. Harbor and gray seals, oblivious to the commotion, cavorted in the water. Dozens of journalists and photographers, Baltimore, Maryland, residents, and government officials searched the seal pool for signs of Baltimore's mayor. The spectators wanted to see him make good on his promise to take a dip in the seal pool if the National Aquarium in Baltimore did not open on schedule. They were not disappointed. On the morning of July 15, 1981, Mayor William Donald Schaefer, dressed in a gay '90s bathing costume complete with straw boater, entered the aquarium's seal exhibit. He instantly made a "splash" for the soon-to-be-opened aquarium.

This playful episode, while an unusual start for one of the world's great aquariums, epitomizes much of what the National Aquarium in Baltimore represents. Dedicated to education through entertainment, this cultural attraction offers its one million annual visitors the opportunity to look through a window on the "world of water" and to see and enjoy its beauty and magic. The goal is a public that can truly respect aquatic animals and realize the need to protect them—and their environments.

Planning and organization

The mayor's involvement in the aquarium actually began long before his famous dip in the seal pool. Under the Schaefer administration, Baltimore's commissioner of housing and community development, Robert Embry, conceived and championed the idea of an aquarium for the city's waterfront. Both he and the mayor visited Boston's New England Aquarium in 1974 and returned to Baltimore convinced that an aquarium could be a vital component of the city's Inner Harbor redevelopment and a major cultural resource for the region.

Schaefer soon formed a citizen's committee—a group of area leaders from the public and private sector—that would later become the aquarium's board of directors; Frank Gunther, Jr., a local businessman,

72

became its chair. This committee educated Baltimore residents about the aquarium and helped win overwhelming public support for the project. That support was demonstrated in 1976, when city residents voted for a $7.5 million bond issue to fund the Baltimore Aquarium. Two years later ground was broken for the $22 million facility.

Even before the three-year construction project was complete, the aquarium's world-class status was recognized by the United States Congress. In November 1979 Congress passed a bill, sponsored by Sen. Charles Mathias (Rep., Md.) and Rep. Barbara Mikulski (Dem., Md.), that gave the aquatic museum its national designation. This bill recognized that the aquarium would be on the level of other national museums, such as the Smithsonian Institution.

Since its opening on Aug. 8, 1981, the aquarium has lived up to its early promise as a world-class facility. The American Association of Zoological Parks and Aquariums and the American Association of Museums praised it as "well-managed" and as "the standard-setter for other zoos and aquariums."

The facility is operated by a nonprofit corporation, National Aquarium in Baltimore, Inc., which consists of a 21-member board of governors, a larger advisory board, and a full-time paid staff of approximately 200. Under the terms of its management agreement with the city of Baltimore, which owns the building and its Pier 3 site, the nonprofit corporation must strive to remain totally self-supporting. It has met that requirement every year since its opening. In fact, the aquarium's attendance and income have far exceeded expectations.

Despite its national designation the aquarium has received only a modest amount of federal funding—a $2.5 million start-up grant from the Economic Development Administration of the Department of Commerce. Approximately 75% of the aquarium's more than $10 million annual operating budget comes from admission fees. The remainder is raised from corporate and individual memberships, public funds grants, private and business donations, and gift shop sales.

Though one of many cultural institutions in the region, the aquarium has had a major economic impact on the state of Maryland. With an average annual attendance of 1.4 million, it is the state's premier tourist attraction. A 1984 study conducted by Economics Research Associates determined that spending by visitors to the aquarium in fiscal 1984 generated a total of $88 million in income for the region. Figures from the Maryland State Department of Economic and Community Development indicate that the aquarium was responsible for the generation of $3.3 million in state tax receipts and $1.9 million in local tax receipts. In addition, the aquarium's success has contributed to the development of almost 3,000 new jobs and more than 3,000 hotel rooms.

The aquarium's major role in Baltimore's revitalization earned it praise from the *Wall Street Journal* as "the model that other cities look to." As news of its success has spread, the aquarium has served as host to officials from dozens of cities around the world that are planning aquariums to help renew their downtown areas.

VICTORIA L. AVERSA is Public Relations Manager of the National Aquarium in Baltimore, Maryland.

(Overleaf) In the Central Space visitors set forth on a continuous one-way path through the National Aquarium in Baltimore. Marine mammals swim below, a skeletal whale dives overhead, and sharks can be seen in the distance. Photograph © Steve Rosenthal; architects and exhibit designers: Cambridge Seven Associates, Inc.

Architecture

The aquarium serves as an economic motor for the city's Inner Harbor area, but it is much more. Designed by Peter Chermayeff of Cambridge Seven Associates (Boston), the aquarium is an award-winning architectural tour de force using innovative exhibitions to introduce visitors to its more than 5,000 inhabitants—fish, birds, reptiles, amphibians, marine mammals, and invertebrates from almost every part of the globe. It acts as a living classroom for scientists, educators, and schoolchildren.

The exuberant, seven-level structure, which *National Geographic* magazine predicted would be one of the most photographed buildings in the world, successfully captures the aquarium's theme to make known the unity of life through water and perfectly suits its Inner Harbor setting. Its pyramid roofs call to mind sails in the wind or the prows of ships. A

(Opposite page) On July 15, 1981, dressed in a "Gay '90s" bathing suit, Baltimore Mayor William Schaefer fulfills a promise to take a dip in the seal pool if the National Aquarium did not open on the scheduled date. At left and below are exterior and aerial views of the aquarium, which is located on Pier 3 of Baltimore's Inner Harbor.

(Opposite page) National Aquarium in Baltimore; photo, Valerie Chase; (this page, left) © Steve Rosenthal; (below) © Ron Haisfield

The seal pool (above), located outside the aquarium building, re-creates the rocky New England coast to provide a suitable habitat for gray and harbor seals. Spiraled ramp (above right) takes visitors through the center of two exhibits, the Atlantic Coral Reef (top) inhabited by more than 1,000 colorful tropical fish and the Open Ocean (bottom) featuring several kinds of sharks.

(Left) © Robert Noonan; (right) © Steve Rosenthal

gaily painted mural on its west side recalls colorful signal flags—like the ones spelling "National Aquarium in Baltimore" at the facility's circular entrance. Viewed from the air, the facility's exterior even bears a striking resemblance to a fish—a fact only recently observed by an imaginative local resident during a helicopter ride.

Exhibits

The aquarium's introduction to the world of water actually begins outside the building. Even before they enter the aquarium, visitors have an opportunity to learn about harbor and gray seals from a 265,000-liter (70,000-gallon) exhibit that re-creates the rocky New England coast. At this free display visitors can discover the unique characteristics of these playful marine mammals during three daily demonstrations.

From the seal pool on the wharf level, visitors ride an escalator to the aquarium's lobby. There, transparent cylinders of bubbling blue water suggest the aquatic environment waiting inside. In the aquarium's central space, visitors get their first glimpse of a different world—the quiet and shadowy ocean depths. Two beluga whales frolic in an enormous pool. Through the window of a nearby tank, sharks glide by at eye level. The sounds of the sea—shore birds, whale songs, and buoy bells—reverberate through the cavernous space. Light, reflected against mirrored surfaces, shifts and shimmers much as it would underwater.

From this mesmerizing introduction visitors move on a continuous one-way path through the building. They walk through galleries and travel on escalators up one side of the building until they reach a rooftop rain forest. Then they wind down again on ramps through the center of two large ring-shaped tanks.

This aquatic journey starts close to home with a look at four Maryland habitats. On the aquarium's second level visitors begin at a freshwater pond in Maryland's Allegheny Mountains, continue to a tidal marsh and a coastal beach, and end at the Atlantic Ocean.

Along the route the exhibits are carefully organized by themes such as adaptation, habitat, and behavior in order to aid in the learning process. Chermayeff and the aquarium staff wanted visitors to understand the interrelationships among ecosystems and marvel at the ways in which animals adapt to their environments—not simply to stare at a collection of fish tanks.

In addition to the thematically arranged displays, the aquarium offers a variety of methods of audiovisual communication—graphics, photos, video, and sound effects—that enhance the illusion of an underwater journey. A striking example is the third-floor gallery, Surviving Through Adaptation. At its entrance a mural of oversized, close-up photographs of animal eyes, beaks, tails, and fins greets the viewer and dramatically introduces the theme of the gallery. By viewing displays such as Feeding, Hiding and Displaying, and Living Together, visitors discover how the giant Pacific octopus evolved a beak to crush the hardest crab shell and how the sightless anemone depends on chance to catch its prey.

The aquarium's fourth-floor gallery takes visitors on a tour of habitats from the North Atlantic to the Pacific. At the Sea Cliffs exhibit visitors can witness how three subarctic seabird species—puffins, murres, and razorbills—"fly" underwater in search of their food. Around the corner is one of the most popular exhibits—the Children's Cove. This re-creation of two tide pools from the Atlantic and Pacific coasts allows children of all ages to touch and hold starfish, horseshoe crabs, and sea urchins.

Photo mural at the entrance to the gallery Surviving Through Adaptation (below left) introduces the gallery's theme with close-up photographs of animal eyes, beaks, tails, and fins. Below, a tidal marsh is re-created as part of an exhibit of four Maryland habitats.

(Left) © Robert Noonan; (right) © Steve Rosenthal

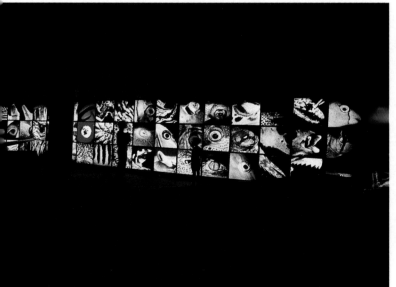

From the fourth floor visitors ride an escalator to the 19.5-meter (64-foot)-high glass pyramid on the roof of the aquarium. Awaiting them there are the sights and sounds of a completely different habitat, the South American rain forest. In this humid jungle visitors can spot a growing collection of free-ranging tropical birds, reptiles, and amphibians amid the lush foliage. Observant explorers might even catch a glimpse of the careful movements of a pair of two-toed sloths or the courtship behaviors of the scarlet ibis.

Not a typical exhibit in most aquariums, the South American rain forest illustrates the theme that all life depends on water. It is there that the aquarium most powerfully demonstrates its growing commitment to conservation by educating the public about the need to save the world's rain forests from destruction.

The adjacent Hidden Life exhibit completes the rain forest experience. This series of naturalistic displays provides visitors with a close-up look at the usually unseen inhabitants of the jungle. There, the aquarium displays the colorful members of its poison arrow frog collection, one of the largest in the country, as well as many other species of small but exotic reptiles and amphibians.

From the heights of the rain forest, travelers descend to the depths of the ocean—the 1.2 million-liter (335,000-gallon), ring-shaped Atlantic Coral Reef exhibit. Through four-meter (13-foot)-high windows, visitors get a diver's view of more than 1,000 beautifully colored tropical fish. A "talking diver" adds to the entertainment and educational value of this exhibit. Volunteer divers suit up in a French-designed helmet that enables them to communicate with people on the other side of the glass. With this new technology a diver can, while feeding the gathering parrotfish and rays, answer questions and describe the characteristics of the hawksbill turtle swimming nearby.

Visitors continue down another level to the 832,700-liter (220,000-gallon) Open Ocean exhibit. The circular design brings them face-to-face with some of the most mysterious and menacing inhabitants of the ocean: sharks. Sand tiger, brown, lemon, and nurse sharks—some as long as 2.7 meters (nine feet)—swim relentlessly past the onlookers. If anyone gets nervous, however, it is an easy escape from the depths of the shark tank—a quick escalator ride back up to the lobby, where the underwater adventure began.

Education programs

Before, during, or after their visit, visitors can increase their understanding of the world of water by taking advantage of the aquarium's many educational opportunities. With quick answers and entertaining anecdotes, volunteer exhibit guides work to make the visitor's experience more meaningful and enjoyable. They invite children and adults to touch such models and artifacts as shark jaws and fan corals. At the information desk receptionists welcome visitors to the aquarium with a newly developed exhibit brochure. Other volunteers help maintain exhibits and conduct discovery sessions. Participating in one of the largest programs

Young visitors join an aquarium guide at the Children's Cove, where they can touch and hold starfish, horseshoe crabs, and sea urchins.

© Robert Noonan

78

A South American rain forest (above left and right) is re-created under a glass pyramid on the roof of the aquarium. Tropical birds, reptiles, and amphibians can be seen amid the lush vegetation of this humid jungle.

of its kind in the country, all of the aquarium's 500 volunteers receive extensive training that equips them to assist every visitor, from the budding scientist to the established marine biologist.

Perhaps inspired by what they have seen or by the enthusiasm of a knowledgeable volunteer, many visitors decide to attend the aquarium's education programs for members, schools, and community groups. Each year the aquarium sponsors dozens of tours, workshops, excursions, performances, and lectures for its 65,000 members as well as for the general public. These innovative programs, which are geared to every age and interest level, range from Breakfast with the Belugas for children to Dolphin Lab for teens and Wilderness Weekends for adults. Whether educational or recreational, all of the programs have an aquatic theme and make use of the aquarium as well as local parks and rivers.

In a partnership with regional school systems, more than 120,000 students from the Middle Atlantic states visit the aquarium on field trips and attend one of three different programs. Offered in the aquarium's classrooms, auditorium, and galleries, these programs focus on specific habitats or animal groups and serve as an invaluable supplement to traditional classroom work.

The aquarium's role as a "living classroom" has also been enhanced by the introduction of a marine science curriculum funded by the National Science Foundation. Developed by the aquarium biologist for elementary school students, the Living in Water curriculum is now being used by educators in Baltimore and in many other schools in the United States.

For several months each year aquarium education staff members also take a little bit of the world of water on the road to dozens of recreation centers, senior citizen homes, hospitals, and schools. Using live animals, artifacts, and other educational materials, these outreach specialists conduct a dozen participatory programs for community residents of all ages.

With a full schedule of special events, discount opportunities, and educational programs, the aquarium continually demonstrates its commitment to improving the quality of life for the Baltimore citizens who helped support it. The Aquarium Cares, an annual event, treats mentally and physically disabled children and adults to exclusive visiting hours, guided tours, and other activities. Dollar Day, the aquarium's popular anniversary celebration, offers free day-long entertainment on the pier and a $1 admission to the exhibits. Fridays after Five, one of approximately 200 discount opportunities, features reduced admission on Friday evenings during the fall and winter months.

These public events are complemented by programs such as the Henry Hall Scholarship Awards. Named after a scientist who donated his fish collection to the aquarium, this endowed program provides minority youth in Baltimore with opportunities to pursue careers in marine biology.

New educational programs at the aquarium aim to educate the public not just about the aquatic environment but also about the need to protect it. Visitors learn about the destruction of the world's rain forests from a newly created fiber-optics exhibit. Animal identification labels

(Opposite page, top to bottom, left and right) Among the many kinds of animals displayed at the National Aquarium are a basilisk lizard, common iguana, sand tiger shark, blue-crowned motmot, gray seal, and a clown fish swimming among the tentacles of a sea anemone. The ring-shaped 1.2 million-liter (335,000-gallon) Atlantic Coral Reef exhibit (above) provides a diver's view of more than 1,000 tropical fish.

and graphics panels highlight endangered species. A multiprojector slide show focuses on the pollution of Chesapeake Bay and discusses action that can be taken to preserve this important resource.

The need for environmental protection has been and will continue to be the focus of lecture series and programs for members. As part of its 1989 Water Planet lecture series, the aquarium brought in such renowned marine biologists as Eugenie Clark to discuss topics including sharks, coral reef ecology, and rain forests. Programs for members have even included several recycling days during which local companies joined forces with the aquarium to create a recycling center.

Breeding and other conservation efforts

The aquarium's growing commitment to conservation education received a behind-the-scenes boost in the late 1980s with the animal care staff's increased efforts to breed rare or threatened rain forest species. In 1988 and 1989 the aquarium became the first zoo or aquarium in the U.S. to breed dusky tree frogs and several species of poison arrow frogs, which, because of the destruction of their habitats, had been designated "threatened" by the Convention on the International Trade of Endangered Species (CITES).

Most notable was the breeding of the rare blue poison arrow frog. Aquarium herpetologists made national headlines with an unusual innovation that was a key to reproducing this brilliantly colored Central and South American species. After years of study scientists found that the bottoms of plastic two-liter soda bottles, when turned upside down, provided much-needed privacy for these diurnal amphibians. The overwhelming success of its frog-breeding program (hundreds of these species have been raised over the years) has enabled the aquarium to send these threatened amphibians to dozens of zoos and aquariums.

Additionally, the aquarium has bred numerous species of tropical birds and reptiles as well as bonnethead sharks and harbor seals. In 1986 the aquatic facility became the first zoo or aquarium in the world to breed the yellow-hooded blackbird. In 1989 a fish-breeding program was in the initial stages of development.

A technician monitors the aquarium's sand filtration system (above right). Sand filters are used to help control water purity for all the aquarium tanks. Below, one of the aquarium's bird specialists prepares food for the puffins.

82

Conservation of species is also a goal of much of the aquarium's research program. Aquarium scientists have undertaken numerous studies with the goal of breeding specific aquatic animals, particularly those whose populations are dwindling in the wild. For example, during the summers of 1988 and 1989 aquarium aviculturists went to Heimay, Iceland, to study the conditions that the Atlantic puffin, a subarctic seabird, needs in order to reproduce. For two weeks on the cliffs of the Westmannjer Islands, aquarium staff worked side by side with volunteers and aquarium members to compile information on the behavior, characteristics, and breeding habits of these fascinating seabirds.

Other research efforts focused on improving the aquarium's conservation practices and increasing the staff's knowledge of aquatic animals in the wild. These efforts gained momentum in 1985, when the aquarium sponsored the first conference of its kind in the world on "Sharks: Recent Advances in Captive Biology." This gathering of scientists from across the United States and several other countries resulted in a major publication that has helped zoos and aquariums improve their care of a variety of shark species.

The aquarium's recent research projects have focused on several species of sharks and frogs. At a newly established shark collection and research station on the North Carolina coast, aquarists—staff who work with the aquarium's fish—tagged numerous species and took blood samples. Back in the aquarium's laboratories, scientists used this information to make comparative studies on blood from sharks in and out of the wild.

Aquarium herpetologists—staff who care for reptiles and amphibians—have initiated a pharmacological research project in conjunction with the National Institutes of Health. Scientists working on this project have traveled to Costa Rica to study the alkaloids in the skin of poison arrow frogs.

Future plans

As the aquarium approaches the end of a spectacular first decade, it is completing an exciting expansion of its ability to present the entire world of water to its visitors. Construction is under way on an 8,750-square

Students participating in a gifted and talented program at the aquarium perform an experiment on a field trip in Maryland (below left). As part of its commitment to save rare or threatened rain forest species, the aquarium succeeded in breeding blue poison arrow frogs (below).

meter (94,000-square foot) addition to the original building. Scheduled to open in the summer of 1990, the $35 million Marine Mammal Pavilion will be one of the most comprehensive whale and dolphin exhibits in the world. This new facility will house the aquarium's current beluga whales along with six Atlantic bottlenose dolphins in a safe and comfortable habitat that melds the needs of the animals with the interests of the visitors.

On the exterior the pavilion is designed to complement and closely resemble the existing aquarium. Its pyramids, angles, materials, and colors will echo those of the original building. The interior space, however, will contrast sharply with the original building's dark and shadowy underwater ambiance. Architect James R. Grieves of Grieves Associates (Baltimore) has re-created the feeling of the outdoors with a large, open atrium, massive windows, and an enormous skylight that offers a panoramic view of the Baltimore harbor.

The centerpiece of the new pavilion will be a cluster of four separate pools that will hold a total of 4.5 million liters (1.2 million gallons) and measure up to seven meters (22 feet) deep. The design of these pools will give the dolphins and whales plenty of room for swimming, diving, and other natural behaviors. Three of the pools will act as resting areas and provide privacy for the animals. The main pool will serve as the site of several daily educational presentations for the public.

Surrounding the pools will be a 1,300-seat amphitheatre that will offer every visitor a close-up look at these fascinating marine mammals. That view will be improved by the exhibit's enormous acrylic windows, believed to be the longest in the world, which will allow spectators to see the animals from both above and below the water. "Slide-out" areas will enable selected visitors to meet and touch the mammals as they "beach" on the exhibit's edge.

The public's interaction with live animals will be augmented by the pavilion's arcade of hands-on exhibits. A variety of educational displays will focus on the physical characteristics and special abilities of dolphins and whales, from baleen and blowholes to songs and sounds. In addition, a life-size model of Scylla, a real humpback whale from the New England coast, will serve as a lesson on whale anatomy. Children and adults will be able to observe Scylla, from her flukes to her tail, through a series of viewer scopes.

Also near completion, the Aquatic Education Resource Center will help the aquarium meet the ever growing demand for educational programs for schoolchildren. It will house two classrooms and a teacher resource room that will make the aquarium's extensive collection of aquatic science materials available to teachers for the first time.

Strengthening the aquarium's commitment to marine mammals will be the pavilion's Animal Care and Research Complex. Destined to be one of the most advanced aquatic animal care centers in the world, the complex will expand the aquarium's program of preventive medicine, enable its staff to provide emergency treatment to stranded animals from the wild, and provide its scientists with the resources to investigate and diagnose diseases in aquatic animals.

Artist's drawings portray the exterior and interior (opposite page, top and bottom) of the Marine Mammal Pavilion, scheduled to open in 1990. The 8,750-square meter (94,000-square foot) addition to the original building will house whales and dolphins in a cluster of four pools. The largest pool will be used as the site of several daily presentations for the public.

Photos, National Aquarium in Baltimore

The impact of the National Aquarium in Baltimore goes beyond its considerable power to entertain and fascinate. With welcoming architecture, stunning exhibits, lively educational programs, and ongoing research, the aquarium teaches visitors to understand and love the world of water. In these days of oil spills and polluted beaches, few lessons seem more important to the future. As the African ecologist Baba Dioum said: "In the end, we will conserve only what we love, we will love only what we understand, we will understand only what we are taught."

DOLPHINS OF SHARK BAY

by Barbara B. Smuts, Richard Connor,
Janet Mann, Andrew Richards,
and Rachel Smolker

A large group of human-habituated wild dolphins living off
the coast of Western Australia is offering marine biologists and
primatologists unprecedented views into dolphin social life, which
shows a striking convergence with that of chimpanzees.

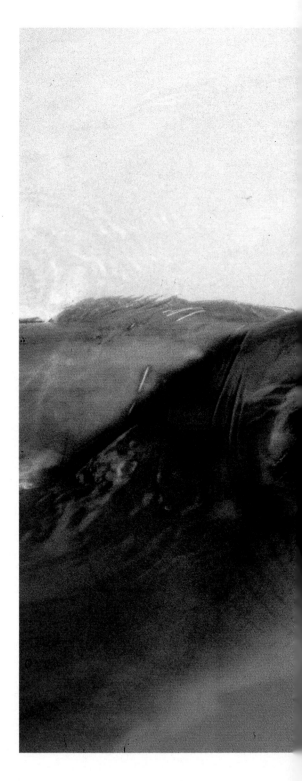

At a remote fishing camp on the shore of Shark Bay, Western Australia,
we emerge from our tents, converge on the beach, and await the gift that
each dawn brings. A grey fin appears in the distance and, moving closer,
resolves into two—one large, one small. Reflecting the first rays of the
Sun, the larger fin curves distinctly to one side. We wade into the cool
water as the adult female dolphin Crooked Fin and her infant, Cookie,
move in graceful synchrony toward shore, surfacing to breathe in the
shallow water. Within moments several other dolphins join Crooked Fin
and Cookie, and we, in turn, are joined by a dozen tourists, each eager
to touch the smooth surface of a dolphin's skin as the animal glides past.
Thus, another day begins at Monkey Mia camp, the only place in the
world where wild dolphins regularly come into shore and accept fish and
physical contact from human beings.

For at least 25 years and perhaps longer, a small number of Monkey
Mia dolphins have been taking fish handouts, at first from local fisher-
men and later from tourists. The same features that attract the tourists—
"tame" wild dolphins—first brought two members of our research team,
Rachel Smolker and Richard Connor, to Monkey Mia in 1982. The tame
dolphins were accustomed to people, and by following them in small
boats offshore, we gradually succeeded in habituating members of their
social network that do not come into shore or interact with people. By
1990 we recognized more than 250 individual dolphins that frequent the
waters near Monkey Mia. As with Crooked Fin, identification is based
on the distinct shape of the dorsal fin and the nicks on it, which are
documented in a photographic catalog.

The ability to distinguish individuals and to observe them at close
quarters has proved critical to our study, which derives inspiration from
the pioneering research of such primate field-workers as Jane Goodall
and Dian Fossey. By observing known individuals for many years, primatologists discovered that nonhuman primates live in highly structured
societies based on long-term social bonds. Compared with most other
mammals, nonhuman primates show a long period of infant dependency,
characterized by the development of enduring attachments to maternal

A bottle-nosed dolphin negotiates the shallow water at Monkey Mia, Western Australia, to accept a food handout from tourists. The unusual habituation of wild dolphins in Shark Bay to human beings has given researchers the unprecedented opportunity to study in detail the social behavior of these large-brained mammals.

Barbara B. Smuts

BARBARA B. SMUTS *is Associate Professor of Psychology and Anthropology at the University of Michigan, Ann Arbor.* **RICHARD CONNOR** *and* **ANDREW RICHARDS** *are Graduate Students in Biology and* **JANET MANN** *and* **RACHEL SMOLKER** *are Graduate Students in Psychology at the University of Michigan. All authors are affiliated with the Evolution and Human Behavior Program of the University of Michigan.*

(Overleaf) Photograph, Barbara B. Smuts

kin and by opportunities to learn a wide variety of skills critical to survival and reproduction. To a greater extent than most other mammals, primates show complex and flexible patterns of competition and cooperation, including opportunistic "political" alliances and long-term friendships between unrelated individuals. Scientists have suggested that these special primate features are linked to their unusually large brains, and some have even argued that natural selection favored large brains in primates, including humans, because of the advantages that a superior intellect afforded in the social domain.

Dolphins and porpoises are particularly interesting in this regard because with the possible exception of elephants, they are the only mammals other than primates that have evolved comparably large and complex brains. Very little is known, however, about the behavior of dolphins in the wild. Our objective at Monkey Mia is to begin to fill this gap by describing in detail the social behavior of wild bottle-nosed dolphins, which are species of *Tursiops*. Ultimately we hope to determine the ways in which dolphin societies resemble and differ from those of nonhuman primates (and of other terrestrial mammals).

The focus on such comparative questions explains why the Shark Bay dolphins have attracted the interest of biologists, primatologists, anthropologists, and psychologists. Barbara Smuts, trained in anthropology and biology, has studied social relationships in rhesus monkeys, chimpanzees, and baboons. Biologist Richard Connor is interested in the evolution of social behavior. Janet Mann, a comparative biopsychologist, has studied mother-infant relationships in human and nonhuman primates. Trained as a mathematician, Andrew Richards was drawn to evolutionary biology through his long-standing interest in dolphins. Rachel Smolker, a psychobiologist, has observed spinner dolphins and killer whales and is particularly interested in animal communication. Together, the members of our group hope to unravel some of the mysteries of dolphin society.

Studying wild dolphins

Since 1984 various team members have spent a minimum of three to four months each year observing the Shark Bay dolphins. We collect data mainly during the austral winter (May through August) but also have done so at other times of the year. We conduct behavioral observations of both the "inshore" tame dolphins that regularly visit Monkey Mia (whose numbers have varied from five to eight over the last six years) and the much larger number of "offshore" dolphins that range within the surrounding waters. Although the behavior of the inshore dolphins is clearly affected by their interactions with tourists, they interact among themselves in ways routinely seen offshore, allowing us to view their social lives in the sort of detail normally possible only in captivity. Thus, the inshore observations provide insight into the behavior of the offshore dolphins. Our research so far has focused on four areas: male relationships, female relationships, infant development, and communication.

Using small boats with outboard motors, we routinely patrol an area of 100 square kilometers (40 square miles) searching for dolphins. When

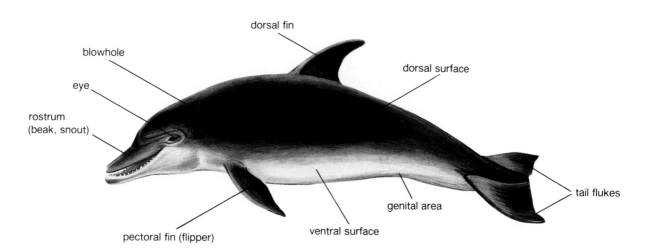

dorsal fin

blowhole

eye

dorsal surface

rostrum
(beak, snout)

tail flukes

genital area

pectoral fin (flipper)

ventral surface

a group, or party, is sighted, we record its activity (*e.g.*, feeding, resting, traveling, socializing) and which individuals are present, and then we move on to search for other parties. This survey method, pioneered in the 1970s by Randall S. Wells, Bernd Würsig, and their colleagues, provides data on dolphin activities, demography, and party composition. Bottle-nosed dolphins in Shark Bay are difficult to sex because males and females look the same and are about the same size, approximately 2.3 meters (7.5 feet) long as adults. Conveniently, however, the Shark Bay dolphins often enjoy riding the bow of our boats upside down, allowing us to view their genitals and record the sex of known individuals. We have also obtained rough estimates of ages by recording the degree of speckling of the ventral surface, which begins around sexual maturity and gradually increases with age.

Detailed information on social interactions is gathered by means of focal sampling techniques derived from primate field studies. During our focal samples, observers follow one individual for as many hours as possible and systematically record specific, clearly defined activities and behaviors, including associations and interactions with other dolphins. The Shark Bay dolphins exhibit a rich repertoire of social interactions, both affiliative and aggressive. Affiliative interactions include rubbing of body parts, called petting, which appears to maintain social bonds in much the same way as does primate grooming. Shark Bay dolphins also show synchronous movement patterns, often indicated by synchronous surfacing. Aggressive interactions include chasing, hitting, and biting.

Ecology

Shark Bay is a large, shallow inlet of the Indian Ocean on the western edge of the Australian continent. Its bottom is covered with extensive sea-grass beds and sandy flats bisected by channels of deeper water. The bay supports a wide variety of marine life, including dugongs, sea turtles, sharks, sea snakes, and numerous seabirds such as cormorants, gulls, and pelicans.

Bottle-nosed dolphins are entirely carnivorous. They eat a wide variety of fish, both schooling and solitary species. We have occasionally seen

The bottle-nosed dolphin (species of Tursiops) is widely distributed in tropical and temperate seas and is the dolphin most often seen performing at aquariums and zoos. It and other cetaceans (members of the whale order) are descended from four-legged, meat-eating, terrestrial ancestors. Over the course of the past 70 million years the front limbs have evolved into paddle-shaped pectoral fins (flippers), the external hind limbs have disappeared, and the tail has developed a pair of horizontal flukes. Powerful vertical movements of the tail produce forward motion, while the pectoral fins help in balancing and steering. All cetaceans must come to the water's surface to breathe through blowholes located on top of their heads. Infant dolphins nurse from mammary slits located on either side of the genital opening of the female.

89

Bibi, a tame male dolphin (right), rolls belly up alongside a research boat in Shark Bay, allowing a view of the animal's genitals and of the ventral speckling, typical of adult dolphins, that gradually increases with age. (Below) Two males from a coalition engage in body rubbing, or petting, activity. Such affiliative interactions appear to maintain social bonds in much the same way as does primate grooming.

(Top) Andrew Richards; (bottom) Barbara B. Smuts

them take squid, rays, and even small sharks. Mixed groups of birds, mostly pelicans and cormorants, often feed in association with dolphins, and both the birds and the dolphins seem to use each other as cues for the presence of fish concentrations. The dolphins often trap smaller fish against the surface and pursue them by swimming rapidly upside down (possibly because a dolphin's best stereoscopic vision is beneath it), a behavior we call snacking. Before consuming a large fish, a dolphin may carry it around and break the head off by rubbing it against the bottom.

A bizarre dolphin behavior, which we think may be a foraging method, involves sponge carrying. Five particular females regularly carry cone-shaped sponges on their snouts for hours at a time in a particular area of the bay. One plausible hypothesis is that they use the sponge as protection from the spines of a poisonous fish known to occur in the area where these females forage.

Patterns of association

The Shark Bay dolphins live in a "fission-fusion" society, one in which individuals associate in small parties whose composition frequently

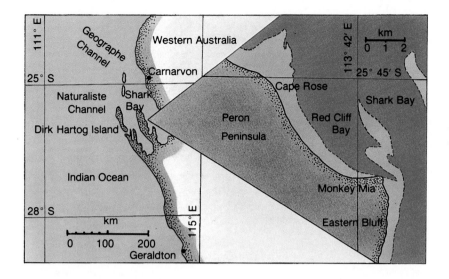

Shark Bay is a large, shallow inlet of the Indian Ocean on the extreme western coast of Australia. It is bisected by the Peron Peninsula, on the eastern shore of which lies Monkey Mia, the fishing camp where small numbers of the bay's dolphins began associating with humans at least a quarter century ago.

changes. (This association pattern is unusual among mammals in general, but intriguingly it is also found in chimpanzees and several other nonhuman primates.) Dolphin parties average 4–5 members excluding dependent infants, but they can vary in size from one to 30. Although the sex ratio of the population is roughly 1:1, only about half of the parties contain both sexes; the remainder are evenly divided between all-female and all-male groups.

Analysis of the association patterns of 50 individuals that we see on a regular basis reveals intriguing sex differences. Males are reliably found in the company of one or two particular other males, and their associations prove stable over several years. Females also associate preferentially with same-sex partners, but these associations are less consistent than the male pairs and triplets. Some females spend considerable time alone.

Male coalitions and herding behavior

We puzzled over these male association patterns. What exactly were the males doing in their tight pairs and triplets, and why did particular groups often travel together? On a calm March morning in 1987, three inshore males, Snubby, Sickle, and Bibi, provided us with a large piece of the puzzle.

The regular dolphins had arrived inshore with a strange dolphin we had never seen before. The stranger, later identified as a female, suddenly turned and bolted seaward, leaving a trail of "flukeprints" in her wake. All three males rocketed after her. A thrashing and splashing some distance offshore signaled an end to the chase, and a few minutes later the new female returned to shore with the males. The stranger did not stay long, though; within seconds she bolted again. Again the males chased her, and again they escorted her back to shore, tightly flanking her. Clearly, the strange female was being brought into Monkey Mia against her will.

In many species of mammals, males attempt to limit or control the movements of females with aggressive behavior termed herding. Herding can be considered a strategy that a male employs to increase his chance

Associating male chimpanzees (above) share prey, while the three male dolphins Snubby, Sickle, and Bibi (right) travel together. Unlike mammals in general, both chimpanzees and the dolphins studied at Shark Bay show complex, flexible patterns of cooperation, including mutually advantageous alliances and long-term friendships.

(Top) David Bygott—Anthro-Photo; (right) Richard Connor

of siring a female's offspring by isolating her from other males. The dolphins' behavior is unusual, however, because herding is performed by males in groups rather than by individuals, as is typical for nonhuman primates and other mammals. We refer to the male pairs and triplets as coalitions, a term used to describe groups of at least two individuals that jointly direct aggression against other members of the same species, in this case the herded female. We are not certain why male dolphins jointly herd single females. It may simply be that a male by himself cannot herd a female. Alternatively, a male herding alone may be unsuccessful in the face of competition from males working together.

In 1987 and 1988 Snubby, Sickle, and Bibi herded females into Mon-

key Mia like clockwork. Observations of more than 200 cases of herding by the inshore triplet, lasting from several minutes to 11 days, enabled us to study the phenomenon in extraordinary detail and, in addition, taught us to recognize cases of herding by other groups of males during offshore observations. Between 1987 and 1989 we documented more than 50 cases of herding by 10 other pairs or triplets, the longest lasting over 28 days. Clearly, herding is a general phenomenon in our study population.

A herding event begins when a coalition of males captures a female. If the female flees during a capture attempt, a long chase or series of chases may result. The longest pursuit we witnessed lasted 85 minutes and covered 7.2 kilometers (4.5 miles). When the female does not attempt to flee, the males rapidly approach her and engage in excited, rapid surfacings and social behavior, including synchronous displays around the female, who then accompanies the males. The displays often involve spectacular aerial acrobatics, such as leaping from the water in opposite directions or leaping toward each other and crossing at the apex of the leaps. It is not clear whether the displays are directed at coalition partners or the female.

As we first saw on that March morning in 1987, herded females often attempt to escape. The males, however, have more to worry about than escaping females. On six occasions we saw two coalitions of males charge another coalition and aggressively take the female that the latter group had been herding. We refer to such combined coalitions as second-order coalitions. Four of the "thefts" were over almost as soon as they began since the outnumbered males were easily vanquished by the combined forces of two coalitions. In the other two cases, however, the coalition under assault was in the company of another coalition that came to its defense. These engagements between two second-order coalitions were protracted affairs, the longer lasting 70 minutes during which the dolphins chased and fought for more than eight kilometers (five miles). Such observations help us to understand why pairs and triplets spend a lot of time engaged in friendly interactions with certain other coalitions. Indeed, during the mating season we often see two coalitions, one or both with herded females, shadowing each other in their travels. They may be hundreds of meters apart, but if one changes direction, so does the other. We suspect that shadowing may be a defensive association that offers protection from potential attacks by other coalitions.

Coalitions between two or more animals are common among primates and some other animals, but second-order coalitions are rare and may depend on sophisticated capacities for social cognition. In addition, the coalitions formed by male pairs and triplets in Shark Bay appear more cooperative and stable than those typical of male nonhuman primates, suggesting that dolphins may equal or in some cases surpass monkeys and apes in their capacity to form mutually advantageous, long-term social bonds.

Female behavior and social relationships

We do not yet understand female behavior as well as that of males. While male association patterns are fairly consistent, those of females are more variable. Female associations appear to be influenced by age and reproductive condition and probably by factors unique to each individual, such as who a female's mother is and how many close female relatives she has. Some Shark Bay females, like one we call Yogi, have been loners for years, rarely associating with other adults. Others, like Square, are consistently more sociable. The association patterns of some females vary a great deal over time and appear to be influenced by reproductive

A coalition consisting of a triplet of males surfaces in tight synchrony behind a herded female (below left). Although the males of many mammalian species attempt to limit or control the movements of females with herding, dolphin behavior is unusual in that herding is done by males in groups rather than by individuals. (Below) Two males perform a synchronous display around a herded female that has not attempted to flee.

Photos, Richard Connor

state. For example, Uhf had more extensive associations with a wider
variety of dolphins both before she gave birth to her most recent infant
and after this infant died than during the two years she was nursing it.

When they do join others, adult females tend to associate preferentially with other females. Some associate regularly with particular female
partners. Even the strongest female-female associations, however, are
less consistent than those of male coalition partners. We know of two
pairs of mothers and daughters who have maintained a strong association
after the daughter reached adulthood. These pairs involved tame inshore
dolphins that were identified before our study began. Because we do
not have information on genetic relatedness for other adult members of
our study population, we do not know whether kinship strongly influences the Shark Bay dolphins' social relationships, as it does those of
nonhuman primates. There are indications, however, from Wells's study
population of *Tursiops* in Florida that female-female associations are
strongest among kin.

A small number of observations indicate that females may cooperate in
the context of sexual harassment by males, for example, during herding
attempts. These incidents range from the possible "hiding" of a recently
herded female between two other females to occasions in which a pair
or triplet of males apparently was swamped by a large female group and
so was prevented from continued harassment. While such incidents are
uncommon, they may be quite significant to the individuals involved.
Intriguingly, female-female cooperation against male harassment also
occurs in nonhuman primates.

On other occasions, sexually receptive females appear to accompany
male coalitions willingly. Dolphin females typically associate with, and
presumably mate with, several different males while sexually receptive.
(We rarely are able to confirm actual copulations, because we cannot
see the dolphins' genital areas clearly enough.) In bottle-nosed dolphins,
as in most other mammals, there is no evidence that males provide any
direct paternal care for young.

94

Mother-infant relationships and infant development

Since 1988 we have conducted detailed observations of 12 mothers with infants ranging in age from five months to five years. We plan to follow these mothers and infants for several years, until the offspring become independent. The life history of Shark Bay dolphins is strikingly like that of chimpanzees, including the age at which females bear their first young (around 12 years), long intervals between births (4–5 years), and long potential life spans (probably around 40–50 years). Given these similarities, our study aims to determine the ways in which the mother-infant relationship and patterns of infant development resemble and differ from those observed among chimpanzees and other primates.

Following a 12-month pregnancy, a single infant is typically born during the austral summer, between September and February. Because

The infants of both apes and dolphins spend much time in maternal contact. While ape infants cling to the mother's belly (above), dolphin infants travel in a "baby position" just beneath the mother's tail (left), where they may receive a hydrodynamic boost from their mother's wake.

(Top) I. Devore—Anthro-Photo; (left) Barbara B. Smuts

newborns arrive with little blubber and the energetic requirements of lactating mothers are high, these warmer months may provide the best chances for infant survival. Even so, infant mortality is high in Shark Bay, at least in part because of predation by sharks. Two infants have been observed with severe injuries apparently inflicted by sharks, and a number of juveniles and adults bear scars from shark attacks.

Although our observations have concentrated on infants over five months of age, we know from captive research that dolphin infants, like ape infants, nurse frequently for the first few months, as often as every half hour. Both ape and dolphin infants spend a great deal of time in contact with their mothers. While ape infants cling to the mother's belly, dolphin infants swim in a "baby position" just beneath the mother's tail.

Despite lengthy maternal contact, dolphin infants approach and leave their mothers frequently, often going to great distances (more than a kilometer, or 0.6 mile) when only a few months old. Such separations would pose great dangers to the ape infant, who seldom leaves the mother's side during the first two years of life. However, features of the marine environment, particularly a lack of barriers to impede travel,

combined with dolphins' superior locomotor abilities, may lessen the risks of mother-infant separation for dolphins. In addition, it is possible that dolphin infants are less vulnerable than primate infants to harassment by other group members.

The ability to wander from the mother enables dolphin infants to explore their physical and social world with relative freedom. When on their own, infants often associate with other dolphins. Some infants develop strong bonds with one another and seek each other out for play and other types of socializing. Sometimes infants will travel with older siblings, adolescents, or adult females. Male infants in particular appear to seek out and associate with adult male coalitions. When socializing with other dolphins, infants engage in social-sexual behaviors commonly seen among adults. During intensive socializing, infants may pet, mount, goose, and chase other dolphins. Adults are frequently seen soliciting interactions and play with infants. An adult male, for example, may lie passively on his side, inviting the infant to mount and rub against him.

Dolphin infants do not live by mother's milk alone. At six to seven months of age, infants begin to catch and consume small fish. The earliest observations of fish catching by infants involve snacking. Often we see the silvery fish skittering about the water surface as the infant visually tracks, echolocates (*i.e.,* locates by means of reflected sound waves), and traps its tiny prey at the surface. The infants must work quickly and skillfully to snap the fish up at just the right moment, and they often falter. Clearly, dolphin babies must learn to snack; sometimes they practice snacking with a piece of seaweed. During these early months they gradually learn to echolocate and capture small prey. We believe these developmental milestones are critical for young dolphins, since echolocation plays such an important role in dolphin life.

Acoustic communication

Sound travels nearly five times faster in water than it does in air, and dolphins are known to hear frequencies as high as 150 kilohertz (150,000 cycles per second), compared with a maximum of about 20 kilohertz for

96

humans. Much of the research on dolphin hearing has focused on their extraordinary echolocation abilities. Given the complexity of dolphin social life and their reliance on acoustics, however, it is not surprising that they also use a wide repertoire of sounds for social communication. Although the water in Shark Bay is sometimes fairly clear, dolphins are often spread too far apart to see one another, necessitating the use of sound to communicate.

Studying dolphin communication at Monkey Mia, as elsewhere, is fraught with difficulties. Because dolphins produce their sounds internally in a series of air sacs below the blowhole, and because sounds are more difficult to localize underwater, it is rare when we can identify the dolphin responsible for producing a particular sound. To obtain recordings of dolphin sounds offshore, we must turn off our noisy boat motors, but since the dolphins generally keep moving, they are soon too far away to be observed in detail. This makes it difficult to correlate vocalizations with behavior.

Fortunately, studying acoustic communication among the tame inshore dolphins is considerably easier. Because they come close to people in extremely shallow water (where their heads are sometimes above the surface), we can often determine which dolphin is responsible for a given sound. One observer tapes the sounds, while another records systematic behavioral information. By listening to the tapes over and over and relating specific sounds to behavioral contexts, we can begin to make sense of the complex repertoire of dolphin sounds.

Dolphin sounds generally fall into three broad categories. One, echolocation click trains, consists of a series of short-duration, wideband clicks emitted in a long sequence that gradually shifts in click repetition rate. When the repetition rate is fast we hear a tone, which may sound something like a rusty door hinge. When the rate is slow we hear distinct clicks. A second category comprises burst-pulse sounds. These also consist of a series of clicks but are emitted in discrete packets with distinctive frequency and repetition-rate characteristics. The third kind comprises pure-tone whistles of long duration, typically changing in frequency and producing a distinctive contour when displayed as a graph.

By evaluating the echoes that return to them as their echolocation clicks bounce off objects in their environment, dolphins are able to use sounds to explore their world in incredible detail; in many ways they rely on this system as humans rely on vision. Since echolocation is so critical to dolphin life, it is expected that echolocation clicks would occur in many different contexts. They are most abundant during feeding activities. Whistles also are common during some types of feeding activities—for example, when pursuit of large schools of fish involves fast traveling and leaping—and during social interactions. Burst-pulse sounds resembling squeaks, growls, chirps, and grunts occur mostly during intimate social interactions, such as when the dolphins are in physical contact, splashing and rolling around.

The nature of a dolphin's vocalizations can provide clues about what the animal is doing out of sight below the water surface. Different kinds

The tamer dolphins at Monkey Mia approach humans on the beach so closely that they sometimes brace their pectoral fins against the bottom and lift their upper bodies out of the water. Because of this proximity, their acoustic communication has been considerably easier to study than that of underwater dolphins offshore.

Rachel Smolker

97

Dolphin sounds can be categorized generally into echolocation clicks, burst-pulse sounds, and whistles. Burst-pulse sounds resembling squeaks, growls, chirps, and grunts are likely to occur during vigorous socializing (top) that involves much splashing and rolling around. (Above) A receptive female mounts a male that has been herding her. When male coalitions herd females, they produce distinctive burst-pulse sounds called pops. Studies in Shark Bay show that a herded female is much more likely to approach a popping male than at other times, apparently to avoid a possible attack by the male.

Photos, Richard Connor

of fish hunting, for instance, sound different. Other noises also can help identify a dolphin's underwater activity. One hunting method involves swatting prey with the tail, which sometimes sends the fish flying out of the water. This behavior is accompanied by loud "bangs," probably produced when the dolphin's tail hits the fish.

Previous research on dolphin whistles, mostly carried out with captive dolphins, has shown that dolphins produce individualized "signature" whistles. While the wild dolphins of Shark Bay do apparently use signature whistles, they often have a repertoire of whistles that may serve other purposes besides individual recognition.

Shark Bay dolphins listen to the vocalizations of distant groups, although just how far away dolphins can hear one another is presently unknown. Often as we follow dolphins, they stop and float near the surface, oriented toward other groups of dolphins, which can be anywhere from a few meters to well over a kilometer away. They may then make a beeline to join the distant group. Feeding sounds may be particularly attractive, as it is common for dolphins to join feeding groups in this manner.

98

Considerable gradation exists among different types of burst-pulse sounds, making it difficult to categorize these sounds in any precise manner. Some classes of sounds, however, can be correlated with classes of behavior. For example, sounds that we call screams, growls, heehaws, and grunts are associated with aggression and are generally accompanied by such behavior as chasing, hitting (with the tail or fins), and biting.

When male coalitions herd females, they produce loud, slowly repetitive burst-pulse sounds we call pops, a kind we have not heard in other contexts. Comparing the herded female's response to a popping male with her behavior toward the same male when he was not popping made it clear that females are much more likely to approach a male during pops than at other times. It also became clear why this is so. Sometimes a popping male suddenly attacks a female that is ignoring his summons, whacking her with his flukes or snout. After the coalition of males and the herded female calm down, the males may engage in a bout of "chimp squeaks," short, comparatively high-frequency burst-pulse sounds that often come in rapid interchanges.

By listening to tape recordings, we have identified more than 30 fairly distinct types of dolphin sounds. With time, we hope to learn more about how these sounds are used, what they mean to the dolphins, and how their use of vocal communication compares with that of other animals.

Future aspirations

Although we have conducted systematic observations at Monkey Mia for several years, we have barely scratched the surface in understanding dolphin society. This is not surprising; many of the more significant finds about the social lives of wild chimpanzees, whose life history is very similar to that of bottle-nosed dolphins, were made only after 15–20 years of continuous study. We plan to pursue our research for years to come.

Despite the fact that we have gained only a preliminary knowledge of dolphin society, it is already clear that we were correct in assuming that dolphins would prove to be valuable subjects for the comparative study of complex social relationships. Our observations, combined with data from other studies of wild dolphins, suggest remarkable similarities between bottle-nosed dolphins and chimpanzees, both as to details of life history and as to social behavior. That dolphins are animals of great intelligence and social complexity is now more apparent than ever; we expect that the future will reveal more of the nature of this complexity and its relation to their intelligence.

Although the dolphins of Shark Bay face no immediate danger of destruction, related species are being slaughtered by the hundreds of thousands as a result of tuna fishing in the Pacific and drift-net fishing around the world. We hope that our continued efforts to understand dolphin society will help people realize the importance of enacting stringent worldwide conservation measures that will end once and for all the human destruction of dolphins and whales.

See also *1987 Yearbook of Science and the Future* Feature Article: THE DYNAMIC AND DIVERSE SOCIETIES OF PRIMATES.

The research described in this article is supported by grants from the National Geographic Society, the National Science Foundation, the Fulbright Foundation, Sigma Xi, the New York Explorer's Club, and the University of Michigan and through private donations to the Dolphins of Shark Bay Research Foundation. Help from the Western Australia Museum, the Department of Anatomy of the University of Western Australia, the Shire of Shark Bay, the Western Australia Department of Conservation and Land Management, the rangers of the Dolphin Information Center at Monkey Mia, and the residents of Denham and Monkey Mia, Western Australia, is gratefully acknowledged by the authors.

Two associating females (below) surface in synchrony. The studies conducted to date at Monkey Mia have only begun to fathom the rich, complex nature of dolphin society. It is hoped that continued research will help in conservation efforts to end the needless destruction of dolphins and whales.

Barbara B. Smuts

THE HELPFUL SPIDER

by Noel D. Vietmeyer

Though regarded with fear and loathing by many people, spiders eat insect pests, help create drugs for pain, and provide silk so strong it may one day be used for bulletproof vests.

Few animals are so universally loathed as spiders. Most people view them as creepy, ugly, and hateful—enemies to be destroyed whenever possible. Even among scientists only a few know much about them. Today, however, spider research is more active than at any previous time, and understanding of these creatures is increasing fast. In fact, a rising number of specialists—from agronomists to engineers—are becoming intrigued by these versatile, skillful animals. A whole new attitude is emerging: Spiders are our friends!

Killing insects is one thing at which spiders are supremely talented. They promise to become major weapons in the worldwide war against pests. They have other talents, too. Already they are helping to create drugs for pain and nervous disorders. Also, they may one day even be helping make automobiles, rockets, and bulletproof vests.

Spiders are not insects. They have soft bodies and eight legs and belong to an entirely different class of invertebrates called arachnids, which also includes scorpions, ticks, and mites. There are over 30,000 known species of spiders, with bodies ranging in length from about 0.5 millimeter (0.02 inch) to about 10 centimeters (3.5 inches).

Spiders are everywhere. They have conquered virtually every ecological niche on land—even such hostile ones as sand dunes, tidal zones, and mountaintops. Their homes range from treetops to underground burrows; at least one lives under water.

Insect killers

All spiders are predators; most feed on insects. (A giant tarantula of the Amazon, whose legs may span as much as 28 centimeters (11 inches), is so big it can catch birds.) In fact, they are the insects' greatest enemies. They kill more insects than all birds combined and far more than do commercial insecticides. Michael Robinson, director of the National Zoo in Washington, D.C., found that 10 female spiders in a New Guinea coffee plantation caught at least 6,039 insects a year. From the number of spiders in the coffee trees, he estimated that in every hectare the

spiders were killing 37 million insects annually (15 million killed per acre). He conjectured that that was why there had never been a major pest outbreak in the local coffee plants.

New Guinea is in the tropics, but in the temperate zones spiders are equally effective. A census of rough meadowland in Sussex, England, revealed a spider population of about five million per hectare (more than two million per acre). It has been estimated that the spiders on open land in temperate countries kill about 40,000 kilograms of insects per hectare (40,000 pounds per acre).

A century ago a U.S. spider expert, Henry C. McCook, pointed out that spiders are vital to humans. Each year they eat a weight of insects that exceeds the weight of the total human population. If those insects were left free to breed and multiply, the effects on crops and human health would be devastating. Indeed, McCook speculated that if spiders were exterminated, a deluge of insects would wipe humankind from the face of the Earth.

The Chinese were the first to harness spider power on a grand scale. They were not following an ancient custom, though. They developed their techniques in the 1970s. Zhao Jinzao (Chao Chin-tsao), vice president of the University of Hubei (Hupeh), one of the founders of the technique, determined that a hectare of ground in his area can harbor more than 1.2 million spiders (500,000 per acre), sometimes even twice that number. Almost half eat crop pests. The main types are wolf spiders, jumping spiders, and crab spiders. These do not spin annoying webs; they pounce on insects, paralyzing them with poison fangs. The wolf spider stays entirely on the ground; the jumping spider prowls all over the plant; and the crab spider hides in flowers.

Zhao found that in only six days spiders can kill 80 to 90% of the harmful insects in cotton fields, even when outnumbered 20 to 1. He learned how to create hospitable environments that boost spider populations. For example, he taught farmers to dig shallow pits every 10 paces throughout their cotton fields and to throw into each an armload of

NOEL D. VIETMEYER *is a Senior Program Officer with the National Research Council in Washington, D.C.*

(Overleaf) Green lynx spider. Photograph, © James H. Robinson— Oxford Scientific Films

straw. The spiders retreat to the straw bundles when the weather turns cold, and there they find a safe haven. Normally, winter kills most spiders, but virtually all the occupants of China's spider "motels" survive. Upon awakening from hibernation, they scuttle across the farmers' fields healthy and ravenous. Any insect trying to suck the life out of the newly planted crops encounters hungry spiders at every turn.

Zhao's ideas proved so successful in practice that within only two years they were being employed on more than 60,000 hectares (150,000 acres). By 1990 such spider enhancement was reportedly used on some 400,000 hectares (one million acres) in China. Partly as a result of this, one province claimed to have cut its pesticide use by 60%.

The rice-growing areas of China use a slight variant of this method. There, farmers set out piles of rice straw on top of the ground. The spiders crawl inside to keep warm, and the farmer picks up the stack and moves the spiders to safety when he floods his fields. Moreover, if insect pests break out in part of his farm, he can carry over "bundles" of spiders to take care of it.

By 1990 such spider pampering was catching on elsewhere. In 1987 Peter Kenmore of the United Nation's Food and Agriculture Organization, persuaded many Indonesian rice farmers to swap insecticides for spiders. It was a daring move. Indonesia was facing the return of the dreaded planthopper, which in the late 1970s had destroyed millions of tons of rice. For five years this insect had been suppressed through the use of a new variety of rice and liberal doses of pesticides, but in the mid-1980s the plants again became infected. In 1986 alone the planthopper destroyed 100,000 hectares (250,000 acres) of rice fields—almost 10% of Indonesia's total. Disaster loomed once more.

Because the insect spends a third of its life inside the stems of plants, it is relatively safe from chemical sprays. However, some spiders manage to squeeze in after it. On these spider-enhanced fields the planthoppers disappeared, and rice yields rose by 20%. Indonesia so strongly embraced the idea of fighting pests with spiders and other biological techniques that

Farmer in China sets out piles of rice straw to attract spiders that will eat insect pests. When the weather turns cold, spiders find shelter in the piles. If insects begin afflicting another part of the farm, the farmer can pick up the bundles and carry them to that area.

Wolf spider with one foot in the water drags a ball-shaped cocoon containing its eggs. These spiders often run across the water to catch insects on the surface; they can also dive beneath the surface to find prey.

in 1988 it saved almost $50 million on pesticide subsidies to farmers. At the same time, average rice yields rose from 6 to 7.4 tons per hectare (2.5 to 3 tons an acre).

For decades Willard H. Whitcomb, former professor of entomology at the University of Florida, has been singing the praises of spiders. Over the years he has identified many useful talents among the various species. Take, for instance, cockroach control. Cockroaches love sheep, and Whitcomb's laboratory was located near a sheep research facility. Nevertheless, he had no cockroaches. Unseen in the darkest crannies in his office, perhaps behind his crowded file cabinets, crawled an unknown number of banana spiders. Harmless to people, these little brownish-gray creatures hate light and leave their burrows only when it is pitch dark. They are aggressive and flat enough to crawl under baseboards in pursuit of their favorite meal—a cockroach.

One of Whitcomb's students kept two banana spiders loose in his van. Another student, Ann Trambarulo, moved into a house that she estimated was infested with 300 adult cockroaches. She released 25 banana spiders and after five weeks realized that the roaches had disappeared. Her laboratory experiments showed that the banana spider releases a scent that attracts cockroaches to their doom.

Trambarulo surveyed residents in the Gainesville area and found that 64% would rather have spiders than roaches. Unfortunately for most of the world, however, the banana spider is tropical and survives only in the warmest climates.

Whitcomb also worked with the green lynx spider, a common field species that throws its hairy front legs over insects like a net. He found that plowing strips around soybean and cotton fields fosters the weedy undergrowth it prefers. From the protection of the weeds hordes of green lynx spiders sally forth, seeking their quarry in the nearby fields.

Whitcomb's other favorites include wolf spiders and jumping spiders—the same type the Chinese use. Wolf spiders are rovers that hunt down their prey. (One dwells along the banks of rivers and lakes and runs across the water to catch insects on the surface; it even dives to grab

Area between road and cotton field in Mississippi (right) is left unmowed in order to allow weedy growth that harbors spiders which will feed on insects that are trying to reach the cotton plants. Clover and other ground cover plants grown between apple trees in California (opposite page, bottom) attract spiders which will prey on insects that can damage the fruit.

tadpoles or small fish it spots beneath the surface.) Like its namesake, this spider depends on fleetness of foot and keen sight—it has three rows of eyes, the last looking backward. Jumping spiders hunt like cats, stalking their prey's every move until close enough for a final pounce. They also flee by jumping but only after attaching a safety thread to the ground—just in case they leap over an edge. They feed on large insects, even boll weevils.

Whitcomb's ideas have been long ignored, but today they are being tested in several places. There are 3,300 species of spiders in North America, more than 600 of them living on crops. Whitcomb's colleagues have, for instance, counted 150 different species in Florida citrus orchards, and it is common to find 90 species in suburban backyards. As with the Chinese, the basic concept in North America is to create environments in which many spiders of a number of species can flourish.

In Tennessee Susan Riechert, an ecologist at the University of Tennessee, found ways to boost the numbers of spiders on garden vegetables. Merely placing a thick layer of grass clippings between rows of broccoli, potatoes, radishes, corn, tomatoes, and beans was enough to increase spider numbers 30-fold. The clippings provided the spiders relief from the summer heat. In turn, the spiders reduced the insect damage by 40 to 70%. For the insects the only safe haven was inside the ears of corn. Apparently, Tennessee spiders will not climb in there.

In Mississippi Orrey Young of the United States Department of Agriculture (USDA) advised cotton farmers not to mow the margins of their fields. Mowing may make farms look neater, he said, but it leaves them wide open to tarnish plant bugs.

These insects suck juices out of young cotton buds and can easily wipe out a whole crop. Most of the year, however, they live outside the cotton fields. By leaving a strip of weeds around a field, a farmer forces the insects to cross a danger zone where hordes of hungry spiders wait in ambush.

In northern California Whitcomb's former graduate student Miguel Altieri tested a similar method of insect control in apple orchards. His

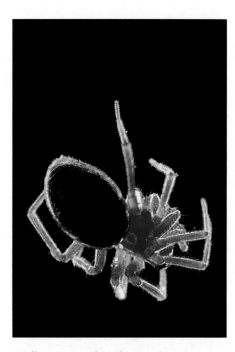

"Ballooning" spider releases a long thread that catches the wind and takes it aloft, often for hundreds of miles. After crops are harvested, spiders leave the fields in this manner, and farmers are seeking ways to prevent them from doing so.

J.A.L. Cooke—Oxford Scientific Films/Animals Animals

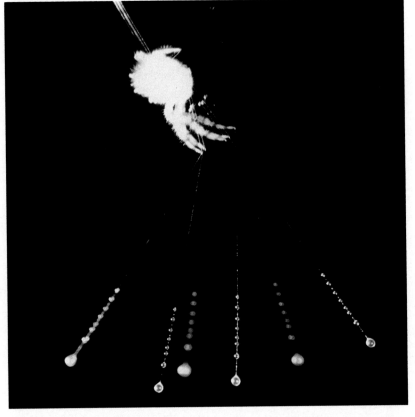

Bolas spider (above) releases a strand of silk tipped with a tiny drop of glue; it then whirls the strand (above right) and captures insects when they become stuck on the glue.

target was the coddling moth, whose larvae become the "worms" in bad apples. By planting clover and other ground cover between the trees, Altieri promoted a dramatic rise in the spider population. To gauge its effect on pests, he put spider "treats" (moth larvae) on small cardboard trays in the trees. In orchards without undergrowth the spider population was big enough to find only 10 to 35% of the tasty morsels within 24 hours, but in those with cover crops the spiders were plentiful enough to find 90 to 100%. The effects on pests would be similar.

In Texas Marvin Harris of Texas A & M University found that spiders can control aphids in pecan orchards. He pointed to the fact that, unlike insect predators such as ladybugs and wasps, spiders will not get up and leave when the hunting turns poor. Spiders can starve for weeks or months. As a result they are present even before insects get a chance to get established. Harris contends that this is one reason why spiders have not been getting the credit they deserve. Their problem is gone before farmers even know they have it.

In Maine Daniel Jennings of the United States Forest Service enlisted spiders in the war against the spruce budworm, the Northeast's most devastating enemy of spruce and fir forests. (Spiders also attack the much-feared gypsy moth.) Jennings found ways to boost the spider population to more than 2.5 million per hectare (one million per acre), half in the trees and half on the ground. Because each spider can eat five or six budworms a day, such numbers can virtually halt an infestation in its tracks.

106

In Missouri Matthew Greenstone of the USDA looked for ways to keep spiders down on the farm. Many spiders take to the air by releasing a long silken thread that catches the wind and carries them aloft. Spiders have been found winging along on these "parachutes" at altitudes above 6,000 meters (20,000 feet); they have landed on ships 320 kilometers (200 miles) at sea; and they undoubtedly travel from continent to continent as some daredevil human balloonists have done. (For this reason the same species are found throughout the world, and spiders are early colonizers of newly formed islands.) To Greenstone this mobility is a major problem. Every time a midwestern farmer harvest his fields, he says, the spiders sling themselves into the thermal updrafts and are lost. He recommended that ways to keep them in the fields be found quickly.

Ingenuity

Spiders have developed some of the most diabolical hunting and killing methods in all of nature. For example, some use gobs of spit. These spitting spiders are so lethargic that one would swear they could never catch anything. Flies (their main targets) seem almost indifferent to the laggardly creatures. Nevertheless, when this kind of spider has crept to within about 2½ centimeters (one inch) of its prey, its body jerks, and the fly suddenly finds itself in a downpour of glue. The spit shoots out so fast that the human eye cannot follow it. It comes out not as single blob but as two thin strands that zigzag and pin down the hapless fly. The spider then saunters over and finishes off the job.

Although most spitting spiders live in the tropics, several species are found in the eastern United States, southern England, and other temperate areas. Their bodies contain glands divided into separate portions that produce gum and poison. However, they squirt the ingredients out together, so that the spit both glues and poisons the victim. It also seems to penetrate the hard skin of insects. If such a property were added to insecticides, a lower dosage of them would be needed to kill the same number of pests.

Spit is certainly a clever weapon, but for pure ingenuity nothing beats the bolas spiders. They spin no webs but instead dangle beneath themselves a strand of silk tipped with a tiny drop of glue. Like a gaucho on the Argentine pampas, they whirl this so-called bola and throw the sticky droplet after a flying insect. They are good at it, too—even in the dark. On average each spider catches two or three moths a night.

Moths and butterflies seldom get caught in normal spider webs; the scales covering their bodies slough off, allowing them to escape. However, the bolas spider's gummy sphere has some sort of "superglue" that in an as-yet-unknown way defeats the moth's quick-release jacket.

It was formerly thought that moths merely blundered into the area near a bolas spider. Recently, however, it was noticed that only male moths are caught. In 1986 Mark Stowe of Harvard University discovered why: the bolas spider produces odors that smell like a female moth's pheromones, chemical substances emitted to attract sexual and other behavioral responses. The male moth, drawn to what seems to be the promise of passion, finds itself instead stuck to a gob of goo. If after about 15 minutes the spider has had no luck whirling its bolas, it draws in the line, bites off the globule, and puts on a fresh one. It seems to know that when the scent dries out a new lure must be attached.

To hunt with the scent of an entirely different species is ingenious, yet the bolas spider's talents go even further. James Tumlinson and Robert Heath of the USDA found that the spider emits a slightly different scent from night to night. This probably takes advantage of the different moths that happen to be most abundant at the time.

Weird webs

The web-weaving spiders also have some great parlor tricks. One Brazilian species makes a web in the middle of the night and then at sunrise detaches it, folds it up, and carries it off to its retreat, where the enmeshed insects are carefully picked out for breakfast. Another in New Guinea builds a brown-colored web curved around tree trunks. It catches insects alighting on what they think is bark.

Quite a number of spiders operate their webs actively. The cribellate spider, for example, builds a triangular web and makes itself a living link between the main strand and the anchorage. Like a boy tugging on a slingshot, it pulls the whole assemblage taut. When an insect strikes the web, the spider lets go and the web snaps back and wraps around the victim.

Others attach silk lines above the hub of the web and pull it up into the shape of a cone. The spider stations itself at the topmost strand, and when an insect flies up into the cone, it jerks the web this way and that until the intruder is hopelessly entangled.

In the eons-long arms race between spiders and moths, some web-building spiders have discovered how to disarm the moth's safety coating. They construct webs like ladders. A moth tumbling down the sticky rings loses so many scales that eventually bare spots are exposed; the web sticks to these spots.

The purseweb spider spins a silken tube that resembles a crooked finger of a glove sticking out of the ground. The spider lurks inside, invisible, and when an insect crawls over the outer surface, the spider chomps through the web. Suddenly, the insect finds jaws attached to its feet.

Among the weirdest devices is that of the ogre-faced spider. This tropical species builds a web about the size of a postage stamp and holds it between its four front legs. When an insect comes within reach, it throws the web over it. Alternatively, it holds up the web like a tiny tennis racket to catch flying insects. Sometimes it claps the web over insects crawling on the ground. For example, it often positions itself over an ant trail, and when an ant marches by, it presses down the web and lifts the ant right off the ground. When the ant is captured in that manner, it cannot leave any scent on the ground to attract help or warn friends.

Each species of web-building spider spins a web that is unique. The web is its game trap, its haven from enemies, and its residence. Some spiders deliberately orient their webs edge-on to the noonday sun, for

108

coolness. A spider knows and remembers every part of its web. If it is taken away from and later returned to its web, it will instantly scurry around on its old territory, fully at home.

Because its web represents a large expenditure of energy and protein, a spider often gathers it up and eats it so that the protein can be recycled. Rain is a major hazard. Many spiders respond to heavy rainfall by cutting out large sections of their webs, thereby quickly collapsing them in order to keep them from washing away. Many others assume "rainfall postures," hanging straight down beneath their webs with their front legs stretched out below them. The rain runs off the webs, down the bodies of the spiders, and drips off their legs.

Masters of disguise

Some Central American spiders have taken the shape of ants, having three body segments instead of two. They walk on six legs, holding their front pair of legs over their heads and wiggling them like antennae. These spiders also mimic the sinuous gait and jerky run of ants. Their mimicry is, in fact, so good that they can get inside ant nests without being suspected. Mostly, though, they line up on ant trails, and when an unsuspecting ant offers its antenna to exchange notes on the neighborhood's tastiest eating-out spots, it finds itself on the menu.

Another tropical spider looks very little like an ant, but it moves like one. It always approaches an ant in short bursts and from the front so

Ogre-faced spider holds between its four front legs a web about the size of a postage stamp (above left); the spider then captures insects by throwing the web over those that come within reach (above).

109

that its body cannot be seen. When the curious ant puts up its antennae, the spider bites it on the head; then it tucks the paralyzed insect under itself and dashes off to a hiding place for a leisurely meal. Dissolving the inner tissues and sucking them up takes just an hour or two. In spiders the stomach acts as a suction pump for taking in food. It is anatomically undefined and can swell and swell without harming the animal or causing it discomfort. As a result spiders can gorge themselves, and they can also fast for a year and a half.

Web-weaving spiders are almost blind. Their actions are ruled by touch. They have vibration receptors and almost certainly know the vibration "fingerprints" of nearly all objects. Michael Robinson has pointed out that they live in a world of melodies played on silk. A potential sex partner, for example, is largely a tune on a thread. One spider has even learned the sex tune of another species. By twanging the seductive melody on the end of a thread, it lures the victim out for a quick supper date.

Venom

Spiders have had a long time to perfect such tricks. They evolved soon after the insects, probably in the Devonian period nearly 400 million years ago. Since their origins spiders have exquisitely refined their venoms to attack an insect's nervous system. Because these venoms paralyze their victims rapidly, chemical companies are studying them for clues to safer and more effective insecticides.

This is not a new idea, but until recently researchers concentrated on venoms from the most poisonous spiders: the black widow, the brown recluse, and the Sydney funnel web. Unfortunately, these venoms proved to be made of molecules too complex to be readily synthesized as insecticides. Lately, however, researchers have found that common garden spiders have much simpler venoms. Indeed, some are now showing considerable potential as insecticides.

Jumping (salticid) spider from Central America mimics an ant. The mimicry of these spiders is so good that they are often able to enter ant nests without being suspected.

© L. West—Photo Researchers

Spider venoms alter the chemical that bridges the gap between the victim's nerve endings and its muscles. After a spider bite an insect's brain continues telegraphing messages down its nerves, but because the instructions never get delivered to the muscles, the insect is powerless to move.

The venom of most spiders has a much milder effect on humans. Most spider fangs are designed to penetrate the thin membrane covering an insect's joints but are too short to punch through human skin. Even those that do penetrate usually have little effect. (Reports of spider bites are greatly exaggerated. One check of 700 cases in California discovered that at least 80% were actually caused by insects, allergic reactions, and diabetes.)

In fact, some components of the venom may benefit human health and are being studied by pharmaceutical companies. The venoms affect the sodium pathway that blocks pain and the calcium pathway that is impor-

Orb web, a type made by several families of spiders, is the most complex and elaborate prey-catching web. It traps insects that fly weakly and cannot see the fine threads. Such webs are usually rebuilt every day.

Kjell B. Sandved

tant in cardiac function. One major company is testing spider chemicals in drugs for epilepsy and Alzheimer's disease.

Stronger than steel

Human uses for spider venoms are fairly new, but spider silk has been used for centuries as cross hairs in gun sights and astronomical telescopes. Also, spider webs have long been placed over bleeding wounds. For this they are effective but probably not because of any special curative powers. The secret is probably purely mechanical: the strands provide a surface that helps blood to clot.

Nevertheless, these uses are nothing compared with what may be coming soon. Though spider silk seems very weak, that is only because it is so fine. In fact, it is so strong that if it were spun into thicker strands it would be ideal for making many modern products.

111

Spiders produce different types of silk. One is for spinning egg-sacs. Another is for the framework of the web. A third is for the sticky spiral of the web, while a fourth is for the anchor that attaches the web to bushes and other objects. A fifth is the "dragline silk" that supports the spider as it hangs in front of one's face or rides the winds. The different silks come out of different glands, and they are not sticky. A separate gland produces the glue. (The spider goes back along a newly laid thread and puts down drops of glue; then it gives the thread a good hard twang to make the glue spread out evenly. Some species never use glue; they comb the threads until they are like microscopic barbed wire or Velcro.)

Dragline silk is the one that interests engineers. At least three spiders produce dragline silk as strong as the fibers used in high-performance aircraft. Near Cambridge, England, one firm is developing methods for producing spider silk commercially. Nick Ashley, one of the company's engineers, pointed out that a fly hitting a spider web is like a fighter jet flying into a piece of fishing net, yet the web absorbs the impact and stops the fly dead. Ashley believes that the web could stop bullets the same way, and he measured its tensile strength as ranging from 1,420 million to 1,550 million newtons per square meter. This compares with the values, in million newtons per square meter, of aramid fiber (2,000), high-tensile nylon (1,600), and carbon fiber (1,750). Furthermore, dragline silk is elastic, while those man-made molecules are not.

Silk can be drawn directly out of spiders and onto spools; one investigator reeled off 137 meters (150 yards) of it in an hour. The process is like milking a cow. The spider cannot stop it; even in nature the silk is pulled out rather than pushed. The animal normally attaches the end to something and then runs or drops away, although it can also pull out its own silk with its legs.

Until recently spider silk could not be produced commercially because 125,000 spiders would be needed to make a kilogram of silk (50,000

Silk is drawn out of a spider and gathered on a spool at the U.S. Army Materials Research Laboratory in Natick, Massachusetts. The silk is then measured for strength and studied by scientists who plan to use it as a basis for making stronger and more extensible fibers.

U.S. Army Natick Research Center, Natick, Mass.

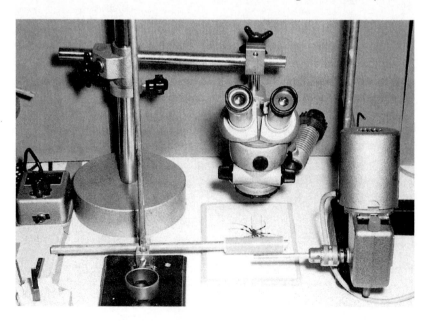

for a pound). The problems of keeping and "milking" them make that impossible. However, biotechnology can now solve this problem. The genes that instruct a spider's cells to make silk protein can be identified, replicated, and spliced into bacteria. The bacteria will then make the same protein. To make tons of the protein the bacteria can be multiplied in large fermentation vats. Then the protein can be separated and forced through fine nozzles to create fibers. (Even in the spider the silk protein is in liquid form until it squirts out through the nozzlelike spinnerets.)

Already, interest in making textiles from this new silk has been expressed. The cloth resembles polished metal more than it does normal silk (which comes from an insect, the silkworm) and is three times stronger. Ashley thinks that it will be used mainly in aircraft, satellites, cables, towlines, and protective clothes that have to be strong, lightweight, and easy to store in a small space.

The U.S. military is also studying spider silk. Beginning with a navy contract in 1983, a company in San Diego, California, worked extensively with spider silk and developed ways of producing it. A navy spokesman said that the material one day will likely be used in membranes, films, and fibers for heart valves, artificial veins, and other surgical implants.

The U.S. Army has also mounted a research effort. At its Materials Research Laboratory in Natick, Massachusetts, biotechnologist David Kaplan expects to be producing spider silk soon in much the same way as Ashley. Kaplan's silk may be even stronger, however, because his group may instruct the bacteria to improve the silk's molecular structure. His goal is to make a bulletproof vest that is far lighter and more comfortable than those now worn by soldiers and police.

Tasty treat

Spider ranching may never overtake cattle ranching, but at least one spider supplies food. Found in the jungles of New Guinea, the world's largest orb-weaving spider (the type that produces circular webs) is big enough to cover the palm of a person's hand. It spins webs the size of bicycle wheels. And it is edible.

Michael Robinson explains that village people gather fat females in a hollow green bamboo stick. Both ends are stoppered, and the stick is placed in hot embers for 10 or 15 minutes until it blackens. When the roasted spiders are taken out, their hard skins have split and they are ready to eat—with or without legs. In village markets New Guineans commonly sell the spiders tied up in bundles with a rubber band. Their region has traditionally been seriously short of protein, and to them (who feel none of the repugnance many other people feel) spiders mean life and health and a good meal.

Spiders probably will never be served at any banquets in the Western world, but many farmers are likely to have armies of spiders running around protecting their fields. As a result grocery bills will be reduced, and soils, waters, and foods will have fewer pesticide residues. People may also be sporting spider-silk cars and spider-silk clothes, and drugs and other products from spiders may be keeping them healthy.

Little Miss Muffet of nursery-rhyme fame is about to have her meal interrupted by an unwanted visitor. She is based on a real person, Patience, daughter of Thomas Muffet (1553–1604), an English physician who was so enamored of spiders that he kept a houseful of them to "beautifie" rooms with their "tapestry and hangings." Patience apparently did not share her father's feelings.

The Granger Collection

113

by John H. Crowe and Lois M. Crowe

Certain plants and animals can
survive long periods of dehydration
in suspended animation. What
scientists have discovered about their
death-defying ability is being turned
to serve human needs in medicine,
agriculture, and other fields.

I took some of this dry sediment which I had taken out of the leaden gutter . . . and put a little of it into glass tubes, wherein I poured some rainwater. . . . As soon as I poured on the water, I stirred the whole about. I examined it, and perceived some animalcules lying closely heaped together. In a short time afterwards they began to extend their bodies, and in half an hour at least a hundred of them were swimming about the glass.

—Antonie van Leeuwenhoek, 1702

The phenomenon first described by pioneering microscopist Antonie van Leeuwenhoek in the quotation above has fascinated biologists for nearly three centuries. It was originally called anabiosis, or "return to life," because for many years biologists studying it believed that the dry but viable organisms had actually died and returned to life when they were moistened. The proposed resurrection was even used as evidence in support of the theory of spontaneous generation, or life from nonliving matter, in the 19th century and sparked the French Academy of Science to appoint a commission to investigate whether the dry organisms were actually dead. To their credit they came to no conclusion, but the fact that the investigation received so much attention in the popular press of the day points up the immense fascination with the idea of a return to life after death.

The phenomenon van Leeuwenhoek witnessed is now called anhydrobiosis, or "life without water," a term coined by the late David Keilin of the University of Cambridge. Keilin also suggested the more general term cryptobiosis, or "hidden life," which includes not only anhydrobiosis but also other instances of suspended animation, such as that seen in frozen organisms. Keilin proposed that even though life processes in anhydrobiotic organisms often are not detectable, thus defying the usual definitions applied to life and death, the dry organisms are hardly dead. Their ability to survive in the dry state until favorable environmental conditions return can be understood in physical and chemical terms. In fact, research into the secrets of "life without water" has advanced such that much of what has been learned is being adapted to serve a variety of human needs in medicine, agriculture, and other fields.

Lives of quiet dehydration

The kinds of organisms that exploit anhydrobiosis include early developmental stages of a wide variety of microbes, plants, and animals, among them the spores of bacteria and fungi, the larvae of certain insects, and the cysts (so-called winter eggs) of brine shrimp. That the seeds of many plants survive drying has been known perhaps for millennia and is a part of everyday experience, particularly in view of its agricultural significance. Another familiar example is ordinary baker's yeast, which is available commercially as dry granules. These dry but living cells rapidly rehydrate when they are placed in water. (Warm water must be used, as every baker knows; the reasons will be discussed below.)

In addition to such commonplace examples, many species of microscopic animals experience anhydrobiosis. The water film around soil grains, for example, harbors a microscopic community that includes

JOHN H. CROWE is Professor of Biophysics and Zoology, and LOIS M. CROWE is Research Biophysicist and Zoologist at the University of California at Davis.

(Overleaf) Illustration by Leon Bishop

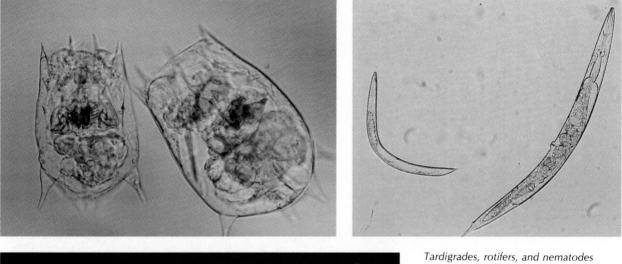

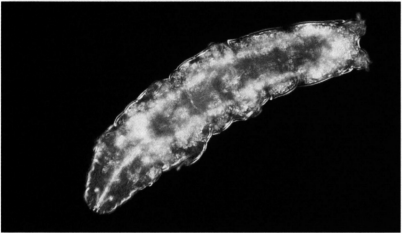

Tardigrades, rotifers, and nematodes (clockwise from bottom left) are numbered among the kinds of microscopic animals that experience anhydrobiosis. In nature many species of these organisms dwell in watery "microenvironments" such as damp moss or lichen or the moisture around soil grains. When the water evaporates, the animals dehydrate, persisting in the dry state for months or years until conditions favorable for active life return.

rotifers, tardigrades, and nematodes. When the water in which they live dries up, the animals shrivel and dry up also. They may persist in this state for months or even years, but when the drought passes and they come in contact with water again, they rapidly swell and resume active life, often within minutes. It is not known how long anhydrobiotic organisms can survive dehydration. Some soil-inhabiting nematodes, which are worms of a class commonly called roundworms, revived after having been kept in a dried state for 39 years, and anecdotal claims suggest that their longevity may be more than a century under specialized conditions. Even in nature anhydrobiosis may extend life span enormously. For instance, tardigrades, which are tiny pond- and soil-dwelling creatures somewhere in evolutionary development between worms and arthropods, probably have a life span of less than a year while they are fully hydrated. Periods in anhydrobiosis under natural conditions, however, may extend that lifetime to 60 years or more.

The longevity of anhydrobiotic plants and plant parts is even more impressive, but controversial. It has been reported that anhydrobiotic seeds may be able to survive 100 years or more, but such figures have been based on samples of seeds collected under field conditions, which makes it difficult to rely on age estimates of the samples. One of the

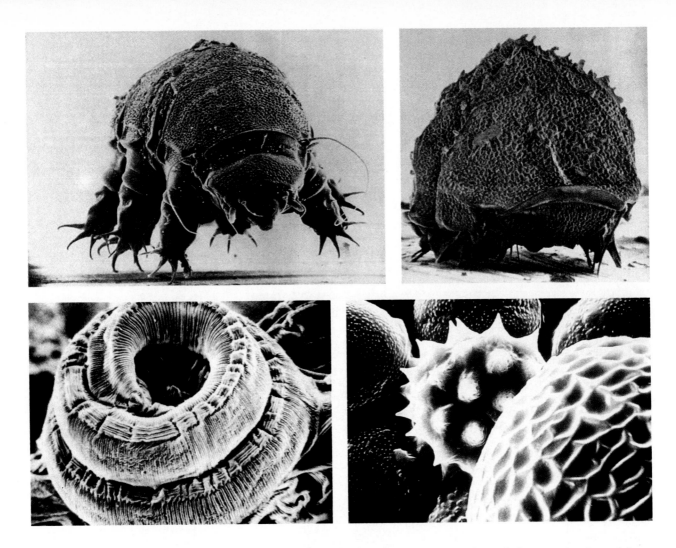

An active, hydrated tardigrade (top left) and one in a drought-induced dry state (top right) are compared in scanning electron micrographs (SEMs). Anhydrobiosis so hardens the animal against extreme heat and cold, high vacuum, and strong radiation that it could conceivably survive in outer space. An anhydrobiotic nematode (shown in the SEM above), whose water content may fall to 2% or less, can endure for months or years until it contacts water again. Also exploiting the dry state for survival are a wide variety of plants and plant parts, including pollen (in the SEM above right), spores, and seeds.

Photos, John H. Crowe

most celebrated of such reports was that of the germination of lotus seeds found buried in a peat bog in Manchuria, where they reputedly had survived for more than 2,000 years. The fact that there emerged strikingly different figures for the actual age of the seeds, depending on the method used to make the estimates, points up the difficulty in assessing the limits of the persistence of life in the anhydrobiotic state. What appears to be the lengthiest laboratory study on longevity of anhydrobiotic organisms deals with the spore-producing bodies of a fungus that was dried in 1909. The last time the samples were examined, in 1962, they still yielded viable spores.

In addition to gains in life span, anhydrobiotic organisms are capable of enduring astonishing environmental extremes that would be lethal if the organisms were fully hydrated. The microscopic water-dwelling invertebrates known as rotifers, for example, are master survivalists in their anhydrobiotic state. In the 1920s P.G. Rahm of the University of Freiburg, Germany, found that they could survive for days at −200° C (−330° F) and for a few minutes at 150° C (300° F), and in the 1950s Henri Becquerel of the University of Paris reported that the same organisms could survive exposure for lengthy periods to temperatures a few thousandths of a degree above absolute zero, −273.15° C (−459.67° F).

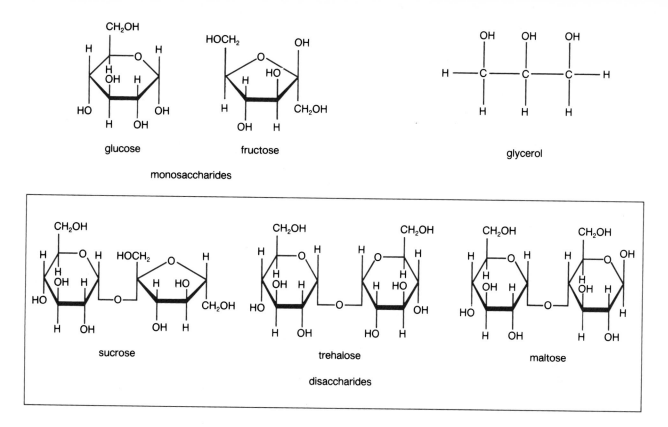

glucose

fructose

glycerol

monosaccharides

sucrose

trehalose

maltose

disaccharides

Working with tardigrades, R.M. May and his colleagues at the University of Paris found that the dose of X-rays required for killing half of a sample in the anhydrobiotic state was 570,000 roentgens. For comparison, the dose required for killing half a population of humans is estimated to be about 500 roentgens. Dry tardigrades also endure exposure to high vacuum for lengthy periods. In short, they could conceivably survive conditions of outer space.

What lets anhydrobiotic organisms defy death?

Since the late 1960s we have been seeking the answer to this question by studying the chemical composition of anhydrobiotic organisms. Such research subsequently led us to explore the mechanisms by which various cellular components of the organisms are preserved in the dry state. We chose early in our studies to focus on adult nematodes as model organisms. One difficulty in working with early life stages, such as the seeds of plants, is that their chemical composition may have as much to do with their future development as with adaptations to dehydration, thus complicating the interpretation of the data gathered. That difficulty is obviated in studies of adult organisms.

In the early 1970s we established laboratory conditions under which one species of nematode that dwells in moist soil can be induced to become anhydrobiotic. We found that the worms must be dried slowly in air that is at first highly humid. While the animals are in moist air, their ability to survive transfer to dry air gradually increases. After three days at high humidity they can be transferred to dry air, in which their water content ultimately falls to 2% or less. Thus dehydrated, they may

Structural formulas are compared for several sugars and glycerol. Sucrose, trehalose, and maltose are all double sugars (disaccharides), made up of two molecules of simple sugars (monosaccharides). Sucrose comprises one molecule each of glucose and fructose, while trehalose comprises two molecules of glucose. Although two glucose molecules also make up maltose, they are linked together in a different way. Over the past two decades researchers have shown that trehalose and sucrose accumulate in high concentrations in anhydrobiotic organisms, where they help cell components maintain their structure during dehydration. Glycerol, whose stabilizing properties during freezing of cells and tissues are well known, was first thought to be a likely stabilizing agent in anhydrobiosis but later was proved to be unessential.

119

Scanning electron micrographs on this page and opposite illustrate the way in which trehalose minimizes dehydration damage to a muscle-cell membrane (sarcoplasmic reticulum) responsible for accumulating calcium ions in the vesicles that it encloses. Freshly prepared vesicles (above) show a spherical shape, while membrane proteins, which appear as tiny surface bumps, are distributed over the vesicles in a characteristic way. When vesicles are dried without trehalose and then rehydrated (below), they fuse into large clumps; moreover, the proteins are displaced from their normal positions into aggregations.

Photos, John H. Crowe

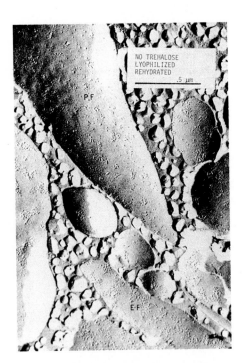

be stored for months without losing the ability to revive. If oxygen is excluded, they may persist for years in this state.

The fact that the animals must be dried slowly suggests that they undergo events that prepare them for the extensive dehydration to come. In the mid-1970s, in collaboration with Katherine Madin and Stephen Loomis, we studied the nematodes' chemical composition and found that the most striking change was in their content of a sugar, trehalose. Trehalose is a disaccharide, or double sugar, composed of two molecules of the simple sugar glucose. The fully hydrated animals possessed only small amounts of trehalose, but during the slow dehydration process they converted up to 20% of their dry mass into it. Its presence was strongly correlated with the ability of the nematodes to survive dehydration.

In addition to trehalose, the nematodes synthesize glycerol (glycerin) during the slow dehydration. Because glycerol's properties are well known as a stabilizing agent during freezing (it is used, for example, as a protective medium for freezing red blood cells), we first regarded it as the most likely candidate for a similar protective role in anhydrobiotic organisms. However, subsequent studies by Christopher Womersley of the University of Hawaii at Manoa established that trehalose is nearly always present at high concentrations in the dried nematodes, whereas glycerol may or may not be. That trehalose is likely to be involved in preserving the cells of anhydrobiotic organisms during dehydration is supported by recent studies by Anita Panek and her colleagues of the Federal University of Rio de Janeiro, who showed that the presence of trehalose is similarly correlated with the ability of yeast cells to survive drying. From studies of comparative biochemistry it is beginning to emerge that trehalose is nearly universally accumulated in large amounts in anhydrobiotic animals and in at least some microbes and lower plants, although the data base is still small.

Trehalose seems to be absent from higher plants, but sucrose, another disaccharide made of one molecule of glucose and one of fructose, may play a similar role here. Recent studies by A.C. Leopold of Cornell University, Ithaca, New York, and F.A. Hoekstra of the Agricultural University of The Netherlands, Wageningen, demonstrated that the presence of sucrose is highly correlated with survival of dehydration by seeds and pollen grains of higher plants.

Does trehalose protect dry proteins and membranes?

In order to investigate the role of trehalose in protecting the cells of anhydrobiotic organisms against damage during dehydration, beginning in 1979 we turned to studies of isolated cell parts: proteins and membranes. Because both of these key components of cells are known to be sensitive to such environmental extremes as drying or freezing, they were chosen to serve as models for the possible protective effects of sugars on cellular components.

As a model protein we chose phosphofructokinase, one of the key enzymes, or biological catalysts, that regulate metabolism in all cells. It serves as an excellent test system since it is extremely sensitive to

120

drying. In fact, in collaboration with John F. Carpenter we found in short order that it is completely denatured—that is, deprived of its biological activity through structural modification—when it is dried without trehalose. When the enzyme is dried in the presence of this sugar (with addition of trace amounts of zinc), however, it is completely stabilized against denaturing. Rehydrating dry preparations of enzyme and sugar produces a fully functional enzyme.

The model membrane we selected is a membrane found within muscle cells that accumulates calcium ions in the water-filled compartment that it encloses. This membrane, called the sarcoplasmic reticulum, is responsible for regulating the contraction and relaxation of muscle by means of the release and uptake of calcium ions. For our purposes the ability of the membrane to accumulate calcium could be used as a convenient marker for its structural stability. Furthermore, when we began this work, it already had been established that the accumulation of calcium is due to the presence of a specific transport protein in the membrane. Molecules of this protein, which function as pumps to move calcium ions across the membrane against a concentration gradient, are distributed in the membrane in a characteristic way. They can be seen with the electron microscope, thus providing a structural marker for whether the membrane remains intact.

When we dried sarcoplasmic reticulum membranes without trehalose, we found that they fused together into a large clump; the transport proteins aggregated and were displaced from their normal positions. When such preparations were rehydrated, they showed extensive structural damage and had completely lost the ability to accumulate calcium. On the other hand, membranes dried in the presence of trehalose showed only minor structural damage. When rehydrated, they accumulated calcium at a rate similar to that seen in membranes that had not been dehydrated.

One would think that the ability of an organism to survive dehydration might involve a myriad array of adaptations that had been evolved over the millions of years that life has existed on Earth, but this does not seem to be the case. The phosphofructokinase used in the studies described above was isolated from rabbits. The enzyme obviously never experiences dehydration in living rabbits, but when dried in the presence of trehalose, it can be stabilized. Similarly, the sarcoplasmic reticulum membranes came from the muscle of a species of lobster. They also clearly do not undergo dehydration in a live lobster. Yet introduction of a single factor, trehalose, is sufficient to protect them completely during dehydration.

Thus, simple studies on fragile parts of cells provided the first evidence that trehalose may play a role in stabilizing the structures of cellular components in anhydrobiotic organisms. But what about other sugars? Do they have similar properties? To some extent they do. In some circumstances sucrose is nearly as effective as trehalose. However, other sugars and a wide variety of other molecules that have been tested are decidedly inferior to either trehalose or sucrose in this regard. This finding is satisfying, as trehalose and sucrose are the molecules that commonly accumulate in high concentrations in anhydrobiotic organisms.

121

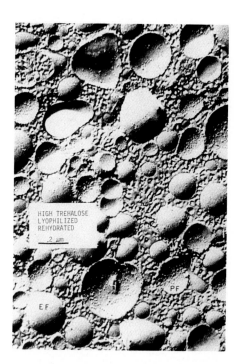

When vesicles enclosed by sarcoplasmic reticulum are dried in the presence of trehalose (above) and then rehydrated (below), they show essentially the same structure that fresh vesicles do. Whereas vesicles dried without trehalose and then rehydrated lose the ability to accumulate calcium, those treated the same way in the presence of trehalose accumulate calcium at a rate similar to that of fresh vesicles.

Photos, John H. Crowe

When cell components dry out

What is special about trehalose and sucrose? What is the mechanism by which they preserve dry cellular components? Before these questions can be answered, one must consider the importance of water to the structure of the living cell.

Cellular life evolved in water billions of years ago. The legacy of that ancestral environment is readily apparent today in even the most land-adapted multicellular organisms, whose cells are filled with a water solution and are bathed in watery tissue fluids. Water is the medium in which the cell's biochemical reactions take place, but, in addition, water plays a key role in maintaining the higher order structure of the cell's constituents. For instance, both proteins and membranes contain hydrophobic, or water-repelling, components that have low solubility in water. As a result, these components tend to associate together, much as oil mixed in water collects on the surface of the water rather than dissolves in it. This phenomenon, which was well documented in the 1960s by Charles Tanford and his colleagues at Duke University, Durham, North Carolina, plays a major role in the assembly of proteins and membranes into their functional configurations. It follows that removal of water might have important consequences for structure and function in proteins and membranes. Furthermore, a significant amount of water is attached by weak chemical bonds (hydrogen bonds) to hydrophilic, or water-attracting, components of proteins and membranes. Removal of that water by dehydration leads to large changes in the physical properties of the protein or membrane.

Consider the following example. Biological membranes comprise a mixture of proteins and fatty molecules called lipids. Phospholipids are one principal type of membrane lipid. Each phospholipid molecule has a hydrophilic, water-soluble head portion linked to two hydrophobic tails made of hydrocarbon chains. It is the hydrophobic association of the tails in a water medium that results in the self-assembly of phospholipid molecules into the basic double-layer (bilayer) structure of biological membranes.

This structure is composed of two sheets of phospholipid molecules with all of the tails of each sheet aligned parallel and facing the tails of the other sheet. The water-soluble heads point outward toward the water, to which they are attracted. In fact, each phospholipid head has associated with it about 10–12 water molecules, which spatially separate the heads, thus limiting contact between adjacent hydrocarbon-chain tails. If the water is removed, as is the case in the cells of a dried organism, the hydrocarbon chains pack more closely and enter a solid, gel phase. This solid phase can be melted by increasing the temperature, rather like the way lard melts in a heated frying pan, an effect that was discovered in the 1960s by Dennis Chapman and his colleagues at Unilever Laboratories in the United Kingdom. They showed that as phospholipids are dehydrated, the temperature at which the hydrocarbon chains melt from a solid to fluid phase increases greatly—by as much as 80° C (144° F). Furthermore, they showed that the effect is fully reversible;

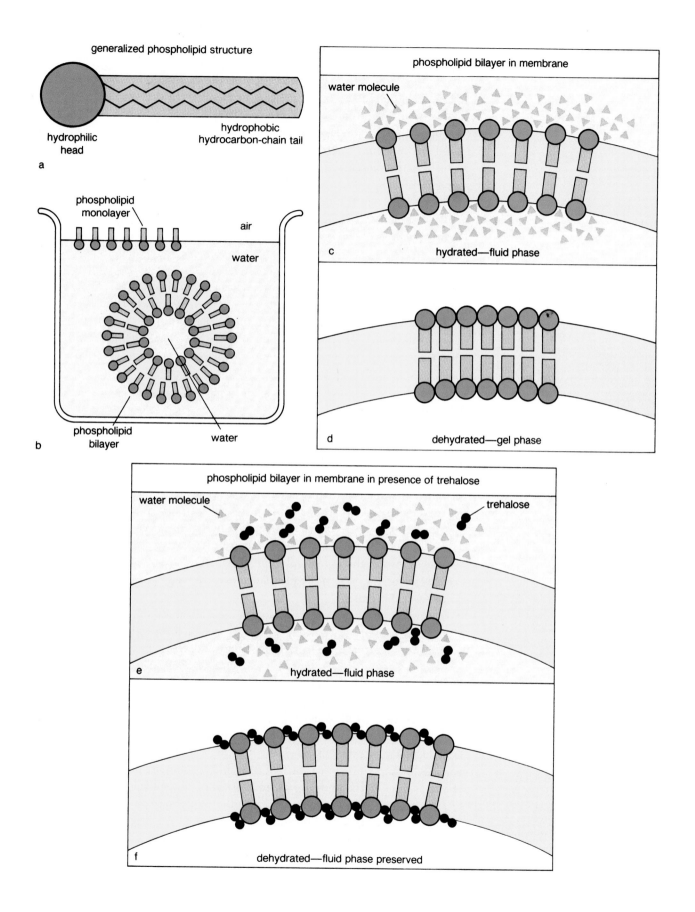

generalized phospholipid structure

hydrophilic head

hydrophobic hydrocarbon-chain tail

a

phospholipid monolayer

air

water

phospholipid bilayer

water

b

phospholipid bilayer in membrane

water molecule

c   hydrated—fluid phase

d   dehydrated—gel phase

phospholipid bilayer in membrane in presence of trehalose

water molecule

trehalose

e   hydrated—fluid phase

f   dehydrated—fluid phase preserved

when the phospholipid is rehydrated, the melting temperature drops to its original value.

We believe the effects of dehydration on the melting temperature of phospholipids to be key to the damage to membranes that results from dehydration, for the following reasons. There is good evidence that as fully hydrated membranes are passed through gel-to-fluid-to-gel phase transitions by being heated and cooled, they become transiently leaky; as a result, the substances enclosed by the membranes leak into the surrounding medium. Because during a dehydration and rehydration cycle the membrane phospholipids undergo a similar series of phase transitions, one might expect them to become leaky.

Furthermore, there is good evidence that in the gel phase the different classes of proteins, phospholipids, and other lipids in a membrane tend to aggregate and exclude each other. Consequently, proteins might be expected to aggregate in membranes during dehydration, and various phospholipid classes to form separate domains. When such a damaged membrane is rehydrated, the proteins might not return to their proper positions in the bilayer, and their functions might be lost. That is indeed what was observed in the dehydrated sarcoplasmic reticulum described above.

A stand-in for water

In the 1960s Sydney J. Webb of the University of Saskatchewan predicted that delicate biomolecules, such as certain proteins and membranes in dry bacterial spores, might be preserved by small molecules that actually substitute for the water around the larger biomolecule. It was not clear just what the chemical nature of the small molecules might be, but it was nevertheless an appealing idea. In the early 1970s we extended this hypothesis and proposed it as a general solution to the problem of stability of biomolecules in anhydrobiotic organisms. This idea subsequently became known as the water-replacement hypothesis. We now have good candidates for the role of small molecules that might replace water—trehalose and sucrose.

At present, all that is known about the mechanism by which trehalose and sucrose stabilize dry proteins is that the sugars form hydrogen bonds with hydrophilic regions on the dry protein molecules. In collaboration with John Carpenter, we showed that hydrogen-bond formation is correlated with the stabilization of the dry protein in a structure similar to that seen in the protein before it was dried.

We know a great deal more about the mechanism by which trehalose and sucrose interact with dry membranes than with proteins. Trehalose is particularly effective at lowering the melting temperature for dry phospholipids, as predicted. In fact, the melting temperature for phospholipids dried in the presence of trehalose is often well below that seen for phospholipids in water. As a result, the phospholipids remain in a fluid state even when fully dehydrated. When they are placed in water, they do not undergo a gel-to-fluid phase transition and thereby avoid the damage caused by the transition.

124

Trehalose exerts its effects on the physical properties of phospholipids by forming hydrogen bonds with the phospholipid heads, an explanation supported by overwhelming evidence from several research groups in North America and Europe. The sugar apparently resides between the phospholipid heads in dry membranes, spatially separating them much as water molecules do in hydrated membranes.

We believe that the available evidence strongly supports the suggestion that trehalose replaces the water around dry biomolecules and that such replacement is the mechanism by which it stabilizes those molecules. Proof that this mechanism underlies the surprising stability of entire anhydrobiotic organisms is still lacking, but progress is being made in this direction.

Anita Panek and her colleagues recently produced direct evidence that trehalose plays a key role in stabilizing intact cells. First, they showed that a mutant of baker's yeast that was unable to synthesize trehalose also was incapable of surviving dehydration. They then showed that if trehalose was added to the outside of the cells, the cells could endure drying. It is not clear whether the trehalose penetrated to the inside of the cells, but what is significant is that a single change—the addition of trehalose—was sufficient to preserve the cells in the absence of water.

Anhydrobiosis and human welfare

While studies of the enhanced survival abilities of dehydrated organisms may be fascinating as a scientific pursuit, they also have significant practical applications. For instance, investigators are learning to apply the secrets of anhydrobiosis to the stabilization of biomolecules of use in the pharmaceutical industry. Previously, it was necessary to ship many proteins that serve as drugs under refrigeration because other means for preserving them were lacking. With the findings outlined above in hand, it is becoming possible to stabilize such proteins in a dry state and ship them at room temperature. For instance, Kevin Hazen of the University of Southwestern Louisiana, Lafayette, and John Carpenter of Cryolife Inc., Marietta, Georgia, recently showed that antibody molecules and insulin, both of which had not proved stable during drying with previous techniques, can be reduced to powders in the presence of trehalose. When the powders are rehydrated, they yield functional molecules. These discoveries are the subject of several patent applications.

Another application is again in the pharmaceutical industry. Liposomes are microscopic vessels whose walls are artificial membranes composed of bilayers of pure phospholipids. Like the cell membrane, liposomes enclose a water-filled compartment. Water-soluble drugs can be trapped in this compartment, and the liposomes can then be injected into a patient's bloodstream. The liposomes subsequently fuse with cell membranes, depositing the drug inside the cell. Numerous efforts are under way to find ways of targeting the liposomes to specific cells and tissues—tumor cells, for instance, into which the liposomes might be used to introduce a poison. One difficulty with such a strategy for drug delivery is that liposomes are not stable for long periods. We have found, however, that

Computer molecular model reveals the way in which trehalose may interact with membrane phospholipids to maintain spacing between the phospholipid heads. A double-ringed trehalose molecule appears in yellow-green, while phospholipid heads appear in blue (with oxygen atoms in red). The spherical starburst patterns represent the relative space occupied by the atoms.

Barbara Rudolph, Naval Research Laboratory

125

liposomes in the presence of trehalose can be freeze-dried and stored as a dry product. After being shipped to its destination, the product simply is mixed with water to obtain rehydrated liposomes with all their contents intact. The University of California owns a patent on this process, which has been licensed to Vestar, Inc., Pasadena, California, a company specializing in clinical uses of liposomes, where the process of drying liposomes is being adapted to industrial applications.

A specialized application of work on preservation of liposomes and proteins has been made by a former student, Alan Rudolph, now of the Naval Research Laboratory, Washington, D.C. Rudolph and co-workers Bruce Gaber and M.C. Farmer demonstrated that if hemoglobin is trapped inside liposomes, the product can be used at least for a short while as a blood substitute, which may be particularly useful under emergency conditions. More recently Rudolph found that liposome-encapsulated hemoglobin can be dehydrated in the presence of trehalose and stored this way for extended periods. This discovery suggests the possibility for a long-lived dry blood substitute that can be rehydrated rapidly when the need arises.

Other applications of work on anhydrobiosis are in the field of food and agriculture. It has been known perhaps for centuries that when dry yeast cells, seeds, or pollen grains are placed in water, they often leak their cellular contents to the surrounding medium and die as a result. It is also well known that these dry organisms leak less and survive rehydration better when they are rehydrated in warm water. In the late 1980s in collaboration with F.A. Hoekstra we established the basis for this phenomenon.

Our studies revealed that when the dry organisms are placed in cool water, their cellular membranes contain some lipids in the gel phase. As the membranes take up water, the lipids undergo a transition to the fluid phase. As discussed above, we know from many studies that fully hydrated membranes become transiently leaky if they are passed through such a phase transition by being heated or cooled. The same kind of leakage might be expected to occur during rehydration.

On the other hand, when dry membranes are heated or cooled, the effects of a phase transition on leakage should be minimal since there is no water available into which the cellular contents can leak. Thus, if dry seeds or yeasts are simply heated before being placed in water, the gel-phase lipids melt before the cells rehydrate. Under these conditions the transition occurs when there is no water outside the cells into which their contents can leak, and they survive rehydration. Even though farmers have long exploited this phenomenon in a practical way—seeds of some species must be planted in warm weather for them to survive— the physical basis had not been known. Similarly, when a baker mixes an envelope of dry yeast cells in warm water to "activate" them, the yeast's membrane lipids in the gel phase melt from the heat before the rehydration process actually gets under way. In other words, at the time the phase transition takes place, water is not yet available to the membranes to allow leakage.

126

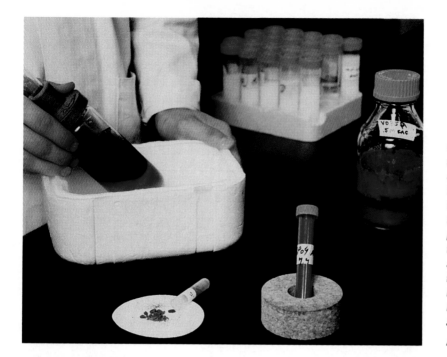

Long-term preservation of hemoglobin as a blood substitute is one medical application of liposome research that is being aided by studies of anhydrobiosis. Hemoglobin that has been trapped in liposomes and dehydrated in the presence of trehalose can be stored dry for extended periods and then rehydrated as needed. In the photo a sample of freeze-dried liposome-encapsulated hemoglobin lies on a paper disk at lower left, while one reconstituted with water appears in the tube at lower right.

Alan Rudolph, Naval Research Laboratory

In all these dry organisms there is good evidence that the transition temperatures in their membranes are depressed by sugars. Baker's yeasts contain as much as 20% of their dry weight in the form of trehalose, and pollen and seeds that survive dehydration commonly contain even greater quantities of sucrose. In pollen of cattail (chosen as an experimental organism because the pollen is so plentiful), we showed that the transition temperature for membrane phospholipids in the dry pollen would be nearly 70° C (158° F) if the pollen did not contain its normal complement of 25% sucrose. The pollen with sucrose has a transition temperature of about 30° C (86° F). Were the sucrose not present, the high temperature needed to avoid leakage would kill the pollen in the process.

One final example from agriculture wherein it is of great interest to preserve living materials is in the field of pest control. Certain nematodes transmit bacteria that are deadly to insects and thus can be used as naturally occurring insecticides if efficient means for storing and distributing the worms can be found. Using our findings described above, researchers at Biosys, Inc., Palo Alto, California, have developed ways of inducing insecticidal nematodes, which are not normally anhydrobiotic, to survive drying. The chances are good that the dry worms can be sprayed directly onto agricultural fields, where they will rehydrate when water becomes available and spread their microbes to insect pests. Similar applications are being explored by several industrial research companies using fungal and bacterial spores as biological control agents.

We envision that the pioneering work being done today on the phenomenon of anhydrobiosis ultimately will be useful in virtually any situation in which it is desirable to stabilize biologically derived molecules, parts of cells, whole cells, or perhaps even complete tissues and organs. The eventual applications are clearly far-reaching.

(Opposite page) Scanning electron micrographs compare freshly prepared liposomes (top) with two samples of liposomes that were put through a dehydration-rehydration cycle—one without trehalose (center) and one in the presence of trehalose (bottom). Liposomes, tiny manufactured spheres having walls of phospholipid bilayers, show potential as drug-delivery systems because they can be made to carry water-soluble substances trapped in their hollow interiors. Unfortunately, they are not stable for long periods in a hydrated state, and like natural membrane-enclosed vesicles, they can be damaged by drying and rehydration such that they leak their contents. In the presence of trehalose, however, liposomes can be dried and then mixed with water to obtain rehydrated liposomes with their contents intact.

(Opposite page) Photos, John H. Crowe

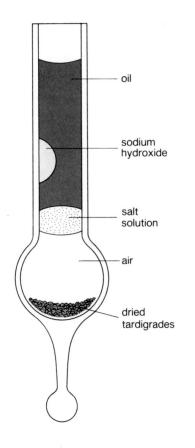

oil

sodium
hydroxide

salt
solution

air

dried
tardigrades

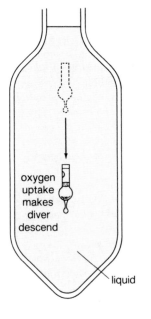

oxygen
uptake
makes
diver
descend

liquid

How "dead" is a dry tardigrade?

Whether metabolism ceases in anhydrobiotic organisms is a question that has preoccupied workers in the field since the time of van Leeuwenhoek. Consequently, heroic efforts have gone into attempts to detect and measure traditional signs of life in the dry organisms directly. For instance, in the early 1950s Andrew Pigon and Barbara Weglarska of the Jagiellonian University, Krakow, Poland, used miniature versions of a science novelty called a Cartesian diver to measure oxygen uptake by anhydrobiotic tardigrades. In their ingenious approach, dry tardigrades were placed in an air pocket at the sealed bottom end of a capillary tube. The neck of the tube was filled with oil, and a droplet of sodium hydroxide was placed in the oil to absorb metabolically produced carbon dioxide. Finally the assembled diver was suspended in a liquid, and the densities of the diver and the liquid were adjusted so that the diver initially had neutral buoyancy, neither rising nor sinking. According to the rationale of the experiment, as oxygen is taken up by the metabolic processes of the tardigrades, carbon dioxide should replace it. Any carbon dioxide will be absorbed by the sodium hydroxide, however, leading to a decrease in the volume of the air space in the diver. As the volume decreases, the buoyancy of the diver declines, and it sinks in the surrounding liquid.

Pigon and Weglarska's extraordinarily sensitive method yielded only equivocal results. At the lowest water content, *i.e.*, the highest level of dehydration, there seemed to be a perceptible oxygen uptake, but the measurements were at the limit of detectability. Nevertheless, the authors could not rule out the possibility that the dry organisms continued to respire even when nearly all their water was removed.

The issue has been further complicated by observations that survival of anhydrobiotic organisms is increased if oxygen is excluded. For example, in the 1960s James S. Clegg, then at the University of Miami, Florida, reported that when dry cysts of the brine shrimp *Artemia* were stored in air for 15 years, virtually none of the cysts survived; when they were stored under vacuum for 10 years followed by storage in air for another 5 years, however, some 22% produced normal animals after rehydration. Such results indicate that the presence of oxygen is, if anything, damaging, an observation inconsistent with occurrence of oxidative metabolism in these organisms. More recently, Clegg produced convincing evidence that full-blown oxidative metabolism does not occur in anhydrobiotic brine shrimp cysts until their water content is elevated to much higher levels (about 40%) than that found in the organisms in dry air (2–5%).

We believe that attempts to measure metabolism directly in very dry organisms are unlikely to produce clear answers, particularly since a lack of detectable metabolism can always be explained by a claim that the technique being used was not sufficiently sensitive. There is an indirect basis, however, for suggesting that metabolism as it is normally understood it is not possible in the dry animals. The argument is as follows: Enzymes, which are crucial to metabolic activity, contain about three-tenths of a gram of water per gram of enzyme that is hydrogen bonded to hydrophilic regions on the molecule. Physical studies of proteins have

128

demonstrated that at lower water contents the proteins are held in a rigid crystalline structure.

Consider the meaning for an anhydrobiotic organism, which contains only 2–5% water. Assuming that it contains about 40% protein and that all the water is associated with protein (an unlikely event), simple calculations show that each gram of protein would contain at most about a tenth of a gram of water. It follows that the enzymes in the dry organism must be in a rigid crystalline structure. Since such a structure does not permit enzymatic activity, metabolism is not possible.

We hasten to add that this reasoning does not imply the impossibility of chemical reactions in dry organisms. Indeed, reactions do proceed, but according to the best evidence available they are adventitious reactions that are actually harmful to the organism, such as the oxidative damage mentioned above. It is possible to construe such reactions as a kind of metabolism, but we believe it unwise to do so, particularly because it would then force one to regard as metabolism similar reactions that go on in objects that are undeniably dead (such as museum specimens or wood furniture). We are forced to conclude, at least until better evidence comes along, that anhydrobiotic organisms exhibit no metabolism when they are reduced to their lowest water content.

In view of this conclusion, one may reiterate the question of the early biologists: are these organisms therefore dead? Suppose one does regard them so. After long-term storage some dried organisms never revive when they are placed in water. Did these nonsurvivors die during storage? But if they are already regarded as dead, then they must have died while they were dead.

There is a way out of logical absurdity. We prefer to think of life and death in terms other than of metabolism. A living thing has organized structure, and implicit in that structure is the capacity for metabolism under favorable conditions. As long as that structural integrity has not been violated, the organism is alive; when the structural integrity breaks down, it is dead. We believe our work on the role of sugars in maintaining structural organization in anhydrobiotic organisms is consistent with that conceptual definition.

FOR ADDITIONAL READING

James S. Clegg, "On the Physical Properties and Potential Roles of Intracellular Water," in G.R. Welch and J.S. Clegg (eds.), *The Organization of Cell Metabolism* (NATO ASI Series, Plenum Press, 1986).

John H. Crowe and James S. Clegg (eds.), *Dry Biological Systems* (Academic Press, 1978).

John H. Crowe, Lois M. Crowe, John F. Carpenter, and Christina Aurell Wistrom, "Stabilization of Dry Phospholipid Bilayers and Proteins by Sugars," *Biochemical Journal* (Feb. 15, 1987, pp. 1–10).

A. Carl Leopold (ed.), *Membranes, Metabolism, and Dry Organisms* (Cornell University Press, 1986).

Stefi Weisburd, "Death Defying Dehydration," *Science News* (Feb. 13, 1988, pp. 97–110).

An attempt in the 1950s by Polish researchers to make direct measurements of metabolic oxygen uptake by anhydrobiotic tardigrades took the form of the experiment illustrated on the opposite page. Dried animals were placed in an air pocket at the sealed bottom of a tiny glass tube (top). In the neck of the tube was added a droplet of salt solution whose concentration maintained the trapped air at a certain humidity level, a filling of oil, and a droplet of sodium hydroxide in the oil to absorb any carbon dioxide produced by the tardigrades. The assembly was then suspended in a liquid in the manner of a Cartesian diver, initially with neutral buoyancy (bottom). Tardigrade metabolism would remove oxygen from the air, while evolved carbon dioxide would be absorbed by the sodium hydroxide. The net result would be a decrease in the volume of air space in the tube and consequent sinking of the diver. This sensitive method yielded equivocal results at the highest level of dehydration. Subsequent attempts to measure metabolism in very dry organisms have not fared much better.

The Yellowstone Fires

by John D. Varley and Paul Schullery

In 1988 Yellowstone National Park experienced fires unprecedented in modern times. In the aftermath scientists have realized that this apparent catastrophe has, as in past centuries, moved the park's ecological systems along to another stage of their ongoing development.

For more than a century Yellowstone National Park, a 2.2 million-acre (900,000-hectare) reserve in Wyoming, Montana, and Idaho, has been known as one of the world's foremost natural laboratories for the study of wild country. National park science and management have often introduced new policies and programs in Yellowstone, constantly putting the park at the center of dialogues and controversy. In recognition of the park's scientific and cultural significance, Yellowstone was named a Biosphere Reserve in 1976 and a World Heritage Site in 1978. Perhaps the world's most famous nature reserve, Yellowstone underwent intense international scrutiny in 1988 when it experienced fires of a magnitude not known in the Rocky Mountains since early in the 20th century and never before experienced in the park's recorded history.

Against the backdrop of this spectacular event, several stories were played out at once. The most newsworthy of these was the political and cultural story, in which the U.S. public reacted to the fires. Depending upon one's perspective, the fires were seen as a simple drama of humans in conflict with powerful natural forces, as a dismal failure of misguided environmental policy, as proof of the wisdom of environmental policy, as a regional economic disaster, as a political hot potato, and in many other ways.

From a purely scientific standpoint, however, the most compelling story was certainly the ecological processes of the fires themselves. Billed by the electronic and print media as a "catastrophe" and a "disaster," the fires were only the latest manifestation of the fundamental ecological forces by which Yellowstone's beloved landscape was created in the first place. Rather than destroying Yellowstone, the fires merely moved the park's ecological systems along to another stage in their ongoing development, a stage not dissimilar to those encountered many times in Yellowstone's prehistoric past. The interweaving of these two major stories—the cultural and the ecological—offers a timely lesson about the changing world of public wildland management.

Yellowstone fire prehistory

Ecologists have long recognized that most North American vegetation communities are in good part the product of periodic fires. In some areas, such as some prairie grasslands, fires were frequent, even annual. In other regions fires occurred infrequently, on a scale of centuries. Prior to the arrival of the European colonists, the two main causes of fire were lightning and American Indians, who seem to have had significant effects on fire frequency in some ecosystems by intentionally or accidentally burning many forest and grassland areas.

Fires performed a variety of natural functions in primitive settings, including opening up closed-canopy forests to new growth, accelerating the buildup of soil by killing live vegetation and by rapidly decomposing dead vegetation, promoting plant succession, and creating a variety of habitat types for wildlife. The colonists, however, disapproved of nature's way of randomly maintaining such natural diversity, and in order to settle and cultivate land they found it expedient to suppress fires.

Most of the Yellowstone plateau is characterized by extensive stands of lodgepole pine, which have experienced relatively long intervals between fires. Research reveals that it typically takes 250 to 400 years for lodgepole forests to reach their most burnable stage, and even then large fires will occur only in extremely dry, windy years. In most years, even with a cool dry climate like that of Yellowstone, most lightning fires cannot find adequate hospitable fuel to burn large acreages.

Thus, the process by which natural fire "recycled" the vegetation communities in Yellowstone was quite irregular. Rather than consistently burning a patch here and there every year, fire burned relatively little most years and then burned huge areas at much longer intervals. Tree-ring studies indicate that the Yellowstone area experienced its last large fire event at the beginning of the 18th century.

The implications of this fire history research became clear in the 1980s, when scientists suggested that park forests were approaching their most volatile life stages. About one-third of Yellowstone's lodgepole forests were between 250 and 350 years old in 1988.

JOHN D. VARLEY *is Chief of Research
and* PAUL SCHULLERY *is a Technical
Writer at Yellowstone National Park,
Wyoming.*

*(Pages 130–131) New grass grows in the
summer of 1989 in an extensively burned
area of Yellowstone National Park.
Photograph © 1990 Gary Braasch*

Fire-management history

For the first few years of Yellowstone Park's institutional life—1872 to
1886—fire fighting was virtually nonexistent. In 1886 the U.S. Cavalry
was assigned to protect the park and, in keeping with the view that fire
was evil, they fought natural and human-generated fires. Their work in
Yellowstone that summer was the first federal involvement in the suppression of natural fires. In 1916, when the National Park Service was
created, its rangers continued to suppress fires whenever possible.

Until World War II fire-suppression efforts in Yellowstone were of
limited effectiveness except on the open shrub-grasslands of the park's
northern range, where natural fires were more readily controlled because of ease of access. In the large forests that cover most of the park,
fires were often difficult to reach and, once burning in the tree crowns,
were often impossible to fight. Some observers wondered if a century of
fire suppression in Yellowstone had caused unnatural fuel buildups, thus
making the fires of 1988 more intense or widespread, but this is unlikely
because fire suppression became consistently effective only after World
War II with the development of aerial fire-fighting technology.

*(Opposite page) Lodgepole pines, the
dominant trees at Yellowstone, begin a
cycle of regrowth amid the fallen trunks
of those destroyed by fire (top right).
After about 150 years the lodgepole
pine forest begins to thin out, and an
understory of such trees as the Engelmann
spruce and subalpine fir appears (top
left). When the forest is about 300 years
old, the original trees begin to die; small
trees and dead branches accumulate,
and the forest once again is vulnerable
to fire (bottom left). The U.S. Cavalry,
grouped at the Mammoth Hot Springs
area in 1911 (above), was assigned to
protect Yellowstone in 1886; they fought
both natural and human-generated fires.
In the 1940s and 1950s the U.S. Forest
Service began to use carefully controlled
fires as a means of improving timber
management (left).*

(Opposite page and this page) photos,
National Park Service

Fire policy in Yellowstone Park often reflected prevailing national trends. In the 1940s and 1950s the U.S. Forest Service and the National Park Service began experimenting with carefully controlled burns, the Forest Service using fire as a tool to improve timber management and the Park Service employing it to restore or re-create more natural replicas of primitive settings.

Yellowstone's 1972 natural fire plan was eventually expanded to include most of the park. Human-generated fires would be fought from time of ignition, and natural fires would be fought if they imperiled park villages, cultural resources, threatened or endangered species, or other special park values. National forests surrounding Yellowstone Park adopted similar plans, though their "ceilings" for allowable burn acreages were much lower than that of Yellowstone Park.

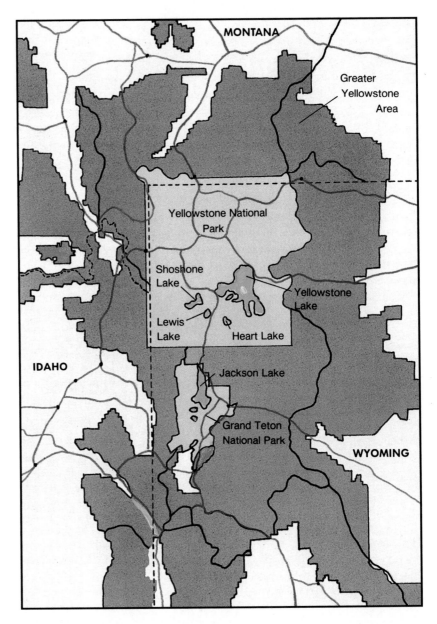

Located mostly in Wyoming, Yellowstone National Park also extends slightly into Montana and Idaho. Covering 2,219,785 acres (898,315 hectares), it is surrounded by national forests (in green), national wildlife refuges (gray), and the John D. Rockefeller, Jr., Memorial Parkway (pink).

Adapted from information obtained from the National Park Service

Image from Landsat 5 satellite, orbiting the Earth at an altitude of 450 miles (725 kilometers), reveals the Yellowstone area in September 1988 when the fires were the most extensive. The red area is that within the burn perimeter, the bright yellow spots along the red border are active fires, and the green and yellow indicate unaffected vegetation. Yellowstone Lake is the dark blue shape on the right; smoke and clouds are shown as white and light blue.

Eros Data Center

During the first 16 years (1972–87) of Yellowstone Park's natural fire program, thousands of lightning strikes started 235 fires that burned 34,157 acres. (One acre equals 0.405 hectare.) Most of these fires burned less than an acre; 15 burned more than 100 acres; the largest of all burned 7,400 acres. The lesson learned from this was that in most years, including those of serious drought, very little would burn in Yellowstone Park. (In 1981, an exceptionally dry year in the West, 21,240 acres— about 1% of the park—burned in natural fires.) The lesson of 1988 was that there is a threshold between a very dry year and an extraordinarily dry year. Once that threshold is crossed, fires no longer increase in acreage at a gradual rate but grow in size much more quickly.

The 1988 fires

The 1988 fires and their environmental effects must be appreciated in the context of longer-term climatic trends. The northern Rocky Mountains experienced a drought from 1982 to 1987, not dry enough to dramatically increase the acreages that were burned but severe enough to have other environmental impacts. In the Greater Yellowstone area, composed of Yellowstone and Grand Teton national parks and six surrounding national forests, the climate was characterized by unusually wet summers and dry winters with little snow. This pattern produced abundant forage for wildlife each summer and also provided wildlife with mild, highly survivable winters. Elk, bison, and other animal populations increased dramatically and were thus set up by nature for the series of environmental shocks provided by the drought and fires of 1988 and the winter conditions of 1988–89.

On the basis of the six previous summers, Greater Yellowstone fire managers had cause to anticipate a continuation in 1988 of the wet-summer pattern. April and May were well above average in precipitation, but by June long-term drought indexes put the area in a "severe drought" classification. (These indexes later were subjected to considerable reinterpretation in the dialogues over whether the fires were fought soon enough.) The summer of 1988 was the driest on record in Yellowstone, but as late as July 11 the National Weather Service was predicting normal precipitation for the region. As the summer and its fires progressed, it became clear that climatic trends even a few days in the future were anybody's guess.

Lightning ignited 20 fires in late May and early June, 11 of which went out on their own. Until late June the others behaved as fires had in previous years, burning relatively small areas. By the first week in July, however, as natural fuels became drier, managers in the national parks and forests recognized that they were encountering fire-hazard conditions not previously experienced. On July 21, though the total area burned in the park was less than 17,000 acres, park managers decided that conditions warranted full suppression of all new and existing fires.

Climatic conditions subsequently grew even more extreme, however, and the threshold for truly large fires was crossed. Six dry-weather fronts passed over Yellowstone in August and September, with high winds and frequent lightning. The fires grew dramatically, and eventually seven major blazes accounted for almost all of the acreage burned.

In Yellowstone Park slightly more than a third of the acreage was affected by some kind of burning. Satellite and aerial mapping revealed about 323,000 acres of "canopy" fire (all needles and small branches burned, all trees killed), the most spectacular form of fire; 281,000 acres of "mixed" burn (a combination of some canopy and some surface vegetation burned); 51,000 acres of shrub-grassland burned; and approximately 138,000 acres of other mixtures of burn types. In all, about 793,000 acres were affected by fire. The total area affected in Greater Yellowstone exceeded one million acres.

The attempt to subdue these fires has been called the largest, most technologically sophisticated fire-fighting effort in U.S. history. It eventually involved more than 25,000 people (as many as 9,000 at one time), dozens of helicopters, retardant-dropping bombers, fire trucks, and other vehicles, and the participation of the Wyoming National Guard and the U.S. Air Force, Army, and Marines. The total cost was estimated at more than $120 million.

Perhaps the two most stunning lessons to emerge from the fires have received very little attention. First, after this huge expense, the fires were finally stopped not by technology but by 0.25 inch (0.62 centimeter) of rain. Second, some fire-behavior experts proposed that though the fire fighters performed heroically in saving almost all structures in the Greater Yellowstone area (67 small buildings, mostly cabins and mobile homes, were destroyed, while many hundreds were saved), the gross acreage burned would have been essentially the same if no money had

A controlled fire deliberately set just inside the northeastern corner of the national park was part of the effort to suppress the Storm Creek fire in early September 1988 (left). The Clover fire on July 21, 1988 (below), ignited by lightning ten days earlier at Clover Creek, joined with the Mist fire on July 22 and burned hundreds of thousands of acres.

been spent at all. Once burning well, under the influence of the extreme climatic conditions, the fires were unstoppable. All fire fighters could hope to do was save property and lives. This they did with remarkable skill and courage.

Fires sent burning embers, carried on high winds, as much as two miles (three kilometers) ahead of the main blaze, starting many "spot fires" that risked the lives of fire fighters and that made any conventional "fire line" dug with shovels or bulldozers useless. Because of high nighttime temperatures and low humidity, fires did not "lie down" at night the way they usually do, and so even in the darkness fire fighters had no advantage over them—and no rest from their labors.

The fires became known as the "Yellowstone Fires," and they were, indeed, all fires in the Greater Yellowstone area. That description was misleading, however, because five of the seven largest fires, including the largest of all, started outside of Yellowstone National Park. Three of those five were human-generated and were fought (without success) from the days they began. The other two were natural fires, initially allowed to burn under the terms of national forest fire-management plans and then fought when they grew too large.

The lesson in this situation was that the Greater Yellowstone area is an ecological unit. The 1988 fires recognized no boundaries and crossed existing ones at will, and although the National Park Service would bear the brunt of public disapproval for the handling of the fires, the entire area would benefit or suffer in the dialogues that followed the fire season.

Ecological effects

Even before the fires were declared extinguished in November 1988, scientific interest in monitoring their effects was great. The fires provided an assortment of scientists with a unique opportunity to examine a massive, landscape-scale perturbation of a wilderness setting.

Soil surveys in the first months following the fires indicated that less than 1% of soils in burned areas were heated enough to kill below-surface vegetation (seeds, roots, tubers, and the like). Regrowth of vegetation in the summer of 1989 varied greatly from site to site, depending upon slope, aspect, soil chemistry, moisture availability, previous vegetation, and other factors. In general, however, regrowth of vegetation, enhanced by ash fertilization and ample precipitation, was considered newsworthy for its lushness, especially the spectacular wildflower shows. Hydrologists and geomorphologists began monitoring soil erosion, which sometimes accelerates when fires reduce vegetative cover on slopes.

A few small fish kills were documented during the fires, some the result of heated water and some caused by airdrops of the fire retardant. The smallest streams were most dramatically affected by fire; larger streams received water from both burned and unburned portions of the watershed and thus were more moderately affected. Fishery researchers predicted that in the short term the fires would improve growing conditions for park fishes until smaller watersheds were revegetated enough to shade streams and reduce the elevated levels of nutrient input.

Plant communities are most directly susceptible to the effects of fire, and landscape ecologists thus showed special interest in monitoring the effects of the fires on the diversity of plant and animal life. The fires, rather than burning vast areas uniformly, created a patchy "mosaic" of burned and nonburned sectors, sometimes on a tiny scale of square inches and sometimes on a grander scale of square miles. This mosaic was imposed over existing mosaics that had resulted from previous fires during the past 300 years, and so Yellowstone continued to provide a more or less infinite variety of potential habitats and conditions for plants and thus for the many animals that live on and with them.

Yellowstone's celebrated lodgepole pine forests are especially adapted to fire. Many of the trees bear cones that are opened only by the intense heat of a fire, thus ensuring the immediate release of seeds onto the open, fertile ground after a fire. Preliminary surveys after the fires revealed pine seed densities on the ground in lodgepole forests ranging from 50,000 to one million per acre. It was expected to take 20 to 30 years for most standing burned trees to fall, 25 to 50 years for a "Christmas tree" forest to appear, and more than a century for the tall forests to regrow.

The effects of the fires on wildlife offered some surprises to observers. Informally (but convincingly) trained by Smokey the Bear and Bambi to believe that forest fires kill all life, the public was slow to grasp a more complicated reality. Except under the most extreme conditions, Yellowstone's famous large animals had little trouble avoiding the flames. Elk, deer, and bison were regularly observed and photographed grazing or bedded down in meadows while forests burned in the background. In

(Opposite page) Efforts to fight the fires included (top to bottom) the use of helicopters to fill buckets with river water, the spraying of fire-retardant foam on buildings, and the clearing of wide strips of land to serve as fire breaks.

(Opposite page) photos, National Park Service; (top) Jeff Henry; (center and bottom) Jim Peaco

Many of the fires did not die down at night, as they often do, because of high nighttime temperatures and low humidity.

(Below) National Park Service; photo, Jim Peaco

Yellowstone Park 246 elk (of a summering population of 31,000), 9 bison (2,700 total population), 4 mule deer, and 2 moose were discovered killed by the fires. Two radiocollared grizzly bears were thought to have died as well, though their remains were not located. Another 137 dead animals (mostly elk and deer) were discovered in burned areas outside the park. On rare occasions the large mammals were trapped when fires were moving rapidly across a broad front. Otherwise, mammals simply stepped aside.

Mortality among smaller mammals was no doubt higher in some areas, as were deaths among reptiles, birds, and insects. Burrowing mammals often escaped the flames by retreating to tunnels, which, if more than an inch or two deep, probably provided adequate insulation from the brief intense heat.

While most ecologists were anxious to point out the positive short-term and intermediate-term effects of fire on wildlife, the important wildlife-related lesson of the Yellowstone fires may be an exercise in taking the long view. Research indicates that Yellowstone Park has been host to very nearly the same assemblage of mammals for at least the past 2,000 years, time enough for several major fire events similar to that of 1988. Clearly, therefore, Greater Yellowstone-area animal populations have been resilient enough to survive such periodic disruptions.

As far as the large mammals were concerned, postfire consequences of recent environmental trends turned out to be more significant and newsworthy than did the fires themselves. The summer of 1988 was the driest in the park's recorded history, resulting in a greatly reduced forage crop, as much as 50% below average on some ranges. This alone would have severely stressed large grazers, but the fires burned substantial portions of some winter ranges, further reducing food supplies. Elk in Yellowstone's famous northern herd (more than 22,000 animals) began their annual migration to winter ranges four to six weeks earlier than usual, and as winter progressed more than half of this herd left the park for unburned winter ranges to the north; usually a much smaller percentage leaves the park.

Adding to the evolutionary challenge facing these elk and other park animals, the winter of 1988–89 was the first in seven years with normal snowfall. Thus, already facing a forage supply reduced by drought and fire, the animals encountered winter conditions that were totally unfamiliar to many of them. Many older animals that would have succumbed if previous winters had been normal were "living on borrowed time," as one biologist put it, and were easy victims of winter stress. By summer several elk herds in Yellowstone Park had been substantially reduced, including about 40% of the northern herd, by a combination of hunting outside the park and winterkill both inside and outside the park. The northern bison herd, one of three main herds in the park, was also severely reduced when the animals migrated into Montana, where more than 500 were killed in a special hunting season. Yellowstone bison carry an organism, brucellosis, that causes domestic livestock to abort, and so the bison are not as welcome on Montana lands as are park elk.

Rather than burning large areas uniformly, the Yellowstone fires produced a patchy "mosaic" of burned and nonburned regions. This will allow the park to continue to provide a wide variety of habitats for plants and the animals that feed on them.

140

Elk graze among singed and burned aspens (left), and a bison finds food in a meadow where sagebrush burned (above). Most large mammals were able to escape the fires, which harmed them most by destroying much of their already drought-reduced food supplies. In the long run, however, the fires will benefit the animals by opening up new fields that will produce grasses for foraging.

National Park Service; photos, Jim Peaco

The environmental lesson of these postfire mortalities may be that every advantage has its price. Ecologists agree that the fires of 1988 will enhance forage production in the park for some years and that the animal populations will benefit from that forage, but first there was a price to be paid in a short-term lack of food.

The political lesson of both the fires and the postfire wildlife mortalities may be that some interest groups and park enthusiasts do not often take the long view. The death of trees in great numbers, even though it has occurred countless times in the Yellowstone area and resulted in the setting so beloved of the public today, was heartbreaking to many people. Some prefer not to see trees die for any reason (almost as if they thought trees were immortal), while others prefer intensive management of one sort or another to keep tree deaths to some aesthetically acceptable minimum. The death of elk, though an event that has occurred annually in Yellowstone for thousands of years, is an emotional issue in modern society. The hunting of bison, one of America's most powerful animal

141

symbols, caused an outcry of national proportions. Though neither the elk nor the bison were threatened with extinction, a large portion of the public did not wish to see them die.

National parks have a long-recognized mission of preserving natural processes. Death is perhaps the least popular, and least understood, of those processes. When Yellowstone's natural system went into its equivalent of evolutionary high gear in 1988—drying and burning the vegetation and trimming the wildlife herds—it was exercising prehistoric prerogatives, as it had many times before.

Though the environmental movement had raised public consciousness much higher than it had been even 20 years before, it appears that for many people, including scientists, managers, and the public, the fires of Yellowstone changed too much too fast. Traditional perspectives on what constitutes a "healthy" forest, based on appearance rather than on ecological realities, surfaced in many circles. While to an ecologist greenery is not scenery, the average American is likely to take a more conservative view, in which forests are expected to stay uniformly picturesque and animals are expected to live indefinitely or die peacefully and out of sight.

Policy prospects

The Yellowstone fires of 1988 generated a national debate not only on federal fire policy but also on other related elements of federal wildland management. In 1990 all U.S. federal agencies with plans concerning natural fires were in the process of reviewing them. Until each management unit—national park, national forest, and so forth—has reviewed and revised its natural-fire-management plan, all fires will be suppressed from the time of ignition. It is hoped that Yellowstone's new plan will be in place by 1991 and that fires will once again be allowed their natural role in park ecosystems.

The debate will no doubt continue for many years; it was under way before the fires, which only highlighted the diversity of opinion over how best to manage federal wildlands. The spectrum of opinion ranges from those who would essentially garden wildlands in order to achieve certain goals—fire prevention and control, safety, aesthetic standards—to those who would let nature do what nature chooses, including the burning of vast areas of wilderness. It already appears that the result of the dialogue will often be compromise, with no viewpoint prevailing. This may satisfy the desire for a democratic process, but it probably will not result in a satisfying wilderness system because it runs the risk of not enacting any one policy consistently, whether that be intensive husbandry or determined avoidance of interference in natural processes.

Much is at stake in these dialogues. Various special interest groups have each claimed that the fires of 1988 proved them right in their goals. Some see the fires as proof that the public domain should be converted to private ownership; others view them as proof that the public domain needs even more extensive federal management. The future promises to be lively and eventful for all involved.

Fireweed and other flowers flourish among trees charred by the fires. Such plants are often the first to appear in a recently burned area of moist forest, and they demonstrate that the cycle of regeneration has begun.

National Park Service; photo, Jim Peaco

REMOTE SENSING

AND ARCHAEOLOGY

by Farouk El-Baz

Advanced space-age tools promise to change the way archaeologists investigate artifacts, explore buried sites without harming their delicate contents, and identify human habitation patterns throughout the world.

Remote sensing is studying an object without having to touch it and also investigating a site from a distance. This broad definition includes such diverse methods as examining an ancient painting with the use of ultraviolet light, probing the subsurface of the Earth with radar waves, and imaging the surface of the Earth from a spacecraft. During the past three decades such methods and techniques were greatly advanced by space exploration. The need to acquire detailed information about the Moon and the planets stimulated important innovations.

It may be difficult to perceive the applications of such high technology to archaeological investigations. The conventional view of an archaeologist is that of a person who handles artifacts, often chemically analyzing them to decipher their origin and that of their context. Furthermore, artifacts are uncovered at a "dig" by excavation using hammers and shovels.

Nevertheless, archaeologists are becoming increasingly aware of the potential value to their work of remote-sensing tools such as hand-held spectrometers, geophysical sensors, and digital imaging systems. Such techniques are assisting modern archaeological investigations in authenticating museum collections, locating hidden burial sites and shipwrecks, evaluating geologic controls on human habitation, deciphering ancient footpaths in the jungle, and revealing the courses of ancient rivers that have long been covered by the sands of time. Combinations of several remote-sensing techniques have been used to study the deterioration of wall paintings of the tomb of Nefertari in Luxor, Egypt, and to investigate nondestructively a sealed chamber at the base of the Great Pyramid of Giza.

Authenticating spectral "signatures"
Researchers at NASA's Jet Propulsion Laboratory (JPL) in Pasadena, California, pioneered the identification of minerals by analyzing the ways by which they reflect sunlight. They recognized that because of

145

Mosaic funeral mask from a Mayan tomb in Guatemala (above) was analyzed for its mineral composition by a portable instantaneous display and analysis spectrometer (above right). Though archaeologists had believed the mask to be jade, the spectrometer revealed that only the two lowest parts of the ears were made of that gemstone.

Photos, Fred Ward—Black Star

FAROUK EL-BAZ is Director of the Center for Remote Sensing at Boston (Mass.) University and President of the Arab Society for Desert Research.

(Overleaf) Photograph by Farouk El-Baz

its unique structure each chemical compound would reflect light rays in a specific way and thus would have a distinct "signature." Therefore, they researched the most practical ways of discriminating those signatures. Their efforts paid off handsomely, and as a result the scientific community has at its disposal several hand-held instruments that can measure the spectral reflectance properties of water, vegetation, soil, rocks, and minerals.

One such instrument, named the portable instantaneous display and analysis spectrometer (PIDAS), weighs 30 kilograms (66 pounds) and can test objects and record their spectral signatures without harming them. Conventional laboratory spectrometers are immobile and require scrapings from the material to be analyzed.

Charles Elachi of JPL mentioned the PIDAS during a meeting that was also attended by Wilbur Garrett, editor of the *National Geographic*. When Garrett heard of the new instrument, his eyes lit up. He knew instantly that it could solve a problem for an article on jade that he was editing. A Mayan masterpiece, a mosaic funeral mask from a tomb in Tikal, Guatemala, was thought by archaeologists to be jade. There was no way to prove it, however, particularly since the delicate mask could not be moved to laboratories or scraped for analysis. Therefore, the PIDAS was taken to the museum in Guatemala City that housed the mask. Its nondestructive measurement confirmed that only the ear flares, the lowest parts of the ears, were made of the mineral jadeite. Other parts were constructed from jade look-alikes.

Ground sensors

Geophysical sensors that probe deep into the Earth have long been used by geologists to study structure and search for mineral resources. Archaeologists have recently increased their use of such hand-held instruments. Foremost among these are magnetometers that measure variations in the local magnetic field and thereby locate buried "anomalies."

Magnetic surveys were conducted by John Weymouth of the University of Nebraska in the Knife River Indian Villages National Historic Site in

North Dakota. The area consists of a series of Native American sites dating back to prehistoric times. The largest archaeological site in the region is the Big Hidatsa Village, which was occupied in the late 1700s and the early 1800s. Having never been plowed, this site exhibits a series of earth lodge depressions and other features. (An earth lodge is a dwelling made of earth that often is built partially below the surface of the ground.)

The magnetic surveys were used to examine the interior features of the visible earth lodges and to discover other lodges not evident by depressions. The typical anomaly at the center of most sites was found to be caused by thermoremanent magnetism (which indicates the strength and direction of the Earth's magnetic field at a former time) in the central fire hearth. Multiple house-construction sequences were inferred from the occurrence of concentric anomalies. Other magnetic anomalies in these houses were caused by a pit, a piece of iron, and a heated boulder. Similar high-magnetic regions were located between houses and were determined to be deep trash middens, where refuse had been discarded. All these anomalies and attributes were confirmed through test excavations at the site.

Similarly, a team led by Philip Hammond of the University of Utah used four proton magnetometers and an instrument that measured resistance to electricity in order to locate anomalies in the floor of the valley of Petra in southern Jordan. Petra, a 2,000-year-old city, is referred to as Sela in the Bible. Carved in the rose-colored sandstone cliffs of Wadi Musa, it was occupied by the Edomites and the Nabataeans, who had their capital there from the 4th century BC until the Roman occupation in AD 106. Only rock-cut tombs and temples line the walls of this vast valley. Few remnants of dwellings, storage bins, etc., have been unearthed. Remote sensing technology came to the rescue to identify habitation sites and other objects.

Standard surveyor's mapping instruments were employed in the valley to establish a baseline, and 72 grids, each measuring 30 × 30 meters (98.4 × 98.4 feet), were laid out. Some 15,975 measurement points,

Research team led by Philip Hammond of the University of Utah uses a proton magnetometer and an instrument that measures resistance to electricity to locate ancient habitation sites and other objects in the valley of Petra in southern Jordan.

P.C. Hammond

Sensors of the subsurface

Geologists have long recognized the value of measuring waves, either emitted or reflected by layers within the Earth, in deciphering subsurface structures. Now it is the archaeologist's turn to benefit from such geophysical sensors as the following:

Electromagnetic conductivity equipment. Electromagnetic equipment measures differences in conductivity between surface and subsurface soils and features. An instrument may provide direct readings of terrain conductivity to a depth of about six meters. Thus, it can be used to map either superimposed layers of soil or subsurface cavities. It is best described as a general-purpose subsurface mapper and is particularly useful where soil conductivity is too high to allow the effective use of ground-penetrating radar.

Ground-penetrating radar. Ground-penetrating radar (GPR) is a special type of low-frequency radar that is capable of "seeing" into the ground. Conventional radars use microwaves, which can penetrate only a few centimeters into the ground. A GPR uses much lower frequencies (close to those used by FM radio or television stations), emitting a brief impulse of radio frequency energy lasting only a few billionths of a second. The radar antenna beams this impulse directly into the ground. Typically, there are three antennae (or transducers): a 500-megaHertz antenna for shallow, high-resolution recording; a 300-megaHertz antenna for general-purpose profiling; and a 120-megaHertz antenna for deeper penetration at less resolution. When the radar impulses travel down into the ground, they pass through various layers of soil, sand, clay, rock, or other natural materials. Each layer produces a reflection, or echo. These echoes return to the surface of the ground, where they are detected by the radar antenna. The deeper the reflecting layer, the longer its echo will take to return to the surface. To make a "picture," the radar antenna is moved along the surface of the ground. The radar echoes are recorded on a chart and may also be viewed on a television screen. The radar picture shows a vertical profile of the subsurface layers along the path covered by the radar antenna.

Seismometer determines subsurface features by measuring the time that artificially generated seismic waves require for traveling to their underground destinations and returning, by refraction, to the surface.

A.C. Roosevelt

Magnetometers. The magnetic field of the Earth is influenced by subsurface features that have a different magnetization than that of the surrounding soil. Small localized features near the surface, such as a metal object, are easily detectable, and deeper geologic structures are observable if the survey is extended across large areas. The effectiveness of the magnetometer depends on the contrast between the surrounding soil and the object of interest. Metals, fired or burned objects, and man-made structures are normally detectable. The "proton magnetometer," the most widely used instrument for measuring magnetic fields in archaeological sites, can measure very small variations in magnetization; this produces a true gradient measurement without interference from diurnal fluctuations or background regional gradients. Measurements are made on a grid of points marked by grids and ropes. For collecting the magnetic measurements, the site is commonly divided into square blocks with 20 grid units on each side. A grid unit one meter in length is preferable, but a two-meter grid may be enough in historic sites with iron anomalies or for preliminary assessments. A microcomputer is often taken into the field to provide real-time information, but more extended processing occurs in the laboratory.

Resistivity instruments. In the resistivity method of prospecting, an electric current is introduced into the ground by two contact electrodes, and the differences in electric potential are measured between them. Electrode arrays may be moved along profiles in order to determine lateral variations in resistivity and, therefore, pinpoint the location of buried anomalies.

Seismometers. Seismometers used by archaeologists are much like the instruments that are used to detect, magnify, and record vibrations caused by earthquakes. They are sensitive to artificially generated elastic waves. The detected motions are recorded in time maps, which show the time it took the wave to travel to its destination and become reflected or refracted back to the surface. These maps are correlated to depth maps to show the depth of the interface that resulted in the reflection. Thus, a "seismic picture" of the subsurface layering and structure emerges.

used for both instruments, were laid out at two-meter (6.6-foot) intervals and read by one or both instruments for a total of 63,900 square meters. Field data were processed by computer and later analyzed with the aid of computers. The resulting contour maps were overlaid to reinforce their information content. Of the 72 grids surveyed, 38 were identified as "high anomaly" areas. These were labeled as sites of high priority for excavation. Thus, remote-sensing techniques were able to pinpoint places that needed further investigation. The alternative would have been a valley eternally pockmarked by "test pits," sites that were investigated without the use of subsurface information.

Stratigraphic profile of hearths in house floors under the Earth's surface (right) was achieved by use of a variety of remote-sensing instruments. Excavations that were made on the basis of the profile uncovered fired-clay hearths (right bottom).

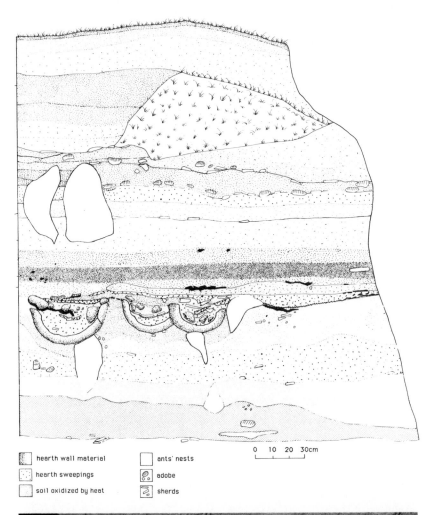

hearth wall material   ants' nests
hearth sweepings   adobe
soil oxidized by heat   sherds

0   10   20   30cm

A mix of instruments

Anna Roosevelt of the American Museum of Natural History and Bruce Bevan of Geosight, Inc., used a variety of instruments to investigate the settlements and lifeways of prehistoric peoples in the lower Amazon region of Brazil. One of the cultures that was investigated was a complex mound-building chiefdom subsisting on fishing and the cultivation and collection of plants.

The instruments detected significant archaeological features that were later verified by excavation. They included baked clay hearths, burned house floors, garbage fill, and earthworks. The geophysical maps, which were checked by excavations, revealed entire layouts of relatively large settlements. For example, in three-hectare (7.4-acre), 7–10-meter (23–33-feet)-high mounds of the Marajoara phase at the mouth of the Amazon (AD 400–1300), proton magnetometers revealed the location of long-houses by detecting their large, fired-clay hearth groups as anomalies. Ground-penetrating radar mapped recent disturbance to soil layers, and electromagnetic equipment revealed conductivity changes in the strata of the Earth. Instruments measuring electrical resistance mapped both horizontal and vertical stratigraphic shifts caused by earthworks, garbage fill, and hearths. Devices that measured the refraction of seismic waves revealed major platform levels in the mound and detected the original ground surface on which the mounds were built.

The effectiveness of the techniques resulted from the ways Roosevelt and Bevan employed them. First, they maintained stricter ground control than usual, using electronic total station theodolites (instruments that electronically record distances, angles, and elevations for surveying a site), and all the work was computerized so that it could be reduced and mapped in the field to check for errors and to be used for planning excavations. They also calculated magnetic data automatically for diurnal changes and checked the interpretations of the geophysical patterns systematically, excavating a sample of each of the different types of features revealed by the surveys.

The view from above

To increase the area of the survey and acquire a bird's-eye view of archaeological sites, instruments must fly into the air. The first step is to load the remote sensors onto a balloon or a blimp. A tethered balloon was first systematically used in 1930 at the excavation of Megiddo (the biblical Armageddon) by Philip Guy and James Breasted. It is a relatively inexpensive platform and can be inflated on site when conditions of light and weather are optimum. A properly fitted camera balloon works well in the range between 10 and 800 meters (2,624 feet) above the ground.

A system developed by J. Wilson Myers of Boston University and used in land areas near the Mediterranean Sea from the mid-1970s included a ten-meter-long, four-finned blimp tethered to the ground and equipped with both a 35-millimeter camera and a Hasselblad camera with FM radio control. A camper van carrying crew and equipment served as a mobile darkroom. A choice of filters and films, including infrared, was

151

A camera on a blimp tethered to the ground (top) took the photograph of the excavated Minoan palace at Mallia, Crete (right). Such aerial views are often essential first steps in archaeological studies of an area.

helpful at sites covered with vegetation and submerged in lakes and seas. The height of the cameras above their target was determined from calibrations on the tether cord and, given the focal length of the lenses, the coverage on the ground could be exactly calculated.

Myers joined two Boston University archaeologists, James Wiseman and Frederick Hemans, to study several sites of the ancient Greek city of Corinth at the northern foot of its fortified mountain citadel, Acrocorinth, and its seaport, Lechaeum. In addition to photographic cameras, a multi-spectral video camera was used. Approximately 500,000 multispectral images were obtained and analyzed at the Boston University Center for Remote Sensing to map the studied sites and reveal details that were otherwise not detectable.

152

A balloon was also used for topographic mapping in support of archaeological investigations in what became known as the "Berkeley map of the Theban Necropolis." In spite of the centuries-old interest in such features as the Valley of the Kings, the Tombs of the Nobles, and other monuments on the east bank of the Nile River at Luxor, no accurate or complete map existed of this "Theban Necropolis." Researchers from the University of California at Berkeley utilized a balloon to acquire the necessary photographs of such features as the Colossi of Memnon, the Mortuary Temple of Hatshepsut, and the Valley of the Queens. These photographs were immediately used in numerous studies, such as the investigation of the deterioration of the wall paintings of the tomb of Nefertari, which is discussed below.

University of Colorado anthropologist Payson Sheets and his student Tom Sever were leafing through some infrared aerial photographs of the Tilaran area of northwestern Costa Rica. The two researchers were familiar enough with the territory to be able to correlate photographed features with places they knew. "What surprised us was an odd, twisting line," wrote Sheets and Sever. "It began near an ancient cemetery, headed straight downhill, made a wide-angle bend around an enigmatic prehistoric rock pile, crossed a stream, headed uphill, and made another bend around another enigmatic rock pile. Because it ran straight across hills and valleys, linking archaeological sites such as cemeteries, villages and sources of stone, we suspected it was not a natural feature, but perhaps a prehistoric road."

Excavation proved that the infrared photographs had revealed a footpath created more than 1,000 years ago that had since been buried by volcanic ash. As people walked to the cemeteries, they compacted the soil and thus formed a shallow trench that channeled rainwater. The compaction also discouraged plant growth, which further encouraged soil erosion. Although the original path may have been 0.5 meter (1.6 feet) or less in width, its present-day traces are nearly four meters (13 feet) deep and more than 10 meters in width. Nonetheless, their discovery had to await the "seeing" powers of aircraft sensors.

Infrared aerial photograph of the Tilaran region in Costa Rica (below) reveals a contemporary road and, above the road in the photo, a 1,000-year-old buried footpath slanting upward from it. Archaeologists used the photograph to make excavations that uncovered the path (below left).

(Left) Payson Sheets; (right) Earth Resources Laboratory, Stennis Space Center, NASA

During the late 1970s Rodman Frates read an article detailing the difficulties archaeologists faced in trying to navigate the dense jungle of the Yucatán Peninsula of Mexico in search of sites. When he found himself in the company of geologists, he asked if there was any way to remedy the situation. The answer was to use Landsat data.

Landsat is a family of imaging satellites that orbit 920 kilometers (572 miles) above the Earth and scan a swath 185 kilometers (115 miles) wide at a time. As sunlight is reflected from the Earth, it is separated into four or seven wavelengths, or spectral bands. The reflected energy is measured by microdetectors and converted into electrical signals for transmission to receiving stations on the ground, where they are recorded on magnetic tapes. When such tapes are manipulated by computers, images are produced that depict variations in the spectral reflectance properties of materials within the scene. These images in green, red, or near-infrared are commonly used to study the surface features of the Earth.

Frates had approached geologists from the Earth Satellite Corp. of Bethesda, Maryland. Their expertise in processing, enhancing, and interpreting Landsat images resulted in the identification of 112 possible Mayan sites and two confirmed Mayan ruins in the Yucatán; one was a previously unknown city, and investigators believed that the other was possibly the "lost" city of Oxpemul. The latter had been discovered in the early 1930s, but problems of navigation in the dense jungle precluded its location on maps.

The Landsat images showed numerous "aquadas," or reservoirs, covering 0.8 to 4 hectares (2 to 10 acres), that the Mayans cut out of limestone surfaces. Furthermore, a 60-meter (197-foot)-long and 5-kilometer (3.1-mile)-wide strip of walled plots was discovered. Field investigations

Imaging systems

In addition to cameras using various types of film, numerous imaging systems are emerging as tools for archaeological research. They include three airborne sensors and three for balloon operations or to be hand held in the field.

Airborne oceanographic lidar. Airborne oceanographic lidar is a laser device that makes "profiles" of the Earth's surface from aircraft altitudes. The laser beam pulses to the ground 400 times per second, striking the surface every 10 centimeters (four inches), and bounces back to its source. In most cases the beam bounces off the top of the vegetation cover and off the ground surface. The difference between the two gives information on forest height or even the height of grass in pastures. For example, as the lidar passes over an ancient, eroded road that still affects the topography, the pathway's indentation is recorded by the laser beam.

Synthetic aperture radar. The synthetic aperture radar, when directed down and sideways from an aircraft, beams energy waves to the ground and records the reflected energy. Radar is sensitive to linear and geometric features on the ground, particularly when different radar wavelengths and different combinations of the horizontal and vertical data are employed. Different wavelengths are sensitive to vegetation or to ground-surface phenomena. In dry, porous soils radar can penetrate the surface.

Thermal infrared multispectral scanner. The thermal infrared multispectral scanner (TIMS) uses six channels to measure the thermal radiation given off by the ground, with accuracy to 0.1° C. The picture element, or "pixel," is the square area being sensed, and the size of the pixel is directly proportional to sensor height. For example, pixels from the newest Landsat satellites are about 30 meters on a side and thus have limited archaeological applications. However, pixels in the TIMS data from an aircraft measure only about one meter on a side, and they can detect small features.

Spectral radiometer. The spectral radiometer is a silicon charge-coupled device (CCD) sensor with spectral sensitivity ranging from 0.4 to 1.1 micrometers. The sensor uses a diffraction grating to take 256 separate readings across the sensitivity range. It is employed to identify the general spectral characteristics of materials and can be used with Landsat multispectral data or the data from any multispectral camera. It is especially useful in the discovery of the locations of the spectral regions and, therefore, identification of those that should be targeted for data collection. The radiometer can also be utilized for "ground-truth" experiments to identify unknown materials and test the degree of accuracy in the interpretation of imagery.

Multispectral camera. The multispectral camera is an imaging system that uses a CCD sensor with six filters mounted on a wheel between the lens and the CCD. Bandpass filters varying from 10 to 100 nanometers of width are available, but the most useful are a configuration of 80–100-nanometer filters centered at 0.45, 0.55, 0.65, 0.75, 0.85, and 1.0 micrometer. This spectral response matches the Landsat multispectral scanner, and filters can be selected to match the same bandwidths. This allows the creation of images, at higher resolution, that can be related to the satellite data. The portability of the system makes it a highly versatile general-purpose multispectral data-collection system.

Ultraviolet and infrared video cameras. The ultraviolet camera is sensitive in the ultraviolet region of the spectrum (0.2–0.4 micrometer), and the infrared camera is sensitive to 1.9 micrometers in the near-infrared region. Both can be used with filters to collect images covering narrow ranges of the spectrum and to provide additional information beyond the spectral range of the multispectral camera. Among other potential uses, the ultraviolet images provide information on paintings and other works of art. Near-infrared images in the spectral region between one and two micrometers are especially useful in soil and mineral analyses.

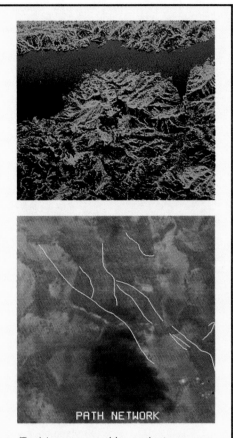

(Top) Image created by synthetic aperture radar shows Lake Arenal in Costa Rica at the top and a cemetery in the lower left corner. Radar beams are directed downward from an airplane, and their reflected energy is recorded. Because heavy vegetation reflects more of the energy, forested areas appear light in color and pastures darker. (Above) The thermal infrared multispectral scanner creates an image by measuring the thermal radiation emitted by the ground. In this case forested areas will be darker than pastures. White lines have been drawn over footpaths, which would actually appear very dark on the original image.

Photos, NASA

Wall painting from the tomb of Nefertari (died about 1280 BC) near Luxor in Egypt reveals deterioration of paint on the seated figure of the goddess Hat-hur. Analysis of the painting indicated that the deterioration affected a thin layer on the surface and might have been caused by moisture in the air.

Farouk El-Baz

showed that the walls surround small farm plots and house mounds. They were made by piled-up stone, much like property "markers" in the New England states. The Oxpemul site, which required a year for a road to be built to it through the jungle, is now being excavated.

Radar rivers

Landsat data have since been used in many cases to reveal archaeological sites and interpret their setting. Another spaceborne method that promises to be as useful is radar imaging. Unlike the "passive" sensors on board the Landsat spacecraft, the imaging radar is "active." It provides a source of electromagnetic energy to "illuminate" the terrain. The returned energy is detected by the imaging system and recorded on photographic film. Thus, radar systems can operate independently of lighting conditions and weather, because radar rays penetrate clouds.

Though the experimenters had no archaeological applications in mind, the imaging radar of the space shuttle *Columbia* in November 1981 obtained images of a featureless tract of the Western Desert of Egypt. Quite unexpectedly, the radar waves penetrated the sand cover in this wasteland; the extreme aridity of the area and thus the dryness of the sand grains allowed this penetration. Uncovered were courses of ancient streams, one 20 kilometers (12.4 miles) across, as wide as today's Nile Valley.

The revelation inspired field investigations to check the potential of human habitation around these ancient watercourses. Digging through sand up to five meters (16.4 feet) in thickness revealed artifacts indicating prehistoric human habitation at these sites dating back to approximately 210,000 years ago.

The finding also sparked interest in the potential for groundwater resources in the region. Some of the water of the ancient rivers must have evaporated, and some must have been supplied to the mouths of the rivers, but some must also have seeped through the underlying rock to be stored as groundwater. After analyzing the images in 1982, the author suggested to the Egyptian government a program of test drilling. Wells drilled to date prove a groundwater reserve that is capable of supporting agriculture on nearly 81,000 hectares (200,000 acres) for 200 years.

Remote sensing in Egyptology

Using the Boston University Center for Remote Sensing as a base, the author during the past two years applied a mix of techniques to two archaeological projects in Egypt: the study of the wall paintings of the tomb of Nefertari in Luxor and the nondestructive investigation of the second boat pit of Pharaoh Khufu (Cheops) in Giza. The study of the wall paintings in the tomb of Nefertari was a joint research effort between the Egyptian Antiquities Organization (EAO) and the Getty Conservation Institute (GCI). The tomb is that of the favorite wife of Pharaoh Ramses the Great, who ruled Egypt for 67 years (1304–1237 BC). When it was unearthed in 1904 by an Italian expedition, it had lost some of its magnificent wall paintings because of salt crystallization behind the plaster

156

layer on which the artisans had applied the paint. Fear of further damage resulted in the closing of the tomb to visitors for the past 50 years.

The objective of the study was to establish the origin of the water that had caused the mobilization of salt and its recrystallization in order to recommend a treatment to conserve the paintings. The author applied remote-sensing methods and techniques to: (1) map the region in the immediate vicinity of the tomb for the establishment of a hydrologic model of the area; (2) establish whether the deterioration was a onetime event or a continuous process; and (3) study the state of various segments of the tomb's walls to locate areas needing emergency treatment.

To establish the drainage pattern in the Valley of the Queens, where the tomb exists, an image obtained by Landsat was studied. It showed the fracture pattern in the region and revealed that a two-kilometer (1.2-mile)-long escarpment separated the valley from the main plateau to the west. This setting allowed the study of the hydrology of the Valley of the Queens as a separate unit. The basic topographic features of the area had been shown in a French map made in 1926. Additional details were mapped by Swiss Air Photo from balloon and aircraft photographs. Also,

Multispectral photography obtained images of a wall painting in the tomb of Nefertari in visible light (left) and ultraviolet light (left bottom). The ultraviolet image shows a detail of the visible-light photograph; it reveals deterioration not detectable by the human eye.

Photos, Farouk El-Baz

Boat made of cedar wood was almost perfectly preserved for 46 centuries in a sealed pit next to the Great Pyramid of the Egyptian pharaoh Khufu at Giza, Egypt. The boat was found disassembled in a pit under a cap of 41 limestone blocks sealed together with gypsum mortar.

Farouk El-Baz

profiles of dry valleys and hill slopes were obtained through the help of Earthwatch volunteers. All such data were integrated in the computer-generated hydrologic model of the area.

To establish the sequence of the deterioration of the wall paintings over time, the author and his colleagues used software that was designed to aid in the study of Landsat images. Photographs of the same wall taken at different times were digitally compared. This indicated that the recent deterioration was mostly physical rather than chemical—pieces that were already separate had fallen down with advanced age. On the basis of this information, it seems unlikely that the chemical deterioration has continued to this day.

The study of the state of various parts of the wall was done with multispectral photography. Instruments were used to obtain photographs in visible, near-infrared, and ultraviolet light. These images indicated which parts of the wall had deteriorated without visible signs. Pockets of air or salt not visible to the human eye were detected and helped in locating areas that required emergency conservation.

The second project involved the nondestructive investigation of a boat pit of Pharaoh Khufu. The pit in question was located in 1954, aligned with another one, 18 meters (59 feet) south of the Great Pyramid of Giza. During the same year the eastern pit was excavated from under a cap of 41 limestone blocks and found to contain a disassembled boat. Gypsum mortar sealed the crevices between the cap blocks. The disassembled boat was made of cedar wood 4,600 years ago. The wood was excavated, and the assembled vessel was placed on exhibit at the Boat Museum, which was built on the site of the discovery. By 1986, however, the boat had shrunk about 0.5 meter since it was assembled in 1966. It was feared that such deterioration may have been caused by the changing environmental conditions inside the museum.

Since the second (western) pit was thought also to contain a boat, it was hoped that the investigation of its environmental surroundings would lead to a better understanding of how best to preserve the ancient wood. This idea was the driving force behind the project. A research plan was developed through an agreement between the EAO and the National Geographic Society to undertake the following steps: (1) geophysically surveying the site; (2) drilling a nine-centimeter (3.5-inch) hole by means of dry rotary drill motion through the limestone cap rock; the drilling and other operations were sealed by an air lock to separate the air inside from that outside; (3) sampling the air in the cavity at different levels; (4) measuring pressure, temperature, and relative humidity inside the chamber; (5) photographing the interior with a video camera using a fiber-optic "cold" light and a 35-millimeter still camera; and (6) sealing the drill hole with material similar to that used by the ancient Egyptian builders.

When the testing of the equipment was completed, site investigation was conducted during October 1987. First, a scaffold was built on top of the selected site, and a tent was set up to protect the imaging equipment. Then one of the blocks of the limestone cap rock was selected

158

and prepared for drilling. The block was 160 centimeters (65 inches) thick, and there appeared to be no change in pressure as the drill bit went through it. This indicated that there may have been communication between the atmosphere inside and that outside the chamber. Seventy liters (18.5 gallons) of air were collected from 18 centimeters (7 inches), 94 centimeters (37 inches), and 145 centimeters (57.1 inches) below the ceiling for analysis by specialists of the National Oceanic and Atmospheric Administration (NOAA) at Boulder, Colorado.

Photography of the interior revealed a disassembled boat. Much like the one that was opened in 1954, the second pit contained stacks of wood with pieces of the cabin arranged on top. This second boat appeared to be smaller than the first and had four small pointed oars. The pressure inside the chamber was identical to that outside. The temperature measured 27° C (81° F), and the relative humidity was 85%.

As the air samples reached NOAA's laboratories, atmospheric scientists and physicists began to monitor the contents of the canisters and analyze their components. Results of freon analyses came first; freon-11 measured 300 parts per trillion, and freon-12 about 540 parts per

Digital image enhancement

Computers are utilized in the processing and enhancement of digital images from hand-held, airborne, or spaceborne remote-sensing instruments to aid the analyst in the extraction and interpretation of pictorial information. The interpretation is impeded by degradations resulting from the imaging, scanning, transmission, or display processes. Enhancement is achieved by the articulation of features or patterns of interest within an image and by a display that is adapted to the properties of human vision. Because the human eye discriminates many more colors than shades of gray, a color display can represent more detailed information than one in shades of gray.

To an image analyst, information significance is definable in terms of the observable parameters of contrast, texture, shape, and color. The characteristics of the data and display method and the properties of the human visual system determine the transformation from the recorded to the enhanced image. They define the range and distribution of the observable parameters in the resulting image for a particular application.

Enhancement operations are applied without quantitative knowledge of the degrading phenomena, which include contrast attenuation, blurring, and noise. The techniques attenuate or discard irrelevant features and at the same time emphasize interesting features or patterns. Typically, the methods include contrast enhancement, edge enhancement, and pseudo-color enhancement performed on monochrome images or on individual components of multi-images. Multi-image enhancement operators generate new features by combining components (channels) of multi-images. For multi-images with more than three components, the dimensionality can be reduced to enable an unambiguous color assignment.

Image of the Middle Orinoco basin in Venezuela taken in infrared light is provided with color enhancement by a computer. The sand and mud banks of the main river channel are cultivated with crops (bright pink). The blue-green of the grasslands north of the river indicates that they are not photosynthesizing, and the mixed red and blue of the gallery forest immediately north of the river reveals that many trees there also are not photosynthesizing. The image was obtained during the peak of the dry season.

A.C. Roosevelt

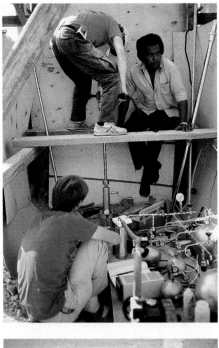

trillion. These values were higher than, but close to, those of the air measured near Cairo.

An unusually high value was that of the content of carbon dioxide, which measured 720 parts per million, double the amount in the surrounding atmosphere. Carbon dioxide might have been produced by degassing from the organic materials inside the pit or even by being driven off the limestone walls of the chamber. A test to date the carbon dioxide gave an age of 2,000 years. This indicated that it was a mixture of ancient air and a modern counterpart.

Three attempts were made to capture from the air organic particles to identify any bacteria or pollen. These samples were completely free of microbial contaminants. This may have been the case because the air was pumped from nearly one meter (3.28 feet) above the contents of the chamber, whereas bacteria or other organisms may have settled at the bottom of the pit or the upper surface of the wood.

Thus, at both sites "video" archaeology was able to aid in the study of delicate artifacts without harming them or affecting their environment. The success of the two projects convincingly established the worldwide applications of remote-sensing technology to archaeological investigations.

A look into the future

In the 1950s carbon-14 age dating transformed archaeology into a more exact science. By 1990 a similar revolution in the archaeological sciences had been achieved through applications of remote-sensing technology. Such applications will expand the use of data from hand-held spectrometers, geophysical sensors, and imaging systems onboard balloons, blimps, aircraft, and spacecraft.

It is conceivable that by the year 2000 remote-sensing instruments may prove more important to archaeologists than shovels. When this happens, it will be assured that information about our human heritage will be collected while the archaeological site is preserved, which may be as significant as preservation of the artifacts they contain. Furthermore, it is being recognized that the excavation of new artifacts is not as important as the conservation of those already discovered. Archaeological objects and sites suffer from recent, human-induced degradation of their environments. Stone carvings, mummies, and even whole temples may weather away if serious attempts are not made to save them.

Remote-sensing technologies promise to play a major role in the nondestructive investigation and monitoring of archaeological sites. This will assist in finding solutions to averting the deterioration of objects and sites alike. Thus, space technology and the most modern of advanced methodologies promise to play a leading role in the preservation of the recorded history of ancient human habitation on the Earth.

160

FOR ADDITIONAL READING

Egyptian Antiquities Organization, "Wall Paintings of the Tomb of Nefertari" (First progress report, Cairo, July 1987).

Farouk El-Baz, "Finding a Pharaoh's Funeral Bark," *National Geographic* (April 1988, pp. 512–533).

Farouk El-Baz, "Origin and Evolution of the Desert," *Interdisciplinary Science Reviews* (December 1988, pp. 331–347).

Alaric Faulkner and Gretchen Fearon Faulkner, *The French at Pentagoet 1635–1674: An Archaeological Portrait of the Acadian Frontier* (New Brunswick Museum, 1987).

Frederick Hemans, J. Wilson Myers, and James Wiseman, "Remote Sensing from a Tethered Blimp in Greece" (Boston University Center for Remote Sensing, Technical Paper No. 2, 1987).

George Rapp and John Gifford, eds., *Archaeological Geology* (Yale University Press, 1985).

Payson Sheets and Tom Sever, "High-Tech Wizardry," *Archaeology* (November–December 1988, pp. 28–35).

Kathy Shirley, "Sensing Spurs Remote Discovery," *AAPG Explorer* (September 1989, pp. 20–21).

University of California, "The Berkeley Map of the Theban Necropolis" (Report of the Fifth Season, 1982).

Fred Ward, "Jade: Stone of Heaven," *National Geographic* (September 1987, pp. 282–315).

John Weymouth, "Magnetic Surveys of Archaeological Sites in the Knife River Indian Villages National Historic Sites: Major Village Sites" (University of Nebraska report submitted to the Midwest Archaeological Center, 1988).

Research team drills a nine-centimeter (3.5-inch) hole through the limestone cap rock covering a second boat pit next to the Great Pyramid of the Pharaoh Khufu (opposite page, top). This was done so that the air inside the pit could be sampled before the cap was broken. When the pit was entered, it was found to contain a disassembled boat (opposite page, bottom) similar to the first boat unearthed nearby in 1954. It was more degraded, however, probably because the airtight seal of the cap had been broken during a construction project in the 1960s. The reconstruction of prehistoric dwellings at the mouth of the Amazon River in Brazil (left) was made possible by remote sensing, which revealed the location, orientation, and shape of the dwellings. Excavation of the site showed that the building materials had been mud, poles, and thatch.

(Left) A.C. Roosevelt; (opposite page, top) Farouk El-Baz; (opposite page, bottom) © 1988 National Geographic Society; photo, Claude E. Petrone

"Smart" Materials:
A Revolution in Technology

by Brian S. Thompson and Mukesh V. Gandhi

Self-diagnosis, self-repair, self-learning, and the ability
to anticipate future problems will characterize new
materials now under development. They are expected
to revolutionize the future at least as dramatically as the
electronic chip has influenced technology today.

BRIAN S. THOMPSON *is Professor and* MUKESH V. GANDHI *is Associate Professor at the Intelligent Materials and Structures Laboratory, Michigan State University, East Lansing.*

(Overleaf) Illustration by Constantino Mitchell

Materials technology has had such a profound impact on the evolution of human civilization that historians have characterized periods in that evolution by such terms as the Stone Age, the Bronze Age, and the Iron Age. Each new era was brought about by the continuing quest for ever better products, a quest that is very much in evidence today. The current "Synthetic Materials Age" has been precipitated by humankind's demand for materials with superior performance characteristics, inspired primarily by the quest to conquer the last frontier of space. The dawn of the 21st century will witness the emergence of the "Smart Materials Age." It will be catalyzed by a technological revolution that will exploit several emerging technologies, such as materials science, biotechnology, biomimetics (the development of synthetic systems by the use of information obtained from biological systems), nanotechnology (the use of molecular-scale objects as components of molecular machines), molecular electronics, neural networks (the electronic simulation of the neural composition of the human brain), and artificial intelligence. These technologies will provide the nervous system, the brains, and the muscles for a new generation of advanced materials and structures that are at present a mere skeleton compared with the anatomy perceived in the not-too-distant future. This quantum jump in materials technology seems certain to revolutionize the future in ways far more dramatic than the way the electronic chip has catalyzed the evolution of our life-styles.

Smart materials will have the capability to select and execute specific functions intelligently in response to changes in environmental stimuli. For example, these innovative multifunctional materials may exhibit homeostasis, the tendency of an organism to maintain normal internal stability by coordinated responses of systems that autonomously compensate for environmental changes. This ability may be complemented by several other capabilities that are characteristic of intelligent systems, such as self-diagnosis, self-repair, self-multiplication, self-degradation, and self-learning. Furthermore, these features may be augmented by capabilities for anticipating future challenges and missions and the ability to recognize and discriminate. It is clearly evident, therefore, that all aspects of our lives will be significantly touched as the development of smart materials impacts industries as diverse as automotive, aerospace, defense, biomedical devices, advanced manufacturing, robotics, industrial machinery, sporting goods, high-precision instruments, highways, buildings, and bridges.

Smart materials and structures

The field of smart materials and structures is broad and draws from a variety of disciplines, including materials science, biotechnology, neural networks, biomimetics, nanotechnology, and artificial intelligence. At this time significant developments have occurred in the area of engineering structures, and it seems certain that the next decade will witness the first successful deployments of smart materials in commercial aerospace applications. This section is focused on current efforts aimed at the development of smart materials and structures for engineering applica-

164

tions. The current generation of smart materials and structures is limited in the scope of its mission since these materials feature only sensing capabilities or actuation capabilities; they are devoid of any adaptive learning capacities.

Ideally this generation of smart materials for structural applications should be characterized by: (1) the ability to respond almost instantaneously to changes in external stimuli; (2) the ability to interface with modern microprocessors and solid-state electronics; and (3) the ability to exploit modern control systems. Typically, these characteristics are achieved through the coherent integration of the following essential ingredients: a structural material, a network of sensors, a network of actuators, microprocessor-based computational capabilities, and real-time control capabilities.

In this novel class of materials and structures, the network of actuators provides the muscle to make things happen; the network of sensors provides the "nervous system" to monitor and communicate the external stimuli; the structural materials provide the skeleton; and the microprocessor-based computational capabilities furnish the brains that ensure the optimal performance of the overall system in the presence of variable and unstructured stimuli. The current generation of smart materials and structures typically exploits the characteristics offered by electrorheological fluids, piezoelectric materials, and shape-memory alloys. These three systems have advantages and disadvantages; by judicious selection a smart-materials designer can synthesize many classes of hybrid actuation systems to satisfy a broad range of performance specifications.

Actuators and sensors

Several sensing technologies may be incorporated in smart materials and structures. For example, the sensing function and the associated electronic data-processing function can be integrated on a single chip. The current practice is to embed piezoelectric sensors or fiber-optic sensors and data links in the structures.

Electrorheological fluids are typically suspensions of micron (millionth of a meter)-sized hydrophilic particles (those having an affinity for water) suspended in suitable hydrophobic (those lacking an affinity for water) carrier liquids, which undergo significant instantaneous reversible changes in material characteristics when subjected to electric fields. The tailoring of the material characteristics by the imposition of suitable electrical potentials can be usefully exploited in a wide range of engineering applications.

Figures 1 and 2 are photomicrographs of an electrorheological fluid that has been subjected to electrical field intensities of zero kilovolts and two kilovolts per millimeter of fluid thickness, respectively. The black regions at the top and bottom of the photomicrographs are images of the electrodes that have been employed to generate the electrical field in the fluid. Figure 1 clearly shows the random structure of the suspension when a potential difference is not generated between the electrodes. Under these conditions the suspension exhibits nominally isotropic global

165

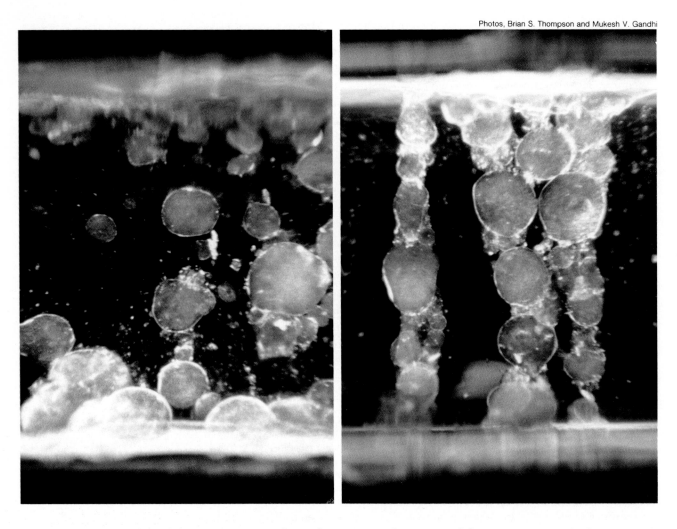

Figure 1 (left); Figure 2 (right).

mechanical properties; that is, it exhibits properties with the same values when measured along axes in all directions. By contrast, Figure 2 reveals the truly dramatic change in the structure of the suspension when there is a potential difference between the electrodes of magnitude two kilovolts per millimeter. Under these conditions the particles in the suspension orient themselves in relatively regular chainlike patterns to form a suspension having properties with different values when measured along axes in different directions. These columnar structures significantly change the local mass distribution, the energy-dissipation characteristics, and the stiffness characteristics of the suspension. Thus, if an appropriate electrical field is imposed upon an electrorheological fluid, the vibrational characteristics of the suspension can be tailored to yield the desired performance characteristics.

The voltages required for activating the phase change in electrorheological fluids are typically in the order of one to four kilovolts per millimeter of fluid thickness, but because current densities are in the order of 10 microamperes per square centimeter, the total power required for triggering this phenomenon is quite low. Furthermore, the response of the fluids to electrical stimuli is typically less than a millisecond.

166

Shape-memory alloys are metals that, when plastically deformed at one temperature, will completely recover their original undeformed state when their temperature is raised above an alloy-specific transition temperature. A characteristic of these alloys is that the crystal structure undergoes a transformation into and out of a martensitic phase when subjected to either prescribed mechanical loads or temperature. (In the martensitic phase martensite, a material characterized by a needlelike pattern, is formed.) During the shape-recovery process these alloys can be engineered to develop prescribed forces or displacements.

The shape-memory phenomenon was originally observed during crystallographic studies of the martensitic phase of brass. Subsequent work focused on alloys of gold-cadmium, copper-zinc-aluminum, indium-cadmium, and nickel-titanium. This nickel-titanium family of alloys became a popular class for shape-memory actuators because the transformation temperature can be selectively tuned over a broad temperature range to suit each application. Typically, deformations as large as 6–8% may be completely recovered by heating these alloys. Furthermore, constraining the alloys from regaining their memorized shape can result in the development of stresses as high as 100,000 pounds per square inch.

Piezoelectric materials are those that either generate an electrical field in response to a mechanical deformation or provide mechanical deformation when subjected to an electrical field. Therefore, such materials can be employed either as actuators or sensors in the development of smart structures. Piezoelectric materials are typically crystals or ceramics; because of the brittle characteristics of those materials, however, piezoelectric sensors are typically made from polymers such as polyvinyldene fluoride. Piezoelectric sensors are typically used for tactile sensing, temperature sensing, and strain sensing. Furthermore, because this class of sensors and actuators generates little heat, it is efficient in many applications when compared with electromechanical devices.

Fiber-optic sensing systems are based on the ability to measure the change in the characteristics of light traveling through an optical fiber that is subjected to various external stimuli. This class of sensing systems offers the following distinct advantages over other sensing technologies: increased sensitivity, geometric versatility, immunity from electromagnetic disturbances, very high rates of data transmission, convenient capabilities of transmitting two or more signals simultaneously on the same circuit or channel, minimal losses and power consumption, and high resistance to adverse environmental conditions.

All fiber-optic sensing systems comprise three major subsystems: the optical transmitter system, the optical modulator system, and the optical receiver system. The transmitter essentially creates an appropriate light signal that is conducted into the fiber and transmitted to the area subjected to such external stimuli as strain, temperature, acceleration, and position. The stimuli then modulate the amplitude, phase, color, or polarization of the light beam, and the modulated light is then detected and analyzed by the receiver in order to extract the relevant information pertaining to the stimuli.

167

(Top and bottom) photos, Brian S. Thompson and Mukesh V. Gandhi

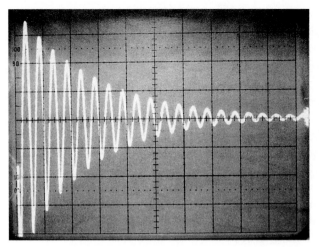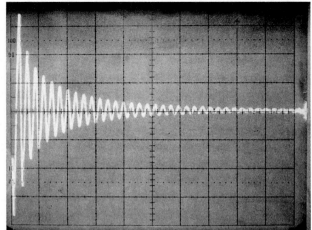

Figure 3 (left); Figure 4 (right).

Synthesis of smart structures: current generation

Research efforts at university laboratories and industrial research and development centers are focused on synthesizing smart structures that feature only one class of embedded actuator or sensing systems. These efforts are aimed at such goals as controlling vibrations, initiating large changes in structural geometry, and assessing damage.

Smart structures have been fabricated from advanced composite laminates through the embedding of electrorheological fluids in macroscopic voids within the laminates. These structures can then dynamically tune their vibrational characteristics in real time by imposing appropriate electrical fields upon the electrorheological fluid domains. Figure 3 shows the vibrational characteristics of a smart beam structure when no electrical field is imposed upon the embedded electrorheological fluid. Figure 4 shows the vibrational characteristics of the same structure subjected to an electrical field of finite strength. It is evident from a comparison of the two figures that the amplitude and frequency of the structure can

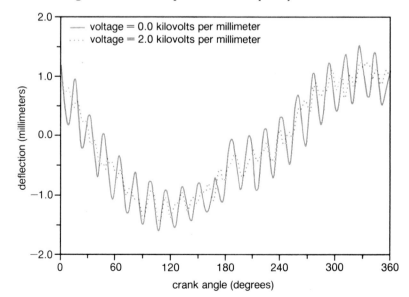

indeed be dynamically tuned. Capabilities of this kind form the kernel of the research and development efforts that have focused on employing smart structures to control autonomous vibrations.

Smart structures have also been fabricated from advanced composite laminates through the embedding of piezoelectric actuators and shape-memory alloy actuators within the laminates. The former can control the vibrational characteristics of the structure and initiate small changes in its geometry, while the latter can initiate large geometrical changes.

Research on smart cantilevered beams and plates that incorporate embedded fiber-optic sensors has yielded promising results in regard to the monitoring of their vibrational behavior in response to dynamical loads. Fiber-optic arrays have also been embedded in advanced composite materials in order to detect damage. These arrays enable critical stress levels to be identified through the monitoring of catastrophic breakage of optical fibers. Developments of this kind have resulted in the successful fabrication of a smart fiber-optic leading edge for a small commercial aircraft. Similar efforts are being undertaken by aerospace industries throughout the world.

Synthesis of smart structures: next generation

The next generation of revolutionary smart structures for the vibrational control of structural and mechanical systems will feature a variety of hybrid actuation and sensing technologies. These smart structures will capitalize on the superior characteristics of advanced composite materials, which will be interfaced with sensors and dynamically tunable actuators. A variety of geometric configurations of the smart actuator domains embedded in structural materials will be employed to optimize the mechanical characteristics of these structures.

The next generation of smart structures will derive its smartness from the merger of sensors that are built into control segments of the smart structural continuum, microprocessors, and dynamically tunable actuator systems. An application of this method of controlling the vibrational response of a smart aircraft wing is schematically represented in Figure 5. The sensors will monitor the relevant characteristics of the smart structure, and the signals from them will be fed to the appropriate microprocessors; these will evaluate the signals prior to determining an appropriate control strategy that will synthesize the desired response characteristics. This will be typically accomplished by controlling the material characteristics of the actuators in the specific control segments. The material changes in a typical control segment will in turn alter the global mass, stiffness, and damping characteristics of the smart structure in order to achieve the desired response.

The next generation of embedded fiber-optic sensing systems will permit the health of the smart structure to be monitored and assessed at all stages of its life, from birth through service to death. Thus, in the case of an aircraft wing, the fiber-optic sensing system will enable the properties of the composite-based smart structure to be carefully monitored during manufacture in order to ensure that the wing structure

Slider-crank mechanism (opposite page, bottom left) features a smart connecting-rod that contains an embedded electrorheological fluid (a suspension of hydrophilic particles in a hydrophobic carrier liquid). When an electrical field is imposed on the fluid (opposite page, bottom right), the deflections of the connecting-rod are reduced. The operating speed of the mechanism is 95 revolutions per minute.

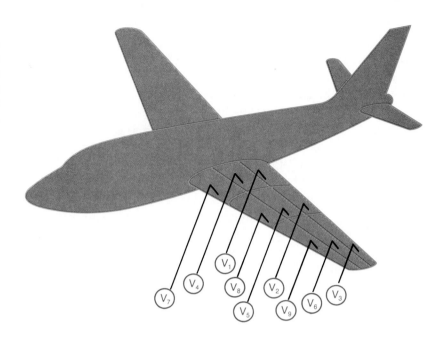

attains desirable characteristics. Subsequently, during the service life of the wing, the embedded sensors will enable the health of the structure to be monitored and assessed. This significant capability may include evaluating the wing's vibrational response, the effect of any loads that might impact on it, the temperature, and the buildup of ice. Furthermore, the sensing system will enable an impending failure of the wing to be detected by integrating the past history of the aircraft.

Synthesis of smart structures: the future

The future of smart structures will clearly be influenced by advances in such areas as materials science, materials design and manufacture, biomimetics, artificial intelligence, nanotechnology, and neural networks. Consider, for example, the vibrational characteristics of combat helicopter rotors fabricated of advanced composite materials. A present-day optimally designed rotor fabricated of advanced composite materials is passive in the sense that it cannot actively respond to external stimuli in an autonomous fashion. It is clearly evident, therefore, that the vibrational response of the rotor is not optimal for all service conditions except the one for which the rotor was "optimally designed." However, if the rotors were fabricated of smart composite materials, their performances could be dynamically tuned to ensure optimal operation under all service conditions and in all unstructured environments.

A helicopter rotor designed and fabricated of smart materials would typically be capable of in-flight structural surveillance, which might include detecting dynamic strains due to changes in payload, in wind gusts, in temperature, and in moisture as well as those caused by battlefield damage. The detection and measurement of changes in the vibrational response characteristics of the rotor, changes in the environment, and the qualitative and quantitative assessment of damage would be undertaken by the sensing network. On the basis of this sensing information, smart

170

structures of the future will be able to initiate appropriate corrective actions almost instantaneously. In a hostile battlefield environment, for example, these activities might involve redistributing loads around highly stressed regions of the rotor structure in order to control the damage that it might sustain.

Another layer of smartness would permit the rotors to "learn" from past experiences and utilize this knowledge in making decisions for future situations. A more sophisticated degree of smartness associated with the rotor would allow the structure to self-diagnose and assess the extent and quality of damage and then make decisions on the abortion or survivability of the mission. Such a rotor could be fabricated from a smart material that could heal and repair itself, thereby compensating for any battlefield damage that might occur. Alternatively, if an automated assessment of the damage revealed that the mission should be aborted, then the smart structure would have the capability of self-degradation. While this discussion has focused on helicopter rotor systems, clearly these capabilities could also have a profound effect on a diverse range of products in the automotive, defense, construction, and advanced manufacturing industries.

The capabilities that will be demanded of smart structures in the future will require substantial advances in various technologies. Advances in nanotechnology would, for example, permit the design and fabrication of structures with embedded sensors, actuators, and processors to be undertaken in a manner that did not compromise structural integrity. This technology would for the first time allow designers the freedom to manipulate individual atoms and molecules in order to fabricate complex structures one atom at a time. Similarly, advances in biomimetics would allow materials and structures to be engineered with self-repair and self-healing capabilities. These structures would be tailored to exhibit substantial toughness and would incorporate redundancy in order to avoid catastrophic failures. Such capabilities in material design and fabrication would render obsolete conventional engineering philosophies that relied on substantial overdesign in order to ensure system integrity under a variety of hostile conditions. Advances in neural networks would facilitate the synthesis of materials and structures with exceptional learning capabilities. These smart systems would capitalize on the architecture of a large number of relatively simple processors connected to one another by variable-memory elements. The neural networks would adjust the weights of these elements by experience in order to ensure self-programming capabilities.

The dawn of the 21st century will certainly witness the emergence of an era in which scientists will learn from biological systems in order to synthesize smart materials. The maturation of various embryonic advanced technologies and their integration will fuel humanity's quest for synthesizing materials whose capabilities may indeed surpass those bestowed by Mother Nature. The journey through these uncharted terrains promises to be an exciting and memorable one.

The Radicals of Chemistry

by M. John Perkins

Atoms and molecules that possess one unpaired electron mediate chemical reactions with effects ranging from ozone depletion to human aging.

To the layperson, it might seem impossible that there could be a common factor linking depletion of the ozone layer, tissue damage following a heart attack, deterioration of the eyesight of cattle treated with a substance widely used to destroy parasitic worms, and some of the elegant laboratory strategies for the synthesis of anticancer drugs. Nevertheless, such a link exists: it is the mediation of a variety of chemical transformations by free radicals.

The term *radical* appears to have been used first in chemistry by Lavoisier, almost 200 years ago, to signify a part of a molecule that remains unchanged in a chemical reaction. A good example of a compound radical (a radical comprising several atoms) was provided by the work of Justus von Liebig and Friedrich Wöhler (1832) on the benzoyl radical (C_6H_5CO-). This radical is unaltered in the reaction of benzoyl chloride (C_6H_5CO-Cl) with water to give benzoic acid (C_6H_5CO-OH). The concept of free radicals recognizes that these groupings may have some discrete, if fleeting, existence during which they are not bound to any other atom or group of atoms. So important has this concept become that the old usage of *radical* is nowadays seldom encountered, and the prefix *free* is often omitted.

Chemists speak of mechanisms of reactions as the description of what happens in the progression from stable reactants to stable products. But the development of such mechanistic understanding in the early decades of this century bypassed free radicals. Electrically charged, ionic, intermediates had been correctly recognized in organic chemistry (the chemistry of carbon compounds) and were believed to participate in many chemical changes, including, for example, the above hydrolysis of benzoyl chloride.

A distinction is drawn between heterolysis and homolysis of chemical bonds. The bonding together of atoms in molecules—for example, water (H_2O) or methane (CH_4; the principal constituent of natural gas)—depends on the sharing of pairs of negatively charged electrons. An input of sufficient energy may split such molecules in one of two ways. In heterolysis H_2O yields the familiar ions H^+ and OH^-; both electrons in one of water's $H-O$ bonds have remained with oxygen to give the negatively charged hydroxide ion, leaving a positive hydrogen ion. Heterolysis of

173

M. JOHN PERKINS is Professor and Department Head, Department of Chemistry, Royal Holloway and Bedford New College, University of London, England.

(Overleaf) Illustration by Ron Villani

liquid water is assisted by the association of the ions with other water molecules; in the gas phase heterolysis of water is much more difficult. Instead, if sufficient thermal energy is provided (at temperatures of several hundred degrees Celsius), homolysis may occur. In this reaction the electron pair divides, a single electron remaining with each fragment— the hydrogen atom, $H \cdot$, and the hydroxyl radical (free radical), $HO \cdot$. (A dot after a chemical notation indicates an unpaired electron.) These fragments are electrically neutral. Similar dissociation of a hydrogen atom from methane yields, at only slightly lower temperatures, the electrically neutral methyl radical, $\cdot CH_3$.

In view of the extreme conditions required for generating these simple radicals, it will come as no surprise that only relatively recently has it been perceived that hydroxyl radicals are implicated in the long-term toxic effects on the body of various chemicals, including alcohol, and that they may play a key role in many other diseases, including, for example, the effects on the heart muscle of coronary thrombosis. Molecular oxygen is essential for nearly all forms of life, yet it is unusual in being a double radical, or biradical ($\cdot O - O \cdot$). The biochemical processes associated with respiration, in which oxygen is reduced to water, can generate compounds capable of liberating hydroxyl radicals under physiological conditions. Hydrogen peroxide (HOOH) is an example. The bond between its central oxygen atoms is weaker (by a factor of approximately three) than the $H - O$ bond in water. Nevertheless, even this does not break spontaneously at normal body temperatures. It can, however, be induced to break, particularly by some iron compounds. Hydroxyl radicals are the result.

Because hydroxyl radicals bond so strongly to hydrogen in forming water molecules, they react almost indiscriminately with any molecule capable of giving up a hydrogen atom:

$$HO \cdot \; + RH \longrightarrow H_2O + R \cdot$$

(RH represents a generalized organic molecule that incorporates a bond from carbon to hydrogen.) In a biological environment the consequence of such a reaction is damage to the cell and, ultimately, cell death.

In the examples of toxicity or heart disease mentioned above, the damage may be localized, but exposure to high-energy ionizing radiation can generate hydroxyl radicals throughout the body by radiolysis of water. Radiation sickness is a short-term consequence. A longer-term possibility, through genetic damage to the cells, is cancer.

A historical perspective

In the mid-19th century the English chemist Edward Frankland sought to liberate radicals from their compounds. In 1849, on discovering that a gaseous substance was liberated from iodomethane (CH_3I) when it was heated with powdered zinc, Frankland believed that he had prepared methyl. However, the gas was later shown to be ethane (C_2H_6), resulting from the pairing (dimerization) of two methyl units.

174

$$2CH_3-I + Zn \longrightarrow \quad H-\overset{\displaystyle H}{\underset{\displaystyle H}{C}}-\overset{\displaystyle H}{\underset{\displaystyle H}{C}}-H + ZnI_2$$

ethane

By the end of the 1850s it was generally recognized that in all molecules containing carbon, the carbon atoms appear to be tetravalent; that is, they have four links to other atoms (as illustrated above for ethane). In the same way, nitrogen is trivalent, oxygen divalent, and hydrogen univalent. Multiple linkages are allowed; for example, molecules of hydrogen cyanide (prussic acid) satisfy the above bonding rules by the incorporation of a triple bond between carbon and nitrogen ($H-C\equiv N$).

The hypothesis that carbon is invariably tetravalent in its compounds was finally overturned by the discovery in 1900 of a trivalent carbon species. Moses Gomberg, attempting to repeat Frankland's experiment but using chlorotriphenylmethane instead of iodomethane, obtained a yellow solution in which he was able to demonstrate that the color was due to the triphenylmethyl free radical in equilibrium with a colorless "dimer":

$$Zn \; + \; 2Ph_3CCl \longrightarrow \quad ZnCl_2 \; + \; 2Ph_3C\cdot \; \rightleftharpoons \; dimer$$

chlorotriphenylmethane   yellow

Despite this demonstration of the existence of a stable species containing trivalent carbon, it was almost three decades before chemists recognized that short-lived free radicals might be important intermediates in a reaction. A major development took place in 1929 with the report by Friedrich Paneth and W. Hofeditz that when tetramethyllead [$Pb(CH_3)_4$] is vaporized and passed through a heated tube, metallic lead is deposited on the side of the tube. Furthermore, a cool lead film, predeposited farther along the tube, is removed, and tetramethyllead is regenerated. The inescapable conclusion was that the lead compound is decomposed by heat to yield methyl radicals, which recombine with the cold lead film:

$$Pb(CH_3)_4 \longrightarrow \quad Pb + 4CH_3\cdot \xrightarrow{\quad Pb \quad} Pb(CH_3)_4$$

Soon afterward Donald Hey and William Grieve at the University of Manchester, England, were carrying out reactions designed to link two benzene molecules together. When one of the molecules was a more complex relative of benzene, such as toluene, the linking reaction led to a mixture of products that was inconsistent with that expected on the basis of contemporary ideas of ionic reactions. This led Grieve and Hey to conclude that the electrically neutral phenyl radical ($C_6H_5\cdot$) must have been the reactive entity.

At almost the same time, Morris Kharasch at the University of Chicago

175

was endeavoring to understand some unusual reactions of hydrogen bromide with alkenes (compounds incorporating a carbon–carbon double bond). Again, results were inconsistent with predictions based on ionic chemistry, in which hydrogen bromide should react as H^+Br^-. Kharasch and his co-workers concluded that the key step involved the addition of a bromine atom, yielding an intermediate carbon-centered radical:

$$Br \cdot + BrCH_2CH{=}CH_2 \longrightarrow BrCH_2\dot{C}HCH_2Br$$

Despite these observations there was a marked reluctance among the scientific community at large to accept the idea that radicals could be important reaction intermediates in solution reactions of organic compounds. This situation finally changed in 1937, however, when a landmark review by Hey and Alec Waters (University of Durham, England) summarized a wealth of experimental data, all of which could be explained in terms of reactive radical intermediates. Particularly important were polymer-forming reactions, which took on a special significance during World War II after the Japanese cut off the supply of natural rubber from Malaya. (A polymer is a chemical compound or mixture of compounds formed when small molecules combine to form larger molecules that contain repeating structural units of the original molecules.) The U.S. production of a polymer made from styrene and butadiene rose from zero in 1941 to outstrip that of natural rubber almost fivefold in 1945. The associated research undoubtedly contributed to the fact that by the late 1940s the qualitative ground rules of our present knowledge of radical reactions were in place, although most of the quantitative understanding was yet to come. Speculation was already under way that radicals might play a role in biology, both in some enzymatic processes and in producing cancer.

From a chemist's viewpoint one of the major misconceptions was that of the indiscriminate reactivity of radicals. In fact, the most reactive radicals, including hydroxyl, phenyl, and the chlorine atom (which plays an important role in a number of industrial chlorination processes), *are* rather unselective in their reactions, but for many other radicals this is not the case.

Generating free radicals

The possibility of generating radicals in a variety of different ways has already been suggested. Thus, the weak O—O linkage in peroxides breaks either on heating or by interaction with reducing agents, including some iron salts, to yield oxygen-centered radicals. Absorption of visible or, more usually, ultraviolet light by a variety of molecules may also result in bond homolysis (termed photolysis) and, of course, ionizing radiation is sufficiently energetic to produce radicals from even the most strongly bonded molecules, such as water.

A variety of reaction types has also been implied, including the coupling of radicals to form a stable compound ($2CH_3 \cdot \rightarrow C_2H_6$) and processes in which the radicals react with stable molecules. The latter category was illustrated by the transfer of a hydrogen atom (*see* equation on page 174) and by the addition to a double bond (page 176). In both of these reactions new radicals are formed. Many transformations mediated by free radicals involve a chain of repeating steps of this kind in which one radical leads to another. Primary radical formation, such as photolysis, is said to initiate a chain reaction. The radical-molecule reactions propagate the chain, and termination occurs only when a pair of radicals interact to give nonradical products. Two principal examples will serve to illustrate this behavior. The first is chlorination of methane:

$$Cl-Cl \xrightarrow[\text{(photolysis)}]{\text{light}} 2Cl\cdot \qquad \text{initiation}$$

$$Cl\cdot + CH_4 \longrightarrow HCl + \cdot CH_3 \qquad \text{(a)}$$

$$\cdot CH_3 + Cl-Cl \longrightarrow CH_3-Cl + Cl\cdot \qquad \text{(b)}$$
$$\text{chloromethane}$$

(a) and (b) bracketed as propagation

Propagation step (b) generates a chlorine atom that reacts again with a methane molecule in step (a). The propagating cycle may repeat many thousands of times with conversion of many thousands of molecules for each molecule of chlorine that is photolyzed. Termination takes place by the recombination of two chlorine atoms (or possibly of two methyl radicals).

Further consideration of step (a) is instructive. The strength of the methane C—H bond that is broken is almost identical to the strength of the Cl—H bond that is formed; that is, the reaction is approximately thermoneutral. Yet the reaction occurs with consummate ease. As the hydrogen atom is transferred from carbon to chlorine, there is little change in total energy. This smooth and energetically economical rebonding is a common feature of radical reactions and contrasts markedly with many other processes in which the end product can be reached only after a substantial injection of energy. The consequence, in the chlorination reaction, is that step (a) is very rapid indeed. Generally, for thermoneutral or exothermic (heat-releasing) steps very little "activation energy" is required. Only for endothermic (heat-absorbing) processes, such as those where the bond being made is significantly weaker than the bond that is broken, is a larger energy input required, resulting in a slower reaction.

Other gas-phase radical chain reactions are encountered in flames and in the depletion of the ozone layer by chlorofluorocarbons. The latter compounds are remarkably stable but are photolyzed in the upper atmosphere to yield chlorine atoms, which then destroy ozone by the following chain-propagating steps:

$$Cl\cdot + O_3 \longrightarrow ClO\cdot + O_2$$

$$2ClO\cdot \longrightarrow 2Cl\cdot + O_2$$

The second representative chain reaction is the formation of a polymer (Plexiglas) from methyl methacrylate. Initiation in this case may take place by the thermal decomposition of a peroxide ROOR:

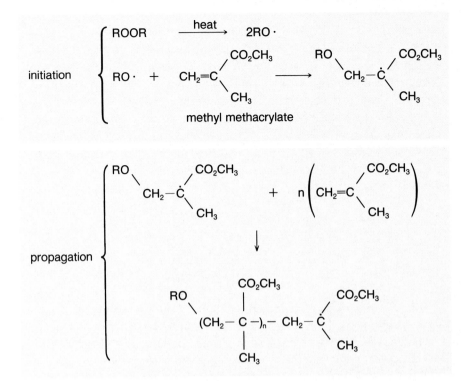

initiation

$$ROOR \xrightarrow{\text{heat}} 2RO\cdot$$

$$RO\cdot + CH_2=C \begin{smallmatrix} CO_2CH_3 \\ \\ CH_3 \end{smallmatrix} \longrightarrow RO-CH_2-\overset{\cdot}{C} \begin{smallmatrix} CO_2CH_3 \\ \\ CH_3 \end{smallmatrix}$$

methyl methacrylate

propagation

$$RO-CH_2-\overset{\cdot}{C} \begin{smallmatrix} CO_2CH_3 \\ \\ CH_3 \end{smallmatrix} + n \left(CH_2=C \begin{smallmatrix} CO_2CH_3 \\ \\ CH_3 \end{smallmatrix} \right)$$

$$\downarrow$$

$$RO-(CH_2-\underset{CH_3}{\overset{CO_2CH_3}{C}})_n- CH_2-\overset{CO_2CH_3}{\underset{CH_3}{C}}$$

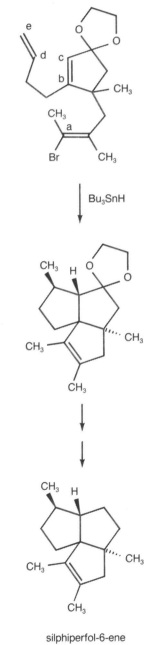

(1)

Bu₃SnH

silphiperfol-6-ene

Once a radical has been formed, additions to the methyl methacrylate monomer occur repetitively, building up a long-chain polymer radical that may incorporate many methacrylate units. (A monomer is a chemical compound that can undergo polymerization.) Termination occurs by interaction between two such growing radicals. The resulting glassy solid is the well-known Plexiglas.

Because individual chain-propagating and chain-terminating steps occur very rapidly, it has proved difficult until relatively recently to measure their reaction rates with any precision. Since the late 1960s, however, quantitative data have been accumulated both on how fast individual radical reactions proceed and on the energies that are injected and released. This has led to a more detailed understanding of radical processes and to the possibility of predicting preferred reaction pathways. Among the techniques employed for rate measurements have been pulse radiolysis and flash photolysis. In each of these, radical processes are monitored after the reaction system has been exposed to an initial pulse of energy that may last for less than a nanosecond. Another important technique is electron paramagnetic resonance spectroscopy (*see* below). The predictability of radical behavior from these quantitative studies is facilitated by the fact that radical reactions are influenced relatively little by the nature of the solvent in which they take place, in contrast to reactions involving electrically charged ionic species.

In the polymerization of methyl methacrylate, the growing polymer radical reacts with a monomer only by addition to the terminal carbon-ation of the double bond and not by the transfer of a hydrogen atom. Clearly, a marked selectivity is occurring that contradicts generalizations about the lack of selectivity that is expected of radical processes. A proper

178

understanding of selectivity and of its origins constitutes the key to the design of transformations that might augment the armory of the synthetic organic chemist. For such a scientist the challenge is to find selective and efficient means of constructing complex molecular frameworks, such as those that may be anticipated to have valuable medicinal properties.

Factors that determine selectivity in radical reactions are quite different from those influencing reactions that proceed via ionic intermediates. This has important implications for the choice of reaction type in various circumstances. One example of the efficiency of a carefully planned synthesis involving radicals is that of the hydrocarbon silphiperfol-6-ene, found in the roots of a South African plant. Central to the method chosen recently for this by Dennis Curran and Shen-Chun Kuo at the University of Pittsburgh, Pennsylvania, was the reaction of compound (1a) with tributyltin hydride to give (1b). A tributyltin radical takes the bromine atom from (1a), leaving a carbon radical center at carbon (a). This adds at (b) to give a new radical at carbon (c). In turn, addition of this to (d) gives a radical at (e), which concludes the sequence by abstracting hydrogen from the tin compound to yield (1b) and generate a new tributyltin radical—which then repeats the sequence. About 65% of the molecules of (1a) followed this route and were transformed into (1b)—a remarkable selectivity in view of the complexity of the process. Subsequent reactions converted (1b) into silphiperfol-6-ene.

A more astonishing example is the reaction devised and executed some years ago by Francesco Minisci and his colleagues in Milan in which four compounds (2a–d) come together in a radical reaction catalyzed by iron salts to give (2e) in excellent yield. In each of the steps of this reaction, only one of the reactants is singled out for attack.

Among the most important of radical reactions, both in organic and in biological chemistry, is that in which compounds of carbon react with the oxygen of the air. The process is called autoxidation. It is largely responsible for the perishing of rubber, the deterioration of lubricating oils, and, more constructively, the "drying" of paints. In living systems it is both destructive and constructive, causing tissue damage yet being essential to the biosynthesis of the prostaglandin hormones.

The generalized autoxidation sequence involves the breaking of a carbon–hydrogen bond R—H to give a carbon-centered radical R·. In the presence of oxygen this reacts with great rapidity to form a peroxyl radical, R—OO·. Chain propagation continues when this reacts with RH to regenerate R· and yield a molecule of hydroperoxide:

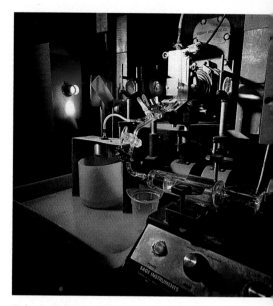

Pulse radiolysis equipment, attached to the linear accelerator at Brunel University in London, is used to measure the formation and decay of short-lived free radicals in solution.

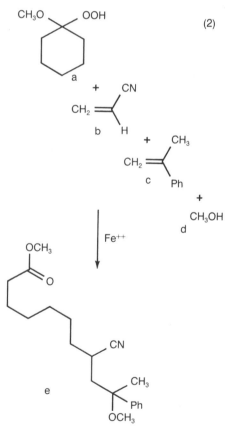

(2)

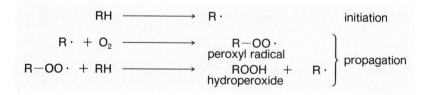

The ease with which autoxidation occurs depends on the strength of the C—H bond in RH. This can vary over a surprisingly wide range, depending on structural features in R. Several important bond strengths (bond dissociation energies) are listed in the table. From this, it will be noted that relatively weak bonds are located adjacent to carbon–carbon double bonds (c) and especially next to two carbon–carbon double bonds in the so-called skipped dienes (d). Skipped diene units occur in many natural materials, notably the vegetable oils such as walnut and linseed that are used in paint formulations. When a film of oil-based paint dries, there is an initial weight increase that reflects absorption of oxygen and hydroperoxide formation. In this case the hydroperoxide group (OOH) attaches in such a way that the double bonds of the diene are repositioned in conjugation (that is, separated by only one carbon–carbon single bond). Subsequently, the conjugated diene

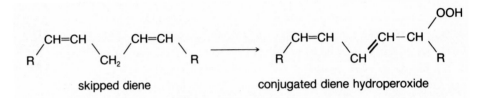

skipped diene   conjugated diene hydroperoxide

is particularly susceptible to radical addition, so that when a radical is generated in one molecule, it is likely to add to a second. This linking together is the beginning of a complex polymerization process wherein the oil sets (dries) to a hard film. It has been known for many centuries that pigments containing metal salts, notably lead and copper, affect the hardening of a paint film when applied to canvas. The conscious incorporation of lead oxide into oil paints to assist drying is commonly attributed to the 15th-century Flemish artist Jan van Eyck. Modern paint technology also uses metal salts to affect the rate of the autoxidation processes in a fashion that, while carefully controlled, is still not fully understood.

Much as autoxidation is desired for the proper hardening of a paint film, it is unwanted in a lubricating oil. Not only is the presence of weak C—H bonds carefully avoided, but additives are present that behave as antioxidants. These compounds, often substituted phenols present only in trace amounts, react rapidly with peroxyl radicals in steps that generate new species that are insufficiently reactive to propagate the autoxidation chains. It will be seen later that nature provides, particularly in the form of vitamins C and E, some effective antioxidants to protect its own molecules from autoxidative decay.

Detection of radicals

Under all but the most exceptional circumstances, production of reactive radicals is initiated quite slowly, yet their destruction is rapid. In solution in a mobile solvent such as water, pairs of radicals will normally combine every time they diffuse (move randomly through the liquid) together. Since the rate of diffusion is known, it can be estimated that the concentration of reactive radicals will seldom rise much above one molecule for every 10^9 molecules of solvent. This makes detection and identification especially difficult. However, one direct technique, under

Bond Dissociation Energies (Bond Strengths) for Some Representative Bonds to Hydrogen

Bond*	Bond Strength (kilocalories/mole)†
(a) CH_3-H	104.3
(b) R\CH—H/R	96.3
(c) RCH=CH\CH—H/R	85
(d) RCH=CH\CH—H/RCH=CH (skipped diene)	76
(e) HO—H	119.3
(f) ROO—H	88

* R = substituent grouping attached through a carbon atom that is connected to other atoms only by single bonds.

† kilocalories = 4.18 kiloJoules

Electron paramagnetic resonance spectrometer detects and identifies free radicals by determining the frequencies at which microwave radiation is absorbed by each radical.

Courtesy, M. John Perkins

special laboratory circumstances of rapid radical production when radical concentrations may be 100 times greater than this, does have sufficient sensitivity. This is electron paramagnetic resonance (EPR) spectroscopy, and it depends on magnetic properties associated with the single (un-paired) electron in a free radical. In the presence of a strong magnetic field, microwave radiation may be absorbed by the radical. This often occurs at several frequencies, the pattern of which gives a "fingerprint" characteristic of the radical.

Other, less direct, techniques have been used, including the decolorization of certain compounds that react selectively with free radicals. Some observations of an indirect kind have led to deductions concerning radicals in biological systems, which are discussed in the following section. Direct observation in a biological environment is very seldom possible. Such exceptions may arise when the radical is so unreactive that it neither combines on every occasion that it meets another of the same kind nor is instantaneously destroyed by antioxidants, etc., in the biological milieu. Particularly interesting in this regard are the nitroxide radicals, $R_2NO\cdot$, some of which are sufficiently unreactive to survive for prolonged periods in a biological environment. These have found application in two techniques referred to as spin labeling and spin trapping.

181

In spin labeling a nitroxide "label" is chemically bonded to a site of interest, such as an enzyme or an antibiotic. Its EPR signature in the biological environment reports to the investigator on the nature of the site of action on this labeled molecule. In spin trapping traces of a "spin trap" are added to the system to be studied. Spin traps are not radicals but compounds that react selectively with reactive radicals to give nitroxides. The spectra of these nitroxides then report on the nature of the reactive radicals that have been trapped. An example is the detection by spin trapping of trichloromethyl radicals ($\cdot CCl_3$) formed in rat liver cells that have been exposed to traces of the toxic degreasing agent tetrachloromethane (CCl_4). Other examples include the trapping of radicals in cigarette smoke and the detection of radicals generated when ultrasound is absorbed by water.

Radicals in biochemistry and biology

Molecular oxygen, O_2, is a biradical; that is, it contains two electrons that are unpaired and that give to the molecule some of the reactivity associated with free radicals. In the normal respiration chain O_2 is reduced by reaction with four electrons and four protons (positive hydrogen ions, H^+) to form two molecules of water:

$$O_2 + 4e + 4H^+ \longrightarrow 2H_2O$$

In animal cells this reduction depends on an enzyme called cytochrome oxidase. The enzyme efficiently avoids releasing radicals; however, linked oxidation-reduction processes are less clean, and up to about 5% of the normal oxygen uptake by the cell results in the formation of the negatively charged superoxide "radical ion" (an electrically charged free radical):

$$O_2 + e \longrightarrow \underset{\text{superoxide}}{O_2^-}$$

Like oxygen itself, superoxide is rather unreactive as a radical, but it can be converted with the aid of another enzyme, superoxide dismutase, into hydrogen peroxide. The hydrogen peroxide can then act as a source of highly reactive and damaging hydroxyl ($\cdot OH$) radicals. Since hydrogen peroxide can diffuse through cell membranes, the hydroxyl radicals may be formed at sites removed from those of hydrogen peroxide production. In particular, reactions of hydrogen peroxide with low-valent iron compounds (Fe^{++}) will induce the production of hydroxyl radicals in a process known as a Fenton reaction:

$$H_2O_2 + Fe^{++} \longrightarrow HO\cdot + HO^- + Fe^{+++}$$

Since pathways exist for converting Fe^{+++} back into Fe^{++}, the effect of iron is catalytic. Not surprisingly, therefore, in healthy cells iron is

182

tightly bound in protein complexes, such as transferrin and hemoglobin, so that this catalytic activity is suppressed. Furthermore, the enzymes catalase and glutathione peroxidase promote the reduction of hydrogen peroxide to water without the formation of free radicals. Thus, nature has designed a system whose efficient operation should minimize radical production. Free iron salts may be released into the body, however—for example, following repeated blood transfusions of patients with one of the inherited anemias known as thalassemia. The patients develop a condition referred to as iron overload, in which all of the iron-complexing proteins are saturated and free iron salts accumulate, notably in the heart and liver; for such persons fatal heart disease is very common after the age of 20. Although injection of iron-complexing drugs that bind free iron, allowing it to be excreted from the body, reduces these adverse effects, the treatment is not a complete solution to the problem. Better alternatives, capable of oral administration, are being sought.

Hydroxyl radicals are highly reactive and can damage essentially any organic molecule, RH. The resulting radicals, R·, are less reactive and eventually seek out only the most weakly bonded molecular fragments, including skipped diene units and thiol (sulfydryl; —SH) groupings. Thiols are found in the cysteine residue of proteins, and their reaction with radicals commonly leads to disulfides.

Skipped dienes in the phospholipids of cell membranes may undergo autoxidation reactions exactly as described earlier in the context of paint chemistry. These are chain reactions and once initiated may lead to the modifications of many molecules of lipids (fats, waxes, and related and derived compounds) in cells. Protection against this type of oxidation is provided by nature's antioxidants, notably the membrane-soluble a-tocopherol (vitamin E; 3a). This reacts with a peroxyl radical much more rapidly than does the diene. The resultant tocopheroxyl radical (3b) is insufficiently reactive to propagate the autoxidation chain. Instead it reacts with a second peroxyl radical, blocking a second chain. Alternatively, it may interact with the water-soluble ascorbate ion (vitamin C) in a process that regenerates a-tocopherol.

The radical oxidation of polyunsaturated fats (those with skipped diene units) in foodstuffs yields hydroperoxides, which, like hydrogen peroxide, can be decomposed to give oxyl radicals:

$$ROOH + Fe^{++} \longrightarrow RO\cdot + HO^- + Fe^{+++}$$

The oxyl radicals may undergo a reaction known as fragmentation, in which stable molecules of low molecular weight are formed. These products are relatively volatile and contribute to rancidity and off-flavors and odors of foods that have been in storage too long.

Concern has been expressed recently that polyunsaturated vegetable oils may not, after all, be a totally satisfactory substitute for saturated animal fats. Oxidation of the oils is inhibited by vitamin E, which is thereby depleted in the diet. Furthermore, the small-fragment molecules may themselves be harmful.

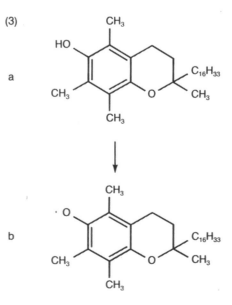

(3)

a

b

183

The use of the antioxidant vitamins C and E as dietary supplements delays the onset of serious symptoms of Parkinson's disease, which has been linked to the localized release of free iron with associated cell damage.

Charles Cegielski

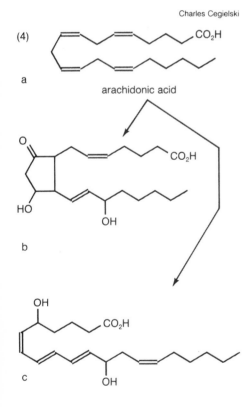

The importance of dietary antioxidants is often coupled with that of the essential trace element selenium. The principal role for the latter is in the enzyme glutathione peroxidase. Because this enzyme was one of the catalysts noted as being capable of achieving harmless destruction of hydrogen peroxide, a link with free radical biology is clear.

Although much of the evidence remains circumstantial, there is a rapidly growing literature that suggests that the formation of hydroxyl radicals followed by lipid peroxidation is important in many disease states. For example, there is compelling evidence that the toxicity to the liver of a variety of chemical poisons, including alcohol, is associated with the production of free radicals. It has become generally accepted that in coronary heart disease, after thrombosis in a coronary artery, it is not the shutting off of the oxygenated blood supply to heart muscle that causes irreversible damage so much as it is its restoration. Under conditions of oxygen depletion (ischemia), enzymic and other changes are believed to take place that, when oxygen supply is restored, result in a massive and uncontrolled surge of radicals. Discoveries related to this belief have indicated that if the reperfusion of the heart tissue by oxygenated blood is accompanied by high concentrations of certain antioxidants, the long-term consequences of a heart attack can be minimized.

In the damaged tissues associated with rheumatoid arthritis, release of free iron is believed to promote local radical production and to aggravate existing cell damage. Recently, localized release of free iron with associated cell damage has also been linked with the development of Parkinson's disease; an encouraging delay of the onset of more serious symptoms of this disease has been achieved by dietary supplement of the antioxidant vitamins C and E.

It has frequently been suggested that damage by free radicals is connected both to cancer and to the processes of aging. In regard to aging it is supposed that the natural enzymic and antioxidant defenses against radical damage are not 100% successful, even in normal cells, and that slow, irreversible changes result as the years go by. Experiments with houseflies suggest that life span may be affected by the rate of oxygen uptake by the body. The respiration rates of these insects are much higher when they are in flight than when they are at rest. Removal of the wings results in a markedly increased life span.

In the case of cancer, epidemiological surveys have revealed that many common cancers occur more frequently in those with low levels of serum vitamin E. Other evidence suggests, more directly, that lipid peroxidation may be involved in mechanisms that influence cell division.

Hydroxyl radicals are so unselective that the natural antioxidants do not interfere appreciably with their reactions. Instead, any hydroxyl involvement in autoxidation must be at the level of initiating the peroxidation chain.

Not all lipid oxidation is detrimental. Arachidonic acid (4a) is a polyunsaturated fatty acid the autoxidation of which leads (in the so-called arachidonic acid cascade) to, among other products, the biologically important prostaglandins and leukotrienes. Under the control of

184

lipoxygenase enzymes, the arachidonic acid is oxidized in directed free-radical processes to yield such products as prostaglandin E_2 (4b) and the leukotriene B_4 (4c).

In addition to this type of directed autoxidation, radicals are evidently produced in a controlled fashion in other enzyme-catalyzed processes from which they can never escape to enjoy a discrete existence or to inflict damage on surrounding molecules. Cytochrome oxidase was mentioned earlier. Another probable example is ribonucleotide reductase, the enzyme responsible for promoting the removal of oxygen from a ribonucleotide (the building block of ribonucleic acid, RNA) to give a deoxyribonucleotide (the building block of DNA).

The interaction of living systems with light under various circumstances is an extensive topic in its own right. The formation and reactions of a reactive form of oxygen called singlet oxygen and its importance in recent developments in laser therapy, the complex chemistry of photosynthesis, and possible radical reactions associated with drug-induced photosensitivity of the skin are all examples. Related to the last is the case of phenothiazine (5a). Although this is still administered to cattle to rid them of parasitic worms, it causes eyesight deterioration. A possible explanation is that the metabolite (5b) associates with water and, on exposure (in the eye) to sunlight, this dissociates to give hydroxyl radicals. Interestingly, the problem is absent in sheep, in which phenothiazine is metabolized by a quite different route.

Summary

Reactive radicals (free radicals) have been recognized as important intermediates in various chemical reactions since the early 1930s, although many aspects of their reactivity have only recently been properly exploited in the laboratory. Reactions proceeding via radical intermediates, either in solution or in the gas phase, are frequently chain processes.

In biological systems mechanisms exist for the production of reactive hydroxyl radicals, although in normal cells this effect is minimized. Hydroxyl radicals, when formed, may initiate the autoxidation of unsaturated lipids, a process that is inhibited by natural antioxidants. A rapidly accumulating literature suggests that radical reactions inflict cell damage and cell death and that many diseases may be associated with cell damage of this kind.

FOR ADDITIONAL READING

Barry Halliwell and John M. Gutteridge, *Free Radicals in Biology and Medicine,* 2nd ed. (Oxford University Press, 1989).

Michael B. McElroy and Ross J. Salawitch, "Changing Composition of the Global Stratosphere," *Science* (Feb. 10, 1989, pp. 763–770).

Kenneth S. Suslick, "Chemical Effects of Ultrasound," *Scientific American* (February 1989, pp. 80–86).

(5)

a

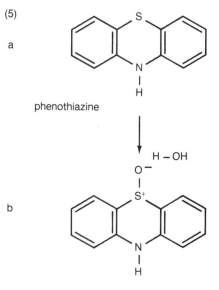

phenothiazine

b

Free radicals may promote aging because natural enzymic and antioxidant defenses against them, even in normal cells, are not completely successful. As the years pass, the body suffers destructive and irreversible changes.

Bill Gallery—Stock, Boston

The Physics of Thrill Rides

by Ronald V. Toomer

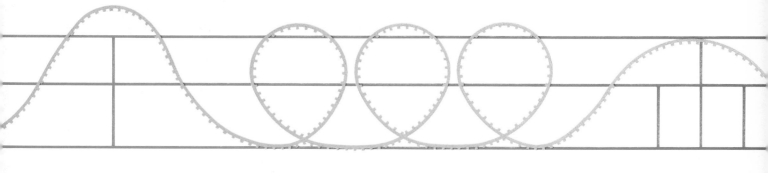

During the last 20 years roller coasters and other amusement park rides have been designed to provide ever increasing thrills.

You see a lot of people waiting in a long line, and as you get closer you see many of them wringing their hands, as if approaching some frightening experience. You get closer still, and it seems that some of the people look quite happy and are telling their not-so-happy companions that it is "O.K." and "it won't do anything to hurt you," while the companions look ready to run off and hide from whatever "it" is. As you get close enough, you can hear things like, "I don't know what I am doing here," "I don't really want to do this," or even "Please tell everyone good-bye for me." Are they waiting to enter the gas chamber? the dentist's office? No, they are waiting to ride a roller coaster.

In 1989 approximately 250 million people visited amusement parks in the United States, and many of these people not only rode roller coasters in the parks they visited but may have come because the coasters were there. What is it that makes so many people visit amusement parks each year to be twisted, turned, thrown, and soaked with water—and

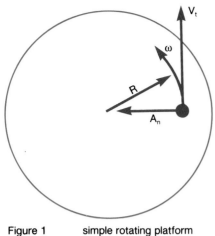

Figure 1   simple rotating platform

R = radius
ω = angular velocity in radians per second
V_t = tangential velocity in feet per second
A_n = acceleration toward center
● = object on platform

why, for the last 100 years, has the roller coaster been the undisputed "king of the park"?

The answers, of course, are within each rider: the challenge associated with the unknown, while knowing one is safe and the danger only imagined; the excitement of the swift and steep fall; the quick turn that causes one to feel heavier than normal; and the light, floating feeling one gets on a fast coaster gliding over the top of a hill.

But why does one not experience the sensation of falling when in an upside-down roller coaster? What is responsible for these and other physical sensations that people experience as they speed up and down, or around and around, on the endless variety of rides offered at amusement parks? The answer is probably easier to understand than one may think, as these phenomena can be explained by some basic fundamentals of physics.

Merry-go-round

When moving through space, one can go only up and down, back and forth, or from side to side and follow either curved or straight paths. It is the combinations of these paths that make all amusement rides work, whether it is a straight drop as on a parachute ride or a complex corkscrew made up of a curved path of steel to guide the train. It is well to consider the forces acting on the passengers of the comparatively simple merry-go-round before proceeding to the more complex rides.

The merry-go-round is basically a platform that is level with respect to the ground and is able to rotate around a vertical axis. An object on the merry-go-round platform, when the platform is not rotating, will feel only one force—that of gravity (+G). This +G force is what people feel at all times and is related to what is called weight. When the platform starts to rotate, another force is added. It is caused by the rotation and is related to the speed of rotation (angular velocity) and the distance from the center of rotation to the object (person) standing or sitting on the platform. This force, which seems to be trying to throw a person outward

RONALD V. TOOMER, a designer of many roller coasters, is President of Arrow Dynamics Inc.

(Overleaf) Photograph © Chad Slattery

188

and off of the platform, is what most people would call centrifugal force, the force that impels things away from the center.

In fact, however, there is no force away from the center. What is being felt is an acceleration toward the center that is known as centripetal force.

Figure 1 shows the relationships that are important for a simple rotating platform. The platform is rotating counterclockwise at a speed ω, and the object on the platform is R distance from the center of rotation. At any given instant the tangential velocity of the object is given as $V_t = R\omega$, where V_t is in feet per second, if R is in feet and ω is radians per second. (A radian is the angle of a circle determined by two radii and an arc joining them, all of the same length.) The acceleration toward the center is A_n, which is given as $A_n = R\omega^2$. It is this acceleration that one feels while on a simple rotating ride like a merry-go-round.

The question remains, however, why one experiences the feeling of being thrown off the platform. Newton's first law of motion helps with the answer. It states that a particle remains at rest or continues to move in a straight line with a uniform velocity if there is no unbalanced force acting on it. In this case the particle, the person on the platform, is at all times trying to follow the line indicated as tangential velocity in Figure 1, and the unbalanced force is the acceleration A_n toward the center of rotation. As long as the persons on a ride are held in place either by a seat or even by the friction between their shoes and the platform, they will follow the curved path of the rotating platform. The force that curves riders away from the straight path, F_n, is shown by $F_n = MA_n$, where M is the mass of the riders and A_n is the acceleration. The force created by the friction between a rider's shoes and the platform can be described as $F_f = W\mu$, where μ is the coefficient of friction between the shoes and the floor and W is the rider's weight. As long as F_f is greater than F_n, a rider stands in place and follows the curved path. As the platform rotates faster, however, F_n increases while F_f remains constant until F_n becomes equal to or greater than F_f. At that time a rider's shoes begin to slide along the path of the tangential velocity, and the rider eventually slides off of the edge of the platform.

Figure 2 shows three positions on the rotating table. Position 1 is the spot at which the shoes begin to slide along the tangential line V_t. As the platform rotates and the slide continues along path V_t, the rider at some time arrives at position 2. At position 2 the rider may think that he or she has moved radially outward from position 1, but that is because position 1 is moving on a circular path while the rider is moving in a straight line; this creates the illusion of sliding radially off the platform. As the starting point moves on its circular path, the rider appears to move farther radially until he or she falls off the platform at position 3, still under the illusion of having slid radially away from the starting point.

The Rotor and the Enterprise

The rotating platform is a simple system that is easy to describe and understand, yet it demonstrates two of the forces that act upon people

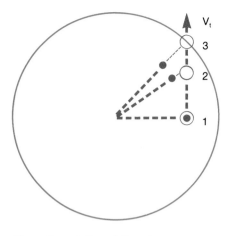

Figure 2   falling off the edge

Merry-go-round (opposite page) is a simple ride consisting basically of a platform that is level with respect to the ground and that rotates around a vertical axis.

(Opposite page) Bill Gallery—Stock, Boston

189

in most amusement rides—the force of gravity and the centripetal force created by traveling on a curved path. It is possible to think of many amusement rides that rely on centripetal force to create the desired sensation. One of the interesting ways to use the force created by a rotating device is demonstrated by an amusement ride called the Rotor. When people enter the Rotor, they find themselves standing in a circular room that is about 4 meters (13 feet) in diameter with a floor and an open top. They stand against the wall, and the room starts to turn around a vertical axis through the center. As the room rotates faster, the riders feel themselves pressed against the wall. At that time the floor drops away, leaving the riders suspended on the wall with nothing to stand on.

Why do the riders not slide down the wall? To explain, we must return to the relationships on the rotating table and apply them in a different manner. The riders are held to the wall by the same force that kept them from sliding off the platform—friction. The forces acting on the riders are gravity (G) and the force F_n caused by the rotation of the room. In this case, gravity is pulling down, trying to cause the riders to slide toward the bottom, and the force holding them against the wall is $F_n\mu$, where F_n is, again, the normal force (toward the center) and μ is the coefficient of friction between a rider's body and the wall.

As the rotation of the room slows down, the riders suddenly realize that at some point they must slide down the wall. The question then is when that will happen.

As the circular room of the Rotor begins to spin fast, the riders are pressed against the wall and the floor beneath them falls away. Because of the centripetal force generated by the spin, the riders do not slide down the wall.

Chance Rides Inc.

Figure 3

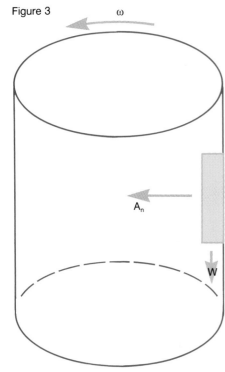

Figure 3 reveals that as long as $F_n\mu$ is larger than W, a rider will stay fastened to the wall; thus, the initial moment of motion down the wall is when $F_n\mu = W$. If the wall is very smooth and polished, the value of μ will be low, and it will take a higher rotational speed to hold people on the wall.

Many amusement rides depend on the simple physical relationships discussed above. One of the most popular rides found in carnivals and amusement parks is often called the Enterprise. It consists of a large wheel with passenger cabins mounted around its perimeter. The wheel is able to rotate about its own center because it is mounted on the end of a pylon that can either lie in a horizontal position or be raised so that it stands vertical to the base. The pylon has the wheel mounted on one end and is fixed to a pivot at the other end; in between, a large hydraulic cylinder is used to raise and lower the pylon.

Each cabin holds two passengers and swings on an axis that is tangent to the rim of the wheel on which it is mounted. When passengers are secured, the wheel begins to rotate about the central axis much like a bicycle wheel lying on its side. As the wheel rotates, the riders first notice that their cabins swing outward, and then the pylon starts to rise so that the wheel is no longer parallel to the ground. The riders now begin to feel new forces acting on their bodies. At first they feel as though they are being pushed harder into their seats as the wheel rotates faster (angular velocity increases). Then, however, as the angle with the ground increases, the force between the riders and their seats varies depending on their position with respect to the ground. Finally, the wheel is vertical and rotating at maximum speed, and riders find themselves feeling light at the top of the wheel and much heavier at the bottom.

What is happening to make their apparent weights vary? Figure 4 shows the forces acting on three of the cabins of the Enterprise. The wheel is rotating at the angular velocity of ω; this provides the force F_n (which is in fact toward the center and not as shown; it is shown as an outward force to aid understanding of how the riders feel). F_n should perhaps be called the "seat force" (SF), because it is felt as the force of the seat pushing against the rider.

In Figure 4, cabin 1 is at the lower side of the wheel, and the two forces W (the riders' weight) and SF are acting in the same direction—down. This makes the riders feel more than twice as heavy as normal if SF is greater than W, which it must be for the ride to work properly. Cabin 2 is on the side of the wheel; riders face the ground with SF of the same magnitude as anywhere on the wheel and the force W seeming to pull them forward out of their seats—but is it? How riders feel in position 2 depends considerably on the magnitude of ω, the angular velocity. If the wheel is turning slowly, riders will slide forward on their seats—and would fall out of the cabin if that were possible. To prevent that, they are held in place by belts. If the wheel is turning at just the correct speed, so that the cabin and the riders are in a free fall together, riders will feel no relative force or motion in the vertical direction between them and their cabin. If the wheel speeds up, it will be turning faster than the riders'

free-fall velocity, and the riders will feel the backs of their seats pushing them downward.

In cabin 3, at the top of the wheel, SF is pointing up and W is pointing down. If SF is regarded as a negative number and W a positive number, they can be added algebraically to determine the forces that the passengers are experiencing. If the number 1 is assigned to both forces so that $W = 1$ and $SF = -1$, and $W + SF =$ net force acting on rider, then $1 + (-1) = 0$. In this case the net force is "0," and riders feel weightless. SF can be altered by changing the speed of rotation ω, but W cannot be changed because it is a function of gravity and the mass (m) of the

192

riders' bodies and can be changed only if the rider loses or gains weight or moves to some other planet or the Moon. If ω is reduced then SF is reduced, and the result is a net force downward that would cause riders to fall out of their seats onto the top of the cabin. If, on the other hand, ω is increased, then the value of SF increases as follows: Let W = 1 and SF = −1.5; then 1 − 1.5 = −0.5.

This means that the net force is upward toward the seat, and riders are held in their seats while upside down. In amusement rides that go upside down, the operators do not want passengers to have to hang onto the restraint devices to keep from falling out of the seat onto the top of the cabin, and so they program the speed so that there is always a net force upward when the car is upside down.

Roller coasters

When people go to an amusement park, the first ride they see on the skyline is truly the king of the park, and it brings together all of the "physics of thrills" that have been discussed so far. This is, of course, the roller coaster or, more precisely, the gravity coaster. Its origins can be traced back nearly 300 years to ice slides in Russia. The first coaster using wheels appeared in France.

The roller coaster as it is known today is about 100 years old, and the first one with a continuous track and a lift was built in the United States. Why is the roller coaster still the most popular ride after more than 100 years? Part of the answer is, of course, because of its applications of the forces described above, while another (and maybe the most important reason) has something to do with the human need to challenge something fearsome.

More than 200 million roller-coaster rides are taken annually in the United States alone. Without a doubt all the riders feel exhilaration or fear brought on by the physical forces to which they are subjected. These forces are the same as those that act on the merry-go-round, the Rotor, and the Enterprise. The roller coaster, however, is built to put these forces to the best possible use—to bombard riders with physical and mental thrills.

Much has been written about very large coasters that are popular today, and some may wonder what size has to do with the ride. Does a coaster have to be large to be a good coaster? The answer to this is no, as there are many very exciting small coasters.

A trip on a roller coaster begins when a rider sits down in the car and pulls the lap bar down to the locked position; the coaster then rolls out of the station. Usually the first thing that happens is that the train comes to a lift and latches onto a moving chain that pulls it up an inclined track. The lift is adding energy to the train, called potential energy, which can be designated by H. At the top of the lift all of the energy that the train will need to complete its trip along the track and back to the station has been added.

The riders, of course, are not thinking about the increase in potential energy or that it is maximum at the top of the first lift, because just

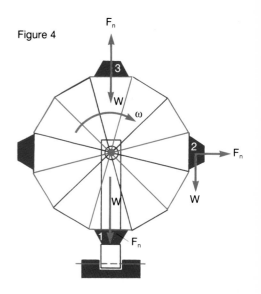

Figure 4

The Enterprise (opposite page) is a large wheel with passenger compartments around its perimeter. The wheel can rotate about its own center because it is mounted on the end of a pylon that can either lie in a horizontal position or be raised so that it stands vertical to the base.

(Opposite page) Intamin AG, Freienbach, Switzerland

193

Ice slides in Russia (above), introduced some 300 years ago, were forerunners of the present-day roller coasters. One of the first wheeled coasters, the Aerial Walk, opened at Beaujon Garden in Paris in 1817 (above right). The Tornado at Coney Island in New York City, seen at the right in 1941, is an example of an early wooden roller coaster.

over the top is a drop that has their complete attention. Figure 5 shows a single coaster car standing motionless with the only force, the riders' weight, acting upon it. The seat force SF is all that the riders feel as they sit in the car. The car is at the top of the lift and starting downhill with a sudden surge, as if it had suddenly been pushed from behind. The train has, in fact, been pushed, or actually pulled, as the force responsible is, of course, gravity.

Figure 6 shows a single coaster car on a downslope with the forces acting on it. Also acting on a coaster is one force that will not be considered at great length, as it does not add to the sensations one feels while riding, but it is real and must be considered by the designer. That force is drag, and it is made up of friction and wind drag. Friction is the sum of the rolling friction of the wheels on the track and the friction of the wheel bearings and oil seals as the wheels rotate. These forces are relatively small in themselves, but there are many wheels on a coaster train, and over a long track the total losses can be high. The wind drag can be very high, as it is a function of the train's velocity squared (V^2); therefore, if the speed doubles, the drag increases by a factor of four.

194

Wind drag can be modified by the shape of the coaches, as a streamlined body will slip through the air easier.

The coaster car heads downhill at a speed that continues to increase as a result of the accelerating force of gravity. It should now become clear that the steepness of the slope must have something to do with how fast the train accelerates. The maximum acceleration will occur if the train is dropping straight down; at this time the applied force is that of gravity. If, however, the angle θ is 90°, then the force acting down the slope, W sin θ, equals G because sin 90° equals 1.00. One notable amusement device, the Free Fall, actually dropped the passenger straight down for a short distance, but to date no real roller coaster has been built with such a steep decline.

In between straight down and the level track shown in Figure 5, the slope can vary widely in steepness, and designers use these variations to make coasters interesting. Because losses from the friction and wind drag are not being considered in this discussion, it can be said that the same speed can be achieved by changing elevation 100 feet (30 meters), whether it is by going down a short and steep drop or a long and gentle decline. No one, however, would be very excited by the long, shallow drop. It is the feeling of rapid acceleration—and if the angle is very steep—the feeling that the rider and the train are indeed falling together rather than coasting along a track that provides the desired thrills.

If the driving force, W sin θ, is related to G, it is possible to understand what happens as the car drops more steeply down the track. If there is a downslope with θ equal to 30°, then W sin θ = W/2, and the seat force will be W cos θ = 0.866 W. This indicates that riders feel a seat force of 86% of their weight and a force along the slope of 50% of their weight; they also feel that their seats are holding them up. To put it another way, the accelerating force is 50% of W.

If there is a downslope with θ equal to 60°, the maximum being used on roller coasters today, then W sin θ = 0.866 W and W cos θ = W/2. This means the forces have been reversed so that riders feel only 50% of their weight on the seat, a very light feeling, and 86% of their weight pulling them down the slope.

Riders do not, however, really feel a force pulling them down the slope, because they are almost in a free fall and consequently feel mostly weightless. Thus, it seems that the speed, the acceleration of the steep slope, and, of course, their own mental condition are all involved in what riders sense—fear, exhilaration, or a mixture of both.

As the train speeds down the drop toward the bottom, the riders are about to experience the next of the forces that they will feel on a roller coaster ride. When their car hits the curved track at the bottom of the dip, they suddenly go from a feeling of lightness to one of extreme heaviness. The seat force has quickly become very high, and all parts of a rider's body feel heavy from what roller coaster enthusiasts call "G's." They may ask, "How many G's do you pull on that dip?" and the answer may be three, four, five, or even greater. What does this mean and what causes it?

Long lines form at the Shock Wave roller coaster at Six Flags Great America near Chicago. After more than 100 years roller coasters continue to be the most popular rides in amusement parks.

Figure 5

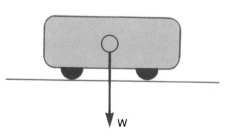

195

Kings Island, near Cincinnati, Ohio, offers a variety of roller coasters. Above, riders descend the first drop on the Beast, a wooden structure. On the opposite page are another traditional wooden coaster, the Racer (top); King Cobra, the world's first stand-up roller coaster, which is made of steel (left); and the Vortex, a steel coaster that takes its riders upside down six times (right).

Figure 6

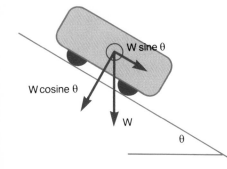

Earlier it was noted that the seat force is related to F_n, which is a force toward the center of rotation. In the present case all of this is still true, but it is calculated in a different manner. Figure 7 shows a coaster car in two different positions on a vertical curve at the bottom of a drop. Position 1 shows the coach as it just enters the curve at the start of the pullout and the force F_n has been added to W, which accounts for a rider's feeling of heaviness. It must be remembered that F_n is the force toward the center of the curve and that it has been equated to seat force. We will now confuse matters further by simplifying the calculation for F_n and giving the answer in "G's," where "G's" are related to seat force divided by W. Thus, "G's" = V^2/gR where V is the velocity in feet per second, g is the gravitational constant 32.2 feet per second squared, and R is the radius of the curve. For example, at the bottom of a 150-foot drop, with the velocity about 97 feet per second and the radius 125 feet, then G's = $97^2/g125$ = 2.33. This is the force that is applied radially along the line F_n of Figure 7, but it does not include the riders' weight W. The necessary values for accomplishing this are W sin θ = component in direction of travel and W cos θ = component through seat, or for $\theta = 50°$: W sin 50° = 0.776 W and W cos 50° = 0.643 W.

Therefore, a force of 0.776 W is pulling the rider down the hill and a force 0.643 W is added to the seat force, which makes the total seat force equal to 2.33 + 0.643 W, or 2.97 W. Consequently, if someone asks, "How many G's does it pull?" the answer is "about three," in which case a rider weighs three times more than normal.

When the car arrives at position 2, the only change in force is that F_n and W are directly added to make a "G" force of 3.33. The train is now speeding uphill, and its riders are feeling themselves pulled back against the seat by the prevailing force of gravity and, again, kinetic energy (the energy of speed and mass) is being changed into the potential energy (the energy of height). Suddenly, the riders are pushed up out of their seats and seem to float as the car hits the crown of the hill and goes over what is commonly called a camel back or speed bump. The forces there are the same as at the bottom of the dip, but they act a bit differently, as can be seen in Figure 8.

At position 1, riders feel the sum of the forces F_n and W cos θ. If V = 40 feet per second and R = 50 feet, then G's = $40^2/g50$ = 1 upward, or −1. If $\theta = 35°$, then W cos θ = 0.819 W. Total seat force then becomes 0.82W −1 = −0.18. If this small quantity is neglected, riders are weightless at this point and feel as if they are floating along the track.

At position 2, if the velocity is the same, F_n and W are equal and opposite and riders are truly weightless. If θ is 30°, W cos θ is 0.866W positive; adding the two gives 0.866 − 1 = −0.134 G. This means that riders feel a small uplift. When the car reaches position 2, it is easy to see that, if the speed remains the same, the two forces are equal and opposite and counteract each other.

There is only one more variation of forces that acts on a roller coaster, that caused by going around curves. When a vehicle follows a curved path, it is influenced by the same forces that were discussed concerning

196

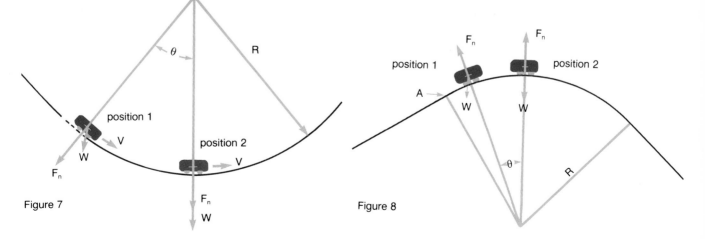

Figure 7

Figure 8

The first roller coaster on which passengers could ride upside down employed the corkscrew, track shaped like a coil spring laid on its side (right); it was developed in the early 1970s. Loops in the shape of teardrops (opposite page, bottom) were found to provide the greatest safety and comfort for riders.

Figure 9

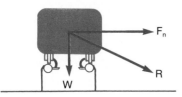

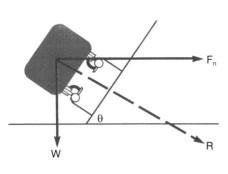

the merry-go-round platform, W and F_n. Figure 9 shows the rear of a coaster car as it makes a turn to the left. In this situation F_n is in the opposite direction so that it really represents the seat force. If the car is traveling 60 feet per second on a curve with a radius of 80 feet, the force F_n is $F_n = G's = V^2/gR = 60^2/g80 = 1.4\ G$; F_n can be combined into the force R, which is what riders actually feel. The direction of R is such that riders would be pulled hard against the side of the car.

Figure 9 also shows the same coach on a curve that is banked. There is one correct bank angle for every combination of velocity and curve radius, and for the case shown the tangent of this angle is numerically equal to the G's—1.4—which is the tangent of 54.5°. This means that if θ on Figure 9 is 54.5°, the resultant R will be straight down through the seat, and a rider may feel heavier but will feel no side force. In reality, when roller coasters are designed, it is not always possible to achieve the optimum bank angle, due to manufacturing constraints and transitions from one curve to another or from a straight track to a curve. Designers compensate for this as much as possible by using varying curve radii to ease the change from a straight to a curved area.

In the early 1970s designers developed and marketed the first roller coaster that was able to go upside down. It utilized an element called the corkscrew, which is track in the shape of a helix laid on its side. (A screw thread is a helix and so is a coil spring.) Before allowing people to ride on the corkscrew, the designers performed extensive testing by using accelerometers attached to the passenger seats. An accelerometer is an electronic device that measures the accelerations applied to it and supplies a signal to a recorder so that the dynamics of an entire ride can be checked and recorded. In all of the upside-down elements that were developed, the speed at the upside-down section prevented riders from feeling as if they were falling out of their seats. (Passengers are restrained from falling out by a mechanical restraint bar.)

The physics of the upside-down elements are the same as those previously discussed. To maintain the proper force while upside down, the familiar equation $F_n = V^2/grR = G's$ is applied. Designers are often asked

198

why the vertical loops are shaped like a teardrop rather than a circle, and this, again, is for passenger comfort and safety.

As the train plunges down a hill toward a vertical loop, it is changing potential energy (elevation) to kinetic energy (speed), and it arrives at the bottom with enough kinetic energy to negotiate the loop ahead. The loop requires a large radius for maintaining the 3.5 maximum G's of seat force. As the train climbs the loop, it changes kinetic energy into elevation and slows down, which requires a smaller radius. The teardrop shape of the loop is, therefore, a function of the decreasing radii; the smallest radius is reached when going over the top.

Coasters of the future

Designers are often asked if there is a limit to how tall a coaster drop can be or if they are approaching some barrier. Many thought that there was a barrier of height that would scare people away from very high rides. With the great popularity of the very large coasters built in the last four years, it would seem that such a limit would exist not from a mechanical or physical standpoint but from an economic one.

The other great question is, ''What does the future hold for roller coasters?'' The usual answer is, ''I don't know.''

Twenty years ago there were no coasters that went upside down. Designers were just starting to talk about the possibility of making such a thing acceptable to the public and would not have been able to imagine what has been accomplished since then. Today designers are in much the same position, talking about new ideas and developing some of them; but without a crystal ball, it is impossible to know what may come along. One thing that is sure is that the roller coasters will continue to be the ''Kings of the Amusement Parks,'' as they have been for more than 100 years, and that they will get bigger and faster. Another is that there are new ideas on the way that will surely make the next 20 years as exciting and challenging as the last 20.

Magnum XL-200, near Sandusky, Ohio, drops 61 meters (200 feet) at a 60° angle at 110 kilometers (70 miles) per hour. As larger and faster roller coasters continue to be built, these rides seem certain to retain their status as ''Kings of the Amusement Park.''

© Chad Slattery

I am thy father's spirit

Technology on STAGE

by Frank E. Wukitsch and John Culbert

Digital recording, synthesized sound, lasers, automated lights, and computerized control are revolutionizing the production and appearance of theatrical plays. Theater people disagree, however, about how much technological infusion is needed or desirable.

FRANK E. WUKITSCH is Professor and Technical Director and **JOHN CULBERT** is Professor and Head of the Lighting Design Program, the Theatre School, DePaul University, Chicago.

(Overleaf) Illustration by M. Renee McGinnis

The overture is coming to a close. Suddenly the unmistakable blare of a steam whistle is heard in the distance. The audience becomes aware of the sound of waves breaking against wooden piers. Blackness slowly evolves into a lush, semitropical forest. A broad wooden dock moves noiselessly across the field of vision, while a Mississippi paddle wheeler, smoke pouring from twin stacks, glides majestically toward her berth. Morning haze dissipates, and oaks dripping with Spanish moss appear on either side of the dock. The river glints in the distance. Light strikes with sunrise colors on the wheelhouse. The giant paddle wheel is slowing. Lines are thrown from the deck to men ashore. A final blast on the whistle, and the title SHOWBOAT blazes across the bright blue sky in lines of fire that remain for one long-held breath before crashing into day-bright explosions of light. The show has begun.

The entertainment is not a Disney motion-picture revival of the musical *Showboat*. It is, rather, a hypothetical production in a state-of-the-art legitimate theater with live actors and technicians working before an audience. This kind of cinematic approach to theater was, to a certain extent, possible even 20 years ago. With enough human minds and muscle working behind the scenes, such an opening moment could have been accomplished, although the cost would have been enormous. Today, however, with the help of new technologies, this same opening might be seen in hundreds of medium-sized theaters throughout the world.

With the advent of computers and digital electronics, it has become possible to control complicated effects in all physical aspects of theatrical production. In the example above, although the music is performed by a live pit orchestra, such sound effects as the whistle and the waves against the pilings are reproduced from recorded sound by an addressable, digital cassette tape deck. Every change of lighting in the scene—the slowly brightening dawn, for example, or the play of direct morning sunlight on the wheelhouse—requires the execution of an assigned cue, at which time numerous individual lighting elements must be varied together. The more changes a particular production requires, the more sophisticated must be the system that controls those changes. Modern computerized lighting control gives the lighting designer an extremely versatile and dependable tool in creating the production. Similarly, boats and docks on rolling platforms, rising and falling backdrops and curtains—in fact, all scenery shifts—can be directed from a single computer by one operator. Centralized computer control improves efficiency, while the computer's ability to repeat programmed activities with precision reduces the danger to the cast and stage crew from collisions with heavy moving scenery.

As in so many other fields, the computer chip and its associated technology is causing a revolution in theater. It is a revolution, however, that is not accepted by all.

Hark! hark! the amplified lark

From the first savage drumbeat that accompanied the telling of an epic myth to the highly directional stage microphones and digitally manipulated music and sound effects of today, hearing has been as important as

202

seeing in theater. Some have argued that for drama, sound in the form of the spoken word is even more important than light.

The most common form of sound in the theater is still the unadorned, unamplified human voice. Though the voice has been called the most versatile of instruments, people have sought ways to improve its quality and volume in theatrical performance probably since prehistoric times. Actors on the modern stage often have not had their voices trained for projection and clarity. Consequently, electronic reinforcement by means of microphones and amplifier-speaker systems is becoming increasingly necessary even in smaller theaters. Amplification is also coming to be expected by the audience, especially in musical production, where it is often used to reinforce live music as well as voice.

Much of the advancement in sound reinforcement in recent years has been due to breakthroughs in microphone technology. For use on stage, microphones must have a highly selective pickup pattern so that they do not catch sounds from either the audience or the offstage crew or recycle sounds coming from the theater's speakers. Microphones with this quality are said to be unidirectional and to have a cardioid, or heart-shaped, pickup pattern. A cardioid microphone is sensitive to sound in front of and somewhat to the sides of the device but virtually dead to sound from the rear. Miniaturization of microphone components has led to a new family of cardioid devices called boundary microphones, which are designed to lie on a smooth, flat surface such as a floor or table (hence *boundary*). Their smallness, typically the size of a pocket calculator, usually makes them the best choice for "miking" a production. For a 1989 production of the musical *Chicago* at the Theatre School of DePaul University, Chicago, three boundary microphones spaced evenly across a 11.6-meter (38-foot) proscenium, or stage front, satisfactorily picked up individual singing voices as far as 10.7 meters (35 feet) away.

Another popular microphone for stage use, although much more expensive than the boundary microphone, is the two-part wireless microphone system. One part, the microphone itself plus a small FM transmitter, travels concealed on the actor's body, while the second part, an FM receiver, puts the transmitted signal into the theater's sound system. In a complex musical production, 6 to 10 actors or more may each be "wired" with a body microphone. In addition to high cost, the wireless microphone has the disadvantages of being bulky and thus hard to hide under skimpy costumes and of being subject to interference; for example, from the competing signal of a local FM radio station.

The same theater sound system that serves for live-sound reinforcement has a second function, sound reproduction. As such, it requires some means of playing back prerecorded music and sound effects. Compared with a professional studio recording system, state-of-the-art theater sound equipment is unsophisticated. The usual playback device is the quarter-inch reel-to-reel tape deck, on which is threaded a specially prepared tape called a show tape.

The process of producing a show tape is simple but time-consuming. Sound effects and music are transferred to the tape from other sources,

Highly sensitive unidirectional microphones that have found use in the theater for sound reinforcement include miniature and boundary styles (left and right, respectively). The diminutive miniature microphone can be suspended inconspicuously over the stage, mounted on a thin floor stand, or hidden in the set. The low-profile boundary microphone, designed to rest on the floor or other flat surface, is usually the best choice for theatrical productions.

Working from a sound plot, a sound technician prepares a show tape for a production. Each tape segment carrying a recorded effect or piece of music is cut on a splicing jig, joined to pieces of colored leader tape, and spliced in its proper order with all the other segments.

Sound equipment at the Blackstone Theatre, Chicago, is representative of the comparatively unsophisticated level of technology found in most theaters. (Above) Two reel-to-reel tape decks and a cassette tape deck stand atop a 24-channel mixer. Output from the mixer feeds into a graphic equalizer (above right), whose horizontally arranged slide controls, each governing the filtering of a third of an octave, provide a visual analogy of how the equalizer is tuned.

Courtesy of the Theatre School, DePaul University, Chicago; photos, Cathy Melloan

which might include recorded sound-effects libraries, recorded incidental music, and recorded commercial music. Other sources are live music and live sound effects recorded specifically for the production. Each piece of tape-recorded sound is edited, the tape being physically cut just before the first note or sound begins and just after the last note or sound has completely decayed. Pieces of colored leader tape are then joined to the ends of each tape segment, and all music and effects are spliced together in proper order. With the junction of the leader tape and audio tape segment immediately behind the playback head on the tape deck, the sound on that segment is said to be "cued up." When the stage manager calls the "go," the technician pushes the play button, and the response is immediate.

For playback through the reproduction system the tape deck is usually connected to a mixer. A mixer is a device that allows a large number of inputs, or incoming signals, to be combined into a small number of outputs, or outgoing signals. In more concrete terms, consider a 24-channel mixer; that is, one having 24 input channels. The channels will be distributed among the particular needs of a hypothetical production.

The production is a musical having both recorded sound and a live mix. *Live mix* designates the use of microphones, musical instruments, or both whose output will be controlled by a sound technician at the mixing board while the performance is in progress. Because of the complexity of the production, the recorded sound effects will require two reel-to-reel tape decks and one cassette deck. If the effects require stereo outputs, two inputs for each tape deck are needed, for a total of six inputs. In addition, there is a wireless microphone on each of the eight principal actors. Only 10 inputs now remain to be divided between the stage and the pit band. Three boundary microphones on the floor will give the coverage needed for the stage at large. The other seven inputs will be divided among microphones in the band.

All 24 inputs are blended in the mixer into one set of stereo program outputs—the signals that will be transformed into amplified sound for the audience. In addition, the input from the pit band's microphones is mixed into a second, monitor output. From the monitor output the signal is shunted through an amplifier to onstage speakers that allow the performers to hear the band at whatever level is required. The program outputs are connected to a one-third-octave graphic equalizer.

204

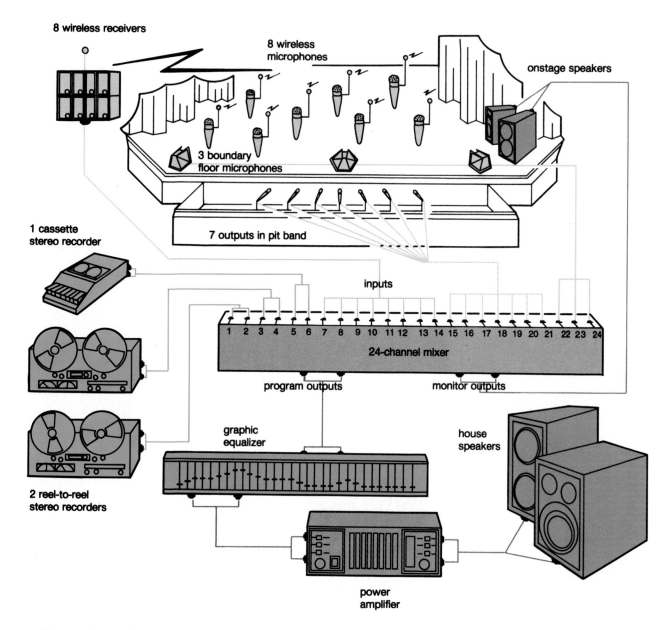

8 wireless receivers

8 wireless microphones

onstage speakers

3 boundary floor microphones

1 cassette stereo recorder

7 outputs in pit band

inputs

1 2 3 4 5 6 7 8 9 10 11 12 13 14 15 16 17 18 19 20 21 22 23 24

24-channel mixer

program outputs

monitor outputs

2 reel-to-reel stereo recorders

graphic equalizer

house speakers

power amplifier

The graphic equalizer is a set of frequency filters, each of which allows the operator control over a narrow band of frequencies. *One-third-octave* refers to the fact that the entire range of audible frequencies is divided into octaves and that each filter covers a third of an octave. The *graphic* nature of the equalizer derives from each filter's having a vertically sliding control. When 30 such controls are placed side by side, the resulting pattern, resembling a graph of frequency versus loudness, gives the operator a visual analogy of how the equalizer is tuned. This instrument is used primarily to adjust the sound system to the peculiarities of the theatrical space and the particular production.

Feedback is the howl that results when a microphone is particularly sensitive to sound at certain frequencies. Those frequencies are am-

The sound setup for the hypothetical musical production described on pages 204–206 is diagramed above. Signals representing live sound from the stage and the pit band as well as prerecorded sound signals are blended in the mixer into one set of program outputs destined for the house speakers. Additionally, the input from the band is mixed into a second set of output signals and routed to other speakers onstage, which allow the performers to hear the band.

Illustration by Robin Faulkner

205

plified preferentially, broadcast as sound, and picked up again by the microphone in a repeating loop until the noise becomes unbearably loud. The graphic equalizer allows the technician to filter out the troublesome frequencies, resulting in less chance for feedback and a subduing of the ringing sound in a system on the verge of feedback.

From the graphic equalizer the stereo signal is routed through power amplifiers to the house speakers. The amplifiers process the signal in such a way that the incoming balance of frequencies is maintained while the overall loudness, or amplitude, is greatly increased. With the advent of the scientific study of speaker enclosure and the development of materials having unique magnetic and electric properties, speakers are becoming both more compact and more efficient. Strong bass response in small speakers requiring less power to drive them is one specific result.

Molding sound like clay

Twenty years ago the notion of a sound designer collaborating on a theater production would have been rare if not unthinkable. The process of gathering the sound for a production usually began with the director's or assistant director's handing a list of music and sounds, or sound plot, to the stage manager. The stage manager would then designate someone to gather together the albums containing the list of items. The music was pirated from the originals by a sound technician who was usually very good at recording from standard phonograph disc to tape. Sound effects were inserted where applicable, and the entire tape was edited and made show ready. The only creativity was on the part of the director in choosing the existing music and effects to fit his or her concept of the production. Today this process has changed. A dynamically evolving concept of the capabilities of sound, spurred on by technologies of digital control and manipulation, has created an important role for sound design in the staging of theatrical works.

Until the early 20th century a tonal statement or sound contained three variables: intensity, pitch, and timbre. Intensity is the relative loudness of the sound; pitch is the frequency or tone of the sound; and timbre is the essential quality of a sound that distinguishes one voice or instrument from any other. An A above middle C played on a piano, within the limitations of the instrument, will always be recognizable as a particular note made by a piano. It will never be mistaken for a note from a trumpet or a bassoon. A human voice will always be recognized as such and will not be confused with a fire siren. Such observations were part of a set of safe assumptions that everyone made about sound. It was also believed that human beings had created all the sounds it was possible to make.

With the advent of electronic music in the late 1930s, these assumptions were all proved to be wrong. The first harbingers of a coming revolution in the music world were the gigantic (by modern standards) vacuum-tube electronic organs that appeared in roller rinks before World War II. The war also gave a boost to the electronic music industry by redefining inductance signal technology, thus leading to the electric guitar's steel strings and inductance pickup. Applying various filters to the electronic signal from the guitar allowed the original vibrations made by the steel strings to be distorted and manipulated to resemble nothing ever heard before. The quality of timbre was no longer a constant.

Synthesizers, machines that generate and modify sounds electronically, became common in the early 1970s. The first ones were clumsy affairs meant to be used with audio recording equipment; unlike modern synthesizers, they did not have a keyboard. Early synthesizers were analog systems—they represented the loudness, pitch, and other characteristics of a sound as a continuous, varying electrical signal in an analogy of the character of real sound waves—and they contained such components as oscillators, filters, chokes, and voltage regulators to generate and modify the analog signal in a way that offered a high degree of creative control over any sound. Today's synthesizers most often are fully digital machines. Digital audio systems, including digital synthesizers and sound-recording and sound-playback devices, handle sound not as a continuous analog signal but as a series of rapid electrical pulses corresponding to the 0's and 1's of binary digits. The pulses represent samplings of the analog signal taken 40,000 times per second, and the binary information contained in the pulses specifies the characteristics of the sound. Digital synthesizers begin either with digitally sampled existing sound or with synthesized sound and use microprocessors to manipulate the binary coding of the signal. A digital-to-analog converter then reads the final output pulses and changes them into analog signals for input into a conventional amplifier.

The synthesizer is becoming an enormously powerful tool for sound design in theatrical production (as well as filmmaking). The sound designer, no longer limited to existing sound effects or music, can actually create new sounds. In addition, he or she can take an existing sound and, by means of sampling and resynthesis, change that sound much as a scene designer might change a paint from purple to violet by adding Prussian blue pigment. The sound designer can combine sounds, stretch them, add or remove harmonics—in general, mold sound as a sculptor molds clay.

Sound designers are often also composers. The synthesizer in conjunction with a computer is allowing them to compose at the keyboard, see the composition on the computer's screen, and manipulate the music on screen by use of either the keyboard or the computer's controls. The composition can then be played for review. When the piece is acceptable, it can be saved on a computer disk and printed out in the form of sheet music.

A new technology that weds digital electronics to lasers is compact disc (CD) recording. The recording medium, a 12-centimeter (4.7-inch) plastic disc, is small, durable, and extremely accurate in its reproduction of sound. The information on the disc is not in the form of an analog signal, such as that on the ridged groove of a standard phonograph disc or on the aligned magnetic particles of a conventional recording tape. Instead, a foil layer inside the plastic of the CD is etched, by means

A sound designer-composer works on a digital synthesizer linked to a computer. The combination allows him to compose at the keyboard, to see the music displayed immediately on the computer screen, to manipulate the composition from either the synthesizer or the computer keyboard, and to store the product on a computer disk. Technologies that allow digital control and manipulation of sound are creating an increasingly important role for sound design in theatrical works.

Pete Addis

207

For theatrical use, sound effects offered on compact disc (CD) albums (top) provide several advantages over their phonograph disc counterparts, including better fidelity, reduced chance for damage, and push-button ease in addressing each separate effect on the album. Multipurpose theaters that depend on high-quality recorded sound without a live mix will find the digital audio tape (DAT) recorder (above) valuable. DAT machines record audio signals as binary-coded samples on a magnetic tape smaller than the standard cassette. Their search function, which can scan a tape that is winding forward or backward at high speed, allows rapid addressing of any moment on the tape.

of a laser beam, with a pattern of holes and unperforated blanks in the language of binary coding: a hole means a 0, and a blank means a 1. The CD's digital encoding has the same function that it does in the synthesizer or computer—the storage of information—and it is translatable by a laser-beamed reading device and digital-to-analog circuitry into an analog signal and then by speakers into sound.

So far, sound designers give CD systems mixed reviews. On the one hand, they are completely free of distortion, wow, and flutter. On the other, their music is unlike any that a theater audience has heard before. With modern microphone technology married to digital recording, CD sound goes beyond the expected orchestra hall experience, producing a sensation somewhat akin to being near every instrument at once. Even a musician in the center of the orchestra never hears music in quite this way. Experiments with CDs employed to supply incidental music for dramatic presentations have been disconcerting to some audience members and distracting to others. The problem can be interpreted either as a failure of a new technology to fit existing conventions or as a failure of the audience to accept a new convention.

Where CD systems unquestionably outstrip their phonograph disc counterparts is in the area of recorded sound effects. By early 1990 there were some 20 CD albums on the market whose contents ranged from standard effects (baby crying, door slam, aircraft taxiing) to environmental sounds (for example, 75 minutes of waves and sea gulls). Even from an inexpensive CD player the sound is incomparable. Because the recording is scanned by a laser beam rather than touched by a solid needle or recording head, there is no wear, scratching, or hiss of dust. Moreover, because the foil layer is encased in tough plastic, the CD, if treated with care, can last many years. By contrast, it is often necessary to replace sound effects records after one use and one careless scratch. Yet another feature that makes CD sound effects important for theater is the ease of addressing and reaching each separate effect on the album. Depending on the sophistication of the CD player, it is possible to move instantly by number to any of as many as 75 effects on the disc. This feature is a particularly valuable timesaver while making the show tape.

Digital tape-recording machines now on the market are studio-quality devices that record audio signals as binary-coded samples on a smaller version of cassette tape. Advantages include digital-quality recording, ability to address any moment on the tape, and high-speed search functions that can scan a tape that is winding in either direction as fast as 100 times the normal playback speed. Digital recorders will be valuable in theaters that are multipurpose and that must depend on high-quality recording without a live mix.

What light on yonder actor breaks?

Until the 20th century humanity depended on ships for long-distance travel and commerce. The ships required lighthouses as navigational aids for safe passage around land. The light source, an oil-fueled flame, was relatively dim, and considerable effort went into finding ways of inten-

208

sifying the light. In the early 1800s the French physicist Augustin-Jean Fresnel developed an efficient, lightweight, and economical lighthouse lens that would concentrate the light from the flame into a strong beam. The same type of lens is still used in a piece of theatrical lighting equipment called, appropriately enough, the Fresnel.

The borrowing of technology from a larger, more financially stable field is typical of the way in which theater acquires new technology. Compared with the motion-picture and television industries, theater is a small enterprise with little capital to support technological research and development. Moreover, those products that do find theatrical use have a relatively small market and thus develop slowly and remain expensive.

For most of its history theater lighting has had one primary purpose: the illumination of performances for the audience. A secondary purpose would have been the creation of spectacular special effects—lightning, fires, and explosions, for example. Around the beginning of the 20th century two theater artists, the Swiss Adolphe Appia and the Englishman Edward Gordon Craig, pursued the use of light as a communicative and emotional means of expression. The implementation of their ideas required devices that could create and control beams of light on stage. This technology (including the Fresnel lens) was being developed in other fields as Appia and Craig developed their philosophies. However, it took decades for the equipment to become feasible for theater use, preventing either theorist from truly implementing his ideas.

As the experience of Appia and Craig suggests, it is impossible to separate the formulation of artistic ideas concerning lighting design from the development of technology to implement the ideas. Lighting designers in modern theater must use available tools and continue to find new ones to adapt to the stage. A recent example of technological borrowing is the automated, computer-controlled, motor-driven, moving lighting device generally known by the brand name VARI*LITE®. The instrument was developed in the early 1980s for the rock music group Genesis to add controllable moving beams of light to its concerts. The lights, now standard for rock concerts and industrial shows, are finding selected theatrical use as well. While the creative potential that these instruments offer would be invaluable to the theatrical lighting designer, the expense is still too great for most establishments.

The strongest possible reason for theaters to invest in new technology is to save money, usually by cutting labor costs or saving time. Since a theatrical production is an event repeated over and over with only slight variations, technology that is precise and accurate in its repeatability is also well received. From the lighting designer's point of view, the most important motivation for investing in new technology is the wish to find more flexible and original ways of lighting a production.

Lighting design is the use of light to create a stage environment that has the appropriate illumination and emotional feel for the action of the production. The tools with which the designer achieves that end can be broken down into four categories: technology used to create washes and beams of light; technology used to control the light once it is created;

The concentrically ringed lens originally developed by Augustin-Jean Fresnel for use in lighthouse lamps (top) eventually found its way into the theater in a piece of lighting equipment appropriately called the Fresnel (above). Such borrowing from a larger, more financially stable field— travel and commerce in the case of the Fresnel lens—is typical of the way theater acquires new technology.

209

Horizontal overhead banks of VARI*LITE®
automated lighting devices play their
beams over the music group Genesis
during a rock concert performance (top).
Developed for Genesis in the early 1980s,
these computer-controlled, motor-driven
instruments have since found selected
theater use, as in the Los Angeles Opera
production of Tristan and Isolde (right).

technology used to set up the working "factory" or theater to make it a
viable space for lighting design; and technology used to keep track of the
other technology—the process of lighting design itself.

Laser pixies, computerized cross fades

Virtually all light used in the theater is created with electricity. Two
elements are involved: the lamp that generates the light and the instrument that controls it. Every instrument is designed to take advantage of
a specific type of lamp. The infusion of lamp technology in the theater
has been quite slow, since a new type of lamp usually requires a new and
expensive instrument as well. Lamp technology developed for television
and film is slowly finding a home in the theater. The new lamps are
more efficient, giving more light and less heat per watt of electricity
consumed, and are physically smaller than the lamps they replace. One
type, a gas-discharge lamp, is found in many theatrical follow spots,

210

MR-16 lamps, long used in carousel slide projectors, were employed extensively for the 1989 Broadway production of Grand Hotel to put strong light in confined spaces. In a set from the play (top), MR-16s are mounted within the ladderlike columns on each side of the stage. In Dreamgirls, which opened on Broadway in 1980, lighting equipment is integrated into the visible scenery in the form of moving towers that carry lights for various scenes of the musical (left).

(Top) Lighting design by Jules Fisher; (bottom) lighting design by Tharon Musser, set design by Robin Wagner; both photos, Martha Swope

spotlights used to keep a beam of light on a moving performer. Rated at 200–300 watts, they provide more light than older units using 1,000-watt lamps. Their theatrical use is limited, however, because they do not allow for electronic dimming, a standard theatrical practice.

Another lamp making inroads into the theater world, the MR-16, has long been a household object; it is commonly found in carousel slide projectors. It is bright, efficient, and small, allowing a designer to generate a lot of light from a tiny space. For the 1989 Broadway production *Grand Hotel*, for example, MR-16s were employed extensively to put light in areas too confined for conventional instruments. In the lighting and set design for the musical *Dreamgirls*, which opened on Broadway in 1980, lighting instruments were incorporated in a highly visual way. The lights used for various scenes of the show were mounted on moving towers visible to the audience, making the exposed technology an integral part of the production.

211

Recently introduced lighting instruments pan, tilt, and focus under the control of a computer that remembers the sequence of thousands of settings. The 2,000-watt Fresnel on the left is designed for television studio work. The smaller 1,200-watt theatrical Fresnel on the right, in addition to its other automated functions, allows a maximum of 11 colored gels to be scrolled in front of its lamp.

The lighting control board for the Blackstone Theatre (below) features a dedicated computer (at lower right) and a pair of monitors that display the commands programmed from the console for the hundreds of individual lighting cues that may constitute a particular production. The data for each production can be saved on a floppy disk and reloaded into the computer as needed.

Lighting designers exert as much control as possible over the properties of light, including color, intensity, direction, and movement, the last of which effects a change in any of the others. They use a number of instruments to light the stage. Any specific instrument has a particular color and, since it is positioned in a fixed location, a particular direction. The amount of light that each instrument emits is regulated from one central location, a lighting control board. To create a sunset, for example, the designer may choose a vertical series of lights to represent incoming sunlight. The first light, fitted with a pale yellow plastic filter, or gel, is installed at a fairly high angle above the horizon. The next instrument, carrying a stronger yellow gel, is positioned at a lower angle, closer to the horizon. The third instrument, carrying an orange gel, is positioned almost horizontally, at the horizon. The designer creates the sunset by turning on the top light, fading it out as the middle one is turned on, and finally fading from the middle one to the bottom one.

A modern theater audience, "trained" by movies, television, and music videos, will become visually bored if it is not treated to a variety of images. Since the designer needs a separate instrument, or group of instruments, for each angle or color of light, hundreds or thousands of instruments may be required for lighting a single production. Designers obviously would have more flexibility and control over light if any one instrument could provide more than one color or direction during a play.

The most common method of coloring a light is to place a colored gel in the path of the light beam. Devices currently on the market allow a series of gels to be scrolled under computer control in front of a lamp, giving multicolor capabilities to a single instrument. Dichroic filters, which have been limited by cost to specialized applications, are now appearing on the market for theater use. Made by applying thin-film coatings to heat-resistant glass, dichroics remove unwanted colors from a light beam by reflection and interference effects rather than by absorption, thus passing colors that are purer and brighter than traditional gels can achieve. Also being developed are new filter materials combining the properties of dichroic filters and liquid crystals in a way that allows their color to be varied electronically. Linked to a computer, such a filter system would provide a highly controllable and repeatable range of colors from a single source.

Altering the direction of a beam of light onstage involves physically moving the instrument. As mentioned above, such recently introduced fixtures as the VARI*LITE® use motors to redirect the beam. Nevertheless, there is still no practical way of varying the angle of the light and changing its color in such a way that the three-light setup for a sunset could be replaced by a single, remote-controlled instrument. In general, most such technology is still too expensive for widespread use but should become part of the theater in the next decade.

The lighting designer today uses a computer to control the intensity of each of the lights used in a production—a job that once relied on people to move specific levers on cue. Previously limited by the number of hands available at any one moment, the designer now can direct

thousands of instruments and their functions (given the limitations of the theater space available for hanging fixtures) with the press of a single button. The 1975 production *A Chorus Line*, the first major Broadway musical to use computerized lighting control, well illustrates the merging of technology and design ideas. The computer allowed movement of huge volumes of light around the stage in precisely timed and repeatable sequences to create the landmark production's different environments and establish its distinctive new look.

The dedicated computer used in conjunction with the lighting control board is the most advanced part of the lighting system in a theater. The direction for future development is to make faster computerized boards that control more instruments and more functions of each instrument—color and direction as well as intensity. Control boards are also being developed that monitor the entire lighting system and can alert the operator if, for example, a lamp is burned out or a circuit breaker is blown. Like computers and computerized systems in general, lighting control boards are becoming smaller, lighter, cheaper, and more powerful.

Lasers—devices that produce brilliant, highly directional beams of light—are recognized as among the most important inventions of the 20th century. Their diverse uses include welding a detached retina to the back of the eye, measuring the distance from the Earth to the Moon, and carrying millions of bits of information simultaneously over a single glass fiber. In the mid-1970s a small number of companies combined lasers with entertainment to create yet another use: the laser light show. The first market was the high-budget rock concert as promoters sought new and exciting effects with which to stimulate teenage audiences. Incor-

Opening in 1975, A Chorus Line *was the first major Broadway musical to use computerized lighting control. The merging of technology and artistry allowed the precise, repeatable movement of huge volumes of light around the stage and created a distinctive new look.*

Lighting design by Tharon Musser; photo, Martha Swope

213

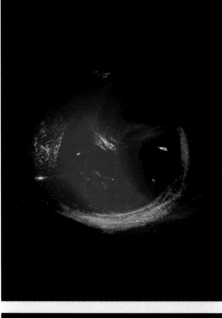

Laser beams directed by quickly moving mirrors and prisms under computer control can be called upon to draw words and pictures, sculpt flowing abstract patterns (top, called lumia), and create a variety of other projected and in-air effects. In 1979 an all-laser Tinker Bell (above) that flitted about, dimmed and brightened, changed shape, and spelled out words was introduced to the stage in a Broadway production of Peter Pan.

porating the narrow beam of the laser with quickly moving prisms and mirrors under the instantaneous control of the computer, laser-effects systems now draw corporate logos and animated characters and create a variety of realistic and abstract imagery.

In 1979 the first computer-controlled all-laser character, Tinker Bell, was introduced to the stage in a Broadway production of *Peter Pan*. Audiences of tomorrow will probably not see many stage characters played by lasers. They are certain, however, to see more of the magical quality of laser light being incorporated into scenic and lighting designs—quite possibly the title SHOWBOAT emblazoned on the morning sky as the curtain goes up.

The theater's space and its systems can be thought of as a factory that is called upon to create a variety of different products, the productions. While each production requires a different lighting setup, certain elements of the lighting system are permanent. Recently the permanent part of the lighting system in most theaters has undergone a major change. The intensity of each lighting instrument is controlled by an electronic dimmer. Because of their size, heat, and noise, the dimmers are located in a central space isolated from the stage. Extension cords, called circuits, are run permanently from the dimmers to various positions in the theater. Lights are connected to these circuits and then controlled by the dimmers.

Before the mid-1970s a theater had comparatively few dimmers, typically fewer than 100, because they were large, hot, and expensive and had to be manually controlled. The system required a mechanical interface between the many circuits and the few dimmers. Today dimmers are small and cheap enough for each circuit in the theater to be permanently wired to a dimmer. Consequently, there may be hundreds of dimmers and circuits, all under computer control. The next evolutionary step will be incorporation of a dimmer in each lighting instrument, simplifying theater wiring and providing even more design flexibility.

The personal computer is ideally suited to helping the lighting designer keep track of all the instruments, colors, locations, circuits, dimmers, and other details of the lighting system. Many software programs exist to assist with the prolific amounts of paperwork created during the process of implementing a production design. The next step in development will be to integrate the computer's design functions with the computerized control board. The designer could then program or alter lighting cues at a computer remote from the theater's control board and transfer the information to the board via a disk or modem.

The adoption of new technology poses a potential danger for any artistic endeavor, lighting design included. To remain an artist, the designer must use and adapt the technology to achieve a desired result rather than let the technology dictate the nature of that result. An example can be found in the way modern control boards have affected the look of theatrical productions. A computerized board remembers particular sets of intensities for particular groups of lights. In a production design each such set is assigned a cue number in consecutive order from start to

214

finish. One of the board's abilities is a "cross fade" from a given cue to the next—fading out the first set of lights while simultaneously fading in the second set to its preset intensities. Computerized boards, in fact, are programmed on the assumption that the cross fade is the desired way to get from one cue to the next; *i.e.*, the cross fade is their "default mode." Before the computer, only a limited number of hands were available for moving levers. The designer had to decide which lights to move first. A cross fade was no easier or more standard than first bringing up one light and then fading out another. Today the computer has made virtually all light cues into cross fades even though most boards will do other types of fades or sequences if the designer exercises those options. Modern technology is allowing more and more flexibility, but the designer must ensure that artistic decisions are still made and that the technology supports, rather than dictates, the choices.

By the pressing of my thumbs, moving scenery this way comes

It is almost certain that Shakespeare wrote all of his plays for the same stage setting. The all-purpose design, the scenic convention of the time, consisted of a wooden architectural facade with numerous doors and other openings. Not all the plays used all the openings, but if a play required a doorway, it was there.

Other historical periods brought other conventions. There were times of ultrarealistic scenery when the stage was covered with three-dimensional architectural and natural elements. At other times the realism lay in the painting technique, and audience members sitting toward the side of the theater saw a distorted view of vanishing points and horizons. Some forms of theater can support very little if any scenery other than props and furniture. Arena theater or theater-in-the-round seats the audience completely around the stage. Any scenery in the usual sense would block someone's view of the stage.

The art of scenic design has undergone a number of changes in the 20th century, changes influenced by certain interwoven elements. First, scenic design has to a great extent followed the evolution of other visual

Rack of solid-state dimmer modules, all under the control of a computerized lighting board, form part of the permanent lighting system at the Blackstone Theatre. A module (one pulled to show detail) contains two dimmers, each of which controls one lighting circuit. Today dimmers are small and cheap enough for every circuit in a theater to be wired permanently to its own dimmer.

Courtesy of the Theatre School, DePaul University, Chicago; photo, Cathy Melloan

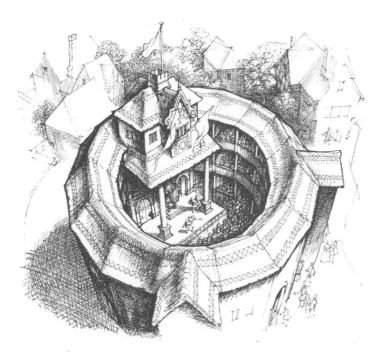

Artist's rendition shows what London's first Globe Theater may have looked like before its destruction by fire in 1613. Shakespeare almost certainly wrote all of his plays for such a stage setting: an all-purpose, fixed wooden facade equipped with numerous doors and other openings. Both before and since that time, different historical periods have brought different conventions for scenic design.

From the Art Collection of the Folger Shakespeare Library

arts. When Expressionism was a popular painting style, it found its way to the stage as well. When Minimalism appeared in the galleries, it permeated the stage in both the dramatic literature and the sensory event. This phenomenon is common in the arts, as a new style usually stems from a new approach to universal or societal issues.

Second, the effect of 20th-century technology on scenic development has paralleled the style changes. Plastics, metals, and other new materials have largely replaced the classic wood and canvas scenery. New methods of construction using modern sheet materials such as fiberboard and lauan mahogany plywood have made for more durable and lighter products.

Third, because of labor costs, the cost of production has skyrocketed. Much of the commercial theater since about 1980 has been produced in England and exported to the U.S. because production costs in England are largely government subsidized.

Finally, motion pictures and television probably have had the most effect on the visual aspects of live theater. Both media introduced the audience to an entirely new way of telling a story. The approach, dubbed the cinematic style, required the instantaneous changing of locations with no disruption in the story line. Stage designers seeking this effect reached back into history to the times when scenery was the most important element in theater. They revived techniques and ideas of the Renaissance and the 19th century, when audiences demanded and received great visual spectacles.

Modern rigging systems, rolling platforms, and mechanical turntables are basically the same pieces of stage machinery they were during the Renaissance. The structure and function of a stage revolve or turntable would in no way confuse Leonardo da Vinci, and he would recognize almost all the other stage machinery in use today. What would give him pause are some of the methods of locomotion and all the methods of electronic control.

The pattern that is emerging for the future of scenic design is the same as that for theatrical technology overall—one of decreasing

New materials and construction methods wrought by 20th-century technology have strongly influenced scenic design, with plastics, metals, and sheet materials largely replacing wood and canvas scenery. Using a metal–inert-gas arc welder, a theater technician (top) builds a set of prison bars from steel tubing. Two technicians (above) carve an element of a topiary from a block of lightweight urethane foam used for insulating refrigerator boxcars. While the trend in modern scenic design is toward increasing mechanization and automation, noncommercial theater will continue to depend on large numbers of people for scenery shifts (right) and other control needs.

manpower and increasing mechanical movement and control. At the noncommercial level, university, community, and regional theaters will remain dependent on a large force of technicians and laborers to control scenery. Commercial theater, which must make a profit, will use more sophisticated technology.

Scenery moves horizontally, vertically, or both. Two special cases are combined vertical and horizontal—*i.e.*, diagonal—movement and circular or rotary motion, which is almost always in a horizontal plane.

For supporting vertical movement many well-designed theaters have a fly loft, a high open space above the stage. Near the top of the fly loft is a platform made of narrow steel planking laid down on a frame of steel I beams that are part of the structure of the building. The gridlike pattern of the planks and I beams has given the platform the name gridiron, or simply grid. There is enough space between the planks to allow steel cable or thick hemp rope to pass through toward the stage below. From these lines hang pipes, or battens, on which scenery and lights are suspended. The opposite ends of the lines go to a counterweight system, which balances the weight of the load on the pipe. If, for instance, there is a 227-kilogram (500-pound) curtain on a certain pipe, the counterweight at the other end will be about 216 kilograms (475 pounds). Consequently, discounting friction, in order to lift the curtain, the technician has to exert a force of 11 kilograms (25 pounds). With the exception of metal to replace natural materials, the system and its operation are exactly the same as that used during the Renaissance.

Attempts to mechanize fly systems have been made since the turn of the century. Whereas some have succeeded, the high initial cost of a large system has made mechanization relatively rare. Today, as the cost of human labor rises sharply, the initial cost of installation is becoming more attractive.

Older mechanized systems used electric winches housed in a winch room remote from the stage. Because early winches were designed for such applications as cranes or tugboats, their noise made it necessary to place them away from the stage. Later, silent electric and hydraulic winches developed specifically for theater use were placed directly on the grid over the pipe to be raised. By ganging a number of winches together electrically in master-slave fashion, an even lift of one long pipe could be effected with three, four, five, or more units. Lift speed on the first winches was constant. Later, the introduction of direct-current motors and three-phase alternating-current motors allowed speed and direction to be controlled with great precision. Winches could be attached semipermanently to the grid, where they would be regarded as permanent rigging for the theater, or they could be moved around and used for "spot lines" on a temporary basis. Some systems allowed their winches to travel on tracks over the grid, expanding their flexibility. Systems became ever more complicated and expensive.

Horizontal movement of scenery has been powered in various ways. For centuries it was much less expensive to hire four unskilled laborers to push a large piece of scenery onto the stage than to hire one skilled

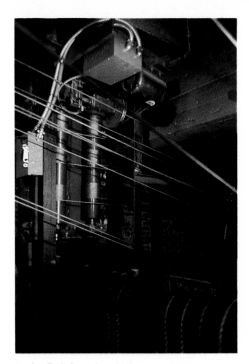

In the fly loft at the Blackstone Theatre, old and new technologies for suspension and vertical movement work together. Visible at the top is a modern dual-drum, six-line electric winch capable of supporting 900 kilograms (2,000 pounds) of scenery or lights over the stage. Near the bottom can be seen some of the pulleys of the theater's hemp system of ropes and sandbags, which, except for the substitution of metal pulleys for wooden ones, is exactly the same as that used during the Renaissance. Crossing diagonally in front of the winch are steel cables for another counterweight system, employing steel weights.

Courtesy of the Theatre School, DePaul University, Chicago; photo, Cathy Melloan

217

craftsman and a number of assistants to build a complicated machine for the task. The great scenery-moving machines designed during the Renaissance likely were built as an end in themselves in spite of the cost. Most theater and scenic designers were architects and practicing engineers. Their work was not merely designing scenery but also designing great machines. Wealthy patrons of the theater paid for the art and the engineering.

Until about the mid-1960s human labor remained the most inexpensive method of moving and controlling scenery. Soon thereafter, labor costs began forcing production expenses—and ticket prices—to intolerable levels. At about the same time, the computer was being introduced for the control of lighting. When it was contemplated for moving heavy, dangerous scenery, however, producers and technicians fearfully eyed the shortcomings of the first lighting computers. A glitch in a lighting computer merely meant that a light might not operate on cue. Were there to be a glitch in a computer controlling the movement of tons of scenery, the producer could face disaster even if there were no injuries.

While computer control of moving scenery remained a concept for some years, other forms of control were developed and refined. Coupled with electric drive units, they did much to cut the operating costs of production. Using a simple set of switches for forward and reverse and

The design of the State Theatre in the Victorian Arts Centre, Melbourne, Australia, assembles several examples of modern power-operated rigging and rolling-platform systems. The stage carries a pair of platforms, or wagons, that move laterally on tracks and a turntable on a another tracked wagon that rolls in from the rear. Electric winches for suspending scenery and lights occupy winch rooms high above the stage on either side of the grid, while several movable spot-line winches rest on the grid itself.

Courtesy of the Peter Albrecht Corporation

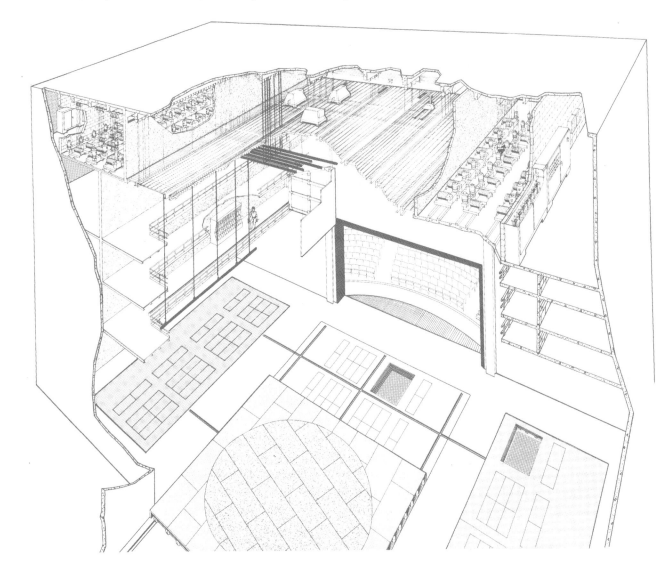

Mechanization and automation of scenery movement have become more and more common in large-budget stage productions. In a scene from the Broadway version of Cats (above), a huge power-driven chandelier of stage lights revolves above the cast. (Left) Aboard a boat guided over the stage by computer, the disfigured Phantom and his beloved glide among horizontally and vertically traveling chandeliers in the London production of Phantom of the Opera.

(Top) Martha Swope; (bottom) © Clive Barda, London

possibly a rheostat for changes in speed, one person could now direct the movement of a single piece of scenery. Because it does require one person for handling each piece of scenery, this type of control is still common where labor is not an issue. In a complicated scenery change involving 10–12 moving pieces, the people at the controls contribute both intelligence and safety.

Recently the computer has made inroads into the mechanization and control of scenery, a trend that is expected to continue in the future.

219

Power-operated rigging and rolling scenery are beginning to replace
manually operated systems even in some medium-sized noncommercial
theaters. Although initially more expensive, they pay for themselves by
replacing large, expensive crews with hydraulic or electric motors controlled by a computer. One technician positioned at a console and using
infrared-sensitive television cameras to monitor the dark stage can shift
scenery quietly, efficiently, and safely. A shift that formerly required 20
people and work lights behind a curtain may now be accomplished by
one person without the curtain and in what the audience perceives as
a total blackout.

Many technicians are still reluctant to relegate the control of moving scenery to the computer. Safety, not reliability, is now the issue.
Interestingly, the safety question has nothing to do with the computer's
proper functioning. The scenery will always be where it should be when
it should be. The actor moving onstage during a scenery shift, however,
might not. The perceived danger is that scenery and actor may try to
occupy the same space at the same time. *Starlight Express,* the most
expensive production in Broadway history when it opened in 1988, was
performed by a company on roller skates interacting with the sets at high
speed. The play owed its commercial success to pure technical spectacle,
satisfying its audience with flashy costumes, motion, lights, and noise.
To move its masses of scenery quickly and safely, its designers relied
on computerized control along with mechanical and electronic interlocks
and human safeties.

To compute, or not to compute

Among practitioners of theater much controversy exists today concerning the ever expanding use of computerized mechanization and control in their art. It arises from four separate arguments regarding practical, financial, pragmatic, and philosophical issues.

The practical argument against computers states that the more sophisticated a system becomes, the more things can and will go wrong with it. It adds that the more complicated a piece of hardware becomes, the less likely it is that its operator will be able to repair it. While both statements in general are true, neither is unassailable.

The first problem can be alleviated by the use of redundancy within the system. Critical components within a computer can be duplicated in such a way that should one component fail, the duplicate would automatically assume its function. Backup control in the form of a second computer outside the system is another type of redundancy, although it often is not financially practical. Finally, building a dependable product with excellent quality control goes far in reducing frequent breakdowns. In response to the second part of the argument, one may note that in most cases the time when the operator could fix a piece of hardware passed many years ago. Most people no longer have the knowledge or the equipment to repair their modern automobiles—a deplorable fact perhaps, but not a reason for discarding automobiles.

The financial argument points out that technology is very expensive. This is especially true when the technology is comparatively young. A good example is the development of computerized lighting control. Many individuals could afford personal computers before most theaters could afford lighting control computers. Although microchip technology was relatively inexpensive in itself, developing it into a dedicated lighting control system was costly. Only the largest theater organizations could afford the product. Consequently, few were built, and price per unit remained high.

Today things have changed somewhat. The specialized package is still expensive; a state-of-the-art computerized lighting controller can cost from $35,000 to $100,000. On the other hand, the generalized technology has become inexpensive enough to allow a number of good alternatives to the large system. Computerized control costing less than $10,000 gives the lighting designer a creative power undreamed of a decade ago. The argument concerning financial feasibility, at least in lighting control, is becoming less important each year.

The pragmatist asks why theater must continually expand its technology. The answer is that it must try to compete with film and television. The pragmatist then asks if it is possible for theater truly to keep up with electronic media. The truth is that attempts to imitate electronic or digital effects live onstage have fallen far short of the competition. The conclusion: theater should stick to the technology it knows lest its art become foolish.

The hypothetical production of *Showboat* described in the introduction suggests that theater within limits can compete with some of the technology of other media. Much of it, however, is beyond reach today. For example, live theater could not do a competitive production of *Star Wars,* nor should it attempt to. The conventions of live theater have little to do with the high adventures of comic-book heroes.

When theater people philosophize about technology in the arts, the conversation invariably turns to the possible adverse effect of mindless control over the artistic environment. Traditionalists see theater in its purest form as an actor speaking in an open space before an audience. They believe that any enhancement of the environment, for whatever purpose, tends to erode that purity. There is no room in their theater for the evolved stylistic conventions that have paralleled the growth of technology. This confrontation between purists and technology has reached new heights with the introduction of computers into production.

Where the technology enthusiast sees the computer as a tool that will make the physical elements of the production more real, the traditionalist believes giving control over to a microprocessor takes the "feel" of human control out of the performance. Moreover, according to the traditionalist, even the actors onstage must become more mechanical as the timing of the production is relinquished to the computer. Before the introduction of the computer into the production, the timing of each cue was directly and literally in the hands of the technicians. Today in many theaters computers have taken over all but the command function. Operation of the equipment, whether it be scenery flying in or lights changing or a complex set of sound cues, is accomplished by the computer after the press of a single button. Here, traditionalists contend, is where art is lost, for the computer never varies its interpretation of the cue. It is that variation in timing contributed by human beings both onstage and off that helps give each performance its artistic uniqueness.

There is a great deal of substance in the traditionalist view, and the danger of forcing the production into a mechanical mold is real. With care, however, the artistic integrity of a production can be maintained. The advantages of computer-operated theater systems, at least for the present, outweigh the disadvantages.

"Tech week" is that week just before the opening performance of a production. It is the time when all the technical elements of the production are brought together in the theater and added to the acting element. Lighting, sound, costumes, props, scenery, special effects, and rigging all must find time for rehearsal during this one week. A complex production may have hundreds of separate cues divided among the above elements. In the noncomputerized theater each cue must be rehearsed until it is perfect, then further rehearsed so that it will be duplicated as exactly as possible in each successive performance. A common rule of thumb states that each cue will use an average of six minutes of rehearsal time. Simple math yields a total of 30 hours for a production with 300 cues. If the tech week is allotted 50–60 hours, as is common, there is little time left to integrate the actors with the technical elements.

On the other hand, computerized cues do not need rehearsal. Once programmed, a cue will be duplicated exactly whenever the correspond-

ing "go" button is pushed. If the director or designer wishes to change or add a cue, the new cue will be executed precisely the first time. When technicians manually operate theater systems, each new change must be practiced to be integrated into the production. Because such changes can devastate a rehearsal, a director often is loath to ask even for appropriate changes, knowing that valuable time will be consumed in their integration. In this respect the computer has added to the artistic freedom of directors and designers by allowing them extra rehearsal time.

Safety is another element in which the computer's ability to duplicate a cue exactly comes into play. When scenery that can weigh as much as a small automobile is moving and actors are present onstage, the slight variations in speed and timing that make each performance artistically unique take on a strong negative aspect. Rehearsal will bring the shifting of scenery to the level of human repeatability, but there will always be the variations that make physical danger a reality. Computerized control systems, with their attendant human monitors and their ability to duplicate movement or change exactly, can remove a great deal of that danger.

Computers and other technologies can no longer be looked upon as passing fancies in the ancient art of theater. The complexity and the cost of modern productions require a move toward the same fruits of research and development that are powerfully affecting so many other elements of human life. It is only by accepting and integrating them into the art that theater will accompany the transition of civilization into the 21st century.

Students of DePaul University's Theatre School participate in a "cue-to-cue" rehearsal during tech week, the week before the opening performance of a play. In a cue-to-cue the actors and production crew jump from one lighting, sound, scenery, or special effects cue to the next, with minimal dialog, in order to integrate and refine all the technical elements of the production. This particularly time-consuming and demanding period has been eased considerably by computer control because computerized cues, once programmed properly, need no rehearsal time for perfecting them.

Courtesy of the Theatre School, DePaul University, Chicago; photo, Cathy Melloan

Oops . . . Eureka!

SERENDIPITY AND SCIENTIFIC DISCOVERY

by George B. Kauffman

The much-touted scientific method notwithstanding,
many discoveries—both old and new—have been made by accident.
Although luck is involved, it is the curious, perceptive, open-minded person
who can convert an unexpected observation into a momentous find.

Courtesy of The Lewis Walpole Library, Yale University

In 1754 Horace Walpole (above), 4th earl of Orford, wrote in a letter of having read a fairy tale, The Three Princes of Serendip, *whose heroes "were always making discoveries, by accidents and sagacity, of things which they were not in quest of." As a name for this faculty Walpole coined the word* serendipity.

What do the following technological advances have in common—fire, cooking, agriculture, the wheel, and weapons? They were all probably stumbled upon by chance rather than as the result of a premeditated search and discovery. In the words of Mark Twain, "Name the greatest of inventors. Accident."

Fire can start in various natural ways, most commonly by lightning. One of humankind's more observant prehistoric ancestors must have realized that this bright, hot, mysterious "force" could be used both for warmth and for keeping wild animals at bay. Before the secret of creating fire at will was discovered, probably the only way to have it on demand was to keep it going continually as a kind of "eternal light," as depicted in Jean M. Auel's 1980 best-seller *The Clan of the Cave Bear* or Jean-Jacques Annaud's 1982 film *Quest for Fire.* The discovery of cooking was also probably accidental, possibly in the manner depicted by Charles Lamb in his charming "A Dissertation on Roast Pig." Similarly, the momentous discovery of agriculture, which transformed humans from nomads into beings living in fixed abodes and which led in turn to the birth of cities and civilization, may have happened when a forager noticed sprouts emerging from grain or seeds that had been spilled accidentally on the ground. The wheel could have been devised by a primitive inventor who had observed a rolling log or stone. Such weapons as spears may have been fashioned by someone who had fallen on a sharp stick.

The common characteristic of these incidents is that in each case an accidental happening became a discovery only when the unknown inventor realized its significance. In the apt words of chemist-turned-microbiologist Louis Pasteur, "In the field of observation, chance favors only the prepared mind."

The above cases are examples of serendipity. The word is more than 235 years old, but it has enjoyed an increased popularity of late, being used in all sorts of contexts. Unfortunately, much of the word's current stylishness can be linked with incorrect and sloppy usage, leading to its application to cases for which it was never intended.

Serendipity's origin

The word was coined and first used by Horace Walpole, 4th earl of Orford, writer, connoisseur, and collector, who is best remembered today as perhaps the most prolific letter writer in the English language. In a letter dated Jan. 28, 1754, to British diplomat Horace Mann, Walpole wrote,

This discovery indeed is almost of that kind which I call *serendipity*, a very expressive word, which as I have nothing better to tell you, I shall endeavour to explain to you: you will understand it better by the derivation than by the definition. I once read a silly fairy tale, called *The Three Princes of Serendip:* as their highnesses travelled, they were always making discoveries, by accidents and sagacity, of things which they were not in quest of: for instance, one of them discovered that a mule blind of the right eye had travelled the same road lately, because the grass was eaten only on the left side, where it was worse than on the right—now do you understand *serendipity*? One of the most remarkable instances of this *accidental sagacity* (for you must observe that *no* discovery of a thing you *are* looking for, comes under this description) was . . .

GEORGE B. KAUFFMAN is Professor of Chemistry at California State University, Fresno. He is a contributing editor to several journals and has written extensively on chemical education and the history of science and technology.

(Overleaf) Illustration by Jane Meredith

226

Yet, despite Walpole's insistence that the discovery be not only accidental but also unsought, the word *serendipity* is often used today as a pretentious synonym for "accidental discovery." Even some unabridged dictionaries do not include the second condition, instead defining it merely as a faculty for making desirable discoveries by accident.

The earliest case of true serendipity recorded in the Judeo-Christian tradition may have been the experience of Saul, son of Kish, who in seeking his father's lost asses, sought counsel from the prophet Samuel, who told him to forget the asses and instead announced to him that he was to reign over Israel. The historical case par excellence is undoubtedly Columbus' discovery of America while seeking a sea route to the East Indies. Columbus, however, was preceded by another serendipitous discoverer, the Norse explorer Leif Eriksson, who is widely held to have landed in eastern Canada about AD 1000 after bad weather had driven him far off his course to Greenland.

Serendipity in science

Scientific inquiry abounds with cases of serendipity, for the phenomenon is more common than generally thought. As illustrations one can cite Luigi Galvani's discovery of "animal electricity" (the bioelectrical nature of nerve impulses); Henri Becquerel's discovery of radioactivity; Wilhelm Conrad Röntgen's discovery of X-rays; Hans Christian Ørsted's discovery that an electrified wire can induce motion in a magnet; Michael Faraday's discovery that a moving magnet can induce an electric current in a wire; Claude Bernard's discovery that the passage of blood into different parts of the body is regulated by the nerves; Charles Richet's discovery of anaphylaxis (a severe immune reaction to a foreign substance following previous sensitization); Arno A. Penzias and Robert W. Wilson's discovery of cosmic microwave background radiation; Samuel C.C. Ting and Burton Richter's discovery of a subatomic particle called the J/psi meson; Luis W. Alvarez, Walter Alvarez, Frank Asaro, and Helen Michel's

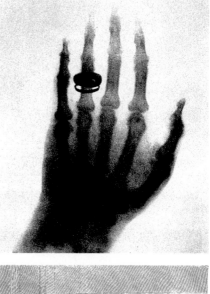

227

discovery of high concentrations of iridium in rock strata, which led to the catastrophic impact hypothesis for explaining mass extinctions at the end of the Cretaceous period; and Anthony Hewish and Jocelyn Bell's discovery of pulsars, or pulsating neutron stars. In these and many other cases of serendipity, the discovery actually made proved to be far more important than the goal originally sought.

On the other hand, the American inventor Charles Goodyear's discovery of the process that marks the birth of the modern rubber industry does not qualify as a serendipitous discovery according to Walpole's definition. In 1839 Goodyear stumbled upon vulcanization when he accidentally brought a sample of rubber mixed with sulfur and litharge (lead monoxide) into contact with a hot stove. Yet this fortuitous occurrence took place only after five years of constant attempts to convert crude rubber from an intractable, smelly substance that became soft and sticky in summer and hard and brittle in winter into a tough, elastic, heat- and cold-stable, commercially useful product.

In order to accommodate such discoveries as that of Goodyear, Royston M. Roberts in his book *Serendipity: Accidental Discoveries in Science* (1989) coined the term *pseudoserendipity* to describe "accidental discoveries of ways to achieve an end sought for." In view of the abundance of examples, the article confines itself to instances of true serendipity.

Charles Goodyear stumbled upon vulcanization when he accidentally brought a mixture of crude rubber, sulfur, and lead monoxide into contact with a hot stove. Because Goodyear had been searching for just such a process for five years, his discovery, although fortuitous, does not meet the terms of Walpole's definition of serendipity and might better be called pseudoserendipity.

Wöhler's synthesis of urea

During the early 19th century few researchers would have ventured to work in the field of organic chemistry, "that jungle," as German chemist Friedrich Wöhler called it. Mysterious forces operated there, forever beyond the reach of scientific scrutiny, for organic chemistry was the chemistry of organized systems, parts of living organisms. It was believed that organic compounds were those that grew within organisms, their design and manufacture made possible by a life force (what French philosopher Henri Bergson was later to call élan vital) that could never be captured in a laboratory flask.

In 1824 Wöhler unintentionally made crystalline urea and in 1828 recognized it as such in a simple laboratory experiment. Until then urea, a waste product of metabolism, had been thought to exist only in organisms and had been crystallized from animal and human urine. Wöhler's genius was not in synthesizing urea but in recognizing that the white crystals indeed were urea. A number of other researchers—and Wöhler himself—had in fact made urea earlier in the laboratory but never guessed what they had made or its significance. Wöhler treated silver cyanate with ammonium chloride solution and obtained a precipitate of silver chloride. He concentrated the solution by heating and obtained white crystals totally unlike the ammonium cyanate that he had anticipated. Ammonium salts liberate ammonia when treated with alkaline substances, and cyanate salts yield cyanic acid with strong acids, the product decomposing further into carbon dioxide and ammonia.

Wöhler's crystals did none of these things. They seemed to do nothing with acids, except for concentrated nitric acid, which "produced at once a precipitate of glistening scales." On observing the behavior of the white crystals with nitric acid, he remembered that the natural urea he had worked with earlier (among hundreds of other white substances) showed uncannily similar behavior. He procured some natural urea, compared the two substances, and found them identical. "Ammonium cyanate is urea," he wrote to his mentor, the great Swedish chemist Jöns Jacob Berzelius. Even the quantitative composition, the percentages of carbon, nitrogen, hydrogen, and oxygen in his crystals, was the same as that published by English chemist William Prout for natural urea.

Urea and the ammonium cyanate that Wöhler had expected to prepare are isomers, a term coined by Berzelius in 1830 to designate two different compounds having the same chemical composition. Whereas ammonium cyanate is a salt made up of two ions, the ammonium ion (NH_4^+) and the cyanate ion (OCN^-), urea is now known to have a totally different structure, that of the covalent molecule shown at right.

Some chemists, in praise of Wöhler, have suggested that he single-handedly lifted organic chemistry out of the darkness, but Wöhler himself wondered at first whether the starting materials from which he had made urea did not themselves still contain some of that vital force believed to be needed for organic synthesis. Both ammonia and cyanic acid were usually made from living materials. However, in 1837 German chemist Justus von Liebig proclaimed, "The extraordinary, and to some extent

Friedrich Wöhler contemplates a pair of kidneys in a contemporary caricature. The German chemist's unintentional laboratory synthesis of urea in 1824 and recognition of the substance as a product of living organisms brought the previously mysterious realm of organic chemistry within the reach of scientific investigation.

Drawing by William B. Jensen, University of Cincinnati

Structural formula for urea.

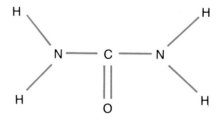

229

inexplicable, production of urea without the assistance of vital functions, for which we are indebted to Wöhler, must be considered one of the discoveries with which a new era in science has commenced." When Wöhler died in 1882, August Wilhelm von Hofmann, the great German chemist and cofounder of the German Chemical Society, claimed that the synthesis of urea "removed at a single blow the artificial barrier which had been raised between organic and inorganic chemistry."

Pittacal, the first synthetic dyestuff

During the 1830s, almost a quarter century before William Henry Perkin's isolation of mauve, the first dyestuff to be produced commercially from coal tar, Karl (or Carl) Ludwig Reichenbach, the discoverer of paraffin and creosote, was engaged in research on compounds isolated from the beechwood tar produced in the charcoal ovens of the metallurgical factories at Blansko in Moravia. One minor but aggravating annoyance of his daily life was the frequent use of the wooden fence around his house by male dogs for a basic function that would later be associated with fire hydrants. Believing that the disagreeable, penetrating odor of creosote would keep the dogs from his property, in 1832 Reichenbach painted his fence with the substance.

Although the creosote failed as a repellent, it did react with the urine, and Reichenbach observed that a blue dyestuff had formed on the fence. He named the new substance pittacal (from Greek words for "tar" and "beautiful"), and by treating beechwood tar with barium oxide he prepared it in a pure state as a blue solid that served as a fabric dye when fixed (mordanted) with alumina. Although sold as a dyestuff, it met with little commercial success.

Reichenbach's discovery is reminiscent of a more significant example of serendipity from the field of physiology. In 1889 German physiologist Oskar Minkowski introduced the concept that diabetes results from the suppression of a substance made in the pancreas (later found to be the hormone insulin). The discovery underlying the concept arose when Minkowski's assistant called to his attention the fact that flies were attracted to the urine of a dog whose pancreas had been removed for an entirely different reason—to study the role of that organ in the digestion of fat. Since urine does not usually draw flies, Minkowski analyzed it and found it to contain unmetabolized sugar. He therefore concluded that the pancreas was involved in breaking down this carbohydrate.

Mauve, the first aniline dye

Another example of serendipity in the dyestuff industry is the discovery of mauve, the first artificial dye produced commercially from coal tar, by William Henry Perkin, then a 17-year-old English youth who was never to complete his college education. To quote English chemist Raphael Meldola, "Seldom, if ever, in the history of science has the discovery of one chemical compound of practical utility led to results of such enormous scientific and industrial importance as the accidental preparation of mauve in 1856."

230

Portrait of William Henry Perkin painted in 1906 shows him holding a skein of material dyed with the aniline dye mauve that he discovered serendipitously a half century earlier while attempting to make quinine. (Above) The original mauve (also called mauveine) synthesized by Perkin is displayed with mauve-dyed yarn and a bottle of alizarin, a synthetic red dye for which Perkin developed an improved manufacturing process.

About the age of 12, Perkin became interested in chemistry, and in 1853, at age 15, he entered London's Royal College of Chemistry, where he attended the lectures of Hofmann. He became Hofmann's assistant two years later. About the same time he set up a laboratory in his home.

As the British Empire expanded into tropical regions where malaria was endemic, quinine, the most useful alkaloid of cinchona bark and the only effective remedy for this mosquito-borne disease, became increasingly important. Hofmann mentioned the desirability of synthesizing quinine to the 17-year-old Perkin, who began work in his home laboratory during the 1856 Easter vacation. Basing his experiments on the then prevalent, incorrect idea that the structure of a chemical compound is determined from the molecular formula alone, Perkin concluded that two molecules of allyltoluidine ($C_{10}H_{13}N$), by taking up oxygen and losing hydrogen in the form of water, would yield a substance with the formula of quinine ($C_{20}H_{24}N_2O_2$) via the reaction $2C_{10}H_{13}N + 3O \longrightarrow C_{20}H_{24}N_2O_2 + H_2O$.

Perkin oxidized a salt of allyltoluidine with potassium dichromate but obtained only a "dirty reddish-brown precipitate." He repeated the experiment with a salt of the simpler molecule aniline ($C_6H_5NH_2$). This reaction produced a very dark precipitate, which he found to have con-

231

siderable dyeing properties. From it he isolated a compound having the molecular formula $C_{27}H_{24}N_4$, which he called aniline purple or Tyrian purple but which is better known by its French name, mauve.

At the time, the goal of organic chemical research was to obtain definite, crystalline compounds. Chemists considered the formation of noncrystalline, and particularly colored, amorphous products an indication of failure. Unlike most of his contemporaries, who would have discarded such a product, especially because the desired substance—quinine—was white, young Perkin possessed a rare combination of scientific and artistic talents that led him to recognize and pursue the implications of his accidental discovery.

With his father's financial support, Perkin began construction of a factory in June 1857 at Greenford Green near Harrow. He later related, "At this time neither I nor my friends had seen the inside of a chemical works, and whatever knowledge I had was obtained from books." Nevertheless, within six months Perkin's dye was being used in London dye houses and soon afterward was being produced by other manufacturers in both England and France. With no previous experience Perkin had worked out, on an industrial scale, two of the most fundamental operations in dyeing: nitration, which involves the conversion of benzene (derived from coal tar) to nitrobenzene, and reduction, the conversion of nitrobenzene to aniline. In one of the smallest synthetic-dye factories in all of Europe, he had overcome what were seemingly impossible odds and transformed his serendipitous discovery into the beginnings of a commercially successful new chemical industry.

Perkin's discovery provided the impetus for research in pure as well as applied chemistry. In the words of chemist and biographer Benjamin Harrow, "The basis for most of the development in organic chemistry since 1856 lies in Perkin's discovery of mauve."

Pasteur's discovery of optical asymmetry

In 1848 Louis Pasteur reported the remarkable discovery that certain chemical compounds could be separated, or resolved, into a "left" constituent and a "right" constituent, one being the mirror-image isomer of the other in the manner of left- and right-handed gloves. Although he later went on to found the field of microbiology, his earliest discovery immortalized his name in the annals of chemistry. His finding that racemic acid, one of the forms of tartaric acid, consists of two isomeric constituents that affect light differently from each other laid the basis for the field of stereochemistry, the study of the spatial arrangement of atoms in molecules. He attributed their differing optical activity to what he called *une dissymétrie dans les molécules* ("molecular dissymmetry"), a phrase selected as the title of the first volume of his collected works and inscribed on his mausoleum at the Institut Pasteur in Paris. Pasteur's resolution of racemic acid has had a profound influence on research in the fields of stereochemistry, crystallography, biology, biochemistry, mineralogy, pharmaceutical chemistry, and organic and inorganic chemistry, among others.

232

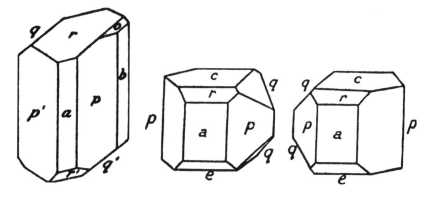

In 1848 young Louis Pasteur (above) embarked on research that was to lay the basis for the field of stereochemistry when he made the "wholly unexpected discovery" of a difference in form between crystals of sodium ammonium tartrate and sodium ammonium racemate. Pasteur then showed that an evaporated solution of sodium ammonium racemate crystallized into a mixture of two distinct mirror-image crystal forms, which he sorted by hand and which proved to be optical isomers of the same compound. He also showed that, like the salt, racemic acid itself comprised two optical isomers. Whereas a solution of an equal mixture of the isomers formed holohedral crystals of racemic acid (left), solutions of the separated isomers crystallized into two hemihedral forms that were mirror images (crystal pair at center). One isomer (the left member of the pair) proved to be identical with the optically active compound tartaric acid obtained from grape fermentation.

Tartaric acid, a simple organic acid found widely in plants, was first isolated in 1769 by Swedish apothecary and chemist Carl Wilhelm Scheele from its potassium acid salt (potassium hydrogen tartrate, or cream of tartar) obtained from fermented grape juice. Sometime around 1819 in France, a second form of tartaric acid was obtained from crude cream of tartar, but it was mistaken for oxalic acid. It was later recognized as a distinct compound, and in 1828 French chemist Joseph-Louis Gay-Lussac gave it its present name, racemic acid (from the Latin *racemus*, "bunch of grapes"), and showed that it has the same chemical composition as tartaric acid.

In 1838 Jean-Baptiste Biot examined racemic acid and found that in solution it failed to rotate the plane of polarized light passed through the solution. Compounds that do not show such a rotation effect are said to be optically inactive, while those that do are termed optically active. Earlier, in 1832 (published in 1835), Biot had recognized that tartaric acid is optically active and showed that in solution it rotates the plane of polarized light to the right. In 1841 French chemist Frédéric Hervé de la Provostaye examined the crystalline forms of tartaric and racemic acids and their salts (tartrates and racemates), and the following year two German chemists, Eilhard (or Eilhardt) Mitscherlich and Carl Remigius Fresenius, prepared, analyzed, and characterized a number of the salts.

Repeating de la Provostaye's work, Pasteur discovered a fact that the other chemist had overlooked. Examined under the microscope, crystals of tartaric acid and its salts were hemihedral—they possessed only half the faces required by the symmetry of the crystal system—whereas crystals of racemic acid and its salts, with one important exception, were holohedral—they possessed the full complement of faces. Pasteur noticed a difference in form between the crystals of sodium ammonium tartrate and those of sodium ammonium racemate, which Mitscherlich in 1844 had claimed to be identical in crystalline form and in all properties except the ability to rotate polarized light.

This anomaly ("a wholly unexpected discovery") so intrigued young Pasteur that he undertook a study of these salts. He treated solutions of equal weights of racemic acid with sodium carbonate and ammonia, combined the solutions, allowed the resultant solution to evaporate, and obtained a salt that was seen to be a mixture of two dissimilar types of hemihedral crystals. By mechanically separating, with tweezers, the two types of crystals, which were mirror images, Pasteur accomplished

233

the first and probably the most famous of all resolutions of optical isomers. He had discovered that although sodium ammonium racemate was hemihedral just like the tartrate, the hemihedral facets were turned sometimes one way, sometimes the other.

Subsequently Pasteur derived the corresponding acid from each group of sorted crystals and showed that solutions of the two acids rotated the plane of polarized light to the same degree but in opposite directions. The acid that rotated light to the right proved to be identical with the tartaric acid from grape fermentation, whereas the one that rotated light to the left was a hitherto unknown optical isomer. Pasteur then completed the cycle of proof by mixing concentrated solutions of equal weights of each acid, which produced optically inactive racemic acid.

Pasteur seems to have been the beneficiary of two elements of sheer luck. First, with the possible exception of the sodium potassium salt, the sodium ammonium salt is the only salt of racemic acid that can be resolved in this manner. The two optical isomers of tartaric acid and of all its other salts combine to form crystalline racemic acid and racemates, which show no hemihedrism or optical activity. Second, had Pasteur carried out his experiments, for example, on the French Riviera rather than in the cool Parisian climate, he probably would not have made his revolutionary discovery, for it was later found that the two optical isomers of sodium ammonium tartrate crystallize as a single holohedral racemate at temperatures above 26° C (79° F). Only below this temperature can they be resolved into the two optically active tartrates.

Pasteur's results, presented to the French Academy of Sciences in 1848, were so startling that the venerable Biot, the reigning French authority on optical activity, demanded to see the evidence. Pasteur repeated his experiment in Biot's own laboratory at the Collège de France with Biot's own reagents and under his supervision. When the 74-year-old scientist witnessed the strong opposing optical activity produced by the solutions of the separated isomers, he embraced the 25-year-old Pasteur and exclaimed with tears in his eyes, "My dear child, I have loved science so much throughout my life that this makes my heart throb with joy."

On the basis of his correlation of crystallographic properties with optical activity, Pasteur proposed that optical activity in a substance is caused by an asymmetric arrangement of atoms in the individual molecule and that molecules of the same substance that rotate the plane of polarized light to the right and those that rotate it to the left are related to each other as mirror images. Nevertheless, the exact relationship eluded him, and he was unable to identify the particular spatial arrangement of the atoms. Not until a generation later, in 1874, did the 27-year-old French chemist Joseph-Achille Le Bel and the 22-year-old Dutch physical chemist Jacobus Henricus van't Hoff show independently that an arrangement of four different atoms or groups of atoms at the corners of a regular tetrahedron having a carbon atom at the center would produce two structures, each a mirror image of the other. By extending the tetrahedral concept to compounds containing more than one so-called asymmetric carbon atom, van't Hoff was able to account for Pasteur's tartaric acid isomers.

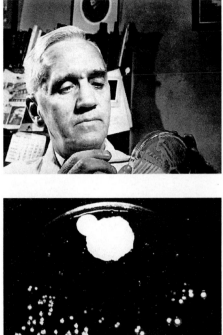

Fleming's discovery of penicillin

The discovery of penicillin, the first of the miracle drugs and the one that French novelist and biographer André Maurois hailed as "the greatest contribution medical science ever made to humanity," stems from an accidental observation made in 1928 by Scottish bacteriologist Alexander Fleming. His fortuitous observation, which was a direct result of his apparently disorderly habit of not discarding culture plates promptly, led to the discovery of a chemical substance that would destroy infectious bacteria without harming tissues or weakening the body's defenses.

Fleming noted that in a petri dish of cultured staphylococcus bacteria a mold that had been introduced by accidental contamination had dissolved the colonies of staphylococci. Such ruining of a pure culture of a bacterium by inadvertent exposure to airborne contaminants is a common annoyance of bacteriologists, for which the customary procedure is to discard the culture and repeat the experiment. In Fleming's own words, however, "It was . . . fortunate that . . . I was always on the lookout for new bacterial inhibitors, and when I noticed on a culture plate that the staphylococcal colonies in the neighborhood of the mold faded away, I was sufficiently interested in the antibacterial substance produced by the mold to pursue the subject."

Fleming's discovery of penicillin depended on a long series of apparently unrelated events. If only one of them had failed to occur, he would

The antibiotic penicillin owes its discovery to the chance observation by Alexander Fleming (top right) of a petri dish (above) in which colonies of staphylococcus bacteria (visible as small dots) were being destroyed in the vicinity of a mold (large white mass) that had been introduced to the culture by accidental contamination. Fleming's momentous find also depended on a long chain of additional, seemingly unrelated circumstances, including the location of Fleming's laboratory (left) directly above that of a mold researcher, a window in the laboratory that was nearly impossible to open, and Fleming's habit of not discarding old cultures promptly.

235

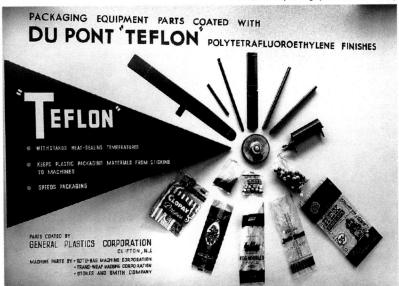

Du Pont chemist Wallace Hume Carothers (above) demonstrates the elasticity of a sample of the synthetic rubber neoprene that he and fellow researcher Arnold Collins unintentionally made in 1931 during other chemical investigations. Seven years later another Du Pont scientist, Roy J. Plunkett, discovered that a tank of tetrafluoroethylene gas being used in refrigerant research had spontaneously polymerized into the slippery, very inert, highly insulating substance Teflon. Industrial applications for Teflon, e.g., as a nonstick finish for packaging-machine parts (right), appeared in the 1950s, some years before its use on cookware made it a household word.

not have made his discovery. Because of his knowledge of staphylococci, Fleming was chosen to contribute a chapter on the topic for a nine-volume *System of Bacteriology* to be published by the Medical Research Council in Great Britain. Late in 1927, while writing the chapter, he read an article that prompted him to study variant colonies of *Staphylococcus aureus*.

Storm van Leeuwen, the eminent Dutch allergist, had gone to London and lectured at St. Thomas Hospital, where he advanced a theory that some asthma patients are allergic to molds growing in the foundations and floorboards of their houses. In attendance was John Freeman, an allergist in charge of routine bacteriological investigations at St. Mary's Hospital, where Fleming worked. Impressed by van Leeuwen's lectures, Freeman persuaded Almroth Wright, head of the inoculation department at St. Mary's Hospital Medical School at Paddington, to appoint a young Irish mycologist, C.J. La Touche, to isolate molds from houses. La Touche was assigned to a makeshift laboratory immediately below Fleming's laboratory. Both laboratories had doors opening onto the same flight of stairs and, because it was virtually impossible to open his window, Fleming usually kept his door open. La Touche was lucky enough to isolate what turned out to be an unusually powerful penicillin-producing strain of mold (*Penicillium notatum*). Because his laboratory had no fume hood under which to work, the atmosphere became contaminated with spores, which probably wafted up to Fleming's laboratory.

After returning from a vacation in September 1928, Fleming discarded some petri dishes that he had left behind. At that time the inoculation department used only shallow enamel trays containing a little antiseptic as disposal containers. If deep buckets filled with antiseptic had been used, as is the case in properly equipped bacteriological laboratories, the evidence for the existence of penicillin would have been destroyed at once, but Fleming placed the dish in question on top of other dishes in

236

the tray. It was only then that he observed the dissolving of the staphylococci by La Touche's mold, and the rest is history.

Ted Thai—Time Magazine

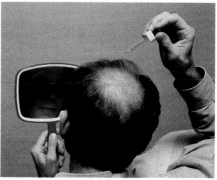

Some modern serendipitous discoveries

With the advent of modern theoretical concepts and the consequent decline of the trial-and-error method made famous by America's preeminent inventor, Thomas A. Edison, it might be thought that the frequency of serendipitous discoveries would have decreased during the 20th century. That this is not the case is illustrated by the following small sampling.

The U.S. synthetic-rubber industry originated with two instances of unsought discovery. In 1922 U.S. chemist Joseph C. Patrick made the polysulfide rubber called Thiokol while trying to break down ethylene dichloride with reagents to obtain ethylene glycol for use as antifreeze. Similarly, a second synthetic rubber, polychloroprene, known better as neoprene, was prepared in 1931 by Arnold Collins and nylon discoverer Wallace Hume Carothers at Du Pont. They produced the rubber while investigating the by-products formed from divinylacetylene.

In 1938 Du Pont chemist Roy J. Plunkett accidentally observed the spontaneous polymerization of tetrafluoroethylene gas while attempting to prepare new chlorofluorocarbons for use as refrigerants. The result was the versatile nonstick substance Teflon, the slipperiest substance known. In 1943 Swiss chemist Albert Hofmann accidentally experienced the psychedelic properties of lysergic acid diethylamide (LSD), a compound prepared during his studies of synthetic derivatives of a toxic substance, ergot, produced in fungal infections of cereal grasses. Hofmann inadvertently ingested some of this potent mind-altering drug, and his bicycle ride home from the Sandoz laboratory in Basel under its influence was the first "acid trip."

Most artificial sweeteners to date have been encountered serendipitously, beginning with the 19th-century discoveries of saccharin and dulcin, both of which were found during basic research on organic compounds. In 1937 U.S. chemist Michael Sveda discovered the cyclamates, later banned in the U.S., when he smoked a cigarette contaminated by a compound that he had recently synthesized. Aspartame (NutraSweet) was isolated from a reacted mixture of amino acids accidentally ingested by G.D. Searle chemist James Schlatter, who was trying to develop a test

A man applies the minoxidil-based drug Rogaine to his balding head. The ability of minoxidil to stimulate hair growth was first observed as a side effect in people who were taking the drug to treat high blood pressure.

Before-and-after photos illustrate the effects of 18 months of therapy with Retin-A (tretinoin) on fine wrinkles in skin prematurely aged by exposure to sunlight. The drug, a derivative of vitamin A, had been available as a topical treatment for acne when some adult users reported the unexpected additional benefit of smoother, less blotchy skin.

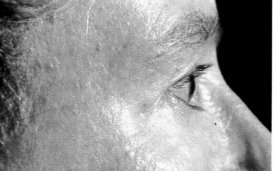

Photos, John J. Voorhees, The University of Michigan Medical Center

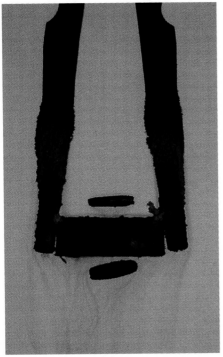

Jim Bailey, University of Arkansas

By virtue of their superconducting properties, two small samples of a metal oxide ceramic that have been cooled in liquid nitrogen hover above and below a permanent magnet. The discovery of high-temperature superconductivity in these materials brought a 1987 Nobel Prize to two physicists who ironically had been searching for new nonconducting substances.

for an ulcer drug. Because these sweeteners are not chemically related to each other or to the naturally occurring sugars, it is not surprising that their sweetness revealed itself only accidentally.

Several serendipitous dermatological discoveries have received recent publicity. The topical action of 5-fluorouracil (Fluoroplex) on precancerous skin lesions (actinic keratosis) was accidentally discovered during its systemic use as an antitumor agent. Minoxidil (Rogaine), the controversial antibaldness and hair-growth drug, was first used for two decades as a treatment for hypertension, while tretinoin, the active ingredient of another controversial drug, the wrinkle-removing Retin-A, was first used as an acne medication beginning in the late 1960s.

Another recent serendipitous find is the drug bupropion (Wellbutrin), originally developed by Burroughs Wellcome Co. as an antidepressant that does not cause weight gain. It was later found to possess libido-enhancing (aphrodisiac) properties. Although approved as an antidepressant by the U.S. Food and Drug Administration in December 1985, the drug caused seizures among several women taking it on an experimental basis for the eating disorder bulimia, and it was withheld from the market until mid-1989 while tests were conducted to demonstrate its safety.

Nobel Prizes frequently have been awarded for serendipitous discoveries. A recent case in point is the 1987 prize for physics bestowed on Johannes Georg Bednorz and Karl Alexander Müller for their celebrated discovery of high-temperature superconductivity in oxide ceramic materials. Paradoxically, the IBM researchers had been searching for a material that would be completely nonconducting.

Giving serendipity its due

As the above accounts demonstrate, an element of luck—being in the right place at the right time—is involved in serendipitous discoveries. In fact, serendipity is probably more prevalent than is generally realized, largely because scientists are reluctant to admit having benefited from chance, even though chance continually enters into the everyday activities of human beings. In view of the editorial practices of most scientific journals requiring that articles be written in an objective, impersonal, third-person, passive-voice style, most scientists report their work in a logical sequence in which the end result appears to follow directly from the initial hypothesis. Thus, they usually omit personal details and chance events, some of which may be quite crucial. Nobel chemistry laureate Roald Hoffmann and others have argued that the scientific article should be "humanized" not only to reflect reality more accurately but also to render the account more intelligible to readers outside the discipline and to dispel the mistaken but common stereotype of science as a boring, passionless activity. Such a change would also make obvious those discoveries in which serendipity is involved.

The origins of serendipity, like those of creativity, lie within the individual and his or her personality traits and work habits rather than in the external situation. The dominant characteristic of scientists who convert accidents into discoveries is curiosity—an ardent desire to understand

238

the accident that they observed. Another related characteristic is perception—taking note of the unexpected phenomenon instead of dismissing it as trivial or annoying. Many scientists had undoubtedly observed dark-colored precipitates, unusually shaped crystals, or contaminated culture plates, yet they did not discover aniline dyes like Perkin, molecular asymmetry like Pasteur, or penicillin like Fleming. In the words of Nobel laureate Albert Szent-Györgyi, "Discovery consists of seeing what everybody has seen and thinking what nobody has thought." Or, as wrote American physicist Joseph Henry, reminiscent of Pasteur's dictum, "The seeds of great discoveries are constantly floating around us, but they only take root in minds well prepared to receive them."

According to chemist Ronald S. Lenox, the desired qualities of curiosity, perception, and open-mindedness can be encouraged and developed. Science students can be trained to make and record observations, including the unexpected ones. Flexibility in thinking and interpreting results can also be encouraged. In Royston M. Roberts' words, "The person who sees only what is expected and discards unexpected results as 'wrong' will make no discoveries." The trait of intuition cannot be taught directly, but a meticulous study of one's field of interest should help the young investigator to recognize the significance of unexpected observations.

Although the common wisdom holds that science progresses in an orderly and systematic way by the so-called scientific method, from earliest times serendipity has been a frequent component of scientific discoveries. Nevertheless, the system for funding research is based on the belief that breakthroughs can be manufactured by giving the money to scientists who promise discoveries according to rational procedures and tidy timetables. In 1988 John F. Christman, Rustum Roy, and Patrick J. Hannan chaired a symposium on "The Role of Chance in Scientific Dis-

"That's Dr. Arnold Moore. He's conducting an experiment to test the theory that most great scientific discoveries were hit on by accident." While it is true that an element of chance is involved in serendipitous discoveries, it is the scientist who embraces the unexpected with a curious, open mind who can turn accidents into breakthroughs.

Drawing by Hoff; © 1957, 1985 The New Yorker Magazine, Inc.

covery" at a meeting of the American Association for the Advancement of Science. They challenged the current method for funding research and invited the official recognition and encouragement of serendipity by the scientific establishment. Christman complained that "research funds are granted only for safe science, not for revolutionary science," and he maintained that "you have to have serendipity for a great discovery. You can't *think* beyond the current paradigm." Indeed, recognition of the role of serendipity in science is long overdue.

FOR ADDITIONAL READING

Otto Theodor Benfey and George B. Kauffman, "The Birthday of Organic Chemistry," *Journal of College Science Teaching* (January 1979, pp. 148–151).

W.I.B. Beveridge, *Seeds of Discovery* (W.W. Norton, 1980).

Alfred B. Garrett, *The Flash of Genius* (D. Van Nostrand Co., 1963).

D.S. Halacy, Jr., *Science and Serendipity* (Macrae Smith Co., 1967).

Patrick J. Hannan, Rustum Roy, and John F. Christman, "Prince Serendip at Work," *Chemtech* (January 1988, pp. 18–21); "Chance and Drug Discovery," *Chemtech* (February 1988, pp. 80–83); "Serendipity in Chemistry, Astronomy, Defense, and Other Useless Fields," *Chemtech* (July 1988, pp. 402–406); "Chance and the Nobel Prize," *Chemtech* (October 1988, pp. 594–598).

George B. Kauffman, "Pittacal—The First Synthetic Dyestuff," *Journal of Chemical Education* (December 1977, p. 753); "Isoniazid—Destroyer of the White Plague," *Journal of Chemical Education* (July 1978, pp. 448–449); "The Discovery of Iproniazid and Its Role in Antidepressant Therapy," *Journal of Chemical Education* (January 1979, pp. 35–36); "The Discovery of Penicillin—Twentieth Century Wonder Drug," *Journal of Chemical Education* (July 1979, pp. 454–455); "Solvents, Serendipity and Seizures," *Education in Chemistry* (November 1982, pp. 168–169); "Teflon—50 Slippery Years," *Education in Chemistry* (November 1988, pp. 173–175); "How the Aniline Dyes Were Discovered," *Industrial Chemist* (March 1988, pp. 26–27); "The Role of Serendipity in Drug Discovery," *Today's Chemist* (June 1989, pp. 13–15).

George B. Kauffman and Paul M. Priebe, "The Discovery of Saccharin," *Ambix* (November 1978, pp. 191–207).

Ronald S. Lenox, "Educating for the Serendipitous Discovery," *Journal of Chemical Education* (April 1985, pp. 282–285).

Charles Panati, *Extraordinary Origins of Everyday Things* (Perennial Library, 1987).

Royston M. Roberts, *Serendipity: Accidental Discoveries in Science* (John Wiley & Sons, 1989).

Robert S. Root-Bernstein, "Setting the Stage for Discovery," *The Sciences* (May–June 1988, pp. 26–34).

Gilbert Shapiro, *A Skeleton in the Darkroom: Stories of Serendipity in Science* (Harper & Row, 1986).

Encyclopædia

Britannica

Science Update

Major Revisions from the 1990 *Macropædia*

The purpose of this section is to introduce to continuing *Yearbook of Science and the Future* subscribers selected *Macropædia* articles or portions of them that have been completely revised or written anew. It is intended to update the *Macropædia* in ways that cannot be accomplished fully by reviewing the year's events or by revising statistics annually, because the *Macropædia* texts themselves—written from a longer perspective than any yearly revision—supply authoritative interpretation and analysis as well as narrative and description.

Two articles have been chosen from the 1990 printing: MOLLUSKS (in part) and Principles of PHYSICAL SCIENCE. Each is the work of distinguished scholars, and each represents the continuing dedication of the *Encyclopædia Britannica* to bringing such works to the general reader.

Mollusks

Bivalves (clams, oysters, mussels, and relatives)

The class Bivalvia, sometimes called Pelecypoda, is characterized by a shell that is divided from front to back into left and right valves. Enclosure in a shell has resulted in loss of the head. Similarly, the adoption of deposit-feeding using labial palps and, later, suspension feeding utilizing the respiratory gills modified into organs of filtration called ctenidia have resulted in loss of the radula from the mouth.

GENERAL FEATURES

Size range and diversity of structure. Bivalves range in size from about one millimetre (0.04 inch) in length to the giant clam of South Pacific coral reefs, *Tridacna gigas,* which may be more than 137 centimetres (54 inches) in length and weigh 264 kilograms (582 pounds). Such an animal may have a life span of about 40 years.

The shell forms are used in classification. In most surface-burrowing species (the hypothetical ancestral habit) the shells are small, spherical or oval, with equal left and right valves (Figure 8). In deeper-burrowing species the shells are laterally compressed, permitting more rapid movement through the sediments. The shells of the most efficient burrowers, the razor clams *Ensis* and *Solen,* are laterally compressed, smooth, and elongated. Surface-burrowing species may have an external shell sculpture of radial ribs and concentric lines, with projections that strengthen the shell against predators and damage.

A triangular form, ventral flattening, and secure attachment to firm substrates by byssal threads (byssus; chitinous threads secreted by the foot) have allowed certain bivalves to colonize hard surfaces. This form, referred to as epibyssate for its byssal attachment to surfaces, has been adopted by many groups, most importantly the true mussels (family Mytilidae) of marine and estuarine shores and the family Dreissenidae of fresh and estuarine waters. Such a shell form and habit evolved first within sediments (endobyssate), where the byssus serves for anchorage and protection when formed into an enclosing nest. The byssus is a larval feature retained by some bivalve groups into adult life. The significance of this is crucial to an understanding of how bivalves have radiated. In addition to the triangular form, other bivalves have used the byssus to attach securely within crevices and thus to assume a laterally flattened, circular shape. The best example of this is the windowpane shell *Placuna.* This form has allowed the close attachment of one valve to a hard surface, and although some groups still retain byssal attachment (family Anomiidae), others have forsaken this for cementation, as in the true oysters (family Ostreidae), where the left valve is cemented to estuarine hard surfaces. Some scallops (family Pectinidae) are also cemented, but others lie on soft sediments in coastal waters and at abyssal depths. By limiting shell thickness to reduce weight, smoothing the shell contours to reduce drag, and assuming an aerofoil-like leading edge, such scallops can swim many metres.

Shell form in the bivalves is thus intimately related to habitat and the relative degree of exposure to predation. From the simple burrowing, equivalve ancestor, the various bivalve groups have repeatedly evolved an elongated, triangular or circular shell; thus, similar body adaptations have been responses to similar modes of life.

Distribution and abundance. Most bivalves are marine and occur at all depths in or upon virtually all substrates. In shallow seas, bivalves are often dominant on rocky and sandy coasts and are also important in offshore sediments.

(margin note: Endo-byssate and epibyssate)

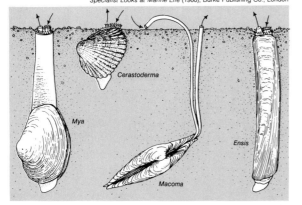

From (Cerastoderma) W. de Haas and F. Knorr, *The Young Specialist Looks at Marine Life* (1966), Burke Publishing Co., London

Figure 8: *Shallow- and deep-burrowing dimayrian bivalves. Cerastoderma lives close to the sediment surface and has limited burrowing powers. When disturbed, Mya retracts its long siphons as does Macoma, but Macoma and Ensis can also dig deeper into the sediment using the muscular foot. Arrows indicate direction of current flow into the mantle cavity via the inhalant and exhalant siphons.*

They occur at abyssal and hadal depths, either burrowing or surface-dwelling, and are important elements of the midoceanic rift fauna. In addition, bivalves bore into soft shales and compacted muds but may be important also in the bioerosion of corals. Bivalves thus occur at all latitudes and depths, although none are planktonic. There are also estuarine bivalves, and two important families, the Unionidae and Corbiculidae, are predominantly freshwater with complicated reproductive cycles. There are no terrestrial bivalves, although some high-intertidal and freshwater species can withstand drought conditions.

To be expected within a class comprising more than 8,000 living species, abundance varies considerably. Commensal and parasitic species are small, often highly host-specific, and comprise some of the rarest animals. Others, such as cockles and clams on soft shores and mussels and oysters on rocky coasts, can occur in densities high enough that they dominate entire habitats and assume important roles in nutrient cycles.

Economic importance

Importance. The total marine catch of mollusks is twice that of crustaceans, and the great majority of this is bivalve. Some three million metric tons (6,615,000,000 pounds) of bivalves are harvested throughout the world each year. Virtually all bivalves, with the possible exception of the thorny oyster *Spondylus*, are edible and fall into the main categories of oysters, mussels, scallops, and clams.

The most important edible oysters are representatives of the genus *Crassostrea*, notably *C. gigas* in the western Pacific, *C. virginica* in North America, and *C. angulata* in Portugal. Most mussels are cultivated on ropes suspended from floats. The European mussel *Mytilus edulis* has been introduced into the northern Pacific, and the practice now flourishes widely in Japan and China. Most scallops, *Pecten, Placopecten,* and *Amusium,* are caught by offshore trawlers, although cultivation is being attempted. A wide variety of clams are cultivated—*e.g., Mya arenaria* and *Mercenaria mercenaria* in the North Atlantic and *Venerupis japonica* and *Tapes philippinarum* in the Pacific. In some parts of the world, red tides, caused by large numbers of toxic protozoan dinoflagellates, are lethal to fish and certain invertebrates. Bivalves, by virtue of their filter-feeding apparatus, concentrate the toxin and, if eaten by humans, can cause paralysis or death.

Pearls

Bivalves of the genera *Pinctada* and *Pteria* have been collected in many tropical seas for the natural pearls they may contain, although in many countries, most notably Japan, pearl oyster fisheries have been developed. The windowpane oyster, *Placuna placenta*, has flat translucent valves that are used, primarily in the Philippines, in the manufacture of lampshades, trays, mats, and bowls, collectively called *tapis*. In developing countries, many kinds of bivalve shells are used in the manufacture of jewelry and ornaments.

Bivalves are important agents in bioerosion, most notably of calcium carbonate rocks and wood in the sea. Piddocks (family Pholadidae) bore into concrete jetties (particularly where the source of obtained lime is coral), timber, and plastics. Shipworms (family Teredinidae) bore softer woods. Date mussels (*Lithophaga*) bore into rocks and corals. Marine mussels (family Mytilidae) foul ships, buoys, and wharves; they may also block seawater intakes into the cooling systems of power stations.

Few bivalves are host to human parasitic infections. Industrial and agricultural effluents—notably trace metals, chlorophenothane (DDT), and chlorinated hydrocarbons—have contaminated bivalves, with subsequent concern over human health.

NATURAL HISTORY

Reproduction and life cycles. Although most bivalves are either male or female (dioecious), some produce both sperm and eggs (hermaphroditic); sexual dimorphism is rare. In dioecious species there is usually an equal division of the sexes. Some groups of bivalves, typically those occupying specialized habitats, have adopted hermaphroditism as a reproductive strategy, although expression of this condition may take various forms (simultaneous, consecutive, rhythmical consecutive, and alternative hemaphroditism). Simultaneous hermaphroditism

occurs when sperm-producing tubules and egg-producing follicles intermingle in the gonads (as in the family Tridacnidae), or the gonads may be developed into a separate ovary and testis, as in all representatives of the subclass Anomalodesmata. In consecutive hermaphroditism, one sex develops first. Typically, this is the male phase (protandry), but in a few cases it is the female (protogyny). This is most clearly seen in the wood-boring family Teredinidae, where a young male becomes a female as it ages. Rhythmical consecutive hermaphroditism is best known in the European oyster, *Ostrea edulis,* in which each individual undergoes periodic changes of sex. Alternative hermaphroditism is characteristic of oysters of the genus *Crassostrea*, in which most young individuals are male. Later the sex ratio becomes about equal, and finally most older individuals become female.

Hermaphroditism

Bivalve sperm have two flagellae. Most eggs are small, and synchronized spawning results in the discharge of both types of gametes into the sea for external fertilization. Hermaphrodites either inhale sperm from another individual or fertilize their own eggs within the ctenidia; the eggs are then brooded, typically also within the ctenidia. There, the fertilized eggs, well endowed with yolk, develop directly (without a larval stage), and the young are released as miniature adults. Although ctenidial incubation is most common, there are other patterns: egg capsules are produced by *Turtonia minuta;* a brood chamber is plastered to the shell of the palaeotaxodont *Nucula delphinodonta;* and in members of the Carditidae the female shell is modified into a brood pouch.

For most marine species, however, the fertilized egg undergoes indirect development first into a swimming trochophore larva and then into a veliger larva in which the embryonic shell and rudiments of other organs are established. The veliger has a ciliated velum for swimming and also for trapping minute particles of food. Following a period in the plankton, the veliger settles to the seafloor, where metamorphosis into the adult takes place: the velum is lost, the foot develops and usually secretes one or two byssal threads for secure attachment, and the ctenidia develop.

Larval stage

In the freshwater Unionidae the released larva, called a glochidium, often has sharp spines projecting inward from each valve. The larva is attracted to fish and attaches to either their gills or fins, where it encysts, is temporarily parasitic, and eventually ruptures the cyst wall and falls to the lake floor. There it metamorphoses into an adult.

Ecology and habitats. The division and lateral compression of the shell into two valves is clearly related to the adoption of a burrowing mode of life, which is achieved by a muscular foot. Primitive forms were detritivorous, whereas modern bivalves are filter feeders that have modified the respiratory gills into complex structures called ctenidia. The burrowing, filter-feeding mode of life restricts bivalves to aquatic environments.

Retention of the larval anchoring byssus into adult life has freed many bivalves from soft substrates, allowing them to colonize hard surfaces. This has also been achieved by cementation, as, for example, in oysters.

There are no pelagic bivalves, except for *Planktomya hensoni,* which is still benthic as an adult but has an unusually long planktonic larval stage. Some bivalves can swim, albeit weakly, when removed from the sediment, as can some file shells. True swimming is, however, seen only in the family Pectinidae but is used mostly as an escape reaction.

Movement

Many representatives of the superfamily Galeommatoidea are commensal, a few are parasitic, and both have thus become miniaturized. Most bivalves are found in coastal seas, but their diversity is greatest on continental landmasses, where large rivers create suitable deltaic habitats and the continental shelf is broad. Except on tropical ones with coral reefs, few bivalves are found on islands.

Of the various subclasses, two are most important ecologically: the Heterodonta, which are modern burrowers that feed primarily on suspended material, and the Pteriomorphia, an older group that is epibyssate and dominates hard substrates. Some of their older representatives are endobyssate, exposing their evolutionary history. Most of these two classes occupy a wide diversity of subhabitats, with simple reproductive strategies, external fertilization, and planktonic larvae to effect wide dispersal. They apportion the shallow-water marine domain virtually everywhere. The Palaeoheterodonta are exclusively fresh water and infaunal although a few in South America are epifaunal, but all have significantly more complicated life cycles.

The Palaeotaxodonta are coastal and deepwater detritivores, always infaunal. They share this diversity of habitat with the Anomalodesmata, which have radiated along two lines: shallow-water species that are highly specialized, are hermaphroditic, occupy narrow niches, and have a short planktonic stage and deep-sea species that are even more specialized, most being predators.

Most bivalves are primary consumers, typically exploiting organic material. The two dominant bivalve subclasses are high in the diet of many predators. Some 60 million years ago great adaptive radiation, notably in the Bivalvia, took place with a similar radiation in predatory crustaceans, starfishes, and snails. It is thought that such predation pressure effectively drove the Bivalvia underground with the resultant evolution of many antipredation devices on the shell—spines, ridges, and teeth—or of the habit of burrowing to great depths. On coral reefs a similar pressure led to deep boring into the fabric of the coral and the evolution of a host–borer intimacy.

Locomotion. Unlike in other molluscan groups, locomotion in bivalves is used only when dislodgement occurs or as a means to escape predation.

The bivalve foot, unlike that of gastropods, does not have a flat creeping sole but is bladelike (laterally compressed) and pointed for digging. The muscles mainly responsible for movement of the foot are the anterior and posterior pedal retractors. They retract the foot and effect back-and-forth movements. The foot is extended as blood is pumped into it, and it is prevented from overinflating by concentric rings of circular, oblique, and longitudinal muscle fibres, which also help to direct pedal extension and permit fine mobility.

Burrowing

During burrowing, the foot is greatly extended anteriorly from between parted shell valves. Taking a grip on the substratum, typically by dilation of the tip, the pedal retractors pull the shell downward. This is accompanied by sharp adduction of the shell valves, forcing water out of the mantle cavity into the burrow, helping to fluidize the sediment, and making movement through it more efficient. So effective is this mechanism that fast burrowers, when removed from the sediment, can swim.

Food and feeding. The primitive bivalve was almost certainly a detritivore (consumer of loose organic materials), and the modern palaeotaxodonts still pursue this mode of life. The posterior leaflike gills serve principally for respiration; feeding is carried out by the palp proboscides, which collect surface detritus.

Evolution of the ctenidia

The vast majority of other bivalves feed on the plant detritus, bacteria, and algae that characterize the sediment surface or cloud coastal and fresh waters. The gills have gradually become adapted as filtering devices called ctenidia. The primitive posterior respiratory gills have enlarged and moved to lie lateral to the body as paired folds, or demibranchs. Further increases in surface area have been achieved by folding the platelike gill lamellae into plicae. Each lamella comprises vertical rows of filaments upon the outer head of which are complex arrays of cilia that create a flow of water through the gill, form a filtration barrier, and transport retained particles to food grooves in the dorsal axes or ventral margins of the ctenidia. Bound in mucus, the food is transported to the mouth via the labial palps, where further selection occurs (see below *Internal features*).

Two groups of bivalves have exploited other food sources. These are the shipworms (family Teredinidae) and giant clams (family Tridacnidae). Shipworms are wood borers and are both protected and nourished by the wood they inhabit. They possess ctenidia and are capable of filtering food from the sea. When elongating the burrow, they digest the wood as well. In the Tridacnidae, symbiotic zooxanthellae (minute algal cells) are contained within the inhalant siphon. The relationship between clam and algae

is probably mutually beneficial, the algae having access to the dissolved waste products of the clam and the clam benefiting from the nutritional value of either culled zooxanthellae or their metabolic products.

A few bivalves are parasitic—*e.g.,* species of *Entovalva,* which live either in the esophagus or upon the body of sea cucumbers (Holothuroidea), and the larvae of freshwater Unionidae, which parasitize fish.

The most exotic adaptations of the basic bivalve feeding plan are found in two groups of deepwater bivalves. These are scallops of the genus *Propeamussium* and the various deepwater families of the Anomalodesmata. In *Propeamussium* what appear to be typical ctenidia are present in the mantle cavity, but on closer examination these prove to be wholly atypical in that the filament heads are internal. The ctenidia are incapable of filtering. The gut is minute, and detected prey is sucked into the mantle cavity by an inrush of water when the valves open. The food is then pushed into the mouth with the foot.

Many deepwater Anomalodesmata have modified the typical bivalve ctenidium into a septum—the "septibranch" ctenidium—that creates pressure changes within the mantle cavity and produces sudden inrushes of water, carrying prey into a funnellike inhalant siphon (*Cuspidaria*). Food is then pushed into the mouth by the palps and foot. Others evert the inhalant siphon, like a hood, over the prey (*Poromya* and *Lyonsiella*). Prey items include small bottom-dwelling crustaceans, polychaete worms, and larvae of other benthic animals.

Associations. The greatest affinity of bivalves is with coral reefs. Indo-Pacific, but not Caribbean, reefs are the habitat of giant clams, *Tridacna.* Dead corals are bored by representatives of the Gastrochaenidae, living corals by species of *Lithophaga.* A greater degree of intimacy between living coral and bivalve borer is now known, some species associating with a single coral.

Adaptations

Similarly with wood borers: piddocks (Pholadidae) are more common in hardwoods, while shipworms (Teredinidae) favour softwoods. In the degradation of wood in the sea, a variety of species may colonize it with time and with depth.

One group of bivalves, the superfamily Galeommatoidea, form highly intimate relationships with other marine invertebrates, particularly on soft shores and coral reefs. Typically less than 10 millimetres (0.4 inch) long, most are commensal; *i.e.,* they form an association in which there is no detriment to the host and exploit it for protection, food, and respiratory currents. On soft shores they share the burrows of polychaete worms and crustaceans, sometimes attaching to the body of the host.

FORM AND FUNCTION

General features. The bivalve body comprises a dorsal visceral mass and a ventral foot, which is enclosed within a thin mantle, or pallium. The mantle secretes from its outer surface a shell divided into left and right valves. Between the body and mantle is the mantle cavity, within which hang the left and right gills, or ctenidia. The ctenidia are divided into two demibranchs, inner and outer, each in turn comprising inner and outer lamellae. Anteriorly, the ctenidia unite with paired (left and right) labial palps, which are food-sorting organs. The mantle margin can be fused at various places leaving medial apertures anteriorly for the extension and retraction of the locomotory foot and, in most bivalves, posteriorly to create inhalant and exhalant apertures that may be formed into siphons of variable length according to habitat. Foot and siphons can be withdrawn between the shell valves into the mantle cavity for protection.

External features. The bivalves occupy a wide variety of habitats and, as a consequence, deviate widely from the basic body plan. The shell form is an obvious adaptation to the environment. Shells of many modern burrowers are ornamented and coloured, and those of near-surface-dwelling cockles are thick and radially ribbed. These adaptations stabilize the animal in the substrate and may confer some degree of protection against predators. Such bivalves are slow burrowers. In contrast, the shells of deep-burrowing species are thin and nonornamented. They are

The shell

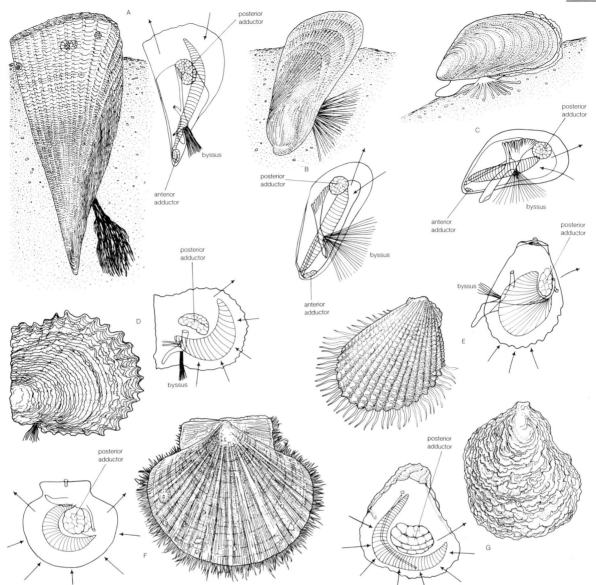

Figure 9: *Anisomyarian and monomyarian bivalves, with sketches of the internal gill and muscle arrangements.*
Arrows indicate inhalant and exhalant water currents. (A) *Pinna*, endobyssate with reduction of the anterior, and enlargement of the posterior, adductor. (B) *Geukensia*, endobyssate with reduction of the anterior, and enlargement of the posterior, adductor. (C) *Mytilus*, epibyssate with reduction of the anterior, and enlargement of the posterior, adductor. (D) *Pinctada*, epibyssate, laterally flattened, with loss of the anterior adductor. (E) *Lima*, epibyssate and monomyarian, with long tentacles and capable of limited swimming. (F) *Pecten*, with loss of the anterior adductor, byssus, foot, and associated musculature and capable of swimming. (G) *Ostrea*, cemented and with loss of the anterior adductor, byssus, foot, and associated musculature.

From (Geukensia) S.M. Stanley, *Relation of Shell Form to Life Habits of the Bivalvia (Mollusca)*, Geological Society of America Memoir no. 125 (1970); (*Mytilus, Pinctada, Lima*) R.C. Moore (ed.), *Treatise on Invertebrate Paleontology. Mollusca 6* (1969), Geological Society of America and University of Kansas Press; (Ostrea) W. de Haas and F. Knorr, *The Young Specialist Looks at Marine Life* (1966), Burke Publishing Co., London

often brightly coloured, as in the Tellinidae. The shell is laterally compressed and thus more bladelike, but the adductor muscles are still of similar size (the isomyarian form). Such structural features adapt the animal for rapid movement through the sand; long siphons project to the surface above. Deep burrowing has been achieved by a different mechanism in the razor shells (e.g., the family Solenidae), where the anterior region of the shell is reduced and the posterior enormously elongate. Because of their short siphons, *Ensis* and *Solen* live close to the sediment surface, but, with the lateral compression of their polished shells, they are among the most proficient burrowers. Other bivalves—*e.g., Mya* (family Myidae)—live at great depths but do not burrow rapidly. The shell is largely unornamented and wider to accommodate the greatly elongated siphons, which can be retracted deeply within its borders.

Rock and wood boring are also specialized consequences

of burrowing—the evolution of borers proceeded from the habitation of stiff muds or from nestling within crevices. Mechanical borers tunnel anterior end first; that face of the shell having a sculpture of spines. Borers derived from a nestling epibyssate ancestor are chemical borers that produce a calcium carbonate chelating secretion from the mantle margin. In such cases the shell is typically smooth, although calcareous encrustations on the posterior shell protect the borer from aperture-attacking predators. Reduction of the anterior adductor (the anisomyarian form) creates a triangular-shaped shell, as in the buried fan shell *Pinna* (Pinnidae) and the mussels (Mytilidae) of rocky coasts. Although such bivalves lack ornamentation, the shell is typically thick and dark.

Loss of the anterior adductor creates a shell with a circular outline, left and right valves being either equal or unequal. In some, lateral flattening and byssal attachment allows occupation of narrow crevices. Cementation

Mechanical versus chemical borers

by either valve is a further consequence of the loss of the anterior adductor muscle (the monomyarian form). Subsequent freedom from attachment, as in the scallops (Pectinidae), is associated with an almost circular outline, flat upper and cup-shaped lower valves, a deep radial sculpture, and, typically, bright coloration (*Pecten*).

Internal features. The general classification of the bivalves is typically based on shell structure and hinge and ligament organization (Figure 9). The internal anatomy is also a tool in classification, particularly the organs of the mantle cavity, the pattern of water movement through it, and the structure and functioning of the ctenidia and labial palps. Early anatomists established a correlation between shell and gill structure that is still often used as a basis for classification but which is now relegated to defining the evolutionary sequence from a deposit-feeding to a filter-feeding mode of life.

The primitive bivalve form

Nucula, from the subclass Protobranchia, reflects the primitive bivalve ancestor. Burrowing close to the sediment surface, *Nucula* is equivalve, anteriorly and posteriorly symmetrical, and isomyarian. The medial foot is wide. There are no mantle fusions ventrally, and the aerating water current passes through the mantle cavity from front to back, a feature not typical of most modern bivalves. The structure of the small gills (Figure 10), located posteriorly, is interpreted as being similar to the earliest mollusks—hence the name protobranch, or "first gills." The paired gills, separated by a central axis, are suspended from the mantle roof. Individual short gill filaments extend outward from either side of the axis, and cilia on their surfaces create an upward respiratory water current that passes from the mantle cavity below the gill (the infrabranchial, or inhalant, chamber) to that area above it (the suprabranchial, or exhalant, chamber). The anus and the urogenital pores also open into the exhalant chamber so that all waste products exit the animal in the exhalant stream. The paired labial palps in the mantle cavity are used in feeding. The outer palp on each side bears a long, extensible proboscis with a ciliated groove that collects organic material, which is then sorted by the inner pair and outer pair of palps. Certain particles are transferred to the mouth by the ciliary currents of the inner pair of palps, while the remaining particles are sent by the outer palps into the mantle cavity as a mucus-bound mass known as pseudofeces, which are ejected by periodic contractions of the adductor muscles.

An important event in the evolution of the modern bivalve from the more primitive form illustrated above was the reorientation of the anterior inhalant stream to the posterior below the exhalant stream so that water both enters and exits the mantle cavity posteriorly. For burrowing bivalves, such a body organization allows deep burrowing in a vertical (head down) orientation, and thus escape from the sediment surface. These changes generally are associated with changes in the method of feeding and, as a consequence, the selective fusion of left and right mantle margins to exclude sediment from the mantle cavity.

The burrowing *Spisula* illustrates these changes. It, like

Nucula, is equivalve and anteriorly and posteriorly symmetrical (isomyarian). The mantle margin is fused ventrally, allowing the foot to extend through an anterior pedal gape. The posterior inhalant and exhalant orifices are formed into tentacle-fringed siphons. The gills are here positioned on either side of the visceral mass. Gill filaments are greatly elongated and folded (forming the shape of a W) to increase their surface area. The central axis of the W joins it to the body, and the outermost arms unite with the visceral body on one side and the mantle on the other. A complex arrangement of cilia on the apex of each filament constituting the gill lamellae draws a water current through the gill, which provides oxygen, but more importantly now sieves food from this current and transfers such material along tracts in the gill axes or their ventral margins (bound in mucus) toward the labial palps. The palps process this food and eliminate the pseudofeces as in *Nucula*.

Evolution of a new gill structure

The modified gill is called a ctenidium, and its structure is best explained by the term lamellibranch. The lamellibranch structure may be further qualified as filibranch, pseudolamellibranch, or eulamellibranch. In filibranchs the filaments are only weakly united by cilia, and often the ctenidium retains some inherent sorting mechanism. Collection and sorting of potential food has not yet been definitively ascribed to gills and labial palps, respectively. In the pseudolamellibranch ctenidium, filaments and lamellae are more securely united, and an inherent sorting mechanism still exists in some. In many, however, the filaments are vertically aggregated into folds, or plicae, that greatly increase the total surface area. In the eulamellibranch ctenidium the filaments and lamellae are closely united, the selection function is lost, and gill structure varies widely. Most modern bivalves are filter feeders, and except in a few members the siphons suck in particles suspended in the water column.

In the deep seas, modification of the lamellibranch ctenidium has allowed the adoption of carnivory. The predatory bivalves of the subclass Anomalodesmata have an inhalant siphon that can be everted rapidly to form a capacious hood beneath which small crustaceans are trapped and brought into the mantle cavity. The eversion of the siphon is assisted by a horizontal septum across the mantle cavity, which is derived from the mantle and the greatly reduced ctenidium. This is the septibranch ctenidium.

The release from a burrowing mode of life has been facilitated by the retention of a larval structure (the byssus) into adult life. The byssus, secreted by a gland in the foot, secures the animal to a hard surface in preparation for burrowing. Its retention and enlargement in the adult has provided a secure means of attachment to the open surfaces of rocks in the intertidal, estuarine, and fresh waters.

Importance of the byssus

In the triangular mussels (Mytilidae) of such habitats the anterior is reduced, and the body and organs of the mantle cavity are contained in the expanded posterior regions of the shell. The reduction of the anterior adductor muscle is matched by a reduction in the size of the anterior pedal retractor muscles (and enlargement of the posterior equivalents). Since such muscles are less concerned with locomotion and more with pulling the shell down against the substrate, they are more correctly redefined as byssal retractors. The ctenidia and palps fulfil the same role as they do in burrowing lamellibranch bivalves, but, because of the triangular cross section of the shell, they come to lie largely underneath the visceral mass instead of beside it.

Further reduction of the anterior adductor, leading to its eventual loss, creates what is called the monomyarian condition. In bivalves with such a configuration, the anterior shell and mantle are confined to a small area; the foot, where present, is always greatly reduced and positioned anteriorly. The visceral mass and organs of the mantle cavity are arranged around the central posterior adductor muscle, and there is extreme reduction or loss of the anterior pedal/byssal retractor muscles. Shell valves may be so compressed that the space between them, as in *Placuna*, the windowpane oyster, is very narrow. Alternatively, as in oysters and scallops, one valve is cup-shaped, with the other fitting against it like a lid. In such a case, the body occupies the former valve, the left in

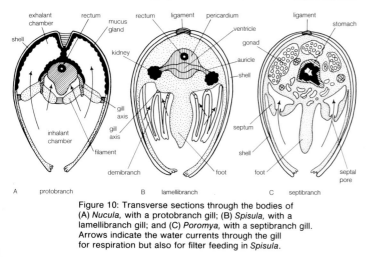

Figure 10: Transverse sections through the bodies of (A) *Nucula*, with a protobranch gill; (B) *Spisula*, with a lamellibranch gill; and (C) *Poromya*, with a septibranch gill. Arrows indicate the water currents through the gill for respiration but also for filter feeding in *Spisula*.

oysters and generally the right in all others, such as the scallops. In these bivalves the bilateral symmetry of the shell and mantle is replaced by a radial symmetry from the midpoint of the hinge line. In these bivalves, too, the adductor muscle is more clearly demarcated into "quick" (striated) and "slow" (smooth) components for rapid and sustained adduction respectively. The capacity for work of the greatly enlarged quick component of the scallop muscle permits rapid adduction that facilitates swimming by directing jets of water out of the mantle cavity to each side of the hinge line characterized by shell auricles.

Shell structure

The shell. The bivalve shell is made of calcium carbonate embedded in an organic matrix secreted by the mantle. The periostracum, the outermost organic layer, is secreted by the inner surface of the outer mantle fold at the mantle margin. It is a substrate upon which calcium carbonate can be deposited by the outer surface of the outer mantle fold. The number of calcareous layers in the shell (in addition to the periostracum), the composition of those layers (aragonite or aragonite and calcite), and the arrangement of these deposits (*e.g.,* in sheets, or foliate) is characteristic for different groups of bivalves. Middorsally an elastic ligament creates the opening thrust that operates against the closing action of the adductor muscles. The ligament typically develops either externally (parivincular) or internally (alivincular) but comprises outer lamellar, and inner fibrous, layers secreted by the mantle crest. The ligament type is generally characteristic of each bivalve group. The hinge plate with ligament also possesses interlocking teeth to enforce valve alignment and locking, when closed, to prevent shear. Many variations in teeth structure occur.

The mantle and musculature. The mantle lobes secrete the shell valves; the mantle crest secretes the ligament and hinge teeth. Growth takes place at the margins, although increases in thickness take place everywhere. The mantle is withdrawn between the shell valves by mantle retractor muscles; their point of attachment to the shell being called the pallial line.

Musculature

The musculature comprises two (dimyarian) primitively equal (isomyarian) adductor muscles; the anterior and the posterior. The anterior of these may be reduced (anisomyarian; heteromyarian) or lost (monomyarian). Only very rarely is the posterior lost and the anterior retained.

Internal to the adductors are paired anterior and posterior pedal retractor muscles. Where the anterior adductor muscle is reduced, so are the anterior pedal retractors. In highly active burrowers, paired anterior pedal protractors and pedal elevator muscles occur—for example, the family Trigonioidea.

In byssally attached bivalves, pedal retractors are reduced and byssal retractors serve to pull the animal down in closer opposition to the rock surface. In oysters, commensurate with the extreme reduction of the foot, pedal retractors are lost. This is also the case in swimming scallops.

The nervous system and organs of sensation. The nervous system is simple, reflecting the sedentary habit. In primitive bivalves (*e.g.,* Palaeotaxodonta) there are four pairs of ganglia—cerebral, pleural, pedal, and visceral. In all other bivalves the cerebral and pleural ganglia are fused into two cerebropleural ganglia, located above and on either side of the esophagus. The pedal ganglia are in the base of the foot, and the visceral ganglia are located under the posterior adductor muscle. Nerve fibres arising from the cerebropleural ganglia extend to the pedal and visceral ganglia. In some bivalves with long siphons, there are accessory siphonal ganglia, and in many swimming bivalves the visceral ganglia are much enlarged, presumably to coordinate complex swimming actions.

Again reflecting the sedentary life, sensory functions are largely taken over by the posterior mantle margins and typically comprise tentacles developed from the middle mantle folds that are mechanoreceptors and chemoreceptors. Scallops (family Pectinidae) have complex eyes with a lens and retina. In other bivalves, eyes are simple ciliated cups, although some variation is possible. In the predatory deepwater septibranchs the inhalant siphon, which captures food, is surrounded by tentacles that have vibration-sensitive papillae for detecting the movements of prey.

Statocysts

Situated close to the pedal ganglia but with direct connections to the cerebropleural ganglia are a pair of statocysts, which comprise a capsule of ciliated sense cells. In the lumen is either a single statolith or numerous crystalline statoconia. Their points of contact with the surrounding cilia yield information about the animal's orientation. Additionally, most bivalves with or without eyes have light-sensitive cells that respond to shadows. Below the posterior adductor muscle an osphradium has been identified in some bivalves that may monitor water flow and quality.

The digestive system and nutrition. The bivalve digestive system comprises a complex stomach and associated structures but an otherwise simple intestine. The various types of stomach have been used to erect an alternative classification. Digestion typically takes place in two phases: extracellular in the stomach and intracellular in the digestive diverticula, opening laterally from the stomach wall. Transport of food particles is effected by cilia, creating an array of tracts and sorting areas within the stomach. The principal organ of extracellular digestion is the crystalline style. It is rotated in its sac by cilia; the head, projecting into the stomach, grinds against a part of the stomach wall lined by a chitinous gastric shield. As it rotates, it dissolves, releasing enzymes and initiating primary extracellular digestion of the mucus-bound food. Products of this process are passed in a fluid suspension into large embayments and thence into the digestive diverticula, where intracellular digestion takes place. Waste material is consolidated in the midgut and rectum and expelled as firm fecal pellets from an anus opening into the exhalant stream. Feeding and digestion are highly coordinated, typically regulated by tidal and diurnal cycles.

The excretory system. Blood is forced through the walls of the heart into the pericardium. From there it passes into the kidneys where wastes are removed, producing urine. The paired kidneys (nephridia) are looped with an opening into the pericardium and another into the suprabranchial chamber. The kidneys may be united. Bivalves also possess pericardial glands lining either the auricles of the heart or the pericardium; they serve as an additional ultrafiltration device.

Gills

The respiratory system. In the primitive bivalves the paired gills are small and located posteriorly. The gills in all other bivalves (save septibranchs, which have lost their gills) are greatly enlarged and possess a huge surface area. While the gills are thought to serve a respiratory function, respiratory demands are low in these mostly inactive animals, and, since the body and mantle are both bathed in water, respiration probably takes place across these surfaces as well. Such a mechanism has been demonstrated for a few bivalves, most notably freshwater species that are exposed to occasional drought. In such species, drying induces slight shell gaping posteriorly, the mantle margins exposing themselves to air. For most intertidal bivalves (which are alternately exposed to wetting and drying), respiration all but ceases during the drying phase.

The vascular system. The heart, enclosed in a pericardium, comprises a medial ventricle with left and right auricles arising from it. Blood oxygenated within the ctenidia flows to the auricles and from there to the ventricle, where it is pumped into anterior and posterior aortas. The blood then enters hemocoelic spaces in the mantle and visceral mass and returns to the heart via the ctenidia or the kidneys. The blood serves both to transport oxygen and metabolic products to tissues deep within the body and as a hydrostatic skeleton (for example, in the extension of the foot during locomotion and siphons during feeding). There are amoeboid corpuscles but, except in a few bivalves, no respiratory pigment.

The reproductive system. The reproductive system is simple and comprises paired gonads. These gonads discharge into the renal duct in primitive bivalves but open by separate gonopores into the suprabranchial chamber in more modern bivalves. Typically, the sexes are separate, but various grades of hermaphroditism are not uncommon. Eggs and sperm are shed into the sea for external fertilization in most bivalves, but inhalation of sperm by a female permits a type of internal fertilization and brooding of young, usually within the ctenidia.

Features of defense and aggression. The most significant adaptation is the earliest division of the shell into two valves within which the animal was wholly contained. Slow components of the adductor muscle permit sustained adduction, while the interlocking hinge teeth prevent shear. In addition, the shell may be strongly ridged, forming an interlocking shell margin, and it may be concentrically ringed with spines or sharp ridges projecting outward. Posterior sense organs, including photophores and eyes, are developed around the siphons and mantle margins. Detection leads to withdrawal deep into the sediment by burrowing species. In such animals the shell is smooth and compressed. Scallops respond to predation by swimming; shallow-burrowing cockles can leap using the foot. In the razor clams the siphons can break off (autotomize) when bitten, to be regenerated later. Similarly, noxious secretions are produced by the similarly autotomizing long tentacles of the Limidae (file shells). The unique pallial organ of fan shells (family Pinnidae) produces a secretion of sulfuric acid when bitten.

Only the deepwater subclass Anomalodesmata (families Verticordiidae, Poromyidae, and Cuspidariidae) and the scallops are predators. Prey is captured either in the sudden rush of water into the mantle cavity or by the rapid eversion of the inhalant siphon.

EVOLUTION AND PALEONTOLOGY

The oldest known bivalves are generally believed to be *Fordilla troyensis,* which is best preserved in the late Early Cambrian rocks of New York (about 550 million years ago), and *Pojetaia runnegari* from the Cambrian rocks of Australia. *Fordilla* is perhaps ancestral to the pteriomorph order Mytiloida, *Pojetaia* to the Palaeotazodonta order Nuculoida.

By the Ordovician period (505 to 438 million years ago) most modern subclasses were represented by definable ancestors. The oldest Ordovician bivalves are, however, the subclass Palaeotaxodonta, which are thought to have given rise to the Cryptodonta by elongation. Modern assessment of their shell structure and body form, notably with the possession of posterior protobranch gills and with palp proboscides for deposit feeding in the Palaeotaxodonta, generally supports this view. An extinct subclass Actinodontia also arose in the Ordovician period and may be represented today by the superfamily Trigonioidea (placed in the subclass Palaeoheterodonta), which are an aberrant group of the subclass Pteriomorphia. The remaining, more typical, members of the Pteriomorphia also arose at this time and persist today, still characteristically occupying a range of substrate types but with byssal attachment and a trend toward loss of the anterior adductor muscle. The common mussels (family Mytilidae) are thought to be derived from an extinct group, the family Modiomorphidae. The subclass Orthonotia also arose in the Ordovician period and are the probable ancestors of the deep-burrowing razor shells (Solenoidea). The origins of the subclass Anomalodesmata are less clear, but they too arose in the Ordovician period and may have links to the order Myoida, which presently includes deep-burrowing forms and borers. Representatives of the superfamily Lucinoidea are very different from all other bivalves, with an exhalant siphon only and an anterior inhalant stream. Some of these deposit feeders also possess, like the subclass Cryptodonta, sulfur-oxidizing bacteria in the ctenidia and are thought to have ancient origins, represented by the fossil *Babinka. Babinka* is itself interesting and is closely related either to *Fordilla,* one of the oldest bivalves or to the ancestors of the molluscan class Tryblidia. Today the superfamily Lucinoidea is generally placed within the subclass Heterodonta, which is a younger group that traces back to the Paleozoic era, when the first radiation of all bivalves took place.

The stamp of modernity was placed upon the Bivalvia in the Mesozoic era (245 to 66.4 million years ago), when virtually all families currently recognized were present. Throughout time, the fortunes of the subclasses have waxed and waned, with repeated modification of form allowing repeated diversification into different habitats. Similarity of habitat is matched by similarity in structure

and form, allowing for various interpretations of the fossil record. It is clear, however, that most modern bivalves can trace their ancestry back a long way and that the inherent plasticity of the bivalve form is responsible for the success of a molluscan experiment in lateral compression of the shell.

CLASSIFICATION

No system of classification erected for the Bivalvia has been accepted by all. Paleontologists interpret bivalves on the basis of shell features, notably shell and ligament structure, arrangement of hinge teeth, and body form as interpreted from internal muscle scars.

Investigators of Recent (Holocene; 10,000 years ago to the present) forms use other anatomic features, such as adductor muscle arrangement, the ctenidia and their junction with the labial palps, the extent and complexity of mantle fusion, and stomach structure. Cluster analysis using many morphological features is effective with lower taxa but less so with higher taxonomic categories because of the many examples of parallel evolution from the basic bivalve plan. The triangular mussel form, for example, has evolved in representatives of virtually every subclass, resulting in similar morphologies. Shell microstructure and mineralogy evidence generally support paleontological conclusions that the class Bivalvia comprises six subclasses, recognizing, however, that some of these taxa may have more than one first ancestor (polyphyletic). In a group with a fossil history extending back to the Cambrian period and occupying a wide range of aquatic habitats, this is not unexpected, particularly since the basic bivalved form permits repeated modification.

Annotated classification.

CLASS BIVALVIA

Laterally symmetrical; left and right calcareous shell valves; dorsal elastic hinge ligament; anterior and posterior adductor muscles; lateral paired filtering ctenidia surrounding the visceral mass; primitively burrowing by means of a muscular foot, but some crawl, some attach to rocks by byssal threads from the foot, some are cemented, and some bore into soft rocks, corals, and wood; some commensal, a few parasitic, and some deepwater species predatory; microphagous feeding; mostly marine, at all depths, also estuarine and freshwater; about 8,000 extant species.

Subclass Palaeotaxodonta

Numerous similar teeth along the hinge plate; isomyarian; unique shell microstructure of aragonitic composite prisms and internal nacre; posterior ctenidia comprising 2 divergent rows of flat, short, filaments; protobranch respiratory gill; food collected by labial palps; mostly near-surface-dwelling marine detritivores; considered to be the most primitive of living bivalves, if not the most ancient.

Order Nuculoida

Equal shell valves with taxodont hinge teeth; isomyarian; posterior protobranch ctenidia; large labial palps usually with palp proboscides, which effect feeding; foot with flat sole; marine; unattached; infaunal.

Subclass Cryptodonta

Hinge either weakly taxodont or edentulous; distinctive shell structure of aragonitic simple prisms and nacre internally; large posterior protobranch ctenidia; small labial palps; of primitive and ancient lineage; marine; unattached; infaunal.

Order Solemyoida

Shell valves equal and elongate, lacking hinge teeth, covered by a shiny periostracum; dimyarian or monomyarian; some with protobranch ctenidia containing symbiotic sulfur-oxidizing bacteria; minute palps; minute or absent gut; foot with flat sole; marginally papillate; marine; deep-burrowing; infaunal.

Subclass Pteriomorphia

Highly variable shell form and structure; dimyarian, anisomyarian, or monomyarian; variable hinge dentition; lateral filibranch ctenidia comprise paired demibranchs of weakly united filaments; mostly marine; some cemented; most epibyssate; some infaunal; representative of the earliest filter-feeding bivalves.

Order Arcoida

Shell solid, elongate or circular-oval, often heavily ribbed; fibrous periostracum with simple crossed-lamellar outer layer and inner complex crossed-lamellar layer, thereby differing from all other pteriomorphs; dimyarian; hinge with vertical denticulations; ctenidia filibranch; mantle margin with uniquely divided outer fold; foot often byssate; marine; epibyssate; infaunal.

Order Trigonioida

Shell valves equal, trigonally oval, strongly ribbed; shell with outer aragonitic prismatic layer and inner nacre layers; strong hinge teeth transversely grooved; typically isomyarian, with pedal elevator and protractor muscles as well as retractors; ctenidia filibranch, without mantle fusions; powerful foot; marine; infaunal; living species confined to Australia.

Order Mytiloida (common mussels)

Shell equivalve, rounded, elongate or triangular depending on habits; anisomyarian tending toward monomyarian; hinge edentulous; shell microstructure of outer calcitic fibrous prisms and inner nacre; ctenidia filibranch; mantle margin lacking fusions; foot creeping; typically byssate; marine, estuarine, rarely freshwater; endobyssate and epibyssate.

Order Pterioida (pearl oysters and fan shells)

Shell equivalve, variably shaped; anisomyarian but often monomyarian; shell structure of outer simple calcitic prisms and inner nacre; ctenidia pseudolamellibranch, often plicate (deeply folded); mantle margin lacking fusions; foot reduced; marine; endobyssate or epibyssate.

Order Limoida

Shell equivalve, ovally elongate, ribbed, often thin and transparent, with outer foliated calcite and inner crossed-lamellar aragonitic layers; hinge short and edentulous; monomyarian; ctenidia pseudolamellibranch, encircling the adductor; palps small and lips of mouth variably fused; mantle margins unfused and often red, with long autotomizing tentacles; some swim weakly; marine; epibyssate with byssus sometimes formed into a nest.

Order Ostreoida (oysters and scallops)

Shell valves unequal, variable, typically lacking hinge teeth; shell structure of foliated calcite, upper valve with outer prismatic calcite; most scallops with inner crossed-lamellar layers; dimyarian but most monomyarian; ctenidia pseudolamellibranch; mantle fusions lacking; foot often lost in adult; scallops capable of swimming; some deepwater scallops predatory; marine; epibyssate; cemented by lower or left valve or free.

Subclass Palaeoheterodonta

Characterized by equal shell valves with a variable hinge dentition; aragonitic shell with outer prismatic and inner layers of nacre; most approximately isomyarian; ctenidia eulamellibranch; mantle fusions lacking, especially ventrally; complicated life cycles; wholly freshwater; nonbyssate; infaunal.

Order Unionoida

Large, equivalve, varying from round to elongate and with equally variable sculpture; shell of outer prismatic layer and inner layers of nacre; hinge schizodont; dimyarian; ctenidia eulamellibranch with either 1 or both demibranchs functioning as an incubatory marsupium; ovoviviparous; parasitically larviparous; freshwater; some cemented and oysterlike; mostly infaunal.

Subclass Heterodonta

Shell highly variable; hinge plate teeth may be reduced or absent; shell comprises crossed-lamellar, complex crossed-lamellar, or prismatic layers, but never nacreous; primitively isomyarian but with wide range of adductor muscle configurations; ctenidia eulamellibranch; mantle margins extensively fused, particularly posteriorly, often to form long inhalant and exhalant siphons; mostly marine but also estuarine and freshwater; some epibyssate, some bore soft rocks and wood; generally infaunal.

Order Veneroida

Shell typically equivalve and of outer crossed-lamellar and inner complex crossed-lamellar layers; hinge comprises radiating cardinal and lateral teeth, often weakly developed; adductor muscles of varying proportions according to habit; ctenidia eulamellibranch, mantle margins extensively fused, often developed into long siphons; most are active burrowers with a large foot; some epibyssate; mostly marine, some estuarine and freshwater; includes the poorly known miniature commensals and parasites; widely divergent, accounting for 50 percent of the extant bivalves.

Order Myoida

Shell typically thin, equivalve, comprising either 2 or 3 layers; hinge plate with cardinal dentition, often degenerate; approximately isomyarian but with much variation; boring forms develop accessory shell plates; ctenidia eulamellibranch, mantle margins extensively fused and covered in periostracum; small foot; marine deep burrowers with long siphons but also rock- and wood-boring.

Subclass Anomalodesmata

Characterized by highly variable shell, either equivalve or inequivalve, often gaping either posteriorly or anteriorly; hinge plate thickened and enrolled but generally edentulous; shell of two or three layers, the inner nacreous; typically isomyarian but with wide variation; ctenidia either eulamellibranch and plicate or septibranch; mantle margins extensively fused, often covered in periostracum; foot reduced; siphons of variable length; consistently hermaphroditic; marine; mostly burrowing; some epibyssate or cemented.

Order Pholadomyoida

Shell more or less equivalve but of widely divergent form; shell comprises aragonitic prisms and nacre or homogeneous structures; typically isomyarian; ctenidia eulamellibranch and plicate but many deepwater species are septibranch; extensive mantle fusions, reduced foot and pedal gape; siphons of variable length; shallow-water forms are burrowing, nestling, epibyssate, or cemented suspension feeders; some deepwater forms are predators with exotic modifications to the bivalve plan.

Critical appraisal. Generally, the classification scheme is accepted up to the level of family and even superfamily. The arrangement of higher categories is, however, still debated. Some authors, for example, combine the subclasses Palaeotaxodonta and Cryptodonta into a single group of primitive detrivores with protobranch gills. Differences in shell structure, however, argue against this. Similarly, the order Arcoida is separated by some from the subclass Pteriomorphia; shell structure again supports this, but other anatomic features do not. The order Trigonioida traditionally has been located within the subclass Palaeoheterodonta, but this has also been disputed, anatomic features suggesting instead an affinity with the subclass Pteriomorphia. This means that the subclass Palaeoheterodonta comprises only the order Unionoida, which has come to occupy the freshwater domain exclusively. Some authors would prefer to relocate the order Myoida from the subclass Heterodonta into the subclass Anomalodesmata, arguing that the edentulous shell, extensive mantle fusions, and deep-burrowing habit are characteristics shared with early ancestors of the order Pholadomyoida. The subclass Anomalodesmata, however, is itself possibly too narrowly demarcated, and some authorities would, for example, separate the deepwater carnivorous septibranchs from the shallow-water pholadomyoids into their own order, the Septibranchoida.

This lack of classificatory agreement is not unusual with regard to a group that has adopted a simple sedentary, filter-feeding mode of life. Simplification and parallel evolution will lead to similarity in form, structure, and function. Debate in creating classificatory trees and reconstructing the historical record is thus about the relative significance of the fossil shell record, as there is little information on tissue morphology, and the importance of morphological data obtained from living representatives.

(Brian Morton)

Principles of Physical Science

Physical science, like all the natural sciences, is concerned with describing and relating to one another those experiences of the surrounding world that are shared by different observers and whose description can be agreed upon. One of its principal fields, physics, deals with the most general properties of matter, such as the behaviour of bodies under the influence of forces, and with the origins of those forces. In the discussion of this question, the mass and shape of a body are the only properties that play a significant role, its composition often being irrelevant. Physics, however, does not focus solely on the gross mechanical behaviour of bodies, but shares with chemistry the goal of understanding how the arrangement of individual atoms into molecules and larger assemblies confers particular properties. Moreover, the atom itself may be analyzed into its more basic constituents and their interactions.

The present opinion, rather generally held by physicists, is that these fundamental particles and forces, treated quantitatively by the methods of quantum mechanics, can reveal in detail the behaviour of all material objects. This is not to say that everything can be deduced mathematically from a small number of fundamental principles, since the complexity of real things defeats the power of mathematics or of the largest computers. Nevertheless, whenever it has been found possible to calculate the relationship between an observed property of a body and its deeper

structure, no evidence has ever emerged to suggest that the more complex objects, even living organisms, require that special new principles be invoked, at least so long as only matter, and not mind, is in question. The physical scientist thus has two very different roles to play: on the one hand, he has to reveal the most basic constituents and the laws that govern them; and, on the other, he must discover techniques for elucidating the peculiar features that arise from complexity of structure without having recourse each time to the fundamentals.

This modern view of a unified science, embracing fundamental particles, everyday phenomena, and the vastness of the Cosmos, is a synthesis of originally independent disciplines, many of which grew out of useful arts. The extraction and refining of metals, the occult manipulations of alchemists, and the astrological interests of priests and politicians all played a part in initiating systematic studies that expanded in scope until their mutual relationships became clear, giving rise to what is customarily recognized as modern physical science.

For a survey of the major fields of physical science and their development, see the articles PHYSICAL SCIENCES, THE; and EARTH SCIENCES, THE. For coverage of various related topics in the *Macropædia* and *Micropædia*, see the *Propædia*, sections 111–133, 10/31, and 10/32, and the *Index*.

This article is divided into the following sections:

The development of quantitative science

Modern physical science is characteristically concerned with numbers—the measurement of quantities and the discovery of the exact relationship between different measurements. Yet this activity would be no more than the compiling of a catalog of facts unless an underlying recognition of uniformities and correlations enabled the investigator to choose what to measure out of an infinite range of choices available. Proverbs purporting to predict weather are relics of science prehistory and constitute evidence of a general belief that the weather is, to a certain degree, subject to rules of behaviour. Modern scientific weather forecasting attempts to refine these rules and relate them to more fundamental physical laws so that measurements of temperature, pressure, and wind velocity at a large number of stations can be assembled into a detailed model of the atmosphere whose subsequent evolution can be predicted—not by any means perfectly but almost always more reliably than was previously possible.

Between proverbial weather lore and scientific meteorol-

ogy lies a wealth of observations that have been classified and roughly systematized into the natural history of the subject—for example, prevailing winds at certain seasons, more or less predictable warm spells such as Indian summer, and correlation between Himalayan snowfall and intensity of monsoon. In every branch of science this preliminary search for regularities is an almost essential background to serious quantitative work, and in what follows it will be taken for granted as having been carried out.

Compared to the caprices of weather, the movements of the stars and planets exhibit almost perfect regularity, and so the study of the heavens became quantitative at a very early date, as evidenced by the oldest records from China and Babylon. Objective recording and analysis of these motions, when stripped of the astrological interpretations that may have motivated them, represent the beginning of scientific astronomy. The heliocentric planetary model (c. 1510) of the Polish astronomer Nicolaus Copernicus, which replaced the Ptolemaic geocentric model, and the precise description of the elliptical orbits of the planets (1609) by the German astronomer Johannes Kepler, based

Initial
achieve-
ments of
modern
quantita-
tive science

on the inspired interpretation of centuries of patient observation that had culminated in the work of Tycho Brahe of Denmark, may be regarded fairly as the first great achievements of modern quantitative science.

A distinction may be drawn between an observational science like astronomy, where the phenomena studied lie entirely outside the control of the observer, and an experimental science such as mechanics or optics, where the investigator sets up the arrangement to his own taste. In the hands of Isaac Newton not only was the study of colours put on a rigorous basis but a firm link also was forged between the experimental science of mechanics and observational astronomy by virtue of his law of universal gravitation and his explanation of Kepler's laws of planetary motion. Before proceeding as far as this, however, attention must be paid to the mechanical studies of Galileo Galilei, the most important of the founding fathers of modern physics, insofar as the central procedure of his work involved the application of mathematical deduction to the results of measurement.

It is nowadays taken for granted by scientists that every measurement is subject to error so that repetitions of apparently the same experiment give different results. In the intellectual climate of Galileo's time, however, when logical syllogisms that admitted no gray area between right and wrong were the accepted means of deducing conclusions, his novel procedures were far from compelling. In judging his work one must remember that the conventions now accepted in reporting scientific results were adopted long after Galileo's time. Thus if, as is said, he stated as a fact that two objects dropped from the leaning tower of Pisa reached the ground together with not so much as a hand's breadth between them, it need not be inferred that he performed the experiment himself or that, if he did, the result was quite so perfect. Some such experiment had indeed been performed a little earlier (1586) by the Flemish mathematician Simon Stevin, but Galileo idealized the result. A light ball and a heavy ball do not reach the ground together, nor is the difference between them always the same, for it is impossible to reproduce the ideal of dropping them exactly at the same instant. Nevertheless, Galileo was satisfied that it came closer to the truth to say that they fell together than that there was a significant difference between their rates. This idealization of imperfect experiments remains an essential scientific process, though nowadays it is considered proper to present (or at least have available for scrutiny) the primary observations, so that others may judge independently whether they are prepared to accept the author's conclusion as to what would have been observed in an ideally conducted experiment.

The principles may be illustrated by repeating, with the advantage of modern instruments, an experiment such as Galileo himself performed—namely, that of measuring the time taken by a ball to roll different distances down a gently inclined channel. The following account is of a real experiment designed to show in a very simple example how the process of idealization proceeds, and how the preliminary conclusions may then be subjected to more searching test.

Lines equally spaced at six centimetres (2.4 inches) were scribed on a brass channel, and the ball was held at rest beside the highest line by means of a card. An electronic timer was started at the instant the card was removed, and the timer was stopped as the ball passed one of the other lines. Seven repetitions of each timing showed that the measurements typically spread over a range of $1/20$ of a second, presumably because of human limitations. In such a case, where a measurement is subject to random error, the average of many repetitions gives an improved estimate of what the result would be if the source of random error were eliminated; the factor by which the estimate is improved is roughly the square root of the number of measurements. Moreover, the theory of errors attributable to the German mathematician Carl Friedrich Gauss allows one to make a quantitative estimate of the reliability of the result, as expressed in the table by the conventional symbol ±. This does not mean that the first result in column 2 is guaranteed to lie between 0.671

The Galileo Experiment		
distance, x (in centimetres)	time, t (in seconds)	$(t + 0.09)/\sqrt{x}$
6	0.678 ± 0.007	0.314
12	0.997 ± 0.006	0.314
18	1.240 ± 0.007	0.313
24	1.444 ± 0.011	0.313
30	1.627 ± 0.010	0.313

and 0.685 but that, if this determination of the average of seven measurements were to be repeated many times, about two-thirds of the determinations would lie within these limits.

Repre-
senting
measure-
ments by
means of
graphs

The representation of measurements by a graph, as in Figure 1, was not available to Galileo but was developed shortly after his time as a consequence of the work of the French mathematician-philosopher René Descartes. The points appear to lie close to a parabola, and the curve that is drawn is defined by the equation $x = 12t^2$. The fit is not quite perfect, and it is worth trying to find a better formula. Since the operations of starting the timer when the card is removed to allow the ball to roll and stopping it as the ball passes a mark are different, there is a possibility that, in addition to random timing errors, a systematic error appears in each measured value of t; that is to say, each measurement t is perhaps to be interpreted as $t + t_0$, where t_0 is an as-yet-unknown constant timing error. If this is so, one might look to see whether the measured times were related to distance not by $x = at^2$, where a is a constant, but by $x = a(t + t_0)^2$. This may also be tested graphically by first rewriting the equation as $\sqrt{x} = \sqrt{a}(t + t_0)$, which states that when the values of $\sqrt{x}$ are plotted against measured values of t they should lie on a straight line. Figure 2 verifies this prediction rather closely; the line does not pass through the origin but rather cuts the horizontal axis at -0.09 second. From this, one deduces that $t_0 = 0.09$ second and that $(t + 0.09)x$ should be the same for all the pairs of measurements given in the table. The third column shows that this is certainly the case. Indeed, the constancy is better than might have been expected in view of the estimated errors. This must be regarded as a statistical accident; it does not imply any greater assurance in the correctness of the formula than if the figures in the last column had ranged, as they might very well have done, between 0.311 and 0.315. One would be surprised if a repetition of the whole experiment again yielded so nearly constant a result.

A possible conclusion, then, is that for some reason—probably observational bias—the measured times underestimate by 0.09 second the real time t it takes a ball, starting from rest, to travel a distance x. If so, under ideal conditions x would be strictly proportional to t^2. Further experiments, in which the channel is set at different but still gentle slopes, suggest that the general rule takes the form $x = at^2$, with a proportional to the slope. This tentative idealization of the experimental measurements may

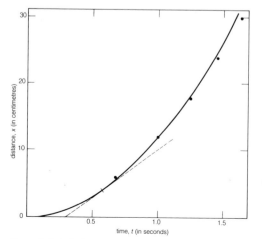

Figure 1: Data in the table of the Galileo experiment. The tangent to the curve is drawn at $t = 0.6$.

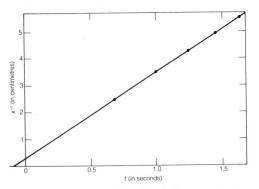

Figure 2: The data in the table of the Galileo experiment plotted differently.

need to be modified, or even discarded, in the light of further experiments. Now that it has been cast into mathematical form, however, it can be analyzed mathematically to reveal what consequences it implies. Also, this will suggest ways of testing it more searchingly.

From a graph such as Figure 1, which shows how x depends on t, one may deduce the instantaneous speed of the ball at any instant. This is the slope of the tangent drawn to the curve at the chosen value of t; at $t = 0.6$ second, for example, the tangent as drawn describes how x would be related to t for a ball moving at a constant speed of about 14 centimetres per second. The lower slope before this instant and the higher slope afterward indicate that the ball is steadily accelerating. One could draw tangents at various values of t and come to the conclusion that the instantaneous speed was roughly proportional to the time that had elapsed since the ball began to roll. This procedure, with its inevitable inaccuracies, is rendered unnecessary by applying elementary calculus to the supposed formula. The instantaneous speed v is the derivative of x with respect to t; if

$$x = at^2, \quad v = \frac{dx}{dt} = 2at.$$

The implication that the velocity is strictly proportional to elapsed time is that a graph of v against t would be a straight line through the origin. On any graph of these quantities, whether straight or not, the slope of the tangent at any point shows how velocity is changing with time at that instant; this is the instantaneous acceleration f. For a straight-line graph of v against t, the slope and therefore the acceleration are the same at all times. Expressed mathematically, $f = dv/dt = d^2x/dt^2$; in the present case, f takes the constant value $2a$.

The preliminary conclusion, then, is that a ball rolling down a straight slope experiences constant acceleration and that the magnitude of the acceleration is proportional to the slope. It is now possible to test the validity of

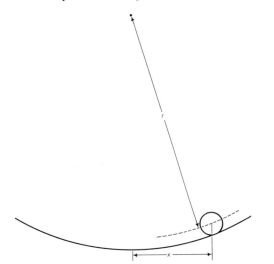

Figure 3: A ball rolling in a curved channel (see text).

the conclusion by finding what it predicts for a different experimental arrangement. If possible, an experiment is set up that allows more accurate measurements than those leading to the preliminary inference. Such a test is provided by a ball rolling in a curved channel so that its centre traces out a circular arc of radius r, as in Figure 3. Provided the arc is shallow, the slope at a distance x from its lowest point is very close to x/r, so that acceleration of the ball toward the lowest point is proportional to x/r. Introducing c to represent the constant of proportionality, this is written as a differential equation

$$\frac{d^2x}{dt^2} = -\frac{cx}{r}.$$

Here it is stated that, on a graph showing how x varies with t, the curvature d^2x/dt^2 is proportional to x and has the opposite sign, as illustrated in Figure 4. As the graph crosses the axis, x and therefore the curvature are zero, and the line is locally straight. This graph represents the oscillations of the ball between extremes of $\pm A$ after it has been released from $x = A$ at $t = 0$. The solution of the differential equation of which the diagram is the graphic representation is

$$x = A\cos(\omega t),$$

where ω, called the angular frequency, is written for $\sqrt{(c/r)}$. The ball takes time $T = 2\pi/\omega = 2\pi\sqrt{(r/c)}$ to return to its original position of rest, after which the oscillation is repeated indefinitely or until friction brings the ball to rest.

According to this analysis, the period, T, is independent of the amplitude of the oscillation, and this rather unexpected prediction is one that may be stringently tested. Instead of letting the ball roll on a curved channel, the same path is more easily and exactly realized by making it the bob of a simple pendulum. To test that the period is independent of amplitude two pendulums may be made as nearly identical as possible, so that they keep in step when swinging with the same amplitude. They are then swung with different amplitudes. It requires considerable care to detect any difference in period unless one amplitude is large, when the period is slightly longer. An observation that very nearly agrees with prediction, but not quite, does not necessarily show the initial supposition to be mistaken. In this case, the differential equation that predicted exact constancy of period was itself an approximation. When it is reformulated with the true expression for the slope replacing x/r, the solution (which involves quite heavy mathematics) shows a variation of period with amplitude that has been rigorously verified. Far from being discredited, the tentative assumption has emerged with enhanced support.

Galileo's law of acceleration, the physical basis of the expression $2\pi\sqrt{(c/r)}$ for the period, is further strengthened by finding that T varies inversely as the square root of r—i.e., the length of the pendulum.

In addition, such measurements allow the value of the constant c to be determined with a high degree of precision, and it is found to coincide with the acceleration g of a freely falling body. In fact, the formula for the period of small oscillations of a simple pendulum of length r, $T = 2\pi\sqrt{(r/g)}$, is at the heart of some of the most precise methods for measuring g. This would not have happened unless the scientific community had accepted Galileo's description of the ideal behaviour and did not expect to be shaken in its belief by small deviations, so long as they could be understood as reflecting inevitable random discrepancies between the ideal and its experimental realization. The development of quantum mechanics in the first quarter of the 20th century was stimulated by the reluctant acceptance that this description systematically failed when applied to objects of atomic size. In this case, it was not a question, as with the variations of period, of translating the physical ideas into mathematics more precisely; the whole physical basis needed radical revision. Yet, the earlier ideas were not thrown out—they had been found to work well in far too many applications to be discarded. What emerged was a clearer understanding of the circumstances in which their absolute validity could safely be assumed.

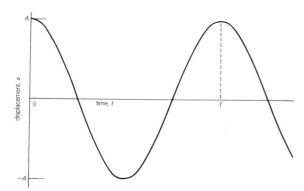

Figure 4: Oscillation of a simple pendulum (see text).

The experiments just described in detail as examples of scientific method were successful in that they agreed with expectation. They would have been just as successful if, in spite of being well conducted, they had disagreed because they would have revealed an error in the primary assumptions. The philosopher Karl Popper's widely accepted criterion for a scientific theory is that it must not simply pass such experimental tests as may be applied but that it must be formulated in such a way that falsification is in principle possible. For all its value as a test of scientific pretensions, however, it must not be supposed that the experimenter normally proceeds with Popper's criterion in mind. Normally he hopes to convince himself that his initial conception is correct. If a succession of tests agrees with (or fails to falsify) a hypothesis, it is regarded as reasonable to treat the hypothesis as true, at all events until it is discredited by a subsequent test. The scientist is not concerned with providing a guarantee of his conclusion, since, however many tests support it, there remains the possibility that the next one will not. His concern is to convince himself and his critical colleagues that a hypothesis has passed enough tests to make it worth accepting until a better one presents itself.

The Newtonian paradigm

Up to this point the investigation has been concerned exclusively with kinetics—that is to say, providing an accurate mathematical description of motion, in this case of a ball on an inclined plane, with no implied explanation of the physical processes responsible. Newton's general dynamic theory, as expounded in his *Philosophiae Naturalis Principia Mathematica* of 1687, laid down in the form of his laws of motion, together with other axioms and postulates, the rules to follow in analyzing the motion of bodies interacting among themselves. This theory of classical mechanics is described in detail in the article MECHANICS, but some general comments may be offered here. For the present purpose, it seems sufficient to consider only bodies moving along a straight line and acted upon by forces parallel to the motion. Newton's laws are, in fact, considerably more general than this and encompass motion in curves as a result of forces deflecting a body from its initial direction.

Newton's first law may more properly be ascribed to Galileo. It states that a body continues at rest or in uniform motion along a straight line unless it is acted upon by a force, and it enables one to recognize when a force is acting. A tennis ball struck by a racket experiences a sudden change in its motion attributable to a force exerted by the racket. The player feels the shock of the impact. According to Newton's third law (action and reaction are equal and opposite), the force that the ball exerts on the racket is equal and opposite to that which the racket exerts on the ball. Moreover, a second balanced action and reaction acts between player and racket.

Newton's second law quantifies the concept of force, as well as that of inertia. A body acted upon by a steady force suffers constant acceleration. Thus a freely falling body or a ball rolling down a plane has constant acceleration, as has been seen, and this is to be interpreted in Newton's terms as evidence that the force of gravity, which causes

the acceleration, is not changed by the body's motion. The same force (*e.g.*, applied by a string which includes a spring balance to check that the force is the same in different experiments) applied to different bodies causes different accelerations; and it is found that, if a chosen strength of force causes twice the acceleration in body *A* as it does in body *B*, then a different force also causes twice as much acceleration in *A* as in *B*. The ratio of accelerations is independent of the force, and is therefore a property of the bodies alone. They are said to have inertia (or inertial mass) in inverse proportion to the accelerations. This experimental fact, which is the essence of Newton's second law, enables one to assign a number to every body that is a measure of its mass. Thus a certain body may be chosen as a standard of mass and assigned the number 1. Another body is said to have mass *m* if the body shows only a fraction $1/m$ of the acceleration of this standard when the two are subjected to the same force. By proceeding in this way, every body may be assigned a mass. It is because experiment allows this definition to be made that a given force causes every body to show acceleration *f* such that *mf* is the same for all bodies. This means that the product *mf* is determined only by the force and not by the particular body on which it acts, and *mf* is defined to be the numerical measure of the force. In this way a consistent set of measures of force and mass is arrived at, having the property that $F = mf$. In this equation *F*, *m*, and *f* are to be interpreted as numbers measuring the strength of the force, the magnitude of the mass, and the rate of acceleration; and the product of the numbers *m* and *f* is always equal to the number *F*. The product *mv*, called *motus* (motion) by Newton, is now termed momentum. Newton's second law states that the rate of change of momentum equals the strength of the applied force.

In order to assign a numerical measure *m* to the mass of a body, a standard of mass must be chosen and assigned the value $m = 1$. Similarly, to measure displacement a unit of length is needed, and for velocity and acceleration a unit of time also must be defined. Given these, the numerical measure of a force follows from *mf* without need to define a unit of force. Thus in the Système Internationale d'Unités (SI), in which the units are the standard kilogram, the standard metre, and the standard second, a force of magnitude unity is one that, applied to a mass of one kilogram, causes its velocity to increase steadily by one metre per second during every second the force is acting.

The idealized observation of Galileo that all bodies in free-fall accelerate equally implies that the gravitational force causing acceleration bears a constant relation to the inertial mass. According to Newton's postulated law of gravitation, two bodies of mass m_1 and m_2, separated by a distance *r*, exert equal attractive forces on each other (the equal action and reaction of the third law of motion) of magnitude proportional to m_1m_2/r^2. The constant of proportionality, *G*, in the gravitational law, $F = Gm_1m_2/r^2$, is thus to the regarded as a universal constant, applying to all bodies, whatever their constitution. The constancy of gravitational acceleration, *g*, at a given point on the Earth is a particular case of this general law.

In the same way that the timing of a pendulum provided a more rigorous test of Galileo's kinematical theory than could be achieved by direct testing with balls rolling down planes, so with Newton's laws the most searching tests are indirect and based on mathematically derived consequences. Kepler's laws of planetary motion are just such an example, and in the two centuries after Newton's *Principia* the laws were applied to elaborate and arduous computations of the motion of all planets, not simply as isolated bodies attracted by the Sun but as a system in which every one perturbs the motion of the others by mutual gravitational interactions. (The work of the French mathematician and astronomer Pierre-Simon, Marquis de Laplace, was especially noteworthy.) Calculations of this kind have made it possible to predict the occurrence of eclipses many years ahead. Indeed, the history of past eclipses may be written with extraordinary precision so that, for instance, Thucydides' account of the lunar eclipse

Popper's criterion for scientific theory

Newton's laws of motion

Newton's law of gravitation

that fatally delayed the Athenian expedition against Syracuse in 413 BC matches the calculations perfectly (see ECLIPSE, OCCULTATION, AND TRANSIT). Similarly, unexplained small departures from theoretical expectation of the motion of Uranus led John Couch Adams of England and Urbain-Jean-Joseph Le Verrier of France to predict in 1845 that a new planet (Neptune) would be seen at a particular point in the heavens. The discovery of Pluto in 1930 was achieved in much the same way.

There is no obvious reason why the inertial mass m that governs the response of a body to an applied force should also determine the gravitational force between two bodies, as described above. Consequently, the period of a pendulum is independent of its material and governed only by its length and the local value of g; this has been verified with an accuracy of a few parts per million. Still more sensitive tests, as originally devised by the Hungarian physicist Roland, Baron von Eötvös (1890), and repeated several times since, have demonstrated clearly that the accelerations of different bodies in a given gravitational environment are identical within a few parts in 10^{12}. An astronaut in free orbit can remain poised motionless in the centre of the cabin of his spacecraft, surrounded by differently constituted objects, all equally motionless (except for their extremely weak mutual attractions) because all of them are identically affected by the gravitational field in which they are moving. He is unaware of the gravitational force, just as those on the Earth are unaware of the Sun's attraction, moving as they do with the Earth in free orbit around the Sun. Albert Einstein made this experimental finding a central feature of his general theory of relativity (see RELATIVITY).

Newton believed that everything moved in relation to a fixed but undetectable spatial frame so that it could be said to have an absolute velocity. Time also flowed at the same steady pace everywhere. Even if there were no matter in the universe, the frame of the universe would still exist, and time would still flow even though there was no one to observe its passage. In Newton's view, when matter is present it is unaffected by its motion through space. If the length of a moving metre stick were compared with the length of one at rest, they would be found to be the same. Clocks keep universal time whether they are moving or not; therefore, two identical clocks, initially synchronized, would still be synchronized after one had been carried into space and brought back. The laws of motion take such a form that they are not changed by uniform motion. They were devised to describe accurately the response of bodies to forces whether in the heavens or on the Earth, and they lose no validity as a result of the Earth's motion at 30 kilometres per second in its orbit around the Sun. This motion, in fact, would not be discernible by an observer in a closed box. The supposed invariance of the laws of motion, in addition to standards of measurement, to uniform translation was called "Galilean invariance" by Einstein.

Galilean invariance

The impossibility of discerning absolute velocity led in Newton's time to critical doubts concerning the necessity of postulating an absolute frame of space and universal time, and the doubts of the philosophers George Berkeley and Gottfried Wilhelm Leibniz, among others, were still more forcibly presented in the severe analysis of the foundations of classical mechanics by the Austrian physicist Ernst Mach in 1883. James Clerk Maxwell's theory of electromagnetic phenomena (1865), including his description of light as electromagnetic waves, brought the problem to a state of crisis. It became clear that if light waves were propagated in the hypothetical ether that filled all space and provided an embodiment of Newton's absolute frame (see below), it would not be logically consistent to accept both Maxwell's theory and the ideas expressed in Galilean invariance, for the speed of light as it passed an observer would reveal how rapidly he was traveling through the ether.

Ingenious attempts by the physicists George FitzGerald of Ireland and Hendrik A. Lorentz of The Netherlands to devise a compromise to salvage the notion of ether were eventually superseded by Einstein's special theory of relativity (see RELATIVITY). Einstein proposed in 1905 that all laws of physics, not solely those of mechanics, must take the same form for observers moving uniformly relative to one another, however rapidly. In particular, if two observers, using identical metre sticks and clocks, set out to measure the speed of a light signal as it passes them, both would obtain the same value no matter what their relative velocity might be; in a Newtonian world, of course, the measured values would differ by the relative velocity of the two observers. This is but one example of the counterintuitive character of relativistic physics, but the deduced consequences of Einstein's postulate have been so frequently and so accurately verified by experiment that it has been incorporated as a fundamental axiom in physical theory.

Special theory of relativity

With the abandonment of the ether hypothesis, there has been a reversion to a philosophical standpoint reluctantly espoused by Newton. To him and to his contemporaries the idea that two bodies could exert gravitational forces on each other across immense distances of empty space was abhorrent. However, attempts to develop Descartes's notion of a space-filling fluid ether as a transmitting medium for forces invariably failed to account for the inverse square law. Newton himself adopted a pragmatic approach, deducing the consequences of his laws and showing how well they agreed with observation; he was by no means satisfied that a mechanical explanation was impossible, but he confessed in the celebrated remark, "Hypotheses non fingo" (Latin: "I frame no hypotheses"), that he had no solution to offer.

A similar reversion to the safety of mathematical description is represented by the rejection, during the early 1900s, of the explanatory ether models of the 19th century and their replacement by model-free analysis in terms of relativity theory. This certainly does not imply giving up the use of models as imaginative aids in extending theories, predicting new effects, or devising interesting experiments; if nothing better is available, however, a mathematical formulation that yields verifiably correct results is to be preferred over an intuitively acceptable model that does not.

Interplay of experiment and theory

The foregoing discussion should have made clear that progress in physics, as in the other sciences, arises from a close interplay of experiment and theory. In a well-established field like classical mechanics, it may appear that experiment is almost unnecessary and all that is needed is the mathematical or computational skill to discover the solutions of the equations of motion. This view, however, overlooks the role of observation or experiment in setting up the problem in the first place. To discover the conditions under which a bicycle is stable in an upright position or can be made to turn a corner, it is first necessary to invent and observe a bicycle. The equations of motion are so general and serve as the basis for describing so extended a range of phenomena that the mathematician must usually look at the behaviour of real objects in order to select those that are both interesting and soluble. His analysis may indeed suggest the existence of interesting related effects that can be examined in the laboratory; thus, the invention or discovery of new things may be initiated by the experimenter or the theoretician. To employ terms such as this has led, especially in the 20th century, to a common assumption that experimentation and theorizing are distinct activities, rarely performed by the same person. It is true that almost all active physicists pursue their vocation primarily in one mode or the other. Nevertheless, the innovative experimenter can hardly make progress without an informed appreciation of the theoretical structure, even if he is not technically competent to find the solution of particular mathematical problems. By the same token, the innovative theorist must be deeply imbued with the way real objects behave, even if he is not technically competent to put together the apparatus to examine the problem. The fundamental unity of physical science should be borne in mind during the following outline of characteristic examples of experimental and theoretical physics.

CHARACTERISTIC EXPERIMENTAL PROCEDURES

Unexpected observation. The discovery of X rays (1895) by Wilhelm Conrad Röntgen of Germany was certainly serendipitous. It began with his noticing that when an electric current was passed through a discharge tube a nearby fluorescent screen lit up, even though the tube was completely wrapped in black paper.

Ernest Marsden, a student engaged on a project, reported to his professor, Ernest Rutherford (then at the University of Manchester in England), that alpha particles from a radioactive source were occasionally deflected more than 90° when they hit a thin metal foil. Astonished at this observation, Rutherford deliberated on the experimental data to formulate his nuclear model of the atom (1911).

Heike Kamerlingh Onnes of The Netherlands, the first to liquefy helium, cooled a thread of mercury to within 4 K of absolute zero (4 K equals −269° C) to test his belief that electrical resistance would tend to vanish at zero. This was what the first experiment seemed to verify, but a more careful repetition showed that instead of falling gradually, as he expected, all trace of resistance disappeared abruptly just above 4 K. This phenomenon of superconductivity, which Kamerlingh Onnes discovered in 1911, defied theoretical explanation until 1957.

The not-so-unexpected chance. From 1807 the Danish physicist and chemist Hans Christian Ørsted came to believe that electrical phenomena could influence magnets, but it was not until 1819 that he turned his investigations to the effects produced by an electric current. On the basis of his tentative models he tried on several occasions to see if a current in a wire caused a magnet needle to turn when it was placed transverse to the wire, but without success. Only when it occurred to him, without forethought, to arrange the needle parallel on the wire did the long-sought effect appear.

A second example of this type of experimental situation involves the discovery of electromagnetic induction by the English physicist and chemist Michael Faraday. Aware that an electrically charged body induces a charge in a nearby body, Faraday sought to determine whether a steady current in a coil of wire would induce such a current in another short-circuited coil close to it. He found no effect except in instances where the current in the first coil was switched on or off, at which time a momentary current appeared in the other. He was in effect led to the concept of electromagnetic induction by changing magnetic fields.

Qualitative tests to distinguish alternative theories. At the time that Augustin-Jean Fresnel presented his wave theory of light to the French Academy (1815), the leading physicists were adherents of Newton's corpuscular theory. It was pointed out by Siméon-Denis Poisson, as a fatal objection, that Fresnel's theory predicted a bright spot at the very centre of the shadow cast by a circular obstacle. When this was in fact observed by François Arago, Fresnel's theory was immediately accepted.

Another qualitative difference between the wave and corpuscular theories concerned the speed of light in a transparent medium. To explain the bending of light rays toward the normal to the surface when light entered the medium, the corpuscular theory demanded that light go faster while the wave theory required that it go slower. Jean-Bernard-Léon Foucault showed that the latter was correct (1850).

The three categories of experiments or observations discussed above are those that do not demand high-precision measurement. The following, however, are categories in which measurement at varying degrees of precision is involved.

Direct comparison of theory and experiment. This is one of the commonest experimental situations. Typically, a theoretical model makes certain specific predictions, perhaps novel in character, perhaps novel only in differing from the predictions of competing theories. There is no fixed standard by which the precision of measurement may be judged adequate. As is usual in science, the essential question is whether the conclusion carries conviction, and this is conditioned by the strength of opinion regarding alternative conclusions.

Where strong prejudice obtains, opponents of a heterodox conclusion may delay acceptance indefinitely by insisting on a degree of scrupulosity in experimental procedure that they would unhesitatingly dispense with in other circumstances. For example, few experiments in paranormal phenomena, such as clairvoyance, which have given positive results under apparently stringent conditions, have made converts among scientists. In the strictly physical domain, the search for ether drift provides an interesting study. At the height of acceptance of the hypothesis that light waves are carried by a pervasive ether, the question of whether the motion of the Earth through space dragged the ether with it was tested (1887) by A.A. Michelson and Edward W. Morley of the United States by looking for variations in the velocity of light as it traveled in different directions in the laboratory. Their conclusion was that there was a small variation, considerably less than the Earth's velocity in its orbit around the Sun, and that the ether was therefore substantially entrained in the Earth's motion. According to Einstein's relativity theory (1905), no variation should have been observed, but during the next 20 years another American investigator, Dayton C. Miller, repeated the experiment many times in different situations and concluded that, at least on a mountaintop, there was a real "ether wind" of about 10 kilometres per second. Although Miller's final presentation was a model of clear exposition, with evidence scrupulously displayed and discussed, it has been set aside and virtually forgotten. This is partly because other experiments failed to show the effect; however, their conditions were not strictly comparable, since few, if any, were conducted on mountaintops. More significantly, other tests of relativity theory supported it in so many different ways as to lead to the consensus that one discrepant set of observations cannot be allowed to weigh against the theory.

At the opposite extreme may be cited the 1919 expedition of the English scientist-mathematician Arthur Stanley Eddington to measure the very small deflection of the light from a star as it passed close to the Sun—a measurement that requires a total eclipse. The theories involved here were Einstein's general theory of relativity and the Newtonian particle theory of light, which predicted only half the relativistic effect. The conclusion of this exceedingly difficult measurement—that Einstein's theory was followed within the experimental limits of error, which amounted to ±30 percent—was the signal for worldwide feting of Einstein. If his theory had not appealed aesthetically to those able to appreciate it and if there had been any passionate adherents to the Newtonian view, the scope for error could well have been made the excuse for a long drawn-out struggle, especially since several repetitions at subsequent eclipses did little to improve the accuracy. In this case, then, the desire to believe was easily satisfied. It is gratifying to note that recent advances in radio astronomy have allowed much greater accuracy to be achieved, and Einstein's prediction is now verified within about 1 percent.

During the decade after his expedition, Eddington developed an extremely abstruse fundamental theory that led him to assert that the quantity $hc/2\pi e^2$ (h is Planck's constant, c the velocity of light, and e the charge on the electron) must take the value 137 exactly. At the time, uncertainties in the values of h and e allowed its measured value to be given as 137.29 ± 0.11; in accordance with the theory of errors, this implies that there was estimated to be about a 1 percent chance that a perfectly precise measurement would give 137. In the light of Eddington's great authority there were many prepared to accede to his belief. Since then the measured value of this quantity has come much closer to Eddington's prediction and is given as 137.03604 ± 0.00011. The discrepancy, though small, is 330 times the estimated error, compared with 2.6 times for the earlier measurement, and therefore a much more weighty indication against Eddington's theory. As the intervening years have cast no light on the virtual impenetrability of his argument, there is now hardly a physicist who takes it seriously.

Compilation of data. Technical design, whether of laboratory instruments or for industry and commerce, depends on knowledge of the properties of materials (density,

Subjectivity

strength, electrical conductivity, etc.), some of which can only be found by very elaborate experiments (*e.g.,* those dealing with the masses and excited states of atomic nuclei). One of the important functions of standards laboratories is to improve and extend the vast body of factual information, but much also arises incidentally rather than as the prime objective of an investigation or may be accumulated in the hope of discovering regularities or to test the theory of a phenomenon against a variety of occurrences.

When chemical compounds are heated in a flame, the resulting colour can be used to diagnose the presence of sodium (orange), copper (green-blue), and many other elements. This procedure has long been used. Spectroscopic examination shows that every element has its characteristic set of spectral lines, and the discovery by the Swiss mathematician Johann Jakob Balmer of a simple arithmetic formula relating the wavelengths of lines in the hydrogen spectrum (1885) proved to be the start of intense activity in precise wavelength measurements of all known elements and the search for general principles. With the Danish physicist Niels Bohr's quantum theory of the hydrogen atom (1913) began an understanding of the basis of Balmer's formula; thenceforward spectroscopic evidence underpinned successive developments toward what is now a successful theory of atomic structure.

Direct and indirect testing

Tests of fundamental concepts. Coulomb's law states that the force between two electric charges varies as the inverse square of their separation. Direct tests, such as those performed with a special torsion balance by the French physicist Charles-Augustin de Coulomb, for whom the law is named, can be at best approximate. A very sensitive indirect test, devised by the English scientist and clergyman Joseph Priestley (following an observation by Benjamin Franklin) but first realized by the English physicist and chemist Henry Cavendish (1771), relies on the mathematical demonstration that no electrical changes occurring outside a closed metal shell—as, for example, by connecting it to a high voltage source—produce any effect inside if the inverse square law holds. Since modern amplifiers can detect minute voltage changes, this test can be made very sensitive. It is typical of the class of null measurements in which only the theoretically expected behaviour leads to no response and any hypothetical departure from theory gives rise to a response of calculated magnitude. It has been shown in this way that if the force between charges, r apart, is proportional not to $1/r^2$ but to $1/r^{2+x}$, then x is less than 2×10^{-9}.

According to the relativistic theory of the hydrogen atom proposed by the English physicist P.A.M. Dirac (1928), there should be two different excited states exactly coinciding in energy. Measurements of spectral lines resulting from transitions in which these states were involved hinted at minute discrepancies, however. Some years later (*c.* 1950) Willis E. Lamb, Jr., and Robert C. Retherford of the United States, employing the novel microwave techniques that wartime radar contributed to peacetime research, were able not only to detect the energy difference between the two levels directly but to measure it rather precisely as well. The difference in energy, compared to the energy above the ground state, amounts to only four parts in 10,000,000, but this was one of the crucial pieces of evidence that led to the development of quantum electrodynamics, a central feature of the modern theory of fundamental particles (see SUBATOMIC PARTICLES: *Quantum electrodynamics*).

CHARACTERISTIC THEORETICAL PROCEDURES

Only at rare intervals in the development of a subject, and then only with the involvement of a few, are theoretical physicists engaged in introducing radically new concepts. The normal practice is to apply established principles to new problems so as to extend the range of phenomena that can be understood in some detail in terms of accepted fundamental ideas. Even when, as with the quantum mechanics of Werner Heisenberg (formulated in terms of matrices; 1925) and of Erwin Schrödinger (developed on the basis of wave functions; 1926), a major revolution is initiated, most of the accompanying theoretical activity

Application of established principles to new problems

involves investigating the consequences of the new hypothesis as if it were fully established in order to discover critical tests against experimental facts. There is little to be gained by attempting to classify the process of revolutionary thought because every case history throws up a different pattern. What follows is a description of typical procedures as normally used in theoretical physics. As in the preceding section, it will be taken for granted that the essential preliminary of coming to grips with the nature of the problem in general descriptive terms has been accomplished, so that the stage is set for systematic, usually mathematical, analysis.

Direct solution of fundamental equations. Insofar as the Sun and planets, with their attendant satellites, can be treated as concentrated masses moving under their mutual gravitational influences, they form a system that has not so overwhelmingly many separate units as to rule out step-by-step calculation of the motion of each. Modern high-speed computers are admirably adapted to this task and are used in this way to plan space missions and to decide on fine adjustments during flight. Most physical systems of interest, however, are either composed of too many units or are governed not by the rules of classical mechanics but rather by quantum mechanics, which is much less suited for direct computation.

Dissection. The mechanical behaviour of a body is analyzed in terms of Newton's laws of motion by imagining it dissected into a number of parts, each of which is directly amenable to the application of the laws or has been separately analyzed by further dissection so that the rules governing its overall behaviour are known. A very simple illustration of the method is given by the arrangement in Figure 5A, where two masses are joined by a light string passing over a pulley. The heavier mass, m_1, falls with constant acceleration, but what is the magnitude of the acceleration? If the string were cut, each mass would experience the force, m_1g or m_2g, due to its gravitational attraction and would fall with acceleration g. The fact that the string prevents this is taken into account by assuming that it is in tension and also acts on each mass. When the string is cut just above m_2, the state of accelerated motion just before the cut can be restored by applying equal and opposite forces (in accordance with Newton's third law) to the cut ends, as in Figure 5B; the string above the cut pulls the string below upward with a force T, while the string below pulls that above downward to the same extent. As yet, the value of T is not known. Now if the string is light, the tension T is sensibly the same everywhere along it, as may be seen by imagining a second cut, higher up,

Figure 5: Dissection of a complex system into elementary parts (see text).

to leave a length of string acted upon by T at the bottom and possibly a different force T' at the second cut. The total force $T - T'$ on the string must be very small if the cut piece is not to accelerate violently, and, if the mass of the string is neglected altogether, T and T' must be equal. This does not apply to the tension on the two sides of the pulley, for some resultant force will be needed to give it the correct accelerative motion as the masses move. This is a case for separate examination, by further dissection, of the forces needed to cause rotational acceleration. To simplify the problem one can assume the pulley to be so light that the difference in tension on the two sides is negligible. Then the problem has been reduced to two elementary parts—on the right the upward force on m_2 is $T - m_2g$, so that its acceleration upward is $T/m_2 - g$; and on the left the downward force on m_1 is $m_1g - T$, so that its acceleration downward is $g - T/m_1$. If the string cannot be extended, these two accelerations must be identical, from which it follows that $T = 2m_1m_2g/(m_1 + m_2)$ and the acceleration of each mass is $g(m_1 - m_2)/(m_1 + m_2)$. Thus if one mass is twice the other ($m_1 = 2m_2$), its acceleration downward is $g/3$.

A liquid may be imagined divided into small volume elements, each of which moves in response to gravity and the forces imposed by its neighbours (pressure and viscous drag). The forces are constrained by the requirement that the elements remain in contact, even though their shapes and relative positions may change with the flow. From such considerations are derived the differential equations that describe fluid motion (see MECHANICS: *Fluid mechanics*).

The dissection of a system into many simple units in order to describe the behaviour of a complex structure in terms of the laws governing the elementary components is sometimes referred to, often with a pejorative implication, as reductionism. Insofar as it may encourage concentration on those properties of the structure that can be explained as the sum of elementary processes to the detriment of properties that arise only from the operation of the complete structure, the criticism must be considered seriously. The physical scientist is, however, well aware of the existence of the problem (see below *Simplicity and complexity*). If he is usually unrepentant about his reductionist stance, it is because this analytical procedure is the only systematic procedure he knows, and it is one that has yielded virtually the whole harvest of scientific inquiry. What is set up as a contrast to reductionism by its critics is commonly called the holistic approach, whose title confers a semblance of high-mindedness while hiding the poverty of tangible results it has produced.

Simplified models. The process of dissection was early taken to its limit in the kinetic theory of gases, which in its modern form essentially started with the suggestion of the Swiss mathematician Daniel Bernoulli (in 1738) that the pressure exerted by a gas on the walls of its container is the sum of innumerable collisions by individual molecules, all moving independently of each other. Boyle's law—that the pressure exerted by a given gas is proportional to its density if the temperature is kept constant as the gas is compressed or expanded—follows immediately from Bernoulli's assumption that the mean speed of the molecules is determined by temperature alone. Departures from Boyle's law require for their explanation the assumption of forces between the molecules. It is very difficult to calculate the magnitude of these forces from first principles, but reasonable guesses about their form led Maxwell (1860) and later workers to explain in some detail the variation with temperature of thermal conductivity and viscosity, while the Dutch physicist Johannes Diederik van der Waals (1873) gave the first theoretical account of the condensation to liquid and the critical temperature above which condensation does not occur.

The first quantum mechanical treatment of electrical conduction in metals was provided in 1928 by the German physicist Arnold Sommerfeld, who used a greatly simplified model in which electrons were assumed to roam freely (much like non-interacting molecules of a gas) within the metal as if it were a hollow container. The most remarkable simplification, justified at the time by its success

rather than by any physical argument, was that the electrical force between electrons could be neglected. Since then, justification—without which the theory would have been impossibly complicated—has been provided in the sense that means have been devised to take account of the interactions whose effect is indeed considerably weaker than might have been supposed. In addition, the influence of the lattice of atoms on electronic motion has been worked out for many different metals. This development involved experimenters and theoreticians working in harness; the results of specially revealing experiments served to check the validity of approximations without which the calculations would have required excessive computing time.

These examples serve to show how real problems almost always demand the invention of models in which, it is hoped, the most important features are correctly incorporated while less-essential features are initially ignored and allowed for later if experiment shows their influence not to be negligible. In almost all branches of mathematical physics there are systematic procedures—namely, perturbation techniques—for adjusting approximately correct models so that they represent the real situation more closely.

Recasting of basic theory. Newton's laws of motion and of gravitation and Coulomb's law for the forces between charged particles lead to the idea of energy as a quantity that is conserved in a wide range of phenomena (see below *Conservation laws and extremal principles*). It is frequently more convenient to use conservation of energy and other quantities than to start an analysis from the primitive laws. Other procedures are based on showing that, of all conceivable outcomes, the one followed is that for which a particular quantity takes a maximum or a minimum value—*e.g.*, entropy change in thermodynamic processes, action in mechanical processes, and optical path length for light rays.

GENERAL OBSERVATIONS

The foregoing accounts of characteristic experimental and theoretical procedures are necessarily far from exhaustive. In particular, they say too little about the technical background to the work of the physical scientist. The mathematical techniques used by the modern theoretical physicist are frequently borrowed from the pure mathematics of past eras. The work of Augustin-Louis Cauchy on functions of a complex variable, of Arthur Cayley and James Joseph Sylvester on matrix algebra, and of Bernhard Riemann on non-Euclidean geometry, to name but a few, were investigations undertaken with little or no thought for practical applications.

The experimental physicist, for his part, has benefited greatly from technological progress and from instrumental developments that were undertaken in full knowledge of their potential research application but were nevertheless the product of single-minded devotion to the perfecting of an instrument as a worthy thing-in-itself. The developments during World War II provide the first outstanding example of technology harnessed on a national scale to meet a national need. Postwar advances in nuclear physics and in electronic circuitry, applied to almost all branches of research, were founded on the incidental results of this unprecedented scientific enterprise. The semiconductor industry sprang from the successes of microwave radar and, in its turn, through the transistor, made possible the development of reliable computers with power undreamed of by the wartime pioneers of electronic computing. From all these, the research scientist has acquired the means to explore otherwise inaccessible problems. Of course, not all of the important tools of modern-day science were the by-products of wartime research. The electron microscope is a good case in point. Moreover, this instrument may be regarded as a typical example of the sophisticated equipment to be found in all physical laboratories, of a complexity that the research-oriented user frequently does not understand in detail, and whose design depended on skills he rarely possesses.

It should not be thought that the physicist does not give a just return for the tools he borrows. Engineering and technology are deeply indebted to pure science, while

Reduction-ism

Recourse to perturbation techniques

Impact of advances in technology and instrumentation

much modern pure mathematics can be traced back to investigations originally undertaken to elucidate a scientific problem.

Concepts fundamental to the attitudes and methods of physical science

FIELDS

Newton's law of gravitation and Coulomb's electrostatic law both give the force between two particles as inversely proportional to the square of their separation and directed along the line joining them. The force acting on one particle is a vector. It can be represented by a line with arrowhead; the length of the line is made proportional to the strength of the force, and the direction of the arrow shows the direction of the force. If a number of particles are acting simultaneously on the one considered, the resultant force is found by vector addition; the vectors representing each separate force are joined head to tail, and the resultant is given by the line joining the first tail to the last head.

In what follows the electrostatic force will be taken as typical, and Coulomb's law is expressed in the form $F = q_1 q_2 r / 4\pi\varepsilon_0 r^3$. The boldface characters F and r are vectors, F being the force which a point charge q_1 exerts on another point charge q_2. The combination r/r^3 is a vector in the direction of r, the line joining q_1 to q_2, with magnitude $1/r^2$ as required by the inverse square law. When r is rendered in lightface, it means simply the magnitude of the vector r, without direction. The combination $4\pi\varepsilon_0$ is a constant whose value is irrelevant to the present discussion. The combination $q_1 r / 4\pi\varepsilon_0 r^3$ is called the electric field strength due to q_1 at a distance r from q_1 and is designated by E; it is clearly a vector parallel to r. At every point in space E takes a different value, determined by r, and the complete specification of $E(r)$—that is, the magnitude and direction of E at every point r—defines the electric field. If there are a number of different fixed charges, each produces its own electric field of inverse square character, and the resultant E at any point is the vector sum of the separate contributions. Thus the magnitude and direction of E may change in a complicated fashion from point to point. Any particle carrying charge q that is put in a place where the field is E experiences a force qE (provided the other charges are not displaced when it is inserted; if they are $E(r)$ must be recalculated for the actual positions of the charges).

A vector field, varying from point to point, is not always easily represented by a diagram, and it is often helpful for this purpose, as well as in mathematical analysis, to introduce the potential φ, from which E may be deduced. To appreciate its significance, the concept of vector gradient must be explained.

Gradient. The contours on a standard map are lines along which the height of the ground above sea level is constant. They usually take a complicated form, but if one imagines contours drawn at very close intervals of height and a small portion of the map to be greatly enlarged, the contours of this local region will become very nearly straight, like the two drawn in Figure 6 for heights h and $h + \delta h$.

Walking along any of these contours, one remains on the level. The slope of the ground is steepest along PQ, and, if the distance from P to Q is δl, the gradient is $\delta h / \delta l$ or dh/dl in the limit when δh and δl are allowed to go to zero. The vector gradient is a vector of this magnitude drawn parallel to PQ and is written as grad h, or ∇h. Walking along any other line PR at an angle θ to PQ, the slope is less in the ratio PQ/PR, or $\cos \theta$. The slope along PR is (grad h) $\cos \theta$ and is the component of the vector grad h along a line at an angle θ to the vector itself. This is an example of the general rule for finding components of vectors. In particular, the components parallel to the x and y directions have magnitude $\partial h/\partial x$ and $\partial h/\partial y$ (the partial derivatives, represented by the symbol ∂, mean, for instance, that $\partial h/\partial x$ is the rate at which h changes with distance in the x direction, if one moves so as to keep y constant; and $\partial h/\partial y$ is the rate of change in the y direction, x being constant). This result is expressed by

$$\text{grad } h = \left[\frac{\partial h}{\partial x}, \frac{\partial h}{\partial y} \right],$$

the quantities in brackets being the components of the vector along the coordinate axes. Vector quantities that vary in three dimensions can similarly be represented by three Cartesian components, along x, y, and z axes; e.g., $V = (V_x, V_y, V_z)$.

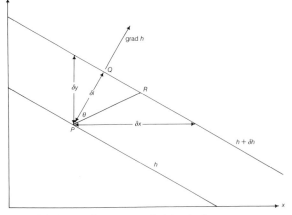

Figure 6: Definition of a vector gradient (see text).

Line integral. Imagine a line, not necessarily straight, drawn between two points A and B and marked off in innumerable small elements like δl in Figure 7, which is to be thought of as a vector. If a vector field takes a value V at this point, the quantity $V\delta l \cdot \cos \theta$ is called the scalar product of the two vectors V and δl and is written as $V \cdot \delta l$. The sum of all similar contributions from the different δl gives, in the limit when the elements are made infinitesimally small, the line integral $\int_A^B V \cdot dl$ along the line chosen.

Reverting to the contour map, it will be seen that $\int_A^B$ (grad h) $\cdot dl$ is just the vertical height of B above A and that the value of the line integral is the same for all choices of line joining the two points. When a scalar quantity φ, having magnitude but not direction, is uniquely defined at every point in space, as h is on a two-dimensional map, the vector grad φ is then said to be irrotational, and $\varphi(r)$ is the potential function from which a vector field grad φ can be derived. Not all vector fields can be derived from a potential function, but the Coulomb and gravitational fields are of this form.

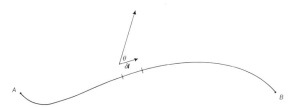

Figure 7: Definition of line integral (see text).

Potential. A potential function $\varphi(r)$ defined by $\varphi = A/r$, where A is a constant, takes a constant value on every sphere centred at the origin. The set of nesting spheres is the analogue in three dimensions of the contours of height on a map, and grad φ at a point r is a vector pointing normal to the sphere that passes through r; it therefore lies along the radius through r, and has magnitude $-A/r^2$. That is to say, grad $\varphi = -Ar/r^3$ and describes a field of inverse square form. If A is set equal to $q_1/4\pi\varepsilon_0$, the electrostatic field due to a charge q_1 at the origin is $E = -$grad φ.

When the field is produced by a number of point charges, each contributes to the potential $\varphi(r)$ in proportion to the size of the charge and inversely as the distance from the charge to the point r. To find the field strength E at r, the potential contributions can be added as numbers and contours of the resultant φ plotted; from these E

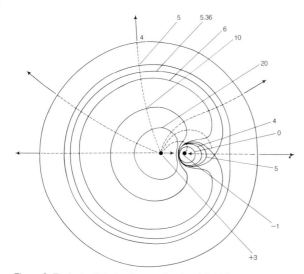

Figure 8: Equipotentials (continuous lines) and field lines (broken lines) around two electric charges of magnitude +3 and −1 (see text).

follows by calculating −grad φ. By the use of the potential, the necessity of vector addition of individual field contributions is avoided. An example of equipotentials is shown in Figure 8. Each is determined by the equation $3/r_1 - 1/r_2 = $ constant, with a different constant value for each, as shown. For any two charges of opposite sign, the equipotential surface, $\varphi = 0$, is a sphere, as no other is.

Conservative forces. The inverse square laws of gravitation and electrostatics are examples of central forces where the force exerted by one particle on another is along the line joining them and is also independent of direction. Whatever the variation of force with distance, a central force can always be represented by a potential; forces for which a potential can be found are called conservative. The work done by the force $\boldsymbol{F}(\boldsymbol{r})$ on a particle as it moves along a line from A to B is the line integral $\int_A^B \boldsymbol{F} \cdot d\boldsymbol{l}$, or $-\int_A^B \text{grad } \varphi \cdot d\boldsymbol{l}$ if $\boldsymbol{F}$ is derived from a potential φ, and this integral is just the difference between φ at A and B.

The ionized hydrogen molecule consists of two protons bound together by a single electron, which spends a large fraction of its time in the region between the protons. Considering the force acting on one of the protons, one sees that it is attracted by the electron, when it is in the middle, more strongly than it is repelled by the other proton. This argument is not precise enough to prove that the resultant force is attractive, but an exact quantum mechanical calculation shows that it is if the protons are not too close together. At close approach proton repulsion dominates, but as one moves the protons apart the attractive force rises to a peak and then soon falls to a low value. The distance, 1.06×10^{-10} metre, at which the force changes sign, corresponds to the potential φ taking its lowest value and is the equilibrium separation of the protons in the ion. This is an example of a central force field that is far from inverse square in character.

A similar attractive force arising from a particle shared between others is found in the strong nuclear force that holds the atomic nucleus together. The simplest example is the deuteron, the nucleus of heavy hydrogen, which consists either of a proton and a neutron or of two neutrons bound by a positive pion (a meson that has a mass 273 times that of an electron when in the free state). There is no repulsive force between the neutrons analogous to the Coulomb repulsion between the protons in the hydrogen ion, and the variation of the attractive force with distance follows the law $F = (g^2/r^2)e^{-r/r_0}$, in which g is a constant analogous to charge in electrostatics and r_0 is a distance of 1.4×10^{-15} metre, which is something like the separation of individual protons and neutrons in a nucleus. At separations closer than r_0, the law of force approximates to an inverse square attraction, but the exponential term kills the attractive force when r is only a few times r_0 (e.g.,

Strong nuclear force

when r is $5r_0$, the exponential reduces the force 150 times).

Since strong nuclear forces at distances less than r_0 share an inverse square law with gravitational and Coulomb forces, a direct comparison of their strengths is possible. The gravitational force between two protons at a given distance is only about 5×10^{-39} times as strong as the Coulomb force at the same separation, which itself is 1,400 times weaker than the strong nuclear force. The nuclear force is therefore able to hold together a nucleus consisting of protons and neutrons in spite of the Coulomb repulsion of the protons. On the scale of nuclei and atoms, gravitational forces are quite negligible; they only make themselves felt when extremely large numbers of electrically neutral atoms are involved, as on a terrestrial or a cosmological scale.

Field lines. The vector field, $V = -\text{grad } \varphi$, associated with a potential φ is always directed normal to the equipotential surfaces, and the variations in space of its direction can be represented by continuous lines drawn accordingly, like those in Figure 8. The arrows show the direction of the force that would act on a positive charge; they thus point away from the charge $+3$ in its vicinity and toward the charge -1. If the field is of inverse square character (gravitational, electrostatic), the field lines may be drawn to represent both direction and strength of field. Thus from an isolated charge q a large number of radial lines may be drawn, filling the solid angle evenly. Since the field strength falls away as $1/r^2$ and the area of a sphere centred on the charge increases as r^2, the number of lines crossing unit area on each sphere varies as $1/r^2$, in the same way as the field strength. In this case, the density of lines crossing an element of area normal to the lines represents the field strength at that point. The result may be generalized to apply to any distribution of point charges. The field lines are drawn so as to be continuous everywhere except at the charges themselves, which act as sources of lines. From every positive charge q, lines emerge (i.e., with outward-pointing arrows) in number proportional to q, while a similarly proportionate number enter negative charge $-q$. The density of lines then gives a measure of the field strength at any point. This elegant construction holds only for inverse square forces.

Gauss's theorem. At any point in space one may define an element of area $d\boldsymbol{S}$ by drawing a small, flat, closed loop. The area contained within the loop gives the magnitude of the vector area $d\boldsymbol{S}$, and the arrow representing its direction is drawn normal to the loop. Then, if the electric field in the region of the elementary area is $\boldsymbol{E}$, the flux through the element is defined as the product of the magnitude $d\boldsymbol{S}$ and the component of $\boldsymbol{E}$ normal to the element—i.e., the scalar product $\boldsymbol{E} \cdot d\boldsymbol{S}$. A charge q at the centre of a sphere of radius r generates a field $\boldsymbol{\varepsilon} = q\boldsymbol{r}/4\pi\varepsilon_0 r^3$ on the surface of the sphere whose area is $4\pi r^2$, and the total flux through the surface is $\int_S \boldsymbol{E} \cdot d\boldsymbol{S} = q/\varepsilon_0$. This is independent of r, and the German mathematician Karl Friedrich Gauss showed that it does not depend on q being at the centre nor even on the surrounding surface being spherical. The total flux of $\boldsymbol{\varepsilon}$ through a closed surface is equal to $1/\varepsilon_0$ times the total charge contained within it, irrespective of how that charge is arranged. It is readily seen that this result is consistent with the statement in the preceding paragraph—if every charge q within the surface is the source of q/ε_0 field lines, and these lines are continuous except at the charges, the total number leaving through the surface is Q/ε_0, where Q is the total charge. Charges outside the surface contribute nothing, since their lines enter and leave again.

Gauss's theorem takes the same form in gravitational theory, the flux of gravitational field lines through a closed surface being determined by the total mass within. This enables a proof to be given immediately of a problem that caused Newton considerable trouble. He was able to show, by direct summation over all the elements, that a uniform sphere of matter attracts bodies outside as if the whole mass of the sphere were concentrated at its centre. Now it is obvious by symmetry that the field has the same magnitude everywhere on the surface of the sphere, and this symmetry is unaltered by collapsing the mass to a point at the centre. According to Gauss's theorem, the

Gauss's theorem in gravitational theory

total flux is unchanged, and the magnitude of the field must therefore be the same. This is an example of the power of a field theory over the earlier point of view by which each interaction between particles was dealt with individually and the result summed.

Images. A second example illustrating the value of field theories arises when the distribution of charges is not initially known, as when a charge q is brought close to a piece of metal or other electrical conductor and experiences a force. When an electric field is applied to a conductor, charge moves in it; so long as the field is maintained and charge can enter or leave, this movement of charge continues and is perceived as a steady electric current. An isolated piece of conductor, however, cannot carry a steady current indefinitely because there is nowhere for the charge to come from or go to. When q is brought close to the metal, its electric field causes a shift of charge in the metal to a new configuration in which its field exactly cancels the field due to q everywhere on and inside the conductor. The force experienced by q is its interaction with the canceling field. It is clearly a serious problem to calculate E everywhere for an arbitrary distribution of charge, and then to adjust the distribution to make it vanish on the conductor. When, however, it is recognized that after the system has settled down, the surface of the conductor must have the same value of φ everywhere, so that $E = -\text{grad } \varphi$ vanishes on the surface, a number of specific solutions can easily be found.

In Figure 8, for instance, the equipotential surface $\varphi = 0$ is a sphere. If a sphere of uncharged metal is built to coincide with this equipotential, it will not disturb the field in any way. Moreover, once it is constructed, the charge -1 inside may be moved around without altering the field pattern outside, which therefore describes what the field lines look like when a charge $+3$ is moved to the appropriate distance away from a conducting sphere carrying charge -1. More usefully, if the conducting sphere is momentarily connected to the Earth (which acts as a large body capable of supplying charge to the sphere without suffering a change in its own potential), the required charge -1 flows to set up this field pattern. This result can be generalized as follows: if a positive charge q is placed at a distance r from the centre of a conducting sphere of radius a connected to the Earth, the resulting field outside the sphere is the same as if, instead of the sphere, a negative charge $q' = -(a/r)q$ had been placed at a distance $r' = r(1 - a^2/r^2)$ from q on a line joining it to the centre of the sphere. And q is consequently attracted toward the sphere with a force $qq'/4\pi\varepsilon_0 r'^2$, or $q^2 ar/4\pi\varepsilon_0(r^2 - a^2)^2$. The fictitious charge $-q'$ behaves somewhat, but not exactly, like the image of q in a spherical mirror, and hence this way of constructing solutions, of which there are many examples, is called the method of images.

Divergence and Laplace's equation. When charges are not isolated points but form a continuous distribution with a local charge density ρ being the ratio of the charge δq in a small cell to the volume δv of the cell, then the flux of E over the surface of the cell is $\rho \delta v/\varepsilon_0$, by Gauss's theorem, and is proportional to δv. The ratio of the flux to δv is called the divergence of E and is written div E. It is related to the charge density by the equation div $E = \rho/\varepsilon_0$. If E is expressed by its Cartesian components (ε_x, ε_y, ε_z),

$$\text{div } E = \frac{\partial \varepsilon_x}{\partial x} + \frac{\partial \varepsilon_y}{\partial y} + \frac{\partial \varepsilon_z}{\partial z}.$$

And since $E_x = -\partial\varphi/\partial x$, etc.,

$$\frac{\partial^2 \varphi}{\partial^2 x} + \frac{\partial^2 \varphi}{\partial^2 y} + \frac{\partial^2 \varphi}{\partial^2 z} = -\frac{\rho}{\varepsilon_0}.$$

The expression on the left side is usually written as $\nabla^2\varphi$ and is called the Laplacian of φ. It has the property, as is obvious from its relationship to ρ, of being unchanged if the Cartesian axes of x, y, and z are turned bodily into any new orientation.

If any region of space is free of charges, $\rho = 0$ and $\nabla^2\varphi = 0$ in this region. The latter is Laplace's equation, for which many methods of solution are available, providing a powerful means of finding electrostatic (or gravitational) field patterns.

Non-conservative fields. The magnetic field B is an example of a vector field that cannot in general be described as the gradient of a scalar potential. There are no isolated poles to provide, as electric charges do, sources for the field lines. Instead, the field is generated by currents and forms vortex patterns around any current-carrying conductor. Figure 9 shows the field lines for a single straight wire. If one forms the line integral $\int B \cdot dl$ around the closed path formed by any one of these field lines, each increment $B \cdot \delta l$ has the same sign and, obviously, the integral cannot vanish as it does for an electrostatic field. The value it takes is proportional to the total current enclosed by the path. Thus every path that encloses the conductor yields the same value for $\int B \cdot dl$; i.e., $\mu_0 I$, where I is the current and μ_0 is a constant for any particular choice of units in which B, l, and I are to be measured.

If no current is enclosed by the path, the line integral vanishes and a potential φ_B may be defined. Indeed, in the example shown in Figure 9, a potential may be defined even for paths that enclose the conductor, but it is many-valued because it increases by a standard increment $\mu_0 I$ every time the path encircles the current. A contour map of height would represent a spiral staircase (or, better, a spiral ramp) by a similar many-valued contour. The conductor carrying I is in this case the axis of the ramp. Like E in a charge-free region, where div $E = 0$, so also div $B = 0$; and where φ_B may be defined, it obeys Laplace's equation, $\nabla^2\varphi_B = 0$.

Magnetic fields

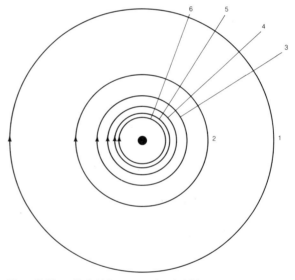

Figure 9: Magnetic field lines around a straight current-carrying wire (see text).

Within a conductor carrying a current or any region in which current is distributed rather than closely confined to a thin wire, no potential φ_B can be defined. For now the change in φ_B after traversing a closed path is no longer zero or an integral multiple of a constant $\mu_0 I$ but is rather μ_0 times the current enclosed in the path and therefore depends on the path chosen. To relate the magnetic field to the current, a new function is needed, the curl, whose name suggests the connection with circulating field lines.

The curl of a vector, say, curl B, is itself a vector quantity. To find the component of curl B along any chosen direction, draw a small closed path of area A lying in the plane normal to that direction, and evaluate the line integral $\int B \cdot dl$ around the path. As the path is shrunk in size, the integral diminishes with the area, and the limit of $A^{-1}\int B \cdot dl$ is the component of curl B in the chosen direction. The direction in which the vector curl B points is the direction in which $A^{-1}\int B \cdot dl$ is largest.

To apply this to the magnetic field in a conductor carrying current, the current density J is defined as a vector pointing along the direction of current flow, and the magnitude of J is such that JA is the total current flowing across a small area A normal to J. Now the line integral of B around the edge of this area is A curl B if A is very small, and this must equal μ_0 times the contained current. It follows that

$$\text{curl } \boldsymbol{B} = \mu_0 \boldsymbol{J}.$$

Expressed in Cartesian coordinates,

$$\frac{\partial B_y}{\partial z} - \frac{\partial B_z}{\partial y} = \mu_0 J_x,$$

with similar expressions for J_y and J_z. These are the differential equations relating the magnetic field to the currents that generate it.

A magnetic field also may be generated by a changing electric field, and an electric field by a changing magnetic field. The description of these physical processes by differential equations relating curl $\boldsymbol{B}$ to $\partial \boldsymbol{E}/\partial t$, and curl $\boldsymbol{E}$ to $\partial \boldsymbol{B}/\partial t$ is the heart of Maxwell's electromagnetic theory and illustrates the power of the mathematical methods characteristic of field theories. Further examples will be found in the mathematical description of fluid motion, in which the local velocity $\boldsymbol{v}(\boldsymbol{r})$ of fluid particles constitutes a field to which the notions of divergence and curl are naturally applicable.

Examples of differential equations for fields. *Continuity.* An incompressible fluid flows so that the net flux of fluid into or out of a given volume within the fluid is zero. Since the divergence of a vector describes the net flux out of an infinitesimal element, divided by the volume of the element, the velocity vector $\boldsymbol{v}$ in an incompressible fluid must obey the equation div $\boldsymbol{v} = 0$. If the fluid is compressible, however, and its density $\rho(\boldsymbol{r})$ varies with position because of pressure or temperature variations, the net outward flux of mass from some small element is determined by div $(\rho\boldsymbol{v})$, and this must be related to the rate at which the density of the fluid within is changing:

$$\text{div } (\rho\boldsymbol{v}) = -\frac{\partial \rho}{\partial t}.$$

Diffusion. A dissolved molecule or a small particle suspended in a fluid is constantly struck at random by molecules of the fluid in its neighbourhood, as a result of which it wanders erratically. This is called Brownian motion in the case of suspended particles. It is usually safe to assume that each one in a cloud of similar particles is moved by collisions from the fluid and not by interaction between the particles themselves. When a dense cloud gradually spreads out, much like a drop of ink in a beaker of water, this diffusive motion is the consequence of random, independent wandering by each particle. Two equations can be written to describe the average behaviour. The first is a continuity equation: if there are $n(\boldsymbol{r})$ particles per unit volume around the point $\boldsymbol{r}$, and the flux of particles across an element of area is described by a vector $\boldsymbol{F}$, meaning the number of particles crossing unit area normal to $\boldsymbol{F}$ in unit time,

$$\text{div } \boldsymbol{F} = -\frac{\partial n}{\partial t}$$

describes the conservation of particles. Secondly, Fick's law states that the random wandering causes an average drift of particles from regions where they are denser to regions where they are rarer, and that the mean drift rate is proportional to the gradient of density and in the opposite sense to the gradient:

$$\boldsymbol{F} = -D \text{ grad } n,$$

where D is a constant—the diffusion constant.

These two equations can be combined into one differential equation for the changes that n will undergo,

$$D\nabla^2 n = \frac{\partial n}{\partial t},$$

which defines uniquely how any initial distribution of particles will develop with time. Thus the spreading of a small drop of ink is rather closely described by the particular solution,

$$n = \left(\frac{C}{t^{3/2}}\right) \exp\left(\frac{-r^2}{4Dt}\right),$$

in which C is a constant determined by the total number

of particles in the ink drop. When t is very small at the start of the process, all the particles are clustered near the origin of r, but, as t increases, the radius of the cluster increases in proportion to the square root of the time, while the density at the centre drops as the three-halves power to keep the total number constant. The distribution of particles with distance from the centre at three different times is shown in Figure 10. From this diagram one may calculate what fraction, after any chosen interval, has moved farther than some chosen distance from the origin. Moreover, since each particle wanders independently of the rest, it also gives the probability that a single particle will migrate farther than this in the same time. Thus a problem relating to the behaviour of a single particle, for which only an average answer can usefully be given, has been converted into a field equation and solved rigorously. This is a widely used technique in physics.

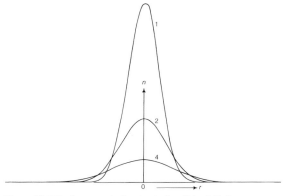

Figure 10: Diffusive spread of a cloud of particles initially concentrated at a point. The value given for each curve represents the time elapsed since n, the particles per unit volume around point r, began to disperse (see text).

Further examples of field equations. The equations describing the propagation of waves (electromagnetic, acoustic, deep water waves, and ripples) are discussed in relevant articles, as is the Schrödinger equation for probability waves that governs particle behaviour in quantum mechanics (see below *Fundamental constituents of matter*). The field equations that embody the special theory of relativity are more elaborate with space and time coordinates no longer independent of each other, though the geometry involved is still Euclidean. In the general theory of relativity, the geometry of this four-dimensional space-time is non-Euclidean (see RELATIVITY).

CONSERVATION LAWS AND EXTREMAL PRINCIPLES

It is a consequence of Newton's laws of motion that the total momentum remains constant in a system completely isolated from external influences. The only forces acting on any part of the system are those exerted by other parts; if these are taken in pairs, according to the third law, A exerts on B a force equal and opposite to that of B on A. Since, according to the second law, the momentum of each changes at a rate equal to the force acting on it, the momentum change of A is exactly equal and opposite to that of B when only mutual forces between these two are considered. Because the effects of separate forces are additive, it follows that for the system as a whole no momentum change occurs. The centre of mass of the whole system obeys the first law in remaining at rest or moving at a constant velocity, so long as no external influences are brought to bear. This is the oldest of the conservation laws and is invoked frequently in solving dynamic problems.

The total angular momentum (also called moment of momentum) of an isolated system about a fixed point is conserved as well. The angular momentum of a particle of mass m moving with velocity $\boldsymbol{v}$ at the instant when it is at a distance $\boldsymbol{r}$ from the fixed point is $m\boldsymbol{r} \wedge \boldsymbol{v}$. The quantity written as $\boldsymbol{r} \wedge \boldsymbol{v}$ is a vector (the vector product of $\boldsymbol{r}$ and $\boldsymbol{v}$) having components with respect to Cartesian axes

$$\boldsymbol{r} \wedge \boldsymbol{v} = (yv_z - zv_y, zv_x - xv_z, xv_y - yv_x).$$

The meaning is more easily appreciated if all the particles

Phenomenon of Brownian motion

Conservation of angular momentum

lie and move in a plane. The angular momentum of any one particle is the product of its momentum mv and the distance of nearest approach of the particle to the fixed point if it were to continue in a straight line. The vector is drawn normal to the plane. Conservation of total angular momentum does not follow immediately from Newton's laws but demands the additional assumption that any pair of forces, action and reaction, are not only equal and opposite but act along the same line. This is always true for central forces, but it holds also for the frictional force developed along sliding surfaces. If angular momentum were not conserved, one might find an isolated body developing a spontaneous rotation with respect to the distant stars or, if rotating like the Earth, changing its rotational speed without any external cause. Such small changes as the Earth experiences are explicable in terms of disturbances from without—*e.g.,* tidal forces exerted by the Moon. The law of conservation of angular momentum is not called into question.

Nevertheless, there are noncentral forces in nature, as, for example, when a charged particle moves past a bar magnet. If the line of motion and the axis of the magnet lie in a plane, the magnet exerts a force on the particle perpendicular to the plane while the magnetic field of the moving particle exerts an equal and opposite force on the magnet. At the same time, it exerts a couple tending to twist the magnet out of the plane. Angular momentum is not conserved unless one imagines that the balance of angular momentum is distributed in the space around the magnet and charge and changes as the particle moves past. The required result is neatly expressed by postulating the possible existence of magnetic poles that would generate a magnetic field analogous to the electric field of a charge (a bar magnet behaves roughly like two such poles of opposite sign, one near each end). Then there is associated with each pair, consisting of a charge q and a pole P, angular momentum $\mu_0 Pq/4\pi$, as if the electric and magnetic fields together acted like a gyroscope spinning about the line joining P and q. With this contribution included in the sum, angular momentum is always conserved.

The device of associating mechanical properties with the fields, which up to this point had appeared merely as convenient mathematical constructions, has even greater implications when conservation of energy is considered. This conservation law, which is regarded as basic to physics, seems at first sight, from an atomic point of view, to be almost trivial. If two particles interact by central forces, for which a potential function φ may be defined such that grad φ gives the magnitude of the force experienced by each, it follows from Newton's laws of motion that the sum of φ and of their separate kinetic energies, defined as $1/2mv^2$, remains constant. This sum is defined to be the total energy of the two particles and, by its definition, is automatically conserved. The argument may be extended to any number of particles interacting by means of central forces; a potential energy function may always be found, depending only on the relative positions of the particles, which may be added to the sum of the kinetic energies (depending only on the velocities) to give a total energy that is conserved.

The concept of potential energy, thus introduced as a formal device, acquires a more concrete appearance when it is expressed in terms of electric and magnetic field strengths for particles interacting by virtue of their charges. The quantities $1/2\varepsilon_0 E^2$ and $B^2/2\mu_0$ may be interpreted as the contributions per unit volume of the electric and magnetic fields to the potential energy, and, when these are integrated over all space and added to the kinetic energy, the total energy thus expressed is a conserved quantity. These expressions were discovered during the heyday of ether theories, according to which all space is permeated by a medium capable of transmitting forces between particles (see above). The electric and magnetic fields were interpreted as descriptions of the state of strain of the ether, so that the location of stored energy throughout space was no more remarkable than it would be in a compressed spring. With the abandonment of the ether theories following the rise of relativity theory, this visualizable model ceased to have validity.

The idea of energy as a real constituent of matter has, however, become too deeply rooted to be abandoned lightly, and most physicists find it useful to continue treating electric and magnetic fields as more than mathematical constructions. Far from being empty, free space is viewed as a storehouse for energy, with E and B providing not only an inventory but expressions for its movements as represented by the momentum carried in the fields. Wherever E and B are both present, and not parallel, there is a flux of energy, amounting to $E \wedge B/\mu_0$, crossing unit area and moving in a direction normal to the plane defined by E and B. This energy in motion confers momentum on the field, $E \wedge B/\mu_0 c$, per unit volume as if there were mass associated with the field energy. Indeed, the English physicist J.J. Thomson showed in 1881 that the energy stored in the fields around a moving charged particle varies as the square of the velocity as if there were extra mass carried with the electric field around the particle. Herein lie the seeds of the general mass–energy relationship developed by Einstein in his special theory of relativity; $E = mc^2$ expresses the association of mass with every form of energy. Neither of two separate conservation laws, that of energy and that of mass (the latter particularly the outcome of countless experiments involving chemical change), is in this view perfectly true, but together they constitute a single conservation law, which may be expressed in two equivalent ways—conservation of mass, if to the total energy E is ascribed mass E/c^2, or conservation of energy, if to each mass m is ascribed energy mc^2. The delicate measurements by Eötvös and later workers (see above) show that the gravitational forces acting on a body do not distinguish different types of mass, whether intrinsic to the fundamental particles or resulting from their kinetic and potential energies. For all its apparently artificial origins, then, this conservation law enshrines a very deep truth about the material universe, one that has not yet been fully explored.

An equally fundamental law, for which no exception is known, is that the total electrical charge in an isolated system is conserved. In the production of a negatively charged electron by an energetic gamma ray, for example, a positively charged positron is produced simultaneously. An isolated electron cannot disappear, though an electron and a positron, whose total charge is zero and whose mass is $2m_e$ (twice the mass of an electron), may simultaneously be annihilated. The energy equivalent of the destroyed mass appears as gamma ray energy $2m_e c^2$.

For macroscopic systems—*i.e.,* those composed of objects massive enough for their atomic structure to be discounted in the analysis of their behaviour—the conservation law for energy assumes a different aspect. In the collision of two perfectly elastic objects, to which billiard balls are a good approximation, momentum and energy are both conserved. Given the paths and velocities before collision, those after collision can be calculated from the conservation laws alone. In reality, however, although momentum is always conserved, the kinetic energy of the separating balls is less than what they had on approach. Soft objects, indeed, may adhere on collision, losing most of their kinetic energy. The lost energy takes the form of heat, raising the temperature (if only imperceptibly) of the colliding objects. From the atomic viewpoint the total energy of a body may be divided into two portions: on the one hand, the external energy consisting of the potential energy associated with its position and the kinetic energy of motion of its centre of mass and its spin; and, on the other, the internal energy due to the arrangement and motion of its constituent atoms. In an inelastic collision the sum of internal and external energies is conserved, but some of the external energy of bodily motion is irretrievably transformed into internal random motions. The conservation of energy is expressed in the macroscopic language of the first law of thermodynamics—namely, energy is conserved provided that heat is taken into account. The irreversible nature of the transfer from external energy of organized motion to random internal energy is a manifestation of the second law of thermodynamics.

The irreversible degradation of external energy into random internal energy also explains the tendency of all

Conservation of energy

Conservation of massenergy

systems to come to rest if left to themselves. If there is a configuration in which the potential energy is less than for any slightly different configuration, the system may find stable equilibrium here because there is no way in which it can lose more external energy, either potential or kinetic. This is an example of an extremal principle—that a state of stable equilibrium is one in which the potential energy is a minimum with respect to any small changes in configuration. It may be regarded as a special case of one of the most fundamental of physical laws, the principle of increase of entropy, which is a statement of the second law of thermodynamics in the form of an extremal principle— the equilibrium state of an isolated physical system is that in which the entropy takes the maximum possible value. This matter is discussed further below and, in particular, in the article THERMODYNAMICS.

The earliest extremal principle to survive in modern physics was formulated by the French mathematician Pierre de Fermat in about 1660. As originally stated, the path taken by a ray of light between two fixed points in an arrangement of mirrors, lenses, and so forth, is that which takes the least time. The laws of reflection and refraction may be deduced from this principle if it is assumed as Fermat did, correctly, that in a medium of refractive index μ light travels more slowly than in free space by a factor μ. Strictly, the time taken along a true ray path is either less or greater than for any neighbouring path. If all paths in the neighbourhood take the same time, the two chosen points are such that light leaving one is focused on the other. The perfect example is exhibited by an elliptical mirror, such as the one in Figure 11; all paths from F_1 to the ellipse and thence to F_2 have the same length. In conventional optical terms, the ellipse has the property that every choice of paths obeys the law of reflection, and every ray from F_1 converges after reflection onto F_2. Also shown in the figure are two reflecting surfaces tangential to the ellipse that do not have the correct curvature to focus light from F_1 onto F_2. A ray is reflected from F_1 to F_2 only at the point of contact. For the flat reflector the path taken is the shortest of all in the vicinity, while for the reflector that is more strongly curved than the ellipse it is the longest. Fermat's principle and its application to focusing by mirrors and lenses finds a natural explanation in the wave theory of light (see LIGHT).

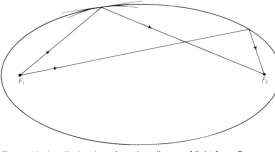

Figure 11: An elliptic mirror focusing all rays of light from F_1 onto F_2 (see text).

A similar extremal principle in mechanics, the principle of least action, was proposed by the French mathematician and astronomer Pierre-Louis Moreau de Maupertuis but rigorously stated only much later, especially by the Irish mathematician and scientist William Rowan Hamilton in 1835. Though very general, it is well enough illustrated by a simple example, the path taken by a particle between two points A and B in a region where the potential $\varphi(\mathbf{r})$ is everywhere defined. Once the total energy E of the particle has been fixed, its kinetic energy T at any point P is the difference between E and the potential energy φ at P. If any path between A and B is assumed to be followed, the velocity at each point may be calculated from T, and hence the time t between the moment of departure from A and passage through P. The action for this path is found by evaluating the integral $\int_A^B (T - \varphi)dt$, and the actual path taken by the particle is that for which the action is minimal. It may be remarked that both Fermat and Maupertuis were guided by Aristotelian notions of economy

in nature that have been found, if not actively misleading, too imprecise to retain a place in modern science.

Fermat's and Hamilton's principles are but two examples out of many whereby a procedure is established for finding the correct solution to a problem by discovering under what conditions a certain function takes an extremal value. The advantages of such an approach are that it brings into play the powerful mathematical techniques of the calculus of variations and, perhaps even more important, that in dealing with very complex situations it may allow a systematic approach by computational means to a solution that may not be exact but is near enough the right answer to be useful.

Fermat's principle, stated as a theorem concerning light rays but later restated in terms of the wave theory, found an almost exact parallel in the development of wave mechanics. The association of a wave with a particle by the physicists Louis-Victor de Broglie and Erwin Schrödinger was made in such a way that the principle of least action followed by an analogous argument.

FUNDAMENTAL CONSTITUENTS OF MATTER

Development of the atomic theory. The idea that matter is composed of atoms goes back to the Greek philosophers, notably Democritus, and has never since been entirely lost sight of, though there have been periods when alternative views were more generally preferred. Newton's contemporaries, Robert Hooke and Robert Boyle, in particular, were atomists, but their interpretation of the sensation of heat as random motion of atoms was overshadowed for more than a century by the conception of heat as a subtle fluid dubbed caloric. It is a tribute to the strength of caloric theory that it enabled the French scientist Sadi Carnot to arrive at his great discoveries in thermodynamics. In the end, however, the numerical rules for the chemical combination of different simple substances, together with the experiments on the conversion of work into heat by Benjamin Thompson (Count Rumford) and James Prescott Joule, led to the downfall of the theory of caloric. Nevertheless, the rise of ether theories to explain the transmission of light and electromagnetic forces through apparently empty space postponed for many decades the general reacceptance of the concept of atoms. The discovery in 1858 by the German scientist and philosopher Hermann von Helmholtz of the permanence of vortex motions in perfectly inviscid fluids encouraged the invention—throughout the latter half of the 19th century and especially in Great Britain—of models in which vortices in a structureless ether played the part otherwise assigned to atoms. In recent years the recognition that certain localized disturbances in a fluid, the so-called solitary waves, might persist for a very long time has led to attempts, so far unsuccessful, to use them as models of fundamental particles.

These attempts to describe the basic constituents of matter in the familiar language of fluid mechanics were at least atomic theories in contrast to the anti-atomistic movement at the end of the 19th century in Germany under the influence of Ernst Mach and Wilhelm Ostwald. For all their scientific eminence, their argument was philosophical rather than scientific, springing as it did from the conviction that the highest aim of science is to describe the relationship between different sensory perceptions without the introduction of unobservable concepts. Nonetheless, an inspection of the success of their contemporaries using atomic models shows why this movement failed. It suffices to mention the systematic construction of a kinetic theory of matter in which the physicists Ludwig Boltzmann of Austria and J. Willard Gibbs of the United States were the two leading figures. To this may be added Hendrik Lorentz's electron theory, which explained in satisfying detail many of the electrical properties of matter; and, as a crushing argument for atomism, the discovery and explanation of X-ray diffraction by Max von Laue of Germany and his collaborators, a discovery that was quickly developed, following the lead of the British physicist William Henry Bragg and his son Lawrence, into a systematic technique for mapping the precise atomic structure of crystals.

While the concept of atoms was thus being made indispensable, the ancient belief that they were probably structureless and certainly indestructible came under devastating attack. J.J. Thomson's discovery of the electron in 1897 soon led to the realization that the mass of an atom largely resides in a positively charged part, electrically neutralized by a cloud of much lighter electrons. A few years later Ernest Rutherford and Frederick Soddy showed how the emission of alpha and beta particles from radioactive elements causes them to be transformed into elements of different chemical properties. By 1913, with Rutherford as the leading figure, the foundations of the modern theory of atomic structure were laid. It was determined that a small, massive nucleus carries all the positive charge whose magnitude, expressed as a multiple of the fundamental charge of the proton, is the atomic number. An equal number of electrons carrying a negative charge numerically equal to that of the proton form a cloud whose diameter is several thousand times that of the nucleus around which they swarm. The atomic number determines the chemical properties of the atom, and in alpha decay a helium nucleus, whose atomic number is 2, is emitted from the radioactive nucleus, leaving one whose atomic number is reduced by 2. In beta decay the nucleus in effect gains one positive charge by emitting a negative electron and thus has its atomic number increased by unity.

The nucleus, itself a composite body, was soon being described in various ways, none completely wrong but none uniquely right. Pivotal was James Chadwick's discovery in 1932 of the neutron, a nuclear particle with very nearly the same mass as the proton but no electric charge. After this discovery, investigators came to view the nucleus as consisting of protons and neutrons, bound together by a force of limited range, which at close quarters was strong enough to overcome the electrical repulsion between the protons. A free neutron survives for only a few minutes before disintegrating into a readily observed proton and electron, along with an elusive neutrino, which has no charge and zero, or at most extremely small, mass. The disintegration of a neutron also may occur inside the nucleus, with the expulsion of the electron and neutrino; this is the beta-decay process. It is common enough among the heavy radioactive nuclei but does not occur with all nuclei because the energy released would be insufficient for the reorganization of the resulting nucleus. Certain nuclei have a higher-than-ideal ratio of protons to neutrons and may adjust the proportion by the reverse process, a proton being converted into a neutron with the expulsion of a positron and an antineutrino. For example, a magnesium nucleus containing 12 protons and 11 neutrons spontaneously changes to a stable sodium nucleus with 11 protons and 12 neutrons. The positron resembles the electron in all respects except for being positively rather than negatively charged. It was the first antiparticle to be discovered. Its existence had been predicted, however, by Dirac after he had formulated the quantum mechanical equations describing the behaviour of an electron (see below). This was one of the most spectacular achievements of a spectacular albeit brief epoch, during which the basic conceptions of physics were revolutionized.

Rise of quantum mechanics. The idea of the quantum was introduced by the German physicist Max Planck in 1900 in response to the problems posed by the spectrum of radiation from a hot body, but the development of quantum theory soon became closely tied to the difficulty of explaining by classical mechanics the stability of Rutherford's nuclear atom. Bohr led the way in 1913 with his model of the hydrogen atom, but it was not until 1925 that the arbitrary postulates of his quantum theory found consistent expression in the new quantum mechanics that was formulated in apparently different but in fact equivalent ways by Heisenberg, Schrödinger, and Dirac (see MECHANICS: *Quantum mechanics*). In Bohr's model the motion of the electron around the proton was analyzed as if it were a classical problem, mathematically the same as that of a planet around the Sun, but it was additionally postulated that, of all the orbits available to the classical particle, only a discrete set was to be allowed, and Bohr devised rules for determining which orbits they were. In Schrödinger's wave mechanics the problem is also written

down in the first place as if it were a classical problem, but, instead of proceeding to a solution of the orbital motion, the equation is transformed by an explicitly laid down procedure from an equation of particle motion to an equation of wave motion. The newly introduced mathematical function Ψ, the amplitude of Schrödinger's hypothetical wave, is used to calculate not how the electron moves but rather what the probability is of finding the electron in any specific place if it is looked for there.

Schrödinger's prescription reproduced in the solutions of the wave equation the postulates of Bohr but went much further. Bohr's theory had come to grief when even two electrons, as in the helium atom, had to be considered together, but the new quantum mechanics encountered no problems in formulating the equations for two or any number of electrons moving around a nucleus. Solving the equations was another matter; yet, numerical procedures were applied with devoted patience to a few of the simpler cases and demonstrated beyond cavil that the only obstacle to solution was calculational and not an error of physical principle. Modern computers have vastly extended the range of application of quantum mechanics not only to heavier atoms but also to molecules and assemblies of atoms in solids, and always with such success as to inspire full confidence in the prescription.

From time to time many physicists feel uneasy that it is necessary first to write down the problem to be solved as though it were a classical problem and them to subject it to an artificial transformation into a problem in quantum mechanics. It must be realized, however, that the world of experience and observation is not the world of electrons and nuclei. When a bright spot on a television screen is interpreted as the arrival of a stream of electrons, it is still only the bright spot that is perceived and not the electrons. The world of experience is described by the physicist in terms of visible objects, occupying definite positions at definite instants of time—in a word, the world of classical mechanics. When the atom is pictured as a nucleus surrounded by electrons, this picture is a necessary concession to human limitations; there is no sense in which one can say that, if only a good enough microscope were available, this picture would be revealed as genuine reality. It is not that such a microscope has not been made; it is actually impossible to make one that will reveal this detail. The process of transformation from a classical description to an equation of quantum mechanics, and from the solution of this equation to the probability that a specified experiment will yield a specified observation, is not to be thought of as a temporary expedient pending the development of a better theory. It is better to accept this process as a technique for predicting the observations that are likely to follow from an earlier set of observations. Whether electrons and nuclei have an objective existence in reality is a metaphysical question to which no definite answer can be given. There is, however, no doubt that to postulate their existence is, in the present state of physics, an inescapable necessity if a consistent theory is to be constructed to describe economically and exactly the enormous variety of observations on the behaviour of matter. The habitual use of the language of particles by physicists induces and reflects the conviction that, even if the particles elude direct observation, they are as real as any everyday object.

Following the initial triumphs of quantum mechanics, Dirac in 1928 extended the theory so that it would be compatible with the special theory of relativity. Among the new and experimentally verified results arising from this work was the seemingly meaningless possibility that an electron of mass m might exist with any negative energy between $-mc^2$ and $-\infty$. Between $-mc^2$ and $+mc^2$, which is in relativistic theory the energy of an electron at rest, no state is possible. It became clear that other predictions of the theory would not agree with experiment if the negative-energy states were brushed aside as an artifact of the theory without physical significance. Eventually Dirac was led to propose that all the states of negative energy, infinite in number, are already occupied with electrons and that these, filling all space evenly, are imperceptible. If, however, one of the negative-energy electrons is given more than $2mc^2$ of energy, it can be raised into a positive-energy state, and the hole it leaves behind will be perceived as an electron-like particle, though carrying a positive charge. Thus this act of excitation leads to the simultaneous appearance of a pair of particles—an ordinary negative electron and a positively charged but otherwise identical positron. This process was observed in cloud-chamber photographs by Carl David Anderson of the United States in 1932. The reverse process was recognized at the same time; it can be visualized either as an electron and a positron mutually annihilating one another, with all their energy (two lots of rest energy, each mc^2, plus their kinetic energy) being converted into gamma rays (electromagnetic quanta), or as an electron losing all this energy as it drops into the vacant negative-energy state that simulates a positive charge. When an exceptionally energetic cosmic-ray particle enters the Earth's atmosphere, it initiates a chain of such processes in which gamma rays generate electron–positron pairs; these in turn emit gamma rays which, though of lower energy, are still capable of creating more pairs, so that what reaches the Earth's surface is a shower of many millions of electrons and positrons.

Not unnaturally, the suggestion that space was filled to infinite density with unobservable particles was not easily accepted in spite of the obvious successes of the theory. It would have seemed even more outrageous had not other developments already forced theoretical physicists to contemplate abandoning the idea of empty space. Quantum mechanics carries the implication that no oscillatory system can lose all its energy; there must always remain at least a "zero-point energy" amounting to $h\nu/2$ for an oscillator with natural frequency ν (h is Planck's constant). This also seemed to be required for the electromagnetic oscillations constituting radio waves, light, X rays, and gamma rays. Since there is no known limit to the frequency ν, their total zero-point energy density is also infinite; like the negative-energy electron states, it is uniformly distributed throughout space, both inside and outside matter, and presumed to produce no observable effects.

Developments in particle physics. It was at about this moment, say 1930, in the history of the physics of fundamental particles that serious attempts to visualize the processes in terms of everyday notions were abandoned in favour of mathematical formalisms. Instead of seeking modified procedures from which the awkward, unobservable infinities had been banished, the thrust was toward devising prescriptions for calculating what observable processes could occur and how frequently and how quickly they would occur. An empty cavity which would be described by a classical physicist as capable of maintaining electromagnetic waves of various frequencies, ν, and arbitrary amplitude now remains empty (zero-point oscillation being set aside as irrelevant) except insofar as photons, of energy $h\nu$, are excited within it. Certain mathematical operators have the power to convert the description of the assembly of photons into the description of a new assembly, the same as the first except for the addition or removal of one. These are called creation or annihilation operators, and it need not be emphasized that the operations are performed on paper and in no way describe a laboratory operation having the same ultimate effect. They serve, however, to express such physical phenomena as the emission of a photon from an atom when it makes a transition to a state of lower energy. The development of these techniques, especially after their supplementation with the procedure of renormalization (which systematically removes from consideration various infinite energies that naive physical models throw up with embarrassing abundance), has resulted in a rigorously defined procedure that has had dramatic successes in predicting numerical results in close agreement with experiment. It is sufficient to cite the example of the magnetic moment of the electron. According to Dirac's relativistic theory, the electron should possess a magnetic moment whose strength he predicted to be exactly one Bohr magneton ($eh/4\pi m$, or 9.27×10^{-24} joule per tesla). In practice, this has been found to be not quite right, as, for instance, in the experiment of Lamb and Retherford mentioned earlier; more recent determi-

nations give 1.0011596522 Bohr magnetons. Calculations by means of the theory of quantum electrodynamics give 1.0011596525 in impressive agreement.

This account represents the state of the theory in about 1950, when it was still primarily concerned with problems related to the stable fundamental particles, the electron and the proton, and their interaction with electromagnetic fields. Meanwhile, studies of cosmic radiation at high altitudes—those conducted on mountains or involving the use of balloon-borne photographic plates—had revealed the existence of the pi-meson (pion), a particle 273 times as massive as the electron, which disintegrates into the mu-meson (muon), 207 times as massive as the electron, and a neutrino. Each muon in turn disintegrates into an electron and two neutrinos. The pion has been identified with the hypothetical particle postulated in 1935 by the Japanese physicist Yukawa Hideki as the particle that serves to bind protons and neutrons in the nucleus. Many more unstable particles have been discovered in recent years. Some of them, just as in the case of the pion and the muon, are lighter than the proton, but many are more massive. An account of such particles is given in the article SUBATOMIC PARTICLES.

The term particle is firmly embedded in the language of physics, yet a precise definition has become harder as more is learned. When examining the tracks in a cloud-chamber or bubble-chamber photograph, one can hardly suspend disbelief in their having been caused by the passage of a small charged object. However, the combination of particle-like and wavelike properties in quantum mechanics is unlike anything in ordinary experience, and, as soon as one attempts to describe in terms of quantum mechanics the behaviour of a group of identical particles (*e.g.*, the electrons in an atom), the problem of visualizing them in concrete terms becomes still more intractable. And this is before one has even tried to include in the picture the unstable particles or to describe the properties of a stable particle like the proton in relation to quarks. These hypothetical entities, worthy of the name particle to the theoretical physicist, are apparently not to be detected in isolation, nor does the mathematics of their behaviour encourage any picture of the proton as a molecule-like composite body constructed of quarks. Similarly, the theory of the muon is not the theory of an object composed, as the word is normally used, of an electron and two neutrinos. The theory does, however, incorporate such features of particle-like behaviour as will account for the observation of the track of a muon coming to an end and that of an electron starting from the end point. At the heart of all fundamental theories is the concept of countability. If a certain number of particles is known to be present inside a certain space, that number will be found there later, unless some have escaped (in which case they could have been detected and counted) or turned into other particles (in which case the change in composition is precisely defined). It is this property, above all, that allows the idea of particles to be preserved.

Undoubtedly, however, the term is being strained when it is applied to photons that can disappear with nothing to show but thermal energy or be generated without limit by a hot body so long as there is energy available. They are a convenience for discussing the properties of a quantized electromagnetic field, so much so that the condensed-matter physicist refers to the analogous quantized elastic vibrations of a solid as phonons without persuading himself that a solid really consists of an empty box with particle-like phonons running about inside. If, however, one is encouraged by this example to abandon belief in photons as physical particles, it is far from clear why the fundamental particles should be treated as significantly more real, and, if a question mark hangs over the existence of electrons and protons, where does one stand with atoms or molecules? The physics of fundamental particles does indeed pose basic metaphysical questions to which neither philosophy nor physics has answers. Nevertheless, the physicist has confidence that his constructs and the mathematical processes for manipulating them represent a technique for correlating the outcomes of observation and experiment with such precision and over so wide a

Electron–positron pairs

Creation and annihilation operators

Concept of the particle

range of phenomena that he can afford to postpone deeper inquiry into the ultimate reality of the material world.

SIMPLICITY AND COMPLEXITY

The search for fundamental particles and the mathematical formalism with which to describe their motions and interactions has in common with the search for the laws governing gravitational, electromagnetic, and other fields of force the aim of finding the most economical basis from which, in principle, theories of all other material processes may be derived. Some of these processes are simple—a single particle moving in a given field of force, for example—if the term refers to the nature of the system studied and not to the mathematical equipment that may sometimes be brought to bear. A complex process, on the other hand, is typically one in which many interacting particles are involved and for which it is hardly ever possible to proceed to a complete mathematical solution. A computer may be able to follow in detail the movement of thousands of atoms interacting in a specified way, but a wholly successful study along these lines does no more than display on a large scale and at an assimilable speed what nature achieves on its own. Much can be learned from these studies, but, if one is primarily concerned with discovering what will happen in given circumstances, it is frequently quicker and cheaper to do the experiment than to model it on a computer. In any case, computer modeling of quantum mechanical, as distinct from Newtonian, behaviour becomes extremely complicated as soon as more than a few particles are involved.

The art of analyzing complex systems is that of finding the means to extract from theory no more information than one needs. It is normally of no value to discover the speed of a given molecule in a gas at a given moment; it is, however, very valuable to know what fraction of the molecules possess a given speed. The correct answer to this question was found by Maxwell, whose argument was ingenious and plausible. More rigorously, Boltzmann showed that it is possible to proceed from the conservation laws governing molecular encounters to general statements, such as the distribution of velocities, which are largely independent of how the molecules interact. In thus laying the foundations of statistical mechanics, Boltzmann provided an object lesson in how to avoid recourse to the fundamental laws, replacing them with a new set of rules appropriate to highly complex systems. This point is discussed further in *Entropy and disorder* below.

Analyzing complex systems by means of simplified models The example of statistical mechanics is but one of many that together build up a hierarchical structure of simplified models whose function is to make practicable the analysis of systems at various levels of complexity. Ideally, the logical relationship between each successive pair of levels should be established so that the analyst may have confidence that the methods he applies to his special problem are buttressed by the enormous corpus of fact and theory that comprises physical knowledge at all levels. It is not in the nature of the subject for every connection to be proved with mathematical rigour, but, where this is lacking, experiment will frequently indicate what trust may be placed in the intuitive steps of the argument.

For instance, it is out of the question to solve completely the quantum mechanical problem of finding the stationary states in which an atomic nucleus containing perhaps 50 protons or neutrons can exist. Nevertheless, the energy of these states can be measured and models devised in which details of particle position are replaced by averages, such that when the simplified model is treated by the methods of quantum mechanics the measured energy levels emerge from the calculations. Success is attained when the rules for setting up the model are found to give the right result for every nucleus. Similar models had been devised earlier by the English physicist Douglas R. Hartree to describe the cloud of electrons around the nucleus. The increase in computing power made it feasible to add extra details to the model so that it agreed even better with the measured properties of atoms. It is worth noting that when the extranuclear electrons are under consideration it is frequently unnecessary to refer to details of the nucleus, which might just as well be a point charge; even if this is too simplistic,

a small number of extra facts usually suffices. In the same way, when the atoms combine chemically and molecules in a gas or a condensed state interact, most of the details of electronic structure within the atom are irrelevant or can be included in the calculation by introducing a few extra parameters; these are often treated as empirical properties. Thus the degree to which an atom is distorted by an electric field is often a significant factor in its behaviour, and the investigator dealing with the properties of assemblies of atoms may prefer to use the measured value rather than the atomic theorist's calculation of what it should be. However, he knows that enough of these calculations have been successfully carried out for his use of measured values in any specific case to be a time-saver rather than a denial of the validity of his model.

These examples from atomic physics can be multiplied at all levels so that a connected hierarchy exists, ranging from fundamental particles and fields, through atoms and molecules, to gases, liquids, and solids that were studied in detail and reduced to quantitative order well before the rise of atomic theory. Beyond this level lie the realms of the Earth sciences, the planetary systems, the interior of stars, galaxies, and the Cosmos as a whole. And with the interior of stars and the hypothetical early universe, the entire range of models must be brought to bear if one is to understand how the chemical elements were built up or to determine what sort of motions are possible in the unimaginably dense, condensed state of neutron stars.

The following sections make no attempt to explore all aspects and interconnections of complex material systems, but they highlight a few ideas which pervade the field and which indicate the existence of principles that find little place in the fundamental laws yet are the outcome of their operation.

SYMMETRY

The normal behaviour of a gas on cooling is to condense into a liquid and then into a solid, though the liquid phase may be left out if the gas starts at a low enough pressure. The solid phase of a pure substance is usually crystalline, having the atoms or molecules arranged in a regular pattern so that a suitable small sample may define the whole. The unit cell is the smallest block out Concept of the unit cell of which the pattern can be formed by stacking replicas. The checkerboard in Figure 12 illustrates the idea; here the unit cell has been chosen out of many possibilities to contain one white square and one black, dissected into quarters. For crystals, of course, the unit cell is three-dimensional. A very wide variety of arrangements is exhibited by different substances, and it is the great triumph of X-ray crystallography to have provided the means for

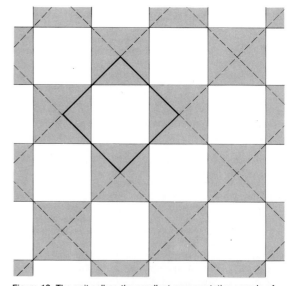

Figure 12: The unit cell as the smallest representative sample of the whole. In the case of this checkerboard, the unit cell consists of one white square, and one shaded square dissected into quarters.

determining experimentally what arrangement is involved in each case.

One may ask whether mathematical techniques exist for deducing the correct result independently of experiment, and the answer is almost always no. An individual sulfur atom, for example, has no features that reflect its preference, in the company of others, for forming rings of eight. This characteristic can only be discovered theoretically by calculating the total energy of different-sized rings and of other patterns and determining after much computation that the ring of eight has the lowest energy of all. Even then the investigator has no assurance that there is no other arrangement which confers still lower energy. In one of the forms taken by solid sulfur, the unit cell contains 128 atoms in a complex of rings. It would be an inspired guess to hit on this fact without the aid of X rays or the expertise of chemists, and mathematics provides no systematic procedure as an alternative to guessing or relying on experiment.

Nevertheless, it may be possible in simpler cases to show that calculations of the energy are in accord with the observed crystal forms. Thus, when silicon is strongly compressed, it passes through a succession of different crystal modifications for each of which the variation with pressure of the energy can be calculated. The pressure at which a given change of crystal form takes place is that at which the energy takes the same value for both modifications involved. As this pressure is reached, one gives way to the other for the possession of the lower energy. The fact that the calculation correctly describes not only the order in which the different forms occur but also the pressures at which the changeovers take place indicates that the physical theory is in good shape; only the power is lacking in the mathematics to predict behaviour from first principles.

The changes in symmetry that occur at the critical points where one modification changes to another are complex examples of a widespread phenomenon for which simple analogues exist. A perfectly straight metal strip, firmly fixed to a base so that it stands perfectly upright, remains straight as an increasing load is placed on its upper end until a critical load is reached. Any further load causes the strip to heel over and assume a bent form, and it only takes a minute disturbance to determine whether it will bend to the left or to the right. The fact that either outcome is equally likely reflects the left–right symmetry

of the arrangement, but once the choice is made the symmetry is broken. The subsequent response to changing load and the small vibrations executed when the strip is struck lightly are characteristic of the new unsymmetrical shape. If one wishes to calculate the behaviour, it is essential to avoid assuming that an arrangement will always remain symmetrical simply because it was initially so. In general, as with the condensation of sulfur atoms or with the crystalline transitions in silicon, the symmetry implicit in the formulation of the theory will be maintained only in the totality of possible solutions, not necessarily in the particular solution that appears in practice. In the case of the condensation of a crystal from individual atoms, the spherical symmetry of each atom tells one no more than that the crystal may be formed equally well with its axis pointing in any direction; and such information provides no help in finding the crystal structure. In general, there is no substitute for experiment. Even with relatively simple systems such as engineering structures, it is all too easy to overlook the possibility of symmetry breaking leading to calamitous failure.

It should not be assumed that the critical behaviour of a loaded strip depends on its being perfectly straight. If the strip is not, it is likely to prefer one direction of bending to the other. As the load is increased, so will the intrinsic bend be exaggerated, and there will be no critical point at which a sudden change occurs. By tilting the base, however, it is possible to compensate for the initial imperfection and to find once more a position where left and right are equally favoured. Then the critical behaviour is restored, and at a certain load the necessity of choice is present as with a perfect strip. The study of this and numerous more complex examples is the province of the

so-called catastrophe theory. A catastrophe, in the special sense used here, is a situation in which a continuously varying input to a system gives rise to a discontinuous change in the response at a critical point. The discontinuities may take many forms, and their character may be sensitive in different ways to small changes in the parameters of the system. Catastrophe theory is the term used to describe the systematic classification, by means of topological mathematics, of these discontinuities. Wide-ranging though the theory may be, it cannot at present include in its scope most of the symmetry-breaking transitions undergone by crystals.

ENTROPY AND DISORDER

As is explained in detail in the article THERMODYNAMICS, the laws of thermodynamics make possible the characterization of a given sample of matter—after it has settled down to equilibrium with all parts at the same temperature—by ascribing numerical measures to a small number of properties (pressure, volume, energy, and so forth). One of these is entropy. As the temperature of the body is raised by adding heat, its entropy as well as its energy is increased. On the other hand, when a volume of gas enclosed in an insulated cylinder is compressed by pushing on the piston, the energy in the gas increases while the entropy stays the same or, usually, increases a little. In atomic terms, the total energy is the sum of all the kinetic and potential energies of the atoms, and the entropy, it is commonly asserted, is a measure of the disorderly state of the constituent atoms. The heating of a crystalline solid until it melts and then vaporizes is a progress from a well-ordered, low-entropy state to a disordered, high-entropy state. The principal deduction from the second law of thermodynamics (or, as some prefer, the actual statement of the law) is that, when an isolated system makes a transition from one state to another, its entropy can never decrease. If a beaker of water with a lump of sodium on a shelf above it is sealed in a thermally insulated container and the sodium is then shaken off the shelf, the system, after a period of great agitation, subsides to a new state in which the beaker contains hot sodium hydroxide solution. The entropy of the resulting state is higher than the initial state, as can be demonstrated quantitatively by suitable measurements.

The idea that a system cannot spontaneously become better ordered but can readily become more disordered, even if left to itself, appeals to one's experience of domestic economy and confers plausibility on the law of increase of entropy. As far as it goes, there is much truth in this naive view of things, but it cannot be pursued beyond this point without a much more precise definition of disorder. Thermodynamic entropy is a numerical measure that can be assigned to a given body by experiment; unless disorder can be defined with equal precision, the relation between the two remains too vague to serve as a basis for deduction. A precise definition is to be found by considering the number, labeled W, of different arrangements that can be taken up by a given collection of atoms, subject to their total energy being fixed. In quantum mechanics, W is the number of different quantum states that are available to the atoms with this total energy (strictly, in a very narrow range of energies). It is so vast for objects of everyday size as to be beyond visualization; for the helium atoms contained in one cubic centimetre of gas at atmospheric pressure and at 0° C the number of different quantum states can be written as 1 followed by 170 million million million zeroes (written out, the zeroes would fill nearly one trillion sets of the *Encyclopædia Britannica*).

The science of statistical mechanics, as founded by the aforementioned Ludwig Boltzmann and J. Willard Gibbs, relates the behaviour of a multitude of atoms to the thermal properties of the material they constitute. Boltzmann and Gibbs, along with Max Planck, established that the entropy, S, as derived through the second law of thermodynamics, is related to W by the formula $S = k \ln W$, where k is the Boltzmann constant (1.380662×10^{-23} joule per kelvin) and $\ln W$ is the natural (Naperian) logarithm of W. By means of this and related formulas it is possible in principle, starting with the quantum mechanics of the constituent atoms, to calculate the measurable thermal properties of the material. Unfortunately, there are rather few systems for which the quantum mechanical problems succumb to mathematical analysis, but among these are gases and many solids, enough to validate the theoretical procedures linking laboratory observations to atomic constitution.

When a gas is thermally isolated and slowly compressed, the individual quantum states change their character and become mixed together, but the total number W does not alter. In this change, called adiabatic, entropy remains constant. On the other hand, if a vessel is divided by a partition, one side of which is filled with gas while the other side is evacuated, piercing the partition to allow the gas to spread throughout the vessel greatly increases the number of states available so that W and the entropy rise. The act of piercing requires little effort and may even happen spontaneously through corrosion. To reverse the process, waiting for the gas to accumulate accidentally on one side and then stopping the leak, would mean waiting for a time compared to which the age of the universe would be imperceptibly short. The chance of finding an observable decrease in entropy for an isolated system can be ruled out.

This does not mean that a part of a system may not decrease in entropy at the expense of at least as great an increase in the rest of the system. Such processes are indeed commonplace but only when the system as a whole is not in thermal equilibrium. Whenever the atmosphere becomes supersaturated with water and condenses into a cloud, the entropy per molecule of water in the droplets is less than it was prior to condensation. The remaining atmosphere is slightly warmed and has a higher entropy. The spontaneous appearance of order is especially obvious when the water vapour condenses into snow crystals. A domestic refrigerator lowers the entropy of its contents while increasing that of its surroundings. Most important of all, the state of nonequilibrium of the Earth irradiated by the much hotter Sun provides an environment in which the cells of plants and animals may build order—*i.e.*, lower their local entropy at the expense of their environment. The Sun provides a motive power that is analogous (though much more complex in detailed operation) to the electric cable connected to the refrigerator. There is no evidence pointing to any ability on the part of living matter to run counter to the principle of increasing (overall) disorder as formulated in the second law of thermodynamics.

Irreversible tendency toward disorder

The irreversible tendency toward disorder provides a sense of direction for time which is absent from space. One may traverse a path between two points in space without feeling that the reverse journey is forbidden by physical laws. The same is not true for time travel, and yet the equations of motion, whether in Newtonian or quantum mechanics, have no such built-in irreversibility. A motion picture of a large number of particles interacting with one another looks equally plausible whether run forward or backward. To illustrate and resolve this paradox it is convenient to return to the example of a gas enclosed in a vessel divided by a pierced partition. This time, however, only 100 atoms are involved (not 3×10^{19} as in one cubic centimetre of helium), and the hole is made so small that atoms pass through only rarely and no more than one at a time. This model is easily simulated on a computer, and Figure 13 shows a typical sequence during which there are 500 transfers of atoms across the partition. The number on one side starts at the mean of 50 and fluctuates randomly while not deviating greatly from the mean. Where the fluctuations are larger than usual, as indicated by the arrows, there is no systematic tendency for their growth to the peak to differ in form from the decay from it. This is in accord with the reversibility of the motions when examined in detail.

If one were to follow the fluctuations for a very long time and single out those rare occasions when a particular number occurred that was considerably greater than 50, say 75, one would find that the next number is more likely to be 74 than 76. Such would be the case because, if there are 75 atoms on one side of the partition, there

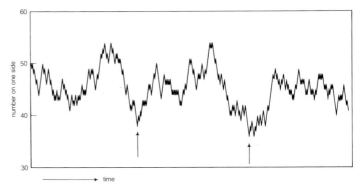

Figure 13: Fluctuations in the number of particles, out of 100, on one side of a perforated partition dividing a box into equal halves (see text).

will be only 25 on the other, and it is three times more likely that one atom will leave the 75 than that one will be gained from the 25. Also, since the detailed motions are reversible, it is three times more likely that the 75 was preceded by a 74 rather than by a 76. In other words, if one finds the system in a state that is far from the mean, it is highly probable that the system has just managed to get there and is on the point of falling back. If the system has momentarily fluctuated into a state of lower entropy, the entropy will be found to increase again immediately.

It might be thought that this argument has already conceded the possibility of entropy decreasing. It has indeed, but only for a system on the minute scale of 100 atoms. The same computation carried out for 3×10^{19} atoms would show that one would have to wait interminably (*i.e.*, enormously longer than the age of the universe) for the number on one side to fluctuate even by as little as one part per million. A physical system as big as the Earth, let alone the entire Galaxy—if set up in thermodynamic equilibrium and given unending time in which to evolve—might eventually have suffered such a huge fluctuation that the condition known today could have come about spontaneously. In that case man would find himself, as he does, in a universe of increasing entropy as the fluctuation recedes. Boltzmann, it seems, was prepared to take this argument seriously on the grounds that sentient creatures could only appear as the aftermath of a large enough fluctuation. What happened during the inconceivably prolonged waiting period is irrelevant. Modern cosmology shows, however, that the universe is ordered on a scale enormously greater than is needed for living creatures to evolve, and Boltzmann's hypothesis is correspondingly rendered improbable in the highest degree. Whatever started the universe in a state from which it could evolve with an increase of entropy, it was not a simple fluctuation from equilibrium. The sensation of time's arrow is thus referred back to the creation of the universe, an act that lies beyond the scrutiny of the physical scientist.

It is possible, however, that in the course of time the universe will suffer "heat death," having attained a condition of maximum entropy, after which tiny fluctuations are all that will happen. If so, these will be reversible, like the graph of Figure 13, and will give no indication of a direction of time. Yet, because this undifferentiated cosmic soup will be devoid of structures necessary for consciousness, the sense of time will in any case have vanished long since.

CHAOS

Many systems can be described in terms of a small number of parameters and behave in a highly predictable manner. Were this not the case, the laws of physics might never have been elucidated. If one maintains the swing of a pendulum by tapping it at regular intervals, say once per swing, it will eventually settle down to a regular oscillation. Now let it be jolted out of its regularity; in due course it will revert to its previous oscillation as if nothing had disturbed it. Systems that respond in this well-behaved manner have been studied extensively and have frequently been taken to define the norm, from which departures are somewhat unusual. It is with such departures that this section is concerned.

An example not unlike the periodically struck pendulum is provided by a ball bouncing repeatedly in a vertical line on a base plate that is caused to vibrate up and down to counteract dissipation and maintain the bounce. With a small but sufficient amplitude of base motion the ball synchronizes with the plate, returning regularly once per cycle of vibration. With larger amplitudes the ball bounces higher but still manages to remain synchronized until eventually this becomes impossible. Two alternatives may then occur: (1) the ball may switch to a new synchronized mode in which it bounces so much higher that it returns only every two, three, or more cycles, or (2) it may become unsynchronized and return at irregular, apparently random, intervals. Yet, the behaviour is not random in the way that raindrops strike a small area of surface at irregular intervals. The arrival of a raindrop allows one to make no prediction of when the next will arrive; the best one can hope for is a statement that there is half a chance that the next will arrive before the lapse of a certain time. By contrast, the bouncing ball is described by a rather simple set of differential equations that can be solved to predict without fail when the next bounce will occur and how fast the ball will be moving on impact, given the time of the last bounce and the speed of that impact. In other words, the system is precisely determinate, yet to the casual observer it is devoid of regularity. Systems that are determinate but irregular in this sense are called chaotic; like so many other scientific terms, this is a technical expression that bears no necessary relation to the word's common usage.

The coexistence of irregularity with strict determinism can be illustrated by an arithmetic example, one that lay behind some of the more fruitful early work in the study of chaos, particularly by the physicist Mitchell J. Feigenbaum following an inspiring exposition by Robert M. May. Suppose one constructs a sequence of numbers starting with an arbitrarily chosen x_0 (between 0 and 1) and writes the next in the sequence, x_1, as $Ax_0(1 - x_0)$; proceeding in the same way to $x_2 = Ax_1(1 - x_1)$, one can continue indefinitely, and the sequence is completely determined by the initial value x_0 and the value chosen for A. Thus, starting from $x_0 = 0.9$ with $A = 2$, the sequence rapidly settles to a constant value: 0.09, 0.18, 0.2952, 0.4161, 0.4859, 0.4996, 0.5000, 0.5000, and so forth.

When A lies between 2 and 3, it also settles to a constant but takes longer to do so. It is when A is increased above 3 that the sequence shows more unexpected features. At first, until A reaches 3.42, the final pattern is an alternation of two numbers, but with further small increments of A it changes to a cycle of 4, followed by 8, 16, and so forth at ever-closer intervals of A. By the time A reaches 3.57, the length of the cycle has grown beyond bounds—it shows no periodicity however long one continues the sequence. This is the most elementary example of chaos, but it is easy to construct other formulas for generating number sequences that can be studied rapidly with the aid of the smallest programmable computer. By such "experimental arithmetic" Feigenbaum found that the transition from regular convergence through cycles of 2, 4, 8, and so forth to chaotic sequences followed strikingly similar courses for all, and he gave an explanation that involved great subtlety of argument and was almost rigorous enough for pure mathematicians.

The chaotic sequence shares with the chaotic bouncing of the ball in the earlier example the property of limited predictability, as distinct from the strong predictability of the periodically driven pendulum and of the regular sequence found when A is less than 3. Just as the pendulum, having been disturbed, eventually settles back to its original routine, so the regular sequence, for a given choice of A, settles to the same final number whatever initial value x_0 may be chosen. By contrast, when A is large enough to generate chaos, the smallest change in x_0 leads eventually to a completely different sequence, and the smallest disturbance to the bouncing ball switches it to a different but equally chaotic pattern. This is illustrated for the number

Determinate yet irregular systems

sequence in Figure 14, where two sequences are plotted (successive points being joined by straight lines) for $A = 3.7$ and x_0 chosen to be 0.9 and 0.9000009, a difference of one part per million. For the first 35 terms the sequences differ by too little to appear on the graph, but a record of the numbers themselves shows them diverging steadily until by the 40th term the sequences are unrelated. Although the sequence is completely determined by the first term, one cannot predict its behaviour for any considerable number of terms without extremely precise knowledge of the first term. The initial divergence of the two sequences is roughly exponential, each pair of terms being different by an amount greater than that of the preceding pair by a roughly constant factor. Put another way, to predict the sequence in this particular case out to n terms, one must know the value of x_0 to better than $n/8$ places of decimals. If this were the record of a chaotic physical system (e.g., the bouncing ball), the initial state would be determined by measurement with an accuracy of perhaps 1 percent (i.e., two decimal places), and prediction would be valueless beyond 16 terms. Different systems, of course, have different measures of their "horizon of predictability," but all chaotic systems share the property that every extra place of decimals in one's knowledge of the starting point only pushes the horizon a small extra distance away. In practical terms, the horizon of predictability is an impassable barrier. Even if it is possible to determine the initial conditions with extremely high precision, every physical system is susceptible to random disturbances from outside that grow exponentially in a chaotic situation until they have swamped any initial prediction. It is highly probable that atmospheric movements, governed by well-defined equations, are in a state of chaos. If so, there can be little hope of extending indefinitely the range of weather forecasting except in the most general terms. There are clearly certain features of climate, such as annual cycles of temperature and rainfall, which are exempt from the ravages of chaos. Other large-scale processes may still allow long-range prediction, but the more detail one asks for in a forecast, the sooner will it lose its validity.

Horizon of predictability

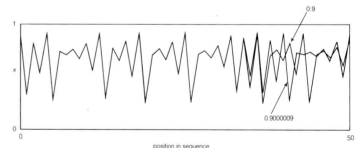

Figure 14: Sensitivity of a chaotic number sequence to initial value, illustrating the horizon of predictability (see text).

Linear systems for which the response to a force is strictly proportional to the magnitude of the force do not show chaotic behaviour. The pendulum, if not too far from the vertical, is a linear system, as are electrical circuits containing resistors that obey Ohm's law or capacitors and inductors for which voltage and current also are proportional. The analysis of linear systems is a well-established technique that plays an important part in the education of a physicist. It is relatively easy to teach, since the range of behaviour exhibited is small and can be encapsulated in a few general rules. Nonlinear systems, on the other hand, are bewilderingly versatile in their modes of behaviour and are, moreover, very commonly unamenable to elegant mathematical analysis. Until large computers became readily available, the natural history of nonlinear systems was little explored and the extraordinary prevalence of chaos unappreciated. To a considerable degree physicists have been persuaded, in their innocence, that predictability is a characteristic of a well-established theoretical structure; given the equations defining a system, it is only a matter of computation to determine how it will behave. However, once it becomes clear how many systems are sufficiently nonlinear to be considered for chaos,

Prevalence of chaos in nonlinear systems

it has to be recognized that prediction may be limited to short stretches set by the horizon of predictability. Full comprehension is not to be achieved by establishing firm fundamentals, important though they are, but must frequently remain a tentative process, a step at a time, with frequent recourse to experiment and observation in the event that prediction and reality have diverged too far.

BIBLIOGRAPHY. ERIC M. ROGERS, *Physics for the Inquiring Mind: The Methods, Nature, and Philosophy of Physical Science* (1960), is especially good on the origins of astronomy and mechanics, with minimal mathematics. Of the many general student texts, the *Berkeley Physics Course,* 5 vol. (1965–71), covering mechanics, electricity and magnetism, waves, quantum physics, and statistical physics; and DAVID HALLIDAY and ROBERT RESNICK, *Fundamentals of Physics,* 3rd ed. (1988), are recommended. *The Feynman Lectures on Physics,* 3 vol. (1963–65), by RICHARD P. FEYNMAN, ROBERT B. LEIGHTON, and MATTHEW SANDS, instructs students and teachers in the whole range of physical concepts, with characteristically revealing insights. See also JEFFERSON HANE WEAVER (ed.), *The World of Physics: A Small Library of the Literature of Physics from Antiquity to the Present,* 3 vol. (1987), an anthology covering the history of the major concepts of physics.

Expositions of more limited scope, reflecting on general principles for the benefit of nonspecialists, include H. BONDI, *Assumption and Myth in Physical Theory* (1967); RICHARD P. FEYNMAN, *The Character of Physical Law* (1965); and J.M. ZIMAN, *Public Knowledge: An Essay Concerning the Social Dimension of Science* (1968). At a more advanced level, M.S. LONGAIR, *Theoretical Concepts in Physics* (1984); and PETER GALISON, *How Experiments End* (1987), illustrate typical research procedures by means of case studies. ERNST MACH, *The Science of Mechanics,* 6th ed. (1974; originally published in German, 9th ed., 1933), is both a detailed history and a classic critique of fundamental assumptions. E.T. WHITTAKER, *A History of the Theories of Aether and Electricity,* vol. 1, *The Classical Theories,* rev. and enlarged ed. (1951, reprinted 1973), is equally detailed but less philosophically oriented.

Special topics in more recent physics are treated by ALBERT EINSTEIN, *Relativity: The Special & the General Theory* (1920; originally published in German, 1917), and many later editions; WOLFGANG RINDLER, *Essential Relativity: Special, General, and Cosmological,* rev. 2nd ed. (1979); STEVEN WEINBERG, *The Discovery of Subatomic Particles* (1983), and *The First Three Minutes: A Modern View of the Origin of the Universe,* updated ed. (1988); NATHAN SPIELBERG and BRYON D. ANDERSON, *Seven Ideas that Shook the Universe* (1985); P.C.W. DAVIES, *The Forces of Nature,* 2nd ed. (1986); A. ZEE, *Fearful Symmetry: The Search for Beauty in Modern Physics* (1986); and TONY HEY and PATRICK WALTERS, *The Quantum Universe* (1987).

The principles of catastrophe theory are presented, without mathematical detail, in V.I. ARNOLD, *Catastrophe Theory,* 2nd rev. and expanded ed. (1986; originally published in Russian, 2nd ed. enlarged, 1983), which is notably scornful of speculative applications. A full treatment is provided in TIM POSTON and IAN STEWART, *Catastrophe Theory and Its Applications* (1978).

Introductions to chaotic processes are found in A.B. PIPPARD, *Response and Stability: An Introduction to the Physical Theory* (1985); and JAMES GLEICK, *Chaos: Making a New Science* (1987). More systematic is J.M.T. THOMPSON and H.B. STEWART, *Nonlinear Dynamics and Chaos: Geometrical Methods for Engineers and Scientists* (1986). Anthologies of influential early papers are BAI-LIN HAO (comp.), *Chaos* (1984); and PREDRAG CVITANOVIĆ (comp.), *Universality in Chaos* (1984).

(Sir A. Brian Pippard)

Science
Year in
Review

Contents

The Year in Science: An Overview

by Robert P. Crease

Science, as British novelist and scientist C.P. Snow reminded us so prominently three decades ago, is a culture as well as a body of technologies and information. Like a culture, it consists of many different kinds of interactions among human beings and between human beings and the world. Also like a culture, there can be many different kinds of perspectives on it. There is, for instance, the perspective of the working scientist who is engaged in pushing forward the knowledge and techniques of a narrowly circumscribed area. Then there is the perspective of the teacher who reads about the advances of working scientists in a wider range of areas and who must synthesize that information for students. Finally, there is the perspective of an outsider who has no interest in becoming a scientist but who is curious about it—like a tourist in a foreign land who has no intention of living in that country but who takes pleasure in seeing its most prominent and public landmarks.

While each such perspective may be valid, each may also produce an entirely different picture. The last year in science is one example. Judged solely by what reached the newspapers, it was not a distinguished period. True, there was the Voyager 2 flyby of Neptune, and the Hubble Space Telescope was finally lifted into orbit after a seven-year delay. For the most part, however, the major science stories involved failures and frauds, deceptions and disagreements. In biology, for instance, the Oversight and Investigations Subcommittee of the U.S. House of Representatives Energy and Commerce Committee conducted a lengthy, controversial, and much-publicized investigation into possible fraud in connection with a paper coauthored by Nobel laureate David Baltimore. DNA (deoxyribonucleic acid) fingerprinting became a widely used tool in criminal investigations by the FBI—but in several court tests late in the year was ruled as insufficiently reliable to be admissible as evidence. And a landmark study conducted in 1987 that claimed to have established a link between manic-depressive illness and a specific gene was shown to be flawed, having been based on a sample that was statistically much less significant than first thought.

ROBERT P. CREASE is an Assistant Professor of Philosophy at the State University of New York, Stony Brook, and Historian at the Brookhaven National Laboratory, Upton, New York.

Other branches of science were embarrassed by similar kinds of stories. In astronomy, evidence for the existence of a bizarre pulsar "discovered" in January 1989—and which made news because it radically upset existing theories about the structure of cosmic explosions—turned out by the end of the year to have been the product of electrical interference between laboratory equipment and a television camera. In meteorology the scientific evidence for global warming—one of the major environmental stories of 1988—came under harsh criticism, as did analyses of nuclear winter. And in physics, who could forget the dramatic announcement of a new form of fusion that gave birth to hopes of revolutionizing energy creation and distribution only to be exposed as at best premature and at worst as a case of self-deception? Hardly any field of science escaped unscathed. One can surely pardon Martha Graham for having commented, in a program distributed during an appearance of her dance company last year, that "even the most brilliant scientific discoveries will in time change and perhaps grow obsolete, as new scientific manifestations emerge. But Art is eternal."

Yet, to paraphrase French writer Antoine de Saint-Exupéry, what is essential is invisible to the public eye. If one were to consider the last year in science not from the perspective of one who seeks landmarks but from the perspective of day-to-day practitioners, the view changes markedly. One then sees a gradual but steady accumulation of understanding about nature and the development of better techniques and practices for engaging with it. Even though this increased ability to know and handle nature might not have culminated, as in previous years, in many dramatic and newsworthy landmarks, it nevertheless continued to grow in important ways. Indeed, if the year was unique in science, its uniqueness was in the size of the gap between the progress of science as viewed by the outsider and that as viewed by the working scientist. Conflicts, errors, and setbacks characterized the year's science from the point of view of those who seek landmarks, but improvements, advances, and even triumphs marked it from the point of view of laboratory researchers. It is interesting to consider three examples of this gap, from the vastly different fields of fusion research, DNA technology, and particle accelerators.

Fusion, hot and cold. The most visible and protracted science story of the year was certainly the flap over cold fusion, allegedly a safe and economical way of tapping nuclear energy. Ever since the atomic nucleus was discovered almost 80 years ago, individuals have dreamed of exploiting the energy it contains. While chemical reactions release energy on the order of electron volts per individual reaction (an electron volt is approximately the amount of energy an electron gains when traversing an ordinary flashlight battery), nuclear reactions release energy on the order of millions of electron volts per reaction. One form of nuclear reaction is fission, in which energy is released when a single atomic nucleus splits into two nuclei; this process is used in conventional nuclear reactors. Another and more efficient reaction, however, is fusion, in which energy is released when two light nuclei are squeezed together; it is the process that powers the Sun. Alas, it is a truth universally acknowledged that it is easier to break things apart than to get them together. Atomic nuclei are positively charged and, therefore, repel each other. Creating nuclear fusion on a large scale would involve heating up a dense swarm of nuclei, called a plasma, to several hundred million degrees—temperatures much hotter than those in the interior of the Sun—and confining it within a magnetic "bottle." Nevertheless, the advantages of fusion over fission as an energy source are such that ever since fusion was first described in detail over 50 years ago, scientists and engineers have hoped to be able to exploit it. The scientific and engineering problems have proven formidable, however. Even though the U.S. has constructed huge facilities and spent $6.1 billion over 35 years, scientists are only now nearing the break-even point—at which more energy comes out than goes in. In the spring of 1989, 37 years after the explosion of the first hydrogen bomb (an uncontrolled fusion reaction), practical fusion energy seemed still to be at least three decades and billions of dollars in the future.

Then, in a sensational news conference on March 23, B. Stanley Pons of the University of Utah and Martin Fleischmann of the University of Southampton, England, announced that they had achieved a shortcut. By passing an electrical current through a solution containing deuterium (an isotope of hydrogen), they had managed to force deuterium nuclei to be absorbed by a palladium electrode. Palladium, like all metals, is a crystal, and once inside it the deuterium atoms were squeezed together between the crystal's interstices. Eventually, Pons and Fleischmann claimed, the deuterium nuclei were crowded in so tightly that they fused, releasing energy in the form of heat. Thus, there was no need to re-create a miniature Sun in the laboratory, no need for the equivalent of a small-scale hydrogen bomb, no need to spend billions of U.S. government dollars on huge, complicated, radiation-producing devices, no need to wait decades. The process was small enough to fit

B. Stanley Pons (left) and Martin Fleischmann display a large-scale model of the bottle in which they claimed in March 1989 to have achieved sustained nuclear fusion reactions.

inside houses and automobiles but, when scaled up, powerful enough to support cities.

It was certainly exciting. For a few weeks the complexities of nuclear physics were being explained in newspapers and magazines and on television. Engineers and businessmen spoke of a new era in energy production; politicians discussed forthcoming geopolitical realignments. As everybody now knows, though, it was not to be. Despite a few initial confirmations, some laboratories had trouble replicating the results; a few that had reported early confirmations later withdrew them. By the end of April, while segments of the chemical community were still optimistic, the overall mood among members of the physics community was skepticism. As more and more laboratories failed to replicate the Utah results, the skeptics triumphed. By July a panel of the U.S. Department of Energy concluded that no persuasive evidence of cold fusion existed. Magazines ran cartoons about achieving fusion by using only room-temperature gin and vermouth, while a prankster marketed a "Cold Fusion Kit" consisting of test tube, electrodes, and Alka-Seltzer. In less than three months the announcement of cold fusion went from epoch-making news to the butt of cruel jokes. Still, the story refused to die. Some scientists continued to pursue the quest for cold fusion, and reports continued to emerge indicating that palladium behaves in mysterious ways when it stores and releases energy. Nevertheless, as of early 1990 no one had been able to describe this process exactly, control it sufficiently to switch it on and off, or demonstrate persuasively that it involves fusion.

The cold fusion extravaganza, however, obscured the slow but real progress that was being made by conventional fusion programs. Progress in such fusion devices is gauged by several parameters. One of the most important of these is β, the ratio of the plasma pressure to the magnetic field pressure in which it is confined. The higher the pressure, the more power can be achieved by a smaller machine; if the pressure is low, the machine may produce power but at a cost too high to be economical. Another important parameter is Q, or the ratio of fusion power produced to the input power; the break-even point, when a reactor creates more power than it uses, can be simply defined as the moment when Q becomes greater than one. Late in 1989 fusion scientists obtained record values for both parameters. At the General Atomics laboratory in San Diego, Calif., scientists achieved a value of 9.3% for β—sufficiently high for an economical fusion reactor. Meanwhile, scientists working at the Joint European Torus in Culham, England (outside of Oxford; a torus is a doughnut-shaped magnetic bottle), obtained a value for Q of between 0.7 and 0.8, tantalizingly close to the break-even value of 1. Next to the dazzling plot developments of the cold fusion story, such developments were too modest to attract the attention of the press. Nevertheless, from the laboratory perspective, they are significant indications of an increased ability to handle plasmas in a way that someday will be required for the operation of fusion energy reactors.

DNA fingerprinting. Disappointed expectations were also the stuff of several front-page stories concerning DNA technology. Near the beginning of 1989 the FBI started to employ a new criminological tool—DNA fingerprinting—that was heralded as the most important advance in forensic science since ordinary fingerprinting. The idea is simple: every human being has a pattern in the DNA of his or her cells that is as unique as that person's fingerprint and that can be "read" from tiny samples of blood, semen, hair, or other tissues. Strands of DNA from the two samples to be compared are cut into specific pieces by a restrictive enzyme, and each is placed at the starting point of a "lane" in a gel covering a flat surface. When an electric field is applied, the fragments of each sample begin to separate and form bands of various lengths in each lane, a process known as electrophoresis. Radioactive probes

and other methods are then used to make the band patterns visible on film; if the two DNA samples were from the same person, the patterns should be identical. Given a reliable enough technology for reading such samples, DNA fingerprinting can be used to make positive identifications or to positively rule out suspects in criminal cases where the evidence includes such samples. DNA fingerprinting was regarded as especially important because blood, semen, hair, or tissue samples are sometimes present in cases where fingerprints are absent, such as in many sex crimes. Following a series of initial tests, the FBI began extensive use of DNA fingerprinting, sending samples to commercial laboratories to perform the readings.

The reliability of such readings was challenged, however, in a series of court tests. In one case that took place in Maine, for instance, a prime suspect in a sexual assault case was released when the DNA profile of his semen failed to match that taken from the victim. A few months later a second suspect—whose physical description was completely unlike that originally provided of the assailant—was put on trial on the basis of a purported matchup between his DNA and that of the semen sample. The trial came to an abrupt halt, however, when the defense lawyer exposed a weakness in the process by which the commercial laboratory had determined the DNA profile, as well as sloppiness in the handling of the data. In a second case that took place in the Bronx, New York City, a judge threw out evidence from the same commercial laboratory that purported to match up the blood of a murder victim with a bloodstain on the suspect's watch.

Nevertheless, in both these cases—and in numerous others where evidence based on DNA fingerprinting has been challenged—the scientific principles behind such fingerprinting have not been doubted. Rather, the disputes have concerned the reliability of the techniques by which such principles have been put into practice. In the Maine case, for example, the commercial laboratory was shown to have run afoul of a phenomenon known as bandshifting—the way that similar DNA fragments may travel at different speeds in their two lanes through the gel and thereby produce different patterns. In other court cases, contamination was thought to have affected the readings. Once technologies become available to reduce or eliminate bandshifting and contamination, there will be no scientific reason why DNA fingerprinting cannot be regarded as a trustworthy tool of criminology. The issue does, however, raise the social problem of how judges and juries (who may have had no scientific training) should decide when a technology is sufficiently reliable to be admitted as evidence and whether the technology has been adequately administered.

Unlike the case of cold fusion, the embarrassments that beset DNA fingerprinting during the past year amounted to the exposure of a hope that was premature rather than a hope falsely raised. That DNA fingerprinting became an issue in criminal proceedings at all testifies to the tremendous strides in biotechnology in recent years; rather than the sign of a failed achievement, the developments of the year were a sign that the pieces of a very remarkable achievement are not yet all in place.

Particle accelerators. A third case of a disappointed expectation that made news concerned the new particle accelerator at the Stanford Linear Accelerator Center (SLAC). Particle accelerators, the basic tools of high-energy physics, boost subatomic particles to high speeds, smash them together, and track the resulting fragments. Over the past 50 years the ability to answer the important questions in high-energy physics generally has gone hand in hand with the development of more powerful particle accelerators. At the beginning of 1989 one key unanswered question concerned the number of families of subatomic particles; three had been discovered, but there was no reason to rule out the possibility of more. The answer bore upon important issues in cosmology and the early structure of the universe.

An answer to this question could be obtained through study of the behavior of a particle known as the Z^0. While the Z^0 was discovered a few years ago at CERN, a laboratory in Geneva, existing accelerators were unable to produce it in sufficient quantities to provide an answer. Two new accelerators, however, held out the promise of doing so: the Large Electron-Positron (LEP) machine at CERN and the Stanford Linear Collider (SLC) at SLAC. The SLC was based on a novel design that collided its particles not by means of beams that continually intersected, as in the LEP, but in tiny segments that had only one chance to intersect with another segment heading in the opposite direction. The SLC was less powerful than LEP but was originally scheduled to become operational a full year and a half earlier—plenty of time to score some discoveries, provided everything went well. The problem of squeezing the particles into tiny enough packages and controlling and aiming them as they moved at speeds close to that of light proved unexpectedly formidable, though, and the SLC experienced serious delays. By the time the problems were solved, its lead over LEP had shrunk to virtually nothing. When in October the two teams announced their preliminary results—three families of particles—the SLAC team had to base its conclusion on a sample of 500 Z^0s, while scientists in Geneva had examined 11,000.

On the surface the episode appeared to be a setback for the SLC and the team of U.S. scientists who had worked on it, but the reality was different. LEP

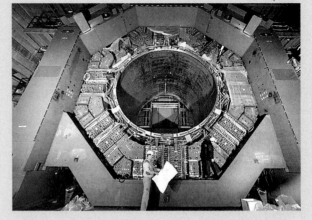

The Mark II detector, a part of the new Stanford Linear Collider at the Stanford (California) Linear Accelerator Center, revealed in April 1989 that the collider had succeeded in producing a Z^0 particle.

was a conventional machine, while the SLC was the prototype of a new accelerator technology. Barring some new and unforeseen development, future particle accelerators after the Superconducting Super Collider will all be based on the principles pioneered in the SLC. The fact that the SLC scientists were able to overcome the difficulties of getting it to work at all was a triumph. Again, what appeared to the public as a setback was from the perspective of the working scientist the crossing of a new frontier.

Multinational science. Even adopting the perspective of the laboratory researcher does not suffice to capture all of the changes taking place in science. During the past several years interactions between the different branches of science have increased as each has incorporated advances that have taken place in others. In the past year, for instance, astronomers began to use computers as tools in scanning for supernovas, archaeologists turned to physicists for help in understanding ancient artifacts, and microbiologists began to call upon mathematicians to assist in understanding the structure of DNA. Still more significantly, however, the scale of the largest scientific projects has grown so enormously that a threshold may have been crossed to a new level of size, complexity, and cost. The culture of science itself, in short, is changing.

Almost 30 years ago physicist Alvin Weinberg coined the phrase "Big Science" to mark a cultural change of his own time between the "Small Science" of previous decades, which had involved mostly investigators working by themselves or in pairs or trios in small university or industry laboratories, and the science of his day, which was beginning to involve groups of dozens of scientists working in nationally funded laboratories. Small Science was typified, perhaps, by the Cavendish Laboratory in

Cambridge, England, a warren of drafty, brick-walled rooms with wooden tables covered with sputtering vacuum pumps and Bunsen burners. The total annual research budget in the late 1800s was about £100, equivalent to a few thousand of today's dollars. The laboratory reached its apex in the 1920s under Ernest Rutherford, a pioneer in the development of nuclear physics. Under Rutherford the budget had inflated to several hundred pounds; still, when someone offered the laboratory a grant of £3,000, he gave the money back because he was shocked by the idea of spending that much on science. Rutherford exemplified scientific leadership of the time. He rarely traveled, and he built all his own equipment; until the third decade of this century, batteries had to be made each morning from scratch. He wore a white coat and worked with one or two assistants assembling complicated little glass-and-metal gizmos. With one of them he discovered that the atom had a nucleus. With another he fired a particle emitted by a bit of radium at some atoms and managed to split a nucleus for the first time.

Rutherford never lived to see the consequences of these achievements, and until the day he died, in 1937, he dismissed as hogwash any suggestion that they would ever have a practical outcome. But not long thereafter, it hardly needs to be recalled, the consequences transformed science. They also transformed modern life. They helped to usher in the cultural change that Weinberg christened "Big Science"—the era when science included collaborations of dozens of scientists, projects requiring months or even a few years to undertake, and machines costing millions of dollars.

Today, however, even the era of Big Science is on the verge of being supplanted by what might be called the era of Multinational Science. Multinational Science might be typified by the LEP experiment headed by Nobel Prize winner Samuel C. C. Ting—possibly the largest single scientific experiment ever performed. Ting won the Nobel Prize in 1976 and spent most of his time after that preparing this single experiment. He amassed a huge international organization to do so; besides several scientific divisions it also has an administrative, an executive, and a financial branch. The organization consists of some 450 Ph.D. physicists and approximately 1,000 supporting technicians and engineers in almost two dozen nations who, in turn, contract to industries and laboratories throughout the world.

The character of Ting's work is a far cry from that of Rutherford. Ting spends the majority of his time traveling to and fro, averting catastrophes, negotiating deals, and smoothing ruffled feathers. He constantly lobbies funding agencies, barters with industrial chiefs, and pleads with government officials for dispensations.

Inevitably, the mere effort to carry off the project has had spin-off effects. Long before the equipment was switched on, the project helped industries to cut costs, increase sales, and open new markets. It caused countries to loosen trade, customs, and employment restrictions. And it enjoined nations with hostile political relations to work together.

Scientific culture. The social, political, and economic impact of Multinational Science makes it all the more imperative that the culture of science be understood. Nevertheless, even as science grows larger and its impact on society stronger, scientific illiteracy has grown. Such illiteracy takes many different forms. One is a simple lack of proficiency in science that in the United States seems to get progressively worse; in 1989 this dismal trend continued, according to the Educational Testing Service, as U.S. teenagers placed last in mathematics and close to last in science in an international study.

Scientific illiteracy also can give rise to openly antiscientific activity, such as the vandalization of a laboratory at the University of Pennsylvania in January 1990. Science plays too important a role in contemporary life for such illiteracy to be maintained, however. "The fear of science is a luxury we cannot afford," wrote Gerald Weissman in a book published in 1990.

Finally, and most ominously, scientific illiteracy is manifested by the lack of a conceptual understanding of science itself. Science tends to be judged by its landmarks—by completed theories or by the creation of products that have socially useful values—rather than by its practice, which may continue for years or decades without culminating in something that is directly useful to or even understandable by the public. This lack of an understanding of the practice of science, in turn, could be damaging to science in quite concrete ways. It would happen if, for instance, public officials were to confuse error and self-deception in science—which, as any working scientist knows, are ordinary consequences of the exploratory nature of the craft—with fraud, which is entirely different. Moreover, misunderstanding the nature of science may lead to misunderstanding the difference between basic and applied research and the different requirements for the management of each.

For this scientific illiteracy to be overcome, it is important that science be recognized as a culture that admits many different perspectives and is not simply a series of landmarks. Last year's landmarks may not have been as dramatic as those of past years. As the following articles reveal, however, the culture of science was just as vital as ever, and it laid the groundwork for activity that in future years will certainly culminate in the creation of significant landmarks.

Anthropology

Developments in anthropology during the past year coincided with major events throughout the world. While ethnic strife was making headlines throughout Europe, Africa, Asia, and the Americas, anthropologists were conducting research on racism and ethnicity on all continents. The work was part of a growing interest in alleviating racial and ethnic problems as well as in advancing knowledge about human relations, the persistence of culture, and the relationship between individuals and their cultures.

In South Africa David Webster, a senior lecturer of social anthropology at the University of the Witwatersrand, was assassinated by terrorists on May 1 because of his concern for justice and his efforts to end apartheid (the government's policy of racial separation). His activism followed earlier ethnographic work on ethnic and tribal relations within South Africa. Such a combination of interest in science and social change was also illustrated by the publication of *South African Keywords: The Uses and Abuses of Political Concepts* (1988), edited by Emile Boonzaier and John Sharp. This book illustrates how the definitions of words such as *community, culture, nation, tribe,* and *ethnic group* have subtly changed in South Africa, depending upon political context. The study of these words in context reveals much about the politics of ethnic relations.

In Germany the use of ethnic studies for political purposes by Adolf Hitler's Nazi regime caused postwar archaeologists and ethnohistorians to avoid the use of certain words and to delay theoretical development in their fields. Instead, scholars limited themselves to a search for factual detail and strict chronology. Six years ago, however, younger scholars in West Germany broke from this tradition, meeting at the town of Unkel. The Unkel Symposium stimulated studies of continuity and discontinuity among European ethnic groups, so that by 1990 generalization and theoretical development were becoming recognized goals in West German archaeology and anthropology, especially in the museums and research commissions. During the past year the young scholars concentrated on the study of how ethnic differences either persist or regularly change.

Eastern Hemisphere. Politics in the Soviet Union also influenced the study of ethnic groups. Marxist thought required that change in ethnicity always be interpreted in terms of social evolution. With the new openness in Soviet society, other theories were now being discussed by ethnographers and anthropologists. At the Institute of Ethnography in Moscow, Valery Tishkov was chosen to succeed Yulian Bromley as director. In addition, the government was encouraging a variety of research techniques that it hoped would provide answers to the problems of

ethnic tensions between Armenians and Azerbaijanis and among smaller groups in the republics of Soviet Central Asia. The emphasis on a practical use for ethnography called for a development in applied anthropology that had been absent in the U.S.S.R.

The new openness to theory was highlighted at a conference in Paris where Soviet anthropologists met with Soviet émigrés and Western scientists in March. Some Soviet representatives continued to insist that history is a science and that various societies represent different levels of an evolutionary continuum. The conference began with an apparent hardening of the differences between Soviets and émigrés, but when a Soviet delegate delivered a paper mocking Stalin's account of evolution, participants realized that the new openness in Soviet society had permeated the Institute of Ethnography. This breakthrough led to discussion of such issues as how Armenians and Azerbaijanis write ethnohistory to justify current political claims; how small, isolated Arctic peoples are creating their own alternative models for future economic development; and, in a major shift of theory, how individual behavior affects collective norms, as among Australian Aborigines. One Soviet participant reported on fieldwork among the Montagnards in Vietnam, reflecting what could be a new development—Soviet research outside the U.S.S.R.

By contrast, Chinese anthropology faced new restrictions following the suppression of student demonstrations in June 1989. Social scientists had led in petitioning the government to listen to student demands. After the crackdown many social scientists were arrested or went into hiding. The building of the Beijing (Peking) Academy of Social Sciences was taken over by the martial law administration, and in early 1990 the state of social science teaching and research in Beijing was unknown.

South Asian ethnicity was analyzed by members of the South Asian Anthropologists' Group meeting at the Institute of Commonwealth Studies in London in September. A major theme of the conference centered on the paradox that as the world has seemed to become a single interconnected system in modern times, increased importance has been attached to dividing up society into ethnic groups. The first day of the conference concentrated on identification by caste and the ways in which the political context influenced such identity; comparisons were also made between the stability of family lineage membership and the flexibility of caste identification. On the second day the focus shifted to the importance of international solidarity of ethnicity as illustrated by the Sikhs since the outbreak of violence between them and the Hindus. A similar growth in solidarity among Muslims was noted after the publication of the controversial book *The Satanic Verses* by Salman Rushdie.

Thousands of Azerbaijanis crowd into Lenin Square in Baku, Azerbaijan, U.S.S.R., on September 7. The rally was one of several in support of a general strike, which resulted from escalating ethnic tensions between Armenians and Azerbaijanis and demands for greater political and economic autonomy.

Among the relatively homogenous Australians, anthropology has emphasized the study of the Aborigines. In recent years special attention had been given to adaptations that these people were making to urban life or to similar adaptations suggesting their acculturation. During the past year, however, the greater focus was placed on relations between the Australian government and the various Aboriginal reserves. One sacred site was returned to a tribe, and others were under consideration. More thought was being given to the likely persistence of Australian Aborigine communities into the future.

Attention to ethnicity in Great Britain has focused on Northern Ireland; it was exemplified during the past year in *Social Anthropology and Public Policy in Northern Ireland*, edited by Hastings Donnan and Graham McFarlane. The study showed how ethnicity shapes perceptions of unemployment applicants in an employment agency, how job seekers use personal networks to seek positions, how family and friends care for the elderly and disabled, and how Protestant shipowners are reluctant to hire Roman Catholic skippers and crews. This research in support of policy-making was in response to governmental pressure to show results from public-sponsored research. The interest in applications of anthropology to public policy was reflected in the invitation to the Society for Applied Anthropology to meet in York in 1990.

Western Hemisphere. In South America during the past year British filmmakers captured the efforts of Indians to preserve their ethnicity when they met in Altamira, Brazil, to protest against outside efforts to seize their traditional homelands. The film *The Kayapo: Out of the Forest* was part of the *Disappearing World* series that portrays the struggle of small,

powerless ethnic groups to protect their land or way of life; it screened in June.

The event depicted in the film took place in February, when Kayapo leaders managed to gather large numbers of unrelated Kayapo and members of other tribes, often hostile to one another, to protest against plans for hydroelectric development that would displace many Indians along the Xingu River in the Amazon region. The Indians finally agreed on a united policy; they were joined by sympathetic outsiders—in particular, those seeking to preserve the rain forest—and explicitly stated their concerns affecting their short-term survival. Brazilian anthropologists joined others working to protect the interests of Indians in Amazonia, but large development agencies, the Brazilian government, and multinational companies combined to advocate damming branches of the Amazon and to locate industry near the hydroelectric generators at the dams.

Such cases of Native Americans being subjected to economic and political demands of the larger society were becoming commonplace. They were regularly documented in *Cultural Survival*, a journal edited by anthropologists in Cambridge, Mass. The journal not only informed the public about peoples threatened with ethnocide but also raised money to help with development and to protect ethnic interests legally, where that was practical. The fall 1989 volume described survival problems of the Miskito, Sumo, and Rama in Nicaragua and Honduras; identification problems for Indians of El Salvador, where they were defined on the basis of poverty rather than cultural tradition; and the struggle for land rights in Panama. Other articles reported some success in protection of rights and improvement of the economy for Caribbean indigenous peoples.

In North America during the past year anthropology focused attention on the ethnic conflict in Arizona, where the Hopi and Navajo disputed the use of what had been common land. A long court case led to the designation of boundaries, and the U.S. government provided funds to relocate the Navajo and Hopi who were living in the joint-use area. During the negotiating process a committee of anthropologists was appointed by the American Anthropological Association to help ameliorate the conflict. The committee urged caution in removing the Hopi and Navajo who refused to relocate; forced removal was likely to result in violence.

This dispute between the Hopi and Navajo was only one of many ethnic conflicts noted by U.S. anthropologists. Interest in race and ethnicity was highlighted in Washington, D.C., where more than 4,500 of the 11,000 members of the American Anthropological Association met in November. Their plenary session was titled "Racism in America: The Divided Society." Panelists included Johnnetta Cole, the first black woman to be president of Spelman College (Atlanta, Ga.), and Niara Sudarkasa, another black woman and president of Lincoln University in Pennsylvania. Others were Carlos Velez-Ibañez (University of Arizona) and Leonard Lieberman (Central Michigan University). They responded to papers given by George Frederickson, a Stanford University historian, and by Derrick Bell of the Harvard University Law School.

The following day was filled by another session on ethnicity, discussing the influence of Vine Deloria, Jr., the Dakota Indian who wrote *Custer Died for Your Sins* 20 years ago. Papers traced the significance of the Deloria family in the study of the Dakota, the influence of Vine Deloria on teaching about American Indians, and especially the effects of the new Native American militancy on anthropological fieldwork. This militancy was an important factor in contemporary efforts to force museums to repatriate skeletal materials of Indian ancestors for burial in their homelands. Eleven states were considering or had passed legislation for repatriation; in 1989 the Nebraska State Historical Society returned more than 200 Native American skeletons to the Pawnee. The Alaska and California legislatures passed resolutions urging the Smithsonian Institution to repatriate skeletal materials requested by tribal descendants. The Smithsonian formulated plans to return much of its collection where materials could be appropriately identified.

The ethnographic collections of the Smithsonian were greatly augmented in May when the Heye Foundation agreed to transfer most of the collection of the Museum of the American Indian in New York City to Washington, D.C., where it was to be housed in a planned National Museum of the American Indian; enabling legislation was passed in November. The Museum of the American Indian had significant Latin-American materials that would supplement the Smithsonian emphasis on North America.

Further concern for ethnic groups was reflected by the American Anthropological Association in creation of a Committee for Anthropology in Predominantly Minority Institutions. This group planned to work to place retired anthropologists in universities or junior colleges where little or no anthropology was taught and where enrollment was largely black, Hispanic, or Native American. The goals of the committee were to offer anthropology to students with limited access to the field and to increase the possibilities that minority students would enter the profession.

—Ernest L. Schusky

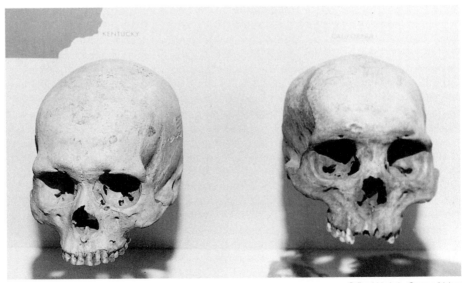

These American Indian skulls are among those in U.S. museums that Native Americans are demanding be returned for burial in their homelands.

Prehistoric art from Western Europe— all approximately 32,000 years old— includes (top left) a wolf's canine tooth, pierced so that it could be worn as a pendant; (top right) a pendant made of soapstone, probably a facsimile of a fossil; and (left) a highly polished woolly mammoth sculpted from a mammoth's ivory tusk, also probably a pendant because of the hole drilled between the front legs.

Archaeology

The final year of the 1980s brought with it several important developments in archaeology from around the world. These included projects and discoveries that shed new light on old problems, some advancements in technology and experimentation, and governmental agreements that may have serious impact on collections from the past.

Earliest European artistic symbols. In Europe new research described the context of the earliest artistic development on the continent, some 35,000 years ago. At that time the first symbolic or artistic objects appear in the archaeological record. Previously, for some 2.5 million years of human prehistory, only utilitarian objects were made.

Randall White of New York University described his research into prehistoric French art and artifacts, most of which were thought to have been lost but had actually been stored for many years in U.S. museums. He began by noting that the appearance of abundant bone beads and pendants and the first known attempts to render nature in two and three dimensions all began about 35,000 years ago. The subsequent period of cultural explosion over large parts of western and eastern Europe is known as the

Aurignacian. For many years the appearance of art and decoration was seen as corresponding with the advent of modern humans, *Homo sapiens sapiens,* in Europe. Now, however, the presence of modern humans has been documented in Africa from about 100,000 years ago and in Europe from about 40,000 years ago. White wanted to know why, after thousands of years with little change in technology, modern humans began to manufacture symbolic and artistic artifacts. He looked to body decoration and the first material images of nature to provide insights into this major cultural turning point.

Several items of interest were noted in the distributions and associations among these kinds of artifacts at European archaeological sites. These included the fact that the earliest beads and pendants were not found in burial contexts, as those dated to about 28,000 years ago were, but in large quantities in various stages of manufacture. Several sites from the 35,000-year-old period were clearly locations of bead and pendant manufacture. Many of these Aurignacian body ornaments were made of materials not found in the general vicinity of the place where they were discovered. This suggests that these early people put great value on these "foreign" materials and that the items were exploited for social dis-

281

play. It is also probable that a few ornament-rich sites were not only manufacturing locations but also places where exchange of valuable items occurred and where social display, possibly associated with status, was important.

Also interesting is the fact that only certain kinds of items were considered valuable. For example, one large class of ornaments comprised pierced animal teeth. When teeth were made into pendants, however, they were usually from carnivores, such as the fox, wolf, hyena, and bear. Perhaps these conferred more likely hunting success on the wearer and also signified an elevated social status.

Sites with abundant body ornaments were also those with the earliest forms of art, such as engraved and painted limestone slabs, mammoth-ivory sculptures, and objects of bone, ivory, antler, and stone with puzzling, but intentional, imagery. White found that many of the latter, previously thought to be marks representing calendrical or other kinds of notations, might in fact be representations of natural markings on shells or animals. The ability to isolate and abstract visual characteristics of natural items and then transfer those to other objects is an evolutionary step of profound significance. By abstracting certain properties of natural objects so that their representations were recognizable to other people, even to modern humans, the Aurignacians were able to convey and store a host of information. By so doing they were also able to make manifest gradations of social status and overall group identities, characteristics that were primarily behavior-related prior to 35,000 years ago. Language must have played a significant role in formulating and perpetuating the transfer and abstraction of natural imagery.

White concluded that the consequences for invention must have been profound after this period. Indeed, the Aurignacian was one of the first great periods of technological and social innovation in all of history. Much of the rapid evolutionary development begun during this period, and continuing today, is based on the forming, manipulating, and sharing of images.

The Mithraic mysteries. Images have played important roles in all religions, and the image of a young man killing a bull in ancient Mediterranean art has been the subject of much speculation by 20th-century archaeologists. The scene is the central icon of a secretive cult known as Mithraism that flourished around the Mediterranean Sea in the centuries near the time of Christ. It began about 100 BC, extended throughout the Mediterranean area in the 3rd century AD, and then succumbed to the expansion of Christianity and the fall of the western Roman Empire late in the 4th century. The bull-slaying, or tauroctony, image is widespread in the region and has long been thought to relate to a particular mythological event. Much energy has been spent in explaining both the antecedents and significance of the tauroctony and its relation to the Mithraic mysteries. David Ulansey of Boston University formulated new hypotheses concerning the image, its relation to the mysteries, and the reasons behind the cult's eclipse by 4th-century Christianity.

Ulansey claimed that, rather than being a representation of mythological events, the tauroctony is actually an astronomical code with strong religious implications. The icon includes an image of Mithras, an adopted early Iranian god; a large bull; and a number of other figures—a dog, a snake, a raven, a scorpion, and sometimes a lion and a cup. While these other figures have often been ignored in past interpretations of the tauroctony, Ulansey argued that they represent the astronomical constellations Taurus, Canis Major, Hydra, Corvus, Scorpio, Leo, and Crater. As such, they represent the key to understanding the image and provide clues to the Mithraic mysteries.

The seven constellations lie along the path of the celestial equator, a projection of the Earth's equator onto the celestial sphere. It is tilted at 23° to the ecliptic, the plane of the Earth's orbit. Extending 9° on either side of the ecliptic is the circle of the zodiac. It is in terms of the zodiac and its importance to ancient astrology that the seven images gain their importance. In antiquity the Earth's location in the center of the universe and the axis of the celestial sphere were believed to be immovable. However, ancient astronomers, beginning with Hipparchus (about 125 BC), also noted that the Earth wobbles on its axis, creating changes in the relative positions of the celestial equator and the ecliptic. This is what causes the precession of the equinoxes, where the position of the Sun in the sky at the equinox moves backward along the ecliptic. The Sun moves through a constellation about every 2,160 years. In 1990 the spring equinox is in Pisces, in 2200 it will be in Aquarius, and during Greco-Roman times it was in Aries. Before about 2000 BC it was in Taurus. All the constellations in the tauroctony except Leo lie on the celestial equator as it would have appeared prior to 2000 BC. Leo marks the Sun's location at the summer solstice of that time. This suggests that the arrangement of constellations in the tauroctony matches the astronomical pattern visible 2,000 years before the advent of Mithraism.

For those holding a view that the Earth was the center of the universe and that all celestial bodies were fixed in relation to all others, the notion that the universe had changed would probably have been shattering. Its meaning to most people of the time, who held that human fates were intimately tied to the stars, would have been doubly significant. It meant, according to Ulansey, that the stable sphere of fixed stars was being upset by a force apparently larger than the cosmos itself. The existence of a powerful, previously unsuspected deity, given the name Mithras, was seen as the force behind the precession.

The tauroctony, then, can be understood as symbolizing the end of the reign of Taurus over the spring equinox and the beginning of the next era. The Sun had already passed through the other constellations in the image, signifying their capitulation to Mithras, the force of the precession. The constellation Perseus, located directly above Taurus, most likely represents Mithras, whose name was changed for several reasons, one of which was the need for secrecy.

Why was secrecy involved in the cult of Mithraic mysteries? There are probably at least two reasons for this. One would be the fear of general public reaction to the complex knowledge. Another would be related to the long period of initiation presumably required for becoming a full member of the cult; it would take a long time to understand the complex astronomical structure underlying the nature of Mithraism.

The secrecy of the group is the key to understanding why it disappeared in the 4th century. Ulansey describes the period around the time of Christ as one of cultural upheaval, in the sense that many local populations were being incorporated into larger, more worldly political bodies. This caused intense pressure on local traditions and religions. Christianity sought to enlighten the world, and it spread rapidly through these groups, bringing a sense of identity, purpose, and significance to generally lower-status people who were thrown into confusion by rapid cultural changes. Mithraism, on the other hand, appealed mostly to intellectuals, merchants, soldiers, and others who were involved in the social order of the Roman Empire. It did not openly seek converts, as did Christianity. As with the power of Mithras, the coming of Jesus was believed to have caused a rupture in the fabric of the cosmos. Both Mithraism and Christianity, along with other religious and philosophical movements of the time, expressed the same desire to identify with a force that could break the boundaries of the universe and provide access to realms outside ordinary experience. The open and outward nature of Christianity allowed it to spread rapidly throughout the Mediterranean world. The secrecy and complexity of Mithraism ensured its decline and disappearance at the end of the western Roman Empire.

The cannibalistic prospector. Archaeological research, in association with forensic anthropology, pathology, and firearms studies, has cast doubt on a Rocky Mountain legend. Folk history in Colorado created a legend around the story of gold prospector Alferd Packer, who was convicted in 1883 of murdering his five companions and eating their flesh during a fierce winter storm in 1874. The legend has it that Packer was wrongly accused and was blamed for the grisly act because he was the only survivor. His story was that another prospector, Shannon Wilson Bell—crazed with hunger—killed and ate the others. Packer claimed he had to kill Bell in self-defense when he himself became the center of Bell's attention upon his return from a hunting trip. Packer then lived through the winter on his companions' remains.

Packer became an icon of folk history after 1901, when a newspaper campaign led the governor of Colorado to release him after only 15 years of his 40-year prison sentence. His legend has grown over the years, to the extent that he is toasted at an annual feast in Boulder, Colo. His bust was displayed in the Colorado state capitol. His fame comes partly from a remark attributed to his sentencing judge, Melville Gerry: "They was sivin Dimmicrats in Hinsdale County, and ye et five of them, God damn ye!"

James Starrs (standing) views two human skeletons excavated from graves in Colorado. Examination of the remains indicated that the two had been killed and butchered by gold prospector Alferd Packer in 1874.

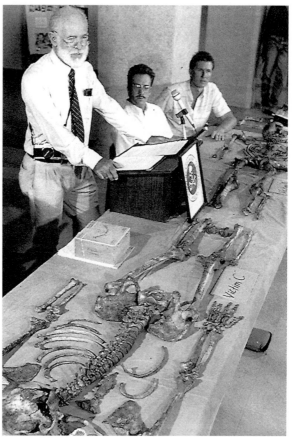

AP/Wide World

In order to find the truth behind the colorful legend, a team of researchers, led by James E. Starrs, law and forensic science professor at George Washington University, Washington, D.C., traveled to Lake City, Colo., to excavate the graves of Packer's five companions. The team also tracked down the origins of Judge Gerry's curse.

Results of the study revealed that Bell was probably killed by surprise, along with the others, and not in self-defense, as Packer had claimed. The skeletal remains showed that the same right-handed ax wielder killed all five prospectors. In addition, all the remains showed evidence of butchering. The researchers concluded that Packer was guilty of the crime and that his story, and subsequent legendary status, is without merit. The curse attributed to Judge Gerry appears to have been made up by a bartender, some time after 1900.

Human colonization of Europe. Archaeologists and paleoanthropologists have long believed that the earliest human remains in Europe were no more than one million years old. It now appears that stone artifacts possibly associated with ancestral humans may be up to 2.5 million years old. These findings were presented by Eugène Bonifay at a 1989 Paris conference of archaeologists, geologists, and paleontologists. Bonifay, from the National Center for Scientific Research in Marseille, brought evidence of simple quartz tools from Saint-Eble, a site at the foot of Mt. Coupet in southern France. These were found in sediments that were well dated by animal fossil remains to between 2.2 million and 2.5 million years ago, extremely old for human-related remains outside of Africa. Major concerns of conference attenders focused on the artifacts themselves and whether they were really made by humans or were merely fortuitous naturally flaked stones.

Many archaeologists and paleoanthropologists were willing to concede that ancestral humans, *Homo erectus*, may have migrated out of Africa possibly as many as 1.5 million years ago, but the extremely old dates of the Saint-Eble site were not supported by dated remains anywhere else in Europe or Asia. Dates older than two million years ago suggest that not *Homo erectus* but the earlier form *Homo habilis* did the migrating. No remains of the latter have ever been found outside of Africa.

Many prominent paleoanthropologists did not even agree that convincing evidence exists for the presence of *Homo erectus* in Europe. The debate continued during the past year, but most researchers gave credit to Bonifay for expanding the discussion, causing reevaluation of other presumed artifact sites with old dates, especially those in southeastern Europe.

Modern images and the reburial issue. A recent movement by Native American rights activists culminated in agreements with institutions holding large collections of prehistoric skeletal material, such as the Smithsonian Institution and the Universities of Minnesota, Nebraska, and South Dakota, as well as Stanford University, to "give back" those remains for ceremonial reburial. No professional archaeologist wanted to hinder the rights of any group of people, but in many of those cases the relationship of the remains to living Native American groups was quite tenuous. In addition, there was now a move to repatriate not only skeletal remains but also other related artifacts.

To many who study the past, the wholesale giveaway of much irreplaceable research material seemed irresponsible. Bones and artifacts are the books of the past. To rebury them is to destroy them, effectively preventing them from helping people understand the past.

—James D. Wilde

See also Feature Article: REMOTE SENSING AND ARCHAEOLOGY.

Architecture and civil engineering

Architecture. Architects continued to examine new ways to create space, express ideas, and respond to issues. Although the past year produced no dramatic aesthetic departures or startling technological breakthroughs, many significant buildings were conceived and built. Additionally, the architectural profession appeared to have paused to assess its current directions and changing priorities as it entered the last decade of the 20th century. It was a year in which nature and social change provided the dramatic impetus for reconsideration of architectural values.

The devastating 1988 earthquake in Soviet Armenia that took approximately 25,000 lives, along with those in San Francisco and Newcastle, Australia, in 1989, focused attention on the intertwined issues of cost-effectiveness, social responsibility, and construction methods. While architects and engineers are capable of designing buildings to withstand most earthquakes and hurricanes, the additional cost, even for the world's most prosperous industrialized countries, often makes earthquake-resistant construction economically unfeasible.

Multiple-dwelling housing, in industrialized and less developed countries alike, has most commonly been constructed with load-supporting, nonreinforced masonry. Load-bearing walls of brick, block, stone, and precast concrete, especially when used to support several floors, are particularly vulnerable to the horizontal shaking forces of an earthquake. The prevalence of such construction is due to the almost universal availability, and relatively low cost, of the material and labor.

Steel-framed glass pyramid, designed by I.M. Pei, serves as the above-ground entrance to the new addition to the Louvre museum in Paris. It generated considerable controversy because of its shape and the materials with which it was built.

Those who ultimately are responsible for the adoption of building codes have been reluctant to create restrictions that could restrain construction, especially in regard to mass housing, where even economically prosperous governments do not have sufficient funds to build so as to meet stringent code requirements. Thus, the stability and safety of housing become a difficult issue of cost-effectiveness. Economic priorities force a choice between building large numbers of inexpensive units (while hoping that an earthquake or high wind will never come to that particular spot) or building disaster-resistant shelter for fewer families. The San Francisco quake demonstrated that this type of trade-off also applies to bridges, expressways, and high-rise structures. However, in terms of the total number of people throughout the world who are put at risk, load-bearing masonry housing dwarfs all other building types in its impact on human life.

The growing number of people who continue to enter the ranks of the homeless is another social problem that affects architecture. As with disaster-resistant housing, this issue also pivots on economic and social priorities. Solutions to the problems of housing the homeless relate far more to the types of projects for which a particular country will allocate its resources than on questions of architectural capacity.

In light of these problems, perhaps the most pressing architectural issue has become that of priorities. Can or should architects compromise quality to better fulfill pressing needs? Is more, quicker, and cheaper best in the long run? How much does society ultimately gain from esoteric nuances of stylistic innovation? What is the real role of architecture?

Perhaps there is a rational balance between the need for economically viable basic shelter and the emotional desire for grand and inspirational spaces.

In conjunction with the 200th anniversary of the French Revolution, several buildings were completed in Paris. Those provoking the strongest responses were a new addition to the Louvre museum, designed by I.M. Pei, and the Arche de la Défense, a 35-story symmetrical office building. The Louvre addition is built almost entirely under the plaza located between the wings of the original Louvre. It is the new above-ground entrance, located within the plaza, that has caused all the furor. The entry is a steel-framed pyramid that measures 38 m (124 ft) on each side and is covered with clear glass. Curved stairs and an elevator lead down to the main levels, which also serve as connections between the Louvre's wings. Both its pyramid form and the metal and glass used to construct it raised questions about the entrance's aesthetic compatibility with the Renaissance original. The result seems to have angered as many as it has pleased.

The Arche de la Défense, designed by the late Danish architect Johan Otto von Spreckelsen, provoked even stronger reactions. Forming a large arch over a boulevard that becomes the Champs Élysées, close to the center of Paris, it is intended to serve as a balance for the Arc de Triomphe. Cable-stayed fabric clouds, constructed within the huge opening, intensified controversy. Both the pyramid and the Arche de la Défense generated vehement responses from the architectural community and general public.

Australia's Sydney Harbor area was revitalized by a major urban redevelopment project. The Sydney Convention Center, designed by John Andrews, along with the Exhibition Center and National Maritime Museum buildings by Philip Cox, are among the most significant architectural works in the approximately 50-ha (225-ac) park.

Among the outstanding new public and civil buildings completed during the year were the 157,500-sq m (1,750,000-sq ft) Convention Center in San Diego, Calif., conceived by a design team led by Arthur Erickson's office. Dallas, Texas, gained an outstanding symphony center, designed by I.M. Pei and Partners, with a glazed cone-shaped lobby. Hong Kong has a new cultural center designed by a team of government architects. Located along the waterfront, the windowless structure has a strong and unusual silhouette.

Several elegant small museums opened in Japan. An exquisitely sensitive museum designed especially for the blind by Hiroshi Naito enriched Tokyo's tradition of providing facilities for the handicapped. Changes in texture, acoustics, and light intensity, perceivable by those with little residual sight, are used to create a variety of intense moods. The museum's collection includes pieces by Rodin, Picasso, and others, which can be touched by visitors. Designed to exhibit "phenomenart" (art work based on natural phenomena interpreted in terms of high

The SAS airline headquarters building near Stockholm, designed by Neils Torp, uses a skylit interior street as its organizing theme.

Courtesy, SAS

technology), the Saibu Gas Museum also displays the tension-rod system used to support its suspended roof and two upper floors, as well as several internal bridges. The Yoh Design Office utilized high-tech techniques to produce a serene mood.

The Canadian Chancery, by Erickson, is a handsome addition to public architecture in Washington, D.C. A modern interpretation of classicism, its strong form frames a large, colonnaded, formally landscaped courtyard and incorporates an open colonnaded rotunda.

As the architectural values of many historic buildings became more respected, the refurbishment and renovation of these older structures was becoming more common. A sophisticated example of the use of high-tech materials within the shell of a venerable structure was Richard Rodgers Partnership's conversion of London's Billingsgate Fishmarket into a sleek banking and trading building.

One of the outstanding office buildings built in the last several years was completed just outside Stockholm. Designed by Neils Torp as the headquarters for the airline SAS, it draws on the concept of the street as its organizing theme. Each of the 1,500 employees enjoys a private daylit room, which shares a common area and kitchen with about 20 other workers. Clusters of these groups form departments. Five major departments, restaurants, meeting rooms, and athletic facilities all in turn relate to a unifying, sunlit, level-changing interior street, which is enriched with trees, waterfalls, bridges, and vistas.

The 1989 International Pritzker Prize, for an entire body of work, was awarded to Frank Gehry for his highly individualistic achievements, which include the Aerospace Museum in Los Angeles and a campus for the Loyola University Law School, also in Los Angeles. The Praemium Imperiale prize, a new international award sponsored by the Japan Art Association, was bestowed upon I.M. Pei in recognition of his worldwide collection of innovative buildings, including the National Gallery in Washington, D.C., and the Bank of China office tower in Hong Kong. The American Institute of Architects awarded its gold medal to Fay Jones in February 1990. His work, noted for its special "Ozark" flavor, is exemplified by Thorncrown Chapel in Eureka Springs, Ark.

Civil engineering. The Suncoast Dome, a cable-roof structure with a clear span of 208 m (688 ft), was completed in St. Petersburg, Fla. It covers an area of 33,500 sq m (372,000 sq ft) and contains a 43,000-seat stadium intended primarily for baseball. Designed by Geiger Engineering, the fabric-covered dome is the world's largest nonair-supported, clear-span roof.

Toronto also boasted a new stadium. Designed by the RAN Consortium, it features a rigid retractable roof that contains both rotating and sliding segments.

The Suncoast Dome, a cable-roof structure in St. Petersburg, Florida, with a clear span of 208 meters (688 feet), covers a 43,000-seat stadium and is the world's largest nonair-supported, clear-span roof.

Stockholm's new Globe Arena, a multipurpose sports and entertainment center, is roofed with a truncated hemispherical space frame 110 m (360 ft) in diameter, 2 m (7 ft) thick, and 85 m (280 ft) high. Designed by Berg Arkitektkontor AB, it claimed to be the world's largest spherical building.

Plans were approved in Chicago for construction of what would become the world's tallest building. To be erected on a small site, the 125-story needle-like structure would soar to a height of 584 m (1,914 ft), 141 m (462 ft) taller than the neighboring Sears Tower, the current record holder.

At 308 m (1,018 ft) the First Interstate World Center was the tallest structure ever built in a seismic-4 (highest-risk) zone. Located in Los Angeles 42 km (26 mi) from the San Andreas Fault, it could sway as much as 1.5 m (5 ft) during an earthquake measuring 8.3 on the Richter scale. The 58-story Two Union Square in Seattle, Wash., became the first major structure to use high-strength concrete, capable of withstanding pressures of 19,000 psi. This was a considerably stronger mix than the 14,000-psi concrete used to construct several Chicago buildings, the prior claimants to the use of the highest-strength concrete for framing a major building.

The Roman Catholic basilica of Our Lady of Peace, nearing completion in the city of Yamoussoukro in Côte d'Ivoire (Ivory Coast), was to be the largest Christian church in the world. Its concrete clad, 90-m (295-ft)-diameter steel dome rose 117 m (387 ft) and enclosed six times the volume of St. Peter's in Rome. Interestingly, only about 15% of the population of Côte d'Ivoire was Roman Catholic, and Yamoussoukro had an approximate population of only 100,000.

Santiago Calatrava's bridge in Barcelona, Spain, and his pedestrian bridge over a highway in Creteil, Paris, spanned the gap between art, architecture, and engineering in a manner not seen since the early 20th-century work of another Spaniard, Antino Gaudi. Calatrava's exotic flowing concrete forms for the Zürich, Switz., railway station are a synthesis of sculptural and engineering skill. The unique quality of his work attracted considerable attention and was exerting a major influence on the architectural and engineering professions.

Despite serious budget overruns work continued on the tunnel under the English Channel. Drilling for the 50-km (31-mi)-long project was proceeding

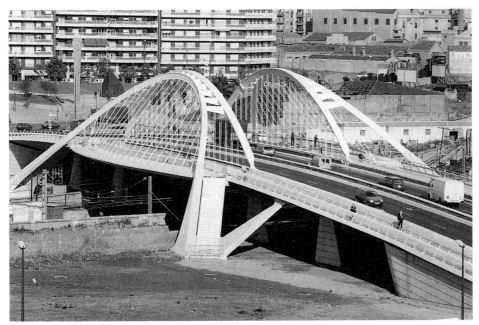

Bridge in Barcelona, Spain, was designed by Santiago Calatrava, whose work was attracting much attention and exerting considerable influence on architects and civil engineers.

at a rate of 4.5 m (14.8 ft) per hour. By 1990 the estimated cost of the project had risen to more than $11.2 billion.

The American Civil Engineering Society bestowed its 1989 Outstanding Achievement Award to the Bullwinkle Project, an offshore oil platform built by Shell Oil Co. At 492 m (1,615 ft), the platform is 49 m (161 ft) taller than the Sears Tower. An Award of Merit was given to the Eklutna Water Project, which was designed to provide treated glacial water for Anchorage, Alaska, and a special citation was awarded for the reerection of an 1898 Waddell A-frame truss bridge in Parkville, Mo.

—David Guise

See also Feature Article: LESSONS FROM THE MASTER BUILDERS.

Astronomy

To many the most exciting astronomical event of the past year was the visit to the planet Neptune and its environs by the U.S. space probe Voyager 2. Among other significant developments, radar imaging was used to reveal the bizarre structure of an asteroid, and a star that may be in the process of becoming a black hole was studied. One of the most distant stars associated with our Galaxy was serendipitously discovered, and a jet emanating from the Galactic center was revealed. New studies of structure in the universe and the uniformity of the cosmic background radiation were announced. And, once again, a new record was established for the most distant object seen in the cosmos.

Solar system. In August 1989, some 12 years and 4.5 billion km (2.8 billion mi) away from Earth, Voyager 2 reached Neptune. The spacecraft returned more than 9,000 images of Neptune and its satellites and rings. In addition, numerous measurements were made of the planet's magnetic field, the plasma around it, and its radio emissions. One of the most interesting features of Voyager's approach was the telecasting of images as they were being received, thus allowing the public to participate in the excitement of the first close-up look at Neptune.

The atmosphere of Neptune provided a number of surprises. A huge persistent storm system, twisting about itself once every 16 days, was discovered. It is about as large as the Earth and was named the Great Dark Spot. It bears considerable similarity to the Great Red Spot of Jupiter. Other features in the atmosphere near the equator move westward relative to the body of Neptune at speeds as great as 325 m per second, making Neptune, along with Saturn, one of the windiest planets in the solar system (1 m per second = 2.2 mph). The thermal energy radiated into space by Neptune implies that there

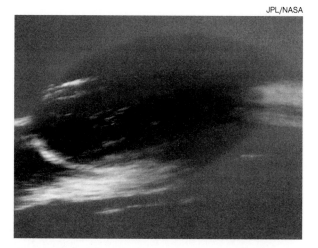

JPL/NASA

Great Dark Spot on the planet Neptune was photographed by Voyager 2. Approximately as large as the Earth, it is a persistent storm system that rotates counterclockwise and twists about itself once every 16 days.

is an internal heat source 2.7 times more powerful than the solar radiation received by the planet. Since the density measured for Neptune is 1.6, it is mostly composed of water ice with a rocky core that is heated by radioactivity. The heat thus generated moves to the planet's surface in a nonuniform way and drives the high winds and atmospheric activity.

While Neptune was known to have a ring system before Voyager began its reconnaissance of the rings, only about 50 stellar occultations had been observed from the Earth, and there were not enough data to describe the rings properly. It was generally accepted from the ground-based observations that Neptune had several narrow ring arcs and not the complete rings associated with Jupiter, Saturn, and Uranus. Voyager, however, discovered that Neptune has two narrow rings and two broad rings with the hint of a possible fifth ring. The known rings are all complete, although the outermost narrow ring does have a pronounced clumping of material into three bright arcs. From measurements of the light-scattering properties of the rings, they appear to consist mostly of dark, microscopic particles. There was no explanation for the stability of the rings since no shepherding satellites like those found for the ring systems of the other planets were discovered.

Voyager 2 discovered that Neptune has a magnetic field with an intensity similar to that of the Earth. The field can be described in terms of a bar magnet that is displaced half a radius from the planet's center and that is inclined 47° to the planet's axis of rotation. In this respect there is considerable similarity to the magnetism of Uranus.

Six new satellites were discovered, all dark chunks of rock ranging from 50 to 400 km in diameter (1 km = 0.62 mi). They all reflect light very poorly, at a rate of only about 6%. The satellite Nereid, discovered from Earth in 1949, was found to have a diameter of only 340 km; however, it reflects light more than twice as well as the newly discovered satellites and also orbits Neptune at nearly five times the distance of the next discovered satellite. Thus, Nereid could be detected from Earth, while the others needed the help of Voyager 2.

Possibly the biggest surprises of the Neptune encounter were provided by Triton, the satellite with a size almost equal to the Earth's moon. It has a density double that of water and, except for the satellites Io and Europa around Jupiter, has the highest density for a satellite of an outer planet. Consequently, it probably has a substantial rocky core with a radius of 1,000 km overlain by an icy mantle of 350 km. Triton has the lowest observed surface temperature, 28 K ($-245°$ C; $-409°$ F), of any natural body in the solar system. A tenuous atmosphere of nitrogen with traces of methane surrounds it, with a surface pressure less than 2% the atmospheric pressure on Earth. Triton's surface appears to be geologically young, much to the surprise of most observers. There are few heavily cratered regions. The impact craters that were seen display sharp rims and bowl-shaped interiors, similar to those seen on other satellites whose crust is thought to be predominantly water ice. There is an extensive area in the equatorial region that has the resemblance of a cantaloupe skin, crisscrossed by ridges that appear to have been formed by erupted material. In contrast to the "cantaloupe terrain," there are plains areas that have large features resembling lakes. In addition, two active geysers were discovered. The plumes above the geysers rise to a height of eight kilometers and appear to be caused by venting nitrogen gas that carries fine, dark particles. The energy to drive the geysers is thought to be either geothermal or localized solar heating.

Voyager 2 is expected to continue to transmit data for the next 25 years. The data will not be images of planets, satellites, and rings but rather measurements of charged particles and the magnetic environment beyond the planets. It is possible that Voyager 2, or the more distant Voyager 1, will be able to report the location where the solar wind finally joins the interstellar medium. And, of course, there is much more work ahead to extract all of the information captured in the tremendous amount of data that the Voyagers returned from Jupiter, Saturn, Uranus, and Neptune. (For additional information *see* Feature Article: THE JOURNEYS OF THE VOYAGERS.)

Steven J. Ostro (Jet Propulsion Laboratory, Pasadena, Calif.), John F. Chandler and Irwin I. Shapiro (Harvard-Smithsonian Center for Astrophysics, Cambridge, Mass.), and Alice A. Hine (Arecibo [P.R.] Observatory) were able to obtain radar images of asteroid 1989 PB, which had been discovered a few months earlier by Eleanor F. Helin of the Jet Propulsion Laboratory. The team had already requested time on the 300-m-diameter radio telescope at Arecibo to make radar measurements of a better known asteroid, not knowing that 1989 PB would pass through the beam of the huge dish on the four days assigned to them. The asteroid proved to be the smallest ever measured by radar, a mere kilometer or so in diameter. The real surprise, however, was its shape; it is a dumbbell with two lobes, each three-quarters of a kilometer in extent, apparently in contact with each other. They were able to measure the distance to the asteroid at 5.7 million km. The observation confirmed earlier predictions of such fused asteroids that had been invoked to explain pairs of impact craters found on the Earth's surface in which the individual craters in the pairs appear to have formed simultaneously.

Stars. Guisa Cayrel de Strobel and Claire Bentolila (Paris Observatory) began searching in the late 1970s for a twin to the Sun, a task that would appear to be easy since the Sun is a very ordinary G2 dwarf star. As of 1990, however, they had not found an identical twin, though they did determine that HD 44594, a fairly bright star visible by telescope in the southern sky, has physical characteristics essentially identical to the Sun. The only significant difference is a slight enrichment in heavy elements in HD 44594 relative to the Sun. The investigators considered this difference significant, however, since a star in the solar neighborhood that is the same age as the Sun but contains more heavy elements implies that the enrichment of heavy elements in the interstellar medium from which the stars were formed began early in the history of the Galaxy. It is interesting to note that the investigators assigned much of their success in identifying HD 44594 as a solar twin to the use of solid-state detectors rather than photographic plates in recording their observational data.

On May 22, 1989, the Japanese Ginga satellite recorded a burst of X-rays that appeared to have originated from a star in the constellation of Cygnus. Brian Marsden, director of the International Astronomical Union's Central Bureau for Astronomical Telegrams (which sent out the announcement of the discovery), noted that the apparent X-ray nova coincided roughly with the visual nova V404 Cygni that had last erupted in 1938. Within days of receiving the telegram, R. Mark Wagner (Ohio State University), Sumner G. Starrfield (Arizona State University), and Angelo Cassatella (European Space Agency) had used the 1.8-m Perkins telescope at Lowell Observatory in Flagstaff, Ariz., and the International Ultraviolet Explorer satellite to confirm that V404 Cygni was in fact having an outburst. The star had increased in brightness a thousandfold over its quiescent state. Wagner, Starrfield, and Cassatella found a 10-minute periodic variation in the star's brightness, implying that the star could be a close binary system. According to the investigators the sudden outburst of X-rays occurred when gas was drawn off from a normal star, compressed and heated to millions of degrees, and fell into an accretion disk flowing around the star's collapsed companion. The random fluctuations seen in the object's brightness arise from clumps in the infalling stream of gas. The rapid changes in high-energy radiation suggest that the companion is a neutron star or, possibly, a black hole. If it is a neutron star, it does not appear that it can remain one for long, since the infalling material will eventually add enough mass to it to make it collapse into a black hole.

Andrew G. Lyne and Jonathan McKenna (University of Manchester), while using the 76-m Lovell radio telescope at the Nuffield Radio Astronomy Laboratories, Jodrell Bank, England, discovered a very different binary pulsar. The system, designated PSR 1820—11, has its pulsar in a highly eccentric orbit with a period of one year around the companion. Most binary pulsars have nearly circular orbits and appear to consist of a neutron star and a white dwarf. There are two other known pulsar binaries with large eccentricities, though smaller than that of PSR 1820—11, that appear to consist of two neutron stars in mutual orbit. They have much shorter orbital periods than one year, however. PSR 1820—11 conforms neither to the previously discovered binary pulsars nor to the accepted evolutionary theory for such systems. Lyne and McKenna speculated that the system they discovered may have formed in an asymmetrical supernova explosion.

Galactic astronomy. Robin Ciardullo and George H. Jacoby (Kitt Peak [Ariz.] National Observatory) and Howard E. Bond (Space Telescope Science Institute, Baltimore, Md.) were using the Canada-France-Hawaii Telescope on Mauna Kea, Hawaii, in a survey to locate planetary nebulae in the Virgo cluster of galaxies, but they ran into difficulties in calibrating the observations photometrically. They traced the difficulty to one of the field stars that they were using in the calibration process; it apparently was variable in brightness. Subsequent observations with telescopes at the Kitt Peak National and Cerro Tololo (Chile) Inter-American observatories confirmed the variability. The observations revealed the star to be an RR Lyrae-type variable with a period of 0.6661 day and a range in brightness (amplitude) of 0.4 magnitude (relative luminance) in visible light. For RR Lyrae variables with similar periods and amplitudes, the absolute brightnesses are known within a range of about 30%. On the basis of this information, the measured apparent brightness of the star places it at a distance of between 155,000 and 180,000 light-years from the center of the Galaxy.

Patricia Reich, Wolfgang Reich, and Yoshiaki Sofue

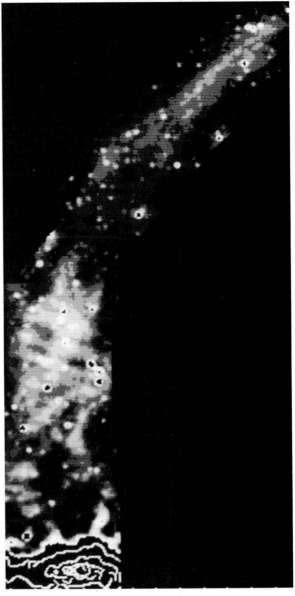

Jet of plasma extends from our Galaxy some 25° across the sky in a direction roughly perpendicular to the Galactic plane. The image was obtained at the 100-meter radio telescope in Effelsberg, West Germany.

The star, not yet given a name or designation, is one of the most distant objects known that is gravitationally bound to the Galaxy. Several other objects have been discovered that may be as distant or more so, but their distances cannot be determined with the same accuracy as can that of the newly found RR Lyrae star. The star may, with further study, prove to be useful in determining the total mass of the Galaxy.

Jets of plasma extending thousands of light-years from the centers of many galaxies have been found through the use of radio-wavelength radiation. It now appears that our Galaxy also has a jet, according to observations made at a wavelength of 21.3 cm by Yoshiaki Sofue (University of Tokyo) and Wolfgang and Patricia Reich (Max Planck Institute for Radio Astronomy, Bonn, West Germany), using the Effelsberg 100-m dish in West Germany. The wavelength in which the observations were made was selected to help discriminate against diffuse background radiation from the Galaxy. The jet extends some 25° across the sky in a direction roughly perpendicular to the Galactic plane and can be traced to within 2° of the direction to the Galactic center.

The observers considered two possible explanations for the apparent jet. It could be an old supernova remnant that happens to lie in the direction of the Galactic center; however, they could find no evidence of the expected optical counterpart on the Palomar Sky Survey charts of the region. In addition, the jet did not display the ridge structure on its outward edge that would be present in an expanding supernova shell. Instead, the researchers concluded that the jet was coming from the Galactic center. If that is, in fact, the case, the jet is roughly 25,000 light-years from the Earth and must be 13,000 light-years long and 1,000 light-years wide to cover as much of the sky as it does. The researchers postulated that the jet may be a high-energy plasma beam ejected from the Galactic center or a "magnetic tornado" produced by differences in the rotation of the disk and halo of the Galaxy in which ionized gas is trapped and ejected outward from the center.

Extragalactic astronomy. There appear to be many different categories of active galactic nuclei, including quasars, radio galaxies, Seyfert galaxies, and others. It has been suggested that except for the level of energy emitted, these seemingly diverse objects may be fundamentally similar and that their observed differences arise because they do not radiate their energies equally in all directions. The differences in their appearances could then result from the directions in which they are viewed. In particular, it has been suggested that Seyfert 2 galaxies, which are characterized by so-called narrow-line emission features, are the same as Seyfert 1 galaxies, which display the so-called broad-line emission features, but that Seyfert 2 galaxies are viewed from directions in which obscuring materials along the line of sight hide the broad-line emitting regions.

Observations of NGC 5252, a Seyfert 2 galaxy in the constellation of Virgo, made by Clive Tadhunter (Royal Greenwich Observatory, Cambridge, England) and Zlatan Tsvetanov (European Southern Observatory, Chile) strongly supported these conjectures. Narrow-band images were obtained of the galaxy in the light of doubly ionized oxygen. The images revealed two sharply defined cones of ionizing radiation that are marked by a series of glowing gas shells that extend to a distance of more than 100,000 light-years on either side of the center of the galaxy. The radiation that is ionizing the glowing gas revealed in the images is obviously not being emitted uniformly in all directions. Images of the galaxy in continuum light, however, reveal the smooth contours and bright central region of a typical S0 galaxy. (Continuum light is light at any wavelength not in an emission or absorption line; an S0 galaxy is one with a shape appropriate to the bulge and disk of a spiral galaxy but without spiral arms.) The axis of symmetry (imaginary line about which a geometric figure is symmetric) of the continuum image is misaligned with respect to the axis of the conical structure seen in the narrow-band image by roughly 30°.

In an effort to probe the central regions of the galaxy, a map was constructed using the ratio of the brightness of doubly ionized oxygen light to hydrogen light seen in the galaxy. The map shows a dark band passing through the center of the galaxy and lying perpendicular to the symmetry axis of the diverging cones. Tadhunter and Tsvetanov proposed that this band marks a disk or ring of obscuring material that collimates (renders parallel to a certain line or direction) the escaping ionizing radiation by permitting it to leave in the two oppositely directed cones. They concluded that their narrow-band images of NGC 5252 support the belief that orientation effects play an important role in the appearances of active galaxies.

Margaret J. Geller and John P. Huchra (Harvard-Smithsonian Center for Astrophysics) published results from their study of the three-dimensional dis-

Image of the Seyfert 2 galaxy NGC 5252 was obtained in the light of doubly ionized oxygen by the 3.6-meter telescope of the European Southern Observatory at La Silla, Chile.

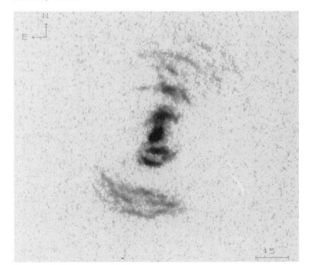

Margaret Geller and John Huchra, Harvard-Smithsonian Center for Astrophysics

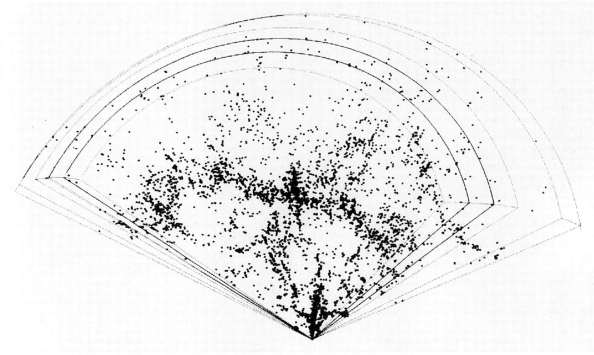

The "Great Wall" of galaxies, the largest coherent structure ever seen in the universe, is at least 500 million light-years wide and contains thousands of galaxies.

tribution of galaxies in space. They pointed out that there have been more than 30,000 galaxies for which good red shifts have been determined by themselves and by others. This three-dimensional mapping covered about 0.00001 of the volume of the visible universe, or, as they put it, an amount about equivalent to the fraction of the Earth covered by the state of Rhode Island. Eventually their survey was to include 15,000 galaxies, but from the more than 10,000 already measured they were able to recognize unexpected structure in the universe. They found the largest coherent structure yet in the universe—a "Great Wall" of galaxies at least 500 million light-years wide containing thousands of galaxies in what can be described as a crumpled membrane stretching halfway across the sky from the vantage point of the Earth. Features on such a grand scale pose large problems for current theories that attempt to describe how galaxies and clusters of galaxies formed. For example, the Great Wall appears to be simply too large and massive, possibly the equivalent of 20 quadrillion solar masses, to have formed from the mutual gravitational attraction between its members operating over the lifetime of the universe.

Researchers from the California Institute of Technology announced the results of their measurements of the cosmic background radiation at a wavelength of 1.5 cm using the 40-m radio telescope at the Owens Valley (Calif.) Radio Observatory between 1984 and 1987. They were looking specifically for differences in temperature of the 2.7 K ($-270°$ C; $-454°$ F) background radiation in 24 patches of sky, each approximately two arc minutes across. They could find no variations in temperature greater than 0.000046 K. This implies that the early universe near the time of the Big Bang was extremely uniform, possibly too uniform to have supplied the clumping that appears to be necessary to explain the formation of the large accumulations of galaxies like those seen in the Great Wall. There appears to be much work to be done to explain how the universe reached its present state from its early beginnings.

The limit of the observable universe was increased by at least 10% with the announcement by Donald P. Schneider (Institute for Advanced Study, Princeton, N.J.), Maarten Schmidt (California Institute of Technology), and James E. Gunn (Princeton University) of a red shift of 4.73 for the quasar PC 1158+4635 in the constellation Ursa Major. The previous record for a large red shift was 4.43. The distance to the quasar cannot be given with assurance because of uncertainties still existing in the distance scale of the universe, but a value between 6 billion and 16 billion light-years would be consistent with a number of current cosmological models.

—W.M. Protheroe

See also Institutions of Science article: THE SPACE TELESCOPE SCIENCE INSTITUTE.

Chemistry

Excitement over the prospect of cheap, abundant energy waxed and waned during the past year as chemists struggled to explain observations purportedly revealing the attainment of nuclear fusion in a simple laboratory apparatus at room temperature. Researchers made significant gains in understanding and applying the properties of spongelike crystalline compounds known as zeolites, assembled the largest single molecule ever made in the laboratory, created an electronic device called a tunnel diode from only a few atoms, squeezed a sample of hydrogen to a semimetallic state, and developed a method for liberating hydrogen from seawater using only sunlight as an energy source.

Inorganic chemistry

The earliest materials worked by human beings were of animal, mineral, or vegetable origin. Examples include animal hair and skins; stone, ceramics, metals, and glass; and wood and plant fiber. Whereas metallurgy remains perhaps the most fundamental materials science of the industrialized world, of increasing importance since the mid-20th century has been the design and synthesis of largely organic substances that mimic and improve upon materials of animal and vegetable origin. Two examples are the host of synthetic fibers that find applications ranging from fishing line to carpet and the countless plastics used in virtually every human endeavor, replacing glass, metal, and even wood in certain applications.

Modern materials science has been driven by several technological advances and the concomitant demands for new materials with heretofore unattainable properties. Advanced technology requires materials that retain their integrity—strength, dimensional stability, and chemical identity—under severe conditions; for example, the extreme temperatures in nuclear reactors and heat engines, the cold and high vacuum of space, and the corrosive environment under the sea or within a reactor cooling circuit. The search for better semiconductors, high-temperature superconductors, light-emitting diodes, solid-state lasers, and other materials and devices has spurred materials research at the molecular level. Concurrently the theoretical description of chemical and physical phenomena has provided a framework within which theoreticians and experimentalists challenge the frontiers of knowledge.

Familiar devices give evidence of the productivity of materials scientists, and no one needs reminders of the value of plastics, synthetic fibers, and high-performance metals. On the other hand, when one thinks of nonmetallic inorganic materials, what often comes to mind is stone—limestone building blocks

from Indiana, marble from Italy, or gemstones from around the world. With the exception of gemstones, it may be difficult to understand the wish to synthesize such materials. Nevertheless, many of the products and processes that distinguish the last quarter of the 20th century from all of recorded history have resulted from advances in inorganic materials.

This article will explore aspects of several classes of inorganic materials and their importance to science and technology through and beyond the end of the 20th century.

Zeolites. Zeolites in the form of naturally occurring minerals have been known for more than two centuries. Natural zeolites effervesce when heated, a consequence of the loss of water from their characteristic hollow molecular structures. If the zeolite is not heated too strongly, the process is reversible, and the mineral will absorb moisture from the air at ordinary temperatures and release moisture when heated, like a molecular sponge. Natural zeolites also have the ability to absorb selectively some "guest" molecules (small ones such as hydrogen sulfide, H_2S) and allow others to pass freely through or around the structure (hydrocarbon fuels, for example). For this reason zeolites are often described as molecular sieves.

Zeolites can also serve as "hosts" for any of a number of chemical reactants, including protons (hydrogen nuclei), small molecules, and catalytically active heavy metals. Zeolites so "activated" have become a cornerstone in the heterogeneous catalytic reactions fundamental to petroleum refining and to the production of many of the starting materials for the synthetic polymer industry.

Zeolites are aluminosilicates and formally can be described by the formula
$$M^{n+}[(AlO_2)_n(SiO_2)_m]^{n-} \cdot xH_2O,$$
in which M is a generalized metal atom, Al is aluminum, Si is silicon, O is oxygen, and H_2O is loosely bound water. In these minerals some of the SiO_4^{4-} tetrahedra of a pure silicate have been replaced by AlO_4^{5-} tetrahedra. Oxygen atoms are shared between silicon atoms or between silicon and aluminum atoms to provide four nearest neighbor oxygens for each silicon or aluminum. The basic building block of the zeolite crystalline lattice is, therefore, a tetrahedron centered on a silicon or aluminum atom. Twenty-four tetrahedral units aggregate to form the so-called sodalite cage, which may be envisioned as an octahedron with each apex removed to leave a square face. In the natural zeolite known as sodalite, these cages are joined at the square faces to form large arrays. In other zeolite minerals and synthetic zeolites, the sodalite cages are joined, through bridges of tetrahedral units, at the square or hexagonal faces, or both. Because an aluminum atom covalently bonded to four oxygens possesses one more donated electron

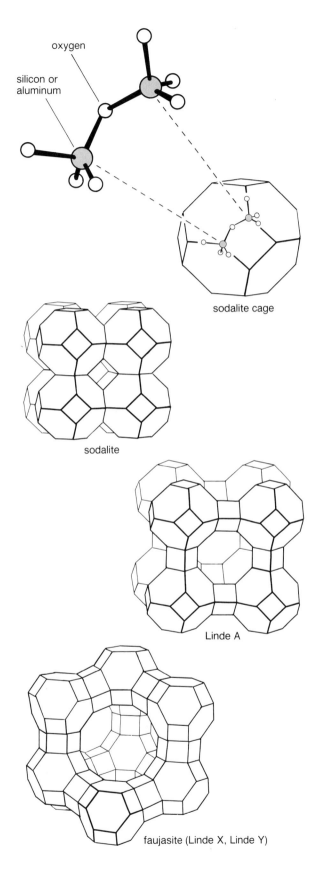

oxygen

silicon or
aluminum

sodalite cage

sodalite

Linde A

faujasite (Linde X, Linde Y)

than its nuclear charge can neutralize, the zeolite framework is an anionic (negatively charged ionic) structure. Consequently, positive charges, usually in the form of metallic cations (positively charged ions; M^{n+} in the general formula), must be present to preserve electrical neutrality.

The useful properties of natural zeolites have encouraged significant research into the synthesis and properties of zeolite analogues. The synthesis is not particularly difficult since the starting material is an alkaline aqueous solution of silica (sand) and aluminum oxide. The reaction is most readily accomplished at high temperature and pressure. Variations in the details of the syntheses produce similar materials having dramatically different properties, the differences being related to the sizes and shapes of the voids within the crystal structure. Recent research has progressed primarily along two paths: the design and synthesis of zeolite structures with internal cavities tailored for specific guest molecules, and studies devoted to a better understanding of the relationships between the zeolite host and activators such as heavy metals and small molecules.

In the early 1960s it was discovered that the addition of an appropriately sized and shaped "template" cation—usually a quaternary ammonium ion (derivatives of the NH_4^+ ion in which the four hydrogens are replaced by organic groups)—to the synthetic reaction mixture will produce a zeolite with internal cavities that accommodate that cation. Moreover, when large template cations with low charge density are used, the results are a decrease in the aluminum content of the product and thus a lowered net negative charge on the aluminosilicate structure. These low-aluminum synthetic zeolites are essentially hydrophobic (water-avoiding) and have enhanced affinities for hydrocarbon molecules.

Two observations enter into the choice of an appropriate size and shape of a template molecule for zeolite synthesis. First, scientists have an increased understanding of the shapes of molecules gained through spectroscopic and crystallographic studies and, to an increasing extent, through computer-based molecular-modeling techniques. Second, many of the template molecules and ions crystallize as hydrates in which the incorporated water molecules assume the geometry that the template would assume if freed from the constraints of the rigid zeolite crystal.

Basic unit of the zeolite crystal lattice is a tetrahedron centered on a silicon or aluminum atom and having oxygen-atom vertexes (top, two units sharing an oxygen are shown). A sodalite cage comprises 24 such units, whereas the structure of the natural zeolite sodalite consists of sodalite cages joined at the square faces. Bridges of tetrahedral units connect sodalite cages to form certain other zeolites, such as the synthetic Linde A, X, and Y, and the mineral faujasite.

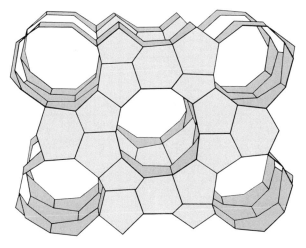

ZSM-5

ZSM-5, marked by large 10-sided cavities, was the first new zeolite to be synthesized by the use of a quaternary ammonium ion as a template. Use of template molecules to guide the structure of the zeolite forming around them gives control over composition and cavity size and shape.

Several techniques are available for determining the sizes and shapes of molecules. X-ray diffraction, often regarded as the ultimate proof of structure, suffers from several limitations when applied to zeolites. First, the unit-cell—one three-dimensional, structurally unique unit—of a zeolite is large. The crystallographic problems associated with zeolites are comparable to those encountered in determining the structures of proteins. Second, the X-ray scattering of silicon atoms and aluminum atoms is almost identical, making it impossible to distinguish between the distribution of these atoms crystallographically. Finally, it is difficult to obtain zeolite crystals appropriate for crystallographic study.

In an effort to overcome these difficulties, C.A. Fyfe and his associates at the University of British Columbia in 1983 used solid-state nuclear magnetic resonance (NMR) spectroscopy to probe the structure of zeolites. Their high-resolution NMR studies of silicon-29 and aluminum-27, taken together, provided substantial insight into local environments within the zeolite cage and made it possible to see interactions between silicon and aluminum atoms and between either silicon or aluminum and an adsorbed molecule. More recently Michael Anderson and Jacek Klinowski of the University of Cambridge applied these techniques to observe the reactions of guest molecules within a zeolite structure. Computer-based molecular-modeling techniques were an integral part of these studies.

Among the theoretical models relating zeolite structure to chemical reactivity, G.O. Brunner and W.M. Meier of the Swiss Federal Institute of Tech-

nology, Zürich, proposed a framework density parameter to describe zeolite structures. Framework density is the number of tetrahedral atoms (aluminum or silicon) per 100 cubic nanometers (a nanometer is a billionth of a meter), ranging from 12.5 to 20.2 for known zeolites and zeolite-type materials. Since the minimum framework density increases with the size of the smallest ring in the tetrahedral networks, there is a relationship between cavity size and framework density. This model is applicable to the choice of template molecules for site-selective zeolite synthesis.

The second major observation relating to the choice of appropriate template molecules had its origins in the extensive structural studies of organic hydrates undertaken by George A. Jeffrey at the University of Pittsburgh, Pa., in the 1960s. In the case of many organic hydrates, a small molecule, frequently a gas at ordinary temperatures and pressures, may be induced to crystallize from aqueous solutions with 20 or more water molecules. The resulting structure is surprisingly similar to that of a zeolite cavity. Unlike organic molecules entrained in a zeolite crystal, the hydrated molecule crystallizes with a "best-fit" arrangement of water molecules, indicative of its preferred cavity size and shape. The structures of organic hydrates, therefore, suggest choices of template cations for site-selective zeolite synthesis.

During the past year a tailor-made zeolite cavity was used as a workbench for the study of small molecules. Galen D. Stucky and his collaborators at the University of California at Santa Barbara and at the Du Pont Co., Wilmington, Del., adopted zeolites for the study of nano-sized clusters. Nano-sized clusters—crystals having nanometer-scale dimensions and containing a few hundred atoms or so—have unusual electronic and optical properties. Such properties differ from those of corresponding macroscopic crystals (those visible to the unaided

Structures show two ways that water molecules organize around an isopropylamine molecule in the crystallization of the hydrate. Such cages are similar to zeolite cavities and thus have helped guide the choices of template molecules for the synthesis of zeolites with desired properties.

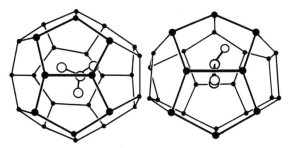

two structures for isopropylamine · 10H$_2$O

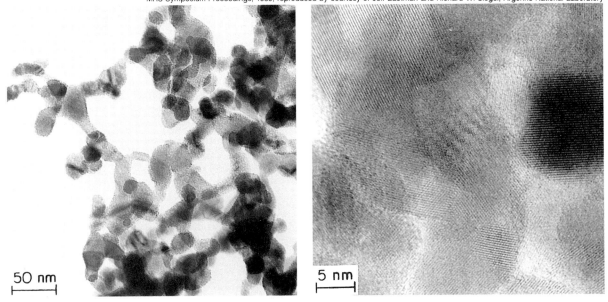

From *Multicomponent Ultrafine Microstructures*, L.E. McCandlish *et al.*, vol. 132, MRS Symposium Proceedings, 1989; reproduced by courtesy of Jeff Eastman and Richard W. Siegel, Argonne National Laboratory

50 nm

5 nm

Transmission electron micrographs show nano-sized particles of titanium dioxide (TiO₂) before (left) and after (right) high-pressure compacting at room temperature and sintering for 30 minutes at 500° C (930° F), which is several hundred degrees lower than the temperature employed to form useful bulk materials from conventionally prepared TiO₂ powders.

eye) and from those of isolated molecules or small ionic clusters in the gas phase.

It had been known for some time that the properties of nano-sized clusters in solution are markedly different from those of macroscopic crystals. Many nano-sized particles luminesce; *i.e.*, reradiate absorbed radiation, usually at an energy lower than that of the absorbed light. Nano-sized particles also exhibit unique size- and structure-dependent light-absorption profiles. These peculiar properties may come from the inability of small atomic assemblies to rid themselves of absorbed radiation through the vibrational mechanisms available to larger crystals. The band structure of these materials ultimately controls their usefulness as electronic or electro-optical materials. The manipulation of absorbed radiation by embedded clusters also suggests that these materials may find use as photocatalysts (materials whose catalytic properties are activated by exposure to light).

Stucky's group implanted nano-sized clusters of several semiconducting compounds in zeolites. Unlike studies in solution, which are complicated by a range of cluster sizes and the instability of the cluster with respect to temperature or time, the size and spatial distribution of zeolite-embedded clusters are controlled by the host lattice. Consequently, zeolite-embedded clusters were providing extraordinary experimental and theoretical insight into the development of the band structure as a function of crystal size. (See *1987 Yearbook of Science and the Future* Feature Article: Zeolites: Solid Service from Hollow Crystals.)

Ceramics. Like zeolites, ceramics are largely aluminosilicate structures. The porous structure that gives zeolites their value, however, is the source of the structural limitation of ceramic materials. In ceramic materials mechanical strength, particularly tensile strength (the ability to resist being pulled apart), is proportional to the density. Voids, therefore, must be eliminated in the synthesis of high-performance engineering ceramics. To use the terms of Brunner and Meier, zeolites have a low framework density, and high-performance ceramics have a high framework density.

Although ceramics can be made from the same simple materials used in zeolite synthesis, the technology for synthesizing and fabricating high-performance ceramics is significantly different from familiar clay-pot techniques. Typically, the chemical components of the ceramic are carefully ground and mixed with little, if any, carrier. Fabrication is accomplished at high temperature and pressure; the precursor is sintered—a solid-state reaction that rearranges the chemical bonds between particles—at temperatures as high as 1,000° C (1,830° F). Recent research at Argonne (Ill.) National Laboratory showed that nano-sized clusters can be fabricated into superior materials at lower energy cost than can the more common micron-sized particles (a micron, or micrometer, is a millionth of a meter).

One driving force for the development of ceramic materials and of technologies for fabricating high-performance ceramics is the continuing evolution of high-temperature superconductors, mixed metal oxide materials that lose all electrical resistance at temperatures above the boiling point of liquid nitrogen (77 K, or −321° F). By 1990 the chemical composition of high-temperature superconducting materials was reasonably well understood, though the mechanism by which superconductivity operates at such temperatures was still debated. Chemically and mechanically, high-temperature superconductors bear a much closer resemblance to the material of flower pots than that of conventional metallic conductors. There was progress, also at Argonne National Laboratory, in fabricating useful superconducting forms such as coils by sintering the superconductor precursor on a silver substrate. Nevertheless, practical application of these materials appeared to depend on ceramic-based technologies.

Diamond thin films. Diamond, one of the allotropes (different forms) of carbon, has unique optical, thermal, and electronic properties in addition to its well-known mechanical properties. The diamond crystal lattice is common to carbon, silicon, germanium, and tin. Of these elements, silicon and germanium have long been used in semiconductor devices because of the convenient band gap and the relative ease with which these materials can be worked. Silicon's electronic properties allow semiconductor devices made of the element to handle greater currents than can germanium devices, and the electronic properties of diamond suggest that it will be an even better material for very-high-current solid-state electronic devices.

The manufacture of solid-state devices involves a sequence of chemical steps in which, typically, chemical precursors for the solid material are introduced in the gas phase and decomposed in the presence of a suitable substrate to form the circuit elements. These processes are known generically as chemical vapor deposition (CVD) techniques. The use of diamond in solid-state electronic devices, therefore, is dependent on technology for manipulating diamond precursors in the gas phase.

Although the best known processes for diamond synthesis involve high temperatures and high pressures acting on a solid precursor, a series of breakthroughs during the 1980s established that diamond can be synthesized via a gas-phase reaction. Current experimental research focuses on the thermal or microwave-induced chemical decomposition of an appropriate hydrocarbon in an excess of hydrogen. A plasma (a mixture of electrons, ions, and excited neutral atoms) is generated at a temperature of about 5,000° C (9,000° F), and a thin film of polycrystalline diamond deposits from the plasma on a substrate maintained typically at about 900° C (1,650° F). To date, the choice of substrate has been limited to graphite and such elements as silicon, molybdenum, tantalum, and tungsten, all of which

form refractory (heat-resistant) carbides. The chemical vapor deposition process is difficult to control. While these techniques do produce diamond, the quality is variable, with small crystallites the dominant product. By 1990 it was possible for chemical vapor deposition technology to produce diamond material suitable for cutting edges and electronic heat sinks, but crystals large and pure enough for use in electronic devices remained in the future.

Concurrent with the development of technology for diamond thin-film synthesis, the mechanism of low-pressure diamond formation was under study. Particular emphasis was being placed on the relationships between the thermodynamic stability of reactants and products under reaction conditions, the rate of deposition, and the crystal morphology of the product.

—George R. Brubaker

Organic chemistry

Advances in organic chemistry during the past year included the development of a new technique for making polycarbonate plastics that would allow their use in high-strength composite materials, the report of a tin-containing propeller-shaped molecule, and the laboratory synthesis of an all-carbon molecule comprising 18 carbon atoms. The discovery of two rare amino acids in 65 million-year-old rocks added support to the catastrophic impact theory for explaining the mass extinction of species that occurred at the end of the Cretaceous period.

Carbonate polymerization. Investigators at the General Electric Research and Development Center, Schenectady, N.Y., announced their development of a technique for polymerizing carbonates that could significantly expand commercial application of the products. Polycarbonates are extremely strong, impact-resistant plastics currently used as windowpanes and in electrical devices and industrial and sporting equipment. Polycarbonates previously could not be used in composites, products in which high-strength fibers of such materials as graphite or glass are embedded in a plastic matrix. Composites are extraordinarily light, strong plastics that have found growing applications in automotive, aerospace, and other industries. In the fabrication of a composite, the liquid plastic resin must flow readily enough to wet the reinforcing fibers thoroughly, filling up all voids to ensure a solid bond between resin and fiber once the resin hardens. Polycarbonates had proved too viscous to penetrate the fiber bundles easily in composite manufacture.

The GE researchers solved the flow problem by using a cyclic (ring-containing) polycarbonate precursor that has the same chemical composition as the polymerized form but only $1/50$ of its molecular

Melted and poured over a fiber mesh, a cyclic polycarbonate precursor developed by GE researchers flows easily enough to penetrate the fibers thoroughly. A catalyst then hardens the precursor to create a tough composite.

weight. When melted, the precursor flows almost as easily as light machine oil, filling tight spaces within the interstices of a fiber network. A special catalyst then is applied to open the cyclic structures and link them together in the long linear chains that account for the great strength of polycarbonates. The researchers believed that the technology could lead to a new generation of ultrastrong polycarbonate composites and also could be applied to aramids, polyarylates, and other resins.

Organometallic chemistry. Organometallic chemistry remained one of the more active fields during the past year. A major motivation was the commercial importance of organometallic compounds, which consist of a metal bonded to an organic molecule and which have found wide application in the production of pharmaceuticals, agricultural chemicals, and fuel additives. A team headed by Robert G. Bergman of the University of California at Berkeley synthesized two new organometallic compounds that exhibit unusual chemical reactivity. One is a ruthenium (Ru) benzyne complex, $Ru[P(CH_3)_3]_4C_6H_4$, that reacts with a wide range of organic substrates that are inert to other organometallic reagents. The other, an iridium-containing pentamethylcyclopentadienyliridium(III) imido complex, undergoes a number of what Bergman and his colleagues characterized as

unprecedented reactions. It was suggested that the compounds could have application in new forms of chemical synthesis.

[1.1.1]Propellanes are compounds formed by the arrangement of five atoms in a conformation resembling a propeller or paddle wheel with three flat triangular blades. Since the synthesis in 1982 of the first [1.1.1]propellane (1a), a carbon-based compound, there had been considerable interest in making structures in which carbon is replaced by atoms of those elements—silicon, germanium, tin, and lead—that are in the same group as carbon in the periodic table. The efforts succeeded in 1989 when the synthesis of a tin-based organometallic compound, a pentastannapropellane (1b), was reported by Lawrence R. Sita and Richard D. Bickerstaff of Carnegie Mellon University, Pittsburgh, Pa. The compound was seen as important in explaining chemical bonding in [1.1.1]propellanes. Sita also believed that it could be used to develop a class of compounds combining the electronic properties of metals with the versatile physical characteristics of polymers.

Bioconjugate chemistry. There was also significant activity in bioconjugate chemistry, an area of research that involves the covalent bonding of small molecules to proteins and other biopolymers to produce new vaccines, medications, and other commercially important products. Advances in the multidisciplinary field came so rapidly that the American Chemical Society established a new scientific journal, *Bioconjugate Chemistry,* to unify publication of research results that previously had appeared in about 200 different journals.

Cretaceous extinction. The mass extinctions at the end of the Cretaceous period 65 million years ago that killed the dinosaurs and perhaps 50–75% of other species on the Earth caught the attention of organic chemists during 1989. Meixun Zhao and Jeffrey L. Bada of the Scripps Institution of Oceanography, La Jolla, Calif., reported evidence in support of the theory that the extinctions were caused by the collision of a comet or asteroid with the Earth. They analyzed sediments from rock strata that marked the boundary between the Cretaceous and Tertiary periods; these layers previously had proved to be rich in iridium, an element rare in the Earth's crust but more common in extraterrestrial material. Zhao and Bada detected α-aminoisobutyric acid and racemic isovaline, two amino acids that are exceedingly rare on the Earth but are major amino acids in meteorites belonging to the carbonaceous chondrite group. Detection of racemic isovaline, which contains both left-handed and right-handed isomers of the compound, further argued for an extraterrestrial origin for the amino acids since only the right-handed form is synthesized by terrestrial organisms.

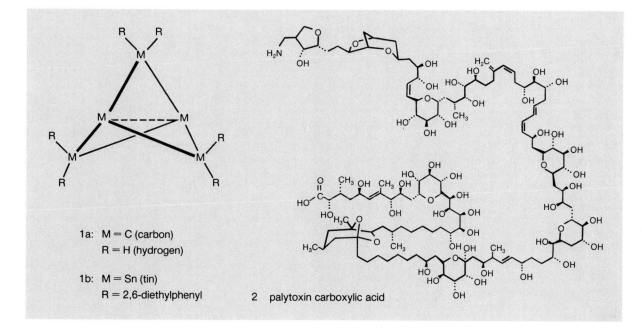

1a: M = C (carbon)
     R = H (hydrogen)

1b: M = Sn (tin)
     R = 2,6-diethylphenyl

2   palytoxin carboxylic acid

Polyene research. Few classes of compounds were attracting more attention in the scientific literature than linear polyenes. Polyenes, compounds that contain many double bonds in their molecular structure, have been important in the development of molecular orbital and valence bond theories of electronic structure, in theories describing human vision, and in understanding links between the color of a compound and the chemical composition of its component molecule. A team headed by J.F. Pfansteil of the University of Pittsburgh, Pa., filled a major gap in knowledge about the extent to which polyenes are distorted after excitation by light. The group obtained the excitation spectrum of a polyene, *all-trans*-1,4-diphenyl-1,3-butadiene using rotational spectroscopy. They found that the molecule remains planar upon excitation, allowing structural changes to be inferred.

Organic syntheses. Demonstrating the power of contemporary organic synthesis, a Harvard University team headed by Yoshito Kishi synthesized palytoxin carboxylic acid (2), the largest single molecule ever made. The highly poisonous compound, first isolated in slightly different form from a Hawaiian coral, has more than 120 carbon atoms and possesses more than one sextillion (10^{21}) isomers, or variations of the same molecular structure, of which only one is the desired isomer. They accomplished the extraordinarily complex synthesis by making eight separate parts of the molecule and then assembling them. The synthesis should permit Kishi and his colleagues to modify portions of the palytoxin molecule systematically to understand its interactions with biological systems.

The total chemical synthesis of an all-carbon molecule, cyclo[18]carbon, was reported by François Diederich and colleagues of the University of California at Los Angeles. All-carbon molecules (C_n) were becoming the topic of an increasing number of experimental and theoretical studies in a variety of fields. They appear in the products of combustion and may be components of interstellar dust. The synthesis was expected to help elucidate the properties of all-carbon molecules by giving investigators the ability to synthesize them in a single size. The traditional technique, laser vaporization of graphite,

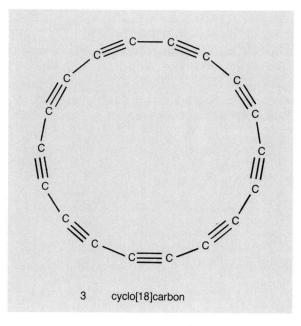

3   cyclo[18]carbon

produces a mixture of cyclic and linear molecules having from 2 to more than 600 atoms. Diederich calculated that cyclo[18]carbon contains alternating single and triple bonds connected to form a monocyclic ring structure (3, on page 299).

—Michael Woods

Physical chemistry

During the past year a major controversy erupted in physical chemistry concerning the possible discovery of "cold," or room-temperature, fusion. A new definition of a basic chemical quantity, electronegativity, led to a proposal for a three-dimensional periodic table of the elements. Researchers continued to increase their ability to manipulate the surfaces of materials at the atomic level.

Cold fusion. When the nuclei of light atoms fuse together, a small amount of matter is lost to the product nuclei, resulting in the release of large amounts of nuclear energy in accord with Einstein's equation $E = mc^2$. For example, nuclei of deuterium (hydrogen-2, or D, a heavy isotope of hydrogen) can fuse to produce tritium (hydrogen-3, or T, another heavy isotope of hydrogen) and a proton (p, an ordinary hydrogen nucleus) with the release of 4 MeV (million electron volts) of energy:

$$(1) \quad D + D \rightarrow T + p \ (4 \ MeV).$$

Such reactions occur inside stars and account for the energy generated by the Sun. If the conditions inside a star could be re-created on the Earth, an abundant energy source might be produced. However, the problems of creating and confining matter at the extremely high temperatures needed for these reactions has seriously hampered attempts to produce power by nuclear fusion.

In light of this difficulty, B. Stanley Pons of the University of Utah and Martin Fleischmann of the University of Southampton, England, created a storm of interest when they announced in March 1989 that they had achieved nuclear fusion in a simple tabletop apparatus at room temperature with a net generation of energy. In view of the long history of failure to obtain sustainable nuclear fusion under conventional high-temperature conditions, the possibility of cold fusion excited immediate worldwide hope of a new, cheap source of renewable energy.

In the process of electrolyzing heavy water, or deuterium oxide (D_2O), in a glass cell containing a platinum anode and a palladium cathode, Fleischmann and Pons claimed to have observed the liberation of heat in excess of the electrical energy supplied, together with the appearance of neutrons, tritium, and helium. They argued that deuterium released electrolytically at the palladium cathode dissolved in the metal, and when the cathode became saturated, the tightly packed deuterium atoms came close enough to fuse. Conventional D-D fusion follows two different pathways, one that yields tritium and a proton (equation 1) and another that forms helium-3 (^{3}He, a light helium isotope) and a neutron (n):

$$(2) \quad D + D \rightarrow {}^3He + n \ (3.3 \ MeV).$$

Hence, D-D fusion should be marked by the appearance of tritium, neutrons, and helium.

During the succeeding months hundreds of laboratories attempted to reproduce the results. Both the nuclear and the calorimetric (heat output) measurements were difficult to perform accurately, and the

U.S. shuttle astronauts aboard a 1988 orbital flight examine a crystal-growing reactor in which lead iodide crystals were formed in microgravity conditions from aqueous solutions of lead acetate and potassium iodide with the aid of a cellulose membrane to orient the growth. In 1989 chemists studying the results reported the space-grown crystals to be purer, more symmetrical, and apparently less dependent on the membrane for formation than crystals grown on Earth.

NASA

results were contradictory. Many groups were unable to measure excess heat or significant levels of nuclear particles above background levels. Long series of experiments conducted at the Lawrence Livermore (Calif.) National Laboratory and the Los Alamos (N.M.) National Laboratory, the Massachusetts Institute of Technology, and the Harwell Nuclear Research Center, Didcot, England, proved negative. Pons and Fleischmann later withdrew many of their nuclear measurement claims but defended their observations of high heat generation.

Other laboratories did find bursts of particle production and, in some cases, excess heat. For example, Runar Kuzmin and co-workers at the University of Moscow claimed neutron levels five times higher than background levels. John O'M. Bockris and co-workers at Texas A&M University measured both tritium and excess heat from the same cell. The measured tritium levels, however, were far below those needed to explain the amount of excess heat.

By early 1990 the status of cold fusion was unclear. The situation was unusual in that even the strongest proponents admitted that the experiments were not reproducible and consistent. Arguments raged as to whether the observations of excess heat and nuclear particles were real or artifacts of a difficult measurement. Even if the heat generation was real, there was no compelling evidence that it was due to nuclear fusion rather than to some as yet unknown cause. As a result, most scientists stopped using the term *cold fusion*, preferring the less colorful *anomalous heat*. The excitement over the initial promise of almost infinite amounts of cheap energy waned, but investigation of the unusual observations continued. (See *Applied chemistry*, below.)

A three-dimensional periodic table. The concept of electronegativity, the tendency of an atom to attract electrons, has been extensively used in chemistry to understand the polarities of bonds in molecules. The first formulation of a comparative scale for the elements was developed by Nobel laureate Linus Pauling in the early 1930s from thermochemical data. (On Pauling's scale fluorine is the most electronegative element and cesium the least.) Since then, other electronegativity scales have been proposed—for example, by Robert S. Mulliken (mid-1930s), Robert T. Sanderson (early 1950s), and Albert L. Allred and Eugene G. Rochow (1950s). More recently Robert G. Parr and co-workers at the University of North Carolina used sophisticated quantum mechanical methods to calculate electronegativities.

In 1989, Princeton University chemist Leland C. Allen proposed that an atom's valence-shell energy, a redefined version of electronegativity, be used as a third dimension to the periodic table. Allen maintained that "energy considerations dominate the structure and properties of matter, yet to date this

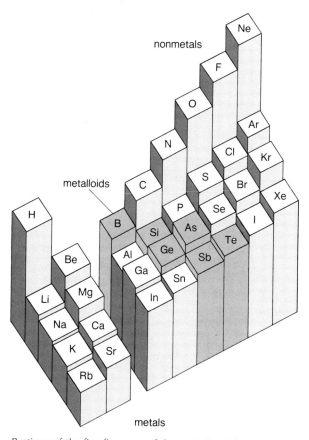

Portions of the first five rows of the periodic table show a proposed new third dimension representing each element's valence-shell energy, a redefined version of electronegativity. The metalloid band separates the metals, with low energies, from the nonmetals, with high energies.

has not been manifest in the periodic table." The valence-shell energy is obtained by averaging the ionization energies of all the *s* and *p* electrons in a neutral atom. (The ionization energy is the energy needed to remove an electron involved in bonding from an atom's valence electron shells.) Allen considered that the diagonal band of metalloid elements of the standard periodic table, which separates the metals, with low valence-shell energies, from the nonmetals, with high valence-shell energies, was in fact a reflection of this previously unrecognized third dimension.

Atomic-scale microdevices. During the past year knowledge of the atomic-scale structure of matter continued to improve, thanks to the new technique of scanning tunneling microscopy (STM) and related methods. (See *1990 Yearbook of Science and the Future* Year in Review: CHEMISTRY: *Physical chemistry*.) One of the more dramatic demonstrations took the form of independent experiments performed by Peter Bedrossian and co-workers at Harvard University and In-Whan Lyo and Phaedon Avouris at IBM's Thomas

J. Watson Research Center, Yorktown Heights, N.Y., which suggested the possibility of building electronic devices as small as a few atoms in size.

In both experiments the researchers positioned the metal tip of an STM very close to the surface of a boron-doped silicon crystal so that quantum mechanical tunneling of electrons between the tip and the surface occurred. A voltage applied between the STM tip and the silicon sets up a tunneling current that, in more conventional applications, can be used to create an image of the atoms at the surface of the silicon crystal. When the microscope was positioned over certain defect sites on the surface, the tunneling current dropped as the tip voltage was increased.

Such electrical behavior, known as negative differential resistance, is opposite to that usually observed. It is characteristic, however, of an electronic device known as a tunnel diode. These types of diodes are important in applications that require high-speed switching, such as digital signal processing and microwave transmission. As is common with electronic devices, the size of a conventional tunnel diode can be decreased only to a certain point before quantum effects dominate the electronic properties; for conventional tunnel diodes the quantum effects are deleterious.

In both experiments quantum tunneling was exploited to create a tunnel diode. It appeared that the STM tunnel diode effect occurred on the surface only at special sites having the correct electron distribution, such as the silicon defect sites encountered. In the future it may be possible to use an STM-based device to create specific sites on a surface that possess the correct electronic characteristics for tunnel diodes or other devices on the scale of individual atoms.

—Philip R. Watson

Applied chemistry

During the past year research in applied chemistry led to developments in "cold" fusion, "hot" fusion, superconductors, metallic hydrogen, hydrogen from seawater, insect control, nitrogen fixation, and polymers.

Cold fusion. Hailed as the greatest scientific event in 40 years, the alleged discovery of cold, or room-temperature, nuclear fusion was without a doubt the most publicized—and most controversial—scientific event of the past year. On March 23, 1989, in a press conference at the University of Utah, chemistry professors B. Stanley Pons of the University of Utah and Martin Fleischmann of the University of Southampton, England, announced that they had achieved nuclear fusion by passing an electric current through a platinum wire electrode coiled around an electrode of palladium (one of the platinum metals) in an electrolyte solution of alkaline heavy water (D_2O—water containing atoms of deuterium [a heavy form of hydrogen] in place of the common hydrogen atoms present in ordinary water, H_2O). By the next day, on the basis of newspaper accounts, scientists in laboratories throughout the world began attempts to replicate Pons and Fleischmann's findings, attempts that continued into 1990 with conflicting results on the detection of the heat, neutrons, and tritium (^3H) that Pons and Fleischmann cited as evidence that fusion was actually occurring.

Nuclear fusion, the process that powers the Sun and stars, occurs when nuclei of the lighter elements, such as hydrogen or deuterium, combine to form nuclei of heavier elements with the release of tremendous amounts of energy—much greater than that released in nuclear fission, the process in which nuclei of heavier elements, such as uranium and plutonium, break down to yield nuclei of lighter elements. The processes may occur rapidly, uncontrolled, and destructively (the atom bomb for fission and the thermonuclear hydrogen bomb for fusion) or

Scientists made an atomic-scale tunnel diode by bringing the tip of a scanning tunneling microscope close to a defect site on the surface of a boron-doped silicon crystal. A voltage applied between the tip and the site created a tunneling current that dropped as the voltage was increased.

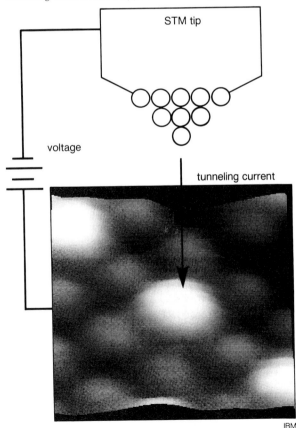

IBM

Apparatus used by University of Utah researchers in the quest for cold fusion comprises a small glass cell holding a platinum wire anode coiled around a palladium cathode. During operation the container is filled with a solution of lithium dissolved in heavy water, and an electric current is passed between the electrodes.

slowly, controlled, and usefully (nuclear reactors for fission and the Sun and stars for fusion). Until Pons and Fleischmann's alleged discovery, using a "simple, table-top apparatus," controlled nuclear fusion, which could furnish an unlimited amount of inexpensive, safe energy, was believed to require temperatures in the millions of degrees and had eluded the most strenuous efforts of the world's greatest nuclear physicists working with the most complicated, multimillion-dollar facilities.

From its unusual beginning, with a press conference announcement in place of the customary peer-reviewed article published in a scholarly journal, the cold fusion controversy involved, to an unprecedented degree, the interaction of science, politics, and the mass media. The world scientific community was polarized into two opposing camps—believers and skeptics.

Articles detailing experiments supporting cold fusion appeared in the scientific literature, by, for example, Pons and Fleischmann; physicists Steven Earl Jones and co-workers from Brigham Young Uni-

versity, Provo, Utah, and Johann Rafelski of the University of Arizona; Noboru Koyama and co-workers at the Tokyo University of Agriculture and Technology; Gyula Csikai and Tibor Staricskoi of the Kossuth Lajos University, Debrecen, Hung.; and Nobuhiko Wada and Kunihide Nishizawa of Nagoya (Japan) University. On the other hand, experimental articles, notably by Nathan S. Lewis and co-workers at the California Institute of Technology (Caltech) and the University of California at Riverside and Moshe Gai and co-workers at Yale University and Brookhaven National Laboratory, Upton, N.Y., reported no evidence for fusion. Alternative explanations, involving "normal" chemistry rather than nuclear reactions, appeared in letters to the editors of various journals, which also featured editorials and articles assessing the latest developments, pro and con, and reporting earlier examples of cold fusion.

To an unusual extent, articles appeared in newspapers and popular magazines, with *Time, Newsweek,* and *Business Week* devoting cover stories to the controversy. By early 1990 full-length books in various languages on the controversy had already been published. As new claims and counterclaims surfaced, the popular, scientific, and educational media had a field day with titles and headlines such as "Science by Press Conference," "Nuclear Tempest in a Test Tube," "Confusion Profusion or Fusion," "Fusion Cools Down," "Fusion Fever," "Political Science," "Cold Fusion Gets a Bruisin' from DOE," and "Fusiomania."

In November 1989 a 22-member U.S. Department of Energy (DOE) advisory panel reported that the positive results obtained at various laboratories "do not present convincing evidence" that the anomalous heat is due to a nuclear reaction, and it recommended against establishing special programs or research centers to develop cold fusion. However, it noted that "some observations attributed to cold fusion are not yet invalidated" and "there remain unresolved issues which may have interesting implications" for geophysics and astrophysics.

Because of its complexity and elusiveness, no consensus had been reached on the cold fusion phenomenon as of early 1990. Work continued in laboratories throughout the world on what may prove to be "the scientific breakthrough of the century" or a self-deluded will-of-the-wisp like René Blondlot's "N-rays" or a misinterpretation like Boris Deryagin's "polywater." At a time when antiscientific prejudice has increased, many people undoubtedly regarded the situation as further evidence of the shortcomings of science. Nevertheless, the controversy, with all its ambiguity, can serve as a case study of the manner in which science progresses and of the provisional nature of scientific "truth" and was already being used as such in undergraduate science courses. Regardless of the final outcome, it is certain to find a place in the history and sociology of science.

Hot fusion. An entirely new method of achieving hot fusion (so-called to differentiate it from the above-discussed room-temperature Utah work) was reported by chemists Robert J. Beuhler, Jr., Gerhart Friedlander, and Lewis Friedman of Brookhaven National Laboratory. Although the work had little in common with cold fusion except that it too was claimed to be a new method and was performed by chemists in a field traditionally the domain of physicists, the scientific community responded cautiously. Caltech physicist Steven E. Koonin, who was critical of Pons and Fleischmann's work, dubbed it "a surprising new opening" and stated that fusion was occurring but that it was still too early to know if the energy could be harnessed.

The Brookhaven researchers bombarded a solid target that contained deuterium (titanium deuteride, zirconium deuteride, or polydeuteroethylene) with clusters of 25 to 1,300 molecules of heavy water (D_2O) produced by an electric discharge. These clusters had a positive charge and were accelerated to 200–300 keV (thousand electron volts) in a meter-long Cockcroft-Walton accelerator for the bombardment. The compression and heating effected by the cluster impacts caused two deuterium nuclei to fuse, producing high-energy protons and ^3H and helium-3 (^3He) nuclei. The researchers' claim for the occurrence of fusion was supported by control experiments with H_2O cluster ions or titanium hydride targets, which produced no fusion. Although the fusion yield would have to be scaled up by a factor of 10 billion to be practical, Brookhaven applied for a patent on this so-called "cluster impact fusion" process. When the voltage was increased from 225 to 300 keV, the fusion rate increased by a factor of 10, and further increases might occur at higher voltages. The Brookhaven researchers are continuing the work with energies up to 5 MeV (million electron volts) under a grant from the DOE's Office of Basic Energy Sciences.

Superconductors. Superconductors are materials that lose all electrical resistance when cooled below a particular critical temperature. Since the discovery in 1986 of high-temperature ceramic superconductors by Johannes Georg Bednorz and Karl Alex Müller (Nobel laureates in physics for 1987), efforts have been directed by physicists, ceramicists, and chemists throughout the world to increase the temperatures at which such materials can operate (currently as high as 125 K, or −235° F) as well as to develop new classes of superconductors.

Superconductors have attracted such widespread attention because of their diverse possible applications and because of the interesting theoretical and experimental problems that they pose. Nevertheless,

as 1989 began, Simon Foner, chief scientist for the Francis Bitter National Magnet Laboratory, Massachusetts Institute of Technology, told a meeting of 300 scientists (January 11) that superconductivity, touted as the biggest advance since the laser, has been "overhyped and oversold," and *Science* magazine reported that recent findings had shown that once-high hopes for high-temperature superconductors were nearly gone because of a possibly insurmountable obstacle to many applications involving high magnetic fields and large electrical currents. The flux lattice—a structure unique to superconductors—creates a resistance to the flow of electrical current that increases with increasing temperature. However, in its December 8 issue *Science* announced that the problem could be overcome and that "the mood among scientists in the field is markedly more upbeat than only a short while ago."

For example, by use of a new technique, Sungho Jin and co-workers at AT&T Bell Laboratories, Murray Hill, N.J., produced bulk samples of $YBa_2Cu_3O_7$ that carried almost 10 times as much current as the best bulk materials prepared by standard techniques. Also, R. Bruce van Dover, E. Michael Gyorgy, Lynn F. Schneemeyer, and co-workers at AT&T Bell Labs, cooperating with two co-workers at the Royal Institute of Technology, Stockholm, demonstrated for the first time that exposure of a single crystal of $YBa_2Cu_3O_7$ to neutron irradiation enabled it to carry 100 times the amount of electric current that had been reported earlier; such large currents had been observed previously in thin films but not in bulk samples.

Another breakthrough, hailed by Du Pont Co. physicist Arthur Sleight as "the biggest news since the original Bednorz-Müller discovery," was made by Y. Tokura, H. Takagi, and S. Uchida of the University of Tokyo, who prepared a new class of superconductors ($Ln_{2-x}Ce_xCuO_{4-y}$, where Ln is one of the lanthanide elements praseodymium, neodymium, or samarium) in which the current is carried by electrons rather than the absence of electrons (electron holes), as in all other known high-temperature superconductors. This new mechanism of current conduction will require new theoretical explanations.

Metallic hydrogen. According to theory, at extremely high pressures hydrogen molecules (H_2) should collapse into tightly packed hydrogen atoms (H) with the electrons freed so as to conduct electricity. Attainment of a condition close to such a "metallic" state for hydrogen—the simplest atom, consisting of a single proton and a single electron—eluded scientists until Ho-Kwang Mao and Russell J. Hemley of the Carnegie Institution, Washington, D.C., squeezed a hydrogen sample less than 20 micrometers wide (one-hundredth the diameter of a human hair) between two gem-quality diamonds at a pressure of more than 2.5 million atmospheres (comparable to pressures near the center of the Earth). Through the transparent diamonds they observed the hydrogen gradually darken and become opaque; this indicated that the hydrogen was becoming semiconducting and then semimetallic, since electrons in semiconductors and conducting metals absorb visible light.

Not only should metallic hydrogen, once fully attained, provide a test of solid-state theory but, according to some theoretical predictions, it should also act as a high-temperature superconductor and conduct electricity with zero resistance near room temperature. Its high energy content, much higher than that of liquid hydrogen, may make it an ideal high explosive or rocket fuel. Metallic hydrogen may exist on Jupiter, Saturn, Uranus, and Neptune, and its discovery there, which remained inconclusive, should add to understanding of these planets.

Hydrogen from seawater. Hydrogen is a non-polluting fuel that produces only water when burned. The subject of much recent research, it may well be the fuel of the future. Ordinary electrolysis of water to produce hydrogen is an uneconomical process, and various scientists have been working to improve it.

Most recently, using natural photosynthesis as a model, H. Ti Tien, professor of physiology and biophysics at Michigan State University, invented an electrochemical-photovoltaic cell that produces hydrogen directly from seawater. Using only visible sunlight with no externally applied voltage, the "semiconductor septum cell" employs a sturdy, inorganic, light-absorbing septum (the counterpart of the fragile biological membrane in a plant) of a thin film of the polycrystalline semiconductor cadmium selenide deposited on nickel foil. When excited by light, electrons in the semiconductor pass into the nickel, where they decompose seawater into hydrogen gas on the dark side of the cell. On the light (semiconductor) side of the cell, electrons from a potassium ferrocyanide/potassium ferricyanide solution in caustic soda (sodium hydroxide) flow into the semiconductor to complete the circuit.

The device, which operated at a conversion efficiency of more than 10% (estimated on the basis of the volume [in milliliters] of hydrogen produced per minute per square centimeter of semiconductor area at normal sunlight intensity, 80–100 milliwatts [mw] per square centimeter, compared with the volume theoretically possible), was the first to produce hydrogen directly from seawater through the use of a cheap polycrystalline semiconductor. Supported by the U.S. National Institutes of Health and the Office of Naval Research, development work was under way to increase the efficiency by employing different semiconductors, metal substrates, catalysts, and electrolytes.

Insect control. Scientists have long been seeking a product to kill or drive away harmful crop pests without harming beneficial insects. Such a substance, which also can be used as a mosquito repellent, in antibacterial toothpaste, and possibly as a male contraceptive, is the limonoid azadirachtin, obtained from seeds of the neem tree (*Azadirachta indica*), which grows in Southeast Asia and Africa. As a natural product widely used in the Third World, it cannot be patented, but chemist Steven Victor Ley of the Imperial College of Science and Technology, London, was working on a total synthesis of the compound in order to determine which part of its complex

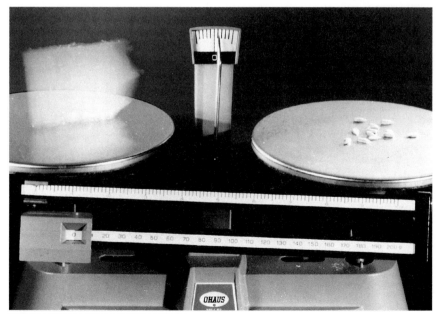

Looking like frozen smoke and weighing less than a few sunflower seeds, the material on the left pan of the balance is a sample of a new silica aerogel developed by researchers at Lawrence Livermore National Laboratory in California. Among the lightest solids known, it is made of tiny spheres of bonded silicon and oxygen atoms joined into long strands that are randomly linked to each other, with air pockets between the strands. The material may find use in traps for sampling cosmic dust from space, in window insulation, and in storing liquid rocket fuels.

Courtesy, Lawrence Livermore National Laboratory

structure is responsible for its biological activity so that more effective analogues could be prepared. As natural products, neem-derived insecticides should be acceptable to the organic farming movement. Although azadirachtin's contraceptive properties were demonstrated only in male rats at very high doses, Ley's group was collaborating with Birkbeck College, London, and Kew Gardens in studying these effects.

The troublesome mite *Varroa jacobsoni* attacks worker bees and drones of the European honeybee (*Apis mellifera*) and causes the loss of hundreds of thousands of hives in Europe and Asia. It first appeared in the U.S. in 1987, where it was controlled by pesticides, but biologists were concerned that it could develop resistance to them. In search of a bait to trap these mites, Guy Ourisson and co-workers of the Institut de Chimie des Substances Naturelles, Gif-sur-Yvette, France, made extracts from drone and worker bee larvae and identified 10 potential mite attractants in them. Although they had not yet field-tested the most potent attractant, an ester called methyl palmitate, they set simple traps in laboratory hives and found that blotting paper impregnated with the ester attracted mites.

Nitrogen fixation. Nitrogen is an important constituent of all plant and animal protein as well as of fertilizers, explosives, and a host of industrial products. Although life literally exists in a sea of this gaseous element, which constitutes about 78% by volume of the Earth's atmosphere, the cells of most living systems cannot assimilate nitrogen from the air for use in making proteins. Notable exceptions are certain bacteria that live in the root nodules of beans, clover, alfalfa, and other legumes, which have long been cultivated to restore depleted nitrogen to the soil—a technique known as rotation of crops.

The conversion of atmospheric nitrogen into nitrogen compounds that can be used by plants, a process called nitrogen fixation, was first accomplished on an industrial scale in 1909 by the German chemist Fritz Haber. This direct combination of nitrogen (N_2) and hydrogen (H_2) to form ammonia (NH_3), however, requires high temperatures and pressures, and through the years scientists have attempted to fix atmospheric nitrogen under less extreme conditions.

During the past year for the first time a complex was synthesized in which diazene (HN=NH), a very unstable molecule, is stabilized by its interaction with two iron atoms. According to chemist Dieter Otto Sellmann and co-workers at the Friedrich Alexander University of Erlangen-Nürnberg, Erlangen, West Germany, the resulting complex is the first that can serve as a model for enzymatic nitrogen fixation.

Polymers. Inorganic chemists Bernard F. Hoskins and Richard Robson of the University of Melbourne, Australia, prepared a new type of potentially useful solid polymer by linking tetrahedral or octahedral bonding centers with rodlike connecting units. The infinite polymeric framework of carbon, nitrogen, and copper atoms crystallizing in a diamondlike lattice contained large interstitial cavities occupying about two-thirds of the lattice's volume and filled with a mixture of nitrobenzene and tetrafluoroborate ions. According to the researchers, such lattices "may show interesting molecular sieve and ion exchange properties . . . [and act as] tailor-made materials for the heterogeneous catalysis of a wide range of transformations."

Ian Manners and Harry R. Allcock of Pennsylvania State University and Gerhard Renner and Oskar Nuyken of the University of Bayreuth, West Germany, prepared poly(carbophosphazenes), a new class of inorganic-organic polymers, by the ring-opening polymerization of cyclocarbophosphazenes (six-membered rings consisting of one carbon, two phosphorus, and three nitrogen atoms). Although the polymer is moisture-sensitive, stable derivatives in which aryloxy or arylamino groups have replaced the chlorine atoms in the original polymer are films or glasses that superficially resemble organic polymers.

Chemist Arnulf-Dieter Schlüter of the Max Planck Institute for Polymer Research, Mainz, West Germany, institute director Gerhard Wegner, and graduate student Karsten Blatter developed a method to synthesize and characterize so-called ladder polymers related to graphite. The chains of such polymers contain carbocyclic rings (containing carbon atoms only), heterocyclic rings (containing carbon and other atoms), or both joined by sharing common sides of the rings. Because at least two bonds per ring must be broken to cut the chain, they are more heat-stable than similar polymers with repeating units joined by single bonds, and they may be used in preparing materials with properties intermediate between those of thermoplastic resins and graphite. Some ladder polymers possess liquid crystalline, electrically conductive, or nonlinear optical properties that may lead to their use as semiconductors and scanners.

Anniversaries. The year 1989 marked the 200th anniversary of the publication of Antoine-Laurent Lavoisier's *Traité élémentaire de chimie* (Paris, March 1789), an event considered the beginning of modern chemistry. It also marked the 150th anniversary of U.S. inventor Charles Goodyear's discovery of the vulcanization of rubber and the 50th anniversary of the discovery of the long-sought element 87 (francium), the heaviest alkali metal and shortest-lived radioactive element below element 102, by 29-year-old French chemical technician Marguerite Perey.

—George B. Kauffman

See also Feature Articles: OOPS . . . EUREKA! SERENDIPITY AND SCIENTIFIC DISCOVERY; THE RADICALS OF CHEMISTRY.

Defense research

The technology of avionics (aviation electronics) achieved two major milestones in 1989: the dedication of the new Photonics Laboratory at Griffiss Air Force Base near Rome, N.Y., to conduct research on postelectronics systems for future aircraft, and the initiation of studies on an advanced avionics "system architecture," the method of integrating these new systems into aircraft, at the Avionics Laboratory at Wright-Patterson Air Force Base near Dayton, Ohio.

The two efforts represented a coordinated approach to harnessing emerging technologies for use in the air and space vehicles of the 21st century. They resulted from a series of previous air force studies known as Project Forecast II.

Those studies predicted that photonics, utilizing the minute energy packet of electromagnetic radiation called the photon, would eventually replace electronics because of its superior information processing capabilities. First, however, a way would have to be found to integrate this technology without disrupting present aircraft operations. That was the purpose of the second effort, which was named the Pave Pace system architecture.

Photonics Laboratory. During formal dedication ceremonies of the Photonics Laboratory on October 24, Gen. Bernard P. Randolph, commander of the U.S. Air Force Systems Command, spelled out the significance of photonics to the Air Force's future defense mission. "The impact that photonics will have on 21st century command, control, communications and intelligence systems was first recognized by Air Force and Department of Defense leaders as a result of Project Forecast II," he said. "The purpose

of the Project Forecast II study, conducted during the summer of 1985, was to determine the 'art of the possible' in future defense systems. It was determined that photonics was one of the major keys to the future."

In simplest terms photonics is the use of neutral photons instead of charged electrons to process, store, and transmit information. Photonic devices have the potential to be lighter, less expensive to build and use, faster, able to carry or store more information, and less susceptible to electromagnetic interference than those based on electronics. From a military standpoint, immunity to interference is critical for secure, jam-resistant communications.

The worldwide consensus among scientists is that photonics may lead to a technological revolution in the 21st century just as electronics revolutionized the 20th. In the United States electronics in 1989 was a $200 billion industry that was growing about 10% annually. Photonics was a $10 billion industry, growing at a rate of about 50% annually. Predictions indicated that the growth rate of the electronics industry would decline, while that of photonics would remain at about 50% annually for the near future. Some already familiar photonics applications include fiber-optic telephone systems, compact discs (the forerunner of which was developed by U.S. Air Force scientists at Rome Air Force Base), supermarket price scanners, and laser scalpels used for precision surgery.

While integrated optics and photonics research was still in an early state of development, major thrusts of photonics research at the Photonics Laboratory during the past year included exploring the feasibility of new photonics applications such

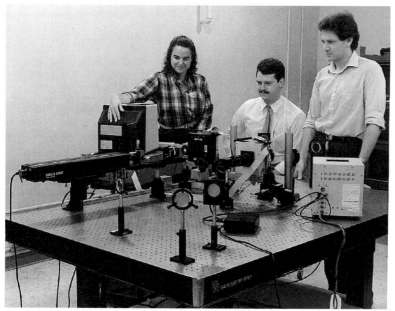

Photonics engineers in the new Photonics Laboratory at Griffiss Air Force Base near Rome, New York, display an optical correlator that can recognize optical patterns. The laboratory is conducting research on the use of photons instead of electrons to process, store, and transmit information; photonic devices are less susceptible to electromagnetic interference than are those based on electrons.

U.S. Air Force/Griffiss Air Force Base

Gallium arsenide (right) and very high speed integrated circuit chips (above) were among the subjects of research in the Pave Pace program at the Avionics Laboratory at Wright-Patterson Air Force Base near Dayton, Ohio. The laboratory was working toward the introduction of advanced technologies into the aerospace vehicles of the 21st century.

as optical signal processing, optical computers, optical communications, optically fed aircraft antennae, integrated adaptive optics for space surveillance, optical mass memory systems, and high-speed optical testing of microcircuits. According to the Air Force, photonic manufacturing processes, competitive with electronic processes, will be necessary for the goal of fully integrated, low-cost photonic systems to be realized.

Photonics research at the new laboratory has begun evolving along three parallel paths—but not necessarily at the same rate. Leading the way are fiber-optic data distribution networks, known as data buses, which convert electronic signals into streams of photons for secure, high-volume traffic within airborne systems. Following behind are analog optical devices to replace sensors such as radar, to further reduce vulnerability to detection, and to increase bandwidth (as measured in bits per second). Bringing up the rear are digital optical devices that would complete the job by processing the information in the form of photons rather than electrons, thus matching the immunity to electromagnetic interference (EMI) and high data rates of the other two. (An analog device is one in which data are represented by continuously variable physical quantities; in a digital device information is represented in the form of discrete digits, ones and zeros.)

Of the three, fiber optics was the most developed in 1990. This technology is to be employed in the generation of weapons systems currently under development, such as the Air Force's Advanced Tactical Fighter (ATF) and the Navy's Advanced Tactical Aircraft (ATA). Fiber-optic data buses were to be the link between two types of advanced electronic systems developed under the sponsorship of the Defense Advanced Research Projects Agency (DARPA); these included powerful sensors for radar that use gallium arsenide (GaAs) analog devices from the microwave and millimeter wave integrated circuit (MIMIC) program, and high-capacity airborne digital computers from the very high speed integrated circuit (VHSIC) program.

The Air Force identified photonics as the technology that would be pervasive throughout future systems because the present-day silicon-based electronics technologies (and even emerging GaAs technologies) are approaching their theoretical limits. The individual elements on the chips, such as transistors, must be made smaller in order to carry the increased data traffic projected for the future. The goal of the VHSIC program was to reduce the diameter of the elements to half a micrometer (one-millionth of a meter; the average human hair is about 100 micrometers in diameter, so it would take 200 of these microminiature transistors to equal that diameter).

That goal was realized, and the VHSIC technology was being inserted into operational weapons systems. MIMIC was expected to be more efficient than VHSIC because electrons can flow through GaAs at least five times faster than through silicon.

Solid-state physicists speculated that another 10-fold reduction in size—down to $\frac{1}{20}$ of a micron—is possible before the elements become jammed so closely together that the required electrical current causes them to overheat and destroy the circuits. At that point optical devices enter the picture. By handling the data traffic as photons, they eliminate the heat- and power-dissipation problems of electronic devices. They also reduce vulnerability to EMI and radiation from nuclear blasts because there are fewer electrical systems to be affected.

As a measure of the seriousness of the Air Force about optical technology, the minimum goal for its next generation of fiber-optic data buses is 10,000 times the data rate of 1990's all-electronic 1553 data bus, which was capable of operating at one million bits per second. The fiber-optic data bus for the ATF and ATA aircraft was designed to operate at 100 million bits per second, but the next generation of networks would start at 10 billion bits per second.

That, however, is only the beginning. By using techniques that maximize the signal-to-noise ratio, the Air Force hopes to reduce the individual pulses to two picoseconds (trillionths of a second) in width and thus increase the data rate to 100 billion bits per second. Such data rates will be needed for other futuristic weapons systems. Reduced weight and increased bandwidth made possible by this technology are expected to enable the Air Force to build advanced phased-array antennae right onto the surface of aircraft of the future, thus, the term *smart skins*. (Phased-array antennae have an array of dipoles in which the signal feeding each dipole is varied so that antenna beams can be formed in space and scanned rapidly in azimuth and elevation.) These powerful new data-distribution systems will also enable the Air Force to create reconfigurable system architectures for mission flexibility on future space platforms, such as the X-30 National Aerospace Plane.

Photonics is inherently more adaptable to analog than digital applications and, consequently, the first optical signal processors to find their way into weapons systems are likely to be analog front-end sensors. This situation is similar to the early days of computers in the late 1940s, when analog systems were briefly competitive until the groundwork was laid for the digital, electronic, stored-program computer. Digital technology has led the way in electronics ever since.

One of the projects at the Photonics Center is an analog acousto-adaptive processor that may greatly reduce the vulnerability of future aircraft to hostile electronic jamming. The rule of thumb is that a radar can be jammed by only one-tenth of its required output power, so the Air Force began looking into optical techniques that would separate out the jamming noise. This noise would be converted into a measurable time delay and subtracted from the total signal in order to negate the jammer.

Another promising analog application of optical processing is pattern recognition, the automatic identification of shapes, forms, and patterns without active human participation in the decision-making process. This is an important military requirement that has strained conventional electronic devices. Consequently, the Air Force was investigating optical filtering in an effort to find the targets faster and with greater resolution. Optical filters partially absorb incident electromagnetic radiation in the visible, ultraviolet, and infrared spectra; the absorption may be selective with respect to wavelength.

Digital optical technologies were being explored for two possible future military requirements: the Strategic Defense Initiative (SDI)—particularly the vexing battle-management problem—and tactical command and control. In each case there was a need for computer output that was many orders of magnitude higher than was possible at present in order to achieve real-time operations. This required parallel processing (performing simultaneously the normally sequential steps of a computer program by using two or more processors), which was being developed for electronic systems, but it also demanded more powerful digital switches. As a result, according to Donald W. Hanson, head of the Photonics Laboratory, there may be a marriage of electronics and optics in which the two technologies would be merged.

System architecture. System architecture is a difficult concept to comprehend. It is not hardware, nor is it software; it is the glue that holds the two together. During the pre-computer days of World War II there was no need for avionics system architecture because there was not much in the way of avionics (airplane electrical and electronic devices) to integrate. Radios, navigation aids, radars, and all the other pieces of first-generation electronic equipment were hung on the airplane anywhere they would fit. Unfortunately, there was a tendency for these black boxes, most of them low-reliability electromechanical and analog systems, to proliferate and take a disproportionately large share of aircraft weight, space, and electrical power.

In 1990 the Avionics Laboratory at Wright-Patterson Air Force Base was working on the system architecture of the 1990s under a program known as Pave Pace (Pave was the Air Force's designation for high-priority programs, and Pace stood for progressive aviation concept engineering). The laboratory was attempting to introduce at least eight advanced technologies into the aerospace vehicles of the 21st century: wafer-scale integration of functions now performed by individual chips; photonics; artificial intelligence; parallel processing; neural networks; radar and other analog functions performed by GaAs chips derived from the MIMIC program; further use of VHSIC; and increased use of computer-aided software engineering (CASE) to attack mounting software costs.

For the purposes of the current round of Pave Pace studies, the Air Force chose to focus on a proposed multirole combat aircraft combining air-to-air and air-to-ground capabilities. The study also was to cover the avionics architecture needs of hypervelocity vehicles to be derived from the X-30 National Aerospace Plane and a new class of unmanned vehicles.

This next generation of vehicles will require not just supercomputers but networks of supercomputers with estimated total processing requirements for each vehicle in excess of 200 billion operations per second. At least 15 supercomputer applications per vehicle are expected for such functions as high-speed image processing for automatic target recognition.

An even more advanced computer architecture is a concept known as neural networks. Such networks attempt to simulate the organization of the human brain. Like electronic computers, the brain is essentially a digital information processing system with about 100 trillion neurons performing the logic and memory functions and organized into subsystems known as synapses. That is equivalent to about a billion of the most powerful VHSIC-class chips available today, but photonics should reduce that number in a few decades.

Where the human brain (and thus neural networks) radically differs from conventional computers is in its ability to operate at a variable speed and thus focus processing power on the most important task at hand. Computers are confined to a fixed operating speed, commonly known as the clock rate; the most powerful supercomputers in 1990 had clock rates of 100 MHz (million cycles per second) or more. A neural network system architecture would theoretically be much more efficient, but it would be extremely difficult to implement with present-day hardware and software.

Another technology effort under way is aimed at reducing the cost of the sensors, such as the radars, which represent more than 60% of avionics hardware costs and which have steadfastly resisted conversion from analog operations to more economical and efficient digital methods. These sensors operate in the radio frequency (RF) domain, and their outputs must be converted to an intermediate frequency (IF) for eventual digital signal processing. Through the use of advanced components, particularly opto-

electronics, these RF signals can be digitized without the need to convert them to IF.

The biggest problem, however, is with the software, which is the least controllable of all the items in an aircraft. Software for the ATF, for example, is projected to require the creation of six million lines of code. (A line of code is a single statement in a programming language.) By comparison, the B-1B bomber required fewer than one million. As a measure of how serious the software problem is, the Air Force estimated that a 10% reduction in its total software spending in 1986 would have bought 26 additional F-16 fighters.

—John Rhea

Earth sciences

Researchers during the past year addressed many aspects of the Earth sciences, including climate change, ozone depletion, mass extinctions, and hydrothermal vents. Several major earthquakes focused particular attention on those destructive events.

Atmospheric sciences

During the past year atmospheric science benefited from continued development and implementation of a range of new measurement systems. There was also heightened concern for environmental degradation associated with air pollution. The scientific and public policy interest in human-caused changes in global climate also became more intense.

Climate change. Possible warming of the Earth's troposphere (the portion of the atmosphere extending outward about 11–16 km (6.8–9.9 mi) from the Earth's surface) due to human-generated increases of carbon dioxide, methane, and other trace gases—referred to as the greenhouse gases—remained a major area of discussion during the year. Increased levels of these gases reduce the amount of heat energy radiated into space, thereby warming the troposphere. The World Meteorological Organization indicated that there was general agreement that unless remedial action was taken, greenhouse gases could cause a global warming of 1.5°–4.5° C (2.7°–8.1° F) by the middle of the next century, resulting in a sea-level rise of 20–140 cm (8–55 in). The degree of warming would be smaller near the equator and greater at the poles. Potential impacts of greenhouse-gas warming could include a collapse of the vast marine ice sheet in West Antarctica, which would result in a 5-m (16.4-ft) rise in global mean sea level.

In the U.S. Congress, legislation was introduced to establish a national energy policy to reduce global warming. The bills included proposals to encourage

The NASA-Ames/Lockheed ER-2 carried instruments to altitudes of more than 21,300 meters (70,000 feet) above the North Pole in 1989 in order to study ozone depletion in the Arctic stratosphere.

the efficient use of energy and to promote the development of solar and renewable sources of energy and other alternatives to fossil fuel.

Donald R. Blake and F. Sherwood Rowland of the University of California at Irvine found that methane concentrations in the troposphere were rising about 1% per year and were 11% higher than 10 years ago. D.C. Lowe, visiting New Zealand scientist at the U.S. National Center for Atmospheric Research (NCAR), concluded that the amount of methane in the troposphere has doubled in the last 150 years. The 1.7 parts per million of methane in 1989 was 2.4 times higher than it had been at any other time during the last 160,000 years, as determined by French and Soviet scientists studying ice cores at Vostok station in Antarctica. Methane is produced from bacteria in such animals as termites and cattle, as well as from decaying organic material in marshes or mines. Paul J. Crutzen and colleagues of the Max Planck Institute in Mainz, West Germany, estimated an increase of 435% in methane from cattle throughout the world since 1890.

Scientists from the University of East Anglia's Climate Research Unit in England determined that 1988 was the warmest throughout the world during the last 100 or so years and that six years during the 1980s were the warmest in the 1900s. They concluded that the Earth's average temperature has risen about 0.5° C (0.9° F) since 1900.

Considerable controversy, however, developed regarding the conclusions about future climate that are based on computer simulations of climate changes due to a long-term increase in the greenhouse gases. Moreover, scientists of the U.S. National Oceanic and Atmospheric Administration (NOAA) questioned the accuracy of the records from the earlier years that the University of East Anglia used in its research. Also, while general-circulation models indi-

cate that greenhouse-gas warming should be greatest in the polar regions, John Sanson in the October 1989 issue of *Journal of Climate* showed that no statistically significant change in average temperature over Antarctica occurred between 1957 and 1987. In the United States Thomas Karl and associates at the National Climatic Data Center compiled surface temperature data that indicate a decrease of nearly 1° C (1.8° F) in the nation's average daily maximum temperature since 1930, while the daily average minimum temperature remained nearly the same as it was during the 1930s.

Kevin Trenberth and colleagues at the NCAR used a numerical model to demonstrate that the drought in the U.S. in the summer of 1988 was due to abnormal sea-surface temperatures in the Pacific Ocean and not to a greenhouse-gas warming. T.N. Palmer and Cedo Brankovic of the European Centre for Medium Range Weather Forecasts concurred with this finding, concluding that strong cooling of the eastern Pacific Ocean near the equator caused the drought. J.J. O'Brien of Florida State University found that unusually cold surface water in the equatorial eastern Pacific, which occurred during the past two years, can contribute to a net global cooling of the atmosphere, thereby slowing up a greenhouse effect by 30 to 35 years.

Natural climate changes that could negate or enhance a greenhouse-gas warming apparently were also occurring. Sunspot activity had been rising during recent years at a rate equal to or greater than any before observed, as reported by Joseph Hirman and Gary Heckman of NOAA's Space Environment Services Center. The maximum activity was expected to peak in late 1989 or early 1990. Previous studies suggested, for reasons that are not understood, that global warming is associated with an increase of solar activity, while cooling is observed during more inactive times. During the so-called Little Ice Age in the 17th century, for example, sunspots nearly vanished in the latter part of that century.

Ozone hole. The observed depletion of ozone in the atmosphere over Antarctica represented another major environmental concern that received considerable attention during the past year, although the ozone hole over Antarctica during the Southern Hemisphere spring was not as extensive as it had been during the same period in 1987, during which the largest ozone depletion was measured. In 1988 the ozone depletion was small. Covering more than 25 million sq km (9.7 million sq mi), the ozone hole occurs when the polar vortex in the stratosphere is isolated and very cold, thereby permitting polar stratospheric clouds to develop. These clouds are believed to be intricately involved with the removal of ozone by active chemical forms of chlorine. Up to 90% of the ozone can be destroyed during this period of the year, with the depleted area migrating toward the equator after the vortex breaks down and begins to mix with air farther north.

Studies of stratospheric ozone also occurred in the Arctic in 1989. The airborne Arctic Stratospheric Expedition, based in Stavanger, Norway, was conducted for about 1½ months beginning on January 1 in order to search for ozone depletion in the Arctic stratosphere. Associated ozone measurements were also made from Barrow, Alaska; Alert, N.W.T.; Lerwick, England; Heiss Island, U.S.S.R.; and elsewhere. While the chemical composition of the Arctic polar stratosphere was highly perturbed, no large ozone hole was observed such as had occurred in Antarctica. One reason for the difference in ozone destruction was warmer winter temperatures in the Arctic, resulting in fewer polar stratospheric clouds.

General acceptance by policymakers of the major impact of chlorofluorocarbons (CFCs) on the depletion of stratospheric ozone was reached in 1989. In early March, for example, environmental ministers of the 12 member nations of the European Communities (EC) agreed to a ban on the production and use of certain CFCs by the end of the century. CFCs release chlorine, resulting in the consumption of stratospheric ozone.

Air quality. The monitoring and inventory of hazardous and toxic chemicals, including their routine and potential accidental release to the atmosphere, continued to become more prominent in national policies in the U.S., Europe, and elsewhere. In the U.S., under Title III of the Superfund Amendments and Reauthorization Act of 1986 (SARA), communities were granted the right to know concerning routine and accidental releases, emergency plans, and other aspects of information concerning these chemicals. In Europe the Seveso Directive was passed in 1980 by the EC in response to two major chemical accidents in the 1970s. The focus of the directive was to provide risk management and emergency planning on a need-to-know basis. Implementation of the SARA Title III requirements in the U.S. during the past year provided effective inventories of toxic and hazardous chemicals for state and local regulatory agencies, as well as for the U.S. Environmental Protection Agency (EPA).

In 1989 the EPA announced rules for reducing the emission of benzene to the atmosphere. Coupled with additional proposed regulations, the plan was to cut benzene emissions by 90%. Benzene, a derivative of petroleum, occurs in a wide range of products, including plastics, insecticides, cigarette smoke, and gasoline. It has been linked to adult leukemia and is classified as a known human carcinogen. In June 1989 environment ministers of the EC agreed to reduce pollution from small cars by about 70% by mid-1992, which will reduce benzene emissions as well those of other air pollutants, including carbon monoxide and nitrogen oxides.

Air pollution also directly affects natural vegetation. As reported by Mike Fosberg of the U.S. Forest Service, air pollution was damaging natural vegetation in a range of locations. In Vermont, maple syrup production had declined 30% since 1985 because of an insect infestation apparently related to trees weakened by ozone or acid deposition or both. In Quebec 15% of the sugar maple trees appeared to have died from the pollution alone. In mountains surrounding the Los Angeles Basin, pines were being replaced by white firs and cedars, which could tolerate the frequent high ozone levels in that area.

Changes in air pollution levels were also shown in 1989 to influence climate. As reported in *Scientific American* in November, clouds downwind of major population centers reflect significantly more of the Sun's radiation back into space than do clouds in a more pristine environment. The presence of contaminants such as sulfate in the cloud droplets could explain this phenomenon. This loss of solar energy to space could compensate for the warming associated with the increase of carbon dioxide and methane in the Earth's atmosphere. The sulfate increase is directly attributable to emissions from fossil-fuel power plants.

Instrumentation for monitoring the atmosphere. The U.S. National Weather Service (NWS) planned to spend $1 billion during the next 10 years to upgrade its forecasting capabilities. Included in the improvement were the installation of 1,000 Automated Surface Observing System (ASOS) stations to measure weather routinely at airports and other NWS sites, 160 Next Generation Weather Doppler Radars (NEXRAD) to monitor severe weather, 30 microwave wind profilers to monitor winds continuously at 72 levels throughout the troposphere in the central U.S., and new higher-resolution polar orbiting and geostationary satellites. Submitted to Congress for approval in 1989, this new observation system—with the current system left in place—was scheduled to be tested in about 1992 at 11 locations in Oklahoma, Kansas, Missouri, and Colorado.

Results from such instrumentation were advancing the understanding of the atmosphere and saving lives. During the summer of 1989 at Stapleton Airport, Denver, Colo., as part of a program to detect dangerous wind shears (which can cause a loss of lift as an aircraft moves from a head wind into a tail wind), a wind-detection system observed a change of velocity across a microburst of up to 175 km/h (110 mph). Microbursts are caused by rapidly descending air that is associated with deep cumulus clouds. The descent results from cooling associated with the evaporation of rainwater and the weight of the rainwater itself. Aircraft aborted landings in response to this information, and the information may have prevented a disaster similar to the airliner crash in Dallas, Texas, on Aug. 2, 1985. The Federal Aviation Administration was developing a procedure for routinely alerting pilots of this danger, and the NEXRAD Doppler radars represent one tool for enhancing this capability.

Instruments on the Earth Radiation Budget Experiment (ERBE) satellite continued to provide a detailed global monitoring of solar and long-wave radiation. In 1989 it was reported by NASA that ERBE data confirmed that clouds cause a net cooling of the Earth; without clouds, and ignoring any changes in other variables, the global temperature would be about 11° C (20° F) warmer than it is now.

Field experiments. From December 1988 to February 1989 the Experiment on Rapidly Intensifying Cyclones over the Atlantic (ERICA) was undertaken off the east coast of North America. Sponsored by the U.S. Office of Naval Research and others, it sought to reveal the mechanisms responsible for explosive winter storm development. During the study the centers of these storms were found to have lower sea-surface barometric pressures and to be more intense than originally suspected. These storms, often referred to as northeasters, can deposit considerable amounts of snow on the northeastern U.S. and eastern Canada when they develop sufficiently close to the coast. On Jan. 4–5, 1989, one of these storms was observed by Mel Shapiro of NOAA's Environmental Research Laboratories in Boulder, Colo., to have surface wind speeds near 182 km/h (113 mph) around a cloud-free eye 100 km (62 mi) in diameter; air temperatures in the storm were about 28° C (50° F) warmer than the surrounding air. These are conditions normally associated with hurricanes.

The first International Satellite Land Surface Climatology Project Field Experiment completed a 20-day field study in late July and early August 1989 in Kansas. Designed to examine how vegetation regulates the flow of soil moisture to space, the experiment documented the significant influence of vegetation on water and carbon dioxide fluxes to the atmosphere.

—Roger A. Pielke

Geologic sciences

Geology and geochemistry. The geologic community, largely because of its intimate association with the petroleum and mining industries, has tended to support national and local policies that have assured the freest possible utilization of natural resources. While contributing dramatically to the economic growth of the industrialized nations, these policies have often been detrimental to environmental quality. Recently the urgent public concern about the deterioration of the environment has been reflected in the activities of both industrial and academic geology. During the past year concern for the environment, perhaps intensified by the disastrous oil spill in Prince William Sound off the coast of Alaska, was especially evident among geologists.

In a commentary published in the July issue of *Geotimes*, Richard J. Proctor, president of the American Institute of Professional Geologists, urged geologists, who, he said, understand natural processes better than anyone else, to become more involved in making national decisions concerning the environment. To that end he directed the Public Affairs Committee of his institute to prepare more position papers and policy statements.

Nuclear waste repository. During 1989 pollution of the atmosphere and the oceans received the greatest share of public attention, but another environmental problem of at least equal urgency continued to evade a satisfactory technical and political solution. With the Nuclear Waste Policy Act of 1982, the U.S. Congress charged the Department of Energy (DOE) with the responsibility of locating a site for a repository that would isolate the damaging radioactive contamination from spent nuclear fuel and high-level radioactive waste for 10,000 years. Geologists became deeply involved in this search because, while 10,000 years is only a brief period geologically speaking, it is long enough for significant, even catastrophic change, to occur. After the DOE had narrowed the search to three possible sites by 1986, Congress in late 1987 directed that, for reasons of economy, a thorough geologic evaluation be confined to the site at Yucca Mountain in Nevada, 160 km (100 mi) northwest of Las Vegas.

Because the contamination of groundwater is a primary hazard, it was proposed that the repository be located in the relatively impermeable welded tuffs

(Above) Researcher studies sample cores from below the Earth's surface in the area of Yucca Mountain in Nevada (right) to determine whether high-level radioactive waste can be safely stored in this material for 10,000 years.

of the Miocene Paintbrush Tuff formation (about 23 million years ago). The welded tuffs, composed of fine-grained volcanic ejecta that were partially fused, were from 500 to 750 m (1,640 to 2,460 ft) thick and were buried 300 m (985 ft) beneath the surface. The flow of water through those rocks was so slow that, according to an estimate of DOE hydrologists, it would take from 9,000 to 80,000 years for water to flow from the proposed repository to the top of the zone of saturation that lies from 200 to 400 m (656 to 1,524 ft) below it.

Although the area under consideration is in a region of low rainfall, the possibility of climatic change during the life of the repository cannot be ruled out. If there were a substantial increase in average annual precipitation, it might result in a rise in the elevation of the water table that marks the top of the zone of saturation and a consequent shortening of the effective life of the repository. William W. Dudley, Jr., of the U.S. Geological Survey expressed the view that the evidence currently available indicates that the hydrologic environment will change little during the projected life of the repository.

Earthquakes present another hazard that would threaten the repository. A number of faults that have been active during the relatively recent past have been recognized in the area of Yucca Mountain, five of them located within eight kilometers (five miles) of the proposed site. There is, moreover, the possibility of the renewal of volcanic activity that has occurred in the region, some as recently as 15,000 to 25,000 years ago. Steps must also be taken to assure that the repository is not breached by future

generations who are unaware of its function or even of its existence.

The DOE was engaged in field and laboratory studies that were intended to assess the suitability of the Yucca Mountain site for a depository. Questions were raised about the quality of these studies by other government agencies, including the Nuclear Regulatory Commission and the Environmental Protection Agency, and by the state of Nevada. For example, Carl A. Johnson of the Nevada Agency for Nuclear Projects, writing in the January 1989 issue of *Geotimes*, expressed concern that, despite assurances to the contrary, the ongoing and projected investigations of the DOE will have taken insufficient account of the complexity of the geology and hydrology of the Yucca Mountain area. He noted that the proximity of the proposed site to the Nevada Test Center will require a greatly increased understanding of the seismic effects of underground nuclear explosions.

The ultimate decision as to whether the DOE will proceed with the construction and operation of the repository rests with the U.S. Nuclear Regulatory Commission, which must not only evaluate a vast amount of relevant technical data but also make difficult decisions involving political, economic, and social issues. Apparently in response to criticism of the quality of the studies undertaken so far, Secretary of Energy James D. Watkins announced in November that the process of site evaluation would be renewed. This decision delayed the planned opening of the repository until 2010 at the earliest.

Petroleum reserves. It has been generally supposed that the discovery of new petroleum reserves in the

314

U.S. will sharply decline in the future, but a more optimistic opinion was recently expressed. A report issued by the American Association of Petroleum Geologists contends that the results of the drilling boom of the 1970s and early 1980s indicate that, for the near future at least, additional reserves can be added to the already proven reserves at a rate proportional to that of exploratory drilling. In addition to new discoveries, improved recovery methods in known fields promise to add further to the growth of reserves. Whether these potentials for growth are realized depends almost wholly upon economic factors. During 1989 drilling activity continued at a low level, with only 14,505 wells being drilled through September, a decline of 15% from the same period in 1988 according to Petroleum Information of Denver, Colo.

In an attempt to encourage the development and application of improved methods of recovery, the U.S. Congress was considering legislation that would restore to 27.5% the depletion allowance for oil and gas produced by more thorough, but more expensive, methods of recovery. Despite such efforts aimed at increasing domestic production and reserves, analysts at Solomon Brothers of New York City concluded that the major U.S. oil companies were accelerating their shift from domestic to worldwide oil exploration and production.

Mass extinctions. Global catastrophes continued to occupy the attention of many geologists and paleontologists during the past year. Controversy diminished over whether such events have occurred. Although the majority of geologists now accepted the fact of catastrophic events in geologic history, some intriguing and difficult questions remained. Perhaps the most prominent among them was the question of periodicity. David Raup and John Sepkoski, both of the University of Chicago, concluded that during the last 250 million years episodes of mass extinction of plants and animals have recurred about every 26 million years. Efforts to link these extinctions with some mechanism that might account for both the cataclysmic events that caused them and their periodicity were not wholly successful, however. The presence of abnormally high concentrations of the element iridium, which the late Luis Alvarez and his colleagues regarded as evidence of the collision of an asteroid with the Earth, had not been unequivocally associated with every inferred episode of mass extinction.

Gene Shoemaker of the U.S. Geological Survey (Flagstaff, Ariz.) and his colleagues made calculations based on observations with the 46-cm (18-in) telescope at Mount Palomar that indicate that asteroids yielding craters with diameters of 100 km (62 mi) or more—the size thought to be capable of causing mass extinctions—might be expected to have encountered the Earth twice in the last 100 million years. This frequency was insufficient to account for the number of postulated mass extinction episodes, let alone their periodicity.

Evidence of intense volcanic activity in the form of flood basalts has been associated with a number of extinction events, but, as in the case of asteroid impact, there is no reason at present to think that such activity might be periodic. Some geologists have suggested that volcanic activity might be triggered by asteroid impacts, but no convincing evidence of such a causal connection has been presented. In a report published in the October 6 issue of *Science*, Mark A. Richards of the University of Oregon and his coauthors assembled evidence that supports the conclusion of W.J. Morgan (reached in 1972) that the eruptions of the vast quantities of lava that have formed flood basalts result from hot spots caused by plumes of molten material rising by convection from the mantle that lies beneath the Earth's crust.

There has been no lack of ingenuity in the attempts to explain mass extinctions. In a letter published in the Jan. 5, 1989, issue of *Nature*, Michal Gruszczynski of the Polish Academy of Sciences and his colleagues suggested that a marked decrease in the concentration of atmospheric oxygen may have caused the extinction at the end of the Permian period (about 245 million years ago). If care is taken to assure that fossil shells have not been altered by postdepositional events, then it can be assumed that the stable isotope composition of the shells is the same as that of the seawater in which the animal lived. The authors determined the stable isotope composition of brachiopod shells from the Kapp Starostin Formation of West Spitsbergen; they found that shells from different horizons within the formation contained different concentrations of carbon-13. They concluded that the changing composition of seawater inferred from the data could be explained by an increase in the rate of burial of organic matter followed by its oxidation. The authors believe that the oxidation of the organic matter could have withdrawn enough oxygen from the atmosphere to have caused the mass extinction at the end of the Permian period.

The periodicity of mass extinctions, or even the occasional occurrence of periods of mass extinction resulting from cataclysmic events, raises some important problems in evolutionary theory. Since Darwin, most U.S. and British paleontologists have held that organisms become adapted to changing conditions through the natural selection of minute variations that favor their survival. Extinction, therefore, occurs when a population of plants or animals fails to meet an environmental challenge, perhaps because the chance variations that might enhance the survival of the organisms are simply not forthcoming. Natural selection, metaphorically speaking, cannot anticipate the future and, consequently, organisms cannot, by means of natural selection, become adapted to changes that have not yet occurred. The survival of a catastrophe of short duration is likely to depend more on the fortuitous possession of characteristics that somehow shield a species from extinction than on adaptation through natural selection to the changes produced by the catastrophe.

Recent studies have called attention to the role of purely contingent factors in the history of life, but the suspicion that accidents, both large and small, may play a significant role in evolution predates the dramatic increase in knowledge of global catastrophes achieved during the past decade. Few would deny the role of adaptation in the history of life, but natural selection as the sole determining factor in evolution was being widely questioned.

Fossil record. In attempts to understand what appear to be recurrent episodes of mass extinction and their influence on the tempo and mode of evolution, paleontology was being called on to provide crucial evidence—a situation that raised, once again, the venerable question of the completeness, or rather the degree of incompleteness, of the fossil record. It is not always clear from the available evidence in the form of fossils whether a sudden extinction has even occurred. Darwin held that evolution is a steady, gradual process and that, consequently, the apparent incompleteness of the fossil record must be the result of an accidental lack of preservation or the destruction of organic remains. However, if the fossil record is to be invoked in the test of evolutionary hypotheses, for example, the hypothesis that evolution was steady and gradual, then judgments about its adequacy cannot be based on the very hypothesis to be tested. Increasingly, paleontologists were attempting to determine the degree of completeness of the fossil record on the basis of research that is independent of the kind of knowledge that it is hoped the fossil record might test.

Paleontologists seek to infer from fossils the composition and structure of the living communities of the past. Assemblages of fossils, however, are death assemblages, which is to say that they consist of remains drawn from living populations according to some geologic process that almost certainly introduces a sampling bias. Taphonomy is the branch of paleontology in which an attempt is made to understand the nature and extent of these sampling biases by studying the events beginning with a community of living organisms and ending with a set of their nonliving remains. It is to be expected, for example, that because of nonbiological factors alone, animals with delicate parts, though they may have played a significant role in a living community, will be underrepresented in a fossil assemblage.

Two recently reported discoveries serve as a dramatic reminder that, however incomplete the fossil record may be, paleontology is not prevented from advancing knowledge of major events in the history of life. In the October 27 issue of *Science,* William A. Shear of Hampden-Sydney (Va.) College and his coauthors described a remarkable fossil from the Middle Devonian rocks (about 385 million to 380 million years ago) near Gilboa, N.Y. The presence of a well-preserved spinneret, the abdominal appendage that contains the spigot through which silk is produced, identified the fossil as belonging to the order Araneae, the spiders. According to the authors this is evidence of the earliest spiders and of the earliest production of silk by animals.

A fossil discovered in the late 1970s in the mudstone of the Lower Devonian Battery Point Formation of Quebec's Gaspé Peninsula by Francis M. Hueber of the Smithsonian Institution's National Museum of Natural History in Washington, D.C., was identified as a primitive insect similar to the living silverfish. Conrad C. Labandeira of the University of Chicago placed the specimen in the order *Archaeognatha,* the most primitive group of insects. The estimated age of the Battery Point Formation is 390 million years, making the fossil 15 million years older than any insect remains previously known. The origin of the insects must be placed even earlier, according to Labandeira, because the newly discovered form, though very primitive, had already evolved beyond the stage that would be expected for the ancestor of all the insects.

Future prospects. The direction of geologic research evident in the 1980s may be expected to be maintained during the next decade. As concern about the environment continues, geologists will be called on to provide a technical foundation to support crucial policy decisions. Following the San Francisco Bay area earthquake of October 17, geophysicists intensified their efforts to improve the precision of earthquake prediction. Geologists, especially through their knowledge of global tectonics and stratigraphy, are expected to make significant contributions to this effort, as they have in the past. It also seems certain that the investigations of global catastrophes and mass extinctions—which have been characterized by remarkable cooperation among geologists, geophysicists, and biologists—will continue.

—David B. Kitts

Geophysics. Earthquakes dominated the geophysical news in 1989. The largest earthquake since 1977 occurred on the Macquarie Ridge southwest of New Zealand but caused no casualties. On the other hand, more than 500 people were killed, more than 10,000 homes were destroyed, and at least 60,000 people were left homeless in 19 other earthquakes, most of them of relatively modest magnitude. In addition to the Macquarie Ridge earthquake, two of the others were of particular interest to geophysicists, one occurring in California and one in Australia. In addition, a swarm of earthquakes near Mammoth Lakes, Calif., was being closely monitored because of its possible relation to the intrusion of molten rock into the Earth's crust.

Macquarie Ridge earthquake. On May 23, 1989, an earthquake with a surface-wave magnitude of 8.2 (its measurement on the Richter scale) occurred at shallow depth on the Macquarie Ridge beneath the ocean southwest of New Zealand and northeast of Macquarie Island. The Macquarie Ridge forms part of the boundary between the Pacific and the Australian tectonic plates. This was the largest earthquake since the 1977 Sumba event in Indonesia. Because of its remote location, the earthquake caused no deaths or damage, but it is particularly interesting for several reasons. It was one of the largest strike-slip earthquakes in the 20th century (the fault rupture was primarily horizontal on a vertical plane), and it had an unusually short duration (about 30 seconds). The short duration was related to an unusually small rupture length of less than 100 km (62 mi). Numerous other earthquakes of smaller magnitude had rupture lengths as long as that. Studies of this and other earthquakes in this active region, reported by U.S., Japanese, French, and New Zealand scientists at the American Geophysical Union meeting in San Francisco in December, suggest that the release of strain energy is 10 times that predicted by plate-tectonic models and that the earthquake may be related to incipient subduction (the downthrusting of one plate beneath another) along this part of the plate boundary.

Loma Prieta earthquake. Not nearly as large as the Macquarie Ridge earthquake but much more damaging and probably more significant in the long run in terms of reducing the hazards of earthquakes was the October 17 quake occurring along the San Andreas Fault near the city of Santa Cruz, Calif. Named after a nearby mountain, the Loma Prieta earthquake had a surface-wave magnitude of 7.1—the largest earthquake to have occurred onshore in California since 1952. It caused 62 confirmed deaths, injuries to more than 3,700 people, and several billion dollars of damage. Most of the deaths occurred in the collapse of a section of freeway at an unusally great distance from the earthquake (about 95 km [59 mi] from the epicenter). Major disruptions to transportation were caused by this and other highway failures and by the partial collapse of the bridge connecting San Francisco and Oakland, which was out of service for a month. Teams of scientists and engineers from many countries converged on the San Francisco and Santa Cruz areas to study the earthquake and its damage.

The earthquake occurred on the best instrumented fault system in the world. It was unusual for events along the San Andreas Fault because of its greater-than-usual depth of 18 km (11 mi) and the nonvertical rupture surface with thrust as well as strike-slip components of slip. Little, if any, of the primary faulting extended to the surface, although a number of complex cracks due to the buried faulting were observed at the surface. The rupture surface dipped about 70° to the southwest and involved slip of about 2.3 m (7.5 ft) over a surface 40 km (25 mi) long and 12 km (7.4 mi) wide. The earthquake occurred on a part of the San Andreas Fault where the fault makes an eastward bend. Because of this bend, the dominantly northwest-southeast relative motions of the Pacific and North American plates produce compression of the crustal rocks and uplift of the mountains. This compression probably explains the thrust components of the slip and the unusual depth. In detail, the faulting and the surface cracking were very complicated, and efforts to understand the observations and inferred slip will take several years.

Earthquakes in well-instrumented regions are always of particular interest because of what scientists can learn about the ongoing efforts to predict earthquakes and their consequences. The Loma Prieta earthquake had much to say in these regards, although the relative lack of dense instrumentation in the epicentral region limited the recording of any premonitory signals connected with the event. Several long-range forecasts of the earthquake had been made, one relying on the historical seismic record in the region over the last century and a half as well as the amount of slip that took place on this section of the San Andreas Fault during the great 1906 earthquake. This forecast was made in a 1988 publication of the Working Group on California Earthquake Probabilities established by the U.S. Geological Survey. For purposes of analysis, the San Andreas and other faults can be broken into segments, with earthquakes of different magnitude and different times of occurrence expected on each segment. The Working Group report identified the segment of the San Andreas Fault that ruptured in the Loma Prieta earthquake as the most likely fault segment to rupture in the San Francisco Bay area in a 30-year period starting in 1988; the report assigned a 30% chance to the occurrence of the event.

A very different forecast was made by a team of eminent Soviet seismologists, geophysicists, and statisticians working at the newly formed International Institute for the Theory of Earthquake Prediction and Mathematical Geophysics in Moscow. This group used a number of measures derived from catalogs containing the time, magnitudes, and locations of earthquakes in particular regions. The group refined their methods by studying earthquakes

Section of the San Francisco–Oakland Bay Bridge collapsed (above) as a result of the Loma Prieta earthquake on Oct. 17, 1989. Measuring 7.1 on the Richter scale, the quake caused considerable damage in San Francisco's Marina District (right), which was vulnerable because it was built on soft landfill.

throughout the world. As applied to the California region, the various measures are computed for all earthquakes within circles whose radii are tied to the magnitude of the earthquakes being forecast (280 km [174 mi] for a magnitude 7 earthquake); the centers of the circles are distributed along the San Andreas Fault. The measures are computed as a function of time, and a time of increased probability (TIP) is announced when a number of measures indicate an unusual pattern in the seismicity within the circles. The TIP remains in effect for five years. Unlike practice by U.S. seismologists, the forecast is not in terms of an earthquake of specific size and location; the forecast is counted a success if any earthquake with a magnitude equal to or larger than the selected one occurs anywhere within the circle within which the TIP has been issued. Beginning in 1975, the method proclaimed a TIP for magnitude 7 earthquakes three times within California, the last being in the region in which the Loma Prieta earthquake occurred. In at least two of the three cases (including the Loma Prieta earthquake), an earthquake of the appropriate size took place. A significant earthquake occurred in the third case, but the magnitude was somewhat lower than 7. As part of a cooperative program between the U.S.S.R. and the U.S., Soviet scientists began collaborating with their U.S. counterparts in further testing and refining of the method.

The forecasts discussed above are rather long-range and do not address short-term forecasts of earthquakes within days or minutes. It seems that real-time monitoring of various geophysical signals and fields, such as the force of gravity, crustal deformation, or electric and magnetic fields, will provide the best hope of achieving short-term predictions. Instruments designed to make such measurements were concentrated along the Cholame–Parkfield section of the San Andreas Fault, where the history of earthquake occurrence suggests that a moderate (magnitude 6) quake has a high probability of occurring within the next decade.

As sometimes happens in science, however, the records from the serendipitous placement of an electromagnetic sensor close to the zone ruptured by the Loma Prieta earthquake produced records that may have significance undreamed of by the designers of the experiment. Anthony Fraser-Smith and colleagues at Stanford University had placed a simple, low-cost electromagnetic sensor near Corralitos, a small town close to the epicenter of the earthquake. The experiment was designed to study low-frequency radio waves, including those in the ultralow-frequency band (frequencies of 0.01 to 10 cycles per second). Such waves may prove useful in communicating with submarines, and the location of the experiment was chosen on the basis of the relative quietness of the site; the Bay Area Rapid Transit

318

(BART) trains produce an unacceptable amount of noise at ultralow frequencies in the San Francisco area. The sensors near Corralitos detected an unusual increase in the amplitudes of these waves in the days before the earthquake, with an exceptionally rapid increase starting a few hours before the event. After the quake the signals decayed slowly (over a span of more than a month) to background levels. Analysis of the records was continuing, as was an evaluation of physical mechanisms for the changes. Similar sensors will almost certainly be placed in other parts of California in which large earthquakes are forecast.

The records from Fraser-Smith's instruments are also significant for what they did not show. A number of reports throughout history have described earthquake-related disturbances in electromagnetic field at frequencies greater than 10 Hz (cycles per second), but no unusual signals were found in the 10 Hz to 3 kHz band from the Corralitos instruments. This finding does not discredit the other observations, of course, but may indicate the complexity of the earthquake process and underscores the need to make many kinds of measurements for the purpose of short-term earthquake prediction.

The seismographic records obtained from the Loma Prieta earthquake are to be used to make predictions of a different sort from the place, time, and magnitude of an earthquake; they will be used to refine the prediction of ground shaking at specified distances from epicenters of earthquakes of a particular magnitude. Such predictions are an essential ingredient in the design of engineered structures. The bounty from the Loma Prieta earthquake is particularly rich in this regard, for it was recorded on more than 100 specially constructed instruments at distances ranging from near the epicenter to more than 100 km from the rupture surface. Of particular importance is the range of geologic materials on which the instruments were sited; these included rock, alluvial fill, and, most important, saturated muds near the edge of San Francisco Bay. This latter material had long been suspected of being particularly unsafe in strong shaking but, until the Loma Prieta quake, few records of strong shaking had been obtained on such sites. During the earthquake such records were obtained from a number of bay-mud sites, and a preliminary analysis of the peak accelerations recorded at the sites indicated that the motions were, on the average, about three times larger than those from rock sites at comparable distances from the earthquake. Continuing analysis of the records was focused on assessing the amplification as a function of the frequency of the ground shaking, and there were indications that the amplifications at some frequencies exceeded a factor of three. Much of the damage near San Francisco seemed to be directly related

to the presence of these sediments, and the lessons learned from an analysis of the records and the damage may well be the most significant outcome of the earthquake.

Other earthquakes. Among the many other damaging and interesting earthquakes during 1989, two will be briefly discussed here (actually, one was a swarm of earthquakes rather than a single event). A magnitude 5.5 earthquake near Sydney, Australia, killed at least 11 people and caused considerable damage. This earthquake occurred in a region that has had few, if any, earthquakes in recorded history and, even though small by worldwide standards, it caused an unusual amount of damage. The importance of the earthquake is the implication it has for other apparently nonseismic regions in the world in which building codes do not include adequate bracing for the horizontal shaking produced by earthquakes. Many such regions, such as the eastern United States, are heavily urbanized and contain facilities such as nuclear power plants whose failure could be catastrophic.

The other event was an unusual swarm of earthquakes occurring beneath Mammoth Mountain (a popular ski resort) near the town of Mammoth Lakes, Calif. This persistent swarm had a number of characteristics, indicating that it was linked to the intrusion of magma into the crust. The area has been recognized in the last decade as one of potential volcanic hazard and was being closely monitored. On the basis of studies of other volcanic areas, the likelihood of a volcanic eruption is small. The last eruption in the region was about 500 to 600 years ago—a short time geologically—and the swarm indicates that the region is still volcanically active and must be closely watched. An eruption on Mammoth Mountain, especially when covered with snow and skiers in the winter, could have severe consequences.

—David M. Boore

Hydrologic sciences

The hydrologic cycle describes the circulation of water between the oceans, atmosphere, and land. Perhaps surprisingly, scientific knowledge about it is quite limited. This cycle is also an important component of the global energy budget. For example, evaporation provides a moisture flux from the ocean to the atmosphere, cooling the ocean in the process. Condensation of water vapor releases heat to the atmosphere, contributing to storm dynamics.

Hydrology. During the past year hydrologists were actively involved in planning activities for the Earth Observing System (EOS), a program of the U.S. National Aeronautics and Space Administration (NASA) to launch a number of space platforms in order to collect extensive satellite data with the objective of better understanding how the Earth functions as an integrated system. While EOS will involve research teams from many disciplines, only those aspects directly related to hydrologic science are noted here. A key feature of EOS will be its broad range of measurements, obtained with a higher resolution than has previously been available. EOS will include a package of instruments that will make passive observations of the electromagnetic spectrum in addition to radar- and laser-based instruments.

Data from EOS will permit improved global-scale definition of some of the fluxes and storage reservoirs within the hydrologic cycle. These fluxes include evaporation from the ocean surface, evapotranspiration from the land surface, the distribution and movement of water vapor in the atmosphere, and precipitation over the oceans. Storage reservoirs that can be better quantified include snowpack, glaciers and icecaps, and wetlands. Data of this kind are essential to a better understanding of the interrelationships between land surface and atmospheric processes, on a range of different spatial and temporal scales. It will be possible for hydrologists to characterize both average values for the fluxes and volumes of water in storage and variations that occur on weekly, seasonal, and yearly time scales. Because the time scale of the EOS mission is planned to be at least 15 years, another objective is to monitor the hydrologic cycle for evidence of global change. If global warming is under way because of emissions of greenhouse gases, the hydrologic cycle should be a sensitive indicator of change.

Hydrologists are working with other scientists to develop methodologies so that the spectral signals recorded by EOS can be translated into reliable estimates of hydrologic fluxes. Under development are computer models that will use the new observational capabilities of EOS to better understand the dynamic behavior of a watershed. One of the greatest challenges of EOS will be the establishment of a data and information system to process and distribute to the international scientific community the immense volumes of data that will be received from the EOS space platforms.

In the year following the 1988 drought in the U.S. Middle West it became possible to place the drought in the perspective of the historical record. Two environmental factors can be used to assess the severity of the drought: the deviation of monthly precipitation from the average and the deviation of daily temperature maximums from expected values. On the basis of those quantities, the drought of 1988 was the worst short-term drought in the Middle West since 1936. The most unusual feature of the drought was the length of the dry period through the spring. About 50% of the area of the nine-state region that was affected experienced the driest May and June on

record. This pattern had a major impact on crop development as soil moisture reserves were depleted in the spring during early plant growth. By July, when crops normally reach the stage of maximum moisture usage, soil moisture had already been severely depleted. It was at this time that many areas experienced their warmest or near-warmest July on record. Impacts of the drought continued to be felt in 1989, a testament to the close link between variability in the hydrologic cycle and socioeconomic activity.

There was growing interest during recent months in the application of new mathematical concepts of chaotic dynamics to problems in hydrologic science. Chaotic dynamics describe physical systems that can be modeled with nonlinear, deterministic equations but, because of a sensitive dependence upon initial conditions, the systems behave in a manner very similar to a stochastic (random) process. (See *1990 Yearbook of Science and the Future* Feature Article: CHAOS: DOES GOD PLAY DICE?) Dynamical analysis and theories of chaos may provide new ways of analyzing hydrologic time series, of identifying underlying order in hydrologic processes that are highly variable in space and time, and for addressing issues related to limits on the capability for hydrologic prediction. Researchers from the Instituto Internacional de Estudios Avanzados in Venezuela and the Iowa Institute of Hydraulic Research published a paper in the journal *Water Resources Research* in which they analyzed erratic variations in rainfall rate collected every 15 seconds during a four-hour rainfall during an October storm in Boston. Evidence was presented to suggest that storm rainfall can be described in terms of deterministic chaos.

The authors pointed out that their analysis really just opened the door to a broad range of questions that can be asked. They analyzed data from one type of storm; the question arises as to whether other types of storms behave in a similar manner. Is the structure of the underlying order in a chaotic process different for different storm types? And what of the structure that emerges when variations in area and duration are considered together? Because rainfall is a basic input to hydrologic simulation models that describe how water moves through a watershed, progress in understanding its nonlinear dynamics has the potential to improve hydrologic analysis in a much broader context.

Atmospheric sulfur emissions are a major contributor to acid rain in eastern North America. Networks monitoring acidic deposition have been in place only since 1965 in the northeastern United States and since the late 1970s in Canada. Atmospheric acidity prior to the mid-1960s must, therefore, be inferred by indirect means. W.D. Robertson, J.A. Cherry, and S.L. Schiff of the University of Waterloo, Ont., demonstrated that by combining data on the spatial distribution of sulfate in a shallow groundwater flow system with accurate groundwater age determinations using tritium measurements, they could infer sulfur deposition for the period from 1950 to 1985 at their study site. Their study was carried out approximately 100 km (62 mi) east of Sudbury, Ont. The nickel-copper smelter operations at Sudbury are the largest point source of atmospheric sulfur emissions in North America.

To apply this methodology they first found it necessary to determine whether the sulfate dissolved in the groundwater is of atmospheric origin rather than the result of chemical reactions with sediments. If the sulfate is primarily of atmospheric origin, carried into the subsurface during recharge of the groundwater flow system, then the concentrations of sulfate can be extrapolated to infer rates of atmospheric deposition. Data indicated that at the field site there has been a 37% decrease in sulfur deposition from the maximum values in the early 1960s. The researchers attributed the decrease to the approximately two-thirds reduction of emissions of sulfate from the Sudbury smelters since the 1960s. In 1990 more than 75% of the sulfate deposition at the field site came from sources more distant than the Sudbury smelters.

A major environmental focus of the past decade was recognition of the extent to which groundwater has been or potentially is at risk of being contaminated by inorganic and synthetic organic chemicals. Groundwater is the source of drinking water for approximately 50% of the population of the U.S. Many serious groundwater-contamination problems have resulted from improper disposal of either liquid or solid chemical wastes at sites underlain by permeable sediments. Such contamination has been found in nearly every region of North America and Europe. It seems likely that tens of millions of dollars may be required for restoration of water quality within a contaminated aquifer or at least for ensuring that water-quality standards are not violated at water-supply wells or by discharge of contaminated groundwater to streams or lakes. For this reason there is considerable interest in research that attempts to develop effective methods for aquifer remediation. One of the most common remedial techniques is the use of purge well systems, in which contaminated groundwater is pumped from the aquifer and treated at the surface. If not properly planned, such a method may be ineffective and very costly. Decisions must be made on the number and location of pumping wells to "capture" the contaminant and at what rate water should be pumped from the wells. Costs escalate with the number of wells, pumping rates, and duration of pumping.

In a 1989 issue of *Water Resources Research*, Brian Wagner and Steven Gorelick of Stanford University published a paper that proposed a methodology for identifying optimal strategies for designing a purge well system. While management models of this kind have been in use for several years, their work represented a major step forward in that they incorporated uncertainty in subsurface geology within the decision-making process. The hydrogeologic properties of aquifers vary through space, and away from measurement points (wells) there can be considerable uncertainty in specifying the values of hydraulic properties that control the rates and directions of groundwater flow. The more field data there are available, the lower this uncertainty is. The reliability of an aquifer remediation design can be properly assessed only if this uncertainty is taken into account. Wagner and Gorelick were able to quantify the relationship between the heterogeneity of porous media, the uncertainty in characterizing subsurface properties of aquifers, and the consequent reliability of a purge well system designed in an attempt to ensure that water-quality standards are not violated. Ultimately, such research will contribute to more cost-effective allocation of resources in efforts to deal with groundwater contamination.

—Leslie Smith

Oceanography. *Oceans and climate.* One of the important environmental topics of the past year was the continuing debate about the effect of increased carbon dioxide in the atmosphere, which could lead to a "greenhouse" warming of the Earth. During the year new results extended scientific understanding of the role of the ocean in this potential climate change. Previous indications and expectations had been that the role of the ocean would be to delay the effect of warming, both by absorbing carbon dioxide and by mixing warmer surface water into the deep ocean.

With a computer-based model that coupled both atmosphere and ocean and that explicitly incorporated heat transport by ocean currents, scientists from the U.S. National Oceanic and Atmospheric Administration (NOAA) found a marked and unexpected asymmetry in temperature between the Northern and Southern hemispheres. In the circumpolar ocean of the Southern Hemisphere, a region of very deep vertical mixing, the increase of surface temperature was very slow. In contrast, in the Northern Hemisphere of the model, the warming of surface air was faster and increased with latitude. After 95 years of an increase of greenhouse gases of 1% per year (doubling by the year 2030), the model air temperature north of latitude 60° N had risen between 6° and 7° C (10.8° and 12.6° F); whereas the model air temperature south of latitude 60° S rose only between 1.5° and 2° C (2.7° and 3.6° F). This remarkable difference was due to the Southern Hemispheric oceans' mixing the warmer water to the bottom and bringing colder water to the surface. Thus, it was clear that early-warning systems would be most effective in the Arctic, rather than the Antarctic, because of the ocean effects.

The global effects of El Niño and the Southern Oscillation, a periodic major climatic event that involves both the atmosphere and the ocean, were the topic of a major international conference held in Liège, Belgium, in May. More than 50 scientists from 14 countries gathered to show results from research models that coupled the atmosphere and the ocean. The models were beginning to have predictive capabilities, which were proving valuable for warning farmers, particularly in the tropics, about climate change associated with El Niño. The tentative projections for the winter of 1989–90 were for no major El Niño/Southern Oscillation event, and in early 1990 this appeared to be accurate. Many difficulties remained with the models, however, particularly with the coupling of the two fluids. Larger computers and better understanding of the physics involved in the interactions will be needed to solve these problems.

On the topic of greenhouse warming and its effect on the ocean, a group of sea level experts announced in December that the ocean will probably not rise as quickly as had been predicted earlier. The best predictions now call for a rise of about one-third of a meter if greenhouse gases are doubled (1 m = about 3.3 ft). The lower predictions for sea level increase reflected new information on how the Antarctic climate will respond to a warmer world. Because Antarctica will not warm as fast as the Arctic, and because greenhouse warming will probably add water vapor to the atmosphere, thus causing more snow to fall on Antarctica, it appears that the net effect will be to decrease sea level rather than to increase it. The group pointed out, however, that the observed rise of about 1.3 mm that has been taking place each year is not fully understood, and that more research was needed.

Hydrothermal vents. The underwater hot springs described as hydrothermal vents support oases of life at the seafloor. Their ecosystems use chemosynthesis (the synthesis of organic compounds by energy derived from chemical reactions) rather than photosynthesis for their energy source. More recently, similar chemosynthetic communities have been discovered around seafloor regions where petroleum and other similar substances seep out. Many vents and seeps have been identified, but most are at mid-ocean ridges and at the margins of continents. In recent months, however, a new set of chemosynthetic ecosystems was found. Investigators from the University of Washington and the Hawaii Institute of Geophysics discovered that the decayed carcasses of whales are surrounded by bacteria, clams, and

mussels similar to those that surround vents and seeps. It appears that the whale skeleton contains enough organic materials to support the ecosystem for at least five years. Deaths among gray whales alone could create at least 500 new deep-sea habitats a year in the North Pacific. The whale carcasses, distributed widely on the sea floor, thus might serve as important "stepping stones" for the dispersal of deep-sea animals that depend on chemosynthesis.

Significant depletions in concentrations of phosphorus have been found in waters above Pacific Ocean seafloor sites where hydrothermal fluids are being emitted. Scientists from NOAA, the Florida Institute of Technology, and the Hawaii Institute of Geophysics used chemical surveys of the Juan de Fuca Ridge, 435 km (270 mi) off the coast of Washington and Oregon, to show that iron oxides that are emitted from the vents react chemically with the waters above. When the metal-enriched fluids are discharged at the seafloor, the most abundant metals, iron and manganese, quickly react and precipitate out as metal-oxide particles. These rapidly scavenge other chemicals from seawater, including phosphorus, and then settle to the seafloor around the vent area, forming sediments that contain metal. The studies help reveal the global cycles of elements important for life on Earth, as well as answer questions about how changes in submarine volcanism have affected the global geochemical cycles of phosphorus and other elements over the course of geologic time.

Hydrothermal vent regions are also of interest for petroleum exploration. A study by U.S. and Chilean scientists showed that petroleum-like hydrocarbons have been detected in hydrothermal vent areas. The hydrothermal oils are similar in structure to conventionally exploited crude oils but have a geologic age of only 5,000 years, much younger than most of the presently exploited petroleum. This might be a relatively rapid, single-step process, but its details were not understood. The new discovery could have a considerable impact on the understanding of petroleum-formation mechanisms and eventually be of aid in tapping resources in new areas.

Chemical and biological oceanography. The Joint Global Ocean Flux Study carried out its first major field study, the North Atlantic Bloom Experiment, in the spring of 1989. Five ships from four nations worked for more than six months to collect more than 300 ship-days of observations. The experiment was planned as a pilot study for a decade-long international investigation aimed at understanding the links between biogeochemical cycles in the ocean and global climate change. It represented the first large-scale exploration of the spring phytoplankton bloom, an annual event thought to affect the cycling of carbon dioxide between the atmosphere and the ocean. The event, analogous to the springtime green-

Scientists with the Joint Global Ocean Flux Study inspect a new map showing the distribution of phytoplankton in the world's oceans. The annual spring phytoplankton bloom is believed to influence the cycling of carbon dioxide between the atmosphere and the ocean.

ing of the land surface, was estimated to account for up to half of the annual transport of oceanic carbon into the deep water by biological processes. Direct measurements of biological, chemical, and physical processes were carried out, and moorings with devices that collect falling particles and sediments in the ocean were set in the spring and recovered in the fall. These "sediment traps" collected samples that showed the progressive rise and fall in total particle flux over the 26 weeks of the experiment. The traps were reset for further studies.

In February NOAA reported that the dolphin deaths on the east coast of the U.S. in 1987 and 1988 were caused by a naturally occurring toxin from "red tide" algae originating in the Gulf of Mexico. The algae were consumed by fish, which were in turn consumed by dolphins. NOAA's CoastWatch program was established to provide warnings and predictions of future occurrences of these types of problems by means of satellite imagery and other relevant information such as wind drift.

Coastal oceanography. Hurricane Hugo, a powerful storm, devastated much of the coast of South Carolina and emphasized the need for further study of the coastal environment. In response to this and other events over the past years, a series of meetings and workshops were held to develop new plans for coastal oceanography. A major interagency workshop focused on understanding and predicting coastal processes.

New initiatives were proposed by a number of nations, and the Intergovernmental Oceanographic Commission sponsored an international planning effort. It was clear that there was considerable interest beyond the research community in improving the understanding and management of the coastal ocean.

Ocean waves. Tsunamis—seismic sea waves caused by undersea earthquakes—can cause destruction and loss of life both near the earthquake source and thousands of kilometers away. Recent work by Japanese scientists revealed that information can be derived from the arrival patterns of tsunamis to show the character of submarine earthquakes, and that these in fact may be more useful than conventional seismometer measurements of the motion of the solid earth.

The new techniques showed that data from previous events could be analyzed and that much more could be learned about the characteristics of the sources of the tsunamis, which was of considerable importance to seismology. For more recent events, additional comparisons between tsunami wave estimates of earthquake slip and those observed by conventional means will better illuminate the advantages and shortcomings of each technique.

Ocean drilling. The international Ocean Drilling Program with the drilling ship *JOIDES Resolution* worked primarily in the western Pacific in 1989. The ship was operated by Texas A&M University for the partnership of 19 countries that support the program (JOIDES is the acronym for Joint Oceanographic Institutions for Deep Earth Sampling).

One of the goals of ocean drilling is to recover samples of material from various stages of the Earth's evolution. The oldest part of the Pacific Ocean crust, from the Jurassic period (208 million–144 million years ago), is in the western Pacific. An area equal to the continental United States is thought to be underlain by Jurassic sediments and oceanic crust, but numerous attempts to recover this material had failed. It had proved to be too difficult to drill and collect samples through the combination of soft and

323

Coast of South Carolina near Charleston reveals some of the destruction from Hurricane Hugo, a powerful storm that caused 71 deaths and billions of dollars of damage in the Caribbean islands and North and South Carolina in September 1989.

hard material in that area. In December, however, the program reported that after a 20-year search, and with the use of new drilling techniques, the Jurassic Pacific had finally been discovered. Measurements of the samples were expected to allow scientists to determine the actual age and latitude of that part of the crust in the Jurassic period, thus furthering knowledge of plate tectonics in that part of the world.

Also in the ocean drilling program, in a unique series of experiments, the scientists on board the ship joined their colleagues from the University of Tokyo's Oceanographic Research Institute to probe deep into Earth's interior. In one experiment scientists placed a newly designed seismometer into a hole 700 m below the seafloor. The instrument was designed to record a wide range of seismic waves generated from large and small earthquakes. In a second experiment a set of electrodes was placed into a hole drilled in the seafloor. A second ship sent electrical signals into the water, setting up currents that penetrated deep into the underlying crust. This allowed scientists to observe the electrical resistivity within this portion of the Earth's interior. These pioneering experiments provided basic research data that were expected to help scientists better understand the collision of crustal plates and the structure of the crust and mantle boundary beneath this unusually dynamic region of the Pacific rim.

Research vessels. A new oceanographic ship completed a world expedition during the past year. The *RRS Charles Darwin,* operated by the U.K. Natural Environment Research Council, returned to Britain in September after a three-year voyage of discovery.

The expedition finished its work with a detailed study of sea-surface temperatures, currents, and salinity in the western Pacific. This El Niño research cruise was one of more than 30 covering a wide spectrum of sciences during the voyage. It was only the third time that a British research ship had made such a journey since Charles Darwin returned on the *HMS Beagle* in 1836. A new Japanese research vessel, the *Hakuho Maru,* began a voyage around the world in 1989.

High technology. New computer technology was allowing the processing and distribution of oceanographic data to become much easier. As a result, a number of new atlases and data sets were being prepared in computer-compatible format. The U.S. National Oceanographic Data Center (NODC) developed a compact disc that contains more than 1.3 million temperature, salinity, and depth profiles taken in the Pacific Ocean between 1900 and 1988. It was the first in a planned series of ocean data compact discs that will hold major portions of NODC's global data archives. The disc was free to researchers who would agree to test it and provide their evaluations to the NODC.

Another computer-related atlas was announced in 1989. An animated atlas designed for use with personal computers and color monitors will graphically display land vegetation, ocean productivity, cloud cover, and precipitation from NOAA satellites, the French SPOT-1 satellite, and the Japanese MOS-1 satellite and will also include other surface-based information. The project was being directed by the Canadian Space Agency.

—D. James Baker

Electronics and information sciences

After a year of strong growth in 1988, the electronics industry posted more moderate gains during the next 12 months. Technological innovations continued in the areas of fiber optics, central processing units, chips, and high-definition television. The transmission of data by facsimile (fax) machines enjoyed another year of rapid expansion.

Communications systems

A major objective of many people throughout the world is to be able to communicate with anybody, in any place, at any time. By 1990 communications technology was providing people with the capability of being paged anywhere in the U.S., of being able to communicate via cellular radio from any highway, of being able to conduct multiparty video conferences with ease, of being able to establish any number of calls by clever use of credit cards, and of leaving a voice message in a "mailbox" when the person who was called was unavailable.

Fiber optics. Fiber optics continued to be one of the most exciting technologies. In 1990 the long-distance telephone network in the U.S. consisted mainly of optical fibers, and the capacity of the network continued to grow. Major advantages of this technology—in which information is transmitted by modulation of a light wave rather than by an electrical signal—are that the glass fiber is capable of carrying virtually any signal and that as more ad-

Cellular radio (car phone) users in the U.S. totaled some 3.5 million at the end of 1989. The use of car phones no longer was confined to executives or professionals but instead extended to a wide range of people.

Cathy Melloan

vanced electronics is developed, it can be applied to an in-place fiber cable. The enormous capacity of a fiber strand can be illustrated by the fact that every telephone conversation taking place in the U.S. during the busiest hour of the day could be placed on a single fiber.

This capacity was being utilized not only on land but also across the sea. A fiber cable that spanned the Atlantic (PTAT-1) was placed in service in December 1988; it was able to carry more telecommunications traffic than all previous cables combined. In 1990 another fiber cable from California to Japan was being laid (see *Electronics,* below). As a result of the huge capacity of optical fibers, the cost of transmission declined.

Although fiber optics in the long-distance network continued to capture much attention, an increasing number of trials of "fiber to the home" were taking place. In most cases these trials combined voice, data, and television; the latter seemed likely to be of greatest interest in the years ahead. It seemed certain that in the near future there would be a single "pipe" to the home in the form of a fiber. It would carry all forms of information.

ISDN. Sufficient bandwidth for high-speed transmission does not reside solely with fiber; it was determined that if reasonable distance limitations are observed, the lowly pair of copper wires is capable of transmitting high-speed digital information. Indeed, this capability is essential to the implementation of the ISDN (Integrated Services Digital Network) as it is deployed throughout the world. ISDN is an attempt to maximize the capabilities of the public switched telephone network. It allows the transmission of voice, data, and image on a single network, regardless of the type of transmitting and receiving terminal. Obviously, in order for such a scheme to be possible, a rigid set of standards must be adhered to. (A telephone, a personal computer, and a facsimile machine cannot be interchangeably plugged into a particular wall jack without telling that wall jack something about the input signal.) Therefore, standards for the various interfaces were being developed. One of the major applications of ISDN was expected to be the interconnection of the hundreds of thousands of private local area networks.

The first configuration of ISDN was called Basic Rate ISDN; it was able to carry two information channels and one data channel. A second configuration, Primary Rate ISDN, could accommodate 23 information channels and one data channel. Beginning in 1989 there was talk of Broadband ISDN; it was so new that its characteristics and capabilities were not yet defined. It was assumed that it would be based on fiber optics, in contrast to the copper-pair transmission facilities of Basic Rate ISDN and Primary Rate ISDN.

Cellular radio and telepoint. The explosive expansion of cellular radio service continued during the past year. At the end of 1988 there were approximately two million cellular radio users in the U.S. At the end of 1989 the number had increased to 3.5 million, and it was expected that by 1995 there would be between 10 million and 20 million, depending on the retail cost of the instruments themselves and the per-minute cost for phone usage. With numbers like these, it was clear that use would not be confined to executives or professionals who find it essential to remain in touch with their offices. Cellular radio was already being used by homemakers who spent a lot of time in their vehicles, by salespersons to check with their offices or plan sales calls without having to search for a pay phone, by construction supervisors who deal with many sites, and, in general, by "people on the move." As prices of conventional vehicle-mounted units continued to drop, units that were smaller, more sophisticated, and more expensive were expected to appear on the market.

Another wireless communications device and service was being tested in Europe. Named telepoint, it was based on the assumption that the standard cordless telephone would not only proliferate but also become smaller and less expensive. Indeed, in parts of Europe and the U.S., more than 50% of all households had a cordless phone. If the phones were small enough, it was argued, owners not only would use them but would carry them. And in that case it seemed to make sense to design them so that they could access stations other than those in one's own home.

For instance, a street corner, hotel lobby, or airport terminal could be equipped with a station that would appear to be a black box with an antenna. It would be the terminal of many telephone lines, and nearby users (who would carry their own cordless telephone) would be able to access those lines and bill the calls to their home phones by keying in appropriate numbers on the touch-tone pad. Because no coin-collection function would be required and because the capital investment of a typical pay station would be avoided, it was expected that the cost of calls from such a telephone would be no more than those from a conventional pay phone. Furthermore, as long as the user was within approximately 200 m (650 ft) of the station, the transmission would be good. In this regard telepoint differs from cellular radio, which does not have that distance limitation. On the positive side, telepoint was expected to cost substantially less.

Facsimile services. A service that witnessed explosive growth during the past year was the transmission of facsimile data. Its slow development was due to the fact that fax machines (which transmit exact representations of the original—whether text

© James Aronovsky—Picture Group

Orders are received on a fax machine at a restaurant in San Diego, California. By 1990 most offices were equipped with at least one such machine.

or numbers or pictures) are useful only if someone else has a fax machine. Thus, a "critical mass" is required before such a service can begin to expand rapidly. By 1990 that had been achieved, and it was an unusual office that was not equipped with at least one fax machine.

It was becoming increasingly obvious that all the telecommunications services are synergistic. That is, not only do the services along with their associated technologies permit better communications but they also facilitate the development of other services and technologies. For instance, optical fiber provides a transmission medium and also stimulates such enhanced services as video conferences. The enhanced telecommunications services that the public was becoming used to require instant contact—and hence there were paging and cellular radio and voice messaging.

—Robert E. Stoffels

Computers and computer science

During the past year one of the oldest packet-switching data networks, the ARPANET, celebrated its 20th anniversary. In addition to providing network services, the ARPANET has been an experimental test-bed for much of the research in computer networking. The government agency responsible for the ARPANET announced that it would follow the advice of computer scientists working in the field to change research directions and discontinue work on the ARPANET. It will begin funding new higher-speed communications technologies and shut down the ARPANET in the near future.

Data communication networks. The need for better telephone service motivated much of the early communications research. Pioneering research at such places as Bell Telephone Laboratories resulted in a well-developed theory of information and helped engineers understand how to sample and encode human voices electronically for transmission. The underlying network technology used by the telephone system is circuit switched because it provides a physical connection (circuit) between two telephones. Much of the early circuit-switched network technology used analog electronics (devices that operate with variables that are represented by continuously measured voltages or other quantities) because the technology was developed before solid-state digital electronic devices became available.

In the 1960s, as companies started to use computers for such tasks as managing airline reservations, it became apparent that new communications network technologies were needed to transmit data between computers. As researchers began to explore ways to interconnect computers, they first encoded data in the same way that the voice networks encoded sounds and then sent the encoded data over conventional telephone circuits. The devices used to convert data from digital form into analog signals appropriate for telephone circuits are called modems. The technique is still used; vendors introduced several new modems during the past year.

Although modems make computer communication over conventional telephone circuits possible, they have limited speed. The first modems operated at rates of 110 bits per second. Within five years modems were available that operated at speeds of 300 or 1,200 bits per second. While modem technology had reached its limits, processor and memory technologies developed throughout the 1960s. In short, computers became faster while circuit-switched communications did not.

In the late 1960s the Advanced Research Projects Agency (ARPA), a U.S. government agency responsible for funding research and development of ideas that could be important to the U.S. Department of Defense (DOD), became aware of the communication problem. DOD used computers to plan strategies, coordinate troop movements, and communicate between military bases throughout the world. Each year the military needed to send more information between agencies, and they needed to send it faster. Slow communication with the circuit-switch technology prevented them from using high-speed computers.

Leaders at ARPA worked with the computer science research community to develop better communications technologies. After surveying the field they turned to a new, unproven technique called packet switching. The idea behind packet switching was

simple: instead of dedicating a high-speed communication circuit to only a pair of computers, many computers should be allowed to share the circuit. If only one pair of machines used the circuit at a given time, they would receive almost 100% of the circuit capacity. If more than two machines decided to communicate at a given time, each pair of machines would receive part of the circuit capacity. Researchers speculated that packet switching could make the allocation of capacity both automatic and fair.

To allow such sharing, packet-switching networks require senders to divide their data into blocks called packets. Each packet contains a short header that specifies the destination. The network accepts packets from multiple senders and routes them to their respective destinations. Because packets traveling between diverse sources and destinations can traverse a single communication circuit, the network does not need separate physical circuits for each pair of communicating computers.

Although the idea of packet switching was commonly accepted in 1990 as the primary technology for computer communication, it was controversial in the 1960s. When ARPA announced that it wanted to build a large, experimental packet-switching network that would eventually span the continental U.S., many communications experts were skeptical. They asked, "What will happen if too many packets enter the system?" and "How will communicating computers tolerate increases in delay that result when many of them try to communicate simultaneously?" Those questions needed to be answered before an efficient packet-switching network could be created.

The ARPANET. ARPA funded research on packet switching, including analytical work with a goal of understanding how packet-switching systems perform and experimental work with the goal of developing a viable packet-switching technology. The analytical work resulted in a group of mathematical techniques commonly referred to as queuing theory; it was used to analyze how the network would perform before any hardware was built. In 1969 the first piece of an operational packet-switching network was installed at the University of California at Los Angeles. The primary contractor was a group at Bolt, Beranek, and Newman (BBN) in Cambridge, Mass. The network BBN developed was called the ARPANET, the name being taken from the agency that funded it. Within two years the ARPANET had grown to 15 sites. The size doubled again by 1973, and the network continued to evolve. By 1982 packet switching had become widely accepted, and the ARPANET technology had become highly reliable. In 1983 the ARPANET was split into two (connected) pieces, one for military sites and the other for computer scientists to use for continuing experimental packet-switching research.

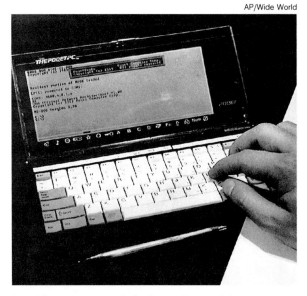

Portable computer made by Poqet Corp. weighs 0.45 kilogram (one pound) and can fit easily into a coat pocket. Comparable to a full-size portable, it has 512-kilobyte random-access memory.

At its peak in 1989 the ARPANET reached hundreds of sites, and computer scientists throughout the world used it daily.

When first built, the ARPANET technology seemed exciting. The circuits interconnecting major switching machines operated at 56,000 bits per second, making them much faster than the typical communication speeds available in the 1960s. Furthermore, because the military required researchers to develop robust technology that could survive simple failures, the ARPANET was designed to automatically detect and accommodate failures of such individual components as a communication line or switching computer. The network was biconnected, meaning that each switching computer had at least two connections to other switches. The switching machines contained programs that automatically changed routes to use working connections whenever a connection failed. Such reconfiguration required much research and made the ARPANET significantly more sophisticated than its predecessors.

To help them manage the ARPANET, BBN developed some of the first network monitoring and control software. The software employed the network itself to carry control information between individual sites and the control center at BBN. From the control center BBN could troubleshoot problems, monitor and control performance, and gather statistics on traffic. The monitoring facility made it possible for BBN to test new ideas and see their effects in a live network.

Within a few years commercial companies began to use the packet-switching technology introduced by the ARPANET. Public data networks such as GTE Telenet used packet switching to provide services that could connect terminals to remote computers. Other vendors offered similar networks. An employee visiting a remote city could carry a portable terminal and modem, use the telephone to dial the local public data network entry point, and connect to a computer back at the home site. While other networks concentrated on providing remote terminal service, researchers used the ARPANET to experiment with direct, high-speed communication from one computer to another.

In addition to the packet-switching hardware technology, ARPANET research produced many software ideas that by 1990 were in common use both in the computer science community and in the commercial world. Probably best known among these is electronic mail. Electronic mail consists of memos sent from one user to others. A user invokes a local mail program that helps to compose a memo and specify recipients. In essence, the mail program is a word processor with a few additional features to handle the formatting of recipients' names. Once a user has composed a memo, the local computer uses network communication facilities to transmit it to each recipient's computer. Later, recipients invoke another program to read the mail. Again, most mail-reading programs are simple modifications of word processors that allow a user to scroll back and forth across the memo or to search for a word or phrase.

Although it seems like a simple idea, computer scientists have come to rely on electronic mail as their primary form of interaction. Because the ARPANET provided reliable, quick mail delivery, computer scientists found that they could depend on it to communicate ideas to colleagues. For example, a computer scientist working on a research paper could send a draft of the paper to a colleague in a few seconds. With high-speed communication it was possible for two computer scientists to cooperate on research even though they were geographically distant from one another.

Encouraged by the success of the ARPANET, ARPA began to explore several other forms of packet switching. The agency developed packet switching for various forms of satellite communication and for mobile radio systems. In the 1970s ARPA researchers had produced several operational packet-switching networks. They then began to ask how these networks could be interconnected so that users on one network could communicate with users on others. With the ARPANET as a central backbone computer scientists experimented with network interconnection. Interestingly, the ARPANET made it possible for geographically dispersed researchers to cooperate in the research and development of interconnection techniques. In essence, the ARPANET was used to build the next generation of networking technologies.

By 1990 the ARPANET formed the backbone of a worldwide collection of interconnected networks called the Internet. The Internet connects universities, government laboratories, military bases, and commercial organizations. During the past year it continued to grow, so that by 1990 it connected more than 1,000 active networks that had over 100,000 computers connected to them. Computer scientists used the Internet every day; other scientists and engineers recently began to use it.

The past year marked a major turning point in the evolution of the ARPANET. Advances in communications technologies (especially in fiber optics) increased communication speeds dramatically. Consequently, the ARPANET, once considered a high-speed network, was slow compared with the available communication speeds of 1.5 million bits per second and 4.5 million bits per second. During the year some parts of the Internet began to adopt the new technologies and operate at speeds of 1.5 million bits per second. Computer scientists expected that it soon would be possible to operate cross-country fiber-optic links at speeds of one gigabit (one billion bits) per second. They recommended that the government stop funding older technologies and use the money to explore higher-speed networking. Thus, during the year the government began to dismantle the ARPANET. Within another year it was expected

to disappear completely. For a generation of computer scientists who depended on the ARPANET for data communication, this change represented a major shift both in the facilities they used and in the research that those facilities made possible.

High-speed processors. Each year it seems that computer vendors announce new machines with central processing units (CPUs) that operate at higher speeds. The past year was no exception. For example, Compaq Computer Corp. announced a "server" machine that executed 40 million instructions per second. Like many companies, Compaq designed its new machines to be used in a client-server configuration. In such configurations a single server handled the processing and storage tasks for a set of several small client computers. Typically, the latter were personal computers (PCs), and the server was a higher speed computer with large disk storage. The clients and server interacted over an inexpensive packet-switching network, making the system easy to expand and easy to integrate with other computers.

Sun Microsystems Inc., one of the leaders in the scientific workstation market, announced a new, more powerful server for its UNIX workstations. Called the SparcServer 490, the new machine was capable of executing 22 million instructions per second (the processor clock ran at 33 MHz). It used a reduced instruction set computer (RISC) design that achieved high speed by eliminating complex instructions that took longer to execute. Although the

The VAX 9000, introduced during the year by Digital Equipment Corp., is a minicomputer that can interact with smaller machines and also can perform large computational tasks for 20–30 users.

Digital Equipment Corporation

underlying processor employed simple instructions, users could not sense this because the software with which the user interacted (such as spread-sheet programs) worked exactly the same as it did on connected complex instruction set computers.

MIPS Computer Systems, Inc., introduced the latest advance in high-speed CPU chips during the past year when it announced a system capable of executing 55 million instructions per second. Like the SparcServer, the MIPS RC6280 system employed a RISC design. The processor chip used in the MIPS was MIPS model R6000, a new, higher-speed version of the MIPS R3000. The R6000 ran at a clock speed of 67 MHz. (By comparison, typical PC processor chips executed at speeds of between 7 and 20 MHz, while a typical scientific workstation processor executed at speeds between 15 and 25 MHz.) In addition to fast instructions for integer arithmetic, the system featured hardware capable of executing 10.3 million floating point operations per second. (Floating point hardware adds, subtracts, multiplies, and divides fractional values used in scientific computations.) The MIPS system was remarkable because it performed at twice the speed of its predecessor while the price did not double.

Like the Compaq computer described earlier, the MIPS system was designed to be a server. Most customers were expected to purchase a single RC6280 system that they would use with a set of smaller client machines.

Digital Equipment Corp. announced several new computers during the year. Like the Compaq, Sun, and MIPS systems, Digital's new VAX 9000 system had significantly more computing power than its predecessors. Furthermore, unlike the workstations intended for an individual or servers intended to support a set of workstations, the VAX 9000 was a minicomputer designed to handle both interactive tasks and large computational tasks for 20–30 users. Because the manufacturer also expected the VAX 9000 to be used in a scientific computing market, it offered an optional processing unit that could perform operations on mathematical matrices quickly. If the processing needs of the users were to outgrow a single VAX 9000 computer, additional machines could be connected to form a cluster of computers that shared storage.

Unlike the Compaq and MIPS systems, some of the Digital announcements focused on price instead of performance. Digital announced a DECstation 3100 with performance in the range of a small minicomputer (3 million–5 million instructions per second) at the price of a high-end personal computer. Thus, improvements in technology continued to allow manufacturers to produce computers that were faster and less expensive than earlier models.
—Douglas E. Comer

Electronics

Electronics in the 1980s experienced many remarkable technological changes combined with healthy economic growth rates. At the close of the decade, however, slow growth rates made for a performance termed "lousy and lackluster" in the opinions of some industry executives.

Predictions for future growth within the industry ranged from flat to only a modest rise during 1990. On the basis of fluctuations of world currencies, the shrinking of military markets, and a lack of capital spending especially in the computer sector of the industry, many of the unfavorable trends of the second half of 1989 were expected to continue into 1990.

Companies began devising different strategies and products to escape the predicted doldrums of the coming year. In one such effort industry experts saw a healthy growth in computer-assisted-engineering (CAD) programs as customers purchased such systems in support of their research and development efforts.

The chip segment of the electronics industry was suffering from overcapacity. Only during the latter half of 1990, as the existing stock of chips was expected to be consumed, were modest growth rates anticipated in that sector. In anticipation of that eventual rise, some companies began to spend large sums on research and development in order to produce new products.

Complicating market predictions and growth rates was the dynamic nature of technological invention and change. While in former times a product cycle lasted for five years, by 1990 it had been shortened to 18 months. So many new features were being introduced at such a fast pace that consumers were unsure of what to buy. Even more inventions and innovations would have to be made in the area of consumer electronics, however, for it was in that sector that many industry observers foresaw growth in 1990. The computer and communications sectors were insufficient to drive the chip business. It was with the intent of revitalizing the consumer portion that the National Advisory Committee on Semiconductors was formed in late 1988.

The technology lag was not the only concern of electronics executives, however. Many of them regarded manufacturing and salesmanship as the most serious problems in the U.S. industry. In particular, the manufacture of electronic equipment was slowly moving overseas.

Funding is a major problem in bringing products to market. In both Japan and Europe government sponsorship of the electronics industry was strong, but it was nonexistent in the U.S. Most projects need a high level of investments, yet in the U.S. the needed funds were not available.

International developments. Compared with 1988, the world's electronics markets showed only a modest growth during 1989, and in certain places and sectors of the industry there was even a slight decline in production. Global consumption of electronic products was near $500 billion, reflecting a growth of less than 10% over the banner year of 1988, when there were growth rates of more than 28% in some areas of industrial production.

The U.S. remained the largest consumer in all categories except consumer electronics, spending about $185 billion in 1989. Next was Japan with $155 billion, though it outpaced the U.S. in electronic consumer goods by $29.1 billion to $24.8 billion. Europe finished third with a total of $124 billion. These figures reflect an important shift for the U.S. While in 1980 the U.S. consumed about half of all electronic goods in the world, by 1989 its portion had been reduced to about one-third.

In all categories of the industry in 1989, Japan showed a larger rate of increase than any other nation. Increases were posted for equipment and software, for industrial equipment and semiconductor manufacturing, and especially for test and measuring equipment. The projected growth rate for that sector was 13%, bringing it to $1.8 billion.

While Japanese consumer electronics shrank as a portion of the overall consumption, that sector nevertheless posted a growth rate of 8%. Camcorders, videodisc players, broadcast satellite antennas, and high-definition television sets were filling up more and more Japanese houses.

The West German electronics industry grew a modest 5% on average for 1989. Among the reasons for the slowdown were indirect taxes that totaled $5 billion for the year. Consumer electronics suffered the greatest decline. Communications equipment experienced a flat growth rate, while computers, at a rate of 7%, were above the average. Even in this relatively slow growth environment, though, certain items stood out for the fast pace of their sales; among them were camcorders and microwave ovens. Mainframe and large central processing units declined in sales. Personal computers sold briskly, with microcomputers leading the pack at a 13% rate that took that sector of the market to $1.4 billion.

Hong Kong profited by its Far Eastern location during much of the 1980s, as that area of the world had the steepest growth rates in electronics and, by mid-1988, surpassed the U.S. in actual sales volume. Parts and components, at 36% of the total, made up its largest share of production, with watches, at 20%, following. Some 35% of its production found its way into the U.S.

Technological development. Intel Corp. produced a new chip, the i860, which packed more than one million transistors onto a single piece of silicon. This, together with its ability to handle 64-bit chunks of data, vastly improved its computing power over that of its predecessors. The chip was placed in workstations that were involved in scientific and engineering applications. Typical tasks included three-dimensional modeling, shading of background, and simulations—all of which had previously been handled by supercomputers and superminicomputers. The new chip was expected to perform these tasks at a much lower price.

On April 18, 1989, a fiber-optic communications cable that was capable of carrying 40,000 simultaneous telephone conversations was placed into service between Point Arena, Calif., and Makaha, Hawaii. From there it extended to an undersea branching station southeast of Japan, where it split with one leg going to Tanguisson, Guam, and the other to Chikura, Japan.

The new cable was the result of the effort of 30 international communications companies. AT&T owned 35% of it, and the Kokusai Denshin Denwa, Japan's international long-distance company, owned 23%; the remainder was split among various other companies, such as RCA and MCI. The cable was laid to meet a growing need for high-speed, high-quality transmission of voice and facsimile communications. For instance, calls by Americans to Japan totaled 14 million minutes in 1977, but by 1987 that figure stood at 175 million minutes.

Fiber-optic cables, which were both cheaper and more efficient to operate than copper cables, were expected to reduce the cost of communications between the two countries. For example, when AT&T opened its first radio channel to Japan in 1934, a three-minute call cost about $30. By 1964 that same call, using the first copper cable across the Pacific, cost $6.34, while in 1989 the call via the fiber-optic cable cost $3.78.

Within the next five years two more fiber-optic cables were planned between the U.S. and Japan. Investment in the technology was expected to total about $8.5 billion by 1995.

Consumer electronics. On June 3, 1989, Japan initiated the world's first broadcast of high-definition-television (HDTV) programs. In a somewhat surprising yet politically astute move, the first image to appear on the 89 giant screens placed across Japan was the Statue of Liberty and New York Harbor. U.S. companies saw HDTV as an area of consumer electronics that would permit them to reenter a consumer market now ceded to the Japanese. Such an effort would not be easy, however, since Japan was well ahead in HDTV development.

HDTV promised a revolutionary change in home entertainment. HDTV receivers were expected to display twice the horizontal and vertical resolutions of present-day television sets together with 10 times the color information details. The picture quality would be that of current 35-mm movie films, and the sound quality would rival that of compact discs.

One of the newest electronic products is the executive organizer. It was made possible by the availability of low-cost memories that require little electrical power. Current models have 32 K bits of memory, weigh about 0.2 kg (0.5 lb), and cost about $300; they consist of a telephone directory, a memo pad, an appointment scheduler, a built-in world clock, and a calculator.

The Pontiac Division of General Motors Corp. planned to introduce a hologram to replace the "high-light" stop sign on its 1990 car models. The hologram will be embedded in the rear windshield and wired up to the brake system. Upon the application of the brakes, it will light up in the shape of a stop sign together with its message. While the display will be clearly visible to anyone driving behind it, the driver can look right through it and not have his or her view impeded in any way.

Ozone depletion and the electronics industry. During most of the 1980s, chlorofluorocarbons, or CFCs, were considered to be the safe and harmless wonder chemicals used in the manufacturing of computer disks, circuit boards, optical fibers, and semiconductors. Electronic manufacturing consumed about 43 million kg (95 million lb) of CFCs in 1988 at a cost of about $128 million. That represented about 12% of the total usage of CFCs in that year.

Scientists had for several years been warning about the possible harmful effects of these chemicals on the ozone layer in the Earth's atmosphere. A report released during 1988 by the U.S. National Aeronautics and Space Administration and the National Oceanographic and Atmospheric Administration documented the existence of high concentrations of ozone-depleting compounds in the stratosphere over Antarctica and the Arctic. The results of such depletions include a possible increase in crop damage and the number of skin cancers.

In consequence, an international agreement, the Montreal Protocol, was ratified; it fixed the consumption of CFCs at 1986 levels. This represented a reduction of about 15 to 20% from 1988 levels. Furthermore, Canada, the U.S., and the European Communities agreed that by the end of the century they would not produce any CFCs.

During the year there was a search to replace CFCs in the electronics industry. IBM, which used 5 million kg (11 million lb) of CFCs in 1987, had already reduced its use by 20% during 1988 and expected an additional 30% reduction in 1989. Water-based detergent solutions seemed suitable for some purposes, though small and complex shapes cannot be cleaned with them.

—Franz J. Monssen

Information systems and services

"Information is the life blood of many Federal Government programs and is essential to the implementation of agency missions and to informed public debate." This statement was made in "Informing the Nation: Federal Information Dissemination in an Electronic Age," a report prepared by the U.S. Office of Technology Assessment. The report concluded that congressional action was urgently needed to resolve issues concerning the dissemination of federal information and to provide direction to existing agencies and institutions so that full advantage could be taken of technological advances in microcomputers, electronic publishing systems, and the many scientific and technical data bases. Among the options for change suggested in the report were that Congress should renew its commitment to public access to information in an electronic age, use a range of techniques for publishing electronic documents, and ensure that federal information is made available expediently to the public.

A Machine-Readable Collections Reading Room was formally opened at the U.S. Library of Congress; more informally this room was called "The Library of Tomorrow." It was part of a pilot program designed to enable the Library of Congress to evaluate methods for acquiring and cataloging machine-readable materials and to study access and security issues. Five workstations with IBM-compatible and Macintosh microcomputers were available for use by the general public, who had access to hundreds of different software programs stored on diskettes, CD-ROM (compact disc-read only memory), and videodiscs. Two librarians were available to assist users. It was anticipated that by the year 2000 the Library of Congress would have the most comprehensive collection of computer software in the world. The Machine-Readable Collections Reading Room was located in the southwest corner of the Thomas Jefferson Building and was open Monday through Friday from 12 noon to 4 PM.

The U.S. National Archives was engaged in a multiyear project to test an optical digital image storage system and explore its applicability for the storage and retrieval of historic documents. Don W. Wilson, the archivist of the U.S., explained that optical digital storage and electronic image enhancement would preserve the original documents and provide scholars with access to previously illegible materials.

The 1990 U.S. decennial census data were to be recorded on CD-ROM and made available to the 1,400 federal depository libraries. The first of these general-use data products provided summary statistics derived from the "100% Questions" asked of all U.S. households. Other products contained data based on the "long form" questionnaires sent to a sample of the population and then statistically weighted to reflect the entire population. A Bureau of the Census report, "1990 Decennial Census of Population and Housing—Tabulation and Publication Program," described the redesigned census tabulation and publication program and contained brief descriptions of all 1990 data products.

The New York City Public Library dug deep below the surface of adjacent Bryant Park to construct an underground storage facility that would double the storage capacity of its main bookstacks. The $16.6 million stack extension should relieve the library's shortage of shelf space by accommodating up to 3.2 million library volumes and 500,000 reels of microforms in the largest known installation of a high-density mobile compact shelving system.

U.S. information systems. Computer data bases collect and organize information gathered from many sources so as to make searching simpler and more efficient. Many new data bases on topics of importance were created during the past year. For example, the Multiple Sclerosis (MS) Research Products data base tracks MS research studies in progress. Input to the data base was provided by the International Federation of Multiple Sclerosis Societies and consisted of information on basic research and clinical and rehabilitation studies that could affect the direction of future research and treatment of MS and its effects.

New data bases related to AIDS (acquired immune deficiency syndrome) were created. CAIN, the Computerized AIDS Information Network, is an electronic forum used by individuals who are committed to checking the spread of the disease by sharing knowledge and experience. CAIN users have access to relevant news abstracts, clinical data, and press releases from a variety of organizations. Also covered are instances of housing and employment discrimination against people with AIDS and information about drugs and treatments that have not yet been federally approved. AIDS in Focus is a file of references about AIDS maintained by the Biological Sciences Information Service (BIOSIS). The data base contains approximately 7,000 records, with about 350 expected to be added to that total each month. The references are to research findings published in journals, books, conference proceedings, and U.S. patents.

A Data Center and Clearinghouse for Drugs and Crime was established by the U.S. Department of Justice in order to provide policymakers and others with ready access to information about drug law violations, drug-related law enforcement, and the impact of drug-related crime on criminal justice administration. The clearinghouse collects data from many federal, state, and local agencies, as well as from the private sector. It answers requests for specific drug enforcement data reports and suggests alternative sources when the requested data are not available. The data analysis and evaluation unit checks all data for statistical reliability and prepares special computer tabulations and analyses on topics of public concern.

Earthquake Database at the National Geophysical Data Center, Boulder, Colo., holds information on more than 500,000 earthquakes and other Earth disturbances recorded worldwide for the period from 2100 BC to 1987. Playbill is a Dartmouth College (Hanover, N.H.) data base that lists some 20,000 theatrical performances from the early 19th century to the present. The theater programs in the collection are indexed by play title, performing company, theater, year of performance, and, in some cases, by the starring actor.

Compton's Multimedia Encyclopedia, © Compton's Learning Company

Compton's MultiMedia Encyclopedia, *introduced in the fall of 1989, includes on one compact disc the 26-volume Compton's* Encyclopedia *with 15,000 illustrations, as well as 60 minutes of speeches, music, and other sounds, a complete dictionary, and 45 animated sequences. Access to the encyclopedia can be gained by using one of the eight paths pictured at the left.*

A microcomputer index is available as a printed publication, issued quarterly, and as an on-line data base, updated monthly, on the Dialog information system. The data base contains more than 75,000 records and covers the 70 most important journals, magazines, and trade publications in the microcomputer field. It also contains a listing of top-selling software packages and books on personal computing and related fields.

International information systems. Six national libraries in Europe formed a consortium for interchanging bibliographic records and increasing access to major research collections. CD-ROM technology was selected as the most cost-effective delivery medium and one that would encourage widespread distribution of cataloging data among countries in the European Communities (EC).

The U.S.S.R. Academy of Sciences and the State Committee for Science and Technology signed a protocol of intent with the U.S. Chemical Abstracts Society (CAS) as a basis for engaging in cooperative projects. The first project established training centers in the Soviet cities of Novosibirsk and Moscow to demonstrate on-line searching of scientific and technical information to Soviet officials and scientists and to train information specialists in on-line searching. CAS agreed to train Soviet chemists in Columbus, Ohio, so that they could serve as demonstrators and trainers in the centers. CAS was primarily interested in gaining prompt U.S. access to scientific and technical information originating in the U.S.S.R.

Unesco encouraged the establishment of the International Chemical Information Network, known by the acronym ChIN, which was designed to promote the exchange of chemical information through shared access to core journals, patents, and translation facilities. The network would also provide a framework for managing cooperative projects involving chemical science and technology, some of which may be supported by Unesco. The network's Secretariat was located at the International Centre for Chemical Studies in Ljubljana, Yugos.

The Commission of the EC supported the creation of a common integrated computer communications infrastructure, or network, that would connect various public and private research centers in Europe and encourage closer cooperation among individual researchers and research teams spread across the region. In addition, the program undertook to improve the dissemination and increase the impact of results derived from scientific and technical research wholly or partly financed by the EC.

The British Library Research and Development Department initiated a program of linked studies to examine the likely impact of technological and other developments on the production, storage, and use of information in the U.K. during the 1990s. The program consists of a series of interrelated forecasting studies, each covering an area of particular interest—such as publishing, bookselling, or library services—and the use of information in the home, in industry, and in education.

The Ulysses project is a multinational data base of tourist information that was collected from France, Portugal, and Ireland. The work was coordinated by an international association of automobile clubs and is available for on-line searching.

An Arab Information Database was conceived by a group of editors based in Dubayy, United Arab Emirates. It contains more than 50,000 articles on such subjects as economics, industry, energy, health, education, culture, religion, and politics as they relate to the Arab world. These articles were translated into English from Arab newspapers and may be searched worldwide via satellite.

Information science research. The U.S. National Science Foundation (NSF) provided funds, equipment, and personnel to enter descriptive data about the Cornell University (Ithaca, N.Y.) Ichthyology Collection of approximately 1.5 million preserved fishes and selected samples of particular species into a computerized data base. The collection regularly receives requests for information from a wide variety of scientific, government, and public users, and thousands of specimens are sent out on loan to scientists at other institutions. However, with only a manual catalog it was impossible, or at least impractical, to answer many of these questions. The NSF grant supported the creation of a computerized data base that would be able to answer questions quickly while increasing the efficiency of all aspects of collection management.

The National Endowment for the Humanities awarded a $1 million multiyear grant to seven member institutions of the Research Libraries Group (Columbia, Cornell, Michigan, Princeton, Stanford, and Yale universities and the New York City Public Library) to help preserve disintegrating materials in their libraries. The subject areas targeted for microfilming included U.S. history, Chinese history, and German literature, along with several others important to research and education in the humanities. By early 1990 more than 50,000 volumes had been microfilmed.

Investigators at New York University received a grant to pursue related studies concerning the role of computers and information in productivity growth. One study investigated the extent to which the rise in employment in information services resulted from a redeployment of the labor force away from manufacturing. A study in occupational mix explored the question of whether the use of computer technology led to an increased level of education and expertise in the labor force or to a reduction in skill level. A third study explored the role of information transmission and technology diffusion on the economic development of nations.

The National Science Foundation awarded a grant to the Disabled Citizens Computer Center to develop, modify, and test educational software in order to produce speech and auditory output for use by visually handicapped individuals. Much of the work was done by students enrolled in computer classes at the Louisville (Ky.) Central High School Computer Technology Career Magnet Program. An important element in this grant was the educational opportunity provided for the students. Teachers received training in the use of the materials and then tested them in the classroom. Finally, the finished products, together with recommendations for their use, were disseminated through the National Education Special Alliance established by Apple Computer and the American Printing House for the Blind.

The University of Sheffield, England, received a grant from the British Library Research and Development Department to study interpersonal skills training in the private sector and in public agencies. Information was gathered through interviews with trainers, observations of training sessions, and reviews and evaluations of methods and materials used in training programs. The knowledge gained was used to further effective development of interpersonal skills training in library and information organizations and to improve the performance of the staff.

A study, jointly sponsored by the EC and Unesco, allowed the Institut de l'Audiovisuel et des Telecommunications in Luxembourg to create a data base designed to improve the flow of information among European experts in communications studies. The data base listed some 200 organizations, 400 researchers and consultants, and 2,000 publications. Searches could identify experts by name, subject matter, and location and could retrieve helpful publications.

—Harold Borko

Satellite systems

Earth-orbiting satellites provide a variety of services of great economic, social, and military value. Called applications satellites, they can be grouped into three general classes: communications, Earth observation, and navigation. These satellites are developed, launched, and operated by individual nations, groups of nations, and private industrial concerns.

In 1989 the U.S. space shuttles *Discovery, Atlantis,* and *Columbia* made five successful flights, three of them deploying large, heavy satellites and two of them deploying probes. An 11-day mission of *Columbia* in January 1990 paved the way for missions of longer duration. A new fourth orbiter under construction, *Endeavour,* will be capable of flights as long as four weeks (*see* SPACE EXPLORATION).

Communications satellites. This largest class of satellites continued during the past year to grow in size, complexity, and performance. Larger, more powerful transmitters, as well as new experimental systems, were orbited by the U.S., Europe, and Japan. The effects of recent deregulation of monopolistic government controls were evident, sparking investment and competition by private industry.

Another development in communications satellite technology was the move toward Very Small Aperture Terminals (VSATs). The increasing power of signals transmitted from orbit permits the use of smaller receiver antennas. This is cost-effective because of the increased number of users for a fixed cost of the orbiting satellite. VSAT antennas are about 1.2 m (4 ft) in diameter, compared with diameters of 3 to 9 m (10 to 30 ft) typically required for business use in 1980.

The International Telecommunications Satellite Organization (Intelsat) is a commercial cooperative owned and operated by 118 member nations. During the year Intelsat operated 13 satellites placed in geostationary orbit above the Atlantic, Pacific, and Indian oceans. (A satellite in a geostationary orbit travels above the equator and at the same speed that the Earth rotates; thus, the satellite seems to remain in the same place.) This global system was the major provider of transoceanic television services. By 1990 total full-time traffic had grown to more than 125,000 channels. At the end of 1989 there were some 900 Earth stations accessing Intelsat. All services offered by the system increased in use; they included transoceanic telephone, television, facsimile, digital data, and telex through 2,100 full-time and on-demand Earth-station-to-Earth-station paths. In addition, many thousand "receive only" small terminals were using Intelsat.

Continuing the organization's steady technological progress, the last seventh-generation-design Intelsat 5-A was launched January 1989; the last fifth-generation 4-A was decommissioned; and the first eighth-generation Intelsat 6 was launched October 1989. In decommissioning the Intelsat 4-A after 10 years of operation, ground controllers directed the satellite to use its remaining fuel to boost it to an orbit 200 km (122 mi) above the geostationary orbit. Thus, the risk of future collision or interference with other operating satellites was greatly lessened.

The Intelsat 6 was the first of five such satellites to be launched over the next two years, replacing aging spacecraft. Placed in geostationary orbit by an Ariane 44-L booster, Intelsat 6 weighed 2,560 kg (5,630 lb) and could relay at least three television channels and 120,000 telephone calls simultaneously. New

An Ariane 44-L rocket launches the first Intelsat 6 into orbit on Oct. 28, 1989. The world's largest telecommunications satellite, it can relay at least three television channels and 120,000 telephone calls simultaneously.

modulation techniques utilizing digital compression resulted in a multiplication factor, greatly increasing the number of simultaneous transmissions. The in-orbit value of an Intelsat 6 was estimated at $250 million.

In addition to the global Intelsat system, the London-based Inmarsat international cooperative continued to grow and diversify. With 55 member nations, Inmarsat had geostationary relay satellites covering most of the Atlantic, Pacific, and Indian ocean regions. High-quality two-way telephone, telex, facsimile, and data communications were provided to more than 8,000 ships at sea. Progress was made in 1989 in offering land mobile communications to Inmarsat member countries.

Inmarsat established an agreement of cooperation with the International Civil Aviation Organization.

This action cleared the way for the eventual use of satellite communications to aircraft throughout the world. Previously all airline communications had been dependent on high-frequency and very high-frequency radio, which was limited in range, capacity, quality, and reliability. The first Inmarsat commercial public telephone calls via satellite from an airliner were made aboard a British Airways 747. A number of major U.S. airlines installed or were planning installation of such telephones. The first of four second-generation Inmarsat 2 satellites was scheduled for launch in mid-1990. These satellites were to carry a transponder with L-band frequency, specifically for aeronautical use.

In 1989 the U.S. Communications Satellite Corp. (Comsat) modified for aeronautical services its coastal Earth stations in Southbury, Conn., and Santa Paula, Calif. By 1990 Comsat's maritime service provided direct-dial telephone via satellite to and from cruise ships.

The U.S. space shuttle *Discovery* launched the third Tracking and Data Relay Satellite (TDRS) in March 1989. Primarily for use by the U.S. National Aeronautics and Space Administration (NASA), the geostationary TDRS network provided communications with the space shuttle and other low-orbit spacecraft. Intelsat concluded an agreement with NASA for the use of the C-band capacity on two TDRS satellites for international telecommunications purposes. The TDRS network was operated and owned by Contel Federal Systems.

In June 1989 an Ariane 44-L launched two broadcast satellites into geostationary orbit, for West Germany and Japan. The West German DFS Kopernicus, owned by the Deutsche Bundespost, was to serve West Germany and West Berlin. The Japanese Superbird, designed for 10 years of service, was to provide communications to Japan and Okinawa. Based on Ford Aerospace's Intelsat 5 design, the Superbirds were large satellites, each one weighing 2,489 kg (5,487 lb). Privately owned by the Japanese Space Communications Corp., Superbird was designed to transmit high-definition television.

A JCSAT-1 direct-broadcast satellite was launched by an Ariane 44-LP rocket on March 6, 1989, from Kourou, French Guiana. (A direct-broadcast satellite transmits the television signals it receives directly to home sets.) Owned by the Japanese Communications Satellite Co. (JCSAT), the satellite was 3.7 m (12.2 ft) in diameter and 10 m (33 ft) long and weighed 1,364 kg (3,000 lb) in geostationary orbit. JCSAT is a joint venture between Itoh Co. and Mitsui Co. of Japan and Hughes Communications Co. of the U.S.

In August 1989 London-based British Satellite Broadcasting (BSB) launched its first direct-broadcast satellite, Marco Polo-1. Built by Hughes Communications Co., a second BSB satellite was scheduled

Syncom communications satellite occupies a geostationary orbit over the Earth after being deployed by the space shuttle Columbia *for the U.S. Navy in January 1990.*

for launch in August 1990. Five channels of television service to the U.K. were expected to be in operation in 1990.

The military forces of major nations use satellites to maintain secure telecommunications between headquarters and land or sea units. On Dec. 31, 1989, the British Defense Ministry communications satellite Skynet 4 was launched into geostationary orbit. Skynet 4, with a lifetime of seven years, was designed to provide jamproof communications for Britain's land- and sea-based military forces. Identical to another Skynet 4 launched in December 1988, it carried a four-channel super-high-frequency transponder for land and sea relays and a two-channel ultra-high-frequency transponder for submarine transmission. Two similar satellites were being built by British Aerospace and Marconi for military and diplomatic communications.

Early in January 1990 the space shuttle *Columbia* deployed into geostationary orbit a 6,700-kg (14,770-lb) Syncom satellite for the U.S. Navy. The Navy also launched the eighth and last in a series of Fleet Satellite Communications (FltSatCom) spacecraft. On board were 23 ultra-high-frequency channels and one extremely high-frequency experimental package for the future generation of military (Milstar) communications satellites. The Milstars were being designed to provide secure command and control during and after a nuclear attack. Users would include national military command centers, navy ships and submarines, and air force strategic forces.

Earth-observation satellites. This category of applications satellites consists of three major types: weather (meteorological), Earth resources, and military reconnaissance.

Weather satellites. Continuous global weather observations were obtained during the past year from U.S., European Space Agency (ESA), Soviet, and Japanese weather satellites in geostationary orbits above the equator. Supplementing this capability were the U.S. and Soviet satellites in polar orbits. Thus, global coverage of weather patterns and movement was provided continuously.

The U.S. normally has two Geostationary Operational Environmental Satellites (GOES) stationed at longitudes 75° W and 135° W to provide eastern and western coverage of the U.S. and the Western Hemisphere. However, GOES-West failed early in 1989. To alleviate this loss of coverage, the U.S. National Oceanic and Atmospheric Administration (NOAA) moved GOES-East to a more westerly position. ESA and EUTEL (NOAA's European counterpart) cooperated by moving one of their two Meteosats to the west to cover the middle of the Atlantic Ocean. Correspondingly, the Japanese Meteorological Agency moved one of its satellites to the east to broaden Pacific Ocean coverage. The first of a new series of five GOES satellites was planned for launch in 1991.

Earth-resources satellites. In the U.S. the Earth Observation Satellite Co. (Eosat) continued to manage the Landsat satellite system under contract from NOAA. However, there was stiff competition from

France's Spot satellites and from Soviet systems. Eosat's customers were primarily the U.S. Agriculture, Commerce, and Defense departments. The images transmitted by the Landsats were used to estimate the size and health of crops, map vegetation, locate mineral and oil deposits, and monitor global climatic changes. The spectral images obtained from Landsat 4 and Landsat 5 satellites are limited to a 30-m (100-ft) resolution of surface features. The French Spot and Soviet Union satellite systems had resolution that was three to five times higher. Furthermore, both countries were developing capabilities to market radar images that could view the Earth through cloud cover and with optical quality.

Military reconnaissance satellites. The prime purpose of this category of satellites is to provide intelligence on movements of troops, tanks, ships, and submarines and also on activity concerning missiles. Such satellites record optical and radar images of the Earth. In addition, emissions of terrestrial and airborne communications and radar systems (called Elint) are recorded and transmitted. Other varieties of reconnaissance satellites record nuclear explosions and detect missile launches by sensing the heat of rocket exhaust plumes.

In June 1989 the first Titan IV, built by Martin Marietta Corp., launched a U.S. Air Force Defense Support Program satellite (DSP) into geostationary orbit. The 2,359-kg (5,200-lb) DSP carried a telescope with 6,000 infrared detectors; it was believed that the satellite could detect even the exhaust heat of military aircraft using afterburners.

In August the space shuttle *Columbia* deployed a new-generation reconnaissance satellite. This was an improved KH-11 design configured in size for launch from the shuttle bay. Weighing 9,344 kg (20,600 lb), the satellite observed most of the Soviet Union landmass as well as the Middle East. It used digital imaging techniques to obtain high resolution.

An Elint satellite was reported deployed by the space shuttle *Discovery* during the November 1989 mission. The satellite was reported to be in geostationary orbit and able to monitor Soviet and Chinese military and diplomatic voice and telemetry transmissions.

Navigation satellites. The Global Positioning System (GPS) of the U.S. Department of Defense made significant progress during 1989. This revolutionary navigation system was to consist of a constellation of 21 satellites in 6,835-km (4,190-mi) circular orbit. In early 1990 10 satellites were in operation. Additional craft were scheduled to be put in orbit on a regular basis by Delta II launch vehicles. It was claimed that GPS would be 10 times more accurate than the existing U.S. Navy Transit system. Horizontal and vertical coordinates, as well as velocity, were provided.

AP/Wide World

The first Titan IV booster rocket launches a U.S. Air Force Defense Support Program satellite into geostationary orbit in June 1989. The satellite carries a telescope with 6,000 infrared detectors.

The U.S. Geostar Corp. was using transponders on the Spacenet 3R and GSTAR 3 satellites to provide position fixes and brief (100 alphanumeric characters) messages to major trucking companies, van lines, and other land vehicles. Positions were automatically given by comparisons of the path of the satellite's transmissions to the Earth with Loran-C units. (Loran-C is a low-frequency radio transmission system using two fixed transmitters.) Onboard equipment was manufactured by Hughes Network Systems and the Sony Corp. Geostar offered this commercial service on an hourly basis, 24 hours a day.

—F.C. Durant III

Energy

As in most of the 1980s, energy developments during the past year primarily involved the normal workings of the industries. Following the trends that started in 1981, governments continued shifting responsibilities back to the private industries. This shift reflected major changes in the influence of alternative, long-debated views about energy. A core of specialists have argued about the subject since the end of World War II. One influential writer, the British consultant Paul Frankel, has long contended that oil must be managed. Others have countered that oil is not so markedly different from other industries that extensive regulations are required.

This dispute was part of a broader one over the proper role of governments in regulating markets. A spectrum of views existed, ranging from proposals that all major industries somehow be supervised to contentions that government intervention is almost always undesirable. The participants in energy debates tended to take a more limited position. The cases for and against intervention usually were justified by appraisals of specific conditions in energy. General philosophies of the desirability of more or less government supervision were rarely invoked.

Whatever the basis, by 1990 energy intervention was in considerable disfavor. The efforts to intervene had disappointing results and, to emphasize the point, improved energy market conditions arose from a decade of deliberate refusals to tinker further with energy markets.

The U.S. was a major example of these tendencies. By 1990 many U.S. government restrictions on the energy industries had been dismantled. The administration of U.S. Pres. Ronald Reagan began this process by speeding the end of oil price controls. The previous administration's subsidies of synthetic fuels were stopped. Pres. Jimmy Carter's complex system of taxes on revenues from oil production was lifted as part of tax reform. In 1989 legislation was enacted to phase out those natural gas price controls that the 1978 Natural Gas Act had made permanent.

However, new energy initiatives were difficult to implement, and many barriers remained in effect. For example, leasing of coal owned by the U.S. government was still suspended in 1990. Discontent had arisen with the way in which leasing was resumed in 1981 after 10 years. A "temporary" moratorium on coal leasing was imposed in 1983. It was supposed to last only for a few months after independent studies were completed. These studies were finished in 1984. However, the U.S. Department of the Interior chose first to undertake a leisurely response to the suggestions of the review groups and then not to employ the revised leasing procedures. Political opposition to offshore oil and gas leasing limited activity in that realm. The financial problems of the utilities were alleviated by some liberalization of rates and by restraint in company capital budgeting. However, regulatory restraints on the utilities remained severe.

OPEC, perestroika, and world oil. The Organization of Petroleum Exporting Countries (OPEC) continued its efforts to control the production and keep up the prices of oil. Enduring agreements among the members were not reached, though, and the end of the Iran-Iraq war created the potential for increased deviation from production control accords. However, prices strengthened somewhat in 1989. Possibly more accord was reached in private than was apparent to the public. Alternatively, unexpectedly strong demand may have offset the effects of producing above OPEC quotas.

In 1989 OPEC output was approximately 22.5 million bbl per day, about 8.5% above the 1988 level. The latter was 11% above 1987 but still below

U.S. Pres. George Bush signs a bill in July that removes federal controls on the price of natural gas at the wellhead. Looking on (from left to right) are Secretary of Energy James Watkins, Sen. Don Nickles (Rep., Okla.), Rep. Joe Barton (Rep., Texas), and Rep. Philip Sharp (Dem., Ind.).

AP/Wide World

A motorist in Canada pumps natural gas into his car through a specially fitted hookup on the engine. The Canadian government was encouraging this use of natural gas on the grounds that it was cleaner and less expensive than gasoline.

the 1979 peak of 31 million bbl per day. Iraq and Iran each raised their outputs but not to the levels reached in the late 1970s.

Saudi Arabia continued to maintain a balancing act of trying to push up prices while not greatly reducing its own output. It increased production from 4.3 million bbl per day in January 1988 to 6.9 million bbl in December, maintained output at about 5 million bbl per day during the first eight months of 1989, and then began increasing production again. Saudi production had reached a peak of about 10 million bbl per day in the late 1970s.

The upheavals in the Soviet Union and Eastern Europe during the past year revived another old energy concern—the evolution of Soviet energy patterns. A major element of the present turmoil related to problems of general mismanagement of the economy. Many were concerned that the reform efforts would flounder until the leaders of the Soviet Union recognized the underlying problems and radically altered the system. The energy implications of the situation were unclear. The Soviet system traditionally overcame its intrinsic inefficiency by devoting large amounts of resources to areas considered critical. Energy had always been such an area, and the result had been energy supplies so ample that exports were extensive. While oil and coal production was unimpressive, this was more than offset by gains in natural gas. The Soviet Union in 1988 accounted for 40% of world natural gas output. Soviet energy problems of sufficient magnitude to put upward pressures on world prices remained a possibility rather than a certainty. Presumably, movements to a more flexible political and economic system would alleviate the problems.

U.S. energy policy. Debates remained intense about air pollution from energy consumption. The major issues continued to be acid rain and global warming. The former, generated by pollution from burning fossil fuels, causes health problems, corrosion of exposed material, and harm to forests and lakes. Originally discussed predominantly in terms of the damage to lakes and forests, acid rain concerns increasingly were concentrated on the other effects. However, these other effects are precisely those that were supposed to have been controlled by the 1977 Clean Air Act Amendments. Future acid rain legislation, therefore, would be based on the belief that the prior policies were inadequate. However, this conclusion remained controversial. Even more controversial was the design of a pollution-control law that could pass both houses of Congress and either be signed by the president or be so strongly supported that a veto could be overridden. Given the lack of a strong consensus, acid rain legislation regularly failed to be reported out of congressional committees during the 1980s.

Any legislation would most heavily affect coal-using states in the Middle West and cause transformations of an unknown sort in coal-production patterns. Proposed laws that would force the citizens of those states to bear all the costs were opposed by members of Congress from those states. Conversely, members of Congress from other states resisted alternatives that would require their states to finance a portion of the reductions. Further debates arose on the appropriate level of emission reduction.

Some proponents of acid rain legislation sought to follow the example of the 1977 law by requiring that pollution be removed in a scrubbing step undertaken between combustion and discharge to the atmosphere. Such a policy was resisted because it reduces options and further increases the costs of control. Moreover, the uncertainties about coal supply preclude accurate estimates of what effects would result from different policies. Were utilities free to use whatever combination of lower sulfur coals and scrubbing that they wanted, the effect necessarily would be more shifting of fuel from one grade to another than would occur if fuel shifting were restricted by law. What was unclear was how much difference this would make and what regions would benefit from the shifts.

The many past studies of impact produced radically different predictions. A combination of differences in beliefs about the details of the policies, the special circumstances that affect individual plants, and relative supplies produced the varying conclusions. One important factor would be the extent to which the plants would be allowed to comply by paying others to reduce pollution.

The differences in expectations also reflected uncertainties about the economics of producing coal that can be burned in existing plants. Boilers are designed for the coals that are expected to be burned. Using radically different coals can cause problems, and some boiler types are less able to accommodate different grades of coal. Also, pollution-control equipment requires additional space.

In regard to coal supply, great uncertainty prevailed about the ability of different mining regions to produce low-sulfur coals that could be used in existing boilers. Different analyses produced radically different results about whether low-sulfur-coal supplies in the Appalachian Mountains or the West were the more attractive source. Moreover, considerable accord existed that any such low-sulfur Appalachian coal would come from southern West Virginia and eastern Kentucky. It was unclear whether states with low production costs, such as Wyoming, could supply the desired types of low-sulfur coal or whether it would be necessary to resort to possibly more expensive coal from Colorado and Utah.

Global warming can be produced by the carbon dioxide produced by fossil fuel burning. However, debates among climatologists about the severity of the threat were becoming more intense. Questions also arose about the effectiveness of unilateral action by the U.S.

Concerns about global warming were used by advocates of nuclear power to justify efforts to reverse the decision of U.S. electric utilities to stop building nuclear reactors. Some proposed facilitating a nuclear revival by fostering research on improving reactors. Many questions were raised about these proposals, among the most important of which was the uncertainty about the relative importance of each of many problems that plagued nuclear power.

In the U.S. nuclear power suffered from an excess of regulation. At least two levels of control were involved. The Nuclear Regulatory Commission (NRC)

was supposed to provide supervision of the safety of plant design and operation. However, it was widely criticized for emphasizing form over substance. This was the one point on which the electric power industry, opponents of nuclear power, and impartial studies agreed. Where the disputes arose was over whether nuclear power would be economical under more rational regulation.

The government investigations after the 1979 Three Mile Island plant accident in Pennsylvania indicated the existence of this problem and the deficiencies of NRC organization that produced it. It was indicated that the commission was split up into excessively autonomous units with inadequate central direction. Moreover, experience in the U.S. and abroad suggested that the importance of new reactor technologies might be limited. The nuclear programs in France and Japan employed adaptations of the technology developed in the U.S. by the Westinghouse Corp. Britain decided to abandon its efforts to employ alternative technologies and use the Westinghouse approach.

Efforts to improve the U.S. nuclear situation were limited by political realities. Reforming the NRC was not a high-priority item. Other, broader influences had become more important than NRC policies in shaping the attitudes of electric utilities. In particular, during the 1970s the historical covenant between electric utilities and their regulators, particularly at the state level, broke down. The implicit accord was that as long as a utility maintained regular service, it would be protected from competition and allowed to earn enough money on its investments to be an attractive place for even the most conservative person to invest. The breakdown of regulation in the 1970s preserved the requirements imposed on the utilities but reduced severely the willingness of regulators to guarantee rates of return. Rate increases were resisted. Elaborate processes were developed to appraise all phases of utility operations. Particular attention was directed at construction and fuel buying.

Recovery by utilities of investments that regulators deemed imprudent were disallowed. The management of construction was appraised. If costs seemed excessive, they also were disallowed. The problems were aggravated by the rise of various interventions by other government agencies. The most systematic was the Energy Commission created in California while Ronald Reagan was governor. The commission was formed to review California's energy needs and determine how best to meet them. Necessary new plants were to be certified. In practice, however, the commission has never certified a traditional large-scale plant. The most recently completed units owned in part by a California utility were in Utah and involved the municipal water and power agency of Los Angeles.

Fuel pellets shown above are made from residential and commercial wastes. When a binding agent is added to the wastes, the pellets remain stable even when stored outdoors for long periods of time.

Given prevailing inherent uncertainties about the growth of demand and construction costs, utilities had considerable incentives to seek alternatives that could be more rapidly built. The desirability of large units was under challenge. Thus, a shift in the nature of electric power investments would have arisen whatever the regulatory climate.

It was unclear, however, that the changes would have been as radical as those that occurred. Examination of the public record on utility expansion plans revealed that the large, company-owned plant that was the traditional backbone of the industry was an endangered species. Virtually all the large-scale plants actually completed or in progress as of 1990 were ones planned during the mid-1970s. Many of the proposed units were not built, and few new large-scale power plants were announced subsequently.

Interest increased in smaller plants, preferably owned by nonutilities or possibly by utilities from another region. This separate ownership brought at least a short-term respite from regulatory pressures. Smaller plants were less subject to delay, cost overruns, and severe regulatory pressures.

Energy and Europe. As the time nears for the much-publicized full integration of the European Communities (EC) in 1992, the conflict between that goal and long-standing energy policies should receive greater attention. Efforts to preserve domestic coal industries in West Germany, the U.K., and Belgium long undermined the commitments to free trade under the European Coal and Steel Commu-

nity Treaty that was a forerunner of the Economic Community Treaty. Since a major element of the preservation policy was guarantees of electric utility markets, free trade in electricity also was hindered.

West Germany often asserted its devotion to free-market concepts, but an actual tendency toward extensive intervention has prevailed since at least the late 19th century. When free markets conflict with welfare state traditions, the latter tend to dominate. Reflecting this tradition, West German protection of coal has been the most unyielding in Western Europe. While France and Belgium reduced the size of their coal industries, West Germany thus far has seemed to be continuing with its historic policy of gradual retreat. Another round of plans to reduce production was announced, but as of 1990 the contract that committed West German utilities to guaranteeing markets for West German hard coal remained in force.

The recent British move to privatize public ventures represented a move toward energy integration thus far absent in West Germany. The latest target for privatization was the Central Electric Generating Board, the organization that long bore the largest share of the burden of providing coal markets in the U.K. Privatization was expected to involve liberating whatever entities emerged after being released from the compulsory contracting with British Coal. The contemplated privatization of British Coal itself would require reducing industry size to a level sustainable by private profit-making firms.

International differences in energy use. In 1989 the Organization for Economic Cooperation and Development (OECD) published a new report that provided more detailed data than available elsewhere on energy consumption for 83 nonmember countries. In particular, efforts were made to provide breakdowns by end use of the consumption of individual fuels. On the basis of what appeared to be a combination of the magnitude of energy use and data availability, the precision of the breakdowns differed. For the most important countries on which information was available, the breakdowns were as detailed as in the annual OECD reports on its 24 members. In other cases coarser breakdowns were provided. In every case at least the roles of the four broad categories (industry, transportation, other, and nonenergy) were reported.

Data on nonmembers were available through 1987, but in some cases information about end uses was available only for earlier years. Given the small role of many of those countries, comparisons of end uses for this article were tabulated only for the countries that were the largest consumers and collectively accounted for 99% of the total.

These data permitted a fuller view of the diversity of world energy consumption. For the leading devel-

342

Table I. Leading Energy-Consuming Countries, 1987
(Percent share of consumption)

Country	World total	Oil	Coal	Gas
United States	24.6	41.1	23.4	22.4
U.S.S.R.	18.0	32.3	22.6	38.3
China	7.8	18.4	75.5	2.3
Japan	4.9	55.9	18.0	9.9
West Germany	3.6	42.2	27.5	17.1
Canada	3.2	31.5	10.7	19.8
United Kingdom	2.7	36.2	32.9	23.8
France	2.7	42.6	9.6	12.4
India	2.0	32.1	55.8	4.2
Italy	2.0	59.3	9.9	21.9
Poland	1.8	13.0	78.9	7.2
Brazil	1.6	52.0	8.8	2.2
Mexico	1.4	70.7	3.4	21.3
East Germany	1.2	17.9	70.4	8.3
South Africa	1.2	13.7	83.7	0.0
Australia	1.1	35.8	39.2	16.0
Czechoslovakia	1.0	21.3	59.9	10.9
Spain	1.0	52.6	23.9	3.4
Romania	1.0	23.9	24.6	47.5

Sources: International Energy Agency, Paris, *Energy Balances of OECD Countries 1986–1987*, 1989; and *World Energy Statistics and Balances 1971–1987*, 1989.

oped economies of the world economic growth has been associated with increased energy use, increased reliance on oil and gas, and greater electrification. Examination of world energy patterns indicates that while larger economies tend to use more energy, the composition of that use is not closely related to the affluence of the country. The availability of fuels seems to be the greatest influence on a country's choice of fuels.

Table I shows the 1987 share of world energy consumption by the 19 largest consumers (those accounting for at least a full percentage point of the world total) and the share of the three chief fossil fuels in their energy supply. Expectedly, the three giants of the world—the U.S., the U.S.S.R., and China—collectively absorb more than half the energy. Eight of the other heavy consumers are the larger OECD countries.

Coal availability was far more important than the level of industrialization in determining 1987 reliance on coal in different countries. A high coal share prevailed in 1987 mainly in countries in which coal was the only significantly developed domestic fuel source. The coal consumers that were not major producers introduced coal because of a desire to reduce dependence on oil or because of the existence of a significant steel industry. In some cases such as in Japan, South Korea, and Taiwan, both influences were operating. The majority of South African coal use was for electricity generation.

A high share of both oil and gas in a nation's energy use was associated either with its lack of domestic energy supplies or with energy output that

was primarily oil or gas. The leading oil-producing countries of the Middle East were examples of the producers that were dependent on oil. Such oil-producing countries usually had gas shares that were higher than the weighted average for the 107-country group. However, the gas share in energy consumption differed widely even among oil-producing nations. Smaller producers such as Oman, Bahrain, and Qatar were likely to use a much higher proportion of gas than of oil. Larger producers such as Saudi Arabia, Iran, and Iraq tended to use more oil than gas. This pattern was not what one would expect if the OPEC members expected sharply rising oil prices. Such expectations would instead encourage substituting gas for oil so that more oil could be sold abroad at high prices.

Predictably, the fuel-poor countries tended to rely most heavily on oil, which is easier to transport than gas, and to have the highest shares of their consumption for oil. Italy, Japan, Brazil, and Mexico were the only countries with oil shares of more than

Table II. Leading Coal-Consuming Economies, 1987

	Total energy use[1]	Coal use[1]	Coal use (percent)	Electric[2]
South Africa	91,208	76,332	83.7	57.8
Poland	133,619	105,445	78.9	58.5
North Korea	41,122	31,244	76.0	21.2
China	593,548	448,165	75.5	19.9
East Germany	94,627	66,639	70.4	72.5
Zimbabwe	4,527	2,859	63.1	52.7
Vietnam	5,071	3,146	62.0	31.3
Czechoslovakia	77,878	46,680	59.9	59.2
India	153,609	85,767	55.8	49.2
Hong Kong	9,560	4,928	51.5	99.9
Bulgaria	40,869	17,277	42.3	63.2
Yugoslavia	46,024	18,551	40.3	66.4
Australia	80,830	31,670	39.2	79.3
Denmark	20,000	7,360	36.8	89.1
South Korea	66,223	23,441	35.4	17.3
Greece	19,300	6,770	35.1	83.5
Luxembourg	3,190	1,060	33.2	10.4
United Kingdom	208,670	68,680	32.9	72.0
Turkey	49,240	14,150	28.7	34.3
Hungary	29,462	8,148	27.7	42.1
West Germany	271,720	74,710	27.5	71.3
Taiwan	37,818	9,592	25.4	54.7
Albania	3,801	962	25.3	47.2
Romania	75,214	18,524	24.6	50.3
Malta	463	112	24.2	100.0
Spain	77,380	18,520	23.9	69.4
Ireland	9,720	2,280	23.5	48.7
United States	1,865,710	436,280	23.4	85.1
Israel	8,924	2,077	23.3	100.0
U.S.S.R.	1,366,014	308,900	22.6	43.4
Belgium	45,380	8,740	19.3	38.7
Japan	371,660	66,840	18.0	32.0

[1]Thousands of tons of oil equivalent.
[2]Percent of coal use for generating electricity.
Sources: International Energy Agency, Paris, *Energy Balances of OECD Countries 1986–1987*, 1989; and *World Energy Statistics and Balances 1971–1987*, 1989.

50% that consumed more than 100 million tons of oil equivalent.

Most countries used the majority of their coal to generate electricity. The exceptions were either less developed or those that used the most coal for making steel. Nations in the latter group included Japan, South Korea, and Belgium.

A high gas share expectedly occurred where gas production was a significant part of energy output. The highest shares were largely in oil-exporting nations, although in a few less developed countries, such as Bangladesh, Burma, and Paraguay, gas was the only significant domestic energy output.

As also should be expected, nuclear power use occurred mostly in those large economies in which the political climate was favorable. The U.S. was by far the largest producer of nuclear power, but because of the large overall size of the U.S. energy market, the share of nuclear power in U.S. energy was less than 6%. The second largest producer of nuclear power, France, had the highest nuclear share of any country. Other large industrial countries that produced other fuels but were also among the top 15 nuclear power producers were the U.S.S.R., Canada, West Germany, and the U.K.

Given the trends in individual countries to use a greater portion of fuel to generate electricity, the differences among countries in the role of electricity might be expected to reflect differences in incomes. In fact, the domestic energy supply again proved a better indicator. A large role for hydroelectric and

nuclear power in energy use indicated a large input into electricity. Thus, the countries with the most relative reliance on electricity included those such as Norway and New Zealand, both of which obtained large proportions of their supply from hydroelectricity. Switzerland, Sweden, and Canada, with high combined nuclear and hydroelectric inputs, exemplified a second type of country with heavy reliance on electricity.

The distribution of final energy uses in the 57 countries examined here was too diverse to be easily understandable. The lowest shares of transportation in energy use were all in Communist countries. However, such low shares prevailed for only 8 of the 11 Communist nations that were studied. Of those eight, five (North Korea, Romania, China, the U.S.S.R., and Czechoslovakia) devoted at least half their energy to industry. The other three (Poland, Hungary, and East Germany) used more energy for nonindustrial and nontransportation uses than for industry.

Three of the four countries using the majority of their energy for transportation were OPEC members; the fourth was Thailand. Among other countries having transportation as their largest energy-consuming sector were Colombia, Algeria, Greece, and the U.S.

The other countries with industrial shares in excess of 50% were South Africa, Taiwan, and India. The remainder of Taiwan's energy was evenly split between transportation and other uses; South Africa and India used more for transportation than for other purposes.

Artist's drawing depicts the $19.6 million laboratory for research on photovoltaic and solar heat technology planned for the U.S. Department of Energy in Golden, Colorado.

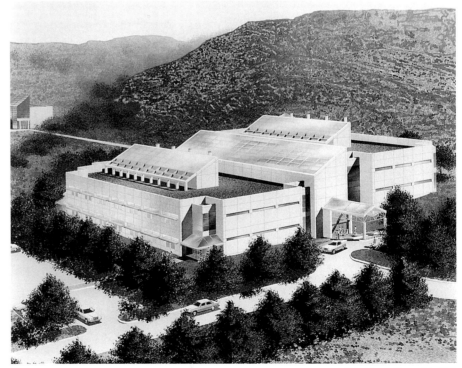

Solar Energy Research Institute

A low share of energy for industry appeared to mean only a low dependence on industry that used large amounts of energy, rather than indicating national poverty. The four lowest shares were in the United Arab Emirates, Iraq, Denmark, and Switzerland. These last two countries, along with Poland and East Germany, were the only nations in which other uses accounted for the majority of energy consumption.

Some complicated mix of forces determined the pattern of consumption for each country. Possible influences included the state of economic development, the supply of different energy sources, the structure of the economy, the transportation system used, and the methodology for generating the data. Considerable further work would be required for determining whether any significant regularities prevailed in these patterns.

—Richard L. Gordon

Environment

Excluding earthquakes and weather, the major environmental incidents of the last 12 months concerned oil spills by two supertankers. The *Exxon Valdez* ran aground in Prince William Sound, Alaska, at 12:04 AM on March 24, 1989, some 40 km (25 mi) outside the harbor at Valdez. Approximately 41.7 million liters (11 million gal) of crude oil were discharged into the sound through a rupture in the hull. The oil gradually spread over 1,930 km (1,100 mi) of Alaskan coastline. It was the worst oil spill ever in United States waters. The environmental consequences in the following weeks appeared calamitous; officials estimated that as many as 100,000 birds and 1,000 sea otters were killed. Also, salmon and herring fisheries were shut down temporarily; the value of the landings from all Alaskan fisheries in recent years had varied between $1 billion and $1.7 billion.

On December 19 the Iranian supertanker *Kharg 5* ruptured after an explosion on board, and by January 2 various news sources were estimating that 72 million to 140 million liters (19 million to 37 million gal) had spilled into the Atlantic Ocean off the coast of Morocco. This was between 1.7 and 3.4 times the volume of the *Exxon Valdez* spill. The resultant oil slick covered 280 sq km (108 sq mi) of ocean by January 2. For a time it appeared that this incident would be a major disaster because in early January winds on the Atlantic Ocean near the tanker were gusting at up to 65 km/h (40 mph), whipping up waves that had the potential to split the vessel in two. If that had happened, the total spill would have been the entire stock of crude oil originally contained in the tanker—273 million liters (72 million gal). To indicate the magnitude of the potential impact, 100,-

Worker uses a special oil-absorbent rag to wipe crude oil from rocks on the beach of an island in Prince William Sound, Alaska. The oil was spilled after the tanker Exxon Valdez *struck a reef in the sound on March 24, 1989.*

000 jobs in fishing and related industries would have been lost in Morocco if this had happened. Within a few days, however, the heavy seas had broken up the oil slick, and the problem appeared to abate.

Terrible as those incidents appeared at the time, their effects were basically short-lived in comparison with those of long-running processes whose consequences are both cumulative and growing. The six major environmental stories of the past year involved such processes. Not only will their effects grow and cumulate for a very long time but their ultimate effects will pervade many aspects of social and biological life on the Earth. Those six stories were the carbon dioxide global-warming theory, the demographic implications of AIDS, the ecological implications of agricultural strategies (agroecology), forests and the environment, the status of planetary fossil fuel resources, and the effect of environmental processes on politics.

Climate. Climate in 1989 would have baffled anyone who was paying close attention. The public had been told repeatedly that the 1980s were the hottest decade in history, containing the four hottest years

345

since measurements were begun. Nevertheless, in December the headlines revealed that record cold temperatures had occurred in 125 cities in the United States. Most people in the U.S. did not know, however, that the cold snap was international; during late December the average temperature for all large cities throughout the world was as much as 0.9° C (1.6° F) below the average of their long-term norms. Florida suffered the fifth freeze of its citrus crop in the "boiling" 1980s, and the temperature fell to 7° C (44° F) at Key West, Fla., the southeastern tip of the U.S., where the previous low had been 8° C (47° F), set in 1906.

The year was replete with climatic ironies. During the week beginning August 7, a large international scientific meeting in Toronto featured several sessions on global warming; the local papers noted that August 7 in the Toronto region was the coldest it had been on that date since record keeping began. Editorializing about the feared warming of the Earth's atmosphere was particularly intense on May 9, 1989. On the previous day it had been colder than normal in 35 of the world's 61 largest cities outside the U.S. In many of those cities it was far colder than normal; furthermore, the cold weather was occurring around the globe. In the U.S. on that day and during the previous week, low temperature records were broken or tied in at least 30 cities in Texas, Virginia, North and South Carolina, Louisiana, Oklahoma, Florida, Georgia, Tennessee, Pennsylvania, Ohio, and New York. In Cincinnati, Ohio, snow fell in May for the first time in nearly a century.

Even as the cool weather continued, however, the popular media and some politicians communicated the following messages about the carbon dioxide issue and climate change to the public during the past year: (1) historical weather data show that warming of the planet has already begun in response to the increased planetary concentration of atmospheric carbon dioxide; (2) computer simulation models show that the climate will warm in the future in response to increased concentrations of carbon dioxide in the global atmosphere; (3) the controversy concerning past and future climate trends is esoteric; fewer than 300 scientists are involved in serious research on climate and the debate about carbon dioxide effects on climate; (4) the notion that warming will occur in the future is shared by almost all scientists qualified to have an opinion; at most about 10 scientists dispute or question this idea; (5) the bulk of the criticisms of the "warming theory" is directed at just two problem areas: the design of the computer climate models and the interpretation of weather data; and (6) both increased concentrations of carbon dioxide in the global atmosphere and future warming of the planet would have alarming consequences.

Each of these contentions could scarcely depart more from the facts. (1) Many scientists in many countries and disciplines showed that the appearance of warming in historical weather records is illusory, due to the "urban heat island effect." Most national temperature data are from thermometers either in the downtown areas of large cities or at airports. Such temperature measurements are contaminated by waste heat from nearby buildings, factories, and vehicles and other local conditions, such as the absence of vegetation, rivers, and lakes from which evaporation could occur. Evaporation of liquids produces cooling because of the latent heat of vaporization, as in refrigerators. To illustrate the illusory nature of temperature trends obtained from weather stations in large cities, J.W.D. Hessell demonstrated that data from the city of Christchurch, N.Z., gave the appearance of a warming trend, whereas data from weather stations in rural or suburban areas around Christchurch showed no such trend. James Goodridge, the former state climatologist of California, showed that the appearance of a warming trend was entirely due to the urban heat island effect. The California average statewide temperature in the 20th century increased about 1.2° C (2.2° F) if one used only the measurements from thermometers in counties with more than 800,000 people. If one estimated the statewide temperature trend by using only the measurements from counties with less than 100,000 people, it declined.

Another way of obtaining estimates of climate trends free of contamination by local urban influences is to use temperature data as measured by the annual growth rings in the trunks of forest trees. D.A. Norton and J. Ogden demonstrated that such measurements from New Zealand showed no long-term warming trend. There was a clear decrease in tree-ring widths in the South African data summarized by P.D. Tyson; R.C. Balling and S.B. Idso showed that when adjusted for population growth in cities, average winter temperatures in the U.S. cooled by almost 3.3° C (5.9° F) from 1920 to 1984.

(2) The popular media have not informed the public that the climate models that project warming are criticized within the scientific community. Nor has the public been informed that when the models are made more complex and realistic, including feedback effects by clouds, as by Erich Roeckner in Hamburg, West Germany, the models project cooling rather than warming in the future. To explain this result one needs to consider the multiple effects of clouds on energy radiation to and from the Earth's surface. For example, changing the ice content of clouds in computer models reduces by 60% the projected warming effect of doubling atmospheric carbon dioxide concentrations. R.S. Lindzen pointed out several reasons for distrusting the models. Perhaps the most compelling argument to most

people is that if the models are correct, there should have been a warming of the Earth's surface over the last century of about 0.5° C (0.9° F). However, no appropriately corrected data series shows any such result. As Goodridge revealed, when really stringent corrections are applied to remove local urban effects, surface temperatures actually declined.

(3) The assertion that this is an esoteric issue about which only 300 scientists are competent to express an opinion can be checked quickly in any large library. During the past year, for example, the Commonwealth Scientific and Industrial Research Organization in Melbourne, Australia, published a large volume on global warming that contained chapters by only a fraction of the Australian experts on this topic; there were 102 authors. A conservative estimate of the number of experts on the carbon dioxide issue in Australia and New Zealand alone would be 300 scientists. Worldwide, there are probably 10,000 scientists who have some expertise on this issue, not just the 300 cited in the popular press.

(4) Politicians and the popular media are incorrect concerning the assertion that only about 10 scientists have raised questions about the warming theory. In fact, more than 3,000 scientists have published books or articles that raise questions about the design or interpretation of the warming models or about the facts concerning or interpretation of the climate record. One of the most convincing findings arose from measurements made of the temperature and carbon dioxide concentration of the Earth's atmosphere throughout its history and comparable pairs of measurements, taken by satellites, of nearby planets. The measurements show that temperature is far less sensitive to variations of carbon dioxide in the planetary atmosphere than had been generally believed. When all the information on this subject was put together, it appeared that, on theoretical grounds, when all the planetary feedback mechanisms are considered, an increase in carbon dioxide concentration in the atmosphere is more likely to cause cooling than warming.

Why have so many scientists written about the global greenhouse warming theory? The explanation is that this is a theory with implications for an extraordinary diversity of other phenomena: the depth of ice cover at the poles, the advance or retreat of glaciers on mountains throughout the world, the change in ocean and lake levels and the increased or decreased exposure of coastal land, the extent and radiation impacts of clouds, the annual growth of trees, and the migration of tree species toward the Equator or the poles. Consequently, scientists in many disciplines were studying and writing about the greenhouse effect, and the theory was consequently being challenged by foresters, geographers, urban ecologists, information scientists, systems analysts,

specialists in satellite data interpretation, meteorologists, geophysicists, glaciologists, dendrochronologists, and tree physiologists, among others.

The question then arises as to why the media, and the larger scientific community, have been unaware of this enormous volume of literature critical of the greenhouse warming theory. Part of the explanation is that these scientists have simply been ignored. For example, the popular media paid little attention to a press conference held at the Marshall Institute in Washington, D.C., at which three distinguished and well-known U.S. scientists—Frederick Seitz, Robert Jastrow, and William Nierenberg—expressed their reservations. Another explanation is that this material was being published in many countries and in a large number of disciplines. Few scientists would have any reason to stumble onto this mass of literature unless they went looking for it. Most importantly, only a small proportion of the publications have titles indicating that the contents are relevant to the carbon dioxide issue. For example, the implications of Norton and Ogden's "Dendrochronology: A Review with Emphasis on New Zealand Applications" in the *New Zealand Journal of Ecology* are not clear. In short, the principal explanation for the failure to notice the literature refuting the warming theory is the fragmentation of modern science and the enormous volume of international scientific literature.

(5) The warming theory was not being criticized simply for deficiencies in the climate models or for the interpretations of historical temperature records. Rather, it was under attack on a wide variety of grounds. Experts on the interpretation of satellite-derived sea-surface temperature data, such as R.W. Reynolds, C.K. Follard, and D.E. Packer, did not see evidence of a warming trend in those data. The

The Iranian tanker Kharg 5 *ruptured after an explosion on board on December 19 and spilled millions of gallons of crude oil into the Atlantic Ocean off the coast of Morocco. The resulting oil slick was broken up by heavy seas.*

Frederic Reglain—Gamma/Liaison

theory predicts that sea levels should be rising; the notion that there is any such rise was being criticized by shore and beach experts. The theory also predicts a decline in levels of lakes in high latitudes; instead, they have risen for most of the last several decades. Experts on glaciers dispute the notion that glaciers are diminishing in size; they are, on average, increasing. Experts on tree growth dispute the notion that growth is increasing because of global warming. The warming theory predicts that tropical trees should be migrating poleward. As the experience of the northern Florida citrus and vegetable industry shows, they are instead migrating toward the Equator.

Finally (6), the popular media have continued to maintain that there is something alarming about an increase of carbon dioxide in the atmosphere and an increase in planetary temperature. As S.B. Idso demonstrated at great length in his book, on closer inspection such increases appear benign and even beneficial. Carbon dioxide is such an important plant nutrient that in Japan it is pumped into greenhouses to speed plant growth.

The carbon dioxide issue has revealed some important messages about modern science. This is a highly complex subject that cries out for an interdisciplinary, as opposed to a specialist, approach. All scientists agree that the carbon dioxide content of the planetary atmosphere is increasing and that this causes surface warming in the tropics. However, high temperatures convert water to water vapor, and this vapor rises to high altitudes where lower temperatures cause condensation of the vapor to water droplets that become rain. The greater the surface warming, the greater will be the altitudes at which heat carried aloft by convection is deposited, as Lindzen noted. Research during the past year suggested a variety of reasons why clouds could have a net cooling effect on the Earth's surface rather than a net heating effect.

Curiously, if the world is cooling rather than warming, the major policy implications are the same: there needs to be much more concern with the efficiency of all energy-transformation processes, from space heating to transportation, and also much more concern about reversing the process of planetary deforestation.

Demographic implications of AIDS. During the year many new studies appeared concerning the epidemiology of AIDS (acquired immune deficiency syndrome) and the implications of the disease for birthrates and death rates and for future population growth. The majority of them suggested that previous estimates of the incidence of AIDS were too low. A number of explanations for this were offered. Studies by the U.S. Government Accounting Office and other agencies suggested that local health de-

partments were having difficulty keeping up with the increasing paperwork engendered by the epidemic. Newly diagnosed cases were not being reported fast enough to allow federal officials to make accurate projections. One experiment by a public health agency showed that when officials made an aggressive effort to gather data from original sources of information, estimates increased markedly. A study by E.O. Laumann, J.H. Gagnon, S. Michaels, R.T. Michael, and J.S. Coleman of the U.S. National Opinion Research Center gave more details on why estimates are too low. The technique they used to check on estimates of AIDS infection rates by other sources was to ask 1,481 randomly selected adults about the number of AIDS cases in their networks of acquaintances. As a check on the validity of the method, the sampled people were also asked about homicide victims in their network of acquaintances. Comparison of the statistics on homicides obtained in this way with official homicide statistics showed that the method was a highly accurate source of social science data. Their study suggested that official statistics on the incidence of AIDS were yielding underestimates for the white population of higher socioeconomic status and also for the Midwest. One explanation for this was that the disease was more likely to escape accurate diagnosis in population subgroups in which the condition was still quite rare. A study at the Centers for Disease Control in Atlanta, Ga., found that only 60% of the AIDS cases in South Carolina were being reported. A consensus, therefore, was developing among AIDS epidemiologists that for a variety of reasons incidence of the disease was being underreported.

By far the most revealing document on AIDS to appear was the Hudson Institute study, *The Catastrophe Ahead: AIDS and the Case for a New Public Policy* by W.R. Johnston and K.R. Hopkins. It probed deeply into the fundamental nature of the AIDS pandemic and its likely future demographic implications. The authors concluded that the focus of concern should not be AIDS, the final expression of a virus-initiated process in the human body that may go on for 10 to 20 years, but rather with the members of the population who have antibodies to the virus in their blood and are therefore highly likely to develop AIDS symptoms some time in the future. This group was much larger than that which already had developed AIDS. The authors also determined that this pandemic must be viewed as a series of epidemics that spread from one population subgroup to another in a wavelike fashion. Some features of the pandemic were similar from one such subgroup to another, while others were different as a consequence of different sexual or drug-using characteristics of the subgroups. One of the most important points they made was that the history of campaigns to change sexual behavior is filled with failures. If the homosexual subgroup in San Francisco can be used as an example, truly dramatic changes in sexual behavior occurred only after members of the subgroup were surrounded by clear evidence that their group was at high risk with respect to AIDS. The problem is that this change had not occurred until about 1986, by which time the virus had already reached more than 60% of the community. If that delayed behavioral response occurs in all subgroups, the end results of the pandemic will be most unfortunate.

The statistical analyses and projections in this study are extremely realistic; the estimates and growth rates are consistent with those from other authoritative sources. Johnston and Hopkins projected the status of the epidemic in the U.S. to the year 2002. They presented three scenarios: worst, middle, and best. Their middle scenario implies annual growth rates of 12.4% in the cumulative number of people infected with the AIDS virus throughout the 14 years. Their worst-case scenario implies average annual growth rates of 20%. These two rates almost exactly enclosed the range of growth rates in 1990 in U.S. cities that already had serious epidemics. In the authors' worst-case scenario, 14.6 million Americans, or 8.2% of the population, will be infected by 2002. In their middle scenario the corresponding statistics are 5.9 million and 2.8%.

The Johnston and Hopkins policy recommendation is unpleasant but appears to be realistic and necessary. The authors state that the only way the natural biological dynamics of the disease can be contained is through limitation of sexual encounters between the infected and the noninfected. Thus, an intense and effective public education campaign is needed. Unfortunately, such a campaign has not yet been mounted.

Agriculture and agroecology. Agriculture in the U.S. in 1990 seemed trapped on a treadmill that involved ever lower profitability coupled with a strategy of farming that led to increased environmental degradation. Furthermore, this highly capital-intensive and resource-consuming approach to agricultural management appeared to be spreading throughout the world. During the year several important publications appeared that attempted to discover the root causes of the present situation in agriculture and to identify policy options that would rectify matters. On the economic side, as H. Ulrich pointed out, an increasing number of other nations were providing U.S. farmers with stiff competition. China could transport its sorghum across the Pacific to Mexico for less than the cost of shipping U.S. sorghum by train. On the environmental side, in order to increase profit per hectare, some farmers were irrigating around the clock, depleting underground aquifers in the process.

During the past year a comprehensive analysis of the problem was presented by 32 experts in the book *Agroecology*. In the book the authors raised the question as to why agriculture evolved toward agrochemically based systems that have adverse environmental side effects. This did not occur because that type of agriculture was inherently technologically superior to other approaches, according to F.H. Buttel. The technological basis for inorganic fertilization was available several decades before 1946, when it began to be employed on a mass scale. Rather, the key driving force behind the present pattern of high-technology agriculture was cheap crude oil. The enormous increase in farm mechanization of the last four decades has been based on direct and indirect use of fossil fuel: to extract and process the metal for farm machinery; to manufacture and fuel the machinery; and to manufacture and transport fertilizer, herbicides, and pesticides.

Mechanization also facilitates and is aided by monoculturing, the dedication of large tracts to single crops. This practice in turn increases the likelihood of problems with insect pests and crop diseases. Mechanization also tends to increase average farm size so that costs of machinery can be spread over more production. That, in turn, reinforces monoculture, dependence on purchased off-farm petrochemicals, and specialization. Specialization moves livestock—producers of organic fertilizer—to farms separate from those that produce crops. Other important forces leading to the present type of agriculture, according to the authors, were low interest rates in the 1970s and a temporary surge in exports before China, India, Indonesia, and others began steep production increases.

AIDS Research Laboratory at the U.S. National Institutes of Health in Bethesda, Maryland, was a major center of work on the deadly disease.

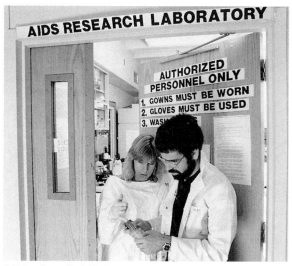

© Nathan Benn—Stock, Boston

Forester displays damage to maple trees in southern Vermont caused by thrips. Reduced maple syrup production was a consequence of the infestation by these insects, which appears to be related to the weakening of the trees by air pollution.

There is a deeper, philosophical problem that is basic to modern agricultural strategy. S.D. Deo and L.E. Swanson analyzed the history of development of new approaches to agriculture in the Third World. As they pointed out, the assumption basic to research at the international agricultural research centers was that increased productivity on the farm was the means to achieve modernity. It is an astonishing goal and one that makes no sense in terms of any body of economic theory. The goal of all enterprises is to maximize net productivity, or net profit, not gross productivity or gross profit. In short, a style of agriculture was developed that encouraged farmers to maximize their production without regard to either the overhead required or the environmental side effects of such necessities for maximum output as fertilizer and pesticides.

The necessary distinction that was not made in regard to maximum production was the one between the interests of farmers and the interests of the entire agricultural sector. As the authors of the study pointed out, only 10% of the value added in modern high-technology agriculture is added on the farm. Of the remaining 90%, approximately 40% is added by production of such farm inputs as machinery and fertilizer and 50% is added after products leave the farm. This strategy therefore maximizes net profit for the entire agricultural sector by maximizing gross productivity on the farm. The more purchased inputs that farmers use to boost their gross productivity, the lower their net profit is and the higher the net profit for the off-farm 90% of the agricultural sector is. The end state of the evolutionary process generated

by this strategic approach to agriculture would be bankruptcy for all farmers.

The solution, according to the authors, is to switch to a new style of agriculture. Maximization of net production would be substituted for maximization of gross output. Diversity of crops instead of monoculture would be a goal, and such diversity would minimize the vulnerability of crops to the invasion of pests. More generally, as Miguel Altieri pointed out, a rational approach to farming can be discovered through analysis of the strategic principles underlying traditional agriculture. Agricultural practice becomes an application of ecological principles.

There is one last irony about the present world situation of agriculture. It has evolved as it has in response to a perception of gradually declining costs of energy, particularly of crude oil. It now appears, however, that oil prices are about to rise as a result of declining reserves in the U.S. and the Soviet Union.

Forestry and ecology. Just as the perception of a crisis in world agriculture was leading to intensive analysis, an obviously excessive rate of global deforestation was producing a reconsideration of the role of trees in society. Most history books do not reveal a central role for forests. There have been only a few such analyses in the past—by geographers, soil scientists, or agriculturalists. However, a new, comprehensive analysis of the relationship of trees to society by John Perlin exposes far more causal pathways than any previous literature. A study of historical documents reveals a crucial role for forests in the balance of trade of a nation, its rate of economic growth, and the waxing and waning of its political power. To illustrate, the availability of abundant, cheap wood in the U.S. in the 19th century was one of the main reasons that American railroads cost so much less to build than those in England. The English had to pay six times more than the Americans to lay track. All English locomotives burned coal. Because so much timber grew along the rights of way of U.S. railroads, up until the Civil War they could burn wood instead of coal. Clearly, differences in the availability and cost of wood can determine which nations have deteriorating balances of trade because of massive timber imports—and, therefore, declining political and military power—and which are in the opposite situation.

Also, forests were crucial in the development of agriculture in the American West. The land for a cattle spread could be purchased for less than $20 at a time when the cost of fencing the spread was about $1,000. Cheap lumber made the fencing possible for poor, young, beginning farmers. Throughout history availability of forests played a hidden role in shifts of political power and relative rates of development of industry. For example, a nation could not become industrialized without metal ores and coal from mines. Mines, in turn, required masses of timbers to support tunnels. The huge advantage enjoyed by England over The Netherlands, Spain, and other possible competitors as they entered the Industrial Revolution resulted in part from its large forests of tall trees suitable for timber.

Fossil fuel reserves. The availability—and therefore the price—of energy has an immense effect on the character of all activities and processes in a nation. Switzerland and Japan have compact, energy-efficient societies because they could not afford to be otherwise. By contrast, Canada, the U.S., and Venezuela have always used more fuel per unit of gross national product than Japan and Switzerland because they had more fuel to use. In 1990, however, both the U.S. and the Soviet Union began to enter an age of significantly lower domestic fossil fuel availability.

In 1969 M. King Hubbert estimated that the ultimate recoverable amount of crude oil under the U.S., including Alaska, was 190 billion bbl. For a long time the U.S. government believed that this estimate was far too low. As recently as 1972 the U.S. Geological Survey believed that the U.S. reserve would be many times that. In 1989, however, the estimate of oil remaining to be discovered in the U.S. plunged to only 35 billion bbl. The economic, political, and environmental implications of this downward revision are expected to be enormous and pervasive throughout society.

Ecology and politics. During the past year an important new international political analysis by Ronald Inglehart appeared. He claimed that the environmental movement had become a major new political force in the world. In West Germany, France, Ireland, Belgium, The Netherlands, and Luxembourg, about half of the electorate said that they might vote for a party that placed its major emphasis on environmental issues.

Inglehart made several significant discoveries through analysis of large numbers of poll results. For example, as people acquire more worldly goods and their material wants become satisfied, other considerations become more important for them, such as the impact of economic growth on the environment. One of his most intriguing findings was that the environmental movement appears to be strengthened rather than weakened by crises that have been generated by the availability and cost of energy. One could interpret this relationship to mean that the reality of limits to growth is made most clear under such circumstances. Given the remarks about fossil energy reserves, the environmental movement may become much more politically important in the near future.

—Kenneth E.F. Watt

See also Feature Article: THE YELLOWSTONE FIRES.

Food and agriculture

The outlook for world agriculture in the 1990s was for rebounding production, rising consumption, and falling stocks of most crops, especially in the early years of the decade. Longer-term changes depended on two critical factors: the physical environment, on which agriculture depends, and the world economy, which determines the use of physical resources in production. Any long-term projections are hazardous, but several developments seemed likely. Even with population growth rates decreasing slightly, adequate food production would remain a challenge, despite occasional problems with surpluses in developed countries. Continuing anxiety over the physical environment would lead to regulation of chemical and other inputs and methods of production, impelling farmers to change their practices. New international trade agreements would alter global markets and might lead to the development of new products and of new uses for existing ones.

Agriculture

Although world crop production was recovering from the drought-reduced levels of the late 1980s, output of most crops in 1990 was not expected to match continued high use. World output of animal products was forecast to rise slightly, led by much higher U.S. poultry production. Following a 5% gain in 1988, world pork production was expected to show little change into the 1990s, while the output of beef and veal, declining in 1989, would hold at about the same levels.

Total U.S. meat production in 1990 was expected to advance about 3% over the previous year's record, with most of the increase coming from the poultry sector. A drop of about 3% in U.S. egg production in 1989 led to rising prices and increased profits for producers. Milk supplies were tight because of poor forage conditions and the high cost of feed concentrates. Prices rose sharply, responding to strong demand for cheese and large commercial exports of nonfat dry milk.

U.S. crop output was expected to increase into 1991 because of higher yields, liberalized acreage-reduction-program requirements, and strong prices for many crops. U.S. crop yields in 1989–90 remained slightly below those of recent years, reflecting drought damage to winter wheat and subnormal conditions for several other crops. However, subsoil moisture in the Corn Belt was improving, and new technology and better practices were expected to continue to boost productivity. The volume of U.S. wheat exports was dropping, primarily because of the recovery in production abroad and tight U.S. supplies.

A technician wearing rubber gloves prepares apples for testing. During the year compound constituents of Alar, a chemical pesticide used on apples, were found to cause cancer in laboratory mice.

Bovine somatotropin. Among scientific issues making news was a dispute over bovine somatotropin (BST), a naturally occurring protein now being made in commercial quantities through the use of genetically engineered bacteria. BST, also referred to as bovine growth hormone, can cause dairy cows to produce as much as 15% more milk. It would seem that such a breakthrough would delight both consumers and dairy farmers, but in fact it was a source of continuing controversy. Some farm groups, including the National Farmers Union, wanted to ban the hormone or at least force milk from treated cows to be labeled, thereby arousing public concern about impure milk. The NFA found an ally in the Foundation on Economic Trends, which opposed all biotechnology.

At least one medical researcher, Samuel Epstein of the University of Illinois Medical Center in Chicago, maintained that BST from milk could be absorbed into the blood, particularly in infants, and produce hormonal and allergic effects. On the other side, Henry Miller, special assistant on biotechnology issues to the head of the Food and Drug Administration (FDA), called Epstein's paper "a gross distortion of scientific facts." The FDA was expected to rule shortly on the safety of the hormone, which had been approved for experimental use. To date no significant safety issue had been raised by its investigation. The FDA said milk produced by treated cows was identical to that produced by untreated cows. (In fact, all milk naturally contains small amounts of the hormone.) Meanwhile, however, several supermarket chains banned dairy products from BST-treated cows.

For farmers, the issue was economic. Owners of small, principally family-farm operations feared that increased production and the resulting lower prices would force them out of business, since they operate with lower profit margins than do large producers. The four multinational companies developing BST argued that its cost (less than a dollar a day per cow) would not give big dairy operations an advantage over small ones. Others noted that small farmers would have the option of producing the same amount of milk with fewer cows or keeping the same number of cows and thereby increasing production.

Alar. While folk wisdom says an apple a day keeps the doctor away, at least one advocacy group warned that apples can kill, precipitating another controversy in which the lines between economic concerns and public health hazards were not clearly drawn. In February 1989 the Natural Resources Defense Council (NRDC) issued a report concluding that apples treated with the pesticide Alar (daminozide) pose an "intolerable risk" to children because certain compounds used to make it cause cancer in laboratory mice. It was implied that children are at risk because they drink large quantities of apple juice. Enlisting the aid of well-known entertainment personalities, the NRDC embarked on a crusade to have Alar banned. As sales of processed apple products fell, the International Apple Institute, representing makers of applesauce and apple juice, joined the call for a ban. In September the Environmental Protection Agency (EPA) ordered Alar to be phased out by May 31, 1991. Prior to its ruling, the EPA reached an agreement with Uniroyal Chemical Co., the sole registrant of daminozide, to stop sales of Alar and to recall all stocks of daminozide food-use products, including those held by users. The agreement applied only to the U.S.

The issue centered on the question of what is a tolerable and what is an intolerable risk to human health. It was true that an ingredient in Alar had been linked to cancer in mice, but only at extremely high levels of consumption. Tests showed that a greater risk was posed by naturally occurring carcinogens in such foods as mushrooms and peanut butter. The issue was not confined to the U.S. A joint announcement by the U.K. Ministry of Agriculture, the Scottish Home and Health Department, the Department of Health, and the Department of the Environment said that there was a wide margin of safety in the use of daminozide and unsymmetrical dimethylhydrazine (UDMH), a contaminant of daminozide. Even so, officials noted that companies making the product were taking it off the market.

Oat bran. On the basis of studies indicating that it could lower a person's blood cholesterol level, oat bran had become the hottest health food of the 1980s. Early in 1990, however, a small study published in the *New England Journal of Medicine* challenged the value of oat bran, claiming that oat fiber is no more effective in lowering cholesterol levels than foods made from low-fiber refined wheat flour. It suggested that people who fill up on oat bran probably eat fewer fatty foods, thus accounting for the earlier findings.

The study was carried out at Boston's Brigham and Women's Hospital. Twenty healthy people ate 87 g of oat bran—about one cup—daily for six weeks. Then, following a two-week return to their normal diets, they ate similar amounts of white flour or cream of wheat for six weeks. They could eat anything else they wanted. Both oat bran and refined wheat cut total cholesterol about 7%. The researchers who conducted the study said the cholesterol-lowering effects of both diets were due not to any direct effect of fiber on cholesterol but rather to the fact that the subjects ate less fat and cholesterol and more polyunsaturated fat during both six-week periods. However, several other studies, including some with as many as 200 participants, indicated that oat bran lowers cholesterol and that the benefits are greater when the cholesterol level is higher. While the debate continued, U.S. Department of Agriculture (USDA) and university researchers showed that both rice bran and barley bran seem to have the same cholesterol-reducing properties as oat bran.

Research. University of Massachusetts researchers using nuclear transplantation successfully produced genetically identical rabbits. Nuclei from early-stage embryos were transplanted to unfertilized eggs from which the chromosomes had been removed. The eggs were then activated to continue development. The technique held promise for large-scale production of mammals. The most important benefit of cloning would be in identifying and multiplying genetically superior farm animals. The rate of genetic progress in farm animals also could be increased, and the sex of clonal lines would be known. Also, because cloned animals are more uniform than random animals, considerably fewer would be needed for research purposes.

A joint team of researchers from the USDA and Mississippi's Alcorn State University found that megadoses of the antioxidant vitamins, vitamins C and E, may reduce health risks under certain circumstances but can also cause problems. Vitamin C supplements of 1,000 g per day significantly reduced blood sodium levels and the ratio of sodium to potassium of 12 men and women with mildly elevated blood pressure. The supplements also lowered systolic—but not diastolic—pressure. However, they had no such effects on eight men and women with normal blood pressure.

The researchers also found that 800 g a day of vitamin E supplements significantly improved the diminishing immune responses of men and women over 60, but another study found that vitamin E

Cathy Melloan

On the basis of studies indicating that it could lower a person's blood cholesterol level, oat bran enjoyed a huge increase in popularity in the 1980s. Research in early 1990, however, raised questions about whether it was any more effective than low-fiber wheat flour.

supplements may adversely affect blood cholesterol. Contrary to reports that vitamin E may help prevent heart disease, a USDA researcher found that it made both "good" and "bad" cholesterol more rigid—the opposite effect of a healthful, low-fat diet. Other researchers found that supplementing the diet of senior citizens with vitamin A—even as little as the Recommended Daily Allowance (RDA)—may cause toxic buildup resulting in liver damage. The findings suggest that the elderly should avoid extended use of supplements containing Vitamin A and should rely instead on dietary sources of beta carotene.

Workers at Virginia Polytechnic Institute and State University uncovered new evidence that biotin (a B-vitamin) deficiency depresses limb-bone metabolism, leading to lameness in poultry. The evidence suggested that metabolism of polyunsaturated fatty acids and/or prostaglandins may be the cause. Further research in this field could enhance understanding of bone mineralization defects, such as osteomalacia and osteoporosis, in humans. Using supercritical carbon dioxide extracting technology, researchers in Nebraska and North Carolina removed about two-thirds of the egg yolk cholesterol and nearly 30% of the lipid triacylglycerols from

USDA; photo, Bruce Fritz

Fengjing boar, bred in China, was taken to the U.S. to breed with domestic swine. Chinese pigs average three to four more offspring per litter than do U.S. hogs.

dried egg yolk without losing desirable functional and sensory properties. The development was significant in that eggs are a nutritionally complete food containing high-quality protein, vitamins, and minerals, but because of their high cholesterol content they have been labeled by some health groups as unwholesome.

USDA scientists developed a new technology in making cotton fabrics as wrinkle resistant as permanent-press cotton-polyester blends. Treating 100% cotton fabrics with certain chemicals produces permanent-press fabrics that dry smooth even after 65 washings. Also, a new cotton fiber called Cellulose III gave promise of improving durable-press cotton's resistance to wear. The fiber is produced by treating plain cotton cellulose with ammonia vapors at high temperatures and pressure until its crystalline structure changes.

The "1890" colleges. The year 1990 marked the 100th anniversary of a second set of land-grant colleges, established by the U.S. Congress in 1890 as institutions that could not restrict entrance on the basis of race or color. Less widely known than their counterparts founded under the first Morrill Act of 1862, they have nevertheless played a significant role in agricultural research. Like the 1862 institutions, they were agriculturally oriented, and they continue to have strong agricultural programs with instructional, research, and extension components. A century later, there were 17 of these historically black institutions.

Although technically not an 1890 institution, as these colleges and universities are called, Tuskegee University in Alabama has been a major contributor to agricultural research since George Washington Carver devised hundreds of uses for the peanut and the sweet potato. Work being carried out at Tuskegee and the 1890 schools in 1990 included research on the productivity and profitability of animal production systems, especially minor livestock species, such as goats and rabbits, which are particularly well suited to small farm operations. Researchers at the 1890 institutions had partially established the nutritional requirements of dairy goats and had identified a milk replacement for kids.

Other 1890 workers were evaluating earthworms as a source of high-quality protein. They found that the amino acid pattern in the earthworm is suitable for incorporation into food for human consumption. This readily available, inexpensive source of high-quality protein has potential for meeting the needs of populations facing famine. The 1890 scientists also described a complete recycling production system using animal wastes as a substrate for producing earthworms. Such a system could be a valuable operation for small farmers.

Work in some traditional areas included the development of practical techniques for screening, propagating, and cataloging rootstocks for peach trees. Workers evaluated survival and production characteristics of various rootstocks and screened and cataloged several new varieties of peach tree with rootstock potential. They also determined the influence of specific hormones on cold hardiness, dormancy regulation, and resistance to short life span.

—John Patrick Jordan

Nutrition

Funding for human nutrition research under the USDA competitive grant program was delayed in Congress in early 1990. The House of Representatives was not threatening to terminate the program, as it had in 1988. However, nutrition research was suffering as a result of across-the-board spending cuts mandated to lower the federal deficit and the diversion of funds to the "war on drugs." Also affecting nutrition research were recent guidelines, a direct result of congressional hearings that brought into question researchers' relationships with commercial producers. Designed to guard against conflict of interest, the 1989 guidelines delve deeply into the personal holdings of researchers and require divestiture of interests where possible conflicts exist.

Objectives for the new century. Objectives for the year 2000, published by the American Institute of Nutrition in December 1989, are summarized as follows:

1. Reduce growth retardation in children by age five with better diets.

2. Reduce iron deficiency among children, especially through age two.

3. Reduce iron deficiency among women aged 20 through 44 by teaching them to choose foods low in fat and sugar.

4. Reduce iron-deficiency anemia, especially in low-income pregnant women who fail to eat their traditional diet of organ meats, "greens," and whole-grain breads.

5. Reduce excess weight among people aged 20 through 74, limiting their excess weight to no more than 20% of the recommendation for their height and build. Also, reduce excess weight among adolescents aged 12 through 17.

6. Ensure that at least 75% of all overweight people have adopted sound dietary practices combined with physical activity to bring their weight within the normal range.

7. Reduce average dietary fat intake to no more than 30% of total caloric intake.

8. Increase the consumption of foods rich in calcium to no less than three servings a day for at least 50% of the population aged 12 and over.

9. Increase the daily intake of dietary fiber by five servings of vegetables, fruits, and whole-grain products.

10. Increase the number of households that restrict the use of salt, soda, and other sources of sodium in food preparation and avoid such highly salted snack-type foods as chips and crackers.

11. Increase the number of mothers who breast-feed their babies and who add no salt or fat to foods fed to infants and children.

12. Increase the percentage of the population who can identify specific nutrients, those foods acceptable to their culture that contain the nutrients, and how much of those foods is needed to prevent abnormal body development, specific symptoms of nutrient deficiency, or the malfunctioning of normal body processes.

Additional objectives include required courses in human nutrition in all medical and dental schools. No multivitamin tablet, even with mineral elements added, can substitute for daily balanced meals.

Nutrition guidelines. The National Research Council's latest RDAs were issued in October 1989 by a subcommittee of the Food and Nutrition Board. The RDA serves as a principal guide for developing nutrition programs and policies. This 10th edition added two nutrients, vitamin K and selenium, and changed the recommended amounts for several vitamins and mineral elements. However, most recommendations in the previous (1980) edition were unchanged or modified only slightly.

The RDAs were defined in the two previous editions as levels of nutrient intake that are "adequate to meet the known nutrient needs of practically all healthy persons." In previous editions the RDAs for adults were based on "ideal heights and weights," but in the current revision they are based on actual heights and weights occurring in the population. The main changes in the new edition are as follows:

Folate: Based on adult populations in the U.S. and Canada who maintain good health on diets with a daily average of 200 micrograms of folate for men and 180 micrograms for women, the committee judged these amounts to be sufficient; the previous RDA was 400 micrograms.

Vitamin B_{12}: The RDA was reduced from 3 micrograms for men and women to 2 micrograms.

Vitamin K: On the basis of new studies, the approximate amounts needed daily were defined as 80 micrograms for men and 65 micrograms for women.

Selenium: Direct evidence for selenium deficiency in humans was discovered in China, where young children and women of childbearing age who lacked selenium developed a heart condition known as Keshan disease. Subsequent research established more precise requirements than the 50–200-microgram range given in the ninth edition. The new RDA is 70 micrograms for men and 55 for women.

Protein: On the basis of new theories about protein accumulation during pregnancy and the efficiency of its conversion to tissues in the mother and fetus, it was determined that an additional increment of 10 g a day during pregnancy is sufficient; the previous recommendation was 30 g.

Iron: The committee lowered the RDA for iron for adolescent girls and premenopausal women to 15 mg. Pregnant women are advised to increase daily iron intake by an additional 15 mg.

The number of overweight people in the U.S. has increased in recent years. Implicated in such diseases as diabetes, cancer, and hypertension, obesity is expected to be a serious problem in the 1990s.

Cary Wolinsky—Stock, Boston

AP/Wide World

Two executives of the NutraSweet Co. sample *Simple Pleasures,* the firm's frozen dessert, which recently won FDA approval. It is made from *Simplesse,* a fat substitute that blends proteins from egg whites and milk.

Vitamin C: Though the RDA of 60 mg for both men and women remained the same, the subcommittee recommended that cigarette smokers continue to consume at least 100 mg daily because they metabolize or excrete vitamin C more rapidly than nonsmokers.

Calcium: Since peak bone mass is not achieved before age 25, even though long bones cease growth at 18, an average daily intake of 1,200 mg is recommended for people up to age 24 (the previous recommendation was up to 18). Optimum calcium intake up to the mid-20s offers the most promising nutritional approach to reducing osteoporosis in later life. Women 25 and older were still urged to consume 800 mg daily.

Vitamin B$_6$: The new RDA was set at 2 mg for men and 1.6 mg for women. This provides a lower intake than previously suggested.

The recommended intake of both magnesium and zinc for women was reduced, based on lower body weight.

Obesity and diet. Increasing evidence justified concern over excessive caloric intake by people whose life-style was becoming more and more sedentary. Despite a life expectancy of 74.9 years in the U.S. in 1987, obesity and management of weight were expected to be serious problems in the 1990s. On the basis of body mass index (the ratio of weight to the square of height), about 25% of adult women and 42% of men in the U.S. were considered overweight, with 14 and 12%, respectively, considered obese. In the first National Health and Nutrition Examination Survey, conducted in 1971–74, 28.8 million Americans were classed as obese and 8.4 million as severely obese. A second survey in 1976–80 found that the number of overweight U.S. adults

had increased to 34 million and the number of severely obese to 13 million. Surveys of children 6–11 years of age in 1963–65 and 1976–80 showed a 54% increase in the incidence of obesity in children. Among adolescents 12–17 years of age, obesity and superobesity rose 39 and 64%, respectively.

Obesity may predispose an individual to a number of diseases, including diabetes, gallstones, cancer, and hypertension. Changes in diet and life-style, including increased exercise, can help control the onset of heart disease, cancer, diabetes, and liver and lung diseases.

Katherine S. Tippett, a home economist with the USDA, reported that women in 1985 had increased their consumption of lowfat milk and ate less meat and fewer eggs. However, higher-income women served more cheese, cream and milk desserts, baked goods, and table fats, reflecting their affluence as well as their lack of knowledge about nutritional recommendations. Barry Popkin and other researchers at the University of North Carolina, comparing the eating habits of 5,400 women in 1977–78 with more than 1,000 women in 1986, reported that major healthful changes had occurred. The more educated women were more likely to make healthful eating choices. However, the consumption of high-fat cheeses increased, as did that of chips, buttered popcorn, ice cream, cake, cookies, pies, doughnuts, and granola bars.

Other developments. To justify the school lunch program as an integral part of the educational system, lunches must contribute to health and to the development of sound eating habits in young children. It was recommended that at least 95% of school lunch and breakfast food service programs use menus that comply with *Dietary Guidelines for Americans.* Too often parents failed to observe and participate in their child's school food service experiences. In an effort to compete with fast-food establishments, many school food services provided foods excessively high in saturated fats, salt, and total calorie content.

Many individuals have regular vitamin B$_{12}$ shots to relieve a "run-down" feeling. A review of the records of 120 people who received regular B$_{12}$ shots, some for as long as 20 years, showed that only 4 actually needed the supplement. People benefit from B$_{12}$ shots when they are not able to absorb enough from their food. Such individuals are deficient in a substance needed to absorb B$_{12}$. People on a very limited diet can assure adequate intake of vitamin B$_{12}$ simply by taking it orally. Vitamin B$_{12}$ does not provide energy or alleviate muscle aches, anxiety, headaches, insomnia, or other problems. In fact, B$_{12}$ deficiencies are rare since it is in many commonly eaten foods.

Foods that are labeled "diet" or "dietetic" are not

necessarily better nutritionally than regular market items. Only a study of the label will indicate how such items differ from the standard product. The specific modification should be identified, indicating which nutrients have been changed in amount or chemical form. Informative labeling continued to be of major concern to consumer protection agencies. Fraudulent, unproven nutritional and health implications were rampant in the marketplace. According to the Tufts University *Diet and Nutrition Letter,* consumers paid up to $25 billion a year for foods that promised health benefits.

—Mina W. Lamb

Life sciences

During the past year the achievements and potentials of genetic research manifested themselves throughout the life sciences. Working genes derived from mouse tissue were transferred to tobacco plants, a new analytical method led to identification of genes whose mutant forms cause cystic fibrosis and Duchenne muscular dystrophy, and the moral and ethical issues of fetal and embryo research continued to stir debate. Other highlights included the ongoing study of plants that generate heat; the discovery of microorganisms living hundreds of meters underground and of photosynthetic bacteria that nodulate the stems, rather than the roots, of plants; the finding of the oldest known dinosaur; and the construction of a robot bee able to communicate with real bees.

Botany

Progress in botany during the past year revealed a number of intriguing relationships among organisms and addressed some controversies. Noteworthy findings emerged from the fields of plant ecology, genetics, reproduction, and forestry.

Plants and environmental temperature. Plant biologists continued to explore the ways in which environmental factors affect the distribution, vigor, and productivity of plants. Two reports of the effects of temperature on plants involved studies conducted under very different conditions. In one, Park S. Nobel of the University of California at Los Angeles found that some plants can tolerate temperatures as low as −16° C (3° F) and as high as 68° C (154° F) for one hour. His investigations were carried out in South Africa on small succulent plants growing close to the soil surface in desert regions. There, by absorbing both direct sunlight and heat conducted from the surrounding soil, they reach very high daytime temperatures. The plants, *Haworthia retusa, H. turgida, Lithops leslei,* and *L. turbiformis,* have temperatures that seldom differ by more than 1° C (1.8°

F) from the surrounding soil. Nobel concluded that whereas the observed low-temperature tolerances are not particularly noteworthy, few vascular plants are able to survive such extreme heat.

The second report focused on the potato (*Solanum tuberosum*), a crop plant of temperate climates, which fails to produce tubers at high temperature. Two researchers from Cornell University, Ithaca, N.Y.—M.P. Reynolds and Elmer E. Ewing—grew potato plants at different air and soil temperatures to determine the effects of high-temperature stress on tuber formation and growth. They observed the effects on shoot, root, and tuber growth of potato plants raised under various combinations of potting soil and air temperature. To observe tuber growth, they prepared leaf-bud cuttings for growth in potting soil, a procedure that normally results in the production of tubers from axillary buds. Raising plants in warm air, even when the soil was cool, produced growth stress in shoots and kept leaf-bud cuttings from producing tubers. Warm soil inhibited the growth of tubers on leaf-bud cuttings. The researchers concluded that the induction of tuberization by leaves is affected mostly by air temperature, although high soil temperature may block tuber development. Keeping soil relatively cool in potato production has been accomplished mainly by mulching.

Epiphytes. Many species of orchids inhabit nutrient-poor habitats in tropical regions of the world. They live perched in the tops of trees in the canopies of forests, unattached to any obvious nutrient source, and are thus called epiphytes. It is not surprising that some of them prove to have unique methods for procurement of nutrients. It has been known for some time that individual plants of some species possess as many as 30 to 40 large hollow pseudobulbs that harbor ants, but plants of the species *Schomburgkia tibicinis* have an unusual relationship with their ant tenants. Although the plants can grow in the absence of ants, uninhabited individuals are quite rare and prove to be small. In ant-inhabited individuals the ants pack some of the pseudobulbs with debris that may include dead ants, a variety of other insects, dead plant material, seeds, and sand.

Victor Rico-Gray of the National Institute for Research on Biological Resources (INIREB), Jalapa, Mexico, and four associates from Tulane University, New Orleans, La., reported that the plants actually absorb and metabolize nutrients from the decaying material through the smooth, black lining of the pseudobulbs. The researchers fed ants radioactive honey and placed dead specimens in hollow pseudobulbs of *S. tibicinis.* After sampling plant tissues for eight weeks, they found increasing radioactivity in leaves over the period. By the eighth week radioactivity in complex molecules in roots had greatly increased, indicating that nutrients derived from the ants not only had traveled to the most distant parts of the plant but also had been incorporated into growing root tissue, the fastest-growing tissues.

Strangler figs also begin their life as epiphytes. They germinate in small depressions in their hosts' trunks and branches, where organic material and other nutrients accumulate. It has been found that such depressions may hold "soil" that is actually richer in nutrients than the true soils of the forest floor. Concentrations of such nutrients as nitrogen, potassium, and phosphorus have been shown to be significantly higher in epiphytic leaves than in the leaves of their host trees. Strangler figs do not remain confined to their lofty perches; as hemiepiphytes they grow downward-reaching roots that eventually contact the soil and thereby supply water and additional nutrients. Although water is probably the primary benefit of downward root growth, nutrients may also be important because the soil roots are associated with special fungi, called mycorrhizae, that are widely involved in plant nutrition. In the llanos of Venezuela, Francis E. Putz and N. Michele Holbrook of the University of Florida studied some strangler figs that begin life in the tops of palm trees. There the figs grow in material trapped behind the palm leaf bases. The investigators found that once the figs' roots reach the ground, they grow upward.

Genetically engineered tobacco plant carries antibody genes derived from mouse tissue. Plants receiving the foreign genes were shown able to synthesize mouse antibodies and, when crossed, to pass on the ability to offspring.

In this way the hemiepiphytes can again take advantage of pockets of nutrient-rich material in the trees, particularly if the roots ascend a tree different from the one on which the fig sprouted. Indeed, Putz and Holbrook noted some instances in which roots did grow into trees that had no epiphytes of their own.

Plant symbiosis. A number of plants from different groups are able to associate with certain bacteria to form nitrogen-fixing nodules on their roots. Both plants and bacteria benefit from this symbiotic alliance: the plants have usable nitrogen compounds made for them from atmospheric nitrogen, and the bacteria presumably have a favorable place to live. The plants most noted for this relationship are members of the pea family, the legumes. They associate with soil bacteria, usually of the genera *Rhizobium* and *Bradyrhizobium*, in a species-specific way. A given strain of bacterium can associate with only certain species of legumes. What determines the specificity has practical importance; its elucidation, for example, may help researchers learn how to inoculate a variety of legumes with the same bacterial strain. Investigators from the State University of Leiden, Neth., Clara L. Díaz and co-workers, confirmed earlier work suggesting that specific carbohydrate-binding proteins called lectins, which are produced by the plant roots, are recognized by the appropriate bacteria and that variability in lectins is a way in which specific host plants attract specific bacteria. To demonstrate such a role for lectins, the researchers transferred the gene for a lectin made by pea plants into clover roots. When exposed to bacteria that normally nodulate pea plants but not clover, the genetically engineered clover roots developed nodules.

Plants and pests. A biologist from Northern Arizona University reported a plant defense against pests that may have practical applications. At two sites in northern Utah, Thomas G. Whitham investigated the relationship of a parasitic aphid, *Pemphigus betae*, to two cottonwood species that interbreed along their common borders. Both *Populus fremontii* and *P. angustifolia* are hosts for the aphid, which produces offspring in galls (growths of tissue made by the leaf following injury from the insects). Whitham observed that the cottonwood hybrids were attacked almost exclusively, as was the case when aphids were introduced experimentally to the various types of trees. He suggested that the presence of the more susceptible hybrids may represent a lowering of selection pressure that would otherwise encourage the aphids to adapt to the purebred cottonwoods' resistance to gall formation. Although the actual genetic basis for the resistance is not known, Whitman suggested that this method for managing some pests may be less harmful than others. For instance, pest-susceptible strains of certain crop plants might be mixed with comparatively resistant ones in order to slow pest adaptation to the latter.

Plant genetics. Two U.S. governmental agencies undertook large projects to map the genes of plants. The National Science Foundation proposed to fund researchers in the U.S. and cooperate with scientists worldwide to map completely the genes of a small plant, *Arabidopsis thaliana*. In view of the plant's recent acceptance as a desirable research organism, a complete map of its genetic endowment, or genome, would be valuable. In addition, the mapping work would serve as a prototype for mapping other plant genomes. The effort was expected to take 10 years and cost $100 million. For the second project, the U.S. Department of Agriculture (USDA) endeavored to begin a 10-year, $500 million study of important crop-plant genes; for example, those related to disease resistance and drought tolerance. The Office of Plant Genome Mapping, a new organization within the USDA's Agricultural Research Service, was to be in charge of the project.

Andrew Hiatt and associates from the Research Institute of Scripps Clinic, La Jolla, Calif., succeeded in introducing functional genes from mouse tissue into tobacco plants. The team used standard techniques for securing the genes and introducing them into cultures of tobacco leaf segments from which mature plants then were regenerated. The plants so transformed produced certain antibodies characteristic of mouse cells and, when crossed, were able to pass on this ability to offspring. The investigators recognized that the antibodies cannot pass through cell walls and thus cannot function as a circulating defense, as they do in animals. It was suggested, however, that they might bind certain substances that enter plant cells. In this way they could immobilize contaminants from the environment.

Plant reproduction. What does it take to keep botanists interested in a plant for more than 200 years? One answer is the plant's ability to use heat and putrescent odors to attract insect pollinators. Several members of the arum family possess this ability, and recently attention has focused on the champion, the voodoo lily (*Sauromatum guttatum*). This tropical relative of the jack-in-the-pulpit has a flowering structure comprising a vase-shaped base called the floral chamber and a protruding, stalk-like spadix. The portion of the spadix hidden in the floral chamber supports the male flowers and, below them, the female flowers. To entice insects into the chamber, the voodoo lily broadcasts such foul-smelling substances as skatole, putrescine, and ammonia. About three to five hours into the day of blooming, the upper spadix, or appendix, liberates heat, increasing its temperature as much as 22° C (40° F) above the surroundings. The burst of heat greatly enhances the stench and the associated

attractiveness to certain insects. Ilya Raskin and associates at the Du Pont Co., Wilmington, Del., reported in 1987 that the heat production is triggered by salicylic acid, which accumulates to as much as 100 times the normal level in the appendix the day before blooming.

In 1989 a new study by Raskin's group described another phase of heating, which takes place in the floral chamber between the male and female flowers and lasts from the night following blooming day to the next dawn. The second phase, which produces a temperature rise about half that of the first phase, stimulates the activity of insects present in the floral chamber. At its peak the male flowers drop their pollen on the insects, which pollinate the female flowers in the chamber and then travel on to cross-pollinate other voodoo lilies. The function of salicylic acid in plants was of continuing interest; it is associated with flowering in plants other than the voodoo lily and seems to be related to the synthesis of ethylene, an important plant hormone.

For some years seed banks have been in operation in several places in the world with the intent of preserving the diversity of germ plasm for economically important plant species. Recently the practice has been extended to pollen preservation, which has certain advantages. Pollen may be used immediately in cross breeding, whereas banked seed first must be grown into flowering plants. In addition, it is believed that pollen can be preserved frozen in liquid nitrogen for prolonged periods. Pollen cryobanks (storage facilities relying on extremely low temperatures for preservation) first were set up in temperate regions of the world, including Japan, Hawaii, and California. More recently a storage laboratory was established in India for preserving the pollen of tropical fruits and vegetables. Good viability has been recorded over five-year storage periods.

Forestry. Perhaps the greatest current controversy in forestry—deciding the destiny of dwindling resources called old-growth forests—remained unresolved. Professional foresters were taking sides over what they saw as conflicting public demands for wood products on one hand and preservation of old trees on the other. The conflict, however, is more complex than the statement implies. Continued supply of wood is linked to jobs, marketable products, and a benefited economy. Safeguarding of ecosystems containing the old trees is linked to preservation of biological diversity, aesthetic considerations, and other projected ecological issues. Some foresters and forest ecologists suggested a middle ground of modified forestry practice. An example was the proposal of Jerry Franklin of the University of Washington and the U.S. Forest Service, who advocated a "new forestry" wherein forest managers, such as the Forest Service, mimic the structure of natural

Cross-sectioned floral chamber of a mature voodoo lily displays the heat-producing spadix with its thick, white collar of male flowers, ring of club-shaped scent organs below, and array of female flowers nearest the base.

forests in parts of their managed stands of timber. This approach would require a significant change in regions like the Pacific Northwest where the clearcutting of large areas was the practice. For their part, environmentalists would have to modify views of old growth as extensive forests several centuries old.

The saga of the relationship between air pollution (quite often acid rain) and the phenomenon of forest decline continued to interest forest ecologists. A recent report from a West German scientist offered a historical explanation for the widespread decline in Norway spruce (*Picea abies*) forests of Europe. E.-D. Schulze of the University of Bayreuth, West Germany, contended that damage is caused by abundance of certain soil nutrients and depletion of others rather than by direct damage from exposure to pollutants or disease organisms. He identified three overlapping phases of deposition from the atmosphere that has led to the present forest decline.

The first phase, to about 1900, consisted mostly of pollution by sulfur compounds, which raised soil acidity somewhat but were largely counteracted. Up to 1960, nitrogen compounds increased steadily and

actually acted as nutrients. Finally, an enormous increase of nitrogen compounds after 1960 led to the decline currently observed. During the last phase, deposition of both nitrates and ammonium compounds in the soil apparently resulted in the preferential uptake of the latter by plants. Thus, accumulating nitrates together with continuing deposit of sulfur compounds elevated soil acidity. Leaching of other nutrients, which is associated with raised acidity, followed. The ensuing nutrient imbalance affected the uptake of nutrients in general as well as water uptake and root development. In Europe the consequences have been needle yellowing, tree loss, and even the death of entire stands.

Donald H. DeHayes and Gary J. Hawley of the University of Vermont offered evidence that genetic uniformity may be behind the observed decline of the red spruce (*Picea rubens*) in eastern North America. Examining 42 gene sites in material taken from red spruce seeds, they found less than 50% of the genetic variation typical of other conifers. Such a condition would be expected from inbreeding among trees in isolated mountain populations.

G. Eriksson of the University of Stockholm and three co-workers reported that they were able to detect increases of certain atmospheric pollutants by examining the contents of the waxy coating, or cuticle, of pine needles. Since individual pine needles persist on trees for a number of years, each tree may bear a record of pollution-releasing events over these years. As an example, a forest-spraying program in East Germany that used increased amounts of the insecticide DDT in 1984 was identified in pine needles collected in Sweden in 1986.

—Albert J. Smith

Microbiology

Scientific progress and new findings often are presented to the public by the news media as "gee-whiz" science. Such reporting, in essence a kind of sensationalism, lends itself well to new and unexpected discoveries, adding interest and romance to basic research. Moreover, professional research scientists can be as excited as anyone else over news of the unusual and unexpected. Such was the case for the discoveries, beginning in 1977, of communities of novel forms of marine life near deep-sea hydrothermal vents in the Pacific and Atlantic oceans. About a decade later astonishing communities were found associated with hydrocarbon cold seeps off the coast of Louisiana. In each instance the primary producers are not photosynthetic organisms that derive energy from sunlight. Instead they are microorganisms that derive energy from the oxidation of simple substances such as dissolved sulfide minerals or methane.

Environmental microbiology. A similar finding was made recently by collaborating researchers from New Mexico and Oregon. Using a one-person submersible, they studied bacterial mats on the bottom of a lake nearly 610 m (2,000 ft) deep located in a volcanic caldera in Oregon. The bacterial communities were those usually associated with anomalously warm, saline waters. The investigators used the term *anomalously* because, although water at this depth ordinarily is about 3° C (38° F), the bacterial mats were found to be about 5.5°–6.5° C (10°–12° F) warmer, which suggested hydrothermal venting into the deep lake as a source of the heat. In this respect there appeared to be a parallel with the heat source of the deep-ocean vent communities. Another parallel was that the bacteria found in the mats gained energy by means of the oxidation of a simple mineral, in this case ferrous iron. Unlike the deep-ocean vent communities, however, there was no evidence of such other forms of life as phytoplankton or zooplankton (minute plants and animals) associated with the mats.

The greenhouse effect is the elevation of the Earth's temperature due to the presence of certain atmospheric trace gases, called greenhouse gases, that trap solar energy near the surface. Methane is considered to be a greenhouse gas and ranks second only to carbon dioxide in its contribution to the greenhouse effect. Nevertheless, methane is increasing in the atmosphere by about 1% each year. The sources of methane are diverse. The gas is produced by cattle and other ruminants, by termites, and in rice fields, wetlands, and peat bogs. In each case the methane is actually generated by microbial activity in the digestive systems of the various animals or in waterlogged soils.

In recent years scientists have taken interest in methane cycling in the environment. Just as microorganisms produce methane, other microorganisms are able to use the gas as a source of energy. Microbiologists have long studied such cyclic metabolic events as the carbon cycle and the nitrogen cycle but know little about the methane cycle.

The interest in cyclical methane processes ties in with discovery of the mostly microbial cold-seep communities that obtain their energy from the oxidation of methane and other hydrocarbons that rise upward from seabed faults. Thus, it seems that food webs of several diverse communities are founded on microorganisms that act as nonphotosynthetic primary producers.

Scientists at the Savannah River Ecology Laboratory, Aiken, S.C., reported finding bacteria that live in the Earth at depths of as much as 520 m (1,700 ft). They isolated numerous microbial species that apparently had never before been described. In fact, few had suspected that bacteria could exist at such depths. The researchers suggested that the microorganisms may have been inhabiting this remote ecological niche for at least 70 million years.

During the past year researchers announced their discovery that the abundance of viruses in aquatic environments is greater than had been thought. The viruses involved are mainly those that infect bacteria. Their presence in such quantity should not have been unexpected, but only recently had scientists made a concerted effort to look for them. The first report came from Norwegian investigators; subsequently others reported similar findings. The discovery suggests that bacterial viruses may be an important factor in the ecological control of populations of planktonic microorganisms. Moreover, it is probable that they play an influential role in genetic exchange among bacteria in natural aquatic environments. One major implication is that the first significant link in the food chain of the oceans may be microbial life rather than planktonic organisms.

The cells of magnetotactic marine bacteria can form and accumulate magnetite, a magnetic iron compound. This substance enables the bacteria to follow lines of the Earth's magnetic field and, in so doing, to seek out favorable ecological niches. In the past such bacteria always had been found in marine sources. Recently scientists from the Woods Hole (Mass.) Oceanographic Institution discovered magnetotactic bacteria that do not require oxygen and exist in salt marshes rather than ocean waters.

A colorful South American leaf-eating bird, the hoatzin, has been nicknamed the stinkbird because it smells like fresh cow manure. In the past year an international group of scientists from the U.S., Venezuela, and Scotland reported that a microbial fermentation of plant material occurs in the bird's foregut, much like the process that takes place in the rumen of cows. Symbiotic bacteria in the crop and esophagus ferment fibrous plant material and release compounds that are important sources of energy for the hoatzin. Scientifically the discovery is the first recorded of a bird to possess a metabolism based on microbial activity similar to that of cattle.

Medical and applied microbiology. In the bacteriological examination of water or food, technicians look for the presence of *Escherichia coli*. *E. coli* inhabits the gut of warm-blooded vertebrates including humans. The presence of *E. coli* in water—whether it be from a lake, river, reservoir, or spring—or in food is an indication of fecal pollution. This is presumptive evidence that the water or food is unfit for consumption since organisms that cause intestinal diseases, such as typhoid fever, cholera, or dysentery, may be present as well.

Scientists in Spain showed that the presence in water of bacterial viruses (bacteriophages) that attack species of *Bacteroides* is also a good indicator

The hoatzin, a South American bird that smells like cow manure, was found to digest its leafy diet with the help of bacteria in its foregut, thus relying on a fermentation process much like that which occurs in the rumen of cattle.

of fecal pollution. *Bacteroides* is the most abundant organism in the human intestinal tract, even more numerous than *E. coli*. Unlike *E. coli*, however, *Bacteroides* is an anaerobic organism (one that grows in the absence of oxygen) that is difficult to culture and identify in the laboratory. For this reason public health workers will continue to rely on *E. coli* as an indicator of fecal contamination of water and food. On the other hand, detection of bacteriophages for *Bacteroides* could be used in special circumstances to extend and confirm *E. coli* tests for fecal pollution.

Shipworms, marine wood-boring mollusks, are detrimental to wooden structures in the marine environment. Interestingly, scientists in Illinois found that enzymes necessary for digestion of the wood consumed by shipworms come from bacteria that live in the mollusks' gut. Whereas the investigators focused primarily on enzymes that digest protein, it is likely that future work will reveal other bacterial enzymes, such as those that break down cellulose.

The infectious bacterium *Vibrio cholerae* often causes outbreaks of cholera, a serious intestinal disease that is particularly widespread in Southeast Asia. The disease is contracted from drinking polluted water or eating contaminated food. *V. cholerae* is beautifully adapted to a marine environment, a

characteristic that was reiterated by the discovery that the bacterium can attach to other resident marine organisms, thus becoming effectively invisible to the usual microbiological means of detecting pathogenic (disease-producing) bacteria. In this manner *V. cholera* often goes undetected in water until it manifests itself in epidemics of cholera, which are usually seasonal. The seasonality appears to be explained by the fact that although *V. cholera* occurs naturally in the environment throughout the year, it can be released in large numbers when zooplankton species seasonally release their exoskeletons, to which the bacteria are attached. This phenomenon, in turn, leads to increases in numbers of *V. cholerae* free in the water and to outbreaks of cholera.

Bacteria can use a variety of substances as nutrients, including organic compounds found in oil spills. Such substances, however, are usually deficient in nitrogen, an element needed in the cellular synthesis of vital compounds. A sensible, low-technology solution was applied recently to cleaning up oil spills. Scientists from California adopted the idea of adding nitrogen fertilizers to the spills to enable indigenous bacteria to better digest the oil, a method that seemed to work.

Adult male and female Ixodes dammini *(top and center), the tick species responsible for transmitting the bacterial agent of Lyme disease, are compared with a common wood tick (bottom) on a U.S. 10-cent coin.*

Scientists from Cornell University, Ithaca, N.Y., reported what appeared to be a new bacterial species that not only can fix atmospheric nitrogen (convert it into useful compounds) but also can obtain energy from sunlight by photosynthesis. The researchers expected that once the metabolic mechanisms used by this bacterium were elucidated, practical applications could be developed and applied to the production of more efficient crop plants.

Another bacterium that is both a nitrogen-fixing and a photosynthetic organism was described by scientists from New York and given the name *Photorhizobium thompsonum*. Although other nitrogen-fixing photosynthetic bacteria were known, the newly isolated bacterium was found to be unique in its ability to establish a symbiotic relationship with certain plants by forming nodules on the plants' stems. Thus, unlike the symbiotic root-nodulating *Rhizobium* species, *Photorhizobium* lives above ground and can use sunlight as an energy source to fix nitrogen. Consequently, it does not have to depend on nutrients from its host plant for this highly energy-demanding task. The practical advantages of such a symbiotic relationship could become available to agriculture provided the organism can be persuaded to form stem nodules on crop plants.

A practical application may also emerge from the recent finding of the sugar L-altrose in the rumen of ruminant animals. The compound, which is produced by bacteria living in the rumen, tastes sweet but is not digestible by human beings, thus making it a potential nonfattening sweetener. It is possible that the bacteria responsible for the production of L-altrose could be used to synthesize it on an industrial scale.

Lyme disease has emerged only recently as a health problem in the U.S. Its name derives from a community in Connecticut where the infection was first recognized in the 1970s as a distinct disease entity, although it may have been first described in Sweden nearly a century ago. Lyme disease is caused by a bacterial agent, *Borrelia burgdorferi*, a spirochete. The organism is transmitted by a tiny tick, *Ixodes dammini*, which in nature is heavily parasitic on the white-footed mouse. The tick, however, is thought to "winter over" on deer (and perhaps other animals as well). The recent high incidence of Lyme disease in the U.S., therefore, appears due to large deer populations, which serve as reservoirs for the disease.

A key to the control of Lyme disease is the control of the tick. A simple approach being tested in 1989 involves cardboard tubes filled with insecticide-impregnated cotton. The tubes are distributed in habitats of white-footed mice, which use the cotton to build nests resistant to tick infestation.

—Robert G. Eagon

Molecular biology

Astonishing technical advances continued to thrust molecular biology deeper into everyday life during the past year, impinging on the worlds of law, medicine, business, and politics. These advances involved DNA—detecting, analyzing, patenting, and field-testing it. One recently developed technology, restriction fragment length polymorphism (RFLP) analysis (see *1989 Yearbook of Science and the Future* Year in Review: LIFE SCIENCES: *Molecular biology*), led to breakthroughs in understanding several major genetic diseases. Moreover, the technology became strengthened with the addition of the DNA polymerase chain reaction.

RFLP analysis. RFLP analysis, one of the new methods that collectively have come to be called DNA (or genetic) fingerprinting, permits a virtually conclusive decision regarding the identity or nonidentity of two DNA samples. It also permits detailed linkage analysis of genes on complex chromosomes such as those of human beings, a capability that was allowing the identification of mutated genes in such diseases as cystic fibrosis and muscular dystrophy.

It should be recalled that each of the paired DNA strands in a chromosome is a linear array of genes, consisting of precise sequences of the nucleotides adenine, cytosine, guanine, and thymine (A, C, G, and T) paired by means of specific hydrogen bonds (A with T; G with C) that link the two strands of the double helix. Any DNA molecule can be cleaved at certain sequences by bacterial enzymes called restriction endonucleases. For example, the enzyme known as *Eco*RI cleaves DNA at the sequence

————————GAATTC————————
————————CTTAAG————————

by cutting the chemical bond between the G and A on each strand. Now consider a long DNA molecule containing many instances of the *Eco*RI target sequence distributed more or less randomly along the length of the molecule. On average, the six-nucleotide-pair sequence occurs once every 5,000 nucleotide pairs. Of course, the distribution is not random: it consists of regions that encode proteins, regions that contain sites for the binding of proteins that regulate gene expression (*i.e.*, transcription of the nucleotide sequence into RNA) and regions of "junk" DNA, the molecular debris of evolution that seems to accumulate inexorably in chromosomes. Some of the junk comprises short sequences repeated in tandem, found in many locations, that may be remnants of viral genes that parked in the chromosomes long ago.

The distribution of target sites for a particular restriction endonuclease, of which there are many, provides a definitive fingerprint of a DNA molecule. A bacterial chromosome, for example, will contain as many as 1,000 target sites for an endonuclease that recognizes a six-nucleotide target sequence. If the collection of fragments resulting from cleavage by the endonuclease is sorted by gel electrophoresis according to the length of the fragments, no clear divisions of fragment lengths can be seen by eye. The restriction fragments range in length from a few tens of nucleotide pairs to many thousands of nucleotide pairs, but there are so many of similar size that the electrophoretogram, a sheet of gel on which the sorted fragments are spread, shows a blur of DNA from one end to the other.

The key to analysis of this blur is a technique called Southern blotting, in which the pattern of fragment sizes on the electrophoretogram is preserved during transfer of the fragments to a supporting membrane (the blot) followed by tagging of the blot with a radioactive DNA fragment (the probe). The probe can be synthesized chemically, or it can be a cloned DNA fragment that corresponds to a particular gene or one of the repeated elements mentioned above. Wherever in the blot a DNA fragment is located whose nucleotide sequence is complementary to that of the probe (complementary in the sense that A pairs with T and G pairs with C), the probe will anneal. After suitable washing, the probe will remain only at those locations where its complementary sequence is found. Autoradiography, the exposure of photographic film to materials to reveal radioactivity, is used to determined where the probe is fixed. Thus, the complex pattern containing thousands of unresolved DNA fragments is simplified to reveal one, two, or a slightly larger number of bands of fragments, depending on the probe.

Consider a probe consisting of 1,000 nucleotides and complementary to a sequence lying entirely within the coding region of a given gene. If the probe has been chosen so that no instances of the sequence GAATTC occur within these 1,000 nucleotides, one can safely assume that the size of a fragment that has been created by EcoRI and revealed by the probe will be determined solely by how distant are the nearest EcoRI sites in that particular chromosome. If the two nearest EcoRI sites, on either side of the probe sequence, are 5,000 nucleotide pairs from each other, then the probe will identify a single band in the EcoRI-digested DNA corresponding to a size of 5,000 nucleotide pairs. If the two closest-flanking EcoRI sites are 7,000 nucleotide pairs apart, then the probe will identify a band corresponding to 7,000 nucleotide pairs, and so on.

If one were to prepare DNA from the blood of any two humans, chosen by chance from a large population, and to run the analysis described above for any gene for which a probe was available, the two samples would differ in the length of their restriction fragments. This difference is due to the fact that the nucleotides in the DNA are subject to mutation. When mutation occurs, a target site may be eliminated, a new one may be created, or the distance between two existing sites may change because of the deletion or insertion of nucleotides. This variation in the distance between restriction sites in individuals is called restriction fragment length polymorphism.

Instead of two individuals chosen by chance from a population, suppose the RFLP for a particular gene in DNA samples taken from a mother, a father, and their children were examined. One would see that each person has two bands of fragments, since an individual carries most of his or her genes in two versions, one from each paired chromosome. In general, those of the mother will differ in fragment size from those of the father because the two individuals are unrelated by blood. But each of the children will have two bands of which one corresponds to one of the mother's two bands and the other to one of the father's two bands. If the description sounds a lot like Mendelian inheritance of genes, it should not be surprising.

The germ cells of humans contain 23 pairs of chromosomes, one of each pair inherited from the mother or the father. During the maturation of sperm and eggs, the germ cells undergo a chromosome-reduction division called meiosis, in which one chromosome of each of the 23 pairs is chosen at random for a particular sperm or egg. Thus, the chromosomes of the parents are scrambled in each offspring. But the genes themselves are not completely scrambled because they are linked together on the chromosomes. To be sure, recombination between members of a chromosome pair occurs during germ-cell maturation, which leads to some reassortment of genes. The likelihood of recombination, however, depends on the distance between the genes on the chromosomes; for genes close together, recombination between them is rare.

RFLPs and genetic disease. What then is the importance of RFLPs to studying genetic disease? The inheritance of an RFLP, revealed by any specific probe, can be followed through a family pedigree by obtaining DNA samples from all members of the family. If linkage of the RFLP to inheritance of a particular genetic disease can be shown through the entire pedigree, then the probe in question must contain a DNA sequence that is very close to the gene affected in the diseased individuals.

This approach to the molecular biology of human disease is extremely labor-intensive. It requires examination of samples from as many informative families as possible—hence the need for wide collaboration among clinical groups. It also requires a vast array of DNA probes that identify particular regions of the human chromosomes. Recently three major diseases were studied by means of these methods:

Duchenne muscular dystrophy, cystic fibrosis, and Huntington's disease. Genes for the first two were identified definitely, and the third seemed on the verge of discovery in early 1990.

Duchenne muscular dystrophy is a degenerative disorder of muscle that affects one of every 3,500 male births, making its first appearance in early childhood. It has long been known to be X-linked; that is, the disease is inherited through the mother. (A male gets his single X chromosome from the mother, while the father contributes a Y chromosome). Very rarely does a girl exhibit Duchenne muscular dystrophy. Researchers found that in such cases a piece of one of the X chromosomes is translocated to another chromosome. In every affected girl examined, the X-chromosome break was found to occur in the same place, so that place became the object of molecular investigation. Eventually, by means of a wide range of experiments involving Southern blots that compared DNA from normal individuals with DNA from persons with muscular dystrophy—and that used probes corresponding to the region of the X chromosome near the break point in the affected girls—a gene was found to be missing in all of the female victims of Duchenne muscular dystrophy. The major contributor to this achievement was Louis M. Kunkel of Harvard Medical School, Boston.

The identified gene is huge (the largest known by a factor of ten), and it encodes a minor muscle protein called dystrophin. It covers more than two million nucleotide pairs, most of which consist of intervening noncoding sequences (introns). The coding segments, when spliced free of introns, give rise to a messenger RNA of 14,000 nucleotides, which in turn encodes a single protein with a molecular mass of 500,000 daltons. This protein is either missing or defective in all persons with Duchenne muscular dystrophy. Most affected persons have deletions of all or part of the dystrophin gene. Investigators found that the deletion frequently begins and ends within one of the short, tandemly repeated junk sequences located between genes or in the introns within genes. This is the first molecular evidence that such junk, far from being an inert passenger, is capable of causing great mischief.

Knowledge of the molecular nature of the disease, unfortunately, will not lead to relief for its current victims. On the other hand, analysis of the DNA of mothers who are carriers of the disease and the DNA of their fetuses should permit unambiguous identification of the X chromosome carried by the fetus. It should no longer be necessary that males with Duchenne muscular dystrophy be born to unwitting parents unless the mutation occurs during egg production in the mother or early in development of the male embryo.

The story of cystic fibrosis (CF) is equally heroic

Adapted from J.R. Riordan et al., Science, vol. 245, no. 4922, pp. 1066–1073; © 1989 AAAS

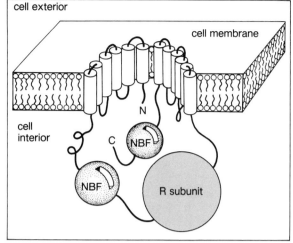

The gene whose defective form is the cause of cystic fibrosis codes for a protein thought to insert in the cell membrane in the manner shown above and to regulate ion flow across the membrane. Parts of the protein (cylinders) span the membrane, while the intracellular regions labeled NBF bind ATP and may be vital to the protein's control of ion flow.

in terms of the magnitude of labor required to find the responsible gene. The disease has many manifestations, but it is the copious production of mucus in the lungs that leads to death before age 30. The mutant CF gene is on chromosome 7. The mutation is recessive; that is, a person with one good gene and one mutant gene is healthy but a carrier. A mutant CF gene is carried by roughly one in 20 Caucasians, resulting in one CF-afflicted offspring in every 2,000 live births in that population.

The CF gene was located largely through the efforts of Lap-Chee Tsui and John R. Riordan of the Hospital for Sick Children, Toronto, and Francis S. Collins of the Howard Hughes Medical Institute at the University of Michigan, Ann Arbor, by analyzing a very large number of DNA samples from families in which cystic fibrosis could be traced through a large pedigree. One Amish population, in which one in 500 births was affected, was particularly informative. The DNA analysis began with the observation that the pursued CF gene was linked to several known genetic loci on chromosome 7. Eventually, by means of the restriction fragments to which they affixed, DNA probes were identified that corresponded to nucleotide sequences lying between the CF gene and the known loci. Finally, a probe that never separated from the CF gene by recombination was found, and it was used to begin DNA sequencing. Ultimately a region of DNA encoding a previously unknown protein of some 1,480 amino acids was sequenced. The protein sequence has several recognizable features and details, which when taken together suggest that the CF protein normally inserts into the cell membrane and controls the flow of ions across it. A mutation of the protein that would result in abnormal control of ion flow is consistent with most of the clinical manifestations of cystic fibrosis. The molecular nature of the mutation is also fascinating. More than 70% of the CF victims examined have exactly the same mutation: a deletion of three nucleotides that results in deletion of the amino acid phenylalanine from a region of the CF protein that binds the energy-supplying compound adenosine triphosphate (ATP).

In the case of cystic fibrosis the contributions of molecular biology are twofold. First, one can begin to think about rational design of therapeutic agents or other therapies for those persons already afflicted with CF. Second, with much greater certainty, one can use DNA probes in both genetic counseling and prenatal diagnosis. In counseling, prospective parents can be evaluated as to the likelihood of their producing an offspring with CF. In prenatal diagnosis, the fetus of a couple at risk (both parents are healthy CF carriers, giving the fetus one chance in four of being afflicted) can be tested and, if found to carry the mutant gene on both chromosome 7s, be considered for abortion.

The polymerase chain reaction. Like RFLP revealed by Southern blotting, the polymerase chain reaction (PCR) was revolutionizing studies of human gene organization, diagnosis, evolution, and the environment. The technique is incredibly simple, so much so that it took a while for the molecular biology community to appreciate its power. The PCR makes it possible to amplify (*i.e.*, produce in quantity) selectively any DNA sequence, starting with as little as a single molecule of DNA.

First developed by Kary Mullis at Cetus Corp., Emeryville, Calif., the procedure requires only the prior knowledge of the nucleotide sequence near the region of interest and the ability to synthesize chemically two short DNA molecules (called oligonu-

cleotides) containing specific sequences. The sample containing the target sequence to be amplified is first heated to denature the DNA, separating the complementary strands. The two oligonucleotides are added in excess of the amount of the target molecule and permitted to bind in complementary fashion (anneal) to the target strands. The sequences of the two oligonucleotides, which will serve as primer for the synthesis of new DNA strands by the enzyme DNA polymerase, are chosen so that they anneal to opposing DNA strands and are oriented toward each other. When DNA polymerase and the four deoxynucleoside triphosphates (dATP, dGTP, dCTP, and dTTP) are added, each of the oligonucleotides are extended to yield two new double-stranded DNA molecules where previously there was only one. If these new DNA molecules are then denatured, the same oligonucleotide primers annealed in place, and the polymerase reaction run again, there will be four DNA molecules. Eventually, if the procedure is recycled many times, a vast number of new DNA molecules will be synthesized, all having the same nucleotide sequence and, just as important, the same length. The latter feature arises from the fact that eventually the majority of template molecules will be those started from the oligonucleotide primers.

The applications of the PCR are staggering. It is possible, for example, to amplify selected regions of DNA from a single human sperm. By determining the frequency with which two RFLPs are found in the same sperm, it will be possible to build a linkage map for human chromosomes without analyzing offspring. Minute amounts of DNA from mummies and other archaeological specimens can be amplified for studies of human evolution. Samples of phytoplankton can be analyzed for the presence of particular genes in order to study the distribution of classes of organisms in the oceans. Individual fish or marine mammals can be sampled, without slaugh-

In the polymerase chain reaction procedure, DNA containing the target sequence to be amplified is heated to separate its complementary strands. The strands are mixed with synthesized short DNA molecules that bind to the target on each strand and serve as primers for the synthesis of new DNA by the enzyme DNA polymerase. After the primers are extended to yield double the original number of DNA strands, the process is repeated until the desired quantity of the target is made.

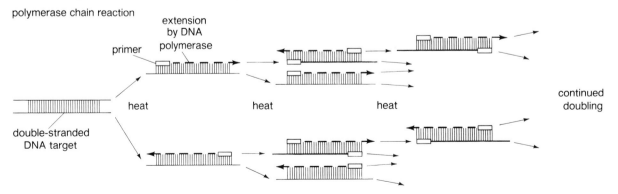

Paleontologist Paul Sereno (left) holds the skull of Herrerasaurus, *the oldest known dinosaur, which was discovered by a joint U.S.-Argentine expedition. The drawing (right) shows the carnivorous reptile as it might have appeared 230 million years ago.*

ter, for their DNA, analysis of which can determine their immediate family. In the case of salmon in the North Atlantic such analysis has revealed where they spawned. The PCR permits exquisitely sensitive monitoring of field tests of genetically engineered plants and microorganisms. Finally, returning to the examples of muscular dystrophy and cystic fibrosis, it permits determination of the presence of disease-linked RFLP in a sample of human placental tissue (which arises from fetal cells) within a day of sampling.

—Robert Haselkorn

Zoology

The environment and the survival of species remained major concerns in 1989. In the face of such environmental calamities and issues as pollution, oil spills, ozone depletion, global warming, tropical deforestation, and endangered organisms, countries were beginning to cooperate in attempts to preserve the water, land, and atmosphere. Other research of special significance in zoology during the past year involved the catastrophic impact theory of extinction, the longest known animal, snake pheromones, fetal tissue research, human speech, and a robot bee.

Paleobiology. Since about 1980 geologists and paleontologists have debated the role of a comet or meteorite impact in the mass extinction of species that occurred 65 million years ago at the boundary separating the Cretaceous and Tertiary geologic periods. Collision of the Earth with a large extraterrestrial body at that time may have disturbed the Earth's surface and climate to the extent that many species of animals and plants could no longer survive. The theory is supported by the abundance of iridium found in the Cretaceous-Tertiary (K-T)

boundary clay of the Earth's crust. Iridium normally is an extremely rare element in the crust but is commonly found in meteorites and comets. Another theory, one that suggests a comparatively abrupt rise in the Earth's volcanic activity, also has been considered as a source of the iridium and an agent of mass extinction at the end of the Cretaceous.

In 1989 the impact theory received support from the detection in K-T clay of two amino acids by Jeffrey L. Bada and Meixun Zhao of the Scripps Institution of Oceanography, La Jolla, Calif. The compounds, racemic isovaline and α-aminoisobutyric acid, are extremely rare in the Earth's crust but are commonly found in certain kinds of meteorites. As part of a five-year study, Bada and Zhao performed detailed analysis using high-performance liquid chromatography and gas chromatography/mass spectrometry of K-T boundary rocks collected in Denmark. Conservatively the scientists stated that although the presence of these compounds supported the idea that an impact did occur at the end of the Cretaceous, the collision was not necessarily the reason for the mass extinction.

Discovery of dinosaur remains always stimulates considerable interest, particularly when the oldest, biggest, or longest is found. Paul Sereno, a University of Chicago paleontologist, reported the discovery of the earliest known dinosaur. In northwestern Argentina two nearly complete skeletons were uncovered in 1988 by a joint U.S.-Argentine expedition led by Alfredo Monetta of the National University of San Juan, Arg., and a report was presented at the 1989 meeting of the Society of Vertebrate Paleontologists in Austin, Texas. The creature was named *Herrerasaurus* after an Argentinian involved in the discovery. Alive, the dinosaur was some 1.8–2.4 m (6–8 ft) long, weighed about 136 kg (300 lb), and was definitely a carnivore although not as fearsome as *Tyrannosaurus rex*. *Herrerasaurus* lived about 230 million years ago, at a time when the Earth's land masses were a single supercontinent, Pangaea.

Tyrannosaurus rex is the epitome of dinosaurs in reigning terror. A full skeleton of the beast, however, had not been discovered until Patrick Leiggi, a paleontologist at the Museum of the Rockies, Bozeman, Mont., uncovered one in the eastern Montana badlands. Leiggi reported that the skeleton is virtually complete from the 1.5-m (5-ft) skull, with teeth the size of bananas, down to the tail.

The longest animal ever described is *Seismosaurus,* a gargantuan dinosaur that was being excavated in 1989 in the desert of central New Mexico. David D. Gillette, Utah's state paleontologist from Salt Lake City, and his team indicated that *Seismosaurus,* or "earth-shaking lizard," may have reached lengths of 37–43 m (120–140 ft). Of particular interest at the excavation site is the unusual method being used to locate bones embedded in the limestone. Alan J. Witten of the Oak Ridge (Tenn.) National Laboratory and his colleagues developed a modified shotgun to penetrate the ground with blasts of vibrations, which are detected on various receivers placed in a borehole. A computer then reconstructs the signals to form a seismic tomographic view somewhat similar to computed tomography (CT) scans used in medical diagnostic procedures. The method was successful in locating *Seismosaurus* vertebrae, which proved to be 10–80% larger than those of the well-known dinosaur *Diplodocus*.

Finding information that allows interpretation of the life-style and activities of the magnificent dinosaurs adds to the spice of discovery. What may be the most extensive group of dinosaur tracks in the eastern North America was discovered in a quarry in Culpeper, Va. "I'm overwhelmed by the magnitude of the information that's available on the floor of this one quarry," stated Robert E. Weems of the U.S. Geological Survey, Reston, Va. "This is the earliest extensive look at dinosaur behavior that we've got." According to Weems and Nicholas Hotton, a vertebrate paleontologist with the Smithsonian Institution, Washington, D.C., the tracks represent the movements of two kinds of bipedal (two-footed) carnivorous dinosaurs and an unidentified quadrupedal (four-footed) reptile that may have resembled a horned crocodile. Most tracks were made by bipedal three-toed carnosaurs (distant relatives of *Tyrannosaurus*) that were about 3.4 m (11 ft) tall. A smaller three-toed coelurosaur (a birdlike biped) about 2.4 m (8 ft) tall made some 10% of the tracks. Scientists were excited about the find because such sets of prints represent movements and activities of the animals while they were living—windows in time that contribute to a knowledge of dinosaur be-

havior. For example, the tracks of the two bipeds in the Culpeper quarry indicate agile animals capable of stopping and starting abruptly.

Discovering and identifying remains of dinosaurs is a time-consuming and important work for paleontologists. The correct mounting of their skeletons, however, is as important. Kenneth Carpenter, a paleontologist at the Denver (Colo.) Museum of Natural History, reported that common mistakes in the preparations of specimens have led to overestimations of weight and underestimations of the agility of the creatures. Preparators often work with a preconceived idea of what a dinosaur looked like. As a result, ribs are often placed in position perpendicular to the vertebral column instead of angling backward, as is seen in living animals. Among other mistakes are spreading the legs too far apart and placing the tail on the ground. According to Carpenter, almost all tracks of dinosaurs indicate that legs were beneath the animal and that tails stuck out behind instead of dragging on the ground.

Endangered species. Significant steps were made in the control of the illicit ivory trade and the protection of the African elephant. Ivory poachers in various countries, including Kenya, Tanzania, and Angola, had developed procedures whereby elephant herds were indiscriminately machine-gunned with AK-47 assault rifles and tusks were collected with axes or chain saws—even the candlestick-sized tusks of juvenile animals. All too often these morbid events appeared to involve the cooperation of people supposedly protecting the elephants. In early June 1989 the U.S. banned all imports of elephant ivory, and by mid-June the European Communities (EC) had banned most imports. The measures, however, were not expected to have much effect on the East Asian countries, for example, Japan, which was consuming 40% of the world ivory supply. *Time* magazine (Oct. 16, 1989) reported that much of the illicit ivory was finding its way into Burundi and eventually to Hong Kong and Japan.

From 1973 to 1989 Kenya's elephant herds had been reduced from 130,000 to 16,000, primarily because of ivory poachers. In April 1989 Richard Leakey, the African-based paleontologist known for his studies of human origins, was appointed director of Kenya's wildlife department. Seven months later, in an address at Buena Vista College, Storm Lake, Iowa, Leakey reported that not a single elephant had been lost inside a national park in nearly half a year. To eliminate the poaching he had worked to enhance park security, bolster personnel morale, and obtain adequate equipment. Another key element was a campaign to persuade Kenyans that wildlife is a national resource and important for the survival not only of elephants but also of many other species. If the elephant became extinct, all species relying

An intact African elephant family (left) has become an increasingly rare sight as poachers slaughter ever younger animals for their ivory. A Kenyan official (right) shows confiscated tusks, part of the stepped-up antipoaching efforts in his country.

on the presence of the elephant would follow suit. For example, adult elephants keep springs open by digging with their tusks, thus providing water to numerous animals that would otherwise perish.

In the past year's most significant step, the delegates to the Convention on International Trade in Endangered Species of Wild Fauna and Flora in Lausanne, Switz., placed the African elephant on the roll of animals perilously close to extinction. This action was supported by 76 nations and resulted in a worldwide ban on the ivory trade. Nations such as Zimbabwe, Botswana, and South Africa that can prove their elephant herds are not in danger may eventually engage in controlled trading. At the end of 1989 the consumer demand for ivory was plummeting, perhaps reducing the danger to the elephant. A future danger, however, may be the lack of cooperation of African farmers who consider the elephant a pest to agricultural crops.

Brazilian forest devastation. Certainly a major concern for the world environment was the accumulation of carbon dioxide and certain other trace gases in the atmosphere and the role of these compounds in raising the mean temperature of the Earth by means of the greenhouse effect. Although the powerful industrial nations of the world had added most to the pollution of the Earth's atmosphere, third world countries were being scrutinized for their contributions. In particular, Brazil received criticism for the ongoing destruction of its rain forest in the Amazon Basin, an area that includes portions of Venezuela, Peru, and Bolivia among other countries and comprises 7 million sq km (2.7 million sq mi)—almost the size of the contiguous U.S. The problems of this

region were bogged down in politics, economics, and social aspects and would require the greatest cooperation of nations for the rain forest to be preserved.

Were the Amazon rain forest to be lost, the effect would be not only a mass accumulation of carbon dioxide in the atmosphere but also a major loss of animals and plants. Of most concern to biologists was that so many species are represented in this region. A 1982 U.S. National Academy of Sciences report estimated that a typical 10.4-sq km (4-sq mi) patch of rain forest may contain 750 species of trees, 125 of mammals, 400 of birds, 100 of reptiles, and 60 of amphibians. A single species of tree may harbor as many as 400 insect species. According to one estimate, if the Amazon forest vanished, more than a million species of plants and animals would disappear. As stated by Thomas Lovejoy of the Smithsonian Institution, "The Amazon is a library for life sciences, the world's greatest pharmaceutical laboratory, and a flywheel of climate."

In a note of encouragement, Brazilian scientists in late 1989 joined forces with those of Italy in a collective assessment of global deforestation. Rain forests in Brazil, Thailand, Nepal, Africa, and other regions were to be observed by the U.S. Landsat remote-sensing satellite system, a yet-to-be-launched Brazilian satellite, the French SPOT satellite, and various ground-based stations. According to Roberto Pereira da Cunha, director of remote sensing at Brazil's space agency, the study would allow researchers to have uniform procedures for examining world deforestation.

Ecology. Increased predation by the crown-of-thorns starfish (*Acanthaster planci*) in the western

Pacific region was believed by many authorities to be a modern phenomenon caused by human interference with the balance of nature through pollution, dredging, and harvesting of the starfish's natural predators. *Acanthaster* preys on coral polyps and during its recent population boom was causing massive damage to coral reefs along the Great Barrier Reef of Australia's northeastern coast.

Studies by Peter D. Walbran and Robert A. Henderson of James Cook University, North Queensland, Australia, A.J. Timothy Jull of the NSF Accelerator Facility for Radioisotope Analysis of the University of Arizona, and M. John Head of Australian National University indicated that the starfish's modern predatory explosion is not necessarily related to human activity and may represent a long history of *Acanthaster* population booms on the Great Barrier Reef. By examining ancient reef sediments and by carbon-14 dating the starfish spines and ossicles found in the sediments, the scientists judged *Acanthaster* to have been present on the reefs for 8,000 years, or from the time the reef began to form. In addition, the varying amounts of the spines and ossicles found at different levels of sediments indicated several fluctuations in population size during this 8,000 years.

Animal behavior. Although sex pheromones, which are secreted chemical substances that elicit sexual responses, are well known in insects, descriptions of similar compounds in vertebrates have been rare. A group of scientists led by Robert T. Mason of the National Heart, Lung, and Blood Institute, Bethesda, Md., and the Institute of Reproductive Biology of the University of Texas isolated, identified, partially synthesized, and field-tested two nonvolatile sex pheromones from the Canadian red-sided garter snake (*Thamnophis sirtalis parietalis*). Although existence of the substances had been suspected, the achievement was the first actual characterization of sex pheromones in reptiles and one of the few in vertebrates.

Male garter snakes of the species aggregate by the thousands in limestone pits in early spring. When a female sporadically appears, 10–100 aggressive males initiate courtship behavior involving rapid tongue flicking and chin rubbing along the female's back. Such behavior eventually leads to the formation of "mating balls" and copulation. After mating, the female immediately leaves the pit. Suspecting that sexual attractive substances may be present in both sexes, Mason and his co-workers collected mature males and females and extracted the lipids (fatty substances) present in the skin. The prepared extracts were placed on paper towels and the responses of sexually active males examined. Only extracts from female skin elicited male courtship behavior. Extracts from male skin did not stimulate such behavior and actually were found to prevent it when added to paper towels containing female skin extracts. The results indicated that the females possess a sex-attractant substance and males a recognition substance that allows them to discriminate other males. In field studies males would sexually investigate snakes of either sex, but male-male courtship would cease, presumably because of the sex-recognition compound in male skin.

Using techniques of analytical chemistry on the extracts, the researchers identified some of the active components. The female sex-attractant pheromone consists of long-chain saturated and monounsaturated methyl ketones. The male sex-recognition pheromone is made up of squalene and other compounds. A sidelight of the study was the discovery that squalene is absent in the skin lipids of "she-males," a small fraction of males in a wild population that are courted by other males. Consequently, she-male skin lipids are more like those of the female than of the male. As suggested by Mason and co-workers, she-males may possess a mating advantage in that they can elicit courtship behavior from other males in the mating balls and thus divert them from true females.

The development of a machine that can faithfully imitate a living organism represents a goal often described in science fiction. Although technology has made great advances, robots that mimic complicated life processes are still fantasy. Nevertheless, the recent development of a robot bee able to communicate with real bees, by bioacoustics researcher Axel Michelsen of the University of Odense, Den., and entomologist Martin Lindauer of the University of Würzburg, West Germany, was expected to make remarkable contributions to the agricultural and behavioral sciences.

German entomologist Karl von Frisch in 1921 described a honeybee dance comprising wing buzzing and abdominal waggling that demonstrated communication between one bee and other members of the hive. Frisch and his students, through diligent and patient experiments, proved that honeybees transmit specific information through the dance. The number of body waggles, the area covered by the dancing activity, the direction of the dance, and the fervor of dancing all convey data concerning the quality of a food source and its distance and direction from the hive. This information first must be encoded by the honeybee dancer and then decoded by her audience. To supplement the message, the dancer periodically regurgitates samples of the food. One characteristic of the dance, the airborne sounds made by wing buzzing, was only recently demonstrated by William F. Towne of Kutztown (Pa.) University and Princeton University and Wolfgang H. Kirchner of the University of Würzburg to be audible to honeybees.

A robot bee would need to demonstrate all of the above qualities in order to convey appropriate information successfully in a dance. The computerized model of Michelsen and Lindauer was a life-sized robot connected to a computer-programmed recorder to control the figure-eight dance pattern, a step motor to allow the body to waggle, a second step motor that pumped scented sugar water from a syringe, and an electromagnetic driver that vibrated the "wing" (a piece of razor blade) at a frequency of 280 hertz (cycles per second). All that remained was to program a dance and observe by video camera and oscilloscope the reactions of the bees. The robot succeeded in imitating a messenger bee well enough to persuade hive mates to fly to specific targets nearly a mile (1.6 km) away.

Future tasks for robot bees may include directing honeybees to agricultural crops for pollination, but the present goal, according to Michelsen, was deciphering the complex bee language. Also, because the robot bee was somewhat clumsy, crashing into unsuspecting bees and regurgitating indiscriminately, polishing its dance steps and the various dance parameters would provide an exciting second project.

Human speech. Controversy is easy to come by when human evolution is being dealt with and even more so when the topic is a complicated human function like the evolutionary development of speech. Anthropologist Baruch Arensburg of Tel Aviv (Israel) University and his colleagues reported finding a small fossil bone called the hyoid from the throat of a Neanderthal skeleton from the Kebara Cave site in northern Israel. The presence of this U-shaped bone, which lies at the base of the tongue, suggested to the anthropologists that Neanderthals could converse as well as modern humans. They based their conclusion on the structure of the Neanderthal hyoid bone and its close similarity to that of modern humans. Because the hyoid bone has attachment sites for muscles of the jaw, larynx, and tongue, the similarity indicated, according to the researchers, that the vocal mechanisms of Neanderthals and modern humans would be practically identical.

Linguist Philip Lieberman of Brown University, Providence, R.I., and anatomist Jeffrey T. Laitman of Mount Sinai School of Medicine, New York City, disagreed with Arensburg's conclusion. They both contended that Neanderthal speech was limited, basing their arguments on the degree of bend in the base (basicranium) of fossil Neanderthal skulls. The position of the vocal tract in humans is dependent on the amount of flexing of the basicranium. A highly flexed basicranium is found in modern humans and is indicative of modern speech. By contrast, that of Neanderthals is straighter and less flexed, thus reducing the capability for producing the wide array of sounds that modern humans can make.

Felled trees stacked for the lumber mill or the charcoal oven represent a small part of the ongoing destruction of the Amazon rain forest, for which Brazil received harsh criticism during the past year.

Neuropsychologist John C. Marshall of Radcliffe Infirmary, Oxford, England, supported Arensburg's conclusion about Neanderthals but pointed out that the reasoning based only on the hyoid bone is "fragile." Marshall observed somewhat cynically that "the argument about their language capacity will undoubtedly run and run until we discover a deep-frozen Neanderthal who is susceptible to resuscitation."

Invertebrate evolution. The phylum Arthropoda has stimulated much interest among invertebrate zoologists concerning the evolutionary relationships of three major living groups—Crustacea (crustaceans), Chelicerata (*e.g.*, scorpions and spiders), and Uniramia (mainly insects)—and a fourth, extinct group, the trilobites. Various investigators have considered these groups either to be separate phyla or to be classes within Arthropoda, thus implying a separate (polyphyletic) or a common (monophyletic) ancestral origin, respectively. Those who favor the polyphyletic view emphasize the obvious differences in functional morphology (form and structure) and embryology among the major groups, while those who support the monophyletic view emphasize the improbability of separate origins for the characteristics that these groups share. Derek E.G. Briggs of the University of Bristol, England, and Richard A. Fortey of the British Museum of Natural History, London, examined the extensive fossil record from the Cambrian geological period (between 570 million and 505 million years ago) and compared it with living representatives. Since the Uniramia are primarily terrestrial and have no Cambrian representative, that group was not considered.

For their comparison Briggs and Fortey selected 23 Cambrian animals and 3 living animals, the latter including the chelicerate *Limulus* (a genus of horseshoe crab) and the crustaceans *Hutchinsoniella* and *Speleonectes*. Also used in their comparison was the well-preserved Ordovician trilobite *Triarthrus* and an extinct eurypterid, *Baltoeurypterus*. From 46 morphological characteristics of these 28 organisms, they developed a cladogram by use of a PAUP (phylogenetic analysis using parsimony) computer program and the morphology of *Marrella*, an accepted primitive Cambrian arthropod, as the primitive base. The cladogram is a flowchart that, in this case, represents the arthropod phylogeny. It arranges selected species on the basis of their chronological divergences from a common ancestral species (*Marrella*).

The approach revealed an adaptive radiation of the many forms of arthropods beginning in the Precambrian period and continuing in the Cambrian. The fossils supported the monophyletic view by showing many intermediate steps, most of which became extinct, thereby leaving the living representatives (*i.e.*, crustaceans and chelicerates) well separated. The study illustrated the way in which evidence from well-preserved fossils can be used to aid understanding of the affinities of living groups.

Physiology. Cold-blooded vertebrates are known to survive at body temperatures below the freezing point of water. No mammal, however, had been observed to maintain such body temperature and survive until Brian M. Barnes and Alison D. York of the University of Alaska at Fairbanks demonstrated the phenomenon in the hibernating Arctic ground squirrel (*Spermophilus parryii*). The squirrels were trapped in their native habitat on the North Slope of Alaska and taken to the Fairbanks laboratory, where miniature temperature-sensitive radio transmitters were implanted in their abdominal cavities. These squirrels were then placed in partially buried outdoor cages, where they hibernated for eight months starting in September. The entire hibernation period comprised stretches of about three weeks of deep sleep alternating with brief arousals. Body temperature dropped below freezing (0° C, or 32° F) during the three-week periods, averaging −1.9° C (28.6° F), and then rose to 0.5° C (32.9° F) before rapidly climbing to normal body levels.

Another group of squirrels, maintained in laboratory chambers at −4.3° C (24.3° F), underwent similar hibernation periods. Temperatures were measured in these animals at several places in the body. Additionally, blood samples were examined for the presence of antifreeze molecules and for blood plasma concentrations. Barnes's team found no special compounds present and no specific changes in blood concentrations. They did find, however, that the temperatures in the brain and heart did not drop to the subzero levels that were measured elsewhere in the body.

Barnes suggested that the animal somehow is able to maintain prolonged supercooling, a below-freezing condition in which body fluids remain free of ice crystals, and that the phenomenon might be common to other Arctic mammals. Survival at such body temperatures could be highly advantageous since energy requirements at subzero temperatures may be as little as a tenth that at above-zero temperatures.

Embryo and fetal research. The ban in the U.S. on federal funding for research involving transplantation of human fetal tissue from induced abortions, in effect since March 1988, was extended by the Department of Health and Human Services (HHS). The reason presented by HHS Secretary Louis W. Sullivan was the likelihood that acceptance of funding of such research by the National Institutes of Health (NIH) would increase the incidence of abortion in the U.S. Other countries (including Mexico and Sweden) allowed such research, and an NIH advisory panel supported it in the belief that it was morally acceptable. According to some observers, the decision reflected the Bush administration's opposition to abortion.

Studies on human embryos (fertilized eggs, blastula stage, and bilaminar embryo stage) also created concerns. European countries, although not without some trepidation, appeared on the way to approving research studies on embryos as old as 14 days. There was broad agreement, however, that a number of areas of research should not be allowed, including human cloning, formation of chimeras between human and animal embryos, genetic engineering of human gametes, and commercial trading of embryos or embryonic materials. A desire for acceptable standards was widespread. As had been stated so well in late 1988 by Karl-Heinz Narjes, then the EC commissioner responsible for industry and scientific research, "We cannot have a situation in which the same research might lead to a Nobel Prize in some member states of the EEC and to prison in others."

—George G. Brown

See also Feature Articles: DOLPHINS OF SHARK BAY; THE HELPFUL SPIDER; LIFE WITHOUT WATER; THE NATIONAL AQUARIUM IN BALTIMORE; THE YELLOWSTONE FIRES.

Materials sciences

Ceramics

Technological advances were made in several major areas of ceramics during the past year. They included structural ceramics, high-temperature superconductors, and diamond-like coatings.

Structural ceramics. Considerable activity continued to be directed toward ceramic materials that can be used reliably for structural applications. Emphasis was placed on the development of composite materials that incorporate "second-phase" constituents (particulates, whiskers—microscopic rods—and chopped or continuous fibers) and also on monolithic materials that have composite-like microstructures created during processing. The appeal of these toughened materials stemmed from their ability to combine the attributes of traditional ceramics, such as strength at high temperatures, oxidation resistance, and low density, with the potential to overcome the Achilles heel of monolithic ceramics—their inherent flaw sensitivity and resultant tendency toward catastrophic structural failure. The forgiving nature of the toughened ceramics made them legitimate candidates for such demanding uses as gas turbine engine components, space vehicle structures, and automotive parts.

An attractive feature of ceramic composites reinforced by continuous fibers (long strands of manufactured fiber) is that the characteristics of the composites can be tailored by choosing the appropriate reinforcing fiber and fiber architecture. This highly desirable attribute assumes, however, that fibers with suitable properties are available for use with any given composite. Unfortunately, this is all too often not the case, especially in applications requiring stable fiber/composite performance to temperatures of 1,100° C (2,012° F) and above. During the past year, however, three new fibers with the potential to meet these qualifications were developed to preproduction status. Each fiber was derived from an organosilicon precursor polymer. The polymer was spun into fiber by extrusion and drawing through a multihole spinneret, a small metal plate, thimble, or cap with fine holes in it. The fibers were cured by polymer crosslinking (connecting parallel chains) to maintain shape and then subjected to a treatment at a high temperature to drive off volatile constituents and convert them to a ceramic. The resulting fiber microstructure is often a mixture of amorphous and microcrystalline material.

The three emerging fibers are: (1) a silicon carbonitride fiber (that is, by weight, 59% silicon, 10% carbon, 28% nitrogen, and 3% oxygen) from Dow Corning in the U.S.; (2) a silicon carbonitride fiber (55% Si, 15% C, 22% N, 8% O by weight) from

Rhône Poulenc in France; and (3) a silicon nitride fiber (59.5% Si, 0.5% C, 39% N, 1% O by weight) from Toa Nenryo Kogyo (Tonen) in Japan. All three fibers have a density in the range of 2.3–2.5 g per cc, exhibit good tensile properties, and are expected to be serious candidates for reinforcement of advanced structural ceramic composites.

Processing of composite articles remained a critical issue. A key concern was uniform distribution and encapsulation of the fibers within the matrix (the material within which the fibers are enclosed) and control of the resulting fiber/matrix interface. Ube Industries of Japan reported a novel approach to tackling this problem. Their method involved complete elimination of the matrix. The starting constituent was Ube's commercially produced Tyranno fiber (51% Si, 30% C, 17% O, 2% titanium by weight; amorphous microstructure). Woven cloth layers of the fiber were consolidated in a hot press. Processing at 1,950° C (3,542° F) for one hour under a pressure of 700 atm yielded a fully dense array of hexagonal columns in place of the original cylindrical fibers. After consolidation the oxygen content of this array dropped from 17 to 0.5%, and the atomic ratio of carbon to silicon-plus-titanium fell from 1.5 to 1.0. A spectroscopic analysis indicated some migration of titanium and, to a lesser extent, oxygen to the boundaries between the hexagonal cells. Most of the array was said to have been converted to SiC and TiC. This "composite," named Tyrannohex by Ube, exhibited excellent mechanical behavior over a wide range of temperatures. Flexural strength (resistance to fracture under bending load) as high as 240 MPa at room temperature was observed with complete retention of this strength after exposure at 1,600° C (2,912° F) in air for one hour. Processing variations, including the use of powder of Tyranno composition

U.S.-made silicon carbonitride fiber tow and woven cloth by weight consist of 59% silicon, 28% nitrogen, 10% carbon, and 3% oxygen. The fibers are expected to be used to reinforce structural ceramic composites.

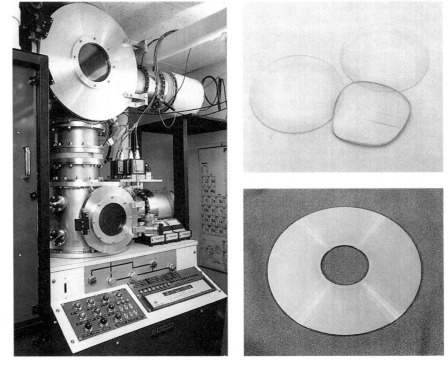

Dual ion beam deposition system (right) sputters beams of carbon ions onto a surface at the same time that the surface is being impinged by a beam of high-energy argon ions. This produces diamond film coatings that can be applied to such consumer items as glass and plastic optical lenses (far right, top) and a rigid magnetic storage disc (far right, bottom).

as a filler between the cloth layers, recently produced composites with 400 MPa flexural strength in air at a temperature as high as 1,500° C (2,732° F). The specimens failed in a tough, noncatastrophic manner. This unique processing approach and resulting composite mechanical behavior bode well for ultimate high-temperature applications.

Although continuous-fiber reinforcement affords the greatest degree of toughening, composites reinforced by whiskers are attractive because they can be processed into complex shapes by such traditional methodologies as injection molding (injecting particulates, whiskers, and molten polymer mixtures into dies) and slip casting (the pouring into porous plaster molds of a liquid suspension of particulates and whiskers). However, whisker agglomeration is a serious problem that can cause significant strength reduction. In addition, concerns have been raised about the possible ill effects of inhaling whiskers. During the past year Allied-Signal Inc. and the Dow Chemical Co. reported the development of toughened silicon nitride through the formation of whisker-like silicon nitride grains during processing. The Dow Chemical material is fabricated by hot pressing and utilizes a glass phase (yttria, magnesia, and calcia additions) to promote formation of needlelike silicon nitride grains. Room-temperature flexural strength as high as 1,300 MPa and fracture toughness of 12 MPa m$^{1/2}$ were achieved, although not in the same specimen. (Fracture toughness is a measure of the size of a flaw a material can tolerate before failing catastrophically under load. Ceramics typically have fracture toughness values of 1–6 MPa m$^{1/2}$, whereas metals exhibit values of 25 or higher.) Toughening was believed to be caused by crack deflection around elongated grains. (This requires more energy than crack propagation through the grains and leads to toughening.) Combinations of strength and toughness can be tailored to given applications by appropriate combinations of chemistry and processing conditions. One composition was evaluated favorably as a cutting tool for cast iron.

The Allied-Signal material is made not by hot pressing but rather by gas pressure sintering (forming a coherent bonded mass by heating under gas pressure without complete melting) of powder compacts formed by cold isostatic pressing. Flexural strength of 550 MPa with fracture toughness of 11 MPa m$^{1/2}$ was achieved. These toughened silicon nitride materials are attractive candidates for a variety of applications, such as automotive turbocharger rotors. Additional companies pursuing this technology included GTE Laboratories in the U.S.

In an exciting development, the first flight demonstration of a ceramic composite gas turbine engine component took place during the past year. Exhaust nozzle flaps made by the Société Européenne de Propulsion (SEP) of France were flown at the Paris Air Show on a Mirage 2000 jet fighter. The flaps were incorporated in a Snecma M-53 engine. The inner flaps were Nicalon (a SiC-type fiber)-reinforced silicon carbide and operated at 845° C

(1,553° F) during cruise and at higher temperatures during afterburner operation. The outer flaps were carbon fiber-reinforced silicon carbide that operated at 510° C (950° F) during cruise and higher during afterburner cycles. The flaps were mounted to the engine using advanced metal/ceramic fittings.

These composites were fabricated by chemical vapor infiltration of fiber preforms (cloth layers fixtured to the desired shape). In this process vapor-phase organometallic species are deposited on a heated preform in a reaction vessel. The chemistry of the deposit is controlled by the species that were chosen, and the matrix is built up around the fibers as the reaction proceeds. This technique is particularly well suited to the fabrication of articles with complex shapes.

High-temperature ceramic superconductors. Research on high-temperature ceramic superconductors focused on three principal chemistries: (1) yttrium-barium-copper oxide, $YBa_2Cu_3O_7$, with a transition temperature (T_c)—the temperature at which it becomes a superconductor—of 93 K (0 K = −273.16° C [−459.68° F]); (2) thallium-barium-calcium-copper oxide, $Tl_2Ba_2Ca_2Cu_3O_{10}$, with T_c of 125 K; and (3) bismuth-based copper oxides with T_c up to 110 K. Besides processing, the most important issue remained improvement of critical current (J_c) capability, especially for bulk materials. (Critical current is the current in a superconducting material above which the material is normal and below which it is superconducting, at a specified temperature and in the absence of external magnetic fields.) Significant understanding of this subject was gained during the past year, particularly as it relates to the role of magnetic flux lattice pinning. This array of magnetic field lines within the superconducting material is formed in the presence of magnetic fields. Movement of the lattice by a sufficiently large current causes resistance to the current flow and destroys the superconductivity. If, however, the field lines can be pinned (stopped or hindered from moving), current capacity will increase.

Thin films have typically exhibited significantly higher J_c than bulk materials. This may relate to the number of defects inherent to thin films that can serve as pinning sites that prevent flux lattice movement. Corroborating evidence was produced recently in bulk materials treated to incorporate defects that could serve as pinning sites. The first such work, at AT&T, involved neutron irradiation. Later experiments at AT&T, the University of Houston, and in Japan used processing techniques to create the defect structure needed for pinning. Critical currents increased two orders of magnitude in the best cases. These results stirred a new degree of optimism for the eventual application of these superconductors in bulk form.

Diamond coatings. Considerable activity continued toward the goal of depositing high-quality diamond films by both chemical vapor deposition and ion-beam-based techniques. Significant progress was reported by Beam Alloy Corp. in the U.S. through use of a dual ion beam method. In this case pure carbon is continuously sputtered by an ion beam from a graphite target onto the sample surface, while the surface is simultaneously impinged by a beam of high-energy argon ions. The end result is a diamond film that is first mechanically mixed into the substrate surface and is subsequently grown out from the surface with a high degree of tetragonal diamond bonding. Since the deposition temperature does not exceed 65° C (149° F), it is possible to diamond face precision tools and engineered components made from ferrous and nonferrous alloys as well as from glasses and crystalline ceramics and from plastics.

—Allan P. Katz

Metallurgy

The search for high-temperature intermetallic alloys continued to be a major focus of efforts in metallurgy. At the recent fall meeting of the Minerals, Metals, and Materials Society in Indianapolis, Ind., more papers were presented on intermetallic alloys than on any other topic. Nearly all of the intermetallic alloys under investigation consisted of aluminum with either iron, niobium, nickel, or titanium. The research effort included measurements of high-temperature deformation, fatigue, thermal stability, oxidation resistance, and processing. Even with those efforts, much of the knowledge of intermetallic systems remained limited. Investigations of intermetallic matrix composites reinforced with stiff metals or ceramics were also under way, as discussed below.

Metal matrix composites. Developments in metal matrix composites (MMCs) spanned a wide range of techniques for the production of metal alloys that are reinforced by the presence of ceramic particulates or fibers. Investigations of aluminum alloys containing silicon carbide particulates were prominent during the past year. Particulates are typically microscopic plates or rods (called whiskers) of silicon carbide single crystals that can be added to the aluminum alloy to enhance its stiffness and strength. Silicon carbide is a very hard ceramic that is often used in place of diamond as a material for cutting and grinding tools. The typical size of particulate additions ranges from 0.5 to 10 micrometers (millionths of a meter). Though these additions are very fine in scale, they are distributed throughout a material to provide properties that are isotropic (the same in all directions), or nearly so. On the other hand, there have been some difficulties of processing these materials, such as attaining a homogeneous dispersion of the particles and maintaining long-term stability.

One potential process for acquiring more uniform and homogeneous properties in MMCs is squeeze casting. This is a relatively new technique wherein pressure is applied to prevent shrinkage porosity during the solidification of castings. Shrinkage porosity consists of small holes that form because the density of the solid metal is usually greater than that of the liquid metal. For its application in MMCs the pressure applied during squeeze casting serves to enhance the infiltration of the molten metal into the reinforcement material prior to solidification. In squeeze casting the metal is poured into a mold made from a material with a higher melting point. Almost immediately the mold is closed, and pressure is applied to the solidifying metal by the mechanical action of the mold. The process can be fine-tuned through variation of the mold temperature, the molten metal temperature, cooling rates, and the squeeze pressure.

As of 1990 squeeze casting had been employed mostly with aluminum or aluminum-based alloys in the production of pistons and other moving parts for the automobile industry. Recent work using Nicalon and Tyranno silicon carbide fibers demonstrated the potential for systems employing a combination of fiber and particulate reinforcement when squeeze casting was employed. These systems produced encouraging mechanical properties at temperatures as high as 350°–400° C (660°–750° F) One drawback of systems using long strands of manufactured fibers was the development of anisotropic properties.

Major hurdles needed to be overcome to prevent damage to fibers during their preparation for squeeze casting. Other issues included ascertaining the stability and retained strength of such reinforcements in other alloy systems. When the molten metal contacts the reinforcement materials, a chemical reaction produces either another phase or the dissolution of the reinforcement material. Small changes in the chemistry of the metal alloy or the process variables (pressure, temperature, etc.) can result in major changes in the interface reaction between the reinforcement and matrix phases. Any phase produced from such a reaction or from dissolution of the reinforcement material can dramatically alter the reliability and performance of the final part.

Efforts to manufacture intermetallic matrix composites reinforced with ceramic materials were quite extensive during the past year. Compared with producing aluminum alloy MMCs, many of the processing and performance problems were greatly magnified by the much higher temperatures required when dealing with ceramics. Processing temperatures were often greater than 2,000° C, and application temperatures higher than 1,000° C. Consequently, much

attention was paid to differences in the thermal and mechanical properties of the materials.

An example of the problems is that of thermal expansion. Not only does the thermal expansion of most materials change with temperature but the thermal expansion coefficients of some matrix and reinforcement materials also can differ by a factor of two or three. (Thermal expansion coefficients are the fractional changes in length or volume of a material for unit changes in temperature.) When this characteristic is displayed during cooling, the ceramic reinforcement material shrinks more slowly than the matrix material surrounding it. Large stresses can develop at the interface between the reinforcement material and the matrix. Considering that the applications for many of these high-temperature materials require constant cycling between low and high temperatures, such repeated cycling can eventually lead to a debonding of the reinforcement material from the matrix; this will cause catastrophic failure. Also, the repeated moves to high temperature will be accompanied by chemical changes that may also weaken the interface between the reinforcement and matrix materials.

Extraction of indium, gallium, and germanium. Interest in electronic applications for semiconductors based on gallium arsenide, indium phosphide, and germanium stimulated research into the extraction and purification of the metals gallium, indium, and germanium. New techniques included the use of organic solutions to recover selectively the desired metals from the residue left from the hydrometallurgical processing of zinc. Researchers designed and synthesized special organic molecules that enable separation of the metal from its ore. Investigators reported a better than 90% recovery of gallium, indium, and germanium when using such a process.

Another technique that showed great promise was the use of microorganisms to accelerate or actually facilitate the separation of gallium and germanium from their ores. One of two processes typically takes place during such biologically assisted extraction of a metal from its ore. The first involves the synthesis by the microorganism of chemicals that assist in leaching out the metal. In the second the microorganism actually ingests or absorbs the metal. The "inoculation" of the ores with thiobacillus ferrooxidans as the added microorganism was found to enhance the amount of germanium extracted in a given time period by a factor greater than five. Another microorganism, the fungus aspergillus niger, was shown to be effective in leaching gallium from the by-products of aluminum processing plants.

Another technique for enhancing the extraction of gallium from aluminum processing by-products was the use of ultrasound along with organic solutions. Many of these solutions are quite effective in recovering gallium, but the rate of recovery is typically quite slow. The application of ultrasound to such a process enhances the recovery rates by more than two to three times. Although the addition of ultrasound thereby substantially increases the rate of gallium production, the expense of applying it could increase the cost of processing gallium. Further investigation revealed that intermittent applications of high-intensity ultrasound to the extraction process are sufficient to increase dramatically the extraction rates without increasing the cost.

American Iron and Steel Institute initiative. A report on a cooperative university and steel industry initiative to investigate novel iron and steel processing was published in the journal *Steel Research* in early 1989. This initiative included visits to steelmaking facilities in Europe and Japan, with an emphasis on ascertaining which emerging steelmaking technologies were most promising.

The consensus of task force members from the U.S. steel industry was that cooperative research and development with particular attention to the "in-bath smelting process" should be pursued. This process involves the simultaneous injection of coal and oxygen during the smelting of iron ore to liquid metal. The report focused on exploiting this new technology by developing a converter-based process for in-bath smelting that would provide a high production rate, reduced coal consumption, direct conversion of iron to steel, and use of a variable quantity of melt scrap. In the report a pilot plant program, a laboratory research program, and a large-scale plant test were proposed.

—Keith J. Bowman

See also Feature Article: "SMART" MATERIALS: A REVOLUTION IN TECHNOLOGY.

Mathematics

In 1989 mathematicians produced a variety of new results. They included a record-large prime number, a record billion digits of pi, a solution to a modern version of the problem of squaring the circle, a striking new approach to "simplify . . ." problems in algebra, and a practical guide for card players on how much shuffling is enough.

New largest prime. A team of mathematicians and computer scientists at Amdahl Corp., which manufactures computers, discovered a new largest number known to be prime; that is, exactly divisible by no positive integers except itself and 1. The number, $391,581 \times 2^{216193} - 1$, has 65,087 decimal digits. The discovery was facilitated by the team's invention of a new algorithm for high-speed convolution (a key ingredient in multidigit multiplication), which itself may have applications in other realms of science.

Digits of pi. Gregory and David Chudnovsky, Soviet immigrants to the U.S., calculated pi to 1,011,-196,691 digits, surpassing the previous records of 134 million (1987) and 201 million digits (1988) by Yasumasa Kanada and the Chudnovsky brothers' own 480 million digits (earlier in 1989).

The Chudnovskys' achievement was based on a faster-converging and more ingenious infinite series than their predecessors had used. Each pass through the Chudnovskys' procedure calculated 14 more correct digits. The greater ingenuity is that the calculation involves arithmetic with integers only and, therefore, eliminates error introduced by rounding off fractions. Previous computations of pi, which involved trying to control error from such rounding, each had to start by regenerating all digits from the first. With the new method the number of digits can be extended by starting from exactly where the Chudnovskys left off.

The Chudnovskys were not motivated by a desire to set a new record. They wanted the billion digits for their research into how closely the digits of pi resemble what is known as a "normal" sequence. In a normal sequence any string of a fixed number of digits has the same likelihood of appearing as any other string of the same length; for example, each of the digits 0 to 9 appears 10% of the time, and each of the two-digit sequences 00 through 99 appears 1% of the time. Mathematicians have long suspected that the digits of pi form a normal sequence but are still unable to prove it. Although no amount of computation will add up to a proof, data on the digits of pi can be used to test ideas and gain insight.

The circle squared, at last (after a new fashion). The ancient Greek problem of squaring the circle was to construct, with a straightedge and compass, a square with the same area as a given circle. The Greeks were unable to solve the problem because the task is impossible, as was shown by Ferdinand von Lindemann in 1882.

Lindemann argued as follows: To square a circle of radius 1 (and hence area pi) would be equivalent to constructing a square with sides the length of the square root of pi ($\sqrt{\pi}$). However, all lengths constructible by a straightedge and compass are algebraic; that is, they are numbers that are solutions to polynomial equations with integer coefficients. For example, $\sqrt{2}$ is algebraic, since it is a solution of $1x^2 - 2 = 0$. Although $\sqrt{\pi}$ is a solution of $1x^2 - \pi = 0$, π is not an integer and, although it is not easy to demonstrate (as Lindemann did), there is no other more complicated polynomial equation with integer coefficients that has $\sqrt{\pi}$ as a solution.

In 1925 Alfred Tarski reformulated the problem by abandoning the ancient construction tools of straightedge and compass and asked simply: Is it possible to dissect a circle (including its interior)

377

"Every once in a while I just like to unwind with a little addition and subtraction."

into a finite number of pieces that can be rearranged in some way whatever to form a square; that is, is a circle *piecewise congruent* to a square? The question is like asking if there is a way to cut a circle up into a jigsaw puzzle and then put the pieces together in a different way to form a square.

The previous year Tarski and Stefan Banach had proved the totally counterintuitive result that a three-dimensional geometric ball is piecewise congruent to a cube—not just to a cube of the same volume but to any cube of any volume whatsoever! The construction, known as the Banach-Tarski paradox, uses nonmeasurable sets, the mathematics of which—contrary to expectations of jigsaw-puzzle pieces—allows them to change total volume in the rearranging.

The paradox led Tarski to ask whether the circle can be reassembled into a square if the pieces must remain the same size and shape; the two figures are then said to be equidecomposable. This restriction would force the square to have the same area as the circle and is closer to how real jigsaw puzzle pieces behave, though Tarski's construction would permit turning a piece over. Until the end of 1988, however, it was not known whether the dissection and reassembly could be done.

Miklos Laczkovich of Eotvos Lorand University in Budapest showed in 1989 that it can be done, and without turning over any of the pieces or even rotating them. The bad news for aficionados of jigsaw puzzles is that the construction would involve 10^{50} pieces.

Simplification of radicals. Many of the problems that students in high-school algebra wrestle with involve the simplification of complicated mathematical expressions, including those that involve square roots, cube roots, etc., that are known collectively as radicals. When radicals are nested (contained) one within another, it may not be apparent whether the expression can be simplified further or what approach one should follow in attempting to do so.

Problems of this type have come to the forefront as mathematicians have analyzed how to instruct computer algebra systems to simplify expressions. Susan Landau of Wesleyan University, Middletown, Conn. (now at the University of Massachusetts at Amherst) found a general method for simplifying nested radicals. The procedure she devised relies on concepts that are 150 years old and have been learned by every mathematician in the past 50 years. Her result is a rare example of a mathematical problem being solved not when it could have been but just when it needed to be.

Seven shuffles suffice. Players of bridge and other card games have all wondered how much shuffling is needed to randomize a deck of cards. In perhaps the year's outstanding practical application of mathematics, Persi Diaconis (Harvard University) and David Bayer (Columbia University, New York City) showed that seven shuffles make the deck reasonably random. Random means that every arrangement of the 52 cards is equally likely or, put another way, that each card is as likely as any other to be in a particular position in the deck. Further shuffles do not significantly improve the mixing of the cards, while doing fewer than seven shuffles runs substantial risk of the cards not being mixed from their original places.

This result exposed a major problem in most gam-

378

ing situations: the cards are not shuffled sufficiently thoroughly, thus allowing knowledgeable gamblers to improve their odds of winning.

Milestones. Richard M. Schoen of Stanford University won the prestigious Bocher Memorial Prize, given every five years for a notable memoir in analysis. Mathematicians received 3 of the 19 National Science Medals awarded in 1989, the highest civic honor for a U.S. scientist. The winners were Samuel Karlin (Stanford University), Saunders Mac Lane (University of Chicago), and Donald Spencer (Princeton University). Karlin made important contributions to several areas that use statistical methodology, most recently to interpretation of DNA sequences. Mac Lane, an algebraist, helped create the fields of homological algebra and category theory and provided sustained leadership in mathematics education. Spencer, a topologist, was recognized for his research on differential and analytic manifolds.

A number of mathematicians famous for both their research and their concern for education died during the past year. Marshall H. Stone (1903–89), formerly of Harvard and the University of Chicago, made memorable contributions to the diverse fields of functional analysis, Boolean algebra, and general topology. E.J. McShane (1904–89) of the University of Virginia was noted for his research in the calculus of variations and was influential in the revitalization of undergraduate mathematics. A member of the National Academy of Sciences, he served as president of both the Mathematical Association of America and the American Mathematical Society. McShane opposed the anti-Communist hysteria of the 1950s and made a memorable reply when asked whether he had ever been involved with organizations that at any time had advocated the overthrow of the U.S. government by force or violence: Yes, he replied, he was an employee of the state of Virginia (which had seceded from the U.S. in the Civil War).

Hassler Whitney (1907–89) of the Institute for Advanced Study in Princeton, N.J., was a pioneer in topology, making major contributions to graph theory, differential topology and surfaces, and cohomology theory (which uses algebraic groups to study the geometric properties of topological spaces); in 1976 he was awarded the National Medal of Science. In retirement he took a keen interest in mathematics education, listening carefully to how children think about problems based on their experiences. From 1979 to 1982 he served as president of the International Commission on Mathematics Education.

Among other notable deaths were those of S.L. Sobolev (1908–89), an eminent Soviet mathematician who made fundamental contributions to solving the wave equation, invented a whole area of functional analysis (Sobolev spaces), and devised the notion of generalized function; J. Barkley Rosser (1907–

89) of the University of Wisconsin, who strengthened Kurt Gödel's incompleteness result and helped establish the theoretical basis in mathematical logic that was later important for the computer language Lisp; and Louise Hay (1935–89), who for nine years had been head of the department of mathematics, statistics, and computer science at the University of Illinois at Chicago. Hay, like Rosser a mathematical logician, was the only female head of a mathematics department at a major research university in the U.S. She was also a founder of the Association for Women in Mathematics and strongly advocated an increased role for women in mathematics.

—Paul J. Campbell

Medical sciences

A new drug showed promise as a treatment for AIDS (acquired immune deficiency syndrome), and researchers continued their efforts to develop a vaccine for the deadly disease. The gene that causes cystic fibrosis was identified. Surgeons developed a method for removing gallstones by inserting a hollow tube through a small incision, and several types of organ transplants were performed for the first time. Dental researchers discovered a drug that is safe and effective for those suffering from dry mouth, and veterinary scientists isolated what appeared to be the smallest known pathogenic animal virus.

General medicine

A protein that was found in the skin of people with Alzheimer's disease could lead to better diagnosis of the degenerative condition. Researchers identified the gene that causes cystic fibrosis, raising the possibility that a cure might be only years away. Several live-donor liver transplants were performed. And U.S. scientists performed the first government-sanctioned transfer of a nonhuman gene into a human being.

AIDS. Scientists inched slowly toward a greater understanding of the AIDS virus and tested possible treatments. Zidovudine (formerly known as azidothymidine, or AZT) continued to demonstrate its ability to stave off death, and researchers searched for similar drugs that, like zidovudine, could slow the action of the AIDS virus but would not have zidovudine's harmful effects on bone marrow. One such drug, dideoxyinosine (DDI) showed promise in experimental trials on people, and its manufacturer received permission from the U.S. government to distribute it pending official approval to market it. Other studies indicated that the dosage of zidovudine could be halved without loss of the drug's benefits. Dextran sulfate, which had shown promise in test-

Antonia Novello (left) is sworn in as surgeon general of the United States by Supreme Court Associate Justice Sandra Day O'Connor, as Pres. George Bush and Novello's husband, Joseph, look on.

tube studies, did not do as well in tests on people and was abandoned as a treatment. Researchers from Genentech, Inc., of South San Francisco, Calif., and from the U.S. National Institutes of Health (NIH) began testing a novel antibody on people with AIDS. It consists of a nonspecific antibody attached to a protein normally found on white blood cells. An AIDS virus hooks onto this protein when the virus enters a cell. In addition, researchers from the Massachusetts Institute of Technology (MIT) discovered a mutant form of HIV (human immunodeficiency virus) that produces an aberrant form of one of the proteins needed by the virus to survive. When they infected cells in culture with the lethal form of the virus and the mutant strain, the mutant strain effectively squelched the lethal virus by tying up the virus-making machinery of infected cells.

On the vaccine front, a project headed by researchers at Tulane University's Delta Regional Primate Research Center in Covington, La., were able to protect monkeys from the simian form of AIDS, caused by the simian immunodeficiency virus (SIV). They chemically inactivated the virus with formalin, injected it repeatedly into monkeys, and then gave the monkeys live SIV. Eight of nine vaccinated monkeys withstood infection, while the virus established itself in all four unvaccinated monkeys. The findings supported previous work that used the same approach at the New England Regional Primate Research Center, Southborough, Mass. While the monkey vaccine will not directly protect against human AIDS, the test provides a model for the treatment of HIV infection. Meanwhile, four patients in the U.K. were given mouse-produced antibodies that

block the virus's entry into cells and spark the production of a second set of antibodies, actually antiantibodies, that bind to the virus itself. The initial results appeared promising. Also, large safety trials in uninfected people of several vaccines consisting of individual AIDS proteins continued at several U.S. institutions. While no one knew whether the vaccines would protect against AIDS, as of early 1990 none of the vaccines under development appeared to have harmed the recipients.

Alzheimer's disease. Determining who has Alzheimer's disease, the rapidly progressing forgetfulness that afflicts some older people, is a matter of guided guesswork. Physicians first rule out nutritional deficits, strokes, and other memory-sapping conditions, and when they can find no other apparent reason for memory loss, they conclude that it must be Alzheimer's disease. Only after a person dies and pathologists can look at brain samples can Alzheimer's disease be diagnosed for certain. During the past year, however, researchers at Boston's Brigham and Women's Hospital may have devised a better method. They found the same protein that clogs the brains of people with Alzheimer's disease in samples of their skin. Further work could result in a simple skin test for Alzheimer's.

Determining how many people have Alzheimer's disease is also problematic. Harvard University researchers canvassed older people in a Boston neighborhood. On the basis of the subjects' performances on psychological and physical testing and the results of blood screening, the researchers concluded that 10% of people over 65 probably have Alzheimer's disease, including nearly 50% of people over 85. Extrapolating from these numbers, the U.S. National Institute on Aging estimated that four million Americans have Alzheimer's disease, a large jump from previous estimates of 2.5 million. Some experts criticized the conclusion, however, because the testing may not have been sufficient to diagnose the disease accurately.

Cancer. Evidence continued to mount that some genes protect against cancer by squelching the activity of cancer-causing genes and that when these protective genes are missing or defective, cancer occurs. Scientists from the Salk Institute for Biological Studies in La Jolla, Calif., announced that, at least in the test tube, an abnormal version of a gene that makes a protein involved in thyroid metabolism manufactures a protein that binds with thyroid hormone. The resulting agglomeration blocks the activity of other genetic material, leading to abnormal growth. Researchers at Princeton University and at Johns Hopkins University, Baltimore, Md., made similar findings with other genes. If this work is validated, it suggests a third way that genes can cause cancer. The other two are by producing proteins that directly spark cell growth and by failing to produce proteins that control cell growth.

Researchers at the University of California at Berkeley linked cancer to a chemical that already had a bad reputation—cholesterol. In laboratory experiments they found that cutting the cholesterol available to a cell that was destined to become cancerous stopped the process. Normally, when a mutant form of the *ras* protein is injected into frog eggs, it spurs the egg cells to divide. When the researchers injected both the mutant *ras* and a cholesterol-blocking drug, however, the process did not occur. If the process is to prove beneficial to people, the researchers must find a way to allow cells to have the cholesterol they need for their cell membranes but keep the levels low enough so that the cells do not begin to divide uncontrollably.

Gallbladders. Surgeons at several U.S. institutions are devising ways to remove gallstones without performing surgery. Instead, they insert a hollow tube through a small incision in a patient's abdomen and then visually guide a device that can pick up small stones. While medication can dissolve some stones, half of those people receiving such treatment develop new stones. Gallbladder removal takes care of the problem, but it is major surgery and requires a large incision. Patients may need five days of hospitalization and weeks of recovery.

Removing the stones through a tube can be done by means of a 1.24-cm (0.5-in) incision on an outpatient basis or with only one day of hospitalization, and patients may be back to work in two or three days. The new procedure joins several others under investigation—laser surgery, dissolving the stones

with a solvent pumped into the gallbladder, and breaking stones up with ultrasound.

Genetics. Studies were beginning to show that all genes are not created equal and that whether they come from one's mother or from one's father makes a difference in how they function. Genes come in pairs, one each from the mother and father. Geneticists during the past year were beginning to identify diseases that result from receiving both genes from the mother or from the father. Judith Hall of the University of British Columbia identified a growth-retardation syndrome that results from inheriting both sets of chromosome 7 from the mother. Some forms of cancer have been linked to defective genes that invariably come from the mother rather than the father. Dutch researchers, however, traced a head-and-neck tumor to the father's genes. Animal studies revealed similar syndromes. What remained to be determined was how a child's cells know the difference between the gene from the mother and its match from the father, and how the difference can affect the cell's function and, ultimately, the child's health.

A U.S.-Canadian collaboration led to a major advance in genetic diagnosis. The team identified the gene that causes cystic fibrosis, the most common birth defect in Caucasians. Roughly one in 20 people in the U.S. is a carrier, and one of every 2,000 white babies in the U.S. is affected with the disease, in which thick mucus lines the lungs and digestive system. It leads to frequent infections and premature death. Researchers from Toronto's Hospital for Sick Children and the University of Michigan announced in September that they had pinpointed the defect to chromosome 7. Defects in both gene pairs account for about 70% of cystic fibrosis cases. By November a Massachusetts company had begun marketing a test to detect fetuses that carry the gene and parents who could pass it on. The previous test for parent carriers required a living relative with cystic fibrosis. The new test, marketed by Integrated Genetics, did not require an affected relative, but because of the difficulty and expense of the test, it was not recommended for routine screening. In the future scientists hope to discover the protein that the gene produces and learn how to cure people with cystic fibrosis by placing a normal version of that protein into their cells.

The news regarding a gene for manic depression was not as good. In 1987 University of Miami, MIT, and Yale University researchers who studied manic depression among an Amish sect announced that they had pinpointed a gene for manic depression to chromosome 11. However, further study by those scientists as well as by researchers from the National Institute of Mental Health, Bethesda, Md., revealed people who had the marker but did not have manic depression and others who did not have the marker yet demonstrated the dramatic mood swings that define the disease. In 1989 the researchers retracted their initial finding, saying that it might have been just a matter of chance.

University of Rome biologists announced in June that they had devised a simple way to put foreign genes into laboratory animals. Currently, scientists insert foreign genes into laboratory animals by carefully injecting the genes into the nuclei of fertilized eggs, a difficult procedure that requires patience and expensive equipment. The Rome researchers said that they had put genes into mice by merely soaking mouse sperm in foreign DNA (deoxyribonucleic acid) and then using the sperm to fertilize female mice. Other scientists were unable to confirm the results, however.

British researchers at the National Institute for Medical Research might have put to rest another genetic discovery first announced in 1987, that of a gene on the Y chromosome that specifically determines maleness by coding for the development of testes. The new work indicated that while the gene is necessary for the development of sperm, it is not required for testes themselves.

After leaping numerous regulatory hurdles, U.S. scientists performed the first government-authorized gene transfer. NIH researchers inserted a marker gene from a bacterium into white blood cells that had been treated with the growth factor interleukin-2. These cells were part of a new form of cancer therapy. The scientists were trying to learn what happens to them after they are injected into a patient's body.

Other gene-manipulating scientists also faced hurdles. The U.K. made it a criminal offense to release a genetically engineered organism without first obtaining government permission to do so. Despite having received government permission, West German scientists bowed to public pressure and postponed their plans to grow genetically engineered petunias. The European Commission decreed a moratorium on the use of bovine growth hormone, a product produced by genetic engineering that stimulates cows to give more milk.

Immunology. Japanese and U.S. immunologists took two key steps toward figuring out how immune cells can custom design an almost infinite number of antibodies with only a finite number of genes. The U.S. researchers, from the Whitehead Institute in Cambridge, Mass., cloned a gene that makes an enzyme that apparently can rearrange antibody-making genes. The Japanese group isolated a protein involved in recombination, as well as the gene that makes it. The Japanese protein binds to genes, flagging the spot where recombination should occur. As of early 1990 the relationship between the Japanese and American genes had yet to be determined.

California researchers, meanwhile, announced a new method of producing monoclonal antibodies, molecules that attack precise targets. Instead of fusing antibody-producing mouse cells with a human tumor line and then screening all the cells for the ones that produce the desired antibodies, Scripps Clinic researchers inserted into bacteria genes that manufacture the basic subunits of antibodies. The bacteria put the subunits together in different ways, producing different and specific antibodies. The researchers then screened clones of millions of those bacteria for the ones making the antibody they wanted. A second advantage of this technique, which was also being worked on by scientists at the United Kingdom's Medical Research Council, was that it might make antibodies that could be used in humans for therapy. As of early 1990 monoclonal antibodies were being used in diagnosis only, because when mouse antibodies are repeatedly injected, humans make antibodies against the antibodies.

Heart disease. A book published in the U.S. contended that dietary cholesterol makes little if any difference to a person's risk of dying of heart disease. Public health experts responded immediately, claiming that author Thomas Moore had ignored studies that showed a higher death rate among people with high levels of blood cholesterol. Moore's critics complained that he focused on short-term studies that did not last long enough to show a difference in death rates.

Nevertheless, it did become easier to avoid death from heart disease. A study by the Institute for Aerobics Research, Dallas, Texas, showed that even a moderate amount of exercise—a daily 30-minute walk, for example—places people in the same low-risk group as those who jog eight kilometers (five miles) a day. The location for that exercise was important, however. A study sponsored by the Health Effects Institute, Cambridge, Mass., showed that carbon monoxide at levels sufficient to bring blood levels up to those found in city dwellers and smokers caused early onset of heart pain in men with coronary artery disease. The U.S. Department of Agriculture made it a little easier to stick to the limit of 300 mg of dietary cholesterol a day set by many public health experts. They used modern laboratory measuring techniques to reanalyze the egg and found only 213 mg instead of the expected 274 mg per average egg.

It may even be possible to reverse heart disease with life-style changes. A study at the University of California at San Diego in 1987 showed that documented artery blockages in men shrank when the men went on drug therapy to lower cholesterol levels, and two other groups demonstrated the same results in 1989. However, Dean Ornish of the Preventive Medicine Research Institute in Sausalito,

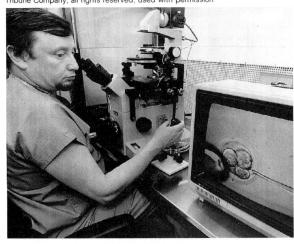

Yury Verlinsky at the Illinois Masonic Medical Center in Chicago removes unneeded genetic material from an unfertilized human egg in order to test it to determine whether a genetic defect is present.

Calif., showed that by intensive dietary and behavior efforts, people can lower their cholesterol levels without drugs. In a small study, when men and women with significantly blocked arteries stopped smoking, adopted a strict vegetarian diet, began exercising, and employed stress-reduction techniques, they were able to reduce their blockages.

Hepatitis. In 1988 researchers from Chiron, a California biotechnology company, announced that they had found an agent that causes non-A, non-B hepatitis, now called hepatitis C. In 1989 they developed a test for the virus, which each year causes hepatitis in about 700,000 people throughout the world, primarily from blood transfusions. Hepatitis C can lead to chronic hepatitis or cirrhosis of the liver. Chiron applied for permission to market the product in several countries.

While there was no cure for hepatitis C, NIH researchers announced that 21 patients with the disease who received alpha interferon three times a week did better, at least during the time they were receiving the therapy, than 20 patients who did not receive interferon.

Obstetrics. During the past decade physicians pushed back the date at which they could determine the health of a fetus. By 1990 researchers were on the way to being able to predict genetic disease even before a human egg was fertilized. Yury Verlinsky and colleagues of the Illinois Masonic Medical Center in Chicago removed unneeded genetic material from five human eggs and subjected them to biochemical analysis. Eggs initially have 23 chromosome pairs. One of each pair is unneeded, and the cell packs them away. Verlinsky devised a way to test the discarded material for the presence of a genetic defect.

If a woman is known to be a carrier, the presence of the defect in the discarded material means that the active gene is not defective.

British researchers from Hammersmith Hospital, London, and the Clinical Research Center, Harrow, England, showed that they could successfully determine the potential sex of three-day-old human embryos. Using a new procedure that creates multiple copies of specific genes, they removed a single cell from each of 30 three-day-old embryos and checked for the presence of the male-determining Y chromosome. They hoped that, should they be able to reimplant such embryos, the procedure would prove useful to parents who carry the genes for certain diseases that occur almost exclusively in males, such as hemophilia and the Duchenne type of muscular dystrophy.

Several groups were working on a totally noninvasive testing technique. It has long been known that fetuses shed some cells into their mother's bloodstream, but the numbers are few. Researchers from Harvard University and several other Boston-area institutions were able to identify fetal cells in the blood of seven pregnant women. They specifically looked for red blood cells that had nuclei. Adult red blood cells do not have nuclei, but fetal cells do. They used a marked strand of DNA to seek out Y-chromosome DNA; the mother's cells do not contain any Y chromosomes.

Neurology. U.S. and Canadian physicians announced the long-awaited results of a trial of deprenyl, an antioxidant that can neutralize cell-damaging chemicals found in the brains of people with Parkinson's disease. While the drug did not totally prevent the degenerative disease, which is marked by progressive tremors and a lack of muscle control, it did significantly delay disability. The discovery came about as a result of an illicit drug experiment gone awry. In 1982 a chemist synthesized a form of heroin that contained a contaminant that produced the same sort of symptoms as Parkinson's disease. Using that drug, researchers were able to set up an experimental system in rats and discovered among other things that some of the early damage of Parkinson's disease came from free radical chemicals that destroy sensitive cells.

University of California at San Diego researchers took a different approach to Parkinson's disease, developing a technique that looked promising in animal trials. They used a virus to transplant genes that make an enzyme that plays a key role in producing L-dopa into skin cells of rats. People with Parkinson's disease do not produce enough dopamine, and L-dopa is a precursor of dopamine. Surgeons in Mexico, Europe, and the U.S. were experimenting with inserting fetal cells that produce L-dopa into adults with Parkinson's. The California scientists injected

The first recipient of a liver transplant by a living donor in the U.S., 21-month-old Alyssa Smith, returns home with her parents. Her mother, Teri, gave up the left lobe of her liver for her daughter.

their genetically engineered cells into the brains of rats with a Parkinson's-like syndrome that caused them to walk in circles. The transplant reduced the frequency of this behavior.

Transplants. Surgeons achieved a number of transplant firsts during the past year. Surgeons at the Washington Hospital Center in Washington, D.C., performed the first heart-pancreas transplant. The recipient was a Silver Spring, Md., diabetic who needed a heart transplant. Because diabetes makes management of a new heart difficult, and because pancreas transplants are known to help diabetics, the surgeons decided to replace both organs at once. University of Chicago surgeons performed the first living-donor liver transplant in the U.S. A 29-year-old mother gave up the left lobe of her liver to her 21-month-old daughter, who had a fatal liver disease. The procedure, made possible by the fact that the liver regenerates, had already been done by surgeons in Brazil, Australia, and Japan.

While live-organ donors will reduce the problem of a shortage of cadaver organs, transplantation requires a major sacrifice by the donor. In an effort to eliminate the need for donors, NIH researchers were working on a way to grow organs in the laboratory. Called organoids or neoorgans, the tissues were grown from the patient's own cells, which were chemically tricked into thinking that they were in the embryo again. The procedure involved growing cells on Gore-Tex, a waterproof material, and soaking them in a growth factor that induces growth of the cells that line vessels within the body; the cells continued to grow. In another development a severely anemic patient who otherwise would have required a bone-marrow transplant received umbilical cord blood instead. French and U.S. researchers developed the procedure, which involved isolating blood-producing cells from the umbilical cord of a newborn.

Transplants in the future might be made easier by two new drugs. One of them, FK-506, was the product of a Japanese company that developed it from a fungus. Thomas Starzl of the University of Pittsburgh, Pa., began using it in his patients in 1989. He found that it was more effective and produced fewer side effects than the currently available drug, cyclosporin, which can damage the kidneys and other organs. The Du Pont Co. began marketing a new solution that matches current kidney preservation times, allowing up to 40 hours before transplant, and triples the eight-hour preservation limit for livers and pancreases. The chemical, called ViaSpan, was tested during the year in several U.S. hospitals. It extended the amount of time a liver can be stored from 8 hours to up to 30 hours, long enough to allow nonemergency operations and the extended transport of organs.

Transplanted cells could be used to deliver chemicals. Scientists led by James Wilson of the University of Michigan harvested from dogs cells that line blood vessels and then inserted a bacterial gene into the cells. These genetically engineered cells were then grown on Dacron tubes and implanted into dogs. The cells produced the hoped-for enzyme, suggesting that drug-producing genes could be transferred as well.

—Joanne Silberner

When placed in ViaSpan, a chemical solution developed by the Du Pont Co., a liver or pancreas being preserved for transplantation into a recipient can be stored three times longer than was previously possible.

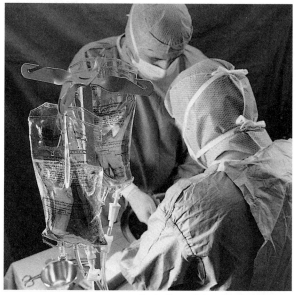

Dentistry

Dentistry entered the 1990s on an upbeat note: tooth decay rates in children were plummeting; toothlessness in middle-aged adults had been nearly eradicated; and older adults were keeping more of their natural teeth longer. The dental health of Americans improved dramatically during the last 40 years, and the 1990s signaled a new era that would change the face of dentistry again, predicted Arthur A. Dugoni, 1989 president of the American Dental Association (ADA) and dean of the University of the Pacific School of Dentistry, San Francisco. "One of the greatest things we have seen is the reduction of restorative needs in our patients. Dental decay and periodontal disease, man's major dental scourges, are now clearly controllable and essentially preventable." The ADA president noted that "in periodontal disease control, we continue to have some of our biggest breakthroughs because we are approaching prevention with chemical as well as mechanical means."

Other good news for dentistry in 1989 was that, according to a Gallup Poll, it was the second most respected profession in America. Dentists were rated higher in terms of honesty and ethical standards than physicians, clergy, and lawyers. Dentists were also driven by the entrepreneurial spirit, as reflected by the statistic that 90% of the 140,000 active practitioners in the U.S. were in private practice. Also, a *USA Today* survey found that more adults were satisfied with services received from dentists than from any other profession.

Sound waves to block pain. Phonophoresis, or high-frequency sound waves, may eliminate the need for anesthetic injections during certain dental treatments. "Phonophoresis is just entering the research phase. If successful, it will direct an anesthetic into the oral tissues through high-frequency sound waves instead of a needle," said Stanley Malamed, professor of anesthesia and medicine at the University of Southern California School of Dentistry.

One new technique already being used was electronic dental anesthesia (EDA), which applies electronic impulses to block the pain signals to the brain. "EDA provides very effective anesthesia for restorative dentistry, periodontal treatment, crown and bridge work, and temporomandibular dysfunction (TMD) problems which involve the jaw hinge joint. Although local anesthetic is still the most effective technique currently, EDA is a viable alternative, especially for needle phobics," Malamed stated.

New use for an old drug. An old drug was performing well in a new way. Pilocarpine, a drug used in prescription eyedrops, recently proved safe and effective as a medication for dry mouth patients in a large clinical trial at the National Institute of Dental Research (NIDR), Bethesda, Md. Dry mouth, also called xerostomia, is not a disease. Rather, it is often a symptom of changes in salivary gland function, either through a reduction in salivary flow or a change in the composition of saliva. Dry mouth also is a common side effect in people who regularly take certain medications—such as antihypertensives and antidepressants—or who have undergone radiation therapy to the head and neck. In addition, it occurs in Sjögren's syndrome, a rheumatic disorder.

According to NIDR scientist Philip C. Fox, pilocarpine—when taken orally three times a day—measurably increased salivary secretions in 20 of 31 dry mouth patients. Traditionally, dry mouth patients have relied on artificial saliva products to relieve the burning pain and other problems often associated with the condition. These products, however, merely wet the surface of the mouth but do not supply the important proteins found in natural saliva. Fox concluded that pilocarpine is a more beneficial therapy because it actually stimulates the salivary glands. He emphasized, however, that the drug is effective only in patients who have some remaining salivary gland function.

Crack-resistant dental crowns. Research on improved ways to make ceramic dental crowns may result in crowns that do not crack as often as those now in use. The research, which was being conducted at the Massachusetts Institute of Technology, stemmed from the recent development of automated systems for carving crowns out of small blocks of ceramic.

Most crowns have been made by layering ceramics over metal foundations. The crown has to be fired after each layer is applied, which can cause defects in the ceramic that later often lead to cracks. The new automated systems use computer-driven milling machines that can carve crowns from solid ceramic blocks that have already been fired. These blocks contain relatively few defects, according to Robert Kelly, a Harvard University School of Dental Medicine scientist.

Nursing bottle syndrome. In West Germany dental scientists renewed the debate over the harmful effects of the nursing bottle syndrome on dental health. Willi-Eckhard Wenzel, a pediatric dentist at Giessen University, sharply criticized the tendency of many parents to feed their infants a sugar-containing tea solution between meals during the daytime and as a "good night" drink before they go to sleep. Made from instant tea and marketed in convenient plastic bottles, it has, according to Wenzel, tempted parents to give children too much tea to drink.

Wenzel's comments were echoed by Swiss medical researchers, who noted that the practice leads not only to serious cavities in children but also to "a physiological liquid burden." Children addicted to the "bottle" in this way may consume up to three

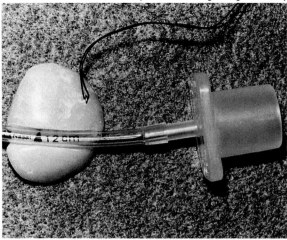

Tiny acrylic device that fits on the palate of a premature infant helps prevent developmental defects while keeping in place the tube that such a baby often needs as a breathing aid. It is held in the mouth by suction and dental adhesive powder.

liters (0.8 gal) per day. Substituting the tea bottle for pacifiers is the wrong way to help children to go to sleep, to counteract their fears and anxieties, and simply to keep them busy, said Wenzel. "Habits are formed that can later be resumed with disastrous effect in conflict situations. Take, for instance, the debate on eating as a pleasure substitute among overweight children. One can just as easily imagine nursing bottle children later become more readily susceptible to drug and alcohol abuse."

Aids for premature infants. A tiny mouthpiece fitting on the palate of a premature newborn infant prevents some problems that result from a tube that is often inserted through the mouth in order to aid breathing. "Advances in neonatology have meant that many more premature infants are surviving than in the recent past," Shahrbanoo Fadavi, assistant professor at the University of Illinois at Chicago College of Dentistry, told the American Association for Dental Research. "The survival rate for extremely low-birthweight infants, weighing as little as one and a half pounds, is about 40%. These newborns need tubes to carry oxygen to their lungs, yet the placement of the tube may exert pressure on the developing palate and teeth and cause defects in these areas."

Fadavi and her colleagues Indru Punwani, Dharmapuri Vidyasagar, Sikendar Adeni, and Kathy Dziedzic found that the small acrylic device, molded in the shape of the roof of the mouth, prevents a groove from forming in the hard palate just behind the teeth. The device also keeps the breathing tube from being dislocated. The mouthpiece is designed with a groove in the center to hold the tubing in place.

It is held in the mouth, just as dentures are, by suction and dental adhesive powder. First tested at the University of Iowa by Arthur Nowak and Allan Erenberg, the device may prevent long-term dental problems, including damage to tooth buds and incorrect alignment of the teeth, both possibly resulting from the insertion of a tube.

Root canal therapy. Once cited as one of the most feared terms in the English language, the root canal is losing its bite and becoming an important procedure to save teeth that might otherwise be lost. Endodontics, or root canal treatment, involves the removal of nerves and tissue inside the tooth when the pulp or tooth nerve is lost because of decay, trauma, infection, or the natural death of the nerve. "We have seen a total revolution in endodontics," said Donald Arens, an associate professor at Indiana University, "covering everything from mechanical techniques to materials used in the process. One of the most exciting advances is the development of a tool that senses the location of the exact tip of the tooth root using electrical resistance." Electrical resistance is a quick, efficient, and very comfortable procedure for the patient, he said.

The use of sonic and ultrasonic instruments also is starting to gain popularity. "Using sonic waves, we are able to clean hard to reach areas of the canal, especially those with unique shapes or curves," Arens said. Gutta-percha, the tough plastic material used to fill the canals, was also undergoing changes, being made more pliable so that it could be fitted to any shape of a tooth root.

Teeth grinders. While most nighttime teeth grinders do not produce a high level of noise, bruxism, as teeth grinding is formally known, can produce more than marital stress. Symptoms range from headache to severe jaw pain, and long-term bruxism can lead to permanent tooth damage. Conventional therapy has been to fit the patient with a plastic mouthpiece that keeps teeth physically separated during sleep. During the past year, however, clinical psychologists Jeff Cassisi and Alan Glaros of the University of Florida and F. Dudley McGlynn of the University of Missouri at Kansas City demonstrated the effectiveness and safety of a new method—an alarm that awakens people when their bruxism reaches damaging levels. The nighttime alarm technique has been found to control teeth grinding without producing undesirable side effects such as sleepiness, tension, or irritability that might result from repeated awakenings.

For 14 nights 10 volunteers with a history of bruxism were monitored as they slept near a "black box" that electronically counted the incidences of jaw tension. An alarm, which the study participant could shut off only after arising, was sounded when jaw pressure reached potentially damaging levels.

Standard psychological tests for fatigue, nervous tension, and irritability were given to the group, which then was monitored for an additional 14 nights without the alarm to check for a reduction in bruxism occurrences. The results showed a significant reduction in teeth grinding with no evidence of adverse side effects.

New adhesive. A new and stronger adhesive system proved to be safe and effective when used to adhere tooth-colored plastics to the surfaces of stained or damaged teeth in a process called bonding. In a study conducted by Rafael Bowen at the NIDR, the system, consisting of three different solutions, was painted on the tooth surfaces of 20 patients. None of the patients experienced any pain or sensitivity, nor did the bonding material stain, discolor, or fall off within four months after the treatment. The tooth pulp also did not seem to be significantly affected by the adhesives.

Previous studies had shown that the new adhesive system was two times stronger than some of the best adhesives commercially available. Another advantage of the new system was that it could be applied to both tooth enamel and the portion of the tooth that underlies the enamel, called dentin.

Oral cancer clue. Using a sensitive genetic probe, University of North Carolina researchers found DNA (deoxyribonucleic acid) traces from several human papilloma viruses (HPVs)—common causes of warts—in squamous cell carcinoma samples taken from patients with oral and pharyngeal cancer. This discovery suggested that HPVs may play a role in the development of this type of oral cancer. Squamous cell carcinomas are cancers that develop in specialized cells of the epithelium, the tissue that covers and lines body surfaces. Typically, they occur in the skin and in the mucous membranes lining the mouth, esophagus, and respiratory tract. Most cancers of the mouth and pharynx—the membranous passage between the mouth, larynx, and esophagus—are squamous cell carcinomas. They often develop as tumors on the inside of the lips, tongue, floor of the mouth, inside of the cheek, and esophageal inlet. If they are left untreated, squamous cell carcinomas can spread to other parts of the body.

Although scientists have long known that HPVs are present in squamous cell carcinomas in some parts of the body, such as the cervix, they had been unable to determine if HPVs are present in oral and pharyngeal squamous cell carcinomas. For that reason the findings could have a significant impact on future research of those cancers. The study found that nearly 60% of the tumor samples taken from patients with oral and pharyngeal squamous cell carcinomas had traces of HPV. These tumors, all malignant, were extracted from the tongue, mouth floor, pharynx, esophageal inlet, sinus, and larynx. All the patients had a history of smoking. Interestingly, there was no evidence of HPV in normal oral tissue or in other types of oral and pharyngeal cancer tissue. However, to clarify this point, additional samples needed to be studied. In future studies the researchers planned to investigate if the HPVs' genetic material actually expresses itself in oral and pharyngeal tumors.

Is it really gum disease? Within the next two years dentists could start using DNA probes to determine whether a patient really had periodontal (gum) disease. Roy Page, a professor of periodontics at the University of Washington, told the annual meeting of the ADA that deep pockets around a tooth do not necessarily mean the patient has gum disease. "Pockets around a tooth used to be a clear signal that the patient had gum disease. What we're finding now is that a patient can have these pockets with no infection. The DNA probe allows us to identify the handful of bacteria in the pockets associated with gum disease from the hundreds of bacteria normally found in the mouth," he said. Traditional treatment of early stages of the disease (gingivitis) includes rigorous home hygiene and regular professional care. Advanced cases, however, may require surgical procedures to scale the surfaces of the tooth's roots and to restructure the tissue around the tooth, thus removing the pockets that hold the bacteria.

In other developments concerning gum disease, Forsyth Dental Center researchers in Boston completed a large-scale controlled clinical trial in which the treatment of periodontal disease by a localized drug delivery system was evaluated. The delivery system consisted of threadlike fibers containing tetracycline. The fibers were inserted into the infected periodontal pocket, where they were maintained for 10 days by means of a colorless adhesive. The tetracycline in the fibers was released at a slow, controlled rate over the therapeutic period. Results indicated that periodontal pockets were reduced in depth and that bleeding on probing decreased to a greater extent than after scaling, the most common form of treatment. Numbers of disease-causing bacteria were also significantly reduced. This localized delivery of an antibiotic was accomplished in a virtually painless, nonsurgical manner in 113 patients in five centers across the U.S.

Investigators at the State University of New York at Buffalo were testing two antibiotics, metronidazole and amoxicillin, to combat localized juvenile periodontitis (LJP), a rare form of gum disease that strikes teenagers and young adults. LJP, which apparently is a genetically linked gum disease that can have disastrous effects on teeth and gums, affects fewer than 1% of U.S. teenagers and young adults. In the study 15 patients with LJP received the drug combination orally three times a day for a week. Prior to using the antibiotic, the patients had their teeth scraped and their tooth roots smoothed. After the treatment all patients showed improvement in the form of decreased gum recession, complete elimination of the harmful bacteria, and a healthier appearance of their gums.

Teeth and hearing loss. A close look at a child's tooth enamel may indicate that a hearing test is in order, according to researchers at Case Western Reserve University School of Dentistry, Cleveland, Ohio. They found that more than 50% of children who had a defect in their tooth enamel also suffered hearing loss. Fetal injury or illness appeared to be the source of the correlation between enamel defects and hearing loss, as teeth and ears develop at about the same time in the womb. The sites of enamel defects, in fact, correlate with the kinds of hearing problems found.

The study indicated that the enamel defect—usually a horizontal line of the tooth—provided clues to the approximate time that an injury to the fetus occurred and to the severity of the hearing loss. When the line was near the tip of the tooth, the injury happened in the early stages of fetal tooth formation and the hearing loss was most severe.

Temporomandibular disorders. Dentists who examine patients with temporomandibular disorders (TMD)—a group of conditions affecting the jaw's temporomandibular joint and chewing muscles that cause pain and dysfunction—often have trouble predicting temporary or long-term TMD conditions. However, a recent study at the University of Washington School of Dentistry indicated that a TMD patient's psychological state may be a better predictor of long-term pain than an examination of the jaw. The researchers noted that their findings did not suggest that dentists should stop examining the jaws of TMD patients to diagnose long-term pain conditions. Rather, they said that it shows that dentists might consider expanding their examinations to assess a patient's psychological state. Millions of people are affected by TMD, and dental researchers were continuing their investigations of the causes of these disorders.

In the study the researchers followed for one year the progress of more than 200 persons seeking treatment for TMD conditions. Findings revealed that 70% of the patients still reported TMD pain after treatment but indicated that their level of pain had no correlation with their physical symptoms. However, the scientists did find a link between patients who continued to suffer high levels of pain and those with anxiety and depression. Samuel Dworkin, the leader of the research team, theorized that the presence of heightened anxiety or depression in TMD patients might indicate a particular vulnerability to suffering a long-term condition.

—Lou Joseph

Veterinary medicine

Veterinary medical education was extensively evaluated in 1989. In the United Kingdom the Riley Working Party report made recommendations for improvements in veterinary education in preparation for the 21st century, many of which were well accepted by the veterinary profession. The recommendations included strengthening basic science courses, improving the quality of teaching, especially in clinical courses, achieving better integration of basic sciences and clinical programs, strengthening clinical and other research programs, and adding residency positions for specialty training. The recommended closing of the Glasgow veterinary school and the clinical and paraclinical departments at the Cambridge school proved to be controversial. The British Veterinary Association (BVA) and the Royal College of Veterinary Surgeons (RCVS) promptly expressed opposition and indicated that all six veterinary schools in the U.K. were needed. Glasgow and Cambridge veterinary schools both conducted campaigns to encourage public opposition to the proposed closures. A petition with over 630,000 signatures was presented in support of the Glasgow school. Since the BVA and the RCVS noted that future manpower needs of the United Kingdom were not adequately defined in recommendations for the closures, a manpower study was to be conducted before a final decision was made on this recommendation.

The 10th Symposium on Veterinary Medical Education was held at Michigan State University in June 1989. The goal of the symposium was identification of methods to implement a national strategy for improving veterinary education in the U.S. The need for a national strategy and the various factors guiding development of the strategy were the subjects of a report entitled "Future Directions for Veterinary Medicine," which was prepared by the Pew National Veterinary Education Program. Some of the factors considered were a shift in emphasis from disease treatment to disease prevention, greater application of computer technology, and increased opportunities for specialization. An important question raised by the Pew Report was whether veterinary medical education was adapting to challenges of a changing society. One of the major changes was the increasing demand for veterinary services for nontraditional patients.

Nontraditional patients. As changing life-styles were making it more difficult for working people to keep a dog or even a cat, exotic pets were becoming more popular. The owners of such pets were looking to the neighborhood veterinarian for medical care, just as they would for standard companion animals. As a result presentations pertaining to exotic animal medicine or treatment of nontraditional patients

Jeff Dunn—Stock, Boston

A parrot is shown to a boy in a pet store. Birds were the fastest growing category of pets in the United States during the past year, and more than 100 U.S. veterinarians specialized in pet-bird medicine.

were appearing with increasing frequency at veterinary meetings and conferences. The British Small Animal Veterinary Association published a text entitled *Manual of Exotic Pets*. While cats were the most popular pets in the U.S. in 1989, the category of birds was the fastest growing one, a trend that was expected to continue for the next several years. It was estimated that more than 100 U.S. veterinarians had practices that were primarily concerned with pet-bird medicine.

Practicing veterinarians were also encountering with increasing frequency requests for health care of reptiles, including snakes, lizards, turtles, and, occasionally, crocodilians. These species provided challenges in health care, *e.g.*, the treatment of middle and inner ear infections in turtles and the evaluation of skin problems in poisonous snakes.

In programs other than practice, veterinary medicine was also becoming more involved with nontraditional patients. A wildlife reproductive specialist at the University of Florida College of Veterinary Medicine was studying ways to improve reproductive efficiency in Florida's wild alligator population,

which was suffering because of urban development. Exotic-animal nutrition was especially important, both in preventive medicine and in the medical treatment of these species. A specialist at Michigan State University worked with veterinarians on such problems as diet to minimize plaque and calculus buildup on the teeth of Siberian tigers and wolves. Veterinary scientists at the University of Florida were gathering information on causes of diseases and reproductive problems in Florida panthers. The panther is a critically endangered animal, and the veterinarians hoped that their efforts would assist in panther population recovery.

Veterinarians working for Alaska's Department of Wildlife Management were concerned with marine mammal biology and wildlife medicine. The bowhead whale was receiving much attention from those veterinarians not only because it is on the rare and endangered species list but also because it is an important source of sustenance for Alaska's Eskimos. Studies on the whale included monitoring population size and conducting anatomic research to improve understanding of its food habits, reproductive cycle, and sensitivity to effects of oil spills. Several U.S. veterinary colleges participated in these studies.

Students. For the seventh year in a row, women outnumbered men in admission applications (62–38%) to U.S. schools and colleges of veterinary medicine. One female veterinary student achieved exceptional personal distinction. As a third-year student at the University of Missouri School of Veterinary Medicine, Debbye Turner had to delay her graduation date by one year after she was crowned Miss America of 1990. In the essay competition she emphasized environmental protection and humane use of animals in biomedical research. During her year-long reign as Miss America, Turner planned to speak to many groups on these issues. She expected to return to the University of Missouri for the 1990–91 school year to complete her courses for the degree of doctor of veterinary medicine.

New facilities. The Smithsonian Institution's National Zoological Park began 1989 by opening its new $3.4 million veterinary hospital. The hospital was designed to provide medical care for the park's 4,000 animals and to facilitate research on improving the health of these animals. The hospital also provided an excellent opportunity for training veterinarians in zoo animal medicine. Texas A&M University dedicated the Shubot Exotic Bird Health Center. The $2 million center represented a state-of-the-art facility for teaching and research in the areas of diagnosis, treatment, and prevention of diseases of pet, exotic, and wild birds and was the first of its kind among the nation's veterinary schools and colleges.

Auburn (Ala.) University started construction on the $1 million Holland Ware Diagnostic Imaging

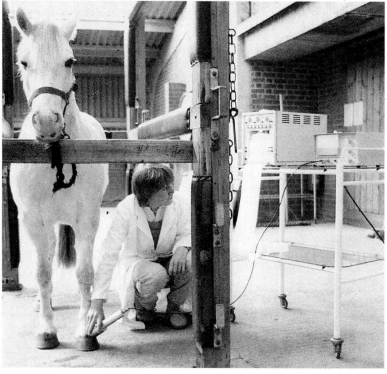

Veterinarian at the new equine lameness referral center of the Royal Veterinary College in London performs a bone scan to locate sources of inflammation. The center could accommodate as many as 20 horses.

Center, which would house oncology (cancer) and nuclear medicine laboratories and associated special diagnostic equipment, including ultrasound, computed tomography, and magnetic resonance. The center would enable utilization of the best technology available for advanced cancer treatment and research in animals. A new equine lameness referral center was opened at the Royal Veterinary College in London. The center was equipped with facilities for as many as 20 horses and included two operating theaters, a covered area for all-weather exercise, and a room with special diagnostic radiology equipment. Funding for the center was obtained through a partnership between industry, charities, and the university.

Emergency medicine. After the Armenian earthquake in December 1988, veterinarians were actively involved in rescuing cattle, sheep, pigs, and poultry from collapsed buildings, in providing treatment to injured animals, and in burying dead animals. In 1989 U.S. veterinarians were confronted by the devastation associated with three major national disasters—the San Francisco Bay area earthquake, Hurricane Hugo, and the Alaskan oil spill. In the aftermath of the earthquake veterinarians reported more cases of psychological trauma to animals than actual injuries caused by falling debris. Several veterinarians were also involved in efforts to find buried people, in some cases with the help of "canine trackers" that had been trained by the Monterey Bay Search Dog

group. There were no reports of serious structural damage to veterinary clinics in the earthquake area.

By contrast, Hurricane Hugo devastated many veterinary clinics in the Charleston, S.C., area. Many veterinary practices were without electrical power for as long as a week, which made medical treatment of patients difficult and necessitated surgery in naturally daylighted areas of clinics. Since many hurricane shelters refused to house pets, officials were encouraged to develop a plan for future disasters that would also offer pet protection.

Veterinarians and biologists worked vigorously and cooperatively to save animals that survived the oil spill in Alaska's Prince William Sound. Many deer, eagles, various other birds, and otters died. It was possible that surviving animals would require veterinary medical assistance for months because of hypothermia, emaciation, dehydration, and toxicity from inhalation and ingestion of the oil. A small veterinary rescue clinic was established soon after the spill but was quickly overcrowded. More than 20 veterinarians donated their time and expertise to help save surviving animals.

Animal disease problems. Bovine spongiform encephalopathy (BSE) continued to be a disease problem threatening cattle health in the U.K. New evidence indicated that the causative agent was similar to that causing scrapie, a spongiform encephalopathy in sheep. The nature of the agent was the subject of a number of theories. To indicate that it is not a conventional viral particle, some termed it a prion, others a virino, and others simply a subviral agent. Human infection appeared unlikely, but as a safety measure the consumption of certain cattle products was banned. The BSE resulted in restrictions on the export of cattle from the U.K. From cockatoos suffering from psittacine beak and feather disease, researchers from the University of Georgia College of Veterinary Medicine isolated a virus that appeared to be the smallest known pathogenic animal virus.

A veterinary research team from the National Animal Disease Center in Ames, Iowa, and Iowa State University College of Veterinary Medicine was awarded a $1 million grant by the National Cancer Institute to evaluate bovine immunodeficiency virus (BIV) as a potential model for human AIDS. The BIV is similar structurally and genetically to the human immunodeficiency virus (HIV). The immune system of cattle is suppressed by BIV, causing the animals to be more susceptible to other infectious diseases. The natural mode of transmission of BIV was unknown. No evidence was found to indicate that BIV is a public health threat.

In Valdez, Alaska, a leg identification band is placed on a pigeon guillemot that became soaked with oil spilled by the Exxon Valdez after the tanker struck a reef in Prince William Sound, Alaska, on March 24, 1989.

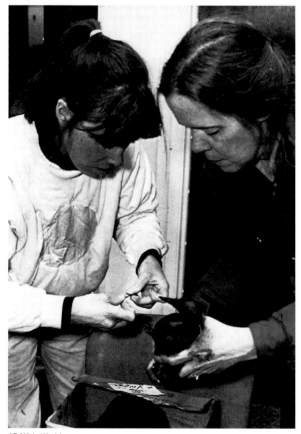

AP/Wide World

A University of Georgia College of Veterinary Medicine pathologist determined that the cause of differential toxicity of pennies swallowed by dogs is related to the year of the pennies' manufacture. Those made before 1983 are 96% copper, while newer pennies are 96% zinc. Stomach acid readily releases the zinc from the newer pennies. The zinc causes destruction of the dog's red blood cells.

—John M. Bowen

Optical engineering

The past year was marked by the acceptance of optical data storage and electronic still cameras in the marketplace. Opportunities for a host of new optical products were opened with the commercial production of visible-wavelength diode lasers. Several other new options for optical devices were noted, but the future for laser weapons and military optics in general was subject to great uncertainty.

In consumer optics the electronic still camera finally began to develop market interest, largely because of the availability of high-resolution image detectors. The cost of such cameras dropped to about $800, competitive with a high-quality photographic camera. Instant photography appeared to have reached market saturation despite the introduction of clever new cameras. The market for 35-mm cameras remained strong, however, as consumer interest in high-quality images appeared to be growing. The integration of electronic controls and optics led to some new compact and lightweight 35-mm cameras with extended-range zoom lenses and to overall camera shapes that deviated markedly from traditional forms.

Wider use and application of lasers continued to be a major driving force in optical engineering. The availability of economical and efficient semiconductor diode lasers continued to push gas lasers, including the familiar helium-neon laser, into a less important position. The major laser development in 1989 centered on the introduction of commercially available visible-wavelength diode lasers having five milliwatts of continuous output power available at a 670-nanometer red-wavelength light. (A nanometer is one one-billionth of a meter). The low driving current requirements and the compact and rugged characteristics of semiconductor light sources indicated that they will supplant many of the other kinds of lasers. Some of their first uses are expected to be in compact bar code readers and optical disc storage devices.

Another approach to obtaining short wavelength light from diode lasers was demonstrated by IBM Corp. with the compact integration of an infrared diode laser and a nonlinear optical device that pro-

Section of a gallium arsenide semiconductor chip is covered with an array of microlasers that have diameters of about 1.5 micrometers (millionths of a meter) and are spaced a similar distance apart from one another.

vided up to 30 mw of blue-wavelength light. (A nonlinear optical device is one based on a class of optical effects that result from the interaction of electromagnetic radiation from lasers with a material in which the radiation produces a response that is not proportional to the influence.) This source would be useful for increasing the allowable storage density in optical memories. High-power diode lasers at wavelengths of 850 nanometers, in the near infrared, were commercially available as continuous 10-output diode arrays. They were finding applications in medical instruments and industrial tooling.

During the past year there was also a significant growth in the number of optical memory devices that reached the marketplace. Reliable magneto-optical disc drives with capacities of several hundred megabytes were available for costs approaching $2,000 for the drive and only a few hundred dollars for each removable disc. (One megabyte equals 1,048,576 bytes.) During the year the gap between magnetic storage and optical storage was narrowed to about a factor of 10 by IBM's announcement of a magnetic storage disc with an information density of one gigabyte per square inch. (One gigabyte equals one billion bytes.) Because of the shorter wavelengths that can be obtained from diode lasers, it seemed certain that the density of optical storage could be increased in the future.

Optical computing did not change significantly during the past year except for the demonstration of a source and a logic gate with potential use by AT&T Bell Laboratories. The source of interest was an array of microlasers, with dimensions of about 1.5 micrometers (millionths of a meter), spaced a

similar distance apart on a gallium arsenide chip. These lasers, of low power and operating in the infrared, can form an array of several million individual sources that can be coupled to various integrated circuit components.

Near the end of 1989 another announcement indicated the fabrication of an array of about 1,000 optically bistable devices on a single chip. Bistable devices can be individually switched between low and high transmission by the intensity of light that is incident upon the element. Thus, they can operate as a two-dimensional array of optical logic switches. The possibility of parallel digital optical computation is clear for these devices. While the existence of these basic source and logic components was demonstrated in the laboratory, their incorporation into workable computers appeared to be several years in the future.

The fabrication of devices incorporating a laser diode and necessary control circuits into a single monolithic chip 1.5 mm square was demonstrated during the past year. This was expected to lead to wider communications applications because of the economic benefit provided by integrated systems.

Applications of lasers in material processing and component fabrication grew. The number of high-power lasers used for material cutting and shaping increased significantly. Their cost approached $40 per watt, greatly widening the possible market for numerically controlled laser welding and cutting devices. Some of the uses reported included the precision trimming of fabric for sailboat sails and welding of double pane windows to aluminum sealing frames, with the welding carried out through the glass windows.

Medical uses of laser and associated optical devices continued to grow slowly, with many surgical applications involving the use of laser energy delivered by optical fibers to various otherwise inaccessible parts of the body. Correcting vision by the use of corneal sculpting with an ultraviolet excimer laser had not reached general application by 1990, but clinical trials of the technique were continuing, and it appeared to be a year away from governmental approval. (An excimer laser is one containing a noble gas, such as helium or neon, that is based on a transaction between an excited state in which a metastable bond exists between two gas atoms and a rapidly dissociating ground state.)

Holographic optics became more important during the past year. The application of holography to storing three-dimensional images was well-established and was even seen on cereal boxes. The use of holograms to store information that would permit the hologram to serve as an optical imaging component has been known for many years but has never enjoyed significant market interest except in specialized scanning applications. Holographic optics are diffraction optics, a hologram consisting of a set of diffraction gratings recorded on a surface. (A diffraction grating is an assembly of narrow slots or grooves that produce a large number of beams that can interfere to produce spectra.) The periodicity, or spacing, of these gratings varies with position on the surface. Redirection of light occurs because of interference between light that passes through adjacent grating regions.

Because diffraction depends on wavelength, the passage of light through holographic optics is wavelength-dependent, and holographic optical components demonstrate considerable variations in image quality. These variations limit the accuracy to which images can be formed and can be corrected only by the use of complex optical systems. They limit the application of holographic optics to single-wavelength sources, such as lasers.

The recent prominence of laser diode sources has led to a renewed interest in commercializing holographic optics. One of the related developments that attracted interest during the past year was the invention of binary optics. These are holographic optics that use discrete digital steps in approximating the continuous grating profile of conventional holography. Because of this digital nature, binary optics can be made by microcircuit fabrication techniques. This melding of two diverse technologies has the possibility of devising unusual optical components that have nontraditional properties and can be used as optical interconnection components in various computer and data-transmission applications.

There were also events of note in more traditional areas of optical engineering. There was an initial move to increase the level of technology used in the production of conventional optical components by the formation of a Center for Optical Manufacturing as a joint activity of the Universities of Rochester (N.Y.); Arizona; and Central Florida, chosen because of their existing programs in applied optics. This move was initiated by several members of the optical industry and appeared to have developed sufficient interest for the U.S. Department of Defense that such a center might become a reality in the near future. Its goal was the unified industrial development of numerically controlled machinery for fabricating and testing lenses, prisms, mirrors, and other precision optical components. Industry leaders hoped that this would make the U.S. precision optics industry competitive with lower cost sources in other parts of the world.

The impetus for the Center for Optical Manufacturing as well as for many of the activities that were taking place in optics was defense. Observers were uncertain about the effect that the prospect of any reductions in defense-related expenditures might have on those portions of the industry committed to working on defense-related projects. Such reductions seemed likely because of the crumbling of the Communist regimes in Eastern Europe. One effect that was felt during the past year was a great reduction of interest in lasers as long-distance weapons, especially for applications in space. The intrinsic difficulties in packaging high-power lasers in compact form led to the cancellation of almost all projects for high-energy laser weapons as well as programs leading to the development of the beam-control systems necessary for projecting these weapons.

At the year's end the plan to launch a satellite with a high-powered chemical laser had been reduced to a ground-based demonstration of the integration of the laser and beam director. This laser, which had appeared during the past few years to have great potential as a very high-power weapon source, yielded to the realities of cost of development, and the demonstration project scheduled for a ground-based beam director at White Sands, N.M. was greatly reduced in power and effective range. The use of optical systems for tracking and acquisition of target information for other purposes did appear to be a necessary goal, and development continued on the design of precision trackers for use in space.

In astronomical optics the European Southern Observatory's plan for an array of four telescopes measuring eight meters in diameter progressed with the selection of a West German firm to produce the mirror blanks and a French firm to polish the large mirrors. The optics for the University of California and the California Institute of Technology 10-m-aperture Keck telescope proceeded with several of the 36 mirror segments completed by the Itek Corp. during the past year. The large telescope program at the University of Arizona continued with the pouring of another 3.5-m-diameter borosilicate glass blank as part of a program leading to a 6.5-m and eventually an 8-m mirror. The 2.4-m-diameter Hubble space telescope, a high-priority space observatory program of the U.S. National Aeronautics and Space Administration, was scheduled for launch in a manned space shuttle at the end of 1990. Significant concerns about the advisability of maintaining such large optics in space were heard during the year as the expense required for meeting such maintenance grew larger than the cost of operating the telescope. In addition, it was believed that the contamination surrounding the shuttle would be detrimental to the high-quality reflective coating on the optics of the telescope. It seemed likely that the emphasis on future space optical observatories would return to long-term operation in unmanned spacecraft. This strengthened interest in the engineering of lightweight optical components that remain stable for lengthy periods of time.

—Robert R. Shannon

Physics

Unprecedentedly precise measurements on two exotic subatomic particles, the antiproton and the Z^0, ranked high on the list of reported achievements in physics during the past year. Analysis of the first large-scale experiments using beams of relativistic-velocity heavy ion beams to bombard stationary targets added to scientific knowledge of the behavior of matter at high temperature and density. Recent theoretical work suggested that a yet-to-be-made crystalline material composed of carbon and nitrogen atoms may have a hardness approaching and perhaps exceeding that of diamond.

General developments

In the past year an international team of scientists working at CERN (European Laboratory for Particle Physics) near Geneva measured the mass of the antiproton with a precision some 2,500 times better than the best previous measurement. Astrophysicists puzzled over the on-again, off-again behavior of a powerful source of gamma rays at the center of our Galaxy. Physicists and psychologists engaged in medical research used measurements of the tiny magnetic fields generated by the human brain to map cortical activity associated with hearing.

Measuring the mass of the antiproton. Modern physics makes allowance for the existence of antimatter, but nature has not seen fit to produce much of it. Positrons, the antimatter counterparts of electrons, were first observed in the 1930s in cosmic-ray showers from space. In the 1950s an accelerator, the Bevatron at the University of California at Berkeley, was built in order to test the hypothesis that antiprotons, if they existed, would have the same mass as protons but opposite electric charge. Antiprotons were duly observed, earning the Berkeley physicists the 1959 Nobel Prize for Physics. Indeed, in subsequent years many other antiparticles were discovered, and interest turned to the measurement of their properties such as mass, magnetic moment, and lifetime.

For scientists to study certain types of physical properties and behavior, particles sometimes must be speeded up (as in tokamaks or particle accelerators) and sometimes have to be slowed down (as in refrigerators or ion traps). When studying antiprotons, one has to do both. First, protons must be accelerated to an energy of billions of electron volts (eV) and then smashed into a chunk of metal, where some of the collision energy is converted into antiprotons. The antiparticles in turn are focused into a beam and then "cooled" to lower energies.

At the low-energy antiproton ring (LEAR) at CERN, antiprotons emerge with an energy of 21 MeV (million electron volts). A team (known as the TRAP collaboration) from Harvard University, the University of Mainz, West Germany, the University of Washington, and the Fermi National Accelerator Laboratory, Batavia, Ill., further reduces the energy of the antiprotons to less than 3 keV (thousand electron volts) by passing them through a thin metal sheet. Finally, some of the antiprotons are captured in a Penning trap, a device consisting of a positively charged ring-shaped electrode and two negatively charged cap electrodes surrounding a central cavity having a volume of about 10 cu cm. There the antiprotons can be cooled, through collisions with an electron gas, to energies below a tenth of an electron volt. Even in this sluggish regime the antiprotons trace out circular orbits (in the trap's magnetic field of 60,000 gauss) 90 million times a second for periods as long as a few days. To keep the antiprotons from meeting and annihilating with ordinary protons, a powerful vacuum system operating at cryogenic (near-absolute-zero) temperatures evacuates the central cavity to a vacuum estimated to be below 10^{-14} torr. Attaining this level of vacuum, among the best in the world, is itself a technological feat.

Using these techniques the team found the mass of the antiproton to be equal to that of the proton within an uncertainty of 2×10^{-8}; the best previous comparison, based on X-ray emissions from atoms excited by antiproton absorption, was only 5×10^{-5}. The TRAP team hopes to improve its mass measurements by an additional factor of 100–1,000. Proton-antiproton mass comparisons at this level of precision would provide an important test of CPT invariance—a principle that holds that the physics describing an interaction between particles is not altered by the combined mathematical operation of charge conjugation (C), which turns particles into their antiparticles; parity (P), which inverts the spatial coordinates of all particles; and time reversal (T), which reverses the order in which the events of the interaction occur.

The TRAP group also hopes to create antimatter atoms by sending a beam of positrons (antimatter counterparts of electrons) in with the stored antiprotons. The resulting cold antihydrogen, a positron orbiting an antiproton nucleus, would make possible a host of spectroscopic tests. A proton-antiproton bound state called protonium and other exotic atoms involving antiprotons are additional potential candidates for creation and study.

Annihilation radiation from the galactic center. Specimens of antimatter can also be found in the more expansive core of the Milky Way Galaxy, 25,000 light-years from Earth. Beginning in the 1970s a series of balloon and satellite observations showed that gamma rays having a characteristic energy of 511 keV are coming from the direction of the galactic center. Such radiation arises from the annihilation of positrons with electrons. Since positrons do not exist in ordinary matter, they must, like antiprotons, be created in a process involving the expenditure of great amounts of energy. Some scientists believe that a black hole may be responsible.

Because of intervening dust clouds, the core of the galaxy cannot be seen at visible wavelengths, but it can be observed in other portions of the electromagnetic spectrum such as the infrared, radio, and gamma-ray regions of the spectrum. Ironically, the same gamma rays that escape the galactic center's dusty shroud cannot penetrate the Earth's atmosphere to the ground, so telescopes must be sent aloft. A collaboration led by Marvin Leventhal of Bell Laboratories (now AT&T Bell Laboratories), Murray Hill, N.J., and involving researchers from Bell Labs and Sandia National Laboratories, Albuquerque, N.M., was the first to detect unambiguously annihilation radiation from the galactic center. In 1977, using a balloon-borne telescope flown over Alice Springs, Australia, that group recorded a gamma-ray rate of 10^{-3} per second per square centimeter of detector surface. This figure corresponds to a positron-electron annihilation rate of 10^{43} per second at the galactic center. The energy released in this colossal mutual destruction is about 10^{37} ergs per second, or about 10,000 times the Sun's luminosity at all wavelengths.

Then something surprising happened. Measurements made in 1979 and 1980 by a group from NASA's Jet Propulsion Laboratory (JPL), Pasadena, Calif., showed that the amount of annihilation radiation was dropping. More balloon flights by the Bell-Sandia group and an independent group at the NASA-Goddard Space Flight Center, Greenbelt, Md., in 1981 and 1984 confirmed that the gamma-ray source had switched off. At the very least this unexpected downturn implied that the source was compact. Based on the principle that no information can travel faster than the speed of light and that an object cannot stop radiating in less time than it takes light to traverse the object, a six-month switch-off time (established by the JPL data) would imply a source no bigger than half a light-year across and perhaps much smaller.

Subsequently and just as surprisingly, the gamma-ray source (or, equivalently, the source of positrons) turned back on. A joint Bell-Sandia-NASA group (known as the GRIS collaboration, for gamma ray imaging spectrometer) made new flights in May and October 1988, the results of which showed the source back up to its old intensity. The 1,680-kg (3,700-lb) GRIS apparatus was carried to an altitude of 40 km (25 mi) by a helium-filled balloon whose volume, when fully inflated to 850 million liters (30 million cu ft), could easily accommodate the Wash-ington Monument. The apparatus employs some of the largest and highest purity germanium crystals in the world to sense incoming gamma radiation. Most recently, in 1989, a French-U.S. team led by James Matteson of the University of California at San Diego recorded evidence that the source was once again declining in intensity.

What is the nature of the positron source, and why is it variable? Reuven Ramaty of NASA-Goddard suggested that the source is a black hole with a mass perhaps as large as a million solar masses. In his model positrons are created when material from nearby stars or dust clouds is drawn by powerful tidal forces down onto an accretion disk swirling around the black hole. The variability of the positron production could be explained by noting that the accretion of matter near black holes is expected to be erratic. Black-hole mechanisms also have been employed to explain the vast energy production in active galaxies and quasars. Thus, it may be that the center of the Milky Way, once thought to be a rather placid galaxy, is serving as a laboratory for studying the most energetic objects in the universe.

Another suggestion, from Leventhal, is that the gamma-ray source may be associated with GX1+4, a binary star system consisting of a neutron star and a red giant and located only 5° from the galactic center. GX1+4 is a powerful X-ray emitter and is one of only four objects in the Milky Way known to have radio-wave-emitting lobes.

The location and identification of the positron source will be aided by better angular resolution (GRIS currently has an angular resolution of 8°). Balloon observations will continue, and the gamma-ray-observing satellites GRO (U.S., scheduled for launch in 1990) and GRANAT (U.S.S.R., launched in December 1989) may add new information.

Neuromagnetism. The electrical activity of the human brain and heart can be studied through placement of electrodes on the skin and by measurement of the small electrical potential differences between various points on the body. The readouts of these measurements in graphic form—electrocardiograms in the case of the heart and electroencephalograms in the case of the brain—can reveal rhythmic patterns in the electrochemical currents flowing inside the body. Since the laws of physics prescribe that wherever there are electrical currents, magnetic fields must arise also, it follows that the brain and heart should have characteristic magnetic properties. Indeed, in recent years scientists have developed techniques for measuring these biomagnetic fields and have begun to apply them on a clinical basis.

The strength of the magnetic fields in question represents the first problem in developing applications. The field produced at the scalp by the currents flowing within active nerve cells (neurons) of the brain, for example, is a billion times weaker than the magnetic field of the Earth. Fortunately, such a weak field can be measured by a device known as a SQUID (superconducting quantum interference device), which is highly sensitive to the presence of magnetic fields and which must be maintained in a liquid-helium bath at a temperature only a few degrees above absolute zero. Although the magnetic field generated by a single neuron is too weak for a SQUID to detect, the field of 10,000 neurons acting simultaneously indeed can be measured.

For study of the magnetism of the brain, arrays of SQUIDs are placed over the scalp; measurement of the field lines that curve up out of the brain and back down again in tight arcs can be used to infer the position of the neuromagnetic source. This information is used for forming not an anatomic map but a functional map of the brain as it responds to various sensory stimuli.

During 1989 Siemans AG, Erlangen, West Germany, introduced a 37-sensor system; Biomagnetic Technologies, Inc., of San Diego, Calif., also produced a 37-sensor system. By reducing sampling time and by sharpening spatial resolution, such multisensor arrays represent a great improvement over single-sensor or even the seven-sensor systems in use only two years earlier. Olli V. Lounasmaa's group at the Low Temperature Laboratory at the Helsinki (Fin.) University of Technology employed a 24-sensor array, which provided the most compact detection surface used to date.

An interdisciplinary team of physicists and psychologists at New York University, led by Samuel J. Williamson and Lloyd Kaufman, embarked on a project to establish a three-dimensional functional map of the brain, with the spatial location of certain types of brain activity, such as hearing, seeing, or touch, determined to a precision of millimeters. They discovered, for example, that different sound tones trigger neural responses in a listener's brain in specific places over the surface of the auditory cortex in a nearly straight line. In fact, a map of the hearing center in the brain looks something like a piano keyboard; for example, the distance between the response areas for low C and middle C is nearly the same as that between the response areas for middle C and high C. Each "octave" occupies a segment of about one centimeter (0.4 in) along the auditory cortex. Furthermore, a West German group led by Mannfried Hoke of the University of Münster discovered that the auditory response to sounds of different intensity do not affect the strength of neural response but shift the location across the cortical surface in a direction nearly perpendicular to the direction corresponding to changes in pitch.

Such research also has implications for the study of tinnitus, the abnormal sensation of a ringing in

O.V. Lounasmaa, Helsinki University of Technology, Finland

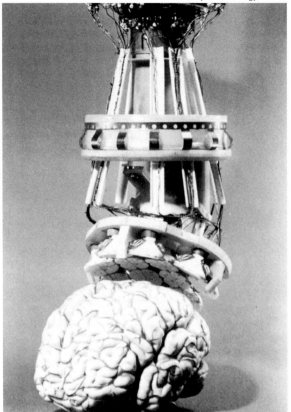

Shown positioned over a model human brain is a neuromagnetometer developed at the Helsinki (Finland) University of Technology. The instrument employs an array of 24 SQUID detectors to map the extremely weak biomagnetic fields generated by the living brain.

the ear. Hoke's group found that the sequence of magnetic-field responses to the onset of a tone was characteristically different for sufferers of tinnitus. Williamson reported that this research allowed for the first time an objective measure of tinnitus.

There is hope that neuromagnetism, which can aid in the location of diseased tissue in the brain, will prove valuable in localizing focal epilepsy prior to surgery and in contributing to the study of Alzheimer's disease. It also may be possible to study the brain region known as the hippocampus (located some five to six centimeters, or 2 to 2.4 in, beneath the scalp), which some scientists believe is associated with memory.

—Phillip F. Schewe

High-energy physics

The most significant development in high-energy physics during the past year was the full-scale operation of two new high-energy colliders that bring together electrons and their antimatter counterparts, positrons. One of them, the Large Electron-Positron Collider (LEP) at CERN (European Laboratory for Particle Physics) near Geneva, is a larger version of standard colliders that have been in operation for some time. At LEP the electron and positron beams counterrotate with equal energies in a ring 27 km (17 mi) in circumference and collide over and over again in several target areas equipped with detectors. Because it used proven technology, LEP had an uneventful history of development and construction. Construction was started in 1983, and operation began on schedule in the summer of 1989. The other machine, the Stanford Linear Collider (SLC) at the Stanford Linear Accelerator Laboratory in California, involves a technology in which two beams of particles are accelerated to high energy along a tube three kilometers (1.9 mi) long. The beams are then shrunk to an area comparable to that of a bacterium and allowed to collide only once. Because this technology is considerably newer and less proven than that used in LEP, the SLC had a much more turbulent history of development. Construction also was begun in 1983, and although the first collisions at SLC were observed in 1987, the collision rate did not reach a level useful for physics observations until the spring of 1989. In early 1990 the rate remained

Officials at the inauguration of CERN's Large Electron-Positron Collider (LEP), near Geneva, in November 1989 stand below a superconducting electromagnet in a portion of the facility's 27-kilometer (17-mile) tunnel.

AP/Wide World

substantially below that originally expected at the SLC and that achieved at LEP. Nevertheless, important results did emerge from the first few months of operation of each accelerator.

Although the energy of the accelerated particles can be varied somewhat, each accelerator was operated such that the sum of the energies of the two colliding particles was equal to about 91 billion electron volts (GeV). This energy was chosen because it approximates the rest energy (rest mass) of a particle known as the Z^0, first produced in 1983 by a proton-antiproton collider at CERN. When an electron and positron with this energy collide and mutually annihilate, there is a relatively high probability that they will convert into the Z^0. A detailed study of the properties of Z^0 particles is currently one of the main goals of physicists at LEP and SLC.

Table I. Gauge Particles of the Electroweak Theory

particle	rest energy
photon	0
W^+, W^-	80 GeV
Z^0	91 GeV

Measuring the Z rest energy. The Z^0 is one of the particles that transmits the weak interactions. Its existence was first predicted by Sheldon Glashow, Steven Weinberg, and Abdus Salam, who independently devised what has come to be known as the unified theory of weak and electromagnetic interactions, or the electroweak theory. According to the theory, there are four particles with closely related interactions: the photon, or light quantum; the Z^0; and the W^+ and W^-, two particles that transmit other aspects of the weak interactions (*see* Table I). These particles are all termed gauge particles, because the equations that describe them are a consequence of a mathematical principle known as local gauge invariance. When the unified theory of weak and electromagnetic interactions is combined with a description of the strong interactions that is also based on local gauge invariance, the result is a theoretical description of almost all known phenomena of particle physics, which has come to be called the standard model.

The electroweak theory allows the rest energy of the Z^0 to be calculated in terms of other quantities involved in weak interactions, such as the charge of the electron, the decay rate of the muon (a charged heavy relative of the electron), and the ratio of the interaction strengths of W and Z. Although these other quantities are not all known precisely, they are known well enough that a prediction of the Z^0 rest energy can be made. If the measured Z^0 rest energy were to be very different from the predicted value, it would mean that something was wrong with

Table II. The Known Fermion Families

families	charged leptons	neutral leptons	quarks with charge 2/3 that of electron	quarks with charge −1/3 that of electron
1	electron	electron neutrino	up quark	down quark
2	muon	muon neutrino	charmed quark	strange quark
3	tau	tau neutrino	top quark	bottom quark

the electroweak theory. Since the predicted value is approximately 91 GeV, the LEP and SLC experimenters knew at what energy to set their beams in order to produce the Z^0. Earlier measurements had shown that the rest energy was close to this value, but the uncertainty in the measurements was several percent, not sufficient for an accurate test of the theory.

In 1989 four different detectors at LEP and one detector at SLC observed large numbers of Z^0 particles and obtained a more accurate value for the rest energy. The average value is 91.1 GeV, with an experimental error of about 0.1 GeV. Future experiments were expected to decrease the error further and perhaps make it possible to determine other quantities that affect prediction of the Z^0 rest energy, such as the mass of the yet unobserved top quark. The reports of the results from LEP on the Z^0 rest energy were published in the journal *Physics Letters* in four articles, each listing hundreds of coauthors from many institutions and countries. A slightly less precise measurement of the rest energy was reported in the journal *Physical Review Letters* by a group of some 200 authors working at the SLC. Moreover, a measurement with a precision similar to that at the SLC was reported in the same issue of *Physical Review Letters* by a similarly large group of physicists working at the Fermi National Accelerator Laboratory (Fermilab), Batavia, Ill. The Z^0 particles at Fermilab were produced in collisions between protons and antiprotons.

Measuring the width of the Z. The Z^0 is an unstable particle with a lifetime of less than 10^{-24} seconds. It is therefore impossible to observe directly. Instead, what is seen are the more stable decay products. The easiest decays to interpret are those that produce a pair of charged leptons, such as an electron and positron or a pair of muons. These modes account for about 10% of the decays. Various combinations of hadrons—strongly interacting particles such as pions (pi mesons)—account for about 70% of the decays. Such hadronic decay modes are indirect manifestations of the direct decay of the Z^0 into quark-antiquark pairs. The quarks and antiquarks do not appear as free particles but instead convert rapidly into the observed hadrons. (*See* Table II.)

The remainder of the decays of the Z^0 particle produces one of several types of neutral particles

called neutrinos. These decay modes are invisible, because neutrinos interact so feebly with other matter that they escape detection even in the massive detectors used with LEP. Nevertheless, it is possible to infer from other measurements how often the Z^0 does decay into neutrinos. This inference is based on the fact that the rest energy of an unstable particle is not precisely defined. Instead each such particle can be produced or can decay over a range of rest energies. This energy range, known as the width of the particle, is proportional to the total decay rate of the particle. A calculation of the decay rate of Z^0 particles into observable products implies that its width is at least 2.1 GeV. By measuring the actual width and comparing it with the sum of the widths due to observable decays, physicists can infer the additional rate of decays into invisible products. In measuring the width, decays via any individual mode (such as into a muon pair) can be used, since according to quantum theory the energy distribution in a single decay mode is governed by the full width due to all decays.

This type of measurement was carried out both at the SLC and at each of the four detectors at

Both the rest energy (the peak near 91 GeV) and the particle width (range of rest energies) of the Z^0 can be inferred from a plot of the energy distribution of muon pairs produced in Z^0 particle decays at LEP.

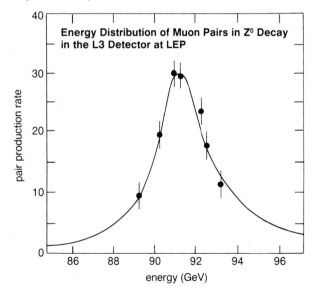

398

LEP. About 12,000 Z^0 decays were observed and the energy of each Z^0 determined. To do this, precise knowledge of the energy and numbers of the colliding electrons and positrons was required. The results of the measurements can be expressed as curves similar to the Figure on the opposite page. From them it is possible to infer both the rest energy and the width of the Z^0. The combined result of the experiments indicates that the width is 2.6 GeV, with a possible error of about 0.1 GeV, a figure that clearly indicates the presence of invisible decay modes.

Such decay modes are expected on the basis of the electroweak theory, which predicts that the Z^0 should sometimes decay into a pair of one of the three known types of neutrino that are associated with the three known charged leptons (Table II). Each neutrino decay mode should contribute 0.17 GeV to the Z^0 width. Therefore, decays into three types of neutrino would increase the width from the calculated minimum of 2.1 GeV to about 2.6 GeV, just about the measured value.

A limit on particle families. The agreement between the measurement of the width and the predictions of the standard model, to within the precision of the measurements, implies that it is highly unlikely that any still unknown invisible modes of decay exist, since those decays would increase the width still further. In particular, it implies that no other neutrinos exist whose rest energy is low enough that the Z^0 can decay into them. This outcome is quite significant within the context of the standard model, as it implies that physicists have discovered all of the particles with low rest energy that exist. The basis of this conclusion lies in the fact that in the standard model particles known as fermions, such as leptons and quarks, occur in families, or generations. Each contains two leptons and two quarks, and there are three such families. The charged leptons and quarks can be produced directly, for example, in collisions between electrons and positrons through the electromagnetic field. However, the rest energies of the quarks and charged leptons rise rapidly from family to family. Consequently, it is possible that other families exist whose members have rest energies so high that they cannot be produced with existing accelerators.

Indeed, by early 1990 one presumed member of a known family, the top quark, remained to be produced and detected because of its high rest energy. Searches for the top quark and for other heavy quarks and charged leptons were being carried out at accelerators such as the Tristan collider at Tsukuba, Japan, which began operation in 1986. At Tristan, electrons and positrons collide at a maximum total energy of about 60 GeV. No new quarks or charged leptons were found in this energy range, which implies that none exist up to a rest energy of about 30 GeV. Other experiments carried out at the proton-antiproton collider at Fermilab, which can collide particles at total energies as high as 1,800 GeV, imply that the rest energy of the top quark must be at least 78 GeV.

On the other hand, the neutrino of each known lepton family has zero, or at least a very small, rest energy. If this characteristic is also true for the neutrinos of hypothetical new families, then those neutrinos would appear as decay products of the Z^0, whereas their charged lepton counterparts might not if their rest energy were very high. The standard model predicts that any additional neutrinos of low rest energy will occur as decay products of Z^0 as often as do the three known neutrinos. If an additional neutrino type did exist, its occurrence in Z^0 decay would increase the width by about 0.17 GeV, which would then disagree with the observations by more than the experimental error. Thus, the conclusion from the measurements of the width—that no other neutrino types exist—is taken to imply that no other families of leptons and quarks exist either.

Assuming that the conclusion is correct, physicists have discovered all of the fermion families similar to the one (the first family) comprising the particles of ordinary matter. It would not be surprising that the number of such families is limited, as nature rarely repeats any specific pattern indefinitely. Physicists, however, now face the problem of understanding why three families of this type exist, rather than some other number. This question is analogous to one that confronted an earlier generation of nuclear physicists, who needed to explain why there are a specific number of stable chemical elements. There are yet no convincing explanations for the existence of exactly three families of fermions. Some theories suggest that other families of fermions exist, all of whose members including the neutrinos have very high rest energy. If so, then some of these particles may be detected when the next generation of accelerators, such as the Superconducting Super Collider planned for construction near Dallas, Texas, begins operation in the 21st century.

—Gerald Feinberg

Nuclear physics

Remarkable progress was made in the past year in understanding many aspects of nuclear dynamics. Analysis of the first large-scale experiments with relativistic heavy ion beams enlarged scientific knowledge of the behavior of nuclear matter under conditions of elevated temperature and density. Significant progress was made toward the development of the Relativistic Heavy Ion Collider (RHIC), the goal of which is the discovery of a new phase of nuclear matter, in which the fundamental constituents,

At the Continuous Electron Beam Accelerator Facility (CEBAF) being built in Virginia, tests are conducted on one of the more than 40 liquid-helium–cooled "cryomodules" whose superconducting accelerating cavities will drive the facility's beams to an energy of 4 GeV. The electron beams will be used to bombard atomic nuclei for a variety of nuclear physics experiments, scheduled to begin in 1994.

namely quarks and gluons, are no longer confined within individual nucleons (neutrons and protons). New insights into the properties of nuclei containing strange particles (hypernuclei) were achieved through analysis of experiments with meson beams.

Relativistic heavy ion collisions. Quantum chromodynamics (QCD), the underlying theory of the strong interactions that hold the nucleons together in the nucleus, led to the remarkable prediction that nuclear matter should exhibit a dramatic change of properties when its energy density is increased approximately by a factor of ten above that characteristic of the interior regions of ordinary atomic nuclei, about $\frac{1}{6}$ GeV/cu fm (1 GeV = one billion electron volts, 1 fm = 10^{-13} centimeters). This profound change reflects a transition from a confined to a deconfined phase of QCD. In the confined phase, as found in ordinary nuclei, the quarks, the basic constituents of matter, are localized in clusters of three within single neutrons or protons. In the deconfined phase, the nucleons in the nucleus dissolve into a plasma of quarks and gluons, the latter being the carriers of the strong interaction.

The prediction of a new phase of matter, the quark-gluon plasma, stimulated a major research direction in nuclear physics. Such a phase of matter may have existed in the first millionth of a second after the big bang and may also reside deep in the cores of neutron stars. The primary impetus for the new research initiative was the realization that the extreme energy densities necessary for quark-gluon plasma formation could be generated in the laboratory through the collisions of relativistic heavy ions. These ions are atomic nuclei stripped of all their electrons and accelerated to velocities close to the speed of light.

In the past year physicists made major progress in the analysis of experiments with relativistic heavy ions. Three large experiments continued at Brookhaven (N.Y.) National Laboratory's Alternating Gradient Synchrotron (AGS), and six more experiments took data at the SPS (Super Proton Synchrotron) at CERN (European Laboratory for Particle Physics) near Geneva. Beams of oxygen, silicon, and sulfur ions were accelerated to energies of 14.5 GeV per nucleon at the AGS (oxygen and sulfur only) and 60 to 200 GeV at CERN and subsequently used to bombard stationary targets.

The measurements fall into two major categories. First, there were measurements of the number of particles (mostly pions, which are light mesons composed of a quark and antiquark) produced in the collision, as well as of the energies carried by these particles. The observations were used to estimate the initial energy density in the collision. The total transverse energy (the energy that all the particles carry off by that component of their motion that is perpendicular to the direction of the incident beam) is a measure of the efficiency of the process for converting the kinetic energy of beam particles into random motion. The production of transverse energy is proportional to the initial energy density attained in the collision. Based on the Brookhaven and CERN data, it was estimated that energy densities of order 1 GeV/cu fm or higher were created, tantalizingly close to theoretical estimates of around 2 GeV/cu fm required for quark-gluon plasma formation.

The second category of measurements probed specific aspects of the collision dynamics. Several striking new phenomena were revealed. For instance, muon pair measurements at CERN demonstrated the suppression of the production of J/psi mesons

400

(bound states of a charmed quark, c, and its antiquark, $\bar{c}$) in heavy ion collisions with large transverse energy. This effect could be a signal of the quark-gluon plasma, but it may also arise from more conventional effects of initial- and final-state interactions; for instance, the dissociation and absorption processes suffered by J/psi particles as they traverse a region of dense nuclear matter. This behavior remained a subject of intense theoretical debate.

A similar controversy surrounded the interpretation of recent measurements of strange particle production. Involved in this case were strange mesons like the positively charged kaon (K^+, which is composed of a strange antiquark, $\bar{s}$, and an up quark, u), and the Λ hyperon (a strange partner of the nucleon that contains three quarks, one of which is an s quark). At Brookhaven the ratio of kaon to pion yields in silicon-gold (^{28}Si-Au) collisions was found to rise dramatically for large transverse momentum, well above the similar ratio observed for proton-proton or proton-nucleus encounters. Results from CERN showed a rapid rise of Λ production with the number of charged particles. This behavior was not predicted by theoretical models that simulate the complicated dynamics of heavy ion collisions.

RHIC progress. The main thrust of the experimental program in high-energy heavy ion physics was the construction of the Relativistic Heavy Ion Collider (RHIC) at Brookhaven. In the 1989 Long Range Plan for Nuclear Physics of the Nuclear Science Advisory Committee (NSAC) of the U.S. Department of Energy (DOE) and the National Science Foundation (NSF), RHIC was given the highest priority for new construction in the nuclear physics program. The collider will consist of two rings of superconducting magnets. Each ring will accelerate a beam of heavy ions to energies as high as 100 GeV per nucleon. The heavy ions will originate in the tandem Van de Graaf accelerator at Brookhaven, proceed into the Accumulator-Booster (under construction in 1989), and then move into the AGS. Next, the ions will be extracted in bunches and transferred to one of the two collider rings, where they will be accelerated in a few minutes to the maximum energy. Once at that energy, the ions will remain in stable orbits in the rings for hours. The RHIC tunnel allows for six intersection areas, where the circulating ion beams cross and collisions occur. The transition from experiments involving an ion beam and a fixed target to ones involving two colliding beams implies an order-of-magnitude increase in the energy available in the center-of-mass system, a big step in providing the energies needed to explore quark-gluon plasma.

A key element in the RHIC design is the system of superconducting electromagnets, about 1,400 of which are required. A prototype dipole magnet is shown in the photo below. This 9.7-m (31.8-ft) magnet produces a uniform magnetic field inside the central pipe where the heavy ions travel. Under operating conditions the iron structure and superconducting coils are kept in liquid helium at a temperature of 4.3 K ($-452°$ F).

The essence of the experimental program at RHIC will be the study of the properties of ultradense matter and the search for quark-gluon plasma formation. This new field of quark matter research was virtually nonexistent as recently as the late 1970s. It arose as a result of the development of quantum chromodynamics as the fundamental theory of strong interactions. By 1989 the search for this new form

Prototype superconducting dipole electromagnet for the Relativistic Heavy Ion Collider (RHIC) under construction at Brookhaven (New York) National Laboratory is 9.7 meters (31.8 feet) long. In operation such magnets will generate a uniform magnetic field to help hold beams of energetic heavy ions on course around RHIC's 3.8-kilometer (2.4-mile) rings.

Brookhaven National Laboratory

of matter had become a cornerstone of research in nuclear physics.

Hypernuclear structure. A hypernucleus is a bound system of ordinary neutrons and protons and a strange baryon (for example, a Λ or Σ hyperon containing a strange quark, s). Such nuclei can be made in accelerator experiments with beams of strange mesons (K^-, for example, which comprises a strange quark and an up antiquark, or $s\bar{u}$) or of pions (π^+, for example, which comprises an up quark and a down antiquark, or $u\bar{d}$) incident on targets of atomic nuclei. A Λ hyperon bound to a nucleus in the lowest lying energy state (the $1s$ orbit of the nuclear shell model with orbital angular momentum of zero) decays by weak interactions with a characteristic lifetime of 260 picoseconds (10^{-12} seconds). For years it had been known that the average Λ interaction with nuclei (the Λ-nucleus potential or mean field) is about half as strong as the nucleon-nucleus interaction, but little was known of the dependence of the interaction on the spin of the Λ.

Recently data from several experiments conducted at the Brookhaven AGS were analyzed, revealing some new features of the Λ-nucleon force. In one of these studies hypernuclei were produced by bombarding nuclear targets with a K^- beam, resulting in the detection of a negatively charged pion ($\pi^- = \bar{u}d$) and a subsequent gamma-ray photon in the final state. Detection of the π^- tags the transfer of a unit of strangeness (the strange quark s) from the kaon to the target, while the gamma ray signifies the energy splitting between two energy levels of the hypernucleus with high precision. The analysis shows that the spin-dependent components of the Λ-nucleon force in the nuclear medium are much smaller than those for two interacting nucleons. These observations were interpreted in the form of models in which the interaction between baryons (the Λ and the nucleon) is mediated by the exchange of mesons, and also, more qualitatively, in terms of a more fundamental picture of quark and gluon exchange.

Recently at the AGS a collaboration of several groups was able to produce hypernuclei with positively charged pion (π^+) beams, the experimental signature being the appearance of a positively charged kaon (K^+) in the final state. The observed energy spectrum of the kaon displays a well-defined sequence of peaks, corresponding to the production of bound states of the Λ. Interpretation of the results suggests a depth of about 28 MeV (million electron volts) for the Λ-nucleus potential well, compared with 50–60 MeV for the nucleon-nucleus well depth. In the center of the nucleus the attractive interactions of the Λ provide it with an effective mass of approximately 0.8 of its mass in free space. In contrast to the case of nucleon orbitals, one can describe both deeply bound and surface localized Λ orbitals with

a single value for the effective mass. The observed Λ spectrum provides a particularly clear example of single particle structure in nuclear physics. The hypernuclear experiments with pion beams opened up a new domain of nuclear spectroscopy. For the future, experiments with kaon beams, in which two units of strangeness are deposited in the nucleus, may be strongly exploited. A high-intensity "kaon factory" was proposed for construction at the TRIUMF meson facility at Vancouver, B.C., and was strongly supported by a recommendation of the 1989 Long Range Plan for Nuclear Physics. Such an accelerator would extend experiments in hypernuclear structure to new levels of precision.

—Carl B. Dover

Condensed-matter physics

During the past year physicists made gains in explaining the unsatisfactory electronic behavior seen in certain doped semiconductor alloys, amassed evidence to support a theory explaining the fractional quantized Hall effect, and made the surprising discovery that boron atoms exposed to a clean silicon surface displace the surface atoms to form a subsurface boron layer. From theoretical work came the intriguing suggestion that crystalline solids made of carbon and nitrogen may eventually replace diamond as the hardest of known materials.

Poor conduction in doped semiconductor alloys. The widespread usefulness of semiconductors in electronics derives primarily from the fact that their electrical properties can be tailored by doping. An ultrapure and, therefore, undoped semiconductor is generally an insulator under normal operating conditions and is not useful for most applications. Doping is achieved through incorporation of minute amounts of specific impurities into the bulk of a semiconductor. Depending on the impurity selected, the semiconductor can be made to display either n-type or p-type conductivity. For example, when the compound gallium arsenide (GaAs) is doped with a so-called donor impurity such as silicon, it shows n-type conductivity. A silicon atom is known to preferentially replace a gallium atom in the GaAs crystal lattice. Since silicon has four outer electrons in its valence shell but gallium only three, the extra electron of the silicon impurity is "donated" to the conduction band, thereby making the sample conducting. Similarly GaAs can be doped as a p-type conductor by replacing some gallium atoms with an acceptor impurity such as beryllium (Be), which has only two electrons in its outer valence shell. To satisfy this electron deficit so as to make strong bonds with their nearest neighbor arsenic atoms, the beryllium atoms "accept" electrons from the filled valence band and thereby create positively charged "holes," or electron deficits, that allow a current to flow in the presence of an electric field.

Because the doping of semiconductors has been intensively studied for more than 40 years, it may seem that no surprises or unsolved problems should remain. This is not the case, however. Since the early 1980s scientific knowledge of impurities has expanded remarkably, and many examples of puzzling electronic behavior have been uncovered. For example, GaAs and aluminum arsenide (AlAs) are structurally identical, have a negligible difference in their atomic spacings, and form a continuous series of alloys, which can be represented by the formula $Al_xGa_{1-x}As$ in which x can have any value between 0 and 1 inclusive. Changing the proportions of the elements in the alloy allows the electronic band gap of the system to be tailored over a range of values depending on the application desired. There is, nevertheless, one problem. Even though GaAs can be easily doped as an n-type conductor by incorporating donor impurities, in $Al_xGa_{1-x}As$ alloys the same process leads to "deep-donor" defects when x exceeds 0.22. The "deepness" of a donor or an acceptor refers to its tendency to resist giving up or accepting electrons, and the deep character of the donors in AlGaAs alloys stands in contrast to the case of "shallow donors" in GaAs. The shallow-to-deep transition of the donors in going from GaAs to AlGaAs alloys results in a sharp reduction in the concentration of electrons in the conduction band, significantly lower conductivity, and interference with many potential applications of this system. Exposing AlGaAs to light has been found to restore the high conductivity, but when the light is turned off, the shallow donors decay back into the deep state. The rate of decay is temperature dependent, occurring very rapidly at room temperature and extremely slowly near absolute zero. Consequently, AlGaAs samples exhibit a phenomenon known as persistent photoconductivity, which means simply that at sufficiently low temperature the samples can be made conductive through exposure to light and that the conductivity persists for a long time (as much as a week or more).

The underlying physical mechanism for the differences in the behavior of impurities in GaAs and the very similar AlGaAs alloys has been a subject of intensive research since the late 1970s. The problem is not limited to the AlGaAs system but has similar manifestations in other III-V and II-VI semiconductors; i.e., semiconductors made from elements in groups IIIa and Va or groups IIb and VIa of the periodic table. The shallow-to-deep transition is not restricted to donors but also is seen in acceptors. For example, zinc selenide (ZnSe) is a wide-band-gap II-VI semiconductor of great interest in creating blue-green light-emitting diodes. However, repeated attempts over many years to induce shallow accep-

tors in the compound have been mostly unsuccessful. The expectation that replacing some selenium atoms with atoms of arsenic or phosphorus (P) should lead to shallow acceptor levels has not been realized despite the use of many different growth techniques.

A significant advance in understanding the origin of these problems at the atomic level took place in the past two years. From the time deep donors were first seen in AlGaAs alloys by Bell Laboratories researchers David Lang and Ralph Logan in 1977, it was theorized that their puzzling properties were the result of a very large atomic relaxation (a physical shift of atoms to a state of lower energy) at the site of the donor impurity. In 1978 the researchers suggested that the impurity atom induced a defect consisting of an arsenic vacancy next to it and that the resulting impurity-vacancy complex could easily accommodate the required large atomic displacements in its vicinity that were necessary to explain the experimental data.

A challenge to this point of view came in 1985 through the experimental work of Masashi Mizuta of NEC Laboratory, Japan, and co-workers. In their studies the ordinary, well-behaved shallow donor in GaAs, in which the impurity atom is known from vibrational spectroscopy to have a normal substitutional geometry with no vacancies around it, was made to go into the deep state by the application of hydrostatic pressure. This result made it difficult to believe that the deep donors were the result of an impurity-vacancy complex. The experimenters concluded that the deep donors must arise from isolated substitutional donors. A model incorporating the new perspective and capable of explaining the properties of these deep donors was put forward in 1988–89 by James Chadi and Kee Joo Chang of the Xerox Palo Alto (Calif.) Research Center. From quantum mechanical calculations the appearance of the deep donor was predicted to be associated with a lattice instability at the site of the donor impurity atom, which caused the atom to break one of its four bonds with its nearest neighbors. The situation for a silicon impurity occupying a gallium site is shown in Figure 1. It was proposed that the impurity gives shallow levels when it is on the fourfold site (1a) but that the level becomes deep when the silicon atom moves off-center into an interstitial position (1b). This implies that the energetically stable state of the silicon impurity is the broken-bond configuration in AlGaAs alloys having an aluminum concentration greater than 22%. Interestingly, the model shows that an isolated impurity, by itself, can undergo a large lattice relaxation and that this phenomenon is an intrinsic property that cannot be modified easily. Heretofore such a possibility had been thought unlikely.

The same ideas also were applied to the problem of p-type doping of ZnSe. In this case, too, a large

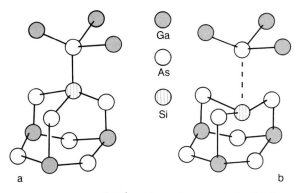

Figure 1. An atom of Si occupies a Ga atom site in the GaAs lattice. A new model proposes that the deep-donor state occurs when the Si impurity shifts from its fourfold-bond position (a) to an interstitial, broken-bond position (b).

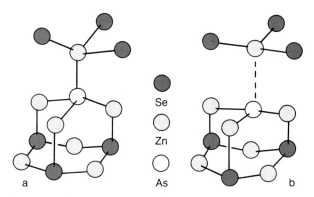

Figure 2. When an As atom replaces an Se atom in ZnSe, theory predicts an atomic relaxation (from a to b) similar to that in Figure 1. In this case, however, both the As impurity and a neighboring Zn move to create the broken bond.

lattice relaxation leading to a shallow-to-deep transition of the acceptor level was predicted to occur as a result of a large atomic relaxation at the impurity site. The relaxations for ZnSe are larger than those in AlGaAs in that both the acceptor and a nearest neighbor zinc atom move significantly away from their expected positions. The situation for an arsenic impurity replacing a selenium atom is shown in Figure 2. For ZnSe the broken-bond geometry in 2b, and not the normal fourfold coordinated substitutional configuration, corresponds to the lower energy state in p-type samples. The theoretical results strongly indicate that these atomic relaxations will make it very difficult, regardless of the growth technique employed, to obtain low-resistivity (or high-conductivity) ZnSe through doping with As. This prediction is consistent with a 30-year failure to do so.

The new insight gained in these studies may lead to the understanding of a number of other problems in semiconductor physics. Much more remains to be done to test the new ideas generated in the past year.

Harder than diamond? Diamond always has been considered the hardest substance in the world, and it sets the standard for absolute hardness. This view was challenged by recent theoretical work at the University of California at Berkeley. On the basis of first-principles quantum mechanical calculations, Amy Liu and Marvin L. Cohen suggested that a crystalline material made out of carbon and nitrogen atoms may have a hardness approaching and possibly surpassing that of diamond. Over the past decade the first-principles approach has proved highly successful in providing accurate information on the bulk properties of many semiconductors. The hardness of a material is inversely proportional to its compressibility and is related to a quantity called the bulk modulus. The bulk modulus can be predicted theoretically by using a physical law that relates it to the variations in the total energy of a system as

a function of its volume. The total-energy variations are determined by the strength, density, and compressibility of the chemical bonds. In particular, the bulk moduli of many known compounds have been obtained to an accuracy of 95% or better. In their theoretical analysis Liu and Cohen applied the same method to predict the bulk modulus of a material that does not yet exist.

The proposed material is beta-C_3N_4, which is structurally and compositionally very similar to the existing compound beta-Si_3N_4. In the latter structure every silicon atom is tetrahedrally bonded to four nitrogen (N) atoms, and every nitrogen atom is bonded to three silicon atoms. With the known beta-Si_3N_4 structure as a base, carbon (C) was substituted for silicon, and the C-N atomic separations were scaled by the ratio of the Si-N to the C-N bond lengths. At this point, first-principles total-energy-minimization calculations were carried out to optimize further the atomic coordinates and determine the equilibrium atomic positions of this new material. The bulk moduli of both beta-Si_3N_4 and beta-C_3N_4 were calculated. The predicted value of the modulus for beta-Si_3N_4 is 2.65 megabars (Mbar), compared with the experimental value of 2.56 Mbar. For beta-C_3N_4 the predicted value is 4.27 Mbar, which is very close to the highest known value of 4.43 Mbar for diamond.

The motivation for suggesting C_3N_4 as a candidate for a superhard material was based on the important observation that the bulk modulus in nearly all group IV, III-V, and II—VI semiconductors having diamond or zinc blende structures increases as the nearest neighbor bond length shortens. Since the C-N bond length is significantly shorter (by about 5%) than the C-C value for diamond, this relation suggests that, in principle, materials with a significantly higher bulk modulus than diamond are possible. In the case of C_3N_4, the bulk modulus falls slightly short of that for diamond even though the individual C-N bonds are stronger than the C-C bonds in diamond. The reason is that because of the threefold coordination of N atoms in C_3N_4, there are fewer bonds to resist deformations. In fact, the average coordination of atoms in C_3N_4 is 3.43, compared with 4 in diamond. The possibility that other covalently bonded networks of C and N (perhaps including some other atoms) may have a higher average coordination of atoms and a higher bulk modulus is exciting and undoubtedly will be pursued in the future. Such superstrong materials can have important technological applications in high-temperature and high-strain environments, such as in engine components and cutting and drilling tools. In early 1990 intensive work at the University of California at Berkeley to synthesize beta-C_3N_4 was in progress. Eugene Haller succeeded in growing a crystalline C-N compound on a silicon substrate, and X-ray tests for determining the exact crystalline structure were under way. Preliminary results seemed to confirm the theoretical predictions for key structural parameters of beta-C_3N_4.

Surface doping of silicon with boron. Chemical adsorption, or chemisorption, is a process in which weak chemical bonds are formed between individual atoms or molecules and a solid surface. For many years physicists have studied the chemisorption of the group III elements boron, aluminum, gallium, and indium on the surface of silicon. All these elements create an ordered arrangement at the surface with a periodicity corresponding to a one-third monolayer coverage on the silicon surface atoms. During the past year, however, it was discovered that boron behaves differently from the other three group III elements in that the periodicity corresponds to that of adatoms (adsorbed atoms) of silicon rather than of boron. Evidence from three independent experimental groups indicates that the addition of boron to the surface leads to its incorporation not over the surface but in the second layer of atoms below the surface. In this process boron atoms substitute for silicon atoms and push them out to the surface layer, where they create a reconstructed surface of silicon adatoms. The peculiar behavior of boron was analyzed and shown to be a result of its smaller covalent radius compared with that of silicon. In contrast, the other three group III elements have covalent radii larger than that of silicon, and their preferred state is over hollow sites above the surface where they bond to three silicon atoms.

The importance of the results for boron lies in the possibility of obtaining surface doping with a highly ordered arrangement of the dopant atoms. If additional silicon can be grown on top of the boron-doped surface without affecting the subsurface borons, then one can achieve bulk doping of silicon with an ordered array of the dopant atoms. The advantage, compared with the normal case of random-site dop-

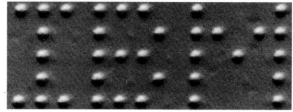

IBM physicists used a scanning tunneling microscope to position individual xenon atoms on a nickel single-crystal surface and then to image the pattern. The achievement suggested the potential for such future applications as building custom-made molecules atom by atom, altering individual molecules, and storing data on an atomic scale.

ing, is that it should allow carriers of electric current to move more freely since the scattering of carriers by disordered atoms is eliminated. Experimental work by R.L. Headrick of AT&T Bell Laboratories, Murray Hill, N.J., and co-workers showed that overgrowth of silicon indeed can be achieved without disturbing the subsurface boron atoms. These results open up new possibilities and potential applications for the bulk doping of silicon.

Fractional charge of quasiparticles. The Hall effect is observed when a magnetic field is applied in a direction normal (perpendicular) to a current flowing in a two-dimensional plane. The field gives rise to a Hall voltage (V), which for classical conduction on a macroscopic scale is proportional to the product of the magnetic field (H) and the current (I). The Hall resistance (R), given by the ratio V/I, thus is proportional to H in this classical regime. In the quantum regime a plot of R versus H shows plateaus where resistance is independent of the magnetic field and, to very high accuracy, is equal to h/ve^2, in which h is Planck's constant, e is the unit charge of the electron, and v is an integer or a rational fraction p/q where q is ordinarily odd; e.g., v has the values $\frac{1}{3}$, $\frac{2}{3}$, $\frac{2}{5}$, and so on. (See *1990 Yearbook of Science and the Future* Year in Review: PHYSICS: *Condensed-matter physics.*) An elegant theory by Robert Laughlin of Stanford University suggests that in the fractional quantized Hall regime, conduction involves the movement of particlelike excitations, called quasiparticles, through a "liquid" of condensed electrons and that the charges of the quasiparticles are nonintegral and equal to $\pm e/q$. Several new experiments during the past year corroborated this prediction of the theory and confirmed a previous experimental result in 1988. Together they strongly support the fractional-charge hypothesis for the quasiparticles involved in the fractional quantized Hall effect.

—D.J. Chadi

See also Feature Articles: THE PHYSICS OF THRILL RIDES; "SMART" MATERIALS: A REVOLUTION IN TECHNOLOGY.

Psychology

Psychology continued to grow during the past year, especially as a health-related profession. Health activities were a major factor in the increase in employed psychologists: professional services were given as their primary work by 40% of doctoral psychologists, up from 25% 10 years earlier.

Development. All behavioral and experiential functions have a developmental history, and in many cases that history contains the key to understanding them. Appreciation of this proposition was one reason for the remarkably accelerated interest in developmental psychology that recently became evident, particularly with respect to cognitive processes.

A major new theoretical approach to cognitive development was advanced by psychologist C.J. Brainerd of the University of Arizona. Called "fuzzy-trace theory," this approach centers on memory for *gist*, contrasted with *verbatim* memory, which is the typical target of classroom efforts. Brainerd offered his concept as an alternative to the two most comprehensive theoretical approaches in the field: the theory of Swiss psychologist Jean Piaget that the mind of a child evolves through a series of set stages to adulthood, and the theory of information processing, both of which he regarded as limited if not incorrect in certain basic features.

Fuzzy-trace theory replaces the deductive logicism of Piagetian theory and the computerlike functions of information processing with an experimentally based concept of intuition. The term *fuzzy trace* was taken from mathematics, where it similarly emphasizes creativity and imagination. The theory was fully described during the year in a paper by Brainerd and his main collaborator, V.F. Reyna. Entitled "The Gist is the Grist: Fuzzy-Trace Theory and the New Intuitionism," the paper was prepared for a special issue of *Development Review*.

The gist of fuzzy-trace theory may be best expressed in the author's own words: "We view human cognition, first and foremost, as a system in which inferences are drawn by constructively processing vague, gist-like representations (fuzzy traces), as well as a system in which previously encoded information is remembered by reconstructively processing these same impoverished representations."

Another, somewhat similar, approach to cognitive development was offered by Harvard University psychologist Jerome Bruner at the biennial meetings of the Society for Research in Child Development. Bruner pointed out that the major cognitive activity of all people is the extraction of meaning from everyday life experiences. He also held that in order to understand development, psychologists must look closely at everyday life and not concentrate simply on experimentally manipulated behaviors.

Psychologist Paul Ekman of the University of California at San Francisco published a book on childhood deception, *Why Kids Lie*. Ekman reported that children invent as many different kinds of lies as adults and stressed that it is important for adults to recognize the differences among kinds of lies and to act accordingly. He cited an early study in England that found eventual convictions for theft in one-third of the children identified as chronic liars by their parents. However, parents were urged to handle lying with caution, because harsh punishment seems to increase rather than reduce it.

Setting a good example by scrupulous avoidance of lies, even the simplest "white" variety, was seen by Ekman as the most important single parental lie-prevention step. For older children family discussions of prominent cases of lying in news stories was also suggested as a means of instilling respect for truthfulness.

U.S. educators have for some time been disheartened by the clear superiority of Asian schoolchildren, especially in mathematics. During the past year a research team headed by psychologist Harold Stevenson of the University of Michigan reported on its intensive comparison of the mathematical skills of first- and fifth-grade students in Beijing (Peking) and Chicago. The results provided a strong confirmation of the superiority of the Chinese children. For first graders the mean scores did not overlap. For fifth graders only a single Chicago school (of the 20 studied, with all socioeconomic levels represented) averaged as high as the lowest Beijing school. Chinese students were found to be both faster and more accurate in their computations.

Nevertheless, U.S. children generally said that they liked math and were pleased with their performance, as were their parents. Stevenson attributed the latter fact to low standards. For example, U.S. parents stated that they would be satisfied with achievement scores a few points above the class average, while Chinese parents wanted to see their children's scores in the 90s (on a 70–100 passing scale). Stevenson suggested that this unrealistically high level of approval of essentially mediocre performance by American parents makes it difficult to work for necessary modifications in teaching practices.

Important differences were also found in teachers' attitudes. U.S. teachers selected sensitivity to individual differences as the most important attribute for a teacher, while Chinese teachers selected the ability to make clear explanations. When the research team members, including both Chinese and U.S. participants, looked closely at classroom activities, they found that Chinese teachers were, in fact, more effective in explaining math functions than their American counterparts. U.S. children were more likely to be given a sheet of problems and left alone to solve them, and their teachers tended to give more convoluted and even misleading instructions.

Memory. For the past several years some memory researchers have been insisting that improvements be made in ecological validity—or, in simple language, that everyday-life experiences replace laboratory conditions in memory research. The most recent expression of this position was in the 1988 book *Remembering Reconsidered: Ecological and Traditional Approaches to the Study of Memory,* edited by Ulric Neisser and Eugene Winograd of Emory University, Atlanta, Ga. During the past year an unusually strong attack on this position was published in *American Psychologist* (September 1989) by Yale University psychologists Mahzarin R. Banaje and Robert G. Crowder. They reviewed reported memory research over the past decade for evidence supporting the claims that significant new discoveries could be made if only more attention were paid to the "real world." They found no new theories, principles of memory, or new methods of data collection. They concluded that the everyday-life movement was "largely bankrupt" and expressed their concern that the unjustified claims, so appealing to many persons both inside and outside the field of psychology, might compromise what they saw as the genuine achievements of traditional memory research.

Efforts by the Chinese government to change the memories of citizens who witnessed the military crushing of the student protests at Tiananmen (T'ien-an-men) Square in June 1989 aroused renewed interest in research on this problem. Psychologist Elizabeth Loftus of the University of Washington, a leading researcher on experimental manipulations of memory, observed during the past year that the methods being used by the Chinese government are those that research has shown to be effective (for example, repeated presentation of slanted and misleading television documentaries).

Loftus also reported the results of a large study of individual differences in susceptibility to memory distortion. Her subjects were nearly 2,000 visitors to the Exploratorium, a science museum in San Francisco. They watched a one-minute film about a political rally showing a man first threatened by people and then attacked by a blue-jacketed man. The subjects then proceeded to walk through the science exhibits, after which they were requested to sit down at a computer keyboard and answer yes or no to 10 questions about the film clip they had watched. Selected questions contained false information, such as reference to the "white-jacketed" attacker.

Loftus found a number of interesting individual differences in her "misinformation effect"—defined as the degree to which the false information was accepted. Perhaps the most important finding was the relatively greater susceptibility to misinforma-

tion in young and old subjects; the group aged 26–35 was clearly the most resistant. Some suggestive occupational differences were also noted. For example, subjects who identified themselves as artists or architects were very accurate when not fed misinformation but were very susceptible to it. Although not usually susceptible to misinformation, the police officers and lawyers who were tested ranked in the lower ranges of accuracy.

The relatively high accuracy scores achieved by college students confirmed the results of many earlier studies raising a question about the common practice of depending so much on these readily available—but in certain respects atypical—subjects for behavioral research in universities. This is the sort of question that has helped to energize the various "everyday-life" arguments discussed above.

Another memory problem in which ecological validity is an active issue is the credibility of children's testimony, particularly in cases involving accusations of sexual abuse. A conference was convened during the year at Cornell University, Ithaca, N.Y., to discuss this problem; it was the first such gathering of psychologists working on the issue, and the hope was that some kind of provisional consensus could be reached. In light of the great diversity of research attitudes and procedures and the complexity of the real-life problem, that proved to be impossible. Nevertheless, some clarification of the issues was achieved.

Studies with some aspects of real-life sex-abuse scenarios—such as a man who wore a "funny mask," took pictures, and played "tickling games"—were reported by Gail Goodman of the State University of New York at Buffalo. Her results generally indicated highly accurate testimony and resistance to misinformation by the children. These findings were, however, vigorously questioned. The major objection was that the children had not been urged to dissemble, as they typically are in the real-life situations.

An experimental manipulation of suggestibility, also within an ecologically valid setting, was reported by Allison Clarke-Stewart of the University of California at Irvine. She found that directly misleading suggestions, even when gently offered, had strong effects on the accuracy of the children's testimony; one-fourth of the subjects answered incorrectly after the first such suggestion, and all but one did so by the end of the second session in which such suggestions were made.

This sampling of results reported at the Cornell conference indicated the difficulties researchers on this problem have in giving legal authorities any kind of definitive propositions with general and immediate applicability. However, they also suggested the viability of the research efforts now under way and permitted some optimism about future developments.

Clinical psychology. One of the most important—and hotly contested—issues in the health field is the role that personality attributes play in physical disorders, such as cancer and heart disease. By far the most dramatic claims thus far made for such a relationship have been advanced by a Yugoslav psychologist, Ronald Grossarth-Maticek. Two features of Grossarth-Maticek's work account for the great amount of attention it has recently been accorded: (1) the long-term follow-up of individuals whose personality profiles had been determined at the start of the study and (2) the spectacular results obtained, indicating a strong association of personality type and disease.

Grossarth-Maticek's diagnostic technique was relatively simple. He used either a short questionnaire or a longer personal interview to place each individual studied into one of four health types: (1) cancer-prone, (2) heart disease-prone, (3) healthy with some unconventionality, and (4) healthy. Cancer-proneness was held to be related to repressed emotions and feelings of helplessness, and heart disease-proneness to the now generally accepted Type A personality characteristics of hostility and aggression. (It should be noted that the latter diagnostic effort was made by Grossarth-Maticek in the 1960s, long before researchers narrowed the Type A attribute list to these two features.)

Three major studies were conducted, the first one starting in the 1960s in Yugoslavia and the latter two carried out in Heidelberg, West Germany. The results were strikingly in accord with predictions. For example, approximately 50% of the type 1 cases died of cancer within 10 years, compared with fewer than 10% in that group who died of heart disease or stroke. About one-third of the type 2 cases died of heart disease or stroke, and one-fifth died from cancer. Few of the type 3 or 4 individuals died within 10 years.

Grossarth-Maticek collaborated with some British and U.S. psychologists in later studies, most notably with University of London psychologist Hans J. Eysenck. Their collaboration focused on attempts to use behavior therapy to teach cancer-prone and heart disease-prone individuals to be more like healthy individuals. Some of their results were as dramatic as those in the original diagnostic studies described above. For example, in one study of 100 individuals diagnosed as cancer-prone on the basis of the short questionnaire, 45 of the 50 who received therapy were still alive after 13 years, compared with only 19 of 50 in the original no-therapy group.

A trip to West Germany in 1987 by a group of U.S. psychologists led to no definitive conclusions concerning Grossarth-Maticek's research. Some minor inconsistencies in the data were uncovered, and some technical questions of a statistical nature were

raised, but the visitors neither rejected nor accepted the results on the basis of their on-the-spot review. Nevertheless, this research must be regarded as unparalleled in its scope (10-year follow-ups after initial diagnosis are not common in the health field), and the results that have been reported cry out for adequate replication.

Research reported during the year by Stanford University psychologist David Spiegel provided an independent confirmation of the way in which participation in group therapy not only can improve the quality of life but also can extend its duration in seriously ill patients. Spiegel studied 86 older women with advanced breast cancer. Compared with patients who did not receive therapy, the women who did showed considerably fewer "maladaptive" coping behaviors and mood disturbances and lived an average of 18 months longer. This study was regarded as a breakthrough by both cancer specialists and clinical psychologists; the results seemed especially impressive because the researchers initially had negative expectations.

An interesting and potentially extremely important message to psychologists and other health workers was delivered by psychologist Fred Frese in a symposium at the 1989 meetings of the American Psychological Association. Frese told the story of his own successful career in clinical psychology "in spite of the fact that my brain episodically functions in a schizophrenic manner." Frese's first mental difficulty occurred at the age of 26 when he was serving as a U.S. Marine Corps officer. He was diagnosed as a paranoid schizophrenic. Nevertheless, over the following 26 years he earned three graduate degrees and worked steadily both as a psychologist and as a hospital administrator in the Ohio Department of Mental Health.

Frese gave a frank, detailed description of how he has managed to handle his psychotic episodes. He compared the world of the psychotic person to the visit of a normal person to a foreign country with its strange language and customs. He described how he was able to take advantage of personal resources, such as an understanding wife, to cope successfully with his periodic disturbances.

This kind of testimony from one who has seen at first hand both sides of the relationship between the psychotic patient and the therapist is unique. Frese's insights should help to break down the barriers that have so long existed between psychotic individuals and those whom he identified as "chronically normal people."

—Melvin H. Marx

International Developments. Within Europe 1992 is the year when many barriers are to be abolished within the European Communities (EC). In preparation for this event a directive of the European Commission was passed into law ensuring the mutual recognition of professional qualifications between member states of the EC. The effect of this legislation will be to facilitate the free movement of psychologists from the country in which they obtained their professional qualifications to work in other countries within the EC. Simultaneously, within many countries the profession of psychology was increasingly being defined within a framework of law. For example, on Feb. 18, 1989, in Italy the Chamber of Deputies enacted legislation that provides significant legal protection to psychology as a profession. Minimum standards were established for training: a period of five years of university education followed by advanced studies of three or four years with particular emphasis on practical training. One feature of this law was that the practice of psychotherapy was restricted to medical or psychology graduates who have taken an additional four-year training in psychotherapy. Within the United Kingdom the British Psychological Society published its first Register of Chartered Psychologists, accompanied by a campaign to inform members of the public that under the provisions whereby professions are recognized within the U.K., only properly qualified psychologists who are in good standing within their profession may use the title Chartered Psychologist once they have had their names entered on the register.

Both the International Union of Psychological Science and the International Social Science Council during the past year were undertaking major programs that focused on the problems of global change. Human activities that lead to large-scale global change were being considered at many levels. Any steps that can be taken, for example, to change individual attitudes and behavior in relation to waste disposal will have important practical consequences. However, environmental problems are typically regarded by governments as technical rather than behavioral. One of the tasks for psychologists has been to convince others that more cost-effective solutions often may be found through concentrating on understanding and then changing the way people behave rather than through focusing on what may be expensive technological solutions.

Research in cognitive psychology has shown biasing effects in which people tend to succumb to wishful thinking. Good outcomes are seen as more probable than bad ones. Thus, if environmental changes such as pollution are slow and gradual and their influences are delayed, many people may ignore them. If such responses are understood and then ways of counteracting their effects are found, real improvements in the prospects for humankind can be forthcoming.

—Colin V. Newman

Space exploration

An active year in space was marked by six missions of the space shuttle, space walks around the manned Soviet station, the launch of a new probe to Jupiter, and a dramatic encounter with Neptune.

Manned flight

The past year was a busy one for manned flight. In addition to launching several space shuttles, the United States began planning manned missions to the Moon and Mars. The Soviet Union continued to center most of its activity on its manned space station but also revealed plans for a manned flight to the Moon.

Space shuttle. The space shuttle continued to be the center of the U.S. manned flight program during the past year. The first of the year's missions, STS-29 (*Discovery*, March 13–18, 1989), carried a Tracking and Data Relay Satellite (TDRS-D) similar to that launched on the STS-26 mission in 1988 and a test model of a heat pipe radiator for the planned U.S. space station. Commander Michael Coats, pilot John Blaha, and mission specialists James Bagian, James Buchli, and Robert Springer made up the crew.

STS-30 (*Atlantis*, May 4–8) reopened U.S. planetary exploration when it launched the Magellan radar mapper to Venus. The mission was crewed by commander David Walker, pilot Ronald Grabe, and mission specialists Norman Thagard, Mary Cleave, and Mark Lee.

STS-28 (*Columbia*, August 8–13) reportedly deployed a large KH-12 reconnaissance satellite and

Marsha Ivins uses an ultrasonic imaging system to conduct medical tests on David Low while Bonnie Dunbar takes notes during the 11-day flight of the space shuttle Columbia *in January 1990.*

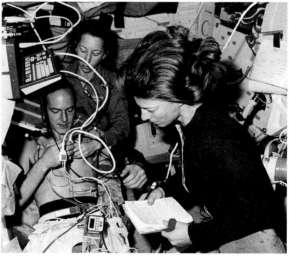

NASA

The Long Duration Exposure Facility (LDEF) unmanned satellite is retrieved by the remote manipulator system on board the space shuttle Columbia in January 1990. The LDEF, in orbit since 1984, carried materials that were to be analyzed for their reactions to the space environment. The shining object in the upper left of the photograph is the Sun.

a smaller electronic "ferret" satellite. The crew comprised commander Brewster Shaw, pilot Richard Richards, and mission specialists David Leestma, James Adamson, and Mark Brown. *Aviation Week & Space Technology* magazine later reported that a short circuit generated some sparks and smoke in the cabin but that there was no serious danger to the crew.

The STS-34 mission (*Atlantis*, October 18–23) carried the Galileo space probe, destined for Jupiter by way of Venus. Commander Don Williams, pilot Michael McCulley, and mission specialists Shannon Lucid, Ellen Baker, and Franklin Chang-Diaz made up the crew. The launch had been scheduled to take place on October 12, the opening of the "window" for Galileo's journey to Jupiter, but a faulty controller on one of the main engines forced a five-day hold. Bad weather near the shuttle landing facility forced another day's delay on October 17, but when it finally took place on October 18 the launch was flawless. Once in orbit, the crew deployed Galileo as scheduled and then turned to a number of secondary experiments, including one designed to monitor ozone depletion in the upper atmosphere and one to measure the concentration and distribution of growth hormone in plants. Antinuclear protesters tried to block the launch because Galileo was carrying electricity generators powered by the heat of decaying plutonium. Fearing that a *Challenger*-like mishap would spew plutonium across central Florida or into the atmosphere, they sued the National Aeronautics and Space Administration (NASA) to halt the launch. Federal courts ruled that NASA was taking proper precautions and allowed the launch to continue. A promised sit-in at the launch pad was called off in favor of a demonstration at the visitor center.

STS-33 (*Discovery*, November 22–27) launched a secret strategic reconnaissance satellite known as Magnum. The crew comprised commander Frederick Gregory, pilot John Blaha, and mission specialists Story Musgrave, Kathryn Thornton, and Manley Carter. Only a brief hold marred the otherwise smooth countdown to a rare nighttime launch. The mission also set a record altitude for the shuttle of 559 km (347 mi).

NASA scheduled nine shuttle missions for 1990. Their payloads were to include two of the Great Observatories for Space Astrophysics (the Hubble Space Telescope and the Gamma Ray Observatory), three Spacelab missions (ASTRO ultraviolet telescopes, Spacelab Life Sciences-1, and International Microgravity Laboratory), the Ulysses solar polar probe, and two Department of Defense missions.

The first mission of 1990 deployed one satellite and recovered another. STS-32 (*Columbia*, January 9–20) was delayed from December first by problems in completing Launch Pad 39A and then by the weather. The crew consisted of commander Daniel Brandenstein, pilot James Wetherbee, and mission specialists Bonnie Dunbar, David Low, and Marsha Ivins. Soon after launch the shuttle deployed a communications satellite. The next four days were spent allowing the shuttle to catch up with the Long Duration Exposure Facility (LDEF), which had been placed in orbit in 1984. LDEF carried samples of various materials being evaluated for their reaction to the space environment. It was to be retrieved in late 1984, but schedule problems and then the *Challenger* tragedy postponed the attempt. In 1989 NASA predicted that LDEF would reenter the atmosphere some time in early 1990. After a textbook approach and retrieval of the satellite by the shuttle, the crew spent about four hours photographing LDEF to start documenting the long-term effects on the materials. The long-term effects on humans were studied, too, with extensive medical experiments on human

The Soviet manned spacecraft Soyuz TM-8 is launched from the Baikonur Cosmodrome in central Asia on September 6 for a rendezvous with the Soviet space station Mir. Aboard the Soyuz spacecraft were cosmonauts Aleksandr Viktorenko and Aleksandr Serebrov. A problem with the craft's guidance system forced them to dock with Mir manually.

adaptation. Reentry was delayed a day by fog at the landing site, and the mission lasted a record 11 days.

Work on successors to the shuttle continued. The National Aerospace Plane (NASP) survived severe budget problems and difficulties in shaping its management. In late 1989 the major contractors involved in studying NASP formed a consortium to assure its continued development. Weight problems led the European Space Agency to redesign its Hermes shuttlecraft so that the resource module would be jettisoned before reentry. Full-scale development was scheduled to be authorized in 1990 and was expected to lead to a first unmanned launch in 1998.

The Soviet space shuttle, *Buran* ("blizzard"), continued to be grounded for lack of funding and computer software. The major activity for *Buran* during the year seemed to be its June visit to the Paris Air Show, where it was flown atop its An-225 carrier jet. This was the first opportunity that most Western observers had to see the spacecraft. Its next unmanned flight was set for 1991 and its first manned launch for 1992. The Soviets conceded that *Buran* and its launcher, *Energia*, were designed for a more ambitious program that had since been scaled back.

Space station. On April 27, 1989, Aleksandr Volkov, Sergey Krikalev, and Valery Polyakov returned from the Soviet space station *Mir*. Volkov and Krikalev, together with French cosmonaut Jean-Loup Chrétien, had been launched to *Mir* aboard Soyuz TM-7 on Nov. 28, 1988. (Polyakov had been launched earlier). Chrétien had returned Dec. 21, 1988, with Vladimir Titov and Musa Manarov, who completed the first yearlong stay in space. For the first time in two years *Mir* was unmanned for several months, leading to speculation that it had been abandoned. The Soviets were in fact resolving technical and management problems.

On September 6 the Soviets returned to *Mir* with the Soyuz TM-8 spacecraft carrying Aleksandr Viktorenko and Aleksandr Serebrov. The two had to resort to a manual docking after a guidance system problem. An early onboard task was to replace *Mir*'s main batteries and computer memory. A new series of unmanned supply craft was introduced with the launch on August 3 of Progress M1; it was separated from *Mir* on December 1. On November 26 the Kvant 2 module (also called Module D or the Reequipment Module) was launched. After some difficulties with the rendezvous computer, it was docked to *Mir* on December 6 and then transferred by a robot arm to a side port. It carried the Icarus "space motorcycle" (comparable to NASA's manned maneuvering unit) and an enlarged airlock to allow cosmonauts to conduct more ambitious space walks. On December 12 Viktorenko and Serebrov reboarded TM-8 to move it from the aft docking port to the forward one. On Dec. 20, 1989, the Progress M2 vehicle was

Soviet cosmonauts Aleksandr Viktorenko (left) and Aleksandr Serebrov are welcomed back to Earth on Feb. 19, 1990, after spending 5¹/₂ months performing research on board the Soviet space station Mir.

launched to *Mir*, with which it docked on December 22. It carried supplies and experiments, including a crystal-growth system developed by a U.S. firm.

Several space walks were conducted around the station to improve its operations. On February 1 Serebrov gave the Icarus unit the first of two flight tests. He moved into space as far as 30 m (100 feet) away from *Mir* while remaining tethered to it. Anatoly Solovyov and Aleksandr Balandin were launched on Soyuz TM-9 on February 11 and soon docked with *Mir;* Viktorenko and Serebrov returned aboard TM-8 on February 19.

In the spring of 1990 a Technology Module carrying advanced materials and life sciences equipment was to be launched to join *Mir*. With the two modules plus Soyuz and Progress spacecraft docked, the *Mir* complex would weigh almost 91,000 kg (200,-000 lb), about half the weight of the planned U.S. space station *Freedom*. Another two modules were to be added in the mid- to late 1990s.

An older Soviet station, Salyut 7, was expected to reenter the atmosphere about 1993–94, and the Soviets wanted to avoid the risks and embarrassment that the U.S. suffered when Skylab broke apart and crashed to the Earth in 1979. Soviet officials were considering docking a Soyuz or Progress spacecraft with Salyut 7 and firing thrusters in order to control reentry over open ocean. The extent of financial woes in the Soviet space program was highlighted by the sale for $10 million of *Mir*'s backup unit to a Japanese trading company after the Soviets displayed it in that nation.

The U.S. space station went through an intense reassessment phase as NASA tried to find components that could be substituted or eliminated in order to meet drastic budget cuts expected from Congress. The schedule called for the station's first element to be launched in March 1995 and the last in Au-

gust 1999. Juggling of launch assignments within that timetable postponed the European and Japanese modules by a year, and proposals to complete them earlier would leave the U.S. laboratory inactive until enough solar panels were attached to power the station fully. The Europeans in particular warned that unilateral actions by the U.S. could jeopardize future ventures.

Within NASA there were other warnings that program changes were curtailing the station's usefulness as a research facility. In early 1990 NASA separated the Earth Observing System and its polar-orbit platforms from the space station program in an apparent attempt to reduce costs and streamline management. At the same time, plans for a privately funded Commercially Developed Space Facility were all but killed when the National Research Council found "no compelling" reasons for it despite a 1988 effort by U.S. Pres. Ronald Reagan to require that part of NASA's research be carried out aboard it.

The Moon and Mars. Returning to the Moon and pressing onward to Mars was endorsed by U.S. Pres. George Bush in remarks delivered commemorating the 20th anniversary of the Apollo 11 first manned landing on the Moon. Following Bush's direction at the Apollo 11 anniversary, NASA conducted a 90-day study to outline several options for the Moon/Mars Initiative to reestablish U.S. preeminence in space. These were reported to the National Space Council. The first option outlined by the study would establish a base on the Moon by the year 2001 and use it to develop techniques for going to Mars by 2018. Other options would put the first human visit to Mars at 2011 and the building of a permanent Mars outpost by 2027.

The Soviets revealed details of their own manned lunar program, which they had denied existed for almost two decades. As Western experts had earlier claimed, various Soviet officials confirmed that their manned lunar effort had faltered for want of a launch vehicle comparable to the U.S. Saturn V. During the year visiting U.S. scientists were given an impromptu viewing of mock-ups of a lander that would have carried one cosmonaut to the surface of the Moon while another stayed in orbit.

Astronauts. NASA received new leadership with the appointment of Richard Truly as administrator, the first astronaut to reach that post. Two other former astronauts were appointed to high positions— William Lenoir as associate administrator for space stations and Robert Crippen as director of the National Space Transportation System. Astronaut S. David Griggs (who was assigned to the upcoming STS-33 mission) was killed while rehearsing aerobatics for an air show.

NASA selected 23 new astronaut candidates for the space shuttle program from among 1,945 qualified applicants, 106 of whom were interviewed. The group comprised 7 pilot candidates and 16 mission specialist candidates, including 11 civilians and 12 military officers; five were women, including the first female pilot candidate.

Japanese, British, and Austrian citizens were given a chance to take a trip to the Soviets' *Mir*. In response, the Tokyo Broadcasting System in March 1989 signed a $20 million contract with Glavkosmos to launch one of their newspersons to the space station in 1991. This caused a furor among Soviet journalists, who finally persuaded the Soviet government to fly one of them to *Mir* in November 1990.

In Britain, Antequera Ltd. was formed to select a Briton for a trip into space on April 12, 1991, the 30th anniversary of Yury Gagarin's first manned space flight. The £16 million cost of "Project Juno" was to be covered by various merchandising arrangements. Two finalists selected from among 16,000 applicants in November were Timothy Mace, a Royal Army Air Corps helicopter pilot, and Helen Sharman, a confectionery research technologist. Two Austrians—Klemens Lothaller, an anesthesiologist, and Franz Fibeck, an electrical engineer—were selected to train for the *Mir* mission in 1991.

Space probes

The launching of a new U.S. probe to Jupiter and an encounter with Neptune were highlights of the past year. The Soviets planned a mission to Mars.

Venus. The first planetary encounter of 1990 was the flyby of Venus by the Galileo spacecraft using the gravitational field of Venus to "crank" the spacecraft outward to Jupiter. Galileo sped past the planet on February 10 at an altitude of only 16,139 km (10,024 mi). The spacecraft's instruments took pictures and obtained other data during the flyby, but these

were not expected to be available until late October, when Galileo would be close enough to the Earth to transmit the data with its low-gain antenna.

A more aggressive exploration of Venus was scheduled to begin when the Magellan spacecraft started orbiting the planet in August 1990. The spacecraft— built largely of spare parts from the Voyager and Galileo programs—was launched on May 4, 1989, by the space shuttle. Magellan was designed to use its radar to peer through the clouds covering Venus and produce detailed maps of the planet's surface. Although such mapping had been conducted before, the resolution from Magellan was expected to be much greater than it had been previously and thus was expected to yield important clues about the formation of Venus and whether plate tectonics (continental drift) is an active phenomenon on the planet.

During Magellan's long cruise to Venus, flight controllers grappled with a number of minor problems. Soon after launch they noted that the temperatures on Magellan's main thrusters were higher than predicted, although within limits. Spurious star scanner signals at times prevented controllers from receiving data needed to keep the navigational system accurate. NASA called these nuisances but said that a "software filter" as well as operations changes would be required for preventing problems during the mapping phase around Venus. An erratic gyroscope that was causing excessive drift in the attitude-control system was switched off, thus reducing the backup capability in that system. The problem appeared to be in a bearing, and engineers believed that the gyroscope could be reactivated if needed.

The Sun took its toll on the solar panels that power the spacecraft as solar flares eroded their output by more than 11%. Intense solar activity had been anticipated, however, and the panels were designed to operate with a loss as great as 35%.

A major problem arose on December 31 when onboard computers detected an error in the privileged memory section. The command system switched to its backup unit, which took control to make sure that the solar panels were properly aligned and that the medium-gain antenna was pointed to Earth, and then canceled the normal cruise activities. A tiny amount of corrosion in the main memory was suspected as the cause—rather than radiation from solar flares— and engineers altered the spacecraft's software to avoid using that block of memory. The spacecraft resumed normal operations on January 18.

Moon. Japan launched the first probe to be sent to the Earth's moon since the Soviet Union's Luna 24 in 1976. It was only the second Japanese mission to another planetary body (a small probe past Halley's comet was the first). The two-in-one Muses spacecraft was launched on Jan. 24, 1990, into a highly elliptical orbit of the Earth that would take

Space exploration

it within 22,550 km (14,000 mi) of the Moon on
March 20. Shortly before that the smaller spacecraft
was scheduled to separate from the larger one and
then fire itself into orbit around the Moon, while the
larger craft would continue in its original orbit. The
two spacecraft were primarily engineering vehicles
whose main purpose was to give Japan experience
for more ambitious missions.

NASA's fiscal 1991 budget included funding to
start work on a Lunar Observer spacecraft. It was
scheduled to study the Moon in the 1990s.

Mars. The second of the Soviet Union's two Phobos probes failed in early 1989 after going into orbit
around Mars. Nevertheless, it collected valuable data
on the planet, which had not been visited since the
Viking landers and orbiters in 1976.

Phobos 1 was lost two months after launch in
July 1988. Despite this the Soviets collected valuable
scientific data from the probe, including 140 X-ray
images of the Sun's corona during the cruise phase,
as well as records of solar wind data and galactic
gamma-ray bursts.

Phobos 2 arrived in Mars orbit on Jan. 29, 1989.
On March 21 it was placed in an orbit around Mars
nearly synchronous with that of the Martian moon
Phobos and took a series of striking, high-resolution
color pictures of the asteroid-like body from distances of 860 to 1,130 km (535 to 700 mi). More
than 80% of the surface was imaged. However, on
March 27, as the probe was being positioned for
closeup pictures of the moon, contact was lost. This
aborted plans to place "hopper" spacecraft on the
surface of Phobos to study it in detail. As of early
1990 the Soviets had not determined what caused
the failure.

Phobos 2 also took a number of measurements
around Mars itself, and these showed that the Martian magnetic field apparently is intertwined with
the solar magnetic field, thus allowing the solar wind
and the Martian ionosphere to mingle. Phobos 2 instruments indicated that Mars was losing about 2 kg
(4.4 lb) of carbon dioxide per second, a significant
amount given the fact that the atmosphere already
was quite thin. One instrument mapped limited portions of the equator in thermal infrared, while others
obtained data that would allow the vertical structure
of the atmosphere to be described.

The Soviet Union's Mars '94 mission was scheduled to launch two Phobos-type spacecraft to Mars in
October 1994. Each was to carry a descent module
equipped with a balloon, two or three small instrument stations, and two or three surface penetrators.
The balloons were to carry instrument packages
across the face of Mars by day (when sunlight would
heat the balloon) and let them sit on the surface for
analyses by night. Meanwhile, the U.S. continued its
preparations for the Mars Observer launch in 1992.

414

Shigeo Kogure—Time Magazine

Japan's Muses space probe is launched to the Moon on Jan.
24, 1990, from the Kagoshima Space Center. It was the first
lunar probe since the Soviet Union's Luna 24 in 1976 and
Japan's second probe to another planetary body.

Jupiter. Galileo was launched by the space shuttle on October 18 on a long path to Jupiter. This
complex planetary spacecraft was designed to drop
a probe into the atmosphere of Jupiter before going
into orbit for almost two years of observations. Original launch plans required the use of high-energy
rocket stages, launched from the shuttle, to send
Galileo on its way, but various technical and safety
problems canceled them. Instead, engineers devised
an innovative and complex means of launching
Galileo with an existing medium-power rocket stage
carried by the shuttle. Although lacking the energy
to place Galileo on a trajectory to Jupiter, the stage
could send it to Venus. Through a series of gravity
assists at Venus (February 1990) and Earth (December 1990 and 1992), Galileo's trajectory could be
"cranked" outward until it was traveling to Jupiter.
Arrival was set for Dec. 7, 1995.

Because the new trajectory would take the spacecraft much closer to the Sun than originally planned
and also cause it to operate longer, solar shades
and other modification were necessary. About five
months before arrival at Jupiter, Galileo was to aim
the probe at Jupiter and then change its own trajectory slightly to miss the planet. The probe was
expected to provide some 20 minutes of data on
winds, chemistry, and lightning before being crushed

by pressures equal to a depth of 180 m (600 ft) of water—while still in the uppermost levels of Jupiter's atmosphere. At the same time, Galileo was to undergo yet another gravity assist—at Jupiter's moon Io—to reduce the energy needed to go into orbit around Jupiter a few hours later. Several more gravity assists were planned over the next 22 months as Galileo explored Jupiter, its four major moons (Io, Europa, Ganymede, and Callisto), and the near-Jovian environment.

Galileo's encounter with Venus appeared to go well, although a software problem had the shutter on the main camera snapping 452 times more often than planned. This did not affect 16 images that were taken but was a problem that would have to be resolved before Jupiter was reached. Engineers switched the shutter off, and a few minutes later the computer stopped sending the erroneous command. Galileo's next planetary encounter was to be with the Earth on Dec. 8, 1990, at a distance of 965 km (600 mi). After that flyby the spacecraft's high-gain antenna could be deployed for normal operations.

Galileo's atmospheric entry probe, imaging system, near-infrared mapping spectrometer, and other science instruments were checked out in October. The heavy-ion counter detected ions with energies up to 130 MeV during an intense solar flare on October 19. There was no damage to the spacecraft.

On January 9 Galileo had its first demonstration of a very long baseline interferometry technique using two Earth tracking stations simultaneously to produce precise-angle tracking data. This would be added to Doppler and ranging to refine spacecraft navigation for the Earth and Jupiter encounters, improving targeting while saving propellant.

Galileo space probe is positioned for its launch toward Jupiter from the space shuttle Atlantis *in October.*

Saturn. NASA's fiscal 1990 budget started funding for the Cassini/Huygens orbiter-and-probe to Saturn and its largest moon, Titan. NASA asked the science community to propose experiments for the Cassini orbiter. The European Space Agency (ESA) was to provide the Huygens probe for Titan. The craft was to be launched in April 1996 by a Titan IV/Centaur on a trajectory that would allow gravity-assist flybys at the Earth in 1998 and Jupiter in 2000. It would also fly by the asteroid 66 Maja in 1999. Arrival at Saturn was scheduled for December 2002. In March 2003 the Huygens probe would descend through the atmosphere of Titan. The orbiter would continue operating for four years and about 60 orbits of Saturn, with most orbits making a gravity-assist flyby of a moon (including 35 of Titan) to shape the trajectory for the next encounter.

In October 1989 NASA asked scientists to propose instrument designs for the Cassini orbiter. Candidates included high-resolution television cameras, plasma instruments, dust analyzers, and scanners to map Saturn and its moons in infrared, visible, and ultraviolet light.

The Huygens probe, to be built by the ESA, was to parachute through the smoglike atmosphere of Titan and land on its surface. Scientists hoped that the probe could survive to operate, at least briefly, on the surface. The probe was to weigh only 193 kg (424 lb) when it entered the Titanian atmosphere, which is poorly understood at this time (pressure is believed to be 1.6 times that of Earth at the surface, while the temperature is only 95 K [−178° C; −288.4° F]). The probe was to have a two-part heat shield that it would jettison in stages and two parachutes to slow its descent to the surface. The probe was designed so that during the descent it would sample the gases and aerosols that make up the atmosphere and relay the data to Earth via the Cassini orbiter. Although it was not designed as a true planetary lander, scientists wanted the probe to operate at least as long as the Cassini orbiter was within radio range.

Neptune. The sole planetary encounter of 1989 was the Voyager 2 flyby of Neptune on August 24, some 12 years after it was launched from the Earth on a mission originally intended to reconnoiter only Jupiter and Saturn. Planetary scientists, however, took advantage of a rare alignment of the planets and aimed Voyager's Saturn encounter so that it would fly past Uranus (1986), then Neptune. As with each prior encounter, Neptune was worth the wait and yielded several surprises, including what might be the fastest winds and the biggest geysers in the solar system. (*See* Feature Article: THE JOURNEYS OF THE VOYAGERS.)

Sun. Ulysses, the first mission to study the Sun from above its poles, was scheduled for launch on

Pockmarked surface of Neptune's moon Triton was photographed from the Voyager 2 space probe from a distance of 40,000 kilometers (25,000 miles) on August 25.

Oct. 5, 1990, aboard the space shuttle *Atlantis*. Although not a planetary mission, the Ulysses probe was expected to be as valuable for the data it was to gather on an unexplored part of the solar system—the regions above and below the orbits of the planets. This information would allow scientists to start building three-dimensional models of the solar wind and magnetic fields on the basis of fact rather than theory.

In order to make a wide loop over the poles of the Sun, Ulysses was scheduled to first fly past Jupiter in February 1992 for a tight U-turn that would redirect its orbit almost at a right angle. This roundabout trajectory was required because it would take far more energy to fire a spacecraft on a solar polar trajectory directly from the Earth than to go to Jupiter, where the planet's intense gravitational field can be used to acquire the additional energy. This route would take Ulysses under the south pole of the Sun in June–October 1994, through the plane of the Earth's orbit in February 1995, and above the north pole of the Sun in June–September 1995.

—Dave Dooling

See also Feature Article: PRESS "UP" FOR SPACE.

Transportation

Automation of transportation in all modes continued to increase during 1989. One important across-the-board effort was the development of a system to permit continuous tracking of containers, truck trailers, and rail freight cars moving in both domestic and international commerce. U.S. railroads in the 1970s spent sizable sums of money and conducted extensive road tests of an automated equipment identification (AEI) system utilizing optical scanners located along the roadbed that read colored bar codes on the rolling stock. Unfortunately, the bar codes soon became unreadable because of dirt, ice, snow, and wear.

New AEI systems were proving to be quite readable, as shown in road tests developed by the Amtech Corp. on Burlington Northern Railroad trains operating in the environmentally rugged Mesabi Iron Range district in northern Minnesota. The railroad installed 1,600 tags on locomotives and taconite freight cars. These tags transmitted equipment location and other tracking data via radio frequency to roadside readers for further transmission to a central point for analysis. Burlington Northern reported that for more than one million reads since April 1988, the accuracy rate was 99.9%; it said that it planned to install more than 4,000 tags and 54 readers by the end of 1990.

Several major U.S. steamship lines installed similar AEI equipment on their containers, many of which interchanged with railroads and truck lines for the domestic portion of international movements of cargo. Unfortunately, the lack of standardization of AEI tags and readers continued to delay widespread use of this technology, especially when more than one form of transportation was involved. This problem was closer to being solved, however, because the International Standards Organization approved interim AEI standards, as did the Association of American Railroads.

An Australian firm in Melbourne, Amskan Ltd., reported that it had developed an electronic tracking system without the risk of microwave radiation. Called the Bartag AIE system, it relied on infrared radiation and FM (frequency modulation) radio signals rather than the microwaves used by most scanning devices. The system used small electronic labels about 3.125 cm (1.25 in) in diameter that were mounted on the transport vehicles and that emitted an encoded signal when scanned by a reader at terminals or interchange transfer points. Amskan claimed that the system could be used at reader distances up to 29 m (32 yd) and when the moving equipment was operating at speeds of up to 100 km/h (62 mph).

Air transport. Despite orders exceeding its capability of early delivery for existing air transports, Boeing began making firm offers to customers for its new B-777, an advanced version of its two-engine B-767. To sell for about $100 million, the new version would retain the new high-technology automated cockpit but might add innovations such as folding wings (to fit into existing airport gates) and so-called fly-by-light (fiber-optic signaling) flight control. Other advanced technology devices such as cockpit flat plate display and passive cooling would provide faster and better information to the two-person crew without placing any additional burden on them. The aircraft was designed to carry about 350 passengers plus supplemental cargo about 7,800 km (4,200 nautical miles), using upgraded Pratt &

The MD-11, McDonnell Douglas's new trijet passenger liner, performs successfully during its first test flight, over Long Beach, California, in January 1990.

Whitney PW4000 engines capable of providing thrust of more than 33,000 kg (74,000 lb). Three engine manufacturers—Pratt & Whitney, Rolls-Royce, and General Electric—planned to offer competing models if the new transport was built.

The extensively used so-called glass cockpits (automated and highly computerized cockpits designed to ease the burdens of pilots and copilots) were subjected to a three-year study by the U.S. National Aeronautics and Space Administration (NASA) to determine how successful they had been in reducing flight-operation burdens without adversely affecting safety. The findings, based on briefings of 200 Boeing 757 pilots throughout that period, were that half of the pilots believed that the workload had been increased and that this tended to decrease their aircraft flight skills. A major concern was the use of the automated flight controls at elevations under 3,000 m (10,000 ft). At these levels, rapid changes in speeds, altitudes, and directions are often required, resulting in the need for pilots to look down in order to reprogram the computers at a time when they are flying in congested traffic.

Heavy worldwide demand for both passenger and freight air transports placed airlines on a long waiting list for new aircraft deliveries. Most orders were for existing models, although in a wide range of variations. Boeing reported that the demand for its advanced-version B-747-400 freighter pushed the price to $120 million per unit, with deliveries not scheduled to begin until 1993. This resulted in many orders for converting older, used 747-200s into freighters at a cost ranging from $46 million to $78 million each. According to Boeing the 747 was in great demand largely because its nose could open to accommodate long loads and also because of its body and wing strength. The advanced 747-400 freighter was designed to fly as far as 12,850 km (8,000 mi)

New Soviet Ilyushin 96-300 jetliner was a featured attraction in August at the first Soviet air show in 22 years.

without refueling and haul 20 more tons of cargo than the existing model.

U.S. combination passenger-cargo air carriers remained unconvinced that they should again start ordering all-cargo freighters. Thus, they remained primarily passenger carriers with sizable but secondary cargo operations in separate aircraft compartments that were designed for rapidly handling containerized cargo so as to minimize interference with passenger schedules. All-freight transports were flown—in converted passenger models—mostly by or for small-package operators such as Federal Express or United Parcel Service (UPS).

A renewed approach for using air transports able to operate as either passenger or cargo aircraft was taken by British Aerospace, which received 174 firm orders for its 146–2000C Convertible transport and delivered 126 of them. The company increased its production rate to 40 a year at its Hatfield plant near London. In less than 30 minutes—using pallet containers loaded and unloaded onto and off a rollerball freight floor—the aircraft can be converted from a passenger version seating 85–94 to a freighter capable of holding 9,100–9,500 kg (20,000–21,000 lb). Passenger seats were likewise loaded and unloaded in multiunit pallets quickly attached to special floor fittings.

British Aerospace officially launched its BAc 1000, a midsize business twin jet designed especially for intercontinental flights, with deliveries scheduled to begin in early 1991. To cost about $10 million, it was to be powered by new Pratt & Whitney Canada PW305 engines, each capable of 2,350 kg (5,200 lb) of thrust and equipped with throttles electronically connected to an automated control to ensure immediate response to the pilot's demands. A five-tube electronic flight instrument system will offer visual screens and integrated radio systems. The aircraft was designed to have a range of up to 6,730 km (3,635 nautical miles), and it would be able to carry 6 to 8 passengers in executive configurations and 15 in a business shuttle version.

A NASA-U.S. aircraft industry program reported a favorable long-term outlook for the development of a U.S. commercial supersonic air transport (SST). Their conclusion was that a U.S.-built SST could be certified as early as the year 2000 if an aggressive research effort was made. Both Boeing and McDonnell Douglas were considering SSTs, focusing on a 250–300 passenger, long-range aircraft that could fly between two and three times the speed of sound. NASA earmarked $25 million for research and development in fiscal 1990, with emphasis on developing the technologies needed to resolve environmental, engine emission, community noise, and sonic boom issues. NASA noted that reduced aircraft weight was a major goal, because that should help significantly

in finding solutions to the problems cited above. If the research efforts prove promising, the program will move into a $284 million, six-year effort.

Highway transport. New, tougher emission standards for diesel engines set by the U.S. Environmental Protection Agency—to apply to urban buses in 1991 and trucks in 1994—put strong pressures on manufacturers to decide which technological path they should take. Since most trucking companies would prefer to stick with diesel engines, the major emphasis was on making them clean. Navistar International Transportation Corp., the largest builder of medium and heavy-duty trucks and diesel engines in the U.S., exhibited its Smokeless 94 Diesel, which it claimed could meet the 1994 EPA standards. The new engine achieved cleaner emissions by refining fuel injection, controlling combustion and lubrication, using low-sulfur fuel, and installing two catalytic converters. Navistar said that the key element was the use of low-sulfur fuel, without which the catalytic converters would fail.

Parker Automotive Corp. claimed that it had developed a system that could clean diesel-fuel carbon emissions. In tests conducted jointly with the American Trucking Associations and the Society of Automotive Engineers, the Carbon Clean Industrial Diesel Tune system produced such results as a 7% increase in fuel economy, a 60% reduction in particulate emissions, a 28% increase in horsepower, and a 30% increase in torque.

Another approach to a cleaner engine for large trucks—the use of methanol fuel—was seriously questioned by the president of the American Trucking Associations. He cited the following disadvantages: methanol can seriously harm people and the environment because its combustion creates gaseous formaldehyde, a suspected cancer-causing agent; its nearly invisible flame creates a risk of severe burns unless colored; it is highly corrosive to conventional materials used in truck fuel lines and storage tanks; and two gallons are required for doing the work of one gallon of diesel fuel.

The fast-approaching 1991 EPA standards for urban buses made natural gas the leading candidate, on the basis of widespread road tests and research activities of engine manufacturers. An added stimulant was the tougher clean-air standards that were being set for metropolitan areas. In September the nation's first urban transit bus specifically designed to use natural gas was placed in regular-route service in Columbus, Ohio. The $200,000 vehicle was developed by a Columbia Gas System Service Corp. subsidiary in Columbus and built by the Flxible Corp., with use of an engine designed by the Cummins Engine Co. specifically to use natural gas. To hold the compressed gas, the engine was equipped with fuel cylinders lined with aluminum and reinforced with fiberglass. Orders for 10 buses powered by such engines were received by Flxible from the Southern California Regional Transit District in Los Angeles. Large-scale orders depended largely on the extent to which the U.S. government, which heavily subsidizes urban bus acquisitions, supported such purchases and whether Congress mandated conversion of urban bus fleets to meet the goals of new clean-air legislation. Tests in Brooklyn, N.Y., of UPS vans powered by natural gas provided the following emissions comparisons with gasoline: natural gas produced 85% less carbon monoxide, 25% less oxides of nitrogen, 23% less carbon dioxide, and 13% less hydrocarbons; natural gas also achieved 12% better fuel economy. In the UPS vans the compressed natural gas was stored in three cylinders installed in the vehicles and was released by driver-controlled regulators on lines moving to a gas-air mixer, carburetor, and the engine. Special solenoid valves prevented the gas from entering the engine when it was turned off.

UPS, the nation's largest domestic freight carrier in terms of revenues, continued to grow rapidly in 1989, not only in the U.S. but also throughout the world. This move toward becoming a truly global carrier in the small-package field was made possible largely through technological innovations. These included a new, centralized computer center, under construction in Mahwah, N.J., for linking every UPS facility throughout its 175–nation network; a futuristic superhub under construction in Chicago, to handle three million packages a day with the help of high-speed optical scanning equipment and a computerized tractor-trailer feeder system; development of postage-stamp-size computer codes able to be read by an optical scanner from a belt moving 152.5 m (500 ft) a minute past it; the development of improved tracking of packages by the use of bar codes and hand-held scanners; and a computer interface

with customs offices to facilitate the clearance of international shipments. During the past year UPS opened a new $128 million facility bordering the Philadelphia International Airport. It featured an aircraft loading ramp capable of handling 50,000 packages an hour at start-up and 78,000 at full capacity between trucks and aircraft via 42 km (26 mi) of conveyors.

Highway traffic congestion, especially in and around major metropolitan areas, stimulated major research efforts aimed at easing congestion through the use of so-called "smart" cars and trucks. Such vehicles would be equipped with computers, transmitters, and dashboard screens capable of receiving and sending data on traffic congestion via linkage to a computer center, which also would collect data from "intelligent" highways equipped with roadside sensors monitoring traffic density and movement. The center could thus advise drivers of traffic bottlenecks ahead and of alternate routes. Backed by a consortium of 16 carmakers, 70 computer/electronic firms, and 6 national governments, an eight-year, $800 million program was under way in Europe. Called Prometheus, it sought not only to facilitate motor vehicle movements but also to make them safer. A more modest U.S. program, called Pathfinder, was being coordinated by the Federal Highway Administration, California Department of Transportation, and General Motors Corp. A pilot test using 25 automobiles began in the Santa Monica, Calif., area.

At the year's end General Motors unveiled what it called the world's first electric-powered auto capable of the acceleration and speed required for operation in today's high-speed, congested traffic. Called Impact, the small experimental car was capable of traveling 190 km (120 mi) at 88.5 km/h (55 mph) on one battery charge—with recharging taking only

General Motors Corporation

The electric-powered Impact, introduced by General Motors Corp. during the past year, was designed to travel 190 kilometers (120 miles) on one battery charge and to accelerate from standing to 95 kilometers per hour (60 miles per hour) in eight seconds.

three hours and using ordinary house current outlets. It could accelerate from standing to 95 km/h (60 mph) in eight seconds. When running at low speeds it was virtually noiseless, and it made only a low whine when accelerating. The Impact uses two AC (alternating current) induction-type motors to drive the front wheels. Its 395-kg (870-lb) lead-acid battery-pack costs $1,500 and must be replaced every two years.

Pipelines. In order to enhance the capabilities of the many electronic data systems used by oil pipeline companies, the American Petroleum Institute (API) developed and published a Pipenet computer program, which provides a standardized format for the direct and rapid transfer of data among carriers, shippers, suppliers, and others. This was expected to help overcome past problems encountered in the interchange of information in the oil pipeline industry, where each company uses its own formatting system and has to reformat any data transferred to it from another firm. According to the API, this proved time-consuming, duplicative, and costly, and often led to error and delay. In the past much of this interchange involved paper documents or postal services. The API claimed that Pipenet should facilitate data exchange in areas such as traffic tracking, schedule conformity, inventories, and pricing and also provide basic carrier information such as locations, types of petroleum handled, points served, and traffic volume capabilities.

The use of waterjet technology specifically designed to remove corrosion and worn coatings from the outside of pipelines was developed by CUPS Inc. The company claimed that waterjets were an improvement over previous methods, such as the use of brushes, scrapers, or sandblasting; these often failed to remove corrosion completely. CUPS also said that such abrasive cleaning reduces the ability of the pipeline walls to perform nondestructive examination of the oil. The firm reported that tests conducted by Oak Ridge (Tenn.) National Laboratory showed that waterjets did not harm the original pipeline metal.

El Paso (Texas) Natural Gas Co. used the CUPS technology to clean about 95 km (60 mi) of its pipelines. The cleaning machine was self-propelled and self-adjusting to allow for variations in the pipe's size and shape, and it could be opened and closed around the pipe so that there was no loose end. The spinning waterjets encompassing the pipe could be adjusted to emit streams with velocities ranging from 18,000 to 35,000 psi, depending on the type of coating or corrosion to be removed. Since the machine travels about 3 m (10 ft) per minute, the dwell time at impact of the jet stream is too short to damage the pipe; tests demonstrated that it would take more than five minutes for any damage to occur even if the stream continued to be trained at the same point on the pipe. The machine could be used on oil as well as gas pipelines.

Rail transport. After several years of study, the U.S. Interstate Commerce Commission ruled that railroads can file their rates electronically, marking the first step toward the eventual elimination of administratively costly and cumbersome paper records containing millions of continuously changing rates. U.S. railroads, already highly computerized, planned not only to computerize rate filings but also to link the data flow with their shippers' computers—covering pricing, billings, payments, and accounting. The railroad industry was to coordinate this effort through a jointly owned Transportation Data Exchange Inc.

Centralized automated freight-train control took another major step forward for both the Union Pacific Railroad (UP) and CSX Rail Transport. The UP announced that its $48 million center in Omaha, Neb., should be fully operational in 1990 and that it would control all of its 37,500 km (23,300 mi) of track and more than 700 trains daily. It would replace 10 regional dispatch centers, and the computers installed in it would also handle labor matters such as train crew assignments, work hours, and paychecks. The $23 million CSX center in Jacksonville, Fla., was designed to control virtually CSX's entire 32,200-km (20,000-mi) rail system. Highlights were to include displays around a wall that would show train location; identification; and signal, switch, and track status for dispatching and monitoring 1,400 trains per day. Color codes used on the screen displays would indicate trains running on schedule (green), trains behind schedule but capable of being expedited (yellow), and trains unable to meet schedules (red).

Canadian National Railway Co. added another train to inspect its lines. Called TEST III and costing $1.8 million, it consisted of an engine, a converted passenger coach containing computers and recording equipment, and an instrumented, ballasted boxcar that simulated a loaded 100-ton freight car. TEST III measured and recorded mileage, superelevation (the vertical distance between the heights of the inner and outer edges of the rails), curvature, gauge, surface profile, and track twist. It produced reports about, for example, track defects and rail wear. Canadian National announced that its TEST technology was being made available to other North American railroads through its subsidiary CANAC International.

Specialized high-speed trains hauling double-stacked containers—the bottom one in a well in the flatcar and the upper one on top locked in place—were taking a rapidly growing share of the total U.S. rail piggyback traffic (combination of tractor trailers and containers)—from 5% of the total in 1984 to 25% in 1988. The shorter trains and more powerful

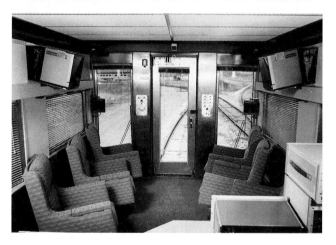

Converted passenger coach (above) houses computers and recording equipment for TEST III, a train devised by the Canadian National Railway Co. to inspect its lines. An observation area on the converted car (left) allows TEST and track-maintenance personnel to inspect the track and right-of-way visually.

locomotives that had become available enabled the specialized trains to operate as a single, articulated unit without the slack that exists between cars in normal freight trains; thus, the specialized trains were relatively damage free in moving general merchandise freight. However, since doublestack trains were most suitable for high-speed service between major, long-distance points, they had to pass through many places that lacked concrete aprons and costly equipment for lifting containers. The Burlington Northern, in an effort to tap the market in such places, began testing RoadRailers (trailers equipped with interchangeable rail and highway wheels) connected at the end of the doublestack trains by a special hitch. The builder of the hitch, Gunderson Inc., claimed that the RoadRailers could be quickly disconnected without any significant slowing down of overall service.

The Burlington Northern announced that in mid-1990 it planned to begin operational tests of diesel locomotives converted to liquefied natural gas (LNG) for power. The tests were to be held with single-commodity trains hauling coal from and returning to the Powder River Basin of Wyoming and Montana; they would operate out of a single LNG storage station. Well-insulated and highly pressurized tanks would be required in order to keep the LNG in a liquid state by holding temperatures below $-162.2°$ C ($-196.6°$ F). This, in turn, would necessitate extensive safety studies by the Los Alamos (N.M.) National Laboratory. Reasons for the Burlington Northern tests included expected stiff environmental (clean-air) regulations on diesel fuels, the approximate 20% saving in costs in comparison with diesel, and maintenance savings because the cleaner-burning LNG reduces carbon buildup in the locomotive engine.

Water transport. The Port of Houston, Texas, already a major U.S. port for handling containers and general cargo, made a major move during the past year to compete for more bagged and boxed freight.

421

A new subway train in Hamburg, West Germany, became operational in 1989. Microcomputers perform almost all control functions, and the water-cooled, three-phase engines are designed to reduce energy consumption by 30%.

This was done by contributing $30 million toward the new $110 million Omniport, an automated terminal featuring the use of four Spiralveyors. Each of these machines weighs 270 tons and is capable of unloading 150 tons of breakbulk (bagged and boxed) freight an hour from the hold of a ship with the aid of only three longshoremen. In the past it took 12 men, using slings and pallets, to move only 60 tons an hour. The longshoremen now can load the freight in the ship's hold onto a platform on the Spiralveyor, which spins the load upward and onto a conveyor belt that carries the freight to the dock, where another machine spins it downward as needed. For outgoing cargo the system is reversed. A transit shed is linked to the dock by conveyor belts that service both railcars and trucks directly and interchangeably. The operations are controlled by a computerized system in the shed. Only two other ports, in Saudi Arabia and Antwerp, Belgium, were said to be using Spiralveyors, although the machines were under construction in New Zealand, a major cargo trader with Houston.

Lloyd's Register of Shipping in London began tests of a computerized "black box"—long standard in the air transport field—to assist in investigating accidents of ships at sea. Called a Voyage Data Recorder, one was installed on the 28,000-deadweight ton containership *Gulf Spirit*, which operated between Europe and the U.S. Gulf Coast. Developed by Lloyd's, the VDR not only continuously records the ship's speed and direction but also is capable of collecting, storing, and analyzing data that can be used to ensure safe loading, maximize fuel efficiency, and improve both navigation and operations. In the event of a sea disaster, the fireproof VDR is automatically released from the ship, after which it floats and transmits a signal to enable rescuers to locate its position. Similar to air carrier devices, the VDR should reduce the

normally large costs of an official inquiry by helping to determine what happened to cause the accident and who was responsible.

Sea-Land Service Inc. unveiled a new, computerized cargo-tracking system that enabled it to monitor closely and continuously the movement of its shipments of wines and spirits throughout the world. Called Cheers, the system could be linked with any IBM-compatible computer of Sea-Land's customers. The type of data automatically given to shippers enables them to know how well the shipment's movement conforms with the plan throughout the many stages of transport. Sea-Land said that half a dozen firms used the new system during the past year and claimed that its acceptance points to widespread use in the near future. Sea-Land predicted expansion of the system to other specialized groups such as chemicals, machinery, and refrigerated cargo.

The U.S. Military Sealift Command (MSC) and Sea-Land Service began the first major test of a containership retrofitted for military contingency planning. The MSC chartered the *Sea-Land Consumer,* a large containership able to carry 1,664 6-m (20-ft) containers, for retrofitting with special cargo devices for handling large military equipment, rolling stock, and other cargo unable to fit into normal marine containers. This included use of multiple flat racks as well as innovative sea sheds, which are open-top units that also provide access through their floors. The tests were slated on trips between New York City, Baltimore, Md., and two undisclosed ports outside the U.S.

The Japan Foundation for Shipbuilding Advancement, a privately financed organization, continued research on the development of commercial vessels propelled by a superconductive propulsion system. The foundation planned to launch in 1990 a $40 million, 30-m (100-ft)-long, 150-ton prototype vessel if its efforts to develop the needed superconducting magnets should succeed. Argonne National Laboratory near Chicago announced a two-year research and development program to develop a propulsion system capable of powering submarines that could operate virtually noiselessly because they would no longer require noise-producing engines and external parts such as propellers. The magnetic waterjet propulsion is based on allowing seawater to flow through a duct surrounded by a superconducting magnet that passes strong electrical currents through the water. This results in an electromagnetic force with virtually no resistance that drives the water out the back of the duct and thereby creates forward motion. The Argonne project was using the world's largest superconducting magnet. Measuring 6.4 m (21 ft) in length and 3.9 m (13 ft) in diameter and weighing 180 tons, it was capable of generating a thrust able to propel a large commercial vessel. If such a system should be successful, ships could operate far more efficiently, at higher speeds, and with greater cargo capacity (because less space would be needed for fuel storage). Obstacles to development included the weight and cost of such magnets as well as the need to keep superconducting materials at extremely low temperatures to achieve zero resistance. Therefore, large-scale commercial utilization appeared to be many years away.

—Frank A. Smith

U.S. science policy

For a few giddy weeks in the spring of 1989, it seemed that the world's energy problems had been solved. Two chemists announced that they had succeeded in producing a fusion reaction in a glass jar at room temperature, a feat formerly restricted to massive, high-temperature reactors costing hundreds of millions of dollars. Physicists and chemists in the United States and around the world dropped what they were doing to try to replicate the astonishing findings, and visionaries imagined scaling up the test-tube fusion reaction to provide the world's energy needs.

As 1989 drew to a close, however, the visions had all but vanished. Most attempts at repeating the experiment were complete failures, and even true believers had only limited success. Cold fusion, it seemed, was a wet firecracker.

The year 1989 did have its share of real science triumphs. The Voyager 2 spacecraft capped a 12-year tour of the solar system with amazing pictures and a bounty of scientific information about the planet Neptune. Researchers discovered the gene that causes cystic fibrosis, a breakthrough that made finding a cure more likely. There was also the first

D. Allan Bromley, Henry Ford II professor of physics at Yale University, was appointed by U.S. Pres. George Bush as an assistant to the president. For many years Bromley wrote the "Nuclear Physics" article in the Yearbook of Science and the Future.

tangible evidence that the massive federal effort to combat AIDS (acquired immune deficiency syndrome) was beginning to have an impact on the disease.

It fell to a new administration to chart the course of science policy in 1989. Although he shared a conservative Republican ideology, Pres. George Bush made it clear that his administration would not be a carbon copy of that of Ronald Reagan, the man he replaced in the White House. Throughout the year Bush's campaign themes of improving education and protecting the environment and his strong pro-life (or, as some preferred to describe it, antiabortion) philosophy began to translate into tangible policies.

Appointments. Bush quickly made good on a campaign promise to raise the role of science adviser to assistant to the president, placing the post on an administrative par with others, such as the national security adviser. Bush's choice for the job was D. Allan Bromley, a physicist from Yale University. Bromley was no stranger to Washington, having served on numerous government advisory panels. (For 20 years he wrote the "Nuclear Physics" article for the YEARBOOK OF SCIENCE AND THE FUTURE.)

Praise for Bush's choice came from all quarters. Scientists were pleased that Bush had chosen a scientist of Bromley's stature. Congressional science committees were pleased that an independent thinker, rather than a political ideologue, was on the job.

Nevertheless, there was some grumbling amid the praise. Bromley's appointment did not come until several months after Bush took office—after the cold fusion news had peaked—and he was not approved by Congress until August. Once on the job, Bromley needed to devote a lot of his time to building up his political capital, and longtime Washington wise men, such as Rep. George Brown (Dem., Calif.), wondered if Bromley would ever really enjoy the access to the president necessary for being effective in shaping policy. When it appeared during the summer that Congress was going to make severe cuts in the administration's budget request for the National Science Foundation, Bromley was too new on the job to help fight for the agency's budget.

The delay in appointing Bromley was not an isolated incident for the Bush administration. Some key science posts in the Departments of Commerce, Defense, Health and Human Services, and Energy were still awaiting appointments at the end of the year.

William Carey, a consultant for the Carnegie Corporation in New York City and a former member of the White House budget office, said in an interview with *Science* magazine that it was always difficult for a new administration to fill all but the very highest government posts, but Bush's difficulties were the worst he had seen in 40 years. "To be at this point in a new administration and still be encountering difficulties in persuading the people you want to come into the system . . . puts the government's ability to do any policy leading in science and technology at an extraordinary disadvantage," said Carey.

The position of under secretary of commerce for technology was a particularly nagging vacancy. The need for a national technology policy became more acute as the United States saw its lead in high-technology areas such as computers and electronics slip away to Japan and Europe. The problem had not gone without notice. The federal government created Sematech, a consortium of computer chip companies aimed at propelling U.S. chip technology back into the international lead. When high-definition television appeared as the next important major commercial electronic technology, however, the government seemed uncertain about the role it should play in developing it. Congress created a new technology agency within the Department of Commerce, but by the end of the year the Bush administration had still not been able to fill the post of under secretary to head the new agency.

Some worried that the Department of Defense was becoming the de facto director of U.S. technology policy. The Defense Advanced Research Projects Agency funded Sematech and had also been supporting projects in high-definition television and high-temperature superconductors. No one was quite sure whether hardware developed with military applications in mind would find its way into the private sector. Also, defense research programs faced cutbacks as the threat from Eastern Europe subsided following the political upheavals in that region.

Abortion. Another job opening that gained some notoriety was that of director of the National Institutes of Health (NIH). With its $7.7 billion budget, the NIH was the primary source of federal funds for biomedical research. James Wyngaarden announced

early in the year that he was leaving as director, and the search got under way for a successor. It became clear that scientific and administrative competence was not the only criterion for a replacement. When William Danforth, chancellor of Washington University, St. Louis, Mo., and one of the candidates, got a call from the White House as part of a background check, he was asked his opinion on abortion. Danforth was incensed, reportedly responding that if that was the only question the Bush administration had for him, they had chosen the wrong man for the job.

Although the White House had made no bones about its antiabortion stance—and joined in the cheering when the U.S. Supreme Court let stand a Missouri law that placed new restrictions on abortion—the outcry over the so-called abortion litmus test prompted a rethinking of the issue. Health and Human Services Secretary Louis Sullivan announced that he was forming a special panel to evaluate the job of NIH director and to determine how to attract the best candidate for the job. Views on abortion, the secretary emphasized, would not be a relevant item in the search.

Another Sullivan decision made it clear, however, that the abortion issue was continuing to have profound effect on federal biomedical research policy. In early November Sullivan announced that he was extending indefinitely a moratorium on the use of federal funds for transplantation research using fetal tissue from induced abortions. The moratorium had been put forward in March 1988 by Assistant Secretary for Health Robert Windom. Windom had asked the NIH to form a special advisory panel to assess the ethical and legal issues of using fetal tissue for transplantation research, including the issue of how demand for fetal tissue would be affected if fetal-tissue transplants could be shown to cure patients with diabetes or Parkinson's disease.

The panel concluded that as long as abortion was legal, the subsequent use of the tissue was morally acceptable and that fetal tissue might someday prove of value for therapy. The panel also concluded that it was essential to separate the decision to have an abortion from the decision of how to dispose of the fetal remains, but that such a separation could be accomplished.

Sullivan rejected the panel's conclusions, arguing that women, already facing a traumatic decision, might ease their consciences by the thought that they might be helping someone else. Although researchers were dismayed by his decision, they were relieved that Sullivan did not extend the ban to cover all research involving fetal tissue. Transplantation research could still proceed in privately funded research programs.

Sullivan declined to move ahead on plans to reconstitute the Ethics Advisory Board, a departmental

Sidney Harris

"I'm sorry it didn't work out, but it really doesn't affect me. I have breakthrough insurance."

body required by statute that had to approve any federally funded research related to such sensitive issues as in vitro fertilization. Without the board the federal government could fund no research in this area, and many saw the United States falling behind in reproductive medicine.

Also remaining off-limits to American women was RU 486, a drug developed in France that induced an abortion without surgery in women less than 10 weeks pregnant. The pill was freely available in France, but its manufacturer, Roussel-Uclaf, refused to permit its export even to countries that had approved it for use. Although RU 486 had been used experimentally in the United States, no company had been willing to take on the political onus of trying to seek a license for it from the Food and Drug Administration.

Genetics. The resolution of one ethical issue opened the door to a new world of medical therapy. In 1988 scientists at the National Institutes of Health received permission to proceed with a gene-therapy experiment, and on May 22, 1989, the first foreign genes were inserted into a human cancer patient. The genes were from a bacterium and were incorporated into the patient's own white blood cells. The transplanted genes conveyed no therapeutic benefit to the patient, but they were not intended to. They were intended as a marker on the white cells to see if the latter successfully infiltrated the patient's cancer. The experiment, which by year's end appeared to be a success, was just the first of numerous planned protocols that would test how genes from other organisms, or from other humans, might be transferred safely into patients to cure otherwise fatal conditions.

If the ethical issues of inserting genes into humans had been well discussed, another ethical problem loomed for research scientists: is it appropriate to test for genetic diseases when no cure can be offered? The discovery of the cystic fibrosis gene meant that scientists could develop a test to show whether a person was a carrier of the disease or whether a fetus would be born with the disease. Until a cure was found, however, that information could force agonizing choices.

Scientific misconduct. Questions on professional ethics also confronted scientists. In the most celebrated case of the year, Nobel Prize-winning scientist David Baltimore went head to head with congressional fraud investigator Rep. John Dingell (Dem., Mich.) over a disputed piece of research. Dingell, as chairman of the Energy and Commerce Committee and its Oversight and Investigations Subcommittee, had challenged the way the data were collected for a paper published by Baltimore and others in the journal *Cell.* The paper looked at how genes transplanted into a mouse affected the expression of genes that the mouse had inherited from its parents.

In an all-day hearing Dingell grilled Secret Service investigators who had uncovered certain discrepancies in the dates contained in lab notebooks of Thereza Imanishi-Kari, the principal author of the paper. Dingell then questioned scientists who had been impaneled by the NIH to investigate the question of misconduct relating to the paper. Finally he took on Baltimore and Imanishi-Kari, but Baltimore struck back, condemning Dingell for conducting what he called a witch-hunt and restating that neither he nor any of his coauthors had anything to apologize for. Dingell seemed to retreat in the face of Baltimore's stinging rebuke, but he vowed that his investigation of the case was not over and that 1990 would bring startling new revelations.

Baltimore was not the only well-known scientist to attract Dingell's interest. Robert Gallo, who with Luc Montagnier had discovered the AIDS virus, caught Dingell's eye when a *Chicago Tribune* investigative reporter dredged up examples of possible misconduct surrounding the pioneering work on the virus. Although most of the issues were settled, the NIH agreed to Dingell's request for an investigation.

Lesser-known scientists also were scrutinized. C. David Bridges was accused of using another scientist's ideas to prepare a paper for *Science* magazine. That inquiry was under way at year's end. The National Institute of Mental Health determined that two Stanford University psychiatrists had used inappropriate controls in studying how certain chemicals behaved in the brains of patients with psychiatric illness. Both subsequently left Stanford.

To clarify what constituted unacceptable behavior in research, the federal government published rules

425

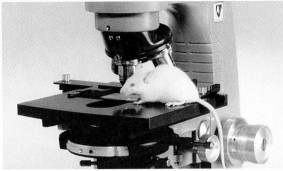

This rare genetic strain of mouse was bred at the Jackson Laboratory in Bar Harbor, Maine. A fire at the laboratory during the past year killed some 500,000 mice.

governing scientific misconduct. The NIH also tried to establish rules regarding conflict of interest. It took up that question under prodding from Congress, most notably from Rep. Ted Weiss (Dem., N.Y.). Weiss wanted to know whether it was appropriate for researchers receiving public money to accept remuneration from commercial interests for the same work. Scientists protested that working with industry was essential in many cases to push research ahead rapidly. Besides, they pointed out, the government had been pushing hard for technology transfer (the movement of academic know-how into commercial applications). It would be unfair, they said, to put on the brakes.

The NIH nonetheless determined that strict guidelines were required. In September it put forward a set of proposals that generated a staggering 700 letters commenting on the proposed guidelines. The broad financial disclosures and prohibitions recommended were in the end deemed excessive, and Secretary Sullivan ordered them withdrawn. Both Congress and the administration, however, seemed intent that the issue of federal rules be kept alive.

Disasters. Three disasters, each involving loss of life, raised important policy questions in 1989. In one, a fire at the Jackson Laboratory in Bar Harbor, Maine, killed some 500,000 mice. The Jackson lab was not only a center of genetic research but also the supplier of a rare genetic strain of mice used in research. Scientists throughout the U.S. were dismayed when they heard of the fire; many of the JAX mice (as they were commonly known) were available only from the Bar Harbor facility. The fire spared the breeding pairs of all strains, however, and work proceeded after some delay.

The second disaster also involved loss of animal life. The *Exxon Valdez* oil tanker struck a reef while leaving the south terminus of the trans-Alaska pipeline and spilled 41.7 million liters (11 million gal) of crude oil into Prince William Sound (*see*

ENVIRONMENT). The accident raised anew the question of the safety of removing oil from otherwise pristine ecosystems. Although the magnitude of the environmental damage caused by the spill was being debated, it clearly cast a pall on efforts to open other areas to exploration for oil, most notably the Alaska National Wildlife Refuge.

The third disaster was not of human origin, but it was far more devastating. The Loma Prieta earthquake, with its epicenter near the coastal town of Aptos, Calif., caused damage and loss of life throughout the San Francisco Bay area (*see* EARTH SCIENCES: *Geophysics*). Later referred to as "not quite the big one," it came as no surprise to seismologists familiar with the San Andreas Fault. Many expected that the neighboring Hayward Fault, which runs along the eastern side of San Francisco Bay, would shift within a matter of years, causing still more destruction.

Environment and education. The Loma Prieta earthquake was a dramatic example of how humans depend on their environment, but a less obvious interaction became a bone of contention in government policy circles. The issue of global environmental change became a hot topic as the environmental movement of the 1970s seemed to be once again in vogue. Two issues drew the most attention. Stratospheric ozone depletion, first noted over Antarctica but appearing in other areas as well, prompted international concern. Chlorofluorocarbons, used as propellants in aerosol cans and as refrigerants and solvents, were clearly a key factor in the ozone depletion, but it was unclear whether the Bush administration would push to reduce their use faster than a 1987 protocol required.

The more vexing issue was whether greenhouse gases were causing an overall rise in global temperatures. Many climate modelers insisted that the buildup of such gases as carbon dioxide would lead inexorably to a global temperature increase of at least 2° to 3° C (3.6° to 5.4° F) and possibly as much as 10° C (18° F) by the year 2100. Environmentalists called for immediate reduction in carbon dioxide output, despite the widespread economic consequences.

Others, however, were less sure the problem was so acute. A report prepared for the George C. Marshall Institute by three preeminent scientists predicted that the change would be less severe, and that report seemed to convince the White House that no dramatic action was needed. (See EARTH SCIENCES: *Atmospheric Sciences.*)

If environmentalists were dismayed that President Bush was not responding more aggressively to the potential threat of global warming, they were unanimous in their praise for his choice as head of the Environmental Protection Agency. William K. Reilly had been president of the Conservation Foundation for 15 years and president of the World Wildlife Fund from 1985. Manuel Lujan, Bush's choice for interior secretary, was less popular with environmentalists. Although it appeared by year's end that Reilly's was not necessarily the predominant voice within the White House on environmental issues, he clearly would have a role in helping Bush fulfill a campaign promise to become the environmental president.

Another Bush promise—that he would be the education president—did not come quite as close to making the grade. National Science Foundation (NSF) Assistant Director Bassam Z. Shakashiri pushed hard for increasing the NSF education budget to $600 million. The 1990 total—closer to $200 million—fell far short of that mark, however, although NSF Director Erich Bloch said that education was the fastest growing part of the NSF budget. International comparisons on the extent of scientific knowledge among young people continued to put U.S. students well down the list in most subjects.

Space. President Bush also addressed the question of where the U.S. space program was headed. He renewed his commitment to a permanently occupied space station and dedicated the U.S. to reestablishing a presence on the Moon and, from there, a foothold on Mars. Laudable goals, said critics, but where would the money come from? Bush offered no answers.

Others were not even thrilled with the goals. To many scientists the space station had become an expensive white elephant, with no clearly defined purpose but ever escalating costs. The price tag reached $30 billion by some estimates and, having spent $2 billion on the project already, the National Aeronautics and Space Administration (NASA) was still attempting to define exactly what the station would do. This did not sit well with NASA's international partners who had made commitments to participate in a project that seemed to be changing shape.

On the other hand, NASA enjoyed a banner year with its unmanned spacecraft. Voyager 2 provided a bounty of information about Neptune; the Cosmic Background Explorer returned key data about the nature of the beginnings of the universe; and two planetary probes—Magellan to Venus and Galileo to Jupiter—finally were launched. With former astronaut Richard Truly as the new NASA administrator, humans appeared to have a secure place in NASA's future plans, but rising costs could ultimately make robotic spacecraft a more appealing alternative.

Budget. In general, the federal science budget did fairly well in 1989. There were big increases for NASA—mostly resulting from the $1.8 billion for the space station—and the AIDS budget continued to climb, reaching $2,930,000,000. In general, though, most science agencies felt that hard times had either arrived or were about to. Despite a budget that reached an all-time high of $7.7 billion, the officials at the NIH were able to fund only about a quarter of new grants deemed worthy of receiving money. Most of the NIH's increase went to previous commitments, and most "new" money went to efforts to combat AIDS and to a newly started project to generate a genetic road map of all the DNA found in human cells. The NSF received a 14% increase to just over $2 billion. This was well below a rate that would double its budget by 1993, a Reagan administration initiative the Bush administration had promised to keep.

At the Department of Energy new money was soaked up by plans for the Superconducting Super Collider (SSC). Congress made a $250 million down payment on the 84-km (52-mi) circular underground particle accelerator. Nevertheless, it was unclear whether the $5.3 billion the Energy Department had budgeted for the project would actually produce a machine capable of generating the energies needed to take high-energy physicists to a new level of understanding about the fundamental properties of matter.

AIDS. The first news that money spent on combating AIDS was having an effect on slowing the pace of the epidemic came toward the end of the year. According to an unreleased Public Health Service document—a copy of which was obtained by *Science* magazine—federal estimates of AIDS for 1993 were between 67,000 and 90,000 cases, a decline of 15% from estimates made one year earlier. In addition, epidemiologists—using a retrospective analysis—saw a dip in the number of expected AIDS cases in 1987, and most believed that this slowdown in the epidemic's spread was the result of either therapy or education.

Epidemiologists were stymied on one important front in predicting the course of the epidemic. Because AIDS is a sexually transmitted disease, researchers argued that they needed to conduct an exhaustive survey on Americans' sexual habits to predict how fast the disease would spread; however, Congress, bowing to pressure from conservative legislators who argued that the federal government had no place in the public's bedrooms, scotched funds for the project.

The Public Health Service also announced that it was planning to make promising new AIDS therapies available at an earlier stage of their development. The "parallel-track" program would enable patients to obtain drugs after a safe dosage level had been determined but before the drug had been shown to be effective. Although the formal details of parallel track were still being worked out, the antiviral therapy dideoxyinosine (ddI) was released in September 1989 under a prototype of the parallel-track scheme.

—Joseph Palca

Scientists of the Year

Honors and awards

The following article discusses recent awards and prizes in science and technology. In the first section the Nobel Prizes for 1989 and the Britannica Awards for 1990 are described in detail. The second section is a selective list of other honors.

Nobel Prize for Chemistry

In the early 1980s two researchers, working independently, made a discovery that reversed a three-quarter-century-old scientific dogma. The dogma was that enzymatic activity—the triggering and acceleration (catalysis) of vital chemical reactions within living cells—was the exclusive domain of protein molecules. The revolutionary find was that ribonucleic acid, or RNA—traditionally thought to be only a passive intracellular carrier of genetic information—could also function as an enzyme. For their discoveries Sidney Altman of Yale University and Thomas R. Cech of the University of Colorado were awarded the 1989 Nobel Prize for Chemistry.

The advance caused scientists to rethink old theories of the way cells function. According to the Royal Swedish Academy of Sciences, the laureates' work would "probably provide a new tool for gene technology, with potential to create a new defense against viral infections." Scientists also speculated that such enzymatic RNA molecules, dubbed ribozymes, may have been the molecules from which sprang the first living organisms on Earth.

Altman's prizewinning work was done with a bacterial enzyme, ribonuclease P, that is composed of both RNA and protein components. Ribonuclease P plays a role in the synthesis of transfer-RNA molecules. Specifically, the enzyme catalyzes a reaction in which one section of a transfer-RNA precursor molecule is cleaved off. Altman originally assumed that it was exclusively the protein part of the ribonuclease P molecule that provided the catalytic action; he believed the RNA component served no active enzymatic function, though it might provide a structural basis for the molecule. His assumption was proved wrong, however, when in 1978 he and his colleagues found that ribonuclease P lost its enzymatic abilities entirely when the RNA portion was removed. By 1983 the roles played by the RNA and protein components had been proved to be exactly the reverse of those Altman had presumed them to be. He and his research team showed that, under certain conditions, the RNA portion alone could act as an enzyme in the cleaving reaction.

Cech was the first person to show that an RNA molecule could catalyze a chemical reaction. (Altman's earlier research had pointed strongly to such a conclusion, but his own demonstration of enzymatic activity by an RNA molecule, as described above, was made in 1983—a year after Cech published his findings.) Cech began his prizewinning work in 1977 by trying to isolate the protein enzyme that was presumed to control a splicing reaction in RNA molecules copied from cellular DNA. In this reaction an intervening segment of 414 nucleotides is selectively removed from the RNA molecule, and the two ends of the molecule are spliced back together to form a new RNA molecule. While studying the reaction in a single-celled microorganism, *Tetrahymena thermophila,* Cech and his team were startled to find that the reaction proceeded whether or not any protein was present. Convinced that there was some sort of error in their procedure, they set the experiment aside. When they returned to the problem, they were prepared to consider the possibility that the RNA molecule was splicing itself. Painstaking experimentation proved this to be the case. The intervening segment of nucleotides twists into a loop and detaches from the two ends of the molecule, which then splice together.

Although Cech's work showed that RNA could catalyze a reaction, the RNA molecule he studied could not be considered a true enzyme because it could perform the catalytic operation only once and was itself changed in the process. True enzymes are defined as molecules that catalyze a reaction repeatedly and emerge from the reaction unchanged. One year later it was Altman who demonstrated true enzymatic activity by an RNA molecule.

Since the prizewinning work of Altman and Cech, scientists have identified about 100 catalytic RNA molecules that are involved in scores of vital reactions. The discovery of catalytic RNA has inspired speculation that enzymatic RNA molecules may have been the key materials that made life on Earth possible. The question of what kind of molecule first sparked life has long puzzled scientists because both catalysis and genetic-information storage are

Sidney Altman
Yale University, Office of Public Information

428

Thomas Cech
University of Colorado at Boulder

considered necessary preconditions for life, but no single biological molecule was known that possessed both capabilities. The laureates' discovery of enzymatic RNA offers to solve the puzzle by supplying a molecule that can both carry genetic information and facilitate chemical reactions.

The laureates' work has also raised the possibility of using ribozymes to manipulate RNA molecules within cells. The discovery led to the development of a new kind of biotechnological tool called gene shears, which can cut RNA molecules at selected points. When the Nobel Prize was announced, Cech was involved in a patent dispute with Australian scientists over the commercial rights to this technology. Gene shears could one day be used to destroy RNA molecules that cause infections and to treat genetic disorders.

Altman was born on May 7, 1939, in Montreal. He left Canada to attend the Massachusetts Institute of Technology, where he received a B.S. in physics in 1960. Seven years later he gained a Ph.D. in biophysics from the University of Colorado, and he subsequently received research fellowships from Harvard University and the Medical Research Council Laboratory for Molecular Biology at the University of Cambridge in England. He joined the faculty of Yale University as an assistant professor in 1971 and became a professor of biology there in 1980. Altman also acted as dean at Yale College from 1985 until 1989. He became a U.S. citizen in 1984, though he retained his Canadian citizenship.

Cech was born in Chicago on Dec. 8, 1947. He received a B.A. from Grinnell (Iowa) College in 1970 and a Ph.D. in chemistry from the University of California at Berkeley in 1975. In 1978, after a stint at the Massachusetts Institute of Technology as a National Cancer Institute fellow in molecular biology, he joined the faculty of the University of Colorado, where he became a full professor in 1983.

Nobel Prize for Physiology or Medicine

The 1989 Nobel Prize for Physiology or Medicine went to two colleagues at the University of California

Medical School in San Francisco for achievements in clarifying the origins of cancer. The researchers, J. Michael Bishop and Harold E. Varmus, discovered that the viral genes that can cause cancer in humans and other animals do not originate within viruses, as had been previously suggested. Instead, they begin as normal genes within healthy cells of the body, where they serve to control cellular growth and division. The laureates' findings indicated that, under certain circumstances, these benign genes can mutate or can be picked up by infecting viruses and then transformed into oncogenes; *i.e.*, genes capable of causing cancer.

The discovery, published in 1976, disproved a theory that cancer is caused by viral genes, distinct from a cell's normal genetic material. According to that theory, these viral genes exist in inactive form in all body cells. It was presumed that cancer results when the dormant viral genes are activated in some way—for example, by exposure to an environmental carcinogen.

Bishop and Varmus set out to test this theory in the mid-1970s. They concentrated on the Rous sarcoma virus—a virus known to cause tumors in chickens. Previous research had shown that the virus' cancer-causing ability is due to a particular gene within the virus. Bishop and Varmus found that, as would be expected, the gene responsible was present in tumor cells. However, they also found that an apparently harmless gene remarkably similar to the guilty gene was present in healthy cells. Continued research led them to conclude that this harmless gene was a precursor to the gene ultimately responsible for the formation of tumors. In 1976 Bishop, Varmus, and two colleagues—Dominique Stehelin and Peter Vogt—published their findings and described the pathway by which they believed the Rous sarcoma virus caused tumors.

In all cases when a virus infects a healthy cell, it does so by first introducing its nucleic acid into the cell. Once inside the host cell, the virus' genes usually "enslave" the cell, altering the cell's metabolic machinery in such a way that the cell begins to produce thousands of new, potentially infective viruses,

J. Michael Bishop
UCSF; photo, Mikkel Aaland

Harold Varmus
UCSF; photo, Mikkel Aaland

called virions. These virions are then discharged from the host cell to infect other cells. Sometimes genes from the original host cell become incorporated into one of these virions and are carried to another host cell.

The researchers concluded that it was this latter process of gene transfer that provided the basic mechanism for the Rous sarcoma virus' carcinogenic effects. The laureates suggested that after the virus had infected a normal cell and begun its usual process of replication, one of the precursor genes became incorporated into a virion offspring. Subsequent research done by Bishop, Varmus, and others showed that once incorporated into a virus, such genes can cause cancer in several ways. The possible pathways to the ultimate carcinogenic end are so varied that Bishop described the precursor genes as "the keyboard on which carcinogens play." For instance, a virus carrying such a gene—which, it should be remembered, normally governs cellular growth and division—may insert the gene into an abnormal place in the DNA of a subsequent host cell, where the gene's action is no longer controlled. If this happens, the gene can cause the inappropriate or uncontrolled cellular growth characteristic of cancer. Even without viral involvement these precursor genes can be converted by certain carcinogens into forms that promote uncontrolled, cancerous growth.

Because the mechanism described by Bishop and Varmus seems to be common to all forms of cancer, their work has proved invaluable to cancer research. Scientists have already identified more than 40 genes that have cancer-causing potential in animals. This work in turn is expected to lead to developments that will help physicians predict, diagnose, treat, and even prevent cancer in their patients.

Bishop, the son of a clergyman, was born in York, Pa., on Feb. 22, 1936. He attended Gettysburg (Pa.) College and graduated in 1957. Although he showed an interest in history, he entered Harvard University Medical School, where he discovered his passion and talent for biomedical science. There he took up the study of animal viruses and arranged with the dean of students to spend his fourth academic year doing research instead of attending classes. After graduating from Harvard with a medical degree in 1962 and spending two years in internship and residency at Massachusetts General Hospital, Boston, he became a researcher in virology at the National Institutes of Health in Bethesda, Md. In 1968 he joined the faculty of the University of California Medical Center in San Francisco, where from 1972 he was a full professor. From 1981 he also served as director of the university's George F. Hooper Research Foundation. Bishop's research won him numerous honors, including the Biomedical Research Award from the American Association of Medical Colleges in 1981, the Albert Lasker Award for Basic Medical Research in 1982, and the American Cancer Society Medal of Honor in 1985.

Varmus was born in Oceanside, N.Y., on Dec. 18, 1939. He earned a B.A. in English from Amherst (Mass.) College in 1961 and studied 17th-century literature at Harvard University, where he graduated with an M.A. in 1962. He attended medical school at Columbia University, New York City, earning a medical degree in 1966, and then joined the National Cancer Institute in Bethesda, Md., where he began to study bacteria. In 1970 he went to the University of California at San Francisco as a postdoctoral fellow. There he met Bishop and soon afterward embarked with him on the work that was to win them the Nobel Prize. Varmus remained on the faculty of the University of California, where he became a professor of biochemistry and biophysics in 1982. He also was made honorary professor of molecular virology by the American Cancer Society.

Nobel Prize for Physics

Half of the 1989 Nobel Prize for Physics was shared by Hans G. Dehmelt of the University of Washington and West German scientist Wolfgang Paul of the University of Bonn for their development of methods for trapping individual electrically charged particles and atoms so that their properties could be studied with unprecedented precision. The remainder of the prize went to Norman F. Ramsey of Harvard University for developing a technique, known as the separated oscillatory fields method, for inducing atoms to shift from one specific energy level to another.

Dehmelt was cited for the development in 1955 of the Penning trap, which uses a strong static magnetic field and a weak static electric field to capture electrons and electrically charged atoms, or ions. The trap confines the electrons and ions in a small space for long periods of time in relative isolation from outside influences so that scientists can better measure their properties. In 1973, by means of his invention, Dehmelt became the first scientist to isolate a single electron for observation.

In 1975 Dehmelt devised a method for "cooling"—reducing the energy of—trapped electrons and ions in order to improve further the accuracy of measurements made on them. His technique uses a laser tuned to a frequency slightly below that of one of the energy-level transitions in the target atoms. Atoms in the trap that are moving toward the laser absorb photons from the laser and reemit them at a slightly higher frequency. The energy difference is taken from the atoms' motion, with the net result that the atoms gradually slow, or "cool." The technique is so successful that Dehmelt was able to cool a magnesium ion to just a few thousandths of a degree above absolute zero—nearly the theoretical limit. The cooling process made it possible for Dehmelt and other physicists to measure atomic frequencies and individual quantum jumps—the transitions between atomic energy levels—with a precision previously unattainable.

Dehmelt and his colleagues used the Penning trap in another ground-breaking procedure when in the 1970s they measured an electron's magnetic moment to an accuracy of four parts in a trillion, the most precise measurement of that quantity at the time. Scientists subsequently used the measurement to test the predictions based on the theory of quantum electrodynamics.

Wolfgang Paul won his share of the Nobel Prize for his development of the Paul trap—the first ion trap invented. Paul's prizewinning work began in the 1950s when he conceived of a means whereby multipolar magnetic fields could be used to focus a beam of ions. He later invented a way of separating ions of different masses—the principle of which is widely used in modern spectrometers—and storing them in what came to be known as the Paul trap. According to the Nobel committee, the Paul trap "developed into a standard method for mass separation, now widely used."

The trap uses a radio-frequency current to maintain an alternating electric field that isolates and confines charged particles and atoms within a small space between three electrodes. The Paul trap "cools" atoms in a manner comparable to Dehmelt's method of laser cooling. Ions moving toward the electromagnetic sources absorb photons and then reemit them at a slightly higher frequency, thereby decreasing their own energy. The result is that the ions are prevented from escaping out of the space between the trap's electrodes.

The traps of Paul and Dehmelt have allowed physicists to study atomic properties and test physical theories with high degrees of precision. They have also become key tools in modern spectroscopy.

For many observers the award to Norman Ramsey of half of the 1989 Nobel Prize for Physics was as much a recognition of his lifetime contribution to science as an acknowledgement of any particular achievement. Ramsey's work on the separated oscillatory fields method, carried out in the late 1940s, provided the basis for modern cesium atomic clocks, which set the international time standard and are used in many exacting applications, including digital telecommunications, satellite navigation, and measurements of continental drift. The Nobel committee also noted Ramsey's contribution to developing the hydrogen maser, a microwave-emitting relative of the laser, which has likewise found applications in the precise measurement of time and frequency. Those specific citations, however, only touched on the highlights of a long, distinguished career.

Ramsey developed his prizewinning separated oscillatory fields method at Harvard University during the late 1940s. His technique uses two separate electromagnetic fields to induce energy-level transitions in atoms. A beam of excited atoms is passed through a magnetic field. As the atoms enter the magnetic field, they are exposed to an electromagnetic field tuned to a frequency equal to one of their energy-level transitions. This induces that specific energy-level transition in the atoms.

Ramsey's achievement lies in his use of a second electromagnetic field—cycling at the same frequency as the first and in phase with it—applied to the atoms as they exit the magnetic field. The effect is to increase the coherence of the photons emitted by the excited atoms, enabling physicists to measure more accurately the energy differences

(From left to right) Hans Dehmelt, Wolfgang Paul, and Norman Ramsey

University of Washington, Seattle; photo, Davis Freeman ©1989

The Nobel Foundation, Stockholm

Harvard University News Office

between specific atomic energy levels and thus to better understand atomic structure.

Ramsey's separated oscillatory fields method was an improvement over earlier techniques for inducing atomic-energy-level transitions. Because those techniques used only one electromagnetic field, their accuracy was limited by the need to keep the magnetic field constant over a relatively large area. Perhaps the most notable application of Ramsey's technique was in the development of cesium atomic clocks, which are used as international time standards—one second is defined as 9,192,631,770 oscillations in the nuclei of excited cesium atoms. Such clocks are accurate to about one part in 10 trillion.

Ramsey later adapted his technique to develop the hydrogen maser, a relative of the laser in which hydrogen atoms are tuned to emit highly coherent microwave radiation at a precise frequency. The hydrogen maser has enabled physicists to study the structure of the hydrogen atom and to make extremely precise measurements of certain atomic properties. It is also widely used in science as a frequency standard.

Dehmelt was born on Sept. 9, 1922, in Görlitz, now part of East Germany. He graduated from the Gymnasium Zum Grauen Kloster, Berlin, in 1940 and for the next six years served as a private in the German Army. Under an army program he studied physics at Breslau Technical University during World War II. In 1945 he was taken prisoner by U.S. military forces near Bastogne, Belgium. After his release in 1946 he took up studies at the University of Göttingen, West Germany, where in 1950 he graduated summa cum laude with a doctoral degree in physics. For the next two years he worked as a research fellow at Göttingen.

Dehmelt traveled to the U.S. in 1952 for postdoctoral work at Duke University, Durham, N.C. In 1955 he joined the faculty of the University of Washington, where he became a full professor in 1961. He also became a U.S. citizen in that year. Dehmelt received numerous awards, including the Davisson-Germer Prize of the American Physical Society in 1970. In 1978 he was elected to the U.S. National Academy of Sciences.

Paul was born on Aug. 10, 1913, in Lorenzkirch, now part of East Germany. He studied at the Munich and Berlin institutes of technology and received a doctorate from the Technical University in Berlin in 1939. In 1944 he became a lecturer at the University of Göttingen, and he was appointed a full professor there in 1950. In 1952 he became director of the Physics Institute and a member of the faculty of mathematical and natural sciences at the University of Bonn, West Germany.

Ramsey was born in Washington, D.C., on Aug. 27, 1915, and attended Columbia University, New York City, where he received a Ph.D. in physics in 1940. Additional studies at the University of Cambridge culminated in a D.Sc. degree in 1954. He also received honorary degrees from Harvard University; Case Western Reserve University, Cleveland, Ohio; Middlebury (Vt.) College; the University of Oxford; and Rockefeller University, New York City. During the 1940s he held positions at the University of Illinois, the Massachusetts Institute of Technology Radiation Laboratory, and Columbia University. At Harvard he was an associate professor from 1947 to 1950, became a full professor in 1950, and in 1966 was named Higgins professor of physics.

In addition to teaching and research, Ramsey accepted numerous advisory and administrative posts, including consultant to the U.S. National Defense Research Committee (1940–45), expert consultant to the U.S. secretary of war (1942–45), science adviser to NATO (1958–59), and member of the general advisory committee of the U.S. Atomic Energy Commission (1960–72). He also served as group leader and associate division head at the Los Alamos (N.M.) Scientific Laboratory (1943–45), head of the physics department at Brookhaven National Laboratory, Upton, N.Y. (1946–47), and chairman of the high-energy physics panel of the Science Advisory Board (1963). In 1989 he cochaired a federal committee to investigate the practical significance of cold nuclear fusion. Ramsey's many awards include the Presidential Order of Merit (1947) for his work in radar development during World War II, the E.O. Lawrence Award of the U.S. Atomic Energy Commission (1960), the Davisson-Germer Prize of the American Physical Society (1974), and the Columbia Award for excellence in science (1980).

—Carolyn D. Newton

Britannica Awards

Britannica Awards for 1990, honoring exceptional excellence in the dissemination of learning, were presented to four persons. Two of them, a British-born U.S. physicist and a U.S. paleontologist, were engaged in scientific research.

Although many medals and prizes mark original contributions to the world's sum of knowledge, the Britannica Awards, presented for the first time in 1986, celebrate both exceptional skills in imparting learning to others and a passion for its dissemination. Candidates for the awards are nominated by members of Britannica's Board of Editors and its Editorial Advisory Committees, drawn from the faculties of great universities in the United States, Canada, Japan, Australia, the United Kingdom, and continental Europe.

Dyson, Freeman John. The distinguished physicist and educator Freeman John Dyson is best known

Freeman Dyson
Courtesy, Freeman Dyson

for his speculative work on the possibility of extraterrestrial civilizations. The son of the musician and composer Sir George Dyson, he was born Dec. 15, 1923, in Crowthorne, Berkshire, England, and was educated at Winchester College and the University of Cambridge. As a boy he was an avid reader of such science fiction writers as Jules Verne and H.G. Wells. As a teenager he developed a passion for mathematics, but his mathematics studies at Cambridge were interrupted in 1943 when he was directed to the operational research section of RAF Bomber Command.

Back at Cambridge, he received a B.A. in 1945 and stayed on as a research fellow of Trinity College. In 1947 he won a Commonwealth Fund fellowship to study physics in the United States, and he spent the next two years at Cornell University, Ithaca, N.Y., and Princeton, N.J., where he studied under J. Robert Oppenheimer, then director of the Institute for Advanced Study. He returned to England in 1949 to become a research fellow at the University of Birmingham, but he was appointed professor of physics at Cornell in 1951 and two years later accepted the professorship of physics at the Institute for Advanced Study. He became a U.S. citizen in 1957.

During a leave of absence in the late 1950s, Dyson joined the Orion Project research team, which was attempting to build a manned spacecraft and send it to Mars. A working model was successfully tested, but for a variety of technological and environmental reasons the government rejected it. A long-time advocate of exploration and colonization by earthlings of the solar system and beyond, Dyson has studied ways of searching for evidence of intelligent life, though he has admitted that too little is known as yet about the universe for scientists to conclude whether the existence of extraterrestrial intelligence is probable. Dyson is the author of several books, including *Disturbing the Universe* (1979), *Weapons and Hope* (1984), *Origins of Life* (1985), and *Infinite in All Directions* (1988).

Gould, Stephen Jay. Paleontologist and teacher of biology, geology, and the history of science at Harvard University, Stephen Jay Gould is also an author known for his gift of explaining scientific phenomena in terms comprehensible and even entertaining to lay readers. His column "This View of Life" in *Natural History* magazine won a National Magazine Award for essays and criticism in 1980, and his books have brought him the National Book Award in science in 1981 (for *The Panda's Thumb*, 1980) and the general nonfiction award of the National Book Critics Circle in 1982 (for *The Mismeasure of Man*, 1981). He was among the first group of MacArthur Foundation fellows in 1981.

Gould was born Sept. 10, 1941, in New York City and was brought up in Queens, where his father was a court stenographer. Taken to the American Museum of Natural History to see his first dinosaur when he was five, Stephen announced that he would become a paleontologist. He earned an A.B. degree from Antioch College, Yellow Springs, Ohio, in 1963 and a Ph.D. in paleontology at Columbia University, New York City, in 1967. He wrote his doctoral dissertation on fossil land snails in Bermuda. He joined the geology faculty at Harvard University in 1967, becoming professor of geology in 1973 and Alexander Agassiz professor of zoology in 1982.

Gould received a number of honorary degrees and fellowships and many distinguished awards, beginning in 1975 with the Schuchert Award of the Paleontological Society, given annually for excellence in research to a paleontologist under 40. In 1985 he was the subject of a profile on the television science program "Nova," which received a Westinghouse Science Film Award. His first book, *Ontogeny and Phylogeny* (1977), although addressed to an academic audience, showed him to be capable of capturing a nonscholarly audience and making complicated subjects understandable to the lay reader. Jeremy Bernstein, writing in *The New Yorker* of April 12, 1982, described his column "This View of Life" as "full of fun, totally without pretentiousness, and absolutely clear." Gould's other books include *Ever Since Darwin* (1977), *Hen's Teeth and Horse's Toes* (1983), *The Flamingo's Smile* (1985), *An Urchin in the Storm* (1987), *Time's Arrow, Time's Cycle* (1987), and *Wonderful Life* (1989).

Stephen Jay Gould
Harvard University News Office

AWARD	WINNER	AFFILIATION
ARCHITECTURE		
Praemium Imperiale	I.M. Pei	I.M. Pei & Partners. New York, N.Y.
ASTRONOMY		
Beatrice M. Tinsley Prize	Edward M. Purcell (Emeritus)	Harvard University, Cambridge, Mass.
Beatrice M. Tinsley Prize	Harold I. Ewen	Ewen Knight Corp.; Ewen Dae Corp.
Dannie Heineman Prize for Astrophysics	Carl Heiles	University of California, Berkeley
Harold C. Urey Prize	Jonathan I. Lunine	University of Arizona, Tucson
Helen B. Warner Prize	Nick Kaiser	Canadian Institute for Theoretical Astrophysics, Toronto, Ont.
Henry Norris Russell Lectureship	Icko Iben, Jr.	Pennsylvania State University, University Park
Herbert C. Pollack Award	Kevin D. Pang	California Institute of Technology, Pasadena
Newton Lacy Pierce Prize	Harriet L. Dinerstein	University of Texas, Austin
Rossi Prize	Rashid Sunyaev	Space Research Institute, Moscow
Rossi Prize	Research Team at Kamioka	Kamioka, Japan
Rossi Prize	Team from University of California, Irvine; University of Michigan, Ann Arbor; and Brookhaven National Laboratory, Upton, N.Y.	
William Bowie Medal	Robert N. Clayton	University of Chicago, Ill.
CHEMISTRY		
Alfred Bader Award	Harry B. Gray	California Institute of Technology, Pasadena
Applied Polymer Science Award	Otto Vogl	Polytechnic University, Brooklyn, N.Y.
Arthur C. Cope Award	Koji Nakanishi	Columbia University, New York, N.Y.
Arthur C. Cope Scholar Award	Edward M. Arnett	Duke University, Durham, N.C.
Arthur C. Cope Scholar Award	Paul A. Grieco	Indiana University, Bloomington
Arthur C. Cope Scholar Award	Robert H. Grubbs	California Institute of Technology, Pasadena
Arthur C. Cope Scholar Award	Clayton H. Heathcock	University of California, Berkeley
Arthur C. Cope Scholar Award	William Jorgensen	Purdue University, W. Lafayette, Ind.
Arthur C. Cope Scholar Award	Peter G. Schultz	University of California, Berkeley
Arthur C. Cope Scholar Award	John K. Stille (Deceased)	Colorado State University, Fort Collins
Arthur C. Cope Scholar Award	Harry H. Wasserman	Yale University, New Haven, Conn.
Arthur C. Cope Scholar Award	Paul A. Wender	Stanford University, Calif.
Charles N. Reilley Award	Theodore Kuwana	University of Kansas, Lawrence
Chemical Education Award	George C. Pimentel (Deceased)	University of California, Berkeley
Colloid or Surface Chemistry Award	J. Michael White	University of Texas, Austin

AWARD	WINNER	AFFILIATION
Creative Invention Award	C.F. Hammer	E.I. du Pont de Nemours
Earl K. Plyler Prize	Richard J. Saykally	University of California, Berkeley
Environmental Science and Technology Award	David M. Golden	SRI International, Menlo Park, Calif.
Ernest Guenther Award	Barry M. Trost	Stanford University, Calif.
Fankuchen Award	David Sayre	IBM Corp.
Fernley H. Banbury Award	John P. Porter	B.F. Goodrich Co.
Frederic Stanley Kipping Award	John L. Speier	Dow Corning Corp.
Fryxell Award	Joseph B. Lambert	Northwestern University, Evanston, Ill.
Garvan Medal	Darleane C. Hoffman	University of California, Berkeley
Gold Medal Award of the American Institute of Chemists	Elias J. Corey	Harvard University, Cambridge, Mass.
International Award for Thermal Analysis	David Dollimore	University of Toledo, Ohio
Irving Langmuir Award	William H. Miller	University of California, Berkeley
James Flack Norris Award	Norman L. Allinger	University of Georgia, Athens
Joel Henry Hildebrand Award	John D. Weeks	AT&T Bell Laboratories
King Faisal International Prize in Science	Ahmed Zewail	California Institute of Technology, Pasadena
Linus Pauling Award	Keith U. Ingold	National Research Council of Canada
Maria Goeppert-Mayer Award	Cherry A. Murray	AT&T Bell Laboratories
National Academy of Sciences Award in Chemical Sciences	Ronald C.D. Breslow	Columbia University, New York, N.Y.
National Medal of Science	Richard B. Bernstein	University of California, Los Angeles
National Medal of Science	Rudolph A. Marcus	California Institute of Technology, Pasadena
National Medal of Science	Harden M. McConnell	Stanford University, Calif.
Nuclear Chemistry Award	Michael J. Welch	Washington University, St. Louis, Mo.
Perkin Medal	Frederick J. Karol	Union Carbide Corp.
Pfizer Award in Enzyme Chemistry	Kenneth A. Johnson	Pennsylvania State University, University Park
Philip Hauge Abelson Prize	John T. Edsall (Emeritus)	Harvard University, Cambridge, Mass.
Photochemistry Award	C. Bradley Moore	University of California, Berkeley
Polymer Chemistry Award	Harold A. Scheraga	Cornell University, Ithaca, N.Y.
Priestley Medal	Roald Hoffmann	Cornell University, Ithaca, N.Y.
Pure Chemistry Award	Peter G. Schultz	University of California, Berkeley
Robert A. Welch Award	Norman R. Davidson	California Institute of Technology, Pasadena
Syntex Award	A. Jerry Kresge	University of Toronto, Ont.
Synthetic Organic Chemistry Award	Clayton Heathcock	University of California, Berkeley
Vannevar Bush Award	Linus C. Pauling (Retired)	Linus Pauling Institute of Science & Medicine, Palo Alto, Calif.
Willard Gibbs Medal	Richard B. Bernstein	University of California, Los Angeles
William M. Burton Award	Delbert H. Meyer	Amoco Chemical Co.

AWARD	WINNER	AFFILIATION
Wolf Prize	Duilio Arigoni	Swiss Federal Institute of Technology, Zürich
Wolf Prize	Alan R. Battersby	University of Cambridge, England

EARTH SCIENCES

Arthur L. Day Medal	Dan P. McKenzie	Bullard Laboratories, England
Donath Medal	Mark P. Cloos	University of Texas, Austin
Harry H. Hess Medal	A.G.W. Cameron	Harvard University, Cambridge, Mass.
Hugh Hammond Bennett Award	Charles F. Bentley (Emeritus)	University of Alberta, Edmonton
John Adam Fleming Medal	Donald A. Gurnett	University of Iowa, Iowa City
John Adam Fleming Medal	Michael W. McElhinny	Australia
Losey Atmospheric Sciences Award	James D. Lawrence, Jr.	NASA Langley Research Center
Macelwane Medal	Richard G. Gordon	Northwestern University, Evanston, Ill.
Macelwane Medal	Seth A. Stein	Northwestern University, Evanston, Ill.
Maurice Ewing Medal	Wolfgang H. Berger	Scripps Institution of Oceanography, La Jolla, Calif.
National Medal of Science	Robert P. Sharp (Emeritus)	California Institute of Technology, Pasadena
National Medal of Science	Henry M. Stommel	Woods Hole Oceanographic Institution, Mass.
Penrose Medal	Warren B. Hamilton	U.S. Geological Survey
Robert E. Horton Medal	Peter S. Eagleson	Massachusetts Institute of Technology, Cambridge
Walter H. Bucher Medal	Arthur H. Lachenbruch	U.S. Geological Survey
William Bowie Medal	Walter H. Munk	Scripps Institution of Oceanography, La Jolla, Calif.

ELECTRONICS AND INFORMATION SCIENCES

Charles Stark Draper Prize	Jack S. Kilby	Dallas, Texas
Charles Stark Draper Prize	Robert N. Noyce	Sematech, Austin, Texas
National Medal of Science	Herbert E. Grier	CER Corp., La Jolla, Calif.
National Medal of Technology	Robert R. Everett	Mitre Corp., Bedford, Mass.
National Medal of Technology	Jay W. Forrester (Emeritus)	Massachusetts Institute of Technology, Cambridge

ENERGY

American Ingenuity Award	Stanford R. Ovshinsky	Energy Conversion Devices, Troy, Mich.
Distinguished Service Award of the Association for Women Geoscientists	Jeanne E. Harris	Equity Oil Co.
Ernest Orlando Lawrence Memorial Award	Alexander Pines	University of California, Berkeley
Homer H. Lowry Award	Irving Wender	University of Pittsburgh, Pa.
John Ericsson Award in Renewable Energy	George T. Tsao	Purdue University, W. Lafayette, Ind.

AWARD	WINNER	AFFILIATION
Petroleum Chemistry Award	Robert K. Grasselli	Mobil Research & Development Corp.

ENVIRONMENT

Albert P. and Blanch Y. Greensfelder Medal	Richard H. Pough (Retired)	Nature Conservancy
Distinguished Service Award	Ralph E. Good	State University of Rutgers, New Brunswick, N.J.
Eminent Ecologist Award	George C. Williams	State University of New York, Stony Brook
George Mercer Award	Russell J. Schmitt	University of California, Santa Barbara
Gerard Piel Award	Paul Erhlich	Stanford University, Calif.
John D. and Catherine T. MacArthur Foundation Award	George D. Davis	Commission on the Adirondacks in the 21st Century
John D. and Catherine T. MacArthur Foundation Award	Daniel H. Janzen	University of Pennsylvania, Philadelphia
John D. and Catherine T. MacArthur Foundation Award	Patricia Chapple Wright	Duke University, Durham, N.C.; Ranomafana National Park, Madagascar
Leo Szilard Award for Physics in the Public Interest	Anthony Nero	Lawrence Berkeley Laboratory, Calif.
Medal of the California Academy of Sciences	Peter H. Raven	Missouri Botanical Garden, St. Louis
National Zoological Park Medal	Sir Peter Scott (Deceased)	England
Tyler Prize for Environmental Achievement	Paul J. Crutzen	Max Planck Institute, W. Germany
Tyler Prize for Environmental Achievement	Edward D. Goldberg	Scripps Institution of Oceanography, La Jolla, Calif.
William S. Cooper Award	David Tilman	University of Minnesota, Minneapolis

FOOD AND AGRICULTURE

Bio-Serv Award in Experimental Animal Nutrition	Roger L. Sunde	University of Arizona, Tucson
Borden Award in Nutrition	Bo Lonnerdal	University of California, Davis
Conrad A. Elvehjem Award for Public Service in Nutrition	Samuel J. Fomon	University of Iowa, Iowa City
Cyrus Hall McCormick Jerome Increase Case Gold Medal	Robert H. Tweedy	Brookfield, Wis.
Distinguished Service Award of the American Institute of Biological Sciences	Alfred E. Harper	University of Wisconsin, Madison
Kenneth A. Spencer Award	Boyd L. O'Dell	University of Missouri, Columbia
King Baudouin Award	International Maize and Wheat Improvement Center	El Batán, Mexico
Lederle Award in Human Nutrition	Ranjit K. Chandra	Memorial University of Newfoundland, St. John's
Mead Johnson Award for Research in Nutrition	Ronald J. Sokol	University of Colorado, Boulder
Osborne and Mendel Award	Anthony W. Norman	University of California, Riverside
Wolf Prize	Peter M. Biggs	Agricultural and Food Research Council, U.K.

AWARD	WINNER	AFFILIATION
Wolf Prize	Michael Elliott	Agricultural and Food Research Council, U.K.
World Food Prize	Verghese Kurien	National Dairy Development Board, India

LIFE SCIENCES

Alfred P. Sloan, Jr., Prize	Donald Metcalf	The Walter and Eliza Hall Institute of Medical Research, Melbourne, Australia
Alfred P. Sloan, Jr., Prize	Leo Sachs	Weizmann Institute of Science, Rehovot, Israel
American College of Physicians Award	Eric R. Kandel	Columbia University, New York, N.Y.
Antonio Feltrinelli International Prize	Giuseppe Attardi	California Institute of Technology, Pasadena
Arthur C. Cope Scholar Award	Paul A. Bartlett	University of California, Berkeley
Charles Valentine Riley Memorial Prize	Toshio Murashige	University of California, Riverside
Crafoord Prize	Paul Ehrlich	Stanford University, Calif.
Crafoord Prize	Edward O. Wilson	Harvard University, Cambridge, Mass.
Eli Lilly Award in Biological Chemistry	Michael M. Cox	University of Wisconsin, Madison
Gairdner Foundation International Award	Mark M. Davis	Stanford University, Calif.
Gairdner Foundation International Award	Tak Mak	Ontario Cancer Institute, Toronto
Gottfried Wilhelm Leibniz Award	Berthold K. Hölldobler	Harvard University, Cambridge, Mass.
John D. and Catherine T. MacArthur Foundation Award	Leo W. Buss	Yale University, New Haven, Conn.; Peabody Museum of Natural History, Mass.
Louisa Gross Horwitz Prize	Thomas Cech	University of Colorado, Boulder
Louisa Gross Horwitz Prize	Phillip Sharp	Massachusetts Institute of Technology, Cambridge
National Biotechnology Award	Herbert Boyer	Stanford University, Calif.
National Biotechnology Award	Stanley Cohen	Stanford University, Calif.
National Medal of Science	Melvin Calvin	University of California, Berkeley
National Medal of Science	Katherine Esau (Emeritus)	University of California, Santa Barbara
National Medal of Science	Viktor Hamburger (Emeritus)	Washington University, St. Louis, Mo.
National Medal of Science	Joshua Lederberg	Rockefeller University, New York, N.Y.
National Medal of Science	Harland G. Wood (Emeritus)	Case Western Reserve University, Cleveland, Ohio
National Medal of Technology	Herbert W. Boyer	University of California, San Francisco
National Medal of Technology	Stanley N. Cohen	Stanford University, Calif.
Nichols Medal	Ronald Breslow	Columbia University, New York, N.Y.
Repligen Medal	Stephen J. Benkovic	Pennsylvania State University, University Park

AWARD	WINNER	AFFILIATION
Research Achievement Award	Kenneth L. Rinehart, Jr.	University of Illinois, Champaign-Urbana
Superior Service Award of the U.S. Department of Agriculture	George P. Georghiou	University of California, Riverside
V.D. Mattia Award	Philip Leder	Harvard Medical School, Boston, Mass.; Howard Hughes Medical Institute
Welch Award	Norman Davidson	California Institute of Technology, Pasadena

MATERIALS SCIENCES

David Adler Lectureship	Robert W. Baluffi	Massachusetts Institute of Technology, Cambridge
Humboldt Prize	Dick Manson	Clemson University, S.C.
International Prize for New Materials	Charles Kao	Chinese University of Hong Kong
International Prize for New Materials	J.B. MacChesney	AT&T Bell Laboratories
International Prize for New Materials	Robert D. Maurer	Corning Glass Works
Woldemar A. Weyl International Glass Science Award	Terry Michalske	Sandia National Laboratories
Wood Prize	David E. Aspnes	AT&T Bell Laboratories

MATHEMATICS

Applied Mathematics and Numerical Analysis Award of the National Academy of Sciences	Martin D. Kruskal	Princeton University, N.J.
MacArthur Award	Simon A. Levin	Cornell University, Ithaca, N.Y.
National Medal of Science	Samuel Karlin	Stanford University, Calif.
National Medal of Science	Saunders Mac Lane (Emeritus)	University of Chicago, Ill.
National Medal of Science	Donald C. Spencer (Emeritus)	Princeton University, N.J.
Wolf Prize	Alberto P. Calderon	University of Chicago, Ill.
Wolf Prize	John W. Milnor	Institute for Advanced Study, Princeton, N.J.

MEDICAL SCIENCES

Albert Lasker Basic Medical Research Award	Michael J. Berridge	Trinity College, University of Cambridge, England
Albert Lasker Basic Medical Research Award	Alfred G. Gilman	University of Texas Southwestern Medical Center, Dallas
Albert Lasker Basic Medical Research Award	Edwin G. Krebs	University of Washington, Seattle
Albert Lasker Basic Medical Research Award	Yasutomi Nishizuka	Kobe University, Japan
Albert Lasker Clinical Medical Research Award	Etienne-Emile Baulieu	National Institute of Health and Medical Research, Bicetre, France
Albert Lasker Public Service Award	Lewis Thomas	Cornell University Medical College, New York, N.Y.
Alfred Burger Award	Arnold Brossi	National Institutes of Health, Bethesda, Md.

AWARD	WINNER	AFFILIATION
American Association for the Advancement of Science-Westinghouse Award	Anthony S. Fauci	National Institutes of Health, Bethesda, Md.
Burroughs Wellcome Toxicology Scholar	Stephen Safe	Texas A & M University, College Station
Charles F. Kettering Prize	Mortimer M. Elkind	Colorado State University, Fort Collins
Charles S. Mott Prize	Peter C. Nowell	University of Pennsylvania, Philadelphia
Charles S. Mott Prize	Janet D. Rowley	University of Chicago, Ill.
Distinguished Scientist of the Year	Janice M. Miller	U.S. Department of Agriculture
Edgar D. Tillyer Award	Joel Pokorny	University of Chicago, Ill.
Edgar D. Tillyer Award	Vivianne C. Smith	University of Chicago, Ill.
Frank H. Field and Joe L. Franklin Award	Marjorie and Evan Horning (Emeritus)	Baylor College of Medicine, Houston, Texas
Gairdner Foundation International Award	Jean-Marie Ghuysen	University of Liège, Belgium
Gairdner Foundation International Award	Louis M. Kunkel	Children's Hospital, Boston, Mass.
Gairdner Foundation International Award	Erwin Neher	Max Planck Institute, W. Germany
Gairdner Foundation International Award	Bert Sakmann	Heidelberg University, West Germany
Gairdner Foundation International Award	Ronald G. Worton	The Hospital for Sick Children, Toronto, Ont.
Hoechst-Roussel Award	David A. Hopwood	John Innes Institute; University of East Anglia, Norwich, U.K.
Izaak Walton Killam Memorial Prize	Jules Hardy	University of Montreal; McGill University; Montreal General Hospital
James D. Bruce Memorial Award	S. Leonard Syme	University of California, Berkeley
John P. McGovern Award	Baruch S. Blumberg	Fox Chase Cancer Center, Philadelphia, Pa.
John Phillips Memorial Award	Kurt J. Isselbacher	Massachusetts General Hospital and Harvard Medical School, Boston
John D. and Catherine T. MacArthur Foundation Award	Byllye Avery	National Black Women's Health Project, Atlanta, Ga.
Medicinal Science Prize	Elias J. Corey	Harvard University, Cambridge, Mass.
National Academy of Sciences Award in Molecular Biology	Kiyoshi Mizuuchi	National Institutes of Health, Bethesda, Md.
National Medal of Science	Philip Leder	Harvard Medical School, Boston, Mass.
Richard and Hinda Rosenthal Foundation Award	Ira D. Goldfine	University of California and Mount Zion Hospital and Medical Center, San Francisco
Right Livelihood Award	Aklilu Lemma	Ethiopia
Right Livelihood Award	Legesse Wolde-Yohannes	Ethiopia
Robert de Villiers Award	Eugene Cronkite	Brookhaven National Laboratory, Upton, N.Y.
Rolla N. Harger Award	Yale H. Caplan	Office of the Chief Medical Examiner, State of Maryland

AWARD	WINNER	AFFILIATION
Wightman Award	Lloyd D. MacLean	McGill University, Montreal, Que.
William C. Menninger Memorial Award	David E. Kuhl	University of Michigan, Ann Arbor
William D. Coolidge Award	John R. Cunningham (Emeritus)	University of Toronto, Ont.
William D. Coolidge Award	William R. Hendee	American Medical Association
Wolf Prize	John B. Gurdon	University of Cambridge, England
Wolf Prize	Edward B. Lewis	California Institute of Technology, Pasadena

OPTICAL ENGINEERING

David Richardson Medal	Jean M. Bennett	Naval Weapons Center, China Lake, Calif.
Engineering Excellence Award	Stanley W. Haskell (Retired)	Polaroid Corp.
Engineering Excellence Award	Robert A. Jones	Itek Optical Systems, Lexington, Mass.
Engineering Excellence Award	David Smithgall	AT&T Bell Laboratories
Engineering Excellence Award	Gary K. Starkweather	Apple Computer
Engineering Excellence Award	Laurence S. Watkins	AT&T Bell Laboratories
Free Electron Laser Prize	John M.J. Madey	Duke University, Durham, N.C.
George E. Pake Prize	John A. Armstrong	IBM Corp.
Harold E. Edgerton Award	Erich P. Ippen	Massachusetts Institute of Technology, Cambridge
John Tyndall Award	Thomas G. Giallorenzi	Naval Research Laboratory, Washington, D.C.
Joseph Fraunhofer Award	Thomas I. Harris	Optical Research Associates, Pasadena, Calif.
Quantum Electronics Award	Anthony Siegman	Stanford University, Calif.
Richardson Medal	John W. Evans (Retired)	Sacramento Peak Observatory, Sun Spot, N.M.

PHYSICS

Adolph Lomb Medal	Andrew M. Weiner	Bellcore
Bernd Matthias Memorial Award	Theodore H. Geballe	Stanford University, Calif.
C.E.K. Mees Medal	Adolf W. Lohmann	Friedrich Alexander University of Erlangen-Nuremberg, W. Germany
Charles Hard Townes Award	Herbert Walther	Max Planck Institute, W. Germany
Dannie Heineman Prize for Mathematical Physics	John S. Bell	European Laboratory for Particle Physics (CERN)
Davisson-Germer Prize	Peter J. Feibelman	Sandia National Laboratories, Albuquerque, N.M.
Dillon Medal	Frank S. Bates	AT&T Bell Laboratories
Dirac Medal	Michael Green	Queen Mary College, University of London
Dirac Medal	John Schwarz	California Institute of Technology, Pasadena
Frederic Ives Medal	Joseph W. Goodman	Stanford University, Calif.
George Sarton Medal	Gerald Holton	Harvard University, Cambridge, Mass.
Gold Medal of the Acoustical Society of America	Arthur H. Benade (Deceased)	Case Western Reserve University, Cleveland, Ohio

Scientists of the Year

AWARD	WINNER	AFFILIATION
Gold Medal of the Acoustical Society of America	Richard K. Cook (Retired)	National Bureau of Standards
Gold Medal of the Acoustical Society of America	Lothar W. Cremer (Emeritus)	Technical University of Berlin, W. Germany
Herbert P. Broida Prize	Stephen R. Leone	Joint Institute for Laboratory Astrophysics, Boulder, Colo.
Hideki Yukawa Prize	Ashoke Sen	Tata Institute for Fundamental Research, Bombay, India
High Energy and Particle Physics Prize	Georges Charpak (Retired)	European Laboratory for Particle Physics (CERN)
High Polymer Physics Prize	Eugene Helfand	AT&T Bell Laboratories
Industrial Applications of Physics Prize	Rowland W. Redington	General Electric Co.
Irving Langmuir Prize in Chemical Physics	Frank H. Stillinger	AT&T Bell Laboratories
John T. Tate International Award	Edoardo Amaldi	University of Rome
Julius Edgar Lilienfeld Prize	N. David Mermin	Cornell University, Ithaca, N.Y.
Joliot-Curie Prize	Daniel Denegri	National Saturne Laboratory, Saclay, France
J.J. Sakurai Prize for Theoretical Particle Physics	Nicola Cabibbo	National Institute for Nuclear Physics, Rome; University of Rome
Max Born Award	Samuel L. McCall	AT&T Bell Laboratories
Max Planck Medal	Bruno Zumino	University of California, Berkeley
National Medal of Science	Harry G. Drickamer	University of Illinois, Champaign-Urbana
National Medal of Science	Eugene N. Parker	University of Chicago, Ill.
National Medal of Science	Robert W. Sperry (Emeritus)	California Institute of Technology, Pasadena
National Medal of Technology	Helen Edwards	Fermi National Accelerator Laboratory, Batavia, Ill.
National Medal of Technology	Richard Lundy	Fermi National Accelerator Laboratory, Batavia, Ill.
National Medal of Technology	J. Ritchie Orr	Fermi National Accelerator Laboratory, Batavia, Ill.
National Medal of Technology	Alvin V. Tollestrup	Fermi National Accelerator Laboratory, Batavia, Ill.
Oersted Medal	Anthony P. French	Massachusetts Institute of Technology, Cambridge
Oliver E. Buckley Prize	Hellmut Fritzsche	University of Chicago, Ill.
Prix Paul Doistau/Emile Blutet	Jean-Marc Gaillard	European Laboratory for Particle Physics (CERN)
R. Bruce Lindsay Award	Mark F. Hamilton	University of Texas, Austin
Richtmyer Memorial Lecture	Robert J. Birgeneau	Massachusetts Institute of Technology, Cambridge
R.W. Wood Prize	Rogers H. Stolen	AT&T Bell Laboratories
Robert R. Wilson Prize	Alvin V. Tollestrup	Fermi National Accelerator Laboratory, Batavia, Ill.
Robert R. Wilson Prize	Martin N. Wilson	Oxford Instruments Ltd., U.K.
Sadi Carnot Award	Sam Berman	University of California, Berkeley
Scientific Reviewing Award	Sidney Coleman	Harvard University, Cambridge, Mass.
Silver Medal in Musical Acoustics	Max V. Mathews	Stanford University, Calif.

AWARD	WINNER	AFFILIATION
Silver Medal in Engineering Acoustics	Joshua E. Greenspon	JG Engineering Research Associates, Baltimore, Md.
Silver Medal of the Acoustical Society of America	Floyd Dunn	University of Illinois, Champaign-Urbana
Tom W. Bonner Prize	Ernest M. Henley	University of Washington, Seattle
William F. Meggers Award	David J. Wineland	National Institute of Standards and Technology
Wolfgang K. H. Panofsky Prize	Jerome I. Friedman	Massachusetts Institute of Technology, Cambridge
Wolfgang K. H. Panofsky Prize	Henry W. Kendall	Massachusetts Institute of Technology, Cambridge
Wolfgang K. H. Panofsky Prize	Richard E. Taylor	Stanford Linear Accelerator Center, Calif.

TRANSPORTATION

Charles Goodyear Medal Award	Jean-Marie Massoubre	Michelin Tire Co., Clermont-Ferrand, France
Clifford W. Henderson Award	Donald D. Engen	Federal Aviation Administration
Dr. Alexander Klemin Award	Joseph Mallen (Retired)	Boeing Co.
Elder Statesman of Aviation	Walter J. Addems (Retired)	United Airlines
Elder Statesman of Aviation	Frank V. Ehling (Retired)	Aircraft Manufacturers Association
Elder Statesman of Aviation	Donald D. Engen (Retired)	U.S. Navy
Elder Statesman of Aviation	Najeeb E. Halaby	Halaby International Corp.
Elder Statesman of Aviation	D.P. Hettermann	Delta Air Lines
Elder Statesman of Aviation	Egbert P. Lott (Retired)	United Air Lines
Elder Statesman of Aviation	Jack G. Real (Retired)	Hughes Aircraft Co.
General Aviation Award	Joseph L. Johnson, Jr.	NASA
Grover E. Bell Award	Shaddow Team	Sikorsky Aircraft, Stratford, Conn.
Harmon Trophy	Anne Baddour	Aero Club of New England, Boston, Mass.
Harmon Trophy	Richard Branson	West Sussex, England
Harmon Trophy	John Iseminger	U.S. Army
Harmon Trophy	Kanellos Kanellopoules	Athens, Greece
Harmon Trophy	Per Lindstrand	Oswestry, England
Harmon Trophy	Musa Manarov and Vladimir Titov	U.S.S.R.
Harmon Trophy	Lois McCallin	Belmont, Mass.
Harmon Trophy	Allen E. Paulson	Gulfstream Aerospace Corp.
Von Karman Medal	K.J. Orlik-Rueckemann	National Aeronautical Establishment, Ottawa, Ont.
Wright Brothers Memorial Trophy	Thomas V. Jones	Northrop Corp.

SCIENCE JOURNALISM

American Association for the Advancement of Science-Newcomb Cleveland Prize	David M. Golden, Ripudaman Malhotra, Michael J. Rossi, Margaret A. Tolbert	*Science,* Nov. 27, 1987
American Association for the Advancement of Science-Newcomb Cleveland Prize	Luisa T. Molina, Mario J. Molina, Tai-Ly Tso, Frank C.Y. Yang	*Science,* Nov. 27, 1987

AWARD	WINNER	AFFILIATION
American Institute of Physics Science-Writing Award in Physics and Astronomy	Michael Riordan	Stanford Linear Accelerator Center, Calif.
Andrew Gemant Award	Gerald Holton	Harvard University, Cambridge, Mass.
James T. Grady-James H. Stack Award for Interpreting Chemistry for the Public	Jerry E. Bishop	*Wall Street Journal*
Science Writing Award in Physics and Astronomy	Mark Littmann	Starmaster Corp.
MISCELLANEOUS		
Distinguished Public Service Award	Jake Garn	U.S. Senate
Distinguished Public Service Award	Doug Walgren	U.S. House of Representatives
Moët Hennessy-Louis Vuitton Prize	Sueo Kawabata	University of Kyoto, Japan
National Medal of Science	Arnold O. Beckman (Emeritus)	California Institute of Technology, Pasadena; Beckman Instruments Inc.
Public Service Award	Mike McCormack	McCormack Associates Inc.
Scientific Freedom and Responsibility Award	Natural Resources Defense Council	Washington, D.C.
Scientific Freedom and Responsibility Award	Robert L. Sprague	University of Illinois, Champaign-Urbana
Vannevar Bush Award	Linus Pauling (Retired)	Linus Pauling Institute of Science and Medicine, Palo Alto, Calif.
Westinghouse Science Talent Search	1. Matthew P. Headrick	University of Chicago Laboratory Schools High School, Ill.
	2. David R. Liu	Polytechnic High School, Riverside, Calif.
	3. David M. Shull	Henry Foss High School, Tacoma, Wash.
	4. Soojin Ryu	Bronx High School of Science, New York, N.Y.
	5. Joshua B. Fischman	Montgomery Blair High School, Silver Springs, Md.
	6. Royce Y.T. Peng	Rolling Hills High School, Rolling Hills, Calif.
	7. Laura A. Ascenzi	Bronx High School of Science, New York, N.Y.
	8. Andrew M. Lines	Yorktown High School, Arlington, Va.
	9. Mina K. Yu	Thomas Jefferson High School for Science and Technology, Alexandria, Va.
	10. Bianca D. Santomasso	Stuyvesant High School, New York, N.Y.

Obituaries

Beadle, George Wells (Oct. 22, 1903—June 9, 1989), U.S. physicist, shared the 1958 Nobel Prize for Physiology or Medicine with Edward L. Tatum and Joshua Lederberg for "fundamental contributions in the field of biochemical and microbial genetics." Specifically, Beadle and Tatum were cited for their work on the genetic regulation of chemical processes, and Lederberg was cited for parallel work in bacterial genetics. After earning B.S. (1926) and M.S. (1927) degrees from the University of Nebraska, Beadle received a Ph.D. in genetics (1931) from Cornell University, Ithaca, N.Y., and in the same year undertook research on the fruit fly, *Drosophila melanogaster,* with Thomas Hunt Morgan at the California Institute of Technology (Caltech). There he concluded that genes influence heredity chemically. As a researcher at the Institut de Biologie in Paris, Beadle worked with Boris Ephrussi and devised a complex technique for determining the nature of these chemical effects in *Drosophila.* After serving (1936–37) as a professor at Harvard University, Beadle joined the faculty at Stanford University, where he conducted his Nobel Prize-winning research with Tatum. There they studied gene action in *Neurospora*, the red bread mold. By exposing the mold to X-rays, the two produced a variety of mutations and discovered that each gene determined the structure of a specific enzyme that, in turn, allowed a single chemical reaction to occur. Their findings revolutionized the production of penicillin and laid the foundations for the field of biochemical genetics. After serving as professor at Caltech from 1946 to 1961, Beadle became president of the University of Chicago in 1961, a post he held until 1968. Beadle was the author of such works as *An Introduction to Genetics* (with A.H. Sturtevant; 1939), *Genetics and Modern Biology* (1963), and *The Language of Life* (with Muriel M. Beadle; 1966). He served as an adviser for the *Yearbook of Science and the Future.*

George Beadle
AP/Wide World

Bond, James (Jan. 4, 1900—Feb. 14, 1989), U.S. ornithologist, reigned as the leading expert on birds of the West Indies for more than half a century and was the author of the authoritative *Birds of the West Indies* (1936; rev. ed., 1960). The book was read by master storyteller Ian Fleming, who adopted Bond's unpretentious name for his fictional British secret agent 007. After graduating from the University of Cambridge, Bond made his first scientific expedition up the Amazon River in 1925; however, the following year he decided to specialize in birds native to the West Indies. He visited some 100 Caribbean islands and collected 294 of the 300 species of birds endemic to the area. His trips produced a bounty of books and scientific papers, as well as field guides and checklists of birds of that region. In 1933 he concluded that the Caribbean birds originated in North America rather than South America, as had been previously believed. Bond spent his entire professional career at the Academy of Natural Sciences in Philadelphia. He joined the academy's scientific staff in 1933 and became curator of ornithology in 1962.

Brodie, Bernard Beryl (Aug. 7, 1909—Feb. 27, 1989), British-born pharmacologist and educator, was credited with being one of the founders of modern pharmacology. His research was instrumental in creating drug therapies used to treat cancer, gout, cardiovascular diseases, and mental and emotional illnesses. Brodie, a free-thinking innovator who generally shunned scientific literature, routinely made scientific breakthroughs in new fields. After graduating from New York University in 1935, he began his pioneering experiments while teaching biochemistry and pharmacology at his alma mater's medical school from 1935 to 1950. He continued his research while serving (1950–70) as director of the chemical pharmacology laboratory at the National Heart Institute of the National Institutes of Health. Among his numerous achievements was the discovery that different species of animals (including humans)—and different members of the same species—respond differently to the same drug because of different rates of metabolism; thus, he concluded that blood drug levels could guide therapeutic dosages. He showed how the neurohormones serotonin and norepinephrine affect the function of the brain—which led to the ability to effectively administer antipsychotic drugs to those suffering from mental and emotional disorders. In addition, Brodie helped develop many drugs, notably acetaminophen (the active ingredient in the painkiller Tylenol) and procainamide (used to treat irregular heartbeats). After his formal retirement in 1970, he remained active as a senior consultant with Hoffman-LaRoche laboratories in Nutley, N.J., and as a professor of pharmacology at Pennsylvania State University. Brodie's illustrious scientific career, marked by several honors, including the prestigious Albert Lasker Basic Medical Research Award in 1967 and the National Medal of Science in 1968, was illuminated in a biography by Robert Kanigel, *Apprentice to Genius.*

Valentin Glushko
Tass/Sovfoto

Glushko, Valentin Petrovich (Sept. 2 [Aug. 20, old style], 1908—Jan. 10, 1989), Soviet engineer, pioneered in the development of rocket propulsion systems and designed the innovative liquid-propellant engines that powered Soviet missiles and space rockets. After graduating (1929) from Leningrad State University, Glushko headed the Gas Dynamics Laboratory in Leningrad and began research on electrothermal, solid-fuel, and liquid-fuel rocket engines. He worked closely with the renowned rocket designer Sergey P. Korolyov from 1932 until Korolyov's death in 1966. Glushko and Korolyov achieved their greatest triumph in 1957 with the launching of the first intercontinental ballistic missile in August and the first successful artificial satellite, Sputnik I, in October. Glushko received many official honors, including the Lenin Prize (1957) and election to the Academy of Sciences of the U.S.S.R. (1958). In 1974 he was named chief designer of the Soviet space program, where he oversaw development of the *Mir* space station.

Golay, Marcel (May 3, 1902—April 27, 1989), Swiss physicist, made important contributions to the development of scientific instrumentation. In the field of gas chromatography (a technique for separating chemical substances on the basis of their relative rates of adsorption from a moving gaseous stream), he demonstrated that constituents of a sample traversed a gas chromatographic column in much the same way that electrical impulses are transmitted over transmission lines. This discovery led him to develop long capillary tubing in which good analyses of the constituents could be achieved with very small samples. Golay, who received his Ph.D. from the University of Chicago in 1931, did much of his work for Perkin-Elmer Corp. in Connecticut beginning in 1955. He also invented the Golay cell, a detector that was capable of measuring the intensity of infrared radiation, and developed the Golay coils,

a system used to improve the resolution of magnetic resonance spectrometers by creating uniform magnetic fields within those instruments.

Hammon, William McDowell (July 20, 1904—Sept. 19, 1989), U.S. epidemiologist, conducted (1951) widespread tests of gamma globulin inoculations on children in Houston, Texas; Sioux City, Iowa; and Provo, Utah, in an effort to prevent polio in those regions; by doing so he was able to reduce the chance of contracting the disease by almost 60%. Hammon left college to spend four years (1926–30) in the Belgian Congo (now Zaire) as director of a medical dispensary. He later earned an undergraduate degree from Allegheny College, Meadville, Pa., in 1932 and was awarded his M.D. in 1936 from Harvard University. In 1940 he joined the faculty of the University of California, and in 1946 he was named dean of the School of Public Health there. During World War II Hammon served as a consultant to the U.S. Army surgeon general; appointed director of the Tropical Diseases Commission in 1946, he traveled to Japan, Korea, and China. From 1950 until his retirement in 1973 he was head of the department of epidemiology and microbiology at the Graduate School of Public Health at the University of Pittsburgh, Pa., where he collaborated with Jonas Salk on the perfection of the Salk antipolio vaccine. After the National Foundation for Infantile Paralysis conducted successful tests on the vaccine, the use of gamma globulin as a polio preventive was discontinued in the U.S. Hammon received the U.S. Medal of Freedom in 1946 for his work with the Okinawa expedition during World War II and was awarded the Outstanding Civilian Service Award from the U.S. Army in 1973.

William Hammon
AP/Wide World

Hodes, Horace Louis (Dec. 21, 1907—April 24, 1989), U.S. pediatrician, isolated the first and most common virus shown to cause gastroenteritis in infants and young children. After earning (1931) his M.D. from the University of Pennsylvania Medical School, Hodes served his internship at Children's Hospital in Philadelphia. As a first-year medical student, he discovered that the primary function of vitamin D is to facilitate the absorption of calcium from the intestines. Hodes was associated with Johns Hopkins Medical Center, Baltimore, Md., and conducted medical research at the Rockefeller Institute, New York City, before becoming medical director of Sydenham Hospital in Baltimore, Johns Hopkins' infectious disease hospital. From 1949 until 1976 he was director of the department of pediatrics at Mount Sinai Medical Center, New York City; he was instrumental in the founding of the Mount Sinai School of Medicine. Hodes was named chairman of pediatrics at Mount Sinai in 1966 and Herbert H. Lehman professor in 1969. In 1978 he became distinguished service professor emeritus. In 1982 he was the recipient of the John Howland Award, the highest honor given by the American Pediatric Society.

Charles Hufnagel
AP/Wide World

Hufnagel, Charles Anthony (Aug. 15, 1916—May 31, 1989), U.S. physician, was a pioneering cardiac surgeon who in the early 1950s designed a plastic artificial heart valve used to replace defective aortic valves. After graduating from the University of Notre Dame in 1937, Hufnagel received a medical degree in 1941 from Harvard University Medical School, where he specialized in the study of heart and organ transplants and devised a technique called multipoint fixation, a vital step in the placement of the artificial aortic valve. In 1947 Hufnagel also participated in the first human kidney transplant at Peter Bent Brigham Hospital in Boston, and he was a contributor to the development of the modern heart-lung machine. While serving (1950–58) as director of the Georgetown University (Washington, D.C.) Medical Center's surgical research laboratory, he implanted (1952) the first artificial heart valve into a human heart. From 1969 to 1979 Hufnagel was chairman of the surgery department at Georgetown's medical school. At the time of his death Hufnagel was professor of surgery at the Uniformed Services University, Bethesda, Md., and clinical professor of surgery at George Washington University Hospital, Washington, D.C.

Jeffreys, Sir Harold (April 22, 1891—March 18, 1989), British scientist, made substantial contribu-

tions in the fields of geophysics, astronomy, and meteorology but was perhaps best known to the general public as a leading opponent of the theory of continental drift. Jeffreys studied at Armstrong College, Newcastle-upon-Tyne (B.S., 1910; D.Sc., 1917), and the University of Cambridge (B.A., 1913; M.A., 1917), where he was elected a fellow at St. John's College in 1914. After working in the Meteorological Office (1917–22), he served on the Cambridge faculty as a lecturer in mathematics (1923–32), a reader in geophysics (1932–46), and Plumian professor of astronomy and experimental philosophy (1946–58). Jeffreys' early research into seismology and the thermal history of the Earth led him to offer the first scientific hypothesis that the Earth's core is fluid, and in 1940 he coauthored the standard tables of travel times for earthquake waves. Jeffreys, who later applied his research to a study of the origin of the solar system, analyzed the long-term effects of tidal friction on planetary shape and devised models for the physical structure of Jupiter, Saturn, Uranus, and Neptune. He also did significant work on atmospheric circulation and on mathematical probabilities. His principal books include *The Earth: Its Origin, History and Physical Constitution* (1924; frequently revised), *Scientific Inference* (1931), *Earthquakes and Mountains* (1935), *Theory of Probability* (1939), and the six-volume *Collected Papers of Sir Harold Jeffreys* (1971–77). Jeffreys was knighted in 1953.

Klots, Alexander Barrett (Dec. 12, 1903—April 18, 1989), U.S. lepidopterist, wrote the authoritative and popular *A Field Guide to the Butterflies of North America, East of the Great Plains*, first published in 1951, which sold more than 100,000 copies. Klots, a recognized expert on butterflies, moths, and other insects, earned a Ph.D. in entomology in 1931 from Cornell University, Ithaca, N.Y. He was a member of the Explorers Club and traveled extensively throughout the U.S., the Canadian Arctic, Puerto Rico, Brazil, and Europe to collect insect specimens. From 1933 to 1967 he served on the biology faculty at City College of New York (now City University of New York), and in 1946 he became a research associate of the American Museum of Natural History in New York City. Klots, the author of more than 100 articles on Lepidoptera, also wrote such books as *The World of Insects* (1966) and *North American Butterflies and Moths* (1967). With his wife, Elsie, he wrote *Living Insects of the World* (1959), *Wildflowers of the Desert* (1960), *1,001 Questions Answered About Insects* (1961), and *Insects of North America* (1971).

Laing, R(onald) D(avid) (Oct. 7, 1927—Aug. 23, 1989), British psychiatrist, polarized the mental health community with his first book, *The Divided Self* (1960), in which he theorized that schizophrenia might be a rational defensive reaction to unbearable pressures from family members and inappropriate psychiatric treatment. Laing rejected the prevailing theory that the symptoms characteristic of schizophrenia arose from genetic or biochemical causes and denounced the use of drugs, lobotomies, and electroshock therapy, then commonly prescribed for schizophrenics. After graduating (1951) in medicine from the University of Glasgow, Laing served (1951–53) as a British army psychiatrist. He taught (1953–56) at the University of Glasgow, received training in psychoanalysis, and conducted research (1956–60) at the Tavistock Clinic in London. He then put his unorthodox theories into practice as an associate of the Tavistock Institute (1960–89), director of the Langham Clinic (1962–65), chairman of the Philadelphia Association (1964–82), and founding director of Kingsley Hall, an experimental community house in London. Laing's approach to mental illness as a form of individual free expression, combined with a series of well-publicized experiments in the therapeutic use of mescaline and LSD, earned him cult status in the antipsychiatry movement of the 1960s. He modified his theories somewhat in his later books, which included *Sanity, Madness and the Family* (1965), *The Politics of Experience* (1967), *The Politics of the Family* (1971), and the autobiographical *Wisdom, Madness and Folly: The Making of a Psychiatrist* (1985).

Leach, Sir Edmund Ronald (Nov. 7, 1910—Jan. 6, 1989), British anthropologist, was a leading figure in the development of cultural anthropology and an early champion of Claude Lévi-Strauss and structuralism (the analysis of cultures through the underlying structural relations of their elements). Leach graduated in engineering from the University of Cambridge in 1932. He was introduced to anthropology while working for a commercial firm in China, and on his return to England in 1937 he studied anthropology at the London School of Economics (LSE) under Bronislaw Malinowski and Raymond Firth. At the outbreak of World War II, Leach was doing field research among the Kachin people in Burma, where he remained as a translator and intelligence worker in the British Burmese Army until 1945. In *Political Systems of Highland Burma* (1954), Leach incorporated both his practical wartime experiences among the Kachin and his study of their history. Although this work was criticized for its lack of ethnographic data, it was highly influential, as were his later ethnographic studies on the peoples of Borneo and Ceylon (Sri Lanka) and his research on patterns of communication, notably the use of animal names in curses and insults. Leach taught social anthropology at LSE (1947–53) and Cambridge (1953–78). As provost of King's College, Cambridge (1966–79), he was instrumental in the admission of women students. His other important books include *Rethinking*

Anthropology (1961), *Culture and Communication* (1976), and *Structuralist Interpretations of Biblical Myth* (1983). Leach was knighted in 1975.

Lorenz, Konrad Zacharias (Nov. 7, 1903—Feb. 27, 1989), Austrian zoologist, along with Nikolaas Tinbergen and Karl von Frisch, was awarded the 1973 Nobel Prize for Physiology or Medicine for the advancement of the science of ethology, the study of animal behavioral patterns. Lorenz was particularly notable for his research into imprinting; he demonstrated that goslings and ducklings would learn to follow almost any conspicuous, moving object if it were presented with the appropriate stimuli during their first days after hatching and that the model established by imprinting would affect the birds' adult behavior. Lorenz studied medicine at Columbia University, New York City (1922–23), before returning to Vienna to study medicine (M.D., 1928) and zoology (Ph.D., 1933). His first paper, on jackdaw behavior, was published (1927) in a prestigious ornithology journal while he was still a student. Lorenz was a lecturer in comparative anatomy and animal psychology at the University of Vienna from 1937

Konrad Lorenz
UPI/Bettmann Newsphotos

until 1940, when he was chosen to head the new institute of comparative psychology at the University of Königsberg. He served as an army physician from 1941, but he was captured in 1944 and interned by the Soviets. After his release in 1948 Lorenz directed Max Planck institutes for behavioral physiology in Altenberg, Austria (1949–51), Buldern, West Germany (1951–54), and Seewiesen, West Germany (1955–73). In 1973 he was named chairman of the department of animal sociology at the Austrian Academy of Sciences' Institute for Comparative Ethology in Altenberg. In perhaps his most controversial book, *Das sogenannte Böse* (1963; *On Aggression*, 1966), Lorenz extended his behavioral theories to explain human aggression as an innate drive. His other influential books include *Er redete mit dem Vieh, den Vögeln und den Fischen* (1949; *King Solomon's Ring*, 1952), *So kam der Mensch auf den Hund* (1950; *Man Meets Dog*, 1954), and *Das Jahr des Graugans* (1979; *The Year of the Greylag Goose*, 1980).

Mangelsdorf, Paul Christoph (July 20, 1899—July 22, 1989), U.S. botanist, was internationally renowned for crossbreeding corn and successfully traced the origins of modern corn to the primitive maize grown by Native Americans. By back breeding, Mangelsdorf produced maize that was akin to 7,000-year-old specimens discovered in Mexico. He was also instrumental in developing a hybrid seed corn that did not require the time-consuming removal of tassels by hand. In 1982 he introduced crossbred seeds, obtained from an Argentine colleague, that produced perennial corn, alleviating the need to plant a crop annually. His research also extended to other grains, and he was credited with being the first to develop winter wheat with rust-resistant stems. Mangelsdorf began his research at Kansas State University. He earned a science degree in genetics from Harvard University in 1925. He returned to Harvard in 1940 as a professor of botany and was named Fisher professor of natural history in 1962. After his formal retirement in 1968, Mangelsdorf continued to conduct cross-pollination experiments at the University of North Carolina at Chapel Hill. He published *Corn: Its Origin, Evolution and Improvement* in 1974.

Patierno, John (Aug. 18, 1934—Feb. 25, 1989), U.S. aerodynamics engineer, as a corporate vice president and general manager of Northrop Corp.'s B-2 division from 1982 to 1989, was instrumental in developing the design and technology that enabled the Air Force's B-2 advanced technology (Stealth) bomber to penetrate enemy radar without detection. Patierno, dubbed "the father of the B-2," was the 1989 recipient of the Reed Aeronautics Award, the highest honor bestowed by the American Institute of Aeronautics and Astronautics. After earning a B.S. in aeronautical engineering at the Massachusetts Institute of Technology, Patierno joined Northrop in 1956 in the aircraft division. During his early years with the firm, Patierno worked on stability and control analyses of the F-89 interceptor, the T-38 trainer, and the F-5 fighter aircraft. From 1962 to 1974 he was in charge of aerodynamics and propulsion work on all Northrop advanced aircraft systems, notably the Air Force's A-9 and YF-17 prototypes. In 1974

John Patierno
Northrop Corporation

Patierno served as deputy program manager for the Air Force's F-17 air combat fighter system, and the following year he was named deputy program manager for the Navy's F/A-18 Hornet strike fighter. He served as manager (1975–78) of advanced systems before his appointment as vice president in charge of advanced planning and systems development of the aircraft division. In all, Patierno devoted 17 years to the highly classified designs and technology required for the B-2 bomber.

Pedersen, Charles John (Oct. 3, 1904—Oct. 26, 1989), U.S. chemist, conducted groundbreaking experiments as an industrial research chemist for E.I. du Pont de Nemours & Co. During the 1960s he synthesized a group of organic compounds that he named crown ethers, a loose flexible ring of carbon atoms punctuated at regular intervals by oxygen atoms. His discoveries were expanded independently by Donald James Cram and Jean-Marie Lehn, and the three shared the 1987 Nobel Prize for Chemistry for their work. Pedersen, the son of a Norwegian seaman who worked in Korea as a mechanical engineer, moved to the U.S. during the 1920s. After earning a B.A. in chemical engineering from the University of Dayton, Ohio, he received an M.A. in organic chemistry from the Massachusetts Institute of Technology. Pedersen joined Du Pont in 1927 as a research chemist, and during his 42 years with the company he wrote 25 technical papers and secured some 65 patents, primarily in petrochemicals. With his promotion in 1960 to the highest research post, that of research associate, Pedersen was given free rein to pursue his own line of investigations. It was then that he embarked on his Nobel Prize-winning research; his 1967 original paper, which detailed his findings, became a classic. His work led to the laboratory synthesis of molecules that could selectively react with other molecules in much the same way that enzymes and other natural biological molecules do. The discovery meant that scientists could design drugs that would be more effective against infections and tumors and that industrial substances could be synthesized in such a way that their release into the environment would be less damaging. Pedersen retired in 1969.

Pimentel, George (May 2, 1922—June 18, 1989), U.S. chemist, gained renown for his discovery of chemical lasers and for devising methods to capture transient molecules in solid rare gases and other inert matrices so that they could be studied spectroscopically. He pioneered in the development of rapid-scan infrared spectrometers and designed those that flew on the Mariner 6 and 7 space probes to Mars. In the early 1960s Pimentel served as the editor of a textbook that revolutionized the study of chemistry in U.S. high schools and was translated into 13 languages. He served as chairman of a 1985

449

National Research Council committee whose report, "Opportunities in Chemistry," argued that chemistry is a central science and ought to be funded as such. Pimentel received many honors, including the National Medal of Science and the American Chemical Society's Priestley Medal, one of the most prestigious in the field of chemistry. From 1959 he was professor of chemistry at the University of California at Berkeley. In addition, he served from 1977 to 1980 as deputy director of the National Science Foundation, and in 1980 he also became associate director of the Lawrence Berkeley Laboratory. He was president of the American Chemical Society in 1986.

Andrey Sakharov
AP/Wide World

Sakharov, Andrey Dmitriyevich (May 21, 1921— Dec. 14, 1989), Soviet nuclear physicist, human rights activist, and intellectual, was the father of the Soviet hydrogen bomb and, as a tireless crusader for human rights, was awarded the 1975 Nobel Prize for Peace. Sakharov enjoyed rare Soviet prerogatives for having helped to create the hydrogen bomb, but then he raised such persistent, acute questions about its use and the flaws he found unconscionable in Soviet society that in 1980 he was exiled. In 1986 Soviet leader Mikhail Gorbachev invited him to return to Moscow. Sakharov, a brilliant student at Moscow State University, graduated in 1942 and worked in a military plant. After pursuing graduate studies (1945–48) in nuclear physics, he joined a top-secret nuclear weapons project. There, as he wrote in *Sakharov Speaks* (1974), he saw the bomb he created in the hands of "people who, though talented in their own way, were cynical." He tried but failed to persuade Nikita Khrushchev to cancel atmospheric tests in the late 1950s and championed the 1963 U.S.-U.S.S.R. treaty banning nuclear tests. In 1968 the Soviet invasion of Czechoslovakia prompted Sakharov to circulate "Progress, Coexistence, and Intellectual Freedom," an essay highly critical of the increasing repression of Soviet dissidents. It was published in the *New York Times* and then broadcast back to the U.S.S.R. by the Voice of America. Sakharov refused to deny authorship and, though he lost top-level security clearance, he was allowed to remain a member of the prestigious Academy of Sciences and to keep his academy-assigned apartment and country house,

car and driver, and a respectable job. In 1970 he and two other dissidents founded the Committee for Human Rights; in 1971 he married physician-dissident Yelena Bonner, gave up his official home, and was increasingly hounded for his outspokenness. When Sakharov was awarded the Nobel Prize, he was not permitted to travel to Oslo, Norway, to receive it; Bonner did, and she delivered his speech, characteristically in support of intellectual freedom. Sakharov waged an increasingly lonely battle that peaked in December 1979, when he urged other nations to protest the Soviet invasion of Afghanistan by boycotting the 1980 Moscow Olympics. He was stopped by Soviet security officers, told he was stripped of state honors, and sent with Bonner to Gorky, an industrial city. Two hunger strikes and occasional letters smuggled by Bonner kept Sakharov in the world's eye until his 1986 return to Moscow. Though he supported Gorbachev's programs, he also warned against giving too much power to any one leader. In March 1989 Sakharov was elected a deputy to the Congress of People's Deputies. He became a leader of dissident deputies and on December 11 called for rallies and petitions to bring about an end to the Communist Party's monopoly of political power; the day he died Sakharov had exhorted fellow deputies to establish another political party. He was named a Hero of Socialist Labour three times and was awarded the Stalin Prize and the Order of Lenin.

Scott, Sir Peter Markham (Sept. 14, 1909— Aug. 29, 1989), British naturalist, was a leading spokesman for wildlife conservation and was both founder of the British Wildfowl Trust (later renamed the Wildfowl and Wetlands Trust) and a founder of the World Wildlife Fund (renamed the World Wide Fund for Nature). Scott, who was the only son of Antarctic explorer Robert Falcon Scott, attended the University of Cambridge and studied art at the Munich (Germany) State Academy and the Royal Academy in London. In the 1930s he gained renown as a painter of wildlife, particularly birds, and as an accomplished single-handed yachtsman, winning the Prince of Wales Cup three times and a bronze medal in the 1936 Olympic Games. After distinguished service in the Royal Navy during World War II, Scott founded (1946) the Slimbridge Refuge, a waterfowl sanctuary on the River Severn in Gloucestershire. He had tremendous success with conservation and breeding programs there, most notably in his efforts to save the Hawaiian goose, which had become nearly extinct by the 1950s. Scott guided the World Wildlife Fund for more than 25 years as chairman (1961–82), council chairman (1983–85), and honorary chairman (1985–89). As a member (1962–81) of the Species Survival Commission of the International Union for Conservation of Nature and Natural Resources, he created the Red Data Books, the

IUCN's official lists of endangered species. He also led expeditions to such far-flung places as Antarctica and the Galápagos Islands, wrote 18 illustrated travel and wildlife books, and promoted conservation issues on the British television series "Look" and "Survival." Scott was knighted in 1973 and made a Companion of Honour in 1987.

Sears, Robert Richardson (Aug. 31, 1908—May 22, 1989), U.S. psychologist, conducted studies on the effects of parental discipline on a child's personality and behavior. While working for the Child Welfare Research Station at the University of Iowa, he discovered that children whose parents disciplined them the most severely for aggression displayed the least openly aggressive behavior but expressed the greatest amount of hidden aggression while engaged in fantasy play with dolls; children whose parents were the most permissive also showed little aggression, and children who were disciplined in a middle range were the most aggressive. After earning a Ph.D. in psychology from Yale University, he combined teaching and research at his alma mater, at the Universities of Illinois and Iowa, and at Harvard University. Sears became director of Harvard's Laboratory of Human Development, where he presided over another study linking child-rearing practices to the behavior and personality of a child. He was also involved in a long-range study, started by Lewis M. Termanand in 1921, that monitored children with high IQs as they grew to maturity and aged. Sears served as head of the psychology department at Stanford University from 1953 to 1961, when he became dean of the School of Humanities and Sciences. In 1970 he was named the David Starr Jordan professor of psychology at Stanford, a post he held until his retirement in 1973. He was the coauthor of such works as *Frustration and Aggression* (1939) and *Patterns of Child Rearing* (1957).

Segrè, Emilio Gino (Feb. 1, 1905—April 22, 1989), Italian-born U.S. physicist, made significant contributions to the science of physics as codiscoverer—with Owen Chamberlain—of the antiproton, the negatively charged particle having the same mass as the proton; the two won the Nobel Prize for Physics in 1959 for their discovery. Segrè studied engineering at the University of Rome but later studied physics under Enrico Fermi and earned a Ph.D. in 1928. His association with Fermi, his mentor, spanned some three decades. Segrè was named assistant professor of physics at the University of Rome and conducted neutron experiments with Fermi, helping to lay the foundation for the development of atomic energy. In 1935 the two discovered slow neutrons, which have properties vital to the operation of nuclear reactors. In 1936 Segrè became director of the physics laboratory at the University of Palermo, and the following year he discovered technetium, the first artificially

produced element. While visiting in California in 1938, Segrè was fired from his university post in Italy by the Fascist government. He decided to remain in the U.S. and became a research associate at the University of California at Berkeley. There in 1940 he and his associates discovered the element astatine and later, with Glenn Seaborg, Segrè discovered plutonium-239, which was used in the atomic bomb dropped on Nagasaki, Japan. From 1943 to 1946 Segrè served as a group leader at the Los Alamos (N.M.) Scientific Laboratory before returning to Berkeley, where he remained a professor until 1972. He was appointed professor of nuclear physics at the University of Rome in 1974 but later returned to California. Segrè was the author of such works as *Nuclei and Particles* (1964), the biographical *Enrico Fermi, Physicist* (1970), *From X-rays to Quarks* (1980), and *From Falling Bodies to Radio Waves* (1984).

William Shockley
UPI/Bettmann Newsphotos

Shockley, William Bradford (Feb. 13, 1910—Aug. 12, 1989), U.S. physicist, had a brilliant career in physics that was later overshadowed by his controversial views on genetics and race. Shockley shared the 1956 Nobel Prize for Physics with John Bardeen and Walter Brattain for the development of the transistor, a tiny semiconductor that was used as a substitute for the bulkier, less efficient, and more expensive vacuum-tube amplifiers then used in radios and other electronics. He later became notorious for his philosophy of "retrogressive evolution," which held that intelligence was genetically transmitted. Shockley argued that blacks were genetically inferior to whites because they scored lower on IQ tests and that, because blacks were reproducing faster than whites, there was a retrogression in human evolution. Shockley graduated from the California Institute of Technology in 1932 and earned a Ph.D. from the Massachusetts Institute of Technology in 1936 before joining the staff of Bell Telephone Laboratories at Murray Hill, N.J. During World War II he served as a director of research in the Antisubmarine Warfare Operations Research Group of the U.S. Navy. After the war he returned to Bell Laboratories as director of the solid-state physics research program, and in 1947 he and his colleagues developed the transistor.

In 1954–55 he was director of evaluation of weapons systems research for the U.S. Department of Defense. Shockley left Bell Labs in 1954 and launched his own semiconductor factory. A rebellion among his employees, who launched their own companies, sparked an electronics boom that created the area near Stanford University known as Silicon Valley. From 1963 to 1975 Shockley served as a professor of electrical engineering at Stanford. During the 1970s he created a stir when, on more than one occasion, he contributed to a sperm bank that was offering to pass along the genes of "geniuses."

Sir Thomas Sopwith
AP/Wide World

Sopwith, Sir Thomas Octave Murdoch (Jan. 18?, 1888—Jan. 27, 1989), British aircraft designer and industrialist, produced the airplanes that helped Britain win three wars over a period of more than 60 years. These planes included the Sopwith Camel, from which some 1,294 enemy aircraft were shot down in World War I; the Hawker Hurricane, which was used in the decisive Battle of Britain (1940) in World War II; and the Harrier, the vertical-takeoff jet fighter used in the 1982 conflict in the Falkland Islands. Sopwith bought his first airplane in the autumn of 1910, taught himself to fly, and received his pilot's license in November. By the end of December he had set British aerial duration and distance records, including one for a prizewinning flight to Belgium. In 1912 Sopwith established a flying school and formed the Sopwith Aviation Co., which supplied thousands of military aircraft—notably the Camel, Pup, and 1½ Strutter—during World War I. When Sopwith Aviation went bankrupt in 1920, he founded H.G. Hawker Engineering Co. Ltd. (from 1935, Hawker Siddeley Aircraft Ltd.), named for his partner and chief test pilot, Harry Hawker, who was killed in 1921. In the 1930s Sopwith anticipated the coming conflict and authorized the construction of hundreds of Hurricanes, with no guarantee of government orders. The Air Ministry did buy them, however, and in the Battle of Britain these fighters shot down more German planes than did the faster and better-known Spitfires. Sopwith retired in 1963 and thereafter held the title of founder and life president. However, he remained on the Hawker Sidde-

ley board of directors until 1978. He also designed yachts and raced the *Endeavour* (1934) and *Endeavour II* (1937) in the America's Cup competition. He was knighted in 1953. In January 1988 the Royal Air Force honored Sopwith's 100th birthday.

Street, Jabez Curry (May 5, 1906—Nov. 7, 1989), U.S. physicist, in 1936 at Harvard University, with E.C. Stevenson, discovered a fundamental particle of matter known as the muon. A subatomic particle similar to the electron but 207 times heavier, the muon has two forms, the negative muon and its positive antiparticle. Street earned a Ph.D. in physics from the University of Virginia in 1931 and then conducted studies on cosmic rays at the Bartol Research Foundation. In 1932 he joined the faculty at Harvard, where he worked intermittently until his 1976 retirement. Street helped develop ground and ship radar systems while working (1940–45) at the Radiation Laboratory of the Massachusetts Institute of Technology. He also directed the production of the prototype loran (long-range navigation) system, used throughout the world for navigating ships and planes. From 1956 to 1960 Street served as chairman of the department of physics at Harvard. He developed a variety of devices used in high-energy physics research, notably the coincidence detector, which can be used to filter out the constant rain of muons when the detection of particles of another type is desired. In addition to his research in high-energy physics, Street conducted investigations into electronic circuits, electrical discharges in gases, ionization and cloud chambers, circuit development, and bubble chambers.

Weiss, Paul Alfred (March 21, 1898—Sept. 8, 1989), Austrian-born biologist, made fundamental discoveries in the field of cellular development, including breakthroughs in embryology, by demonstrating that an embryo's organization and growth are determined by the physical and chemical environment surrounding the newly multiplied cells. He also helped achieve greater understanding of the mechanics of nervous system development, nerve regeneration, and nerve repair. Weiss earned a Ph.D. at the University of Vienna in 1922 and, with the publication of his doctoral thesis, *Animal Behavior as System Reaction*, introduced the landmark "systems" approach, which diverged from the mechanists' view that animal behavior followed a rigid pattern of cause and effect. From 1922 to 1929 Weiss served as assistant director of the Biological Research Institute of the Vienna Academy of Sciences, where he conducted pioneering studies of cell movement, tissue organization, and organ formation. In 1931 he immigrated to the U.S. to join the Yale University Laboratory, but in 1933 he moved to the University of Chicago, where he conducted experiments in embryology and in differentiation, the process by which tissues and organs develop from a single cell. His tenure there (1933–54) was interrupted during World War II, when he was recruited by the U.S. government to improve methods of surgical nerve repair. He devised a technique for the sutureless splicing of severed nerves, a feat that earned him a merit citation from the U.S. War and Navy departments. From 1954 to 1964 Weiss served as professor at the laboratory of developmental biology at the Rockefeller Institute, New York City, where he showed that, after being pulverized, individual cells from complex organs can reconstitute themselves. In 1962, together with A. Cecil Taylor, Weiss for the first time photographed nerve fiber under a powerful phase-contrast microscope and found that it was a living, changing, adaptable tissue. In further experimentation he discovered that nerves could regenerate themselves. A prolific author of some 350 scientific articles, he also published 11 books, including *Principles of Development: A Text in Experimental Embryology* (1939) and *The Science of Life* (1973). In 1980 Weiss was awarded the National Medal of Science.

Wolman, Abel (June 10, 1892—Feb. 22, 1989), U.S. sanitary engineer and educator, together with Linn H. Enslow, developed in 1918 a formula for purifying drinking water with chlorine in specific amounts that would destroy pathogens yet be safe for human consumption. Wolman graduated from Johns Hopkins University, Baltimore, Md., in 1913, and in 1915 he became one of the first students to earn a B.S. degree from the university's newly established School of Engineering. Wolman worked for the U.S. Public Health Service and was chief engineer of the Maryland Department of Health before he joined the faculty of his alma mater in 1937 as chairman of the department of sanitary engineering. His expertise was widely sought, and Wolman advised more than 50 foreign governments on their water supplies. After World War II he conducted studies for the National Research Council to determine the public-health impact of radioactive wastes. His accomplishments were honored in 1975, when he received the National Medal of Science, and in 1976, when he shared the prestigious Tyler Ecology Award with two other scientists.

Yakovlev, Aleksandr Sergeyevich (April 1 [March 19, old style], 1906—Aug. 22, 1989), Soviet aeronautical engineer, designed the Yak series of aircraft, the most important of which constituted more than half of the Soviet Union's World War II fighters. Yakovlev built his own glider in 1924 while working for aircraft designer Sergey V. Ilyushin as an engine mechanic. By the time Yakovlev entered the Zhukovsky Air Force Engineering Academy in 1927, he had designed and built the AIR-1, a light plane that later flew from Sevastopol to Moscow in world-

Aleksandr Yakovlev
Tass/Sovfoto

record time. He completed his studies in 1931, and the next year he organized the Yak design bureau. As deputy aviation minister (1940–46), Yakovlev produced both piston- and jet-engine fighters, bombers, helicopters, and support aircraft. In 1957 he was named chief designer of the Soviet Ministry of the Aircraft Industry. Yakovlev built more than 70 types of aircraft, but in later years he concentrated mainly on the Yak-38 (Forger) jump jet and on commercial and sport planes.

ZoBell, Claude E. (Aug. 22, 1904—March 14, 1989), U.S. marine microbiologist, conducted pioneering studies on living organisms at ocean depths in excess of 6,050 m (20,000 ft) and became the first researcher to recover and cultivate living organisms at extreme ocean depths. After earning his Ph.D. at the University of California in 1931, ZoBell joined the Scripps Institution of Oceanography at the University of California at San Diego the following year. He held the post of professor of marine microbiology there from 1948 to 1972, when he became professor emeritus. ZoBell specialized in the study of deep-sea bacteria, those that survive and thrive under pressures some 1,000 times greater than those found at sea level. He became an expert in barobiology (high-pressure biology) and was credited with coining *barophilic*, a term applied to bacteria that require pressure. Besides winning numerous awards, ZoBell published some 300 scholarly papers and the book *Marine Microbiology* (1946), about his work with the microbial processes associated with the formation and transformation of petroleum.

Claude ZoBell
Scripps Institution of Oceanography,
University of California, San Diego

Contributors to the Science Year in Review

D. James Baker *Earth sciences: Oceanography.* President, Joint Oceanographic Institutions Inc., Washington, D.C.

David M. Boore *Earth sciences: Geophysics.* Geophysicist, U.S. Geological Survey, Menlo Park, Calif.

Harold Borko *Electronics and information sciences: Information systems and services.* Professor, Graduate School of Library and Information Science, University of California, Los Angeles.

John M. Bowen *Medical sciences: Veterinary medicine.* Associate Dean for Research and Graduate Affairs and Professor of Pharmacology and Toxicology, College of Veterinary Medicine, University of Georgia, Athens.

Keith J. Bowman *Materials sciences: Metallurgy.* Assistant Professor of Materials Engineering, Purdue University, West Lafayette, Ind.

George G. Brown *Life sciences: Zoology.* Professor of Zoology, Iowa State University, Ames.

George R. Brubaker *Chemistry: Inorganic chemistry.* Supervisory Chemist, U.S. Food and Drug Administration, Chicago District Laboratory, Chicago.

Paul J. Campbell *Mathematics.* Professor of Mathematics and Computer Science, and Director of Academic Computing, Beloit College, Beloit, Wis.

D.J. Chadi *Physics: Condensed-matter physics.* Principal Scientist, Xerox Palo Alto Research Center, Palo Alto, Calif.

Douglas E. Comer *Electronics and information sciences: Computers and computer science.* Professor of Computer Science, Purdue University, West Lafayette, Ind.

Dave Dooling *Space exploration.* D² Associates, Freelance Science Writing and Aerospace Consulting, Huntsville, Ala.

Carl B. Dover *Physics: Nuclear physics.* Senior Scientist, Brookhaven National Laboratory, Upton, N.Y.

F.C. Durant III *Electronics and information sciences: Satellite systems.* Aerospace Historian and Consultant, Chevy Chase, Md.

Robert G. Eagon *Life sciences: Microbiology.* Franklin Professor of Microbiology, University of Georgia, Athens.

Gerald Feinberg *Physics: High-energy physics.* Professor of Physics, Columbia University, New York, N.Y.

Richard L. Gordon *Energy.* Professor of Mineral Economics and Director of the Center for Energy and Mineral Policy Research, Pennsylvania State University, University Park.

David Guise *Architecture and civil engineering.* Professor of Architecture, City College of New York, and private practice of architecture, New York, N.Y.

Robert Haselkorn *Life sciences: Molecular biology.* F.L. Pritzker Distinguished Service Professor, Department of Molecular Genetics and Cell Biology, University of Chicago, Ill.

John Patrick Jordan *Food and agriculture: Agriculture.* Administrator, Cooperative State Research Service, U.S. Department of Agriculture, Washington, D.C.

Lou Joseph *Medical sciences: Dentistry.* Senior Science Writer, Hill and Knowlton, Inc., Chicago.

Allan P. Katz *Materials sciences: Ceramics.* Technical Manager for Structural Ceramics, Materials Laboratory, Wright-Patterson Air Force Base, Ohio.

George B. Kauffman *Chemistry: Applied chemistry.* Professor of Chemistry, California State University, Fresno.

A
Science
Classic

Benjamin Franklin

Selections from his *Autobiography*

Next to George Washington, Benjamin Franklin (1706–1790) was probably the most famous 18th-century American. Philosopher, politician, businessman, and public servant, he also gained renown for his scientific investigations. His experiments with electricity led to the development of the lightning rod, and he also invented bifocal eyeglasses and a stove that provided more warmth than open fireplaces. Reprinted below, in chronological order, are excerpts from his *Autobiography* (1771–88) in which he describes some of his scientific endeavors.

Beginnings in Electricity

[Franklin was in Philadelphia by the first of January, 1747, and was almost at once absorbed in the special studies in electricity which diverted him from his plans for general science, for the American Philosophical Society, and for his Philosophical Miscellany. In three months he had begun his reports to Peter Collinson in London, who had sent an electric tube to the Library Company of which Franklin was the leading member.]

Philadelphia, March 28, 1747.

Sir:

Your kind present of an electric tube, with directions for using it, has put several of us on making electrical experiments, in which we have observed some particular phenomena that we look upon to be new. I shall therefore communicate them to you in my next, though possibly they may not be new to you, as among the numbers daily employed in those experiments on your side the water, 'tis probable some one or other has hit on the same observations. For my own part, I never was before engaged in any study that so totally engrossed my attention and my time as this has lately done; for what with making experiments when I can be alone, and repeating them to my friends and acquaintance who, from the novelty of the thing, come continually in crowds to see them, I have, during some months past, had little leisure for anything else.

Origin of North-East Storms

[Franklin's observation on the direction of storms, with which the modern study of weather may be said to have begun, was reported to Jared Eliot, along with various other matters which interested Franklin in 1750. The eclipse mentioned in the letter took place on the evening of October 21, 1743.]

Philadelphia, February 13, 1750.

Dear Sir:

You desire to know my thoughts about the northeast storms beginning to leeward. Some years since, there was an eclipse of the moon at nine o'clock in the evening, which I intended to observe; but before night a storm blew up at north-east, and continued violent all night and all next day; the sky thickclouded, dark, and rainy, so that neither moon nor stars could be seen. The storm did a great deal of damage all along the coast, for we had accounts of it in the newspapers from Boston, Newport, New York, Maryland, and Virginia; but what surprised me was to find in the Boston newspapers an account of an observation of that eclipse made there; for I thought, as the storm came from the north-east, it must have begun sooner at Boston than with us, and consequently have prevented such observation. I wrote to my brother about it, and he informed me that the eclipse was over there an hour before the storm began. Since which I have made inquiries from time to time of travellers, and of my correspondents north-eastward and south-westward, and observed the accounts in the newspapers from New England, New York, Maryland, Virginia, and South Carolina; and I find it to be a constant fact that north-east storms begin to leeward and are often more violent there then farther to windward. Thus the last October storm, which with you was on the 8th, began on the 7th in Virginia and North Carolina, and was most violent there.

As to the reason of this, I can only give you my conjectures. Suppose a great tract of country, land and sea, to wit, Florida and the Bay of Mexico, to have clear weather for several days, and to be heated by the sun, and its air thereby exceedingly rarefied. Suppose the country north-eastward, as Pennsylvania, New England, Nova Scotia, and Newfoundland, to be at the same time covered with clouds, and its air chilled and condensed. The rarefied air being lighter must rise, and the denser air next to it will press into its place; that will be followed by the next denser air, that by the next, and so on. Thus, when I have a fire in my chimney, there is a current of air constantly flowing from the door to the chimney; but the beginning of the motion was at the chimney, where the air being rarefied by the fire rising, its place was supplied by the cooler air that was next to it, and the place of that by the next, and so on to the door. So the water in a long sluice or mill-race, being stopped by a gate, is at rest like the air in a calm; but as soon as you open the gate at one end to let it out, the water next the gate begins first to move, that which is next to it follows; and so, though the water proceeds forward to the gate, the motion which began there runs backwards, if one may so speak, to the upper end of the race, where the water is last in motion. We have on this continent a long ridge of mountains running from north-east to south-west, and the coast runs the' same course. These may, perhaps, contribute towards the direction of the winds, or at least influence them in some degree. If these conjectures do not satisfy you, I wish to have yours on the subject.

I doubt not but those mountains which you mention contain valuable mines, which time will discover. I know of but one valuable copper mine in this country, which is that of Schuyler's in the Jerseys. This yields good copper, and has turned out vast wealth to the owners. I was at it last fall, but they were not then at work. The water is grown too hard for them, and they waited for a fire-engine from England to drain their pits. I suppose they will have that at work next summer; it costs them one thousand pounds sterling.

Colonel John Schuyler, one of the owners, has a deer park five miles round, fenced with cedar logs five logs high, with blocks of wood between. It con-

Benjamin Franklin with his lightning detector
The Granger Collection, New York

tains a variety of land, high and low, woodland and clear. There are a great many deer in it, and he expects in a few years to kill two hundred head a year, which will be a very profitable thing. He has likewise six hundred acres of meadow, all within bank. The mine is not far from Passaic Falls, which I went also to see. They are very curious; the water falls seventy feet perpendicularly, as we are told; but we had nothing to measure with.

It will be agreeable to you to hear that our subscription goes on with great success, and we suppose will exceed five thousand pounds of our currency. We have bought for the Academy the house that was built for itinerant preaching, which stands on a large lot of ground capable of receiving more buildings to lodge the scholars, if it should come to be a regular college. The house is one hundred feet long and seventy wide, built of brick, very strong, and sufficiently high for three lofty stories. I suppose the building did not cost less than two thousand pounds but we bought it for seven hundred and seventy-five pounds, eighteen shillings, eleven pence, and three farthings; though it will cost us three and perhaps four hundred more to make the partitions and floors and fit up the rooms. I send you inclosed a copy of our present constitution but we expect a charter from our Proprietaries this summer, when they may probably receive considerable alterations. The paper admonishes me that it is time to conclude. I am, sir, your obliged humble servant. . . .

The Experiment Proposed

[In November 1749 Franklin thought an experiment should be made to prove that lightning and electricity were the same. By July 29, 1750, he had worked out the details of such an experiment. On that date he sent Peter Collinson the famous *Opinions and Conjectures concerning the Properties and Effects of the Electrical Matter, and the Means of Preserving Buildings, Ships, &c., from Lightning, arising from Experiments and Observations made at Philadelphia, 1749,* from which the following extract is taken.]

These explanations of the power and operation of points when they first occurred to me, and while they first floated in my mind, appeared perfectly satisfactory; but now I have written them, and considered them more closely, I must own I have some doubts about them; yet, as I have at present nothing better to offer in their stead, I do not cross them out; for, even a bad solution read, and its faults discovered, has often given rise to a good one, in the mind of an ingenious reader.

19. Nor is it of much importance to us to know the manner in which Nature executes her laws; it is enough if we know the laws themselves. It is of real use to know that china left in the air unsupported will fall and break; but *how* it comes to fall, and *why* it breaks, are matters of speculation. It is a pleasure indeed to know them, but we can preserve our china without it.

20. Thus, in the present case, to know this power of points may possibly be of some use to mankind, though we should never be able to explain it. The following experiments, as well as those in my first paper, show this power. I have a large prime conductor, made of several thin sheets of clothier's pasteboard, formed into a tube, near ten feet long and a foot diameter. It is covered with Dutch embossed paper, almost totally gilt. This large metallic surface supports a much greater electrical atmosphere than a rod or iron of fifty times the weight would do. It is suspended by silk lines, and when charged will strike, at near two inches distance, a pretty hard stroke, so as to make one's knuckle ache. Let a person standing on the floor present the point of a needle, at twelve or more inches distance from it, and while the needle is so presented, the conductor cannot be charged, the point drawing off the fire as fast as it is thrown on by the electrical globe. Let it be charged, and then present the point at the same distance, and it will suddenly be discharged. In the dark you may see the light on the point, when the experiment is made. And if the person holding the point stands upon wax, he will be electrified by receiving the fire at that distance. Attempt to draw off the electricity with a blunt body, as a bolt of iron round at the end, and smooth (a silversmith's iron punch, inch thick, is what I use), and you must bring it within the distance of three inches before you can do it, and then it is done with a stroke and crack. As the pasteboard tube hangs loose on silk lines, when you approach it with the punch-iron, it likewise will move towards the punch, being attracted while it is charged; but if, at the same instant, a point be presented as before, it retires again, for the point discharges it. Take a pair of large brass scales, of two or more feet beam, the cords of the scales being silk. Suspend the beam by a pack-thread from the ceiling, so that the bottom of the scales may be about a foot from the floor; the scales will move round in a circle by the untwisting of the pack-thread. Set the iron punch on the end upon the floor, in such a place as that the scales may pass over it in making their circle; then electrify one scale by applying the wire of a charged phial to it. As they move round, you see that scale draw nigher to the floor, and dip more when it comes over the punch; and if that be placed at a proper distance, the scale will snap and discharge its fire into it. But if a needle be stuck on the end of the punch, its point upwards, the scale, instead of drawing nigh to the punch and snapping, discharges its fire silently through the point, and rises higher from the punch. Nay, even if the needle be placed upon the floor near the punch, its point upwards, the end of the punch, though so much higher than the needle, will not attract the scale and receive its fire, for the needle will get it and convey it away before it comes nigh enough for the punch to act. And this is constantly observable in these experiments, that the greater the quantity of electricity on the pasteboard tube, the farther it strikes or discharges its fire, and the point likewise will draw it off at a still greater distance.

Now if the fire of electricity and that of lightning be the same, as I have endeavoured to show at large in a former paper, this pasteboard tube and these scales may represent electrified clouds. If a tube of only ten feet long will strike and discharge its fire on the punch at two or three inches distance, an electrified cloud of perhaps ten thousand acres may strike and discharge on the earth at a proportionably greater distance. The horizontal motion of the scales over the floor may represent the motion of the clouds over the earth; and the erect iron punch, a hill or high building; and then we see how electrified clouds, passing over hills or high buildings at too great a height to strike, may be attracted lower till within their striking distance. And lastly, if a needle fixed on the punch with its point upright, or even on the floor below the punch, will draw the fire from the scale silently at a much greater than the striking distance, and so prevent its descending towards the punch; or if in its course it would have come nigh enough to strike, yet being first deprived of its fire it cannot, and the punch is thereby secured from the stroke; I say, if these things are so, may not the knowledge of this power of points be of use to mankind in preserving houses, churches, ships, etc., from the stroke of lightning, by directing us to fix on the highest parts of those edifices upright rods of iron made sharp as a needle, and gilt to prevent rusting, and from the foot of those rods a wire down the outside of the building into the ground, or down round one of the shrouds of a ship, and down her side till it reaches the water? Would not these pointed rods probably draw the electrical fire silently out of a cloud before it came nigh enough to strike, and thereby secure us from that most sudden and terrible mischief?

21. To determine the question whether the clouds that contain lightning are electrified or not, I would propose an experiment to be tried where it may be done conveniently. On the top of some high tower or steeple, place a kind of sentry-box, big enough to contain a man and an electrical stand. From the middle of the stand let an iron rod rise and pass bending out of the door, and then upright twenty or thirty feet, pointed very sharp at the end. If the electrical stand be kept clean and dry, a man standing on it when such clouds are passing low might be electrified and afford sparks, the rod drawing fire to him from a cloud. If any danger to the man should be apprehended (though I think there would be none), let him stand on the floor of his box, and now and then bring near to the rod the loop of a wire that has one end fastened to the leads, he holding it by a wax handle, so the sparks, if the rod is electrified, will strike from the rod to the wire and not affect him.

Two Electric Shocks

[Two days before Christmas 1750 Franklin suffered a heavy electric shock about which he wrote a well-known letter on Christmas Day to an unidentified friend in Boston. In February 1751 he wrote, to Peter Collinson in London, a letter which was long thought to be missing but which was finally printed by A. H. Church in The Royal Society. Some Account of the 'Letters and Papers' of the Period 1741–1806, in the Archives, Oxford, 1908.]

Dear Sir:

I received yours of October 4, *via* New England, with the account of what you have laid out in books and mathematical instruments for the Academy, by which I perceive there is but about twenty pounds in your hands, much too little, I fear, for the philosophical apparatus. And the misfortune is that our other expenses in purchasing, building, etc., are like to pinch us so in the beginning that we cannot soon afford an addition to that sum; so that if our good proprietors do not see fit to help us, we must wait for those valuable advantages till we are better able to afford them. The Academy was opened the beginning of this year, and goes on well. Mr. Secretary Peters preached an excellent sermon on the occasion, which he will not suffer to be printed. I long for the letter you mention on Academy affairs, which you intended to send me by Reeves.

By Ouchterlony I sent you my last piece on electricity, and have nothing new to add, except that Mr. Kinnersley, an ingenious gentleman of this place, has applied my horizontal self-moving wheel with success to the playing of tunes on chimes, which it does very prettily. I will get Mr. Evans to make a draft of his machine, and send it to you.

My respects to Mr. Watson. He desired you to inquire what success we had in our attempts to kill a turkey by the electrical strokes. Please to acquaint him that we made several experiments on fowls this winter; that we found two large thin glass jars, gilt (holding each about six gallons and taking two thousand turns of a globe of nine inches diameter to charge them full, when the globe works very well and will charge a common half-pint phial with fifty turns) were sufficient to kill common hens outright; but the turkeys, though thrown into violent convulsions, and then lying as dead for some minutes, would recover in less than a quarter of an hour. However, having added Mr. Kinnersley's jars and mine together, in all five though not fully charged, we killed a turkey with them of about ten-pound weight, and suppose they would have killed a much larger. I conceit that the birds killed in this manner eat uncommonly tender.

In making these experiments I found that a man can without great detriment bear a much greater electrical shock than I imagined. For I inadvertently took the stroke of two of those jars through my arms and body, when they were very near full charged. It seemed an universal blow from head to foot throughout the body, and followed by a violent quick trembling in the trunk, which gradually went off in a few seconds. It was some minutes before I could collect my thoughts so as to know what was the matter; for I did not see the flash though my eye was on the spot of the prime conductor from which it struck the back of my hand, nor did I hear the crack though the by-standers say it was a loud one; nor did I particularly feel the stroke on my hand though I afterwards found it had raised a swelling there the bigness of half a swan shot or pistol bullet. My arms and back of my neck felt somewhat numb the remainder of the evening, and my breastbone was sore for a week after, as if it had been bruised. What the consequences would be if such a shock were taken through the head I do not know. . . .

Our friend, Mr. Kalm, goes home in this ship, with a great cargo of curious things. I love the man and admire his indefatigable industry. I shall do my best endeavour to have the study of natural history established in the Academy, as what I am convinced is a Science of more real worth and usefulness than several of the others we propose to teach, put together. I am, with great respect, dear Sir, your obliged and most humble servant. . . .

Philadelphia, February 4, 1750/1
Please to send for the Library a large glass globe for an electrical machine; a large glass cylinder for ditto. My respects to Dr. Fothergill, and to Dr. Mitchell to whom I purpose to write per next ship.

[Franklin's second shock occurred after 1750, and presumably soon after, while he was still absorbed in electricity; but he did not tell the story till April 29, 1785, in a letter to Jan Ingenhousz.]

. . . YOU will find an account of the first great stroke I received, in pages 161, 162 of my book, 5th edition, 1774. The second I will now give you. I had a paralytic patient in my chamber, whose friends brought him to receive some electric shocks. I made them join hands so as to receive the shock at the same time, and I charged two large jars to give it. By the number of those people I was obliged to quit my usual standing and placed myself inadvertently under an iron hook which hung from the ceiling down to within two inches of my head and communicated by a wire with the outside of the jars. I attempted to discharge them, and in fact did so; but I did not perceive it, though the charge went through me and not through the persons I intended it for. I neither saw the flash, heard the report, nor felt the stroke. When my senses returned, I found myself on the floor. I got up, not knowing how that had happened. I then again attempted to discharge the jars; but one of the company told me they were already discharged, which I could not at first believe, but on trial found it true. They told me they had not felt it, but they saw I was knocked down by it, which had greatly surprised them. On recollecting myself, and examining my situation, I found the case clear. A small swelling rose on the top of my head, which continued sore for some days; but I do not remember any other effect good or bad. . . .

Electrotherapy

[Franklin's experiments in electrotherapy were probably performed about 1751 or shortly after, but his principal account of them was not written till 1757 in a letter to John Pringle.]

Craven Street, December 21, 1757.
Sir:
In compliance with your request, I send you the following account of what I can at present recollect relating to the effects of electricity in paralytic cases which have fallen under my observation.

Some years since, when the newspapers made mention of great cures performed in Italy and Germany by means of electricity, a number of paralytics were brought to me from different parts of Pennsylvania and the neighbouring provinces, to be electrized, which I did for them at their request. My method was to place the patient first in a chair, on an electric stool, and draw a number of large strong sparks from all parts of the affected limb or side. Then I fully charged two six-gallon glass jars, each of which had about three square feet of surface coated; and I sent the united shock of these through the affected limb or limbs, repeating the stroke commonly three times each day. The first thing observed was an immediate greater sensible warmth in the lame limbs that had received the stroke than in the others; and the next morning the patients usually related that they had in the night felt a pricking sensation in the flesh of the paralytic limbs; and would sometimes show a number of small red spots which they supposed were occasioned by those prickings. The limbs, too, were found more capable of voluntary motion, and seemed to receive strength. A man, for instance, who could not the first day lift the lame hand from off his knee, would the next day raise it four or five inches, the third day higher; and on the fifth day was able, but with a feeble languid motion, to take off his hat. These appearances gave great spirits to the patients, and made them hope a perfect cure, but I do not remember that I ever saw any amendment after the fifth day; which the patients perceiving, and finding the shocks pretty severe, they became discouraged, went home, and in a short time relapsed; so that I never knew any advantage from electricity in palsies that was permanent. And how far the apparent temporary advantage might arise from the exercise in the patients' journey, and coming daily to my house, or from the spirits given by the hope of success, enabling them to exert more strength in moving their limbs, I will not pretend to say.

Perhaps some permanent advantage might have been obtained if the electric shocks had been accompanied with proper medicine and regimen, under the direction of a skillful physician. It may be, too, that a few great strokes, as given in my method, may not be so proper as many small ones; since by the account from Scotland of a case in which two hundred shocks from a phial were given daily, it seems that a perfect cure has been made. As to any uncommon strength supposed to be in the machine used in that case, I imagine it could have no share in the effect produced; since the strength of the shock from charged glass is in proportion to the quantity of surface of the glass coated; so that my shocks from those large jars must have been much greater than any that could be received from a phial held in the hand. I am, with great respect, Sir, your most obedient servant. . . .

The Kite

[The experiment Franklin proposed as a means of making certain that lightning was identical with electricity was carried out in France by Dalibard on May 10, 1752; and in June Franklin, who had not yet heard of the success of the experiment, established a similar proof with his famous kite. But he never wrote an autobiographical account of what he had done. His original letter about it to Peter Collinson, dated October 1, 1752, and published in the *Pennsylvania Gazette* on the 19th, was an impersonal announcement intended for the Royal Society. In the Autobiography Franklin passed over both experiments as already familiar. "I will not swell this narrative with an account of that capital experiment"—Dalibard's—"nor of the infinite pleasure I received in the success of a similar one I made soon after in Philadelphia, as both are to be found in the histories of electricity." But Joseph Priestley's *History and Present State of Electricity* published in 1767 was written directly under Franklin's eye and contains precise details about the kite experiment which Priestley could have had only from Franklin, to whom Priestley refers as "the best authority." Priestley's account is therefore almost an autobiographical account by Franklin, and it is here reprinted from pp. 171-72 of Priestley's *History*.]

AS every circumstance relating to so capital a discovery (the greatest, perhaps, since the time of Sir Isaac Newton) cannot but give pleasure to all my readers, I shall endeavour to gratify them with the communication of a few particulars which I have from the best authority.

The Doctor, having published his method of verifying his hypothesis concerning the sameness of electricity with the matter of lightning, was waiting for the erection of a spire in Philadelphia to carry his views into execution, not imagining that a pointed rod of a moderate height could answer the purpose, when it occurred to him that by means of a common kite he could have better access to the regions of thunder than by any spire whatever. Preparing, therefore, a large silk handkerchief and two crosssticks of a proper length on which to extend it, he took the opportunity of the first approaching thunder-storm to take a walk in the fields, in which there was a shed convenient for his purpose. But, dreading the ridicule which too commonly attends unsuccessful attempts in science, he communicated his intended experiment to nobody but his son who assisted him in raising the kite.

The kite being raised, a considerable time elapsed before there was any appearance of its being electrified. One very promising cloud had passed over it without any effect, when, at length, just as he was beginning to despair of his contrivance, he observed some loose threads of the hempen string to stand erect and to avoid one another, just as if they had been suspended on a common conductor. Struck with this promising appearance, he immediately presented his knuckle to the key, and (let the reader judge of the exquisite pleasure he must have felt at that moment) the discovery was complete. He perceived a very evident electric spark. Others succeeded, even before the string was wet, so as to put the matter past all dispute, and when the rain had wet the string he collected electric fire very copiously. This happened in June 1752, a month after the electricians in France had verified the same theory, but before he heard of anything they had done.

Lightning Strikes Upward

[Franklin's further experiments on lightning in a letter to Peter Collinson.]

Philadelphia, September, 1753.

Sir:

In my former paper on this subject, written first in 1747, enlarged and sent to England in 1749, I considered the sea as the grand source of lightning, imagining its luminous appearance to be owing to electric fire, produced by friction between the particles of water and those of salt. Living far from the sea, I had then no opportunity of making experiments on the sea-water, and so embraced this opinion too hastily.

For in 1750 and 1751, being occasionally on the sea coast, I found by experiments that sea-water in a bottle, though at first it would by agitation appear luminous, yet in a few hours it lost that virtue; hence and from this, that I could not by agitating a solution of sea-salt in water produce any light, I first began to doubt of my former hypothesis, and to suspect that the luminous appearance in sea-water must be owing to some other principles.

I then considered whether it were not possible that the particles of air, being electrics *per se*, might, in hard gales of wind, by their friction against trees, hills, buildings, etc., as so many minute electric globes rubbing against non-electric cushions, draw the electric fire from the earth, and that the rising vapours might receive that power from the air, and by such means the clouds become electrified.

If this were so, I imagined that by forcing a constant violent stream of air against my prime conductor, by bellows, I should electrify it *negatively*; the rubbing particles of air drawing from it part of its natural quantity of the electric fluid. I accordingly made the experiment, but it did not succeed.

In September 1752 I erected an iron rod to draw the lightning down into my house, in order to make some experiments on it, with two bells to give notice when the rod should be electrified: a contrivance obvious to every electrician.

I found the bells rang sometimes when there was no lightning or thunder, but only a dark cloud over the rod; that sometimes, after a flash of lightning, they would suddenly stop; and at other times, when they had not rung before, they would, after a flash, suddenly begin to ring; that the electricity was sometimes very faint, so that when a small spark was obtained, another could not be got for some time after; at other times the sparks would follow extremely quick, and once I had a continual stream from bell to bell, the size of a crow-quill; even during the same gust there were considerable variations.

In the winter following I conceived an experiment, to try whether the clouds were electrified *positively* or *negatively;* but my pointed rod, with its apparatus, becoming out of order, I did not refit it till towards the spring, when I expected the warm weather would bring on more frequent thunder-clouds.

The experiment was this: to take two phials; charge one of them with lightning from the iron rod, and give the other an equal charge by the electric glass globe, through the prime conductor; when charged, to place them on a table within three or four inches of each other, a small cork ball being suspended by a fine silk thread from the ceiling so as it might play between the wires. If both bottles then were electrified *positively*, the ball, being attracted and repelled by one, must be also repelled by the other. If the one *positively*, and the other *negatively*, then the ball would be attracted and repelled alternately by each, and continue to play between them as long as any considerable charge remained.

Being very intent on making this experiment, it was no small mortification to me that I happened to be abroad during two of the greatest thunder-storms we had early in the spring; and though I had given orders in the family that if the bells rang when I was from home they should catch some of the lightning for me in electrical phials, and they did so, yet it was mostly dissipated before my return; and in some of the other gusts, the quantity of lightning I was able to obtain was so small, and the charge so weak, that I could not satisfy myself; yet I sometimes saw what heightened my suspicions and inflamed my curiosity.

At last, on the 12th of April, 1753, there being a smart gust of some continuance, I charged one phial pretty well with lightning, and the other equally, as near as I could judge, with electricity from my glass globe; and, having placed them properly, I beheld, with great surprise and pleasure, the cork ball play briskly between them, and was convinced that one bottle was electrized *negatively*.

I repeated this experiment several times during the gust, and in eight succeeding gusts, always with the same success; and being of opinion (for reasons I formerly gave in my letter to Mr. Kinnersley, since printed in London), that the glass globe electrizes *positively*, I concluded that the clouds are *always* electrized *negatively*, or have always in them less than their natural quantity of the electric fluid.

Yet, notwithstanding so many experiments, it seems I concluded too soon; for at last, June the 6th, in a gust which continued from five o'clock P.M., to seven, I met with one cloud that was electrized *positively*, though several that passed over my rod before, during the same gust, were in the *negative* state. This was thus discovered.

I had another concurring experiment, which I often repeated, to prove the negative state of the clouds, viz. while the bells were ringing, I took the phial charged from the glass globe, and applied its wire to the erected rod, considering that if the clouds were electrized *positively*, the rod, which received its electricity from them, must be so too; and then the additional *positive* electricity of the phial would make the bells ring faster; but if the clouds were in a *negative* state, they must exhaust the electric fluid from my rod, and bring that into the same negative state with themselves, and then the wire of a positively charged phial, supplying the rod with what is wanted (which it was obliged otherwise to draw from the earth by means of the pendulous brass ball playing between the two bells), the ringing would cease till the bottle was discharged.

In this manner I quite discharged into the rod several phials that were charged from the glass globe, the electric fluid streaming from the wire to the rod till the wire would receive no spark from the finger; and during this supply to the rod from the phial, the bells stopped ringing; but by continuing the application of the phial wire to the rod, I exhausted the natural quantity from the inside surface of the same phials, or, as I call it, charged them *negatively*.

At length, while I was charging a phial by my glass globe, to repeat the experiment, my bells of themselves stopped ringing, and, after some pause, began to ring again. But now, when I approached the wire of the charged phial to the rod, instead of the usual stream that I expected from the wire to the rod, there was no spark—not even when I brought the wire and the rod to touch; yet the bells continued ringing vigorously, which proved to me that the rod was then *positively* electrified, as well as the wire of the phial, and equally so; and, consequently, that the particular cloud then over the rod was in the same positive state. This was near the end of the gust.

But this was a single experiment, which, however, destroys my first too general conclusion, and reduces me to this: *That the clouds of a thunder-gust are most commonly in a negative state of electricity, but sometimes in a positive state.*

The latter I believe is rare; for, though I, soon

after the last experiment, set out on a journey to Boston, and was from home most part of the summer, which prevented my making further trials and observations, yet Mr. Kinnersley, returning from the Islands just as I left home, pursued the experiments during my absence, and informs me that he always found the clouds in the *negative* state.

So that, for the most part, in thunder-strokes, *it is the earth that strikes into the clouds, and not the clouds that strike into the earth.*

Those who are versed in electric experiments will easily conceive that the effects and appearances must be nearly the same in either case: the same explosion and the same flash between one cloud and another, and between the clouds and mountains, etc.; the same rending of trees, walls, etc., which the electric fluid meets with in its passage; and the same fatal shock to animal bodies; and that pointed rods fixed on buildings or masts of ships, and communicating with the earth or sea, must be of the same service in restoring the equilibrium silently between the earth and clouds, or in conducting a flash or stroke, if one should be, so as to save harmless the house or vessel; for points have equal power to throw off as to draw on the electric fire, and rods will conduct up as well as down.

But though the light gained from these experiments makes no alteration in the practice, it makes a considerable one in the theory. And now we as much need an hypothesis to explain by what means the clouds become negatively, as before to show how they become positively, electrified.

I cannot forbear venturing some few conjectures on this occasion. They are what occur to me at present, and though future discoveries should prove them not wholly right, yet they may in the meantime be of some use, by stirring up the curious to make more experiments, and occasion more exact disquisitions. . . .

These thoughts, my dear friend, are many of them crude and hasty; and if I were merely ambitious of acquiring some reputation in philosophy, I ought to keep them by me till corrected and improved by time and further experience. But since even short hints and imperfect experiments in any new branch of science, being communicated, have oftentimes a good effect in exciting the attention of the ingenious to the subject, and so become the occasion of more exact disquisition and more complete discoveries, you are at liberty to communicate this paper to whom you please; it being of more importance that knowledge should increase than that your friend should be thought an accurate philosopher. . . .

Note on the Conduction of Heat by Different Substances

[On December 6, 1753, Franklin sent Cadwallader Colden a paper of Observations on meteorological matters in which first appeared Franklin's original and pioneer idea on the conduction of heat—an idea later developed at greater length in a letter to John Lining dated April 14, 1757.]

. . . DAMP winds, though not colder by the thermometer, give a more uneasy sensation of cold than dry ones. Because, to speak like an electrician, they conduct better: that is, are better fitted to convey the heat away from our bodies. The body cannot feel *without* itself; our sensation of cold is not in the air *without* the body, but in those parts of the body that have been deprived of their heat by the air. My desk and its lock are, I suppose, of the same temperature when they have been long exposed to the same air; but now, if I lay my hand on the wood, it does not seem so cold to me as the lock; because, as I imagine, wood is not so good a conductor, to receive and convey away the heat from my skin and the adjacent flesh, as metal is. Take a piece of wood of the size and shape of a dollar between the thumb and fingers of one hand, and a dollar in like manner with the other hand; place the edges of both at the same time in the flame of a candle; and though the edge of the wooden piece takes flame, and the metal piece does not, yet you will be obliged to drop the latter before the former, it conducting the heat more suddenly to your fingers. Thus we can without pain handle glass and china cups filled with hot liquors, as tea, etc., but not silver ones. A silver teapot must have wooden handle. Perhaps it is for the same reason that woollen garments keep the body warmer than linen ones equally thick: woollen keeping the natural heat in, or, in other words, not conducting it out to the air. . . .

Institutions
of
Science

THE SPACE TELESCOPE SCIENCE INSTITUTE

BY NAOMI PASACHOFF

"The building with a cosmic observation deck" aptly describes the Baltimore, Maryland, institute that exists to support the largest, most complex astronomical satellite ever built.

A major advantage of an Earth-orbiting telescope becomes apparent when the wavelengths potentially accessible to the HST—ranging from the ultraviolet to the far-infrared—are compared with those that can be observed with the unaided eye and with Palomar's five-meter (200-inch) Hale telescope.

NAOMI PASACHOFF is a Research Associate in the Department of Astronomy, Williams College, Williamstown, Massachusetts, and coauthor of several science textbooks.

(Overleaf) Painting by Robert T. McCall—Space Art International

No self-respecting professor of astronomy would dream of teaching that the universe has a center. Still, more than one distinguished scientist has been heard to call a modern low-rise building on the campus of Johns Hopkins University in Baltimore, Maryland, the center of the astronomical universe. At the time that Johns Hopkins was selected to house the Space Telescope Science Institute (STScI), the president of that university made a somewhat lesser claim. Baltimore, he said, would now become the world capital of astronomy. Whichever sobriquet may be closer to the truth, why is the Space Telescope Science Institute the focus of such interest? Much of the answer lies in the instrument whose scientific management the U.S. National Aeronautics and Space Administration (NASA) has delegated to the institute.

The Hubble Space Telescope (HST) is the world's first major optical telescope intended to be a long-lived fixture in orbit around the Earth. Named for Edwin P. Hubble, the American astronomer whose discovery in the early 20th century that the universe is expanding is considered one of the great milestones in the history of science, the telescope is designed to see objects of a given brightness up to seven times farther in space than can the best telescope on Earth. Further, this orbiting eye in space will work at wavelengths shorter than those accessible from the ground as well as detect objects 50 times fainter and observe them 10 times more clearly.

Instrument with a troubled history

Astronomers are given to analogies to describe their worldview. A favorite in justifying the need for a telescope in space is to ask the skeptic whether a bird-watcher would be satisfied making observations from the bottom of a murky pond, for Earth's bright and turbulent atmosphere limits astronomers' view of the heavens in much that way. In addition,

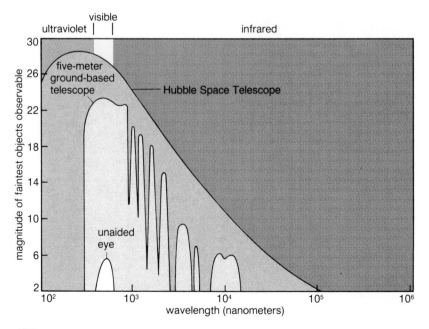

celestial objects give off a wide range of electromagnetic waves having differing energies, but the Earth's atmosphere lets in only light and radio waves. Just as Galileo's first telescope dramatically changed human understanding of the heavens, hitherto limited to what the naked eye could see, astronomers point out that a space telescope will once again revolutionize that understanding. Despite the enormous technological advances since Galileo's time, only a telescope high above the Earth's surface can overcome the basic limitations that the atmosphere imposes.

The first person credited with envisioning a space telescope was German scientist Hermann Oberth, who in 1923 suggested that rockets would someday be powerful enough to launch such an instrument above the atmosphere. Although little notice was taken of his predictions, some quarter century later it was captured German V-2 rockets, taken to the U.S. after the end of World War II, that were used to make the first astronomical observations from space. These peeks lasted only minutes, but they set the stage for the development of small rockets specifically designed for scientific observations and of high-altitude balloons for lifting telescopes.

Princeton University astrophysicist Lyman Spitzer, Jr., is generally acknowledged to be the father of the HST. In 1946, for a classified U.S. Air Force study, Spitzer wrote "Astronomical Advantages of an Extraterrestrial Observatory." Nearly two decades later, as head of a National Academy of Sciences (NAS) group organized to evaluate the future of space science for NASA, Spitzer promoted the idea of a Large Orbiting Telescope.

The name Large Space Telescope (LST) soon evolved and persisted through many feasibility studies and working groups. However, both the name and the size of the telescope mirror eventually grew smaller. In part so the telescope could fit in the cargo bay of a space shuttle, Spitzer's

Positioned above most of the turbulent atmosphere, the HST will observe objects 10 times more clearly than ground-based telescopes. The simulated views below depict the Pleiades star cluster as it might appear were it located in the Large Magellanic Cloud some 160,000 light-years distant. An image of the cluster made with the HST's wide-field–planetary camera (right) would show much more detail than a similar image made with a five-meter telescope on the Earth's surface (left).

Photos, courtesy, Space Telescope Science Institute

original proposal for a 3-meter (120-inch) telescope mirror was amended to call for a 2.4-meter (94-inch) one. To convince the U.S. Congress that the project was worth funding, the word *Large* was dropped in hopes that the connotation "expensive" would fade. Congress finally authorized construction in 1977, although not without an extraordinary lobbying effort on the part of American astronomers. Launch date, via the space shuttle, still under construction itself, was to be in late 1983. (In the early 1980s the instrument received its final name when the decision to honor Hubble's memory with it was made.)

With the benefit of hindsight, one can identify several fateful decisions made in the early days of the project. The original LST was not intimately linked with the space shuttle; a Titan III rocket could have been used to launch it just as easily. Once the decision was made to design the telescope so that it had to be shuttle-launched, the spacecrafts' fates became entwined. A series of problems with the HST's mirrors and instruments caused its launch schedule to slip to 1986. Then the explosion of the shuttle *Challenger* in January of that year began a period of agonizing, expensive further delay. (NASA has since decided that most science missions following 1993 will be launched by expendable rockets. The shuttle will be used only when an astronaut's presence is necessary, as in servicing.)

Perhaps as important in causing the many delays that were to afflict the project even before the *Challenger* disaster was NASA's decision to divide the responsibility for the space telescope project. In 1972 NASA

470

chose Marshall Space Flight Center, Huntsville, Alabama, as "lead center" for the project. Once congressional approval came in 1977, NASA gave responsibility for development of the instruments and of post-launch operations to Goddard Space Flight Center, Greenbelt, Maryland. Marshall, on the other hand, was to direct day-to-day management of the project and oversee the spacecraft engineering. In turn, Marshall chose two contractors—Perkin-Elmer Corp., Wilton, Connecticut, to build the main mirror and the rest of the optical assembly, and Lockheed Missiles and Space Co., Sunnyvale, California, to build the spacecraft and assemble all the components. In addition, the European Space Agency (ESA) was involved in the development of certain parts and instruments.

Rumors abounded about the reasons for the divisions, but all too soon the effects showed themselves. By the end of 1980 it became apparent that Perkin-Elmer could not meet the deadlines for the 1983 launch, and the launch date slipped to 1985. By early 1983 other problems had surfaced that threatened to stall the launch again. When it became clear that the company was falling behind schedule at the rate of one month for every month, NASA officials had to admit to Congress that things

On the day in 1986 that the space shuttle Challenger *exploded, the HST (above) was undergoing vibration tests at Lockheed Missiles and Space Co. to assess its ability to endure the stresses of a shuttle launch. The* Challenger *disaster was but one of several fateful events that contributed to delaying the space telescope's launch schedule.*

NASA/Goddard Space Flight Center

471

were out of hand. NASA made some much-needed changes in management both at Marshall and at the contractors' plants, but to enable it to pay for the overruns, the rest of its 1984 space science program had to be squeezed.

Costs and benefits of the delay

Fortunately, the optical telescope assembly, when finally completed, exceeded NASA's specifications and expectations. In late 1984 it was shipped from Perkin-Elmer to Lockheed. Plans were for Lockheed to assemble the HST and ship it through the Panama Canal from California to Cape Canaveral, Florida, in March 1986 for launch later that year. After the *Challenger* explosion, however, the HST was destined to remain in Sunnyvale for several years. Only in 1989 did it reach Florida—by plane.

The costs required for maintaining the HST during the wait averaged about $7 million a month. Even the most die-hard HST supporters realized that such sums were not trivial—a whole permanent ground-based observatory complete with the world's largest telescope could be built for less than the cost of a year's delay. In addition, scientific opportunities were being lost. The HST would not observe Halley's Comet in its 1986 apparition, nor would it do preliminary observations to support Voyager 2's flyby of Uranus in January 1986 or of Neptune in August 1989. More distressingly, the HST missed the chance to study the early phases of the supernova that appeared in 1987.

On the other hand, it became clear that in many ways the long wait was a blessing in disguise. For example, when Lockheed performed tests on the Hubble telescope in a giant thermal-vacuum chamber in 1986, they found problems with its ability to regulate its internal temperature. Because of the delay, technicians were able to address the problem by replacing thermostats and adding insulation blankets. The postponements also enabled engineers from NASA and ESA to implement solutions to problems with the HST's power supply by installing new solar arrays 10% more powerful than the originals and by replacing the nickel-cadmium batteries for charging in sunlight with more potent nickel-hydrogen batteries. (As NASA's partner in the space telescope project, ESA was responsible for providing the solar array to power the spacecraft. It also designed and built one of the instruments and has several astronomers and other specialists on the STScI staff. In exchange, ESA scientists were guaranteed at least 15% of observing time on the telescope.)

Another unforeseen benefit of the launch delay was that the HST was able to avoid some of the effects of the record-breaking hyperactivity of the Sun that began in 1988–89. High solar activity heats up and expands the Earth's upper atmosphere and thus increases the drag on satellites. Had the HST been launched on one of the earlier dates at orbits as low as then planned (ranging from 555 to 596 kilometers, or 345 to 370 miles), it would almost certainly have required another shuttle mission to lift it to a higher orbit before the end of the 1980s.

NASA and the STScI decided to put the spacecraft into a circular orbit at 611 kilometers (380 miles). The higher altitude not only reduces

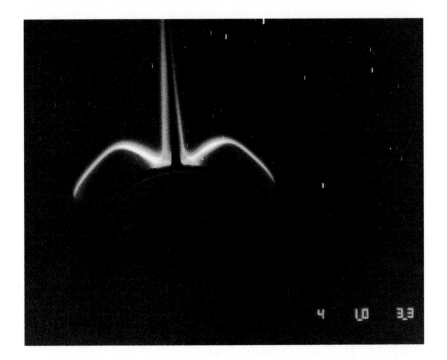

A faint light termed shuttle glow outlines the tail and engine pods of an orbiting space shuttle in a photo taken from the flight deck of the spacecraft. The higher orbit planned for the Hubble telescope should reduce the chances that the phenomenon, caused by reactions between gases of the tenuous upper atmosphere on the leading surfaces of orbiting objects, will interfere with the HST's observations.

NASA

the possibility of premature reentry but also helps counteract another problem that has troubled space researchers since they detected it during early shuttle missions. A mysterious light, dubbed shuttle glow, forms on orbiting spacecraft surfaces as they face into the direction of motion. Although it may still affect the HST, shuttle glow decreases markedly with altitude.

How the STScI came to be

Just as the Hubble Space Telescope has a history that has already entered astronomical lore, so the STScI has an interesting story behind it. The 1965 NAS study that called for a Large Orbiting Telescope also called for a separate service institute. In the mid-1970s, when NASA began to develop plans for the space telescope, it was obvious that for the instrument to function effectively as a research tool, some organization would have to handle many tasks. These included evaluating proposals for observations, scheduling those observations, assisting the observers, and processing and archiving data.

NASA originally intended that Goddard fulfill those functions, just as the Jet Propulsion Laboratory was to handle the Voyager planetary exploration missions. It saw no reason why Goddard's already existing staff of capable professional astronomers should not run the telescope. Non-NASA astronomers, however, took a dim view of those intentions. In their eyes the space telescope was not just another scientific spacecraft but a major observatory, to be used internationally over decades by thousands of scientists. They believed that it should be run in a way similar, for example, to the way Kitt Peak National Observatory in Arizona is operated—by a university consortium, staffed by astronomers who are encouraged to do their own research as well as provide service to visiting astronomers.

473

To avoid an embarrassing public confrontation, NASA decided in 1976 to put the question once again to the NAS. The ensuing report confirmed the conclusion of the previous study: the space telescope should be run like other major optical observatories and not directly by NASA.

In early 1980 NASA solicited bids for the management contract, asking that each applicant indicate a choice of site for the location of the STScI. Numerous institutions with potential sites jumped at the opportunity to become a world center of astronomy. In the end five groups bid for the manager's job, proposing three sites.

The Association of Universities for Research in Astronomy (AURA)— a consortium of over a dozen universities that already managed Kitt Peak, the Cerro Tololo Inter-American Observatory in Chile, and the Sacramento Peak Observatory in New Mexico—submitted the winning bid. Its ultimate choice of site was Johns Hopkins University, whose Baltimore location was convenient. Goddard, which would handle communications with the telescope, was only a short drive away, making the movement of staff nearly as speedy as that of data. The choice of AURA and Johns Hopkins was made official in early 1981.

The chairman of the board of AURA, Arthur Code, taking a leave of absence from the University of Wisconsin to become acting head of the STScI, immediately began looking for a permanent director. From a list of 60 candidates, an AURA board committee selected Riccardo Giacconi of the Harvard-Smithsonian Center for Astrophysics, who was also a professor of astronomy at Harvard.

The announcement of Giacconi's appointment in June 1981 raised eyebrows at NASA. The space telescope, first of all, was an optical observatory, and Giacconi, though a distinguished X-ray astronomer, had not done optical astronomy. Further, Giacconi had hardly impressed many at NASA as a team player when working on the Uhuru and Einstein X-ray satellites. From AURA's point of view, however, Giacconi's experience with NASA and with handling space observatories from the ground were points in his favor. In addition, his administrative abilities and the loyalty

The appointment of astronomer Riccardo Giacconi to head the Space Telescope Science Institute reflected his administrative abilities and previous scientific experience with space observatories. Under Giacconi's leadership the STScI developed into an institution whose responsibilities and high quality few had foreseen.

of his colleagues were unquestioned. Most important, perhaps, Giacconi had already run the Einstein satellite as a national observatory. Although he was principal investigator of the Einstein project, he welcomed involvement of the astronomical community in a way that struck the AURA committee as auspicious.

While NASA may have intended the STScI as little more than a service institution, Giacconi's vision was quite different. Convinced that it should be a first-rank research institute, he pursued a first-rate staff. Some outsiders grumbled that under his leadership the STScI was outgrowing its britches and consequently that it was absorbing too much of NASA's funds for all space research.

The general consensus, however, was that with Giacconi at the helm the institute was succeeding at a task whose immensity had not been anticipated. For example, NASA had not meant for the STScI to develop the software and computers to operate the telescope, plan the observa-

The HST's launch delay gave STScI staff members time to complete largest sky survey in astronomical history. The resulting Guide Star Catalog (top) fits on just two CD-ROMs (compact disc-read only memories) accessible on a personal computer, but it contains information on the positions and brightnesses of almost 19 million celestial objects. Computer screen (above) displays one field of view from the Guide Star Catalog and matches objects (via orange circles) with a display, in the right foreground, of a digitized Palomar sky survey plate.

(Top) Charles Cegielski; (bottom) from NASA, AURA, Caltech, and STScI Plates; photo, Jay M. Pasachoff

tions, and reduce the data (*i.e.*, transform the raw data into condensed, useful forms). The fledgling institute, however, on finding that the outside contractor chosen by NASA to perform these tasks was falling short of the mark, took it upon itself to right the shortcomings. Another task for the new institute was development of the guide star selection system to enable the telescope to hold steady while making observations.

Just as the HST's long launch delay benefited the instrument itself, those years also helped the STScI. In that time astronomers were able to refine their observing proposals. Some STScI staff members developed algorithms, or step-by-step mathematical procedures, to maximize observing time. Others, working on the guide star selection system, completed the largest sky survey in astronomical history. The resulting catalog, about 60 times larger than any of its predecessors, contains information about the positions and brightness of nearly 19 million celestial objects. The Guide Star Catalog not only will enable the HST to locate and track objects under observation but will also assist astronomers using ground-based telescopes. In general, by 1989 the astronomical community agreed that the years of postponements had given the STScI the time to develop into the high-quality institution that Giacconi had foreseen.

A spacecraft of superlatives

As its mandate from NASA, the STScI has the responsibility to "conduct" an observing program on the HST and "to provide the tools for the most efficient utilization of the Edwin P. Hubble Space Telescope by the astronomical community." To comprehend the immense task facing STScI, one must first understand the nature of the most complex astronomical satellite ever built.

Though the HST is the size of a commuter bus, takes up the entire cargo bay of a space shuttle, and weighs 12 tons, it is an incredibly precise instrument. The following "gee-whiz" analogies—and more—have been used to describe its capabilities. (1) It can bring into focus the stars on an American flag seen from 4,800 kilometers (3,000 miles) away. (2) It can hold its aim for 24 hours on a target no bigger than a dime seen at the distance from New York to Washington. (3) It can detect the light of a firefly at a range of 16,000 kilometers (10,000 miles), the distance separating Washington, D.C., and Sydney, Australia.

Despite the superlatives, there are undeniable limits to what the Hubble telescope can do. Designed for astronomical purposes, it cannot make images of or measure phenomena on the Earth. The Sun and the lighted portion of the Moon are too bright for its instruments; likewise, the Earth's brightness can ruin its exposures of the deep sky. Its aperture door automatically closes and the science instruments are automatically turned off if the telescope senses the Sun.

What are the components of the HST that make it at once both so massive and so precise? Essentially the telescope consists of two mirrors and six scientific instruments. The main optics comprise a 2.4-meter (94-inch) concave primary mirror and a 32-centimeter (12½-inch) convex secondary mirror in front of it. The primary mirror, positioned toward

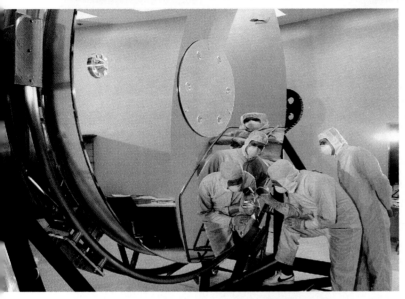

Heart of the HST is its primary mirror, made of fused silica and having a lightweight cellular core sandwiched between two facing surfaces (top left). A microscopically thin coating of aluminum vacuum-deposited on the front surface gives the mirror its high reflectivity (top right and center left). Tube-shaped truss (above), a graphite-epoxy–composite skeleton that spans the middle third of the telescope's length, maintains the relative positions of the primary and secondary mirrors with high accuracy. Completed telescope (left) undergoes preparations at Lockheed for shipment to Florida. The two dark cylinders running parallel to the upper part of the main tube are the solar arrays, which unfurl in space.

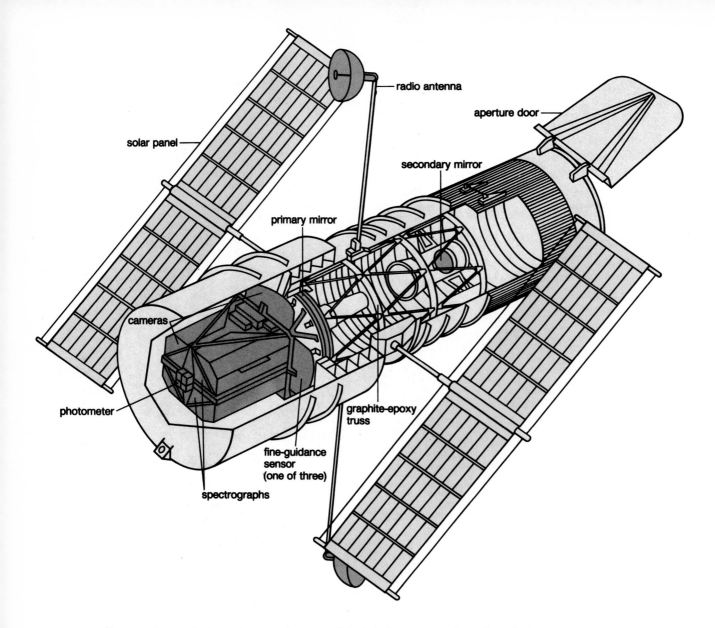

radio antenna

aperture door

solar panel

secondary mirror

primary mirror

cameras

photometer

graphite-epoxy
truss

fine-guidance
sensor
(one of three)

spectrographs

Cutaway diagram depicts various elements of the Hubble Space Telescope, which is approximately 13 meters (43 feet) long and weighs 12 tons. Main components are its two mirrors located in the central third of the cylindrical body and the scientific instruments, in the rear section, which analyze the light gathered by the optics. The solar panels, antennas, and aperture door are deployed into their operating positions after the HST is released from the space shuttle's cargo bay.

the rear of the tubular spacecraft, gathers light from celestial objects and bounces it forward to the secondary mirror. The secondary then redirects the light back to a hole in the primary, where it enters the scientific instrument section.

Perkin-Elmer Corp. extended modern optical technology to its limits in order to produce the mirrors, and the story of their production has made for suspenseful reading in more than one popular magazine. Figuring, polishing, and testing the mirrors to meet, and ultimately to exceed, specifications were all extremely demanding assignments. Zero-gravity simulators were needed so that the mirrors could be figured and polished in an environment similar to what they would experience in orbit. Polishing runs were followed by computerized laser measurements to indicate where the polishing tool should concentrate on each successive run.

Coating and mounting the primary mirror were also difficult tasks. In order to make the mirror reflect not only visible light but also far-ultraviolet, aluminum coatings had to be applied extremely quickly under very high vacuum. Although it took only four minutes to coat the mirrors perfectly, four years of preparation preceded the process. Mounting the mirror took another year and a half.

Although snags at Perkin-Elmer caused delays in the launch schedule, no one faults the mirrors that its engineers turned out. According to all assessments the primary is the finest large astronomical mirror to date. In fact, "gee-whiz" analogies abound in its descriptions as well. For example, if the mirror were as wide as the continental U.S., its surface would be so nearly flat that the highest peak would be less than 10 centimeters (four inches) above the deepest valley. Its shape, necessary for bringing images to a focus, is so nearly perfect that if the mirror's area equaled that of the Earth, it would deviate from that shape by no more than 13 centimeters (five inches). The mirror, made of a fused silica glass disk specially designed by Corning Glass Co., has an extremely lightweight cellular core and weighs only one ton. By contrast, Palomar's five-meter (200-inch) mirror weighs more than the HST in its entirety.

NASA technicians from the astronaut program test in-orbit servicing techniques on a mock-up of the HST in a neutral buoyancy tank at Marshall Space Flight Center. The telescope's modular construction will allow visiting shuttle astronauts to remove the scientific instruments and other components individually for repair or for replacement with next-generation designs.

NASA

Among celestial objects that astronomers hope to study with the space telescope are white dwarf stars and black holes, shown in an artist's conceptions. The white dwarf visualized at the top, part of a binary star system, gravitationally draws material from a red companion star into a pancake-shaped accretion disk around the dwarf. The HST's faint-object camera should be able to detect distant white dwarfs and study their properties. Above, a black hole powers the core of an active galaxy, sending superheated material out along its rotational axis for hundreds of thousands of light-years. The ability of the HST's high-speed photometer to measure fast changes in brightness should allow it to distinguish objects as small as black holes and perhaps amass more evidence for their existence.

To analyze the data gathered by its optics, the HST has six onboard instruments. Intense competition among proposals by different would-be principal investigators culminated in the choice of two cameras, two spectrographs, and a photometer. In addition, as part of the optical telescope assembly, Perkin-Elmer provided fine-guidance sensors that could also be used for astrometry—the accurate measurement of the positions of stars. Each instrument was many years in the making. Since the instruments are modular, space shuttle astronauts can remove them individually for repairs. Instruments can also be switched for other, state-of-the-art replacements over the HST's expected minimum 15-year lifetime. (Two next-generation instruments have already been chosen, at least one of which is to be installed about five years after launch. A near-infrared camera being developed by a group based at the University of Arizona will cover a part of the spectrum not observed by the original set of instruments. An imaging spectrograph from a group based at Goddard is to work over a wide range of wavelengths, from ultraviolet through near-infrared, and will provide images as well as spectra. An improved wide-field–planetary camera is also being prepared.)

The spacecraft has sufficient electricity to allow two instruments to be used at any given time. Sometimes observers will choose to use two instruments simultaneously. Other projects, however, will require only one. In that case other scientists can use a second instrument to scrutinize objects slightly to the side of the main object under study. This "serendipity mode" of parallel observations on Giacconi's X-ray Einstein satellite led to the chance discovery of a large class of quasars, extremely distant but very luminous objects whose exact nature is still a mystery. Undoubtedly, parallel observations with the HST will also prove fruitful.

Each of the HST's instruments was designed to help unlock answers to some questions about the universe that have continued to elude astronomers. The wide-field–planetary camera consists of eight CCDs (charge-coupled devices), electronic chips that change incoming light into electrical signals. The camera's name only begins to suggest its versatility; it can be used in either the wide-field mode for a broad view of a particular region of space or in the high-resolution mode, which is useful not only for observing bodies in our solar system but also for studying extended galactic and extragalactic objects. Among the many types of observations planned for this instrument, astronomers hope to determine whether certain nearby stars have planetary systems of their own. Having been limited in their study of quasars by the fuzzy images obtainable from terrestrial telescopes, astronomers also hope that this camera will help resolve questions about current theories of the way those compact sources can emit as much as 100 times the energy of an entire bright galaxy.

The faint-object camera, the HST's only European-made instrument, yields high-resolution images of very dim objects and gathers data on their chemical makeup. Astronomers expect to use it to expand their understanding of stellar evolution. Ground-based instruments, for example, cannot detect distant white dwarfs, the final stages of certain stars that have used up their nuclear fuel. The faint-object camera should be able both to detect these white dwarfs and to study their properties. Its ability to block out an image's bright portion to uncover very faint objects may also reveal a star's planetary companion. Designed to examine the composition and motion of dim or remote objects, the faint-object spectrograph should help answer questions about the early stages of the universe. Information it gathers from the spectra of distant quasars may provide clues about what matter was like more than 10 billion years ago.

The high-resolution spectrograph, designed to look only at the ultraviolet region of the spectrum, studies light that cannot reach the Earth because of atmospheric absorption. It can detect objects 1,000 times dimmer than those observed by earlier spacecraft launched to study this spectral region. Among other areas of interest, this instrument should help astronomers study the physical composition of active galaxies and quasars and to observe interstellar gas clouds.

Atmospheric turbulence makes it nearly impossible for ground-based telescopes to detect extremely rapid fluctuations in the brightness of stars and other astronomical sources. In space, however, the HST's high-speed photometer, a deceptively simple instrument with no moving parts, will be able to measure these fast changes; it can distinguish events separated by only 10 microseconds; *i.e.*, a hundred-thousandth of a second. Because light takes a finite time to travel from the far side of a star to the side nearest the Earth, the ability to distinguish between such closely spaced events implies that the high-speed photometer could detect fluctuations in brightness of a star as small as three kilometers (1.9 miles) across, about the diameter of a black hole. Accordingly, astronomers hope to use this instrument to collect more evidence for black holes as well as to identify less exotic faint objects.

The fine guidance sensors, which control the pointing of the telescope, also serve as an instrument for astrometry, enabling the HST to measure star positions precisely. While two sensors locate and lock onto two guide stars for the observed target, a third views stars in the vicinity and makes precise measurements of their positions vis-à-vis the guide stars. The HST's measurement of stellar parallax—the change in the apparent position of a star due to the Earth's revolution about the Sun—should be about 5 to 10 times better than measurements made from ground-based telescopes. The fine-guidance sensors should help refine the distance scale of the Milky Way Galaxy and indirectly of the entire universe. Such information may contribute to an answer to what the future of the universe will be. Accurate measurements of star positions might also uncover stars that wobble in their paths through space because of the gravitational pull of hidden planets.

Going beyond the expected

While astronomers have defined ways to use the unique capabilities of each of the HST's instruments to answer long-standing questions, from the outset they have been aware how foolhardy it would be to try to predict just what the telescope would discover. They fully expect that

481

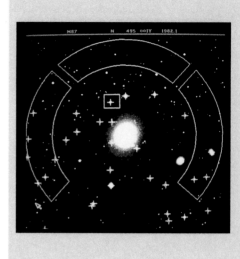

Once the HST is aimed in the general direction of a target, its fine-guidance sensors refine the pointing, searching for guide stars to match against star locations in the Guide Star Catalog. In the simulated image above, in which galaxy M87 is the target, the arc-shaped fields of view of two of the three sensors enclose guide star locations (identified by small crosses). After two of the sensors have acquired and locked onto the correct guide stars, the HST is properly aligned and can begin observations.

Courtesy, Space Telescope Science Institute

Member of the space telescope's guide star selection team holds one of 400 optical discs that together contain images of the entire sky digitized from nearly 1,500 photographic survey plates. Representing the largest sky survey in astronomical history, they form part of the STScI's data archives.

Courtesy, Space Telescope Science Institute

the most exciting finds will be unanticipated ones. The new capabilities of the HST should truly revolutionize astronomy, while its observations should raise at least as many new questions as they answer. Scientists would not be shocked if what they learn demands a revision in their understanding of how the laws of physics work throughout the universe.

As to the perennial question of whether the benefits of the HST will justify the expense, one scientist makes an interesting argument based on the project's entertainment value. She estimates that the HST's total cost will approximate that of a night at the movies for each U.S. resident. Unlike one night out, however, the HST will continue to provide spectacular pictures, not to mention a lot of information, for more than a decade.

How soon the public will be treated to the spectacular returns of the HST is a complicated issue, related to the way science is done. During the first half year or so after launch, the telescope's instruments will be calibrated. The only observations during this period of "commissioning" will be those by the guaranteed time observers (GTOs), the astronomers on the six teams who developed the instruments and those who contributed to the HST's overall design. The STScI will publish some images during this period, but they are supposed to be merely "pretty pictures." Releasing images with much scientific content might enable other scientists to analyze the data and write papers before the GTOs get their much-delayed chance to leave their mark on the advancement of scientific knowledge.

How the STScI operates

Thus, the complexity that the STScI faces in overseeing the operation of the HST extends even to publicizing the initial images and data. In order to handle the various aspects of running the telescope as a major international observatory, the institute has been broken down into several divisions.

The Science Computing and Research Support (SCARS) Division has had the responsibility for developing the Space Telescope Science Data Analysis System. The system contains all the necessary computer software facilities for processing HST data. In addition, HST observers will be able to use the same programs to reduce and analyze data from other observatories. The software has been designed to enable users to work with HST data at their home institutions. To make the system user-friendly, "cookbooks" are available describing standard procedures for different types of data analysis, as well as explaining each of the HST's instruments and its graphics and image displays.

SCARS also operates the data archives. The STScI is the first observatory to try to keep every binary bit of data. Observers formerly concentrated on regions of photographic plates of interest to them and ignored the rest of the data on the plates. While in theory all of this other information is available on the plates filed away in plate vaults, there has been no efficient way for subsequent investigators to access and retrieve it. At the STScI the digital data from the HST's instruments will be stored on optical discs. Specially designed retrieval software will

enable investigators to find what they want and extract it in usable form.
Unlike observers wishing to use the telescope itself, who have to submit
proposals to the STScI for review, researchers interested in the archives
will need to submit proposals only if they want financial or technical
support. The institute's archival function alone could revolutionize the
way astronomy is done. By 1989 digitized versions of photographic sky
surveys carried out on the ground were already available; full-sky coverage takes up 400 optical discs.

SCARS further supports HST users with a photographic laboratory,
the guide star selection system, and the guide star astrometric support
program.

A second component of the institute is its Science and Engineering
Systems Division (SESD). More than a million lines of computer code
are needed to command and control the HST. In a single day of observing, the telescope relays back to Earth more information than would fill
the *Encyclopædia Britannica*. It is the job of the SESD to maintain, and
further develop as necessary, the systems and software to operate the
HST and to keep the flow of data smooth. This division also analyzes
observatory systems and gives engineering support at the STScI.

About one-fourth of the STScI staff are members of Operations Division (OPS), whose responsibility is to carry out the daily operations of
the science operations ground system, which involves setting up weekly
planning and scheduling.

Part of OPS, the Observation Science Support Branch, serves as "mission control" for HST observations. It transmits to the space telescope's
Operations Control Center at Goddard the commands that the science instruments and related instruments aboard the HST follow automatically.
A sequence of such commands might be: move rapidly across the sky
to a certain position; fix steadily on a guide star; open a shutter. (The
Operations Control Center at Goddard checks the commands, since it has

*From the control room of STScI's
Observation Science Support Branch,
the institute transmits to Goddard
the commands that the HST follows
automatically in making observations.
Computer displays in the control room
also allow visiting scientists to see
incoming data.*

Courtesy, Space Telescope Science Institute

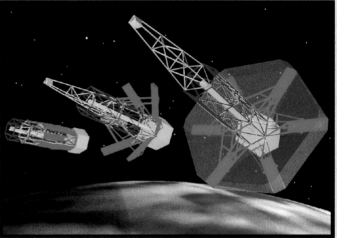
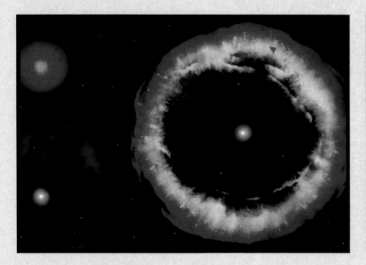
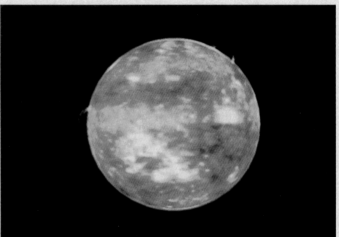

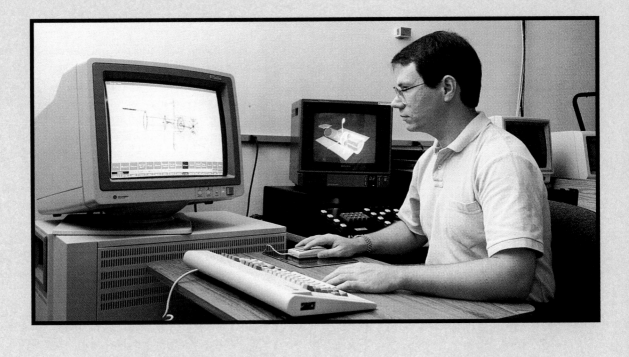

basic responsibility for all commands to the telescope and for the general safety of the instrument.) The Observation Science Support Branch also receives engineering data about the telescope's onboard instruments in order to troubleshoot any problems.

The Academic Affairs (AA) Division helps to provide the intellectual environment necessary to maintain Giacconi's vision of the STScI as a major research institution. AA's responsibilities include keeping the institute's library and organizing workshops, colloquia, and weekly lectures. Among the graduate student, postdoctoral, and visiting fellow programs run by the division is the Hubble Fellowship Program, which aims to give as many as 15 highly capable recent postdoctoral scientists each year the opportunity to work for two to three years on problems related to the HST science program.

The Educational and Public Affairs (EPA) Office keeps the public, news media, and educators up to date on HST projects and research. EPA runs noon lectures, teacher workshops, and monthly astronomy open nights. It includes STScI's Astronomy Visualization Laboratory, which uses computer graphics to translate spacecraft operation and scientists' findings into images that are popularly understandable.

The institute's Science Programs Division (SPD) comprises several branches. The Science Planning Branch is charged with the complex task of arranging the HST's long-term observing program in ways that maximize the telescope's efficiency to ensure the greatest scientific return. For example, observations using the same instrument and directed at the same celestial region are scheduled consecutively so as not to waste valuable time in shifting the telescope. (A number of scientists have their observing proposals "fly standby" on the HST in the sense that if the observations can be fit into late schedule changes, they will be executed.)

The Astronomy Visualization Laboratory, part of the STScI's Educational and Public Affairs Office, employs computer graphics and traditional artistic media to help the public better understand concepts, goals, and findings related to the HST and to other astronomical and space missions. A selection of its images, by artist Dana Berry (above), appears on the opposite page (left to right, top to bottom): a descending Mars lander; the deployment of a proposed orbiting high-angular-resolution interferometer; a white dwarf ringed by a planetary nebula; the remnants of an unusual self-induced nova; a dim, long-lived flare star; a close binary star system with part of an orbiting planet in the foreground; and a comet nucleus.

(Opposite page and above) Courtesy, Space Telescope Science Institute; illustrations by Dana Berry

The SPD's User Support Branch is vital not only in assisting visitors to the institute in making their observations but also in helping aspiring observers prepare proposals. The SPD also provides an electronic news facility to keep HST users abreast of current news, such as schedules and deadlines, information on proposal preparation, and the latest telescope and instrument information. The institute's resident instrument scientists, providing both instrument and calibration expertise, comprise the SPD's Telescope Instrument Branch.

The Science Program Selection Office (SPSO) established the guidelines for the selection of observing proposals. An obvious criterion, for example, is that the HST cannot be used for projects that can be done with ground-based telescopes. It now uses a peer-review system to evaluate proposals primarily on the basis of their scientific importance but also on their technical feasibility (one consideration is the availability of the guide stars needed to aim the telescope in space).

To select the first set of HST observations, 62 scientists, including 10 from ESA countries, took part in the peer review under the direction of Neta Bahcall, now professor of astrophysics at Princeton. STScI director Giacconi made the final selection of proposals, some of which will make use of the telescope to search for nearby planets, for black holes in neighboring galaxies, and for neutron stars that may emit gamma ray bursts. Out of a total of 556 proposals submitted, 162 were accepted.

Since only a small fraction of applicants can be awarded observing time, HST may radically alter the way optical astronomers approach major issues in astronomy. More and more, large teams will work together, as opposed to the solitary astronomer or small group working on a project.

In order to make sure that the telescope's results benefit both the few who get to observe with it and all other concerned parties, the STScI has set up a one-year moratorium from the time of data reduction. During this period the observers have proprietary rights to their data. Except for extenuating scientific reasons, after that year has elapsed, the data will become available both to the astronomical community at large and to the general public.

In addition to the observing time allocated to professional astronomers, Giacconi has reserved some small fraction of the HST's time to be used at his (and subsequent directors') discretion. He intends the time to be used to keep the instruments working at peak efficiency, to support other missions, to take advantage of unscheduled events (such as a comet or supernova), to allow for the pursuit of innovative projects that might never pass peer review, and to involve amateur astronomers. Giacconi points out that Hubble did his pioneering work in collaboration with an amateur, Milton Humason, a high-school dropout whose career included stints as an observatory janitor and a mule driver.

While about 2,500 hours of the HST's first 12-month observing cycle will be devoted to professional observations, an additional 17 hours from the director's discretionary time have been made available for amateur astronomers' use. Several hundred amateurs across the U.S. submitted proposals, in which they were asked to demonstrate the scientific impor-

tance of their ideas and the ways in which they would make use of the HST's unique capabilities. Of these, five were chosen by a committee of representatives from the major American amateur astronomical organizations. STScI astronomers will provide exactly the same services to the amateur observers as to the professionals.

STScI and future space telescopes

In September 1989, the STScI's Academic Affairs Division held a workshop called "The Next Generation: A 10-Meter Ultraviolet-Visible-Infrared Successor to the Hubble Space Telescope." The scientists and engineers who participated were aware of the fact that while the HST was designed as a long-lived observatory, it would take at least as long as its projected life span to develop and construct its successor.

Although both the popular press and official astronomical survey committees have sometimes used *the ultimate* to describe the Hubble telescope, astronomers never meant it to be the greatest possible research tool but only one whose time would eventually come. After all, the HST's mirror is considerably smaller than that of the originally proposed LST. It has only about 6% the area of the Keck 10-meter (394-inch) ground-based telescope scheduled for completion in 1990. Compared with the HST, a 10-meter space telescope would have four times better resolution of fine detail in each direction on every image. It would be able to collect light more than 16 times faster. If it were placed in high Earth orbit, it could be used much more effectively than the HST, which often has to change targets as it swings around the Earth once every 90 minutes. The next generation of telescope might even be a 16-meter (630-inch) mirror on the Moon. Such a lunar-based instrument would be easier to point, would yield even finer images, and would collect light an additional three times faster. The cold lunar conditions would make infrared observations, in particular, much more accurate. Furthermore, a position so far from the Earth's atmosphere, which contains ozone, would allow a lunar-based telescope to search for ozone in distant sources. The discovery of ozone

One concept being contemplated as a successor to the Hubble telescope is a Moon-based version having a mirror as large as 16 meters (630 inches) in diameter. Such an instrument would be easier to point than the HST and would resolve objects several times better.

Courtesy, Space Telescope Science Institute; illustration by Dana Berry

487

might indicate the presence of a planet with an oxygen atmosphere, which would be an encouraging sign of life elsewhere in the universe.

Scientific realizations made too late to implement changes in the HST can also benefit the development of the next generation of space telescopes. For example, an STScI study of the unanticipated effects of artificial Earth satellites and orbiting debris on the HST should help developers of its successors. The study indicates that, at the very least, many images made by the wide-field–planetary camera will be streaked by light from other satellites crossing the HST's field of view. Further, it estimates a 1% chance that the Hubble telescope will be destroyed over a 17-year mission by collision with either a pea-sized fragment of debris or an even tinier piece of natural meteoroid traveling about 10 kilometers per second (more than 22,000 miles per hour) relative to the telescope. The study suggests that both problems can be alleviated by the placement of the next generation of space telescopes in geosynchronous orbits, above most satellites and fragments.

Five years after being chosen first director of the STScI, Giacconi alluded to the astronomical community's sense that the HST was not the final word in space science. Articulating his vision of the institute as a major international observatory, he suggested that the STScI would still be around in 20 years, managing the complexities of the "Son of the Hubble Space Telescope."

It remains to be seen whether the taxpayers' response to astronomers' requests for the next generation of space telescope will be generous or a tightfisted "We already gave you one."

FOR ADDITIONAL READING

John N. Bahcall and Lyman Spitzer, Jr., "The Space Telescope," *Scientific American* (July 1982, pp. 40–51).

J. Kelly Beatty, "HST: Astronomy's Greatest Gambit," *Sky & Telescope* (May 1985, pp. 409–414).

Terry Dunkle, "The Big Glass," *Discover* (July 1989, pp. 69–81).

George B. Field and Donald W. Goldsmith, *Space Telescope: Eyes Above the Atmosphere* (Contemporary Books, 1989).

Richard Tresch Fienberg, "The New, Improved Space Telescope," *Sky & Telescope* (February 1989, pp. 153–155).

Malcolm Longair, "The Scientific Challenge of Space Telescope," *Sky & Telescope* (April 1985, pp. 306–311).

Robert W. Smith, *The Space Telescope: A Study of NASA, Science, Technology, and Politics* (Cambridge University Press, 1989).

Wallace Tucker, "The Space Telescope Science Institute," *Sky & Telescope* (April 1985, pp. 295–299).

M. Mitchell Waldrop, "Space Telescope (I): Implications for Astronomy," *Science* (July 15, 1983, pp. 249–251).

M. Mitchell Waldrop, "Space Telescope (II): A Science Institute," *Science* (Aug. 5, 1983, pp. 534–536).

Index

This is a three-year cumulative index. Index entries for review articles in this and previous editions of the *Yearbook of Science and the Future* are set in boldface type, *e.g.,* **Archaeology. Feature articles appear under the article title and are identified as such. Entries to other subjects are set in lightface type,** *e.g.,* radiation. Additional information on any of these subjects is identified with a subheading and indented under the entry heading. Subheadings in quotes refer to feature articles on that topic. The numbers following headings and subheadings indicate the year (boldface) of the edition and the page number (lightface) on which the information appears. The abbreviation "*il.*" indicates an illustration.

Archaeology 91–281; **90**–288; **89**–278
    field research **89**–233
    honors **90**–438
    "Lessons from the Master Builders" **91**–56

All entry headings are alphabetized word by word. Hyphenated words and words separated by dashes or slashes are treated as two words. When one word differs from another only by the presence of additional characters at the end, the shorter precedes the longer. In inverted names, the words following the comma are considered only after the preceding part of the name has been alphabetized. Names beginning with "Mc" and "Mac" are alphabetized as "Mac"; "St." is alphabetized as "Saint." Examples:

    Lake
    Lake, Simon
    Lake Placid
    Lakeland

a

A-12: *see* Advanced Tactical Aircraft
A-320 jet **90**–421
A. W. Wright Nuclear Structure Laboratory
  (New Haven, Conn., U.S.) **90**–406
AAPG: *see* American Association of
  Petroleum Geologists
Aaronson, Marc Arnold **89**–434
ABC: *see* Apply By Computer system
Abies lasiocarpa: *see* subalpine fir
ABM: *see* antiballistic missile
Aborigine, Australian: *see* Australian
  Aborigine
abortion
  U.S. science policy **91**–424; **90**–430
Abrahamson, James **90**–427
Abu Hureyra, Tell (Syr.)
  excavations **89**–279
abzyme
  catalysis research **90**–307
AC Josephson effect: *see* alternating
  current Josephson effect
Acanthaster planci: *see* crown-of-thorns
  starfish
acceleration
  "The Physics of Thrill Rides" **91**–186
accelerator, particle: *see* particle
  accelerator
accident and safety
  aircraft **89**–306
  explosives **89**–122
  freight vehicles **89**–409
  see also disaster
ACDS: *see* Advanced Combat Direction
  System
acetic acid **90**–154
acetolactate synthase, *or* ALS **90**–313
Acheulean industry **89**–279
acid
  paper deterioration **89**–216, *il.* 220
acid rain
  atmospheric sciences **89**–307
  bacterial control **89**–354
  deforestation studies **89**–341
  energy consumption **91**–340
  hydrologic research **91**–320
acoustic impedance
  seismology **90**–187
acoustics
  pipeline maintenance **90**–424
acquired immune deficiency syndrome: *see*
  AIDS
ACRIM, *or* active cavity radiometer
  irradiance monitor
  solar constant monitoring **89**–76, *il.*
Across North America Tracer Experiment
  89–307
Actinomycetales
  anticancer drugs **89**–293
activator
  genetic regulation **90**–369
active cavity radiometer irradiance monitor:
  see ACRIM

actuator
  materials technology **91**–165
Acuvue **90**–313, *il.* 314
ADA: *see* American Dental Association
ADA deficiency **89**–374
Adams, Pat **89**–25, *il.* 26
adaptive radiation
  shark evolution **90**–77
adatoms, *or* adsorbed atoms
  surface doping **91**–405
adenine
  host-guest chemistry **90**–305
adenosine diphosphate, *or* ADP
  Thoroughbred horse physiology **89**–183
adenosine triphosphate, *or* ATP
  animal metabolism **89**–183, *il.* 184
adhesive
  dental bonding **91**–387
ADP: *see* adenosine diphosphate
Adrastea **91**–33
adsorbed atoms: *see* adatoms
adsorption, chemical: *see* chemical
  adsorption
Advanced Combat Direction System, *or*
  ACDS **89**–305
Advanced Research Projects Agency: *see*
  ARPA
Advanced Tactical Aircraft, *or* A-12, *or* ATA
  90–314; **89**–302
Advanced Tactical Fighter, *or* ATF **90**–314;
  89–302
Advanced Train Control System: *see*
  automatic train control
advertising **89**–16
AEC: *see* Atomic Energy Commission
Aedes sierrensis
  protozoan predation **90**–374
Aegean Sea
  mountain formation **90**–197
AEI: *see* automated equipment
  identification
Aerial Walk *il.* **91**–194
Aeronautical Radio, Inc., *or* Arinc
  satellite communications **90**–344
aerospace plane
  "The National Aerospace Plane" **90**–26
aflatoxin
  shark research *il.* **90**–90
African burrowing viper, *or* Atractaspis
  engaddensis
  sarafotoxin **90**–375
African elephant
  poaching devastation **91**–368, *il.* 369
Afrotarsius: *see* tarsier
Agar, Thomas A. **89**–360
Ageline (data base) **89**–330
aging
  free radical chemistry **91**–184
  memory research **89**–398
  see also senior citizen
"Agricultural Biotechnology: Strategies for
  National Competitiveness"
  (sci. pub.) **89**–346

agriculture: *see* Food and agriculture
Agriculture, U.S. Department of, *or* USDA
  biotechnology guidelines **90**–357
  meat prices **89**–344
  nutrition research grant program **91**–354
  research data base **89**–330
  veterinary medicine **89**–381
Agrobacterium tumefaciens **89**–351
"Agroecology" (sci. pub.) **91**–349
AGS: *see* Alternating Gradient Synchrotron
AGU: *see* American Geophysical Union
Agulhas Current **90**–331
AHA: *see* American Heart Association
Ahlqvist, Raymond **90**–434
AIDS, *or* acquired immune deficiency
  syndrome
  behavioral aspects **90**–413
  dental diagnosis **89**–167
  feline retrovirus similarities **89**–381
  global population influence **91**–348;
    90–353; **89**–341
  information services **91**–333
  medical research **91**–379; **90**–387;
    89–375
  prevention efforts **89**–401
  recombinant DNA research **89**–356
  U.S. government programs **91**–427;
    90–428
AIDS in Focus (data base) **91**–333
AIDS-NET (data base) **90**–342
AIDS Research Laboratory (Bethesda,
  Md., U.S.) **91**–349
'Ain Ghazal (Jor.) **90**–290, *il.*
air conditioning **89**–110
air gun *il.* **90**–185
air plant: *see* epiphyte
air pollution: *see* pollution
air traffic control: *see* aviation
air transport, *or* aircraft: *see* aviation
Airborne Laser Laboratory **90**–397
airborne oceanographic lidar
  archaeological methods **91**–154
airship
  defense research **90**–317
Alar, *or* daminozide
  apples **91**–352
albedo **89**–308
Albertini, Tullio **90**–390
alcohol
  breast cancer link **89**–373
  toxic effects **91**–184
Aleksandrov, Aleksandr **89**–404
Alfvén wave **89**–79
algae **89**–351, 352
  scallop devastation **89**–317
  see also individual genera and species
  by name
algebraic number
  squaring the circle **91**–377
Ali, Salim **89**–434
alkane
  organometallic activation **90**–150
alkynal cation
  elemental transmutation **90**–308
all-carbon molecule
  organic synthesis **91**–299
all-trans-1,4-diphenyl-1,3-butadiene: *see*
  1,4-diphenyl-1,3-butadiene
Allen, Clabon Walter **89**–434
Allen, Leland C. **91**–301
Alliant Computer Systems Corp.
  FX/8 model computer **89**–324
Allied-Signal Inc. (U.S.)
  structural ceramics **91**–374
allopurinol
  uric acid treatment **90**–433
alloy **89**–368
  doped semiconductors **91**–403
alpha aminoisobutyric acid
  mass extinction evidence **91**–298, 367
alpha interferon
  hepatitis C treatment **91**–383
alpha tocopherol: *see* vitamin E
alpine region
  stone circles **89**–88
ALS: *see* acetolactate synthase
alternating current Josephson effect, *or*
  AC Josephson effect **89**–140
Alternating Gradient Synchrotron, *or* AGS
  Fermilab comparisons **89**–476
  relativistic heavy ion collisions **91**–400
Altman, Lawrence K. **89**–417
Altman, Sidney
  Nobel Prize **91**–428, *il.*
alum, *or* aluminum potassium sulfate
  papermaking **89**–216
alumazine **90**–301
aluminum
  alloy development **91**–375; **90**–37;
    89–368
  explosives manipulation **89**–118, 124
  ocean thermal energy conversion
    89–106
  zeolites **91**–293
aluminum-26 **89**–287
aluminum potassium sulfate: *see* alum
aluminum arsenide
  doped semiconductor alloys **91**–403
aluminum sulfate: *see* papermaker's alum

aluminum sulfate: *see* papermaker's alum
Alvarez, Luis Walter **90**–449, *il.*; **89**–359
Alvarez, Walter **89**–359
alvinellid polychaete
  hydrothermal system **90**–330
Alzheimer's disease **89**–374
  diagnosis **91**–380
Amazon Boundary Layer Experiment
  atmospheric research **89**–308
Amazon River region (S.Am.)
  archaeological investigations **91**–151,
    il. 161
  deforestation **91**–369
  forest system studies **89**–308
  health program **89**–235
Ambicin-N
  salmonella **90**–389
"Ambroise Vollard" (paint.) *il.* **89**–21
Amdahl, Gene **90**–335
American Anthropological Association
  91–280; **90**–286
American Association of Petroleum
  Geologists, *or* AAPG **89**–309
  petroleum reserves **91**–315
American Association of Retired Persons
  89–330
American Association of Retired
  Veterinarians **89**–380
American Dental Association, *or* ADA
  89–376
American Ethnological Society **90**–286
American Geophysical Union, *or* AGU
  non-Newtonian gravitation **90**–326
American Heart Association, *or* AHA
  dietary recommendations **89**–347
American Indian, *or* Native American
  anthropology **91**–279; **89**–276
  archaeology **91**–284; **90**–289
  Knife River magnetic surveys **91**–147
  microlivestock raising **89**–200
  Peruvian excavation *il.* **90**–289
  skeletal remains reburial *il.* 280
  Tierra del Fuego field research **89**–238
American Institute of Nutrition **91**–354
"American Landscape" (paint.) *il.* **89**–22
American linden
  pollen grains *il.* **90**–101
American Mobile Veterinary Association
  89–380
American Physical Society, *or* APS
  U.S. science policy **89**–416
American President Companies
  transportation **90**–421
American Psychoanalytic Association
  training controversy **90**–412
American Psychological Association
  90–412; **89**–400
"American Psychologist" (journ.) **89**–398
American Telephone & Telegraph (co.,
  U.S.): *see* AT&T
American Veterinary Medical Association,
  or AVMA **90**–392; **89**–378
amino acid
  hydrothermal vent **90**–330
  mass extinction evidence **91**–298
  molecular biology **90**–370
Amish
  depression study **90**–413, *il.* 414
ammonium cyanate
  Wöhler's discovery **91**–229
amorphous carbon **89**–395
amphibian
  fossil discovery **90**–376
amphora
  fossil pollen studies *il.* **90**–109
amplifier
  theatrical performance **91**–204
Amskan Ltd. (Austr.)
  electronic tracking systems **91**–416
Amtrak (ry., U.S.)
  train design **90**–424
amusement park
  "The Physics of Thrill Rides" **91**–186
Anabaena
  cellular differentiation **90**–366
analog optical device
  defense research **91**–308
analog system
  cellular radio **90**–333
  photonics **91**–309
anaplasmosis
  vaccine research **90**–394
Andean condor **90**–373
Anders, Mark H. **89**–360
Anderson, Herbert Lawrence **90**–449
Anderson, Michael
  zeolite structure **91**–295
Anderson, W. French **90**–430
André Malraux Cultural Center (Chambéry,
  Fr.) **90**–293
Andrews, Peter **90**–376
andrimid **89**–294
Andromeda Galaxy
  black hole theory **90**–297
anemia
  umbilical cord blood treatment **91**–384
anesthesia
  dentistry **91**–385; **89**–168, 376

Uhlenbeck/white

Uhlenbeck, George Eugene **90**–455
Ulansey, David
archaeology **91**–282
ulcer **90**–434
Ultra-Reliable Radar **90**–317
ultrahigh-bypass engine, *or* UHB engine
fuel efficiency **90**–422, *il.* 421
ultrasound
dentistry **89**–175
metal extraction **91**–377
Thoroughbred horses **89**–195
veterinary medicine **89**–381
ultraviolet light
archaeological applications **91**–155
DNA exposure **89**–295
liquid crystalline polymers **89**–300
Ulysses, *or* International Solar Polar Mission, *or* ISPM
solar probe **91**–415; **90**–420; **89**–406
Ulysses project (internat.)
tourist information service **91**–334
umbilical cord **91**–384
Umbriel
Uranus' moons **91**–37
"Underwood Typewriter 1898" (paint.) *il.* **89**–25
Unesco, *or* United Nations Educational, Scientific and Cultural Organization
European science laboratory **89**–461
information science **91**–334; **90**–342
unified theory of weak and electromagnetic interactions: *see* electroweak theory
UNILAC
electron-positron pair research **89**–393
Union of Soviet Socialist Republics
anthropology **91**–278
cooperative seismic experiment **89**–314
space program
manned flight **91**–411; **89**–403
satellites **89**–332
space probes **91**–414; **90**–417; **89**–405
U.S.-U.S.S.R. information project **91**–334
Union Pacific Railroad, *or* UP (U.S.)
automation **91**–420; **89**–411
Union Square (bldg., Seattle, Wash., U.S.)
architecture **89**–283
Union Station (Wash., D.C., U.S.)
restoration **90**–293, *il.*
unit cell
superconducting material **89**–136, *il.* 135
United Kingdom, *or* Great Britain
manned space flight **91**–413
United Nations Educational, Scientific and Cultural Organization: *see* Unesco
United Parcel Service, *or* UPS (co., U.S.) **91**–419
United States
cooperative seismic experiment **89**–314
electronic import tariff **89**–326
mathematics achievement **89**–369
satellite systems **89**–332
space exploration **91**–409; **89**–401, 405
universe: *see* cosmology
universities: *see* colleges and universities
Universities Research Association, *or* URA
Fermilab **89**–475
University Research Expeditions Program, *or* UREP (Berkeley, Calif., U.S.)
fieldwork **89**–226
UNK
high-energy physics research **90**–402
Unkel Symposium
anthropological studies **91**–278
unsymmetrical dimethylhydrazine, *or* UDMH
Alar **91**–352
UP: *see* Union Pacific Railroad
"Upper Paleolithic: A Human Revolution, The" (feature article) **89**–30
UPS: *see* United Parcel Service
URA: *see* Universities Research Association
uranium
purchasing arrangements **89**–337
Uranus
Voyager mission **91**–36, *il.*
urban planning
Tsukuba Science City **90**–477
urea
Wöhler's discovery **91**–229, *il.*
UREP: *see* University Research Expeditions Program
uric acid
allopurinol **90**–433
Uromyces appendiculatus: *see* bean rust fungus
U.S. Capitol building *il.* **91**–71
U.S. Air Force
computerized cockpit **89**–328
defense research **91**–307; **89**–302
U.S. Army
training effectiveness research **89**–399
U.S. Geological Survey, *or* USGS **89**–313
U.S. Naval Undersea Research and Development Center (Calif., U.S.)
shark attack studies **90**–87
U.S. Navy
computerized submarines **89**–328
defense research **89**–302
U.S. Military Sealift Command
military containerships **91**–422
U.S. Occupational Safety and Health Administration
chemical safety **89**–330
U.S. Office of Technology Assessment
DNA sequencing project **90**–385
U.S. science policy 91–423; **90**–426; **89**–413
US Sprint Communications: *see* Sprint Communications
USDA: *see* Agriculture, U.S. Department of
USGS: *see* U.S. Geological Survey
Utah Avocational Archaeologist Certification Program **90**–288
utility, public: *see* public utility

V

V200 **89**–194
V404 Cygni
X-ray outburst **91**–289
vaccine **89**–372
AIDS research **91**–380
genetic engineering **90**–367
malaria research **90**–388
oral diseases **89**–176
swine pseudorabies **89**–381
Tonegawa's research **89**–421
vacuum
CERN research **89**–464
Vacuum Tower Telescope *il.* **89**–69
Vaenget Nord (Den.)
archaeological research **89**–280
"Valdez" (ship): *see* "Exxon Valdez"
valence
radical chemistry **91**–175
valence-shell energy
physical chemistry **91**–301
Valhalla
Voyager discoveries **91**–33, *il.* 31
validity
memory research **91**–407
Valley of the Queens (Egy.)
archaeological investigations **91**–157
van der Meer, Simon **89**–464, *il.* 467
van der Waals forces
nanotechnology *il.* **90**–173
Van Dyk, Drew **90**–313
Vanarsdall, Robert L. **90**–391
Vandiver, Pamela **89**–45
vapor laser **89**–384
Varghese, Sam **89**–211
Vari Eze
Rutan's design **89**–147
VARI*LITE® **91**–209, *il.* 210
Varmus, Harold E.
Nobel Prize **91**–429, *il.* 430
Varo, Remedios **89**–22, *ils.* 10, 24
Varroa jacobsoni
pesticides **91**–306
VAX 9000 system **91**–330, *il.* 329
VDR: *see* Voyage Data Recorder
vector processor
computer architecture **89**–324
Vedder, Elizabeth J. **90**–352, 376
vegetation: *see* botany
vehicle, motor: *see* motor vehicle
velocity
"The Physics of Thrill Rides" **91**–186
venom
pesticide research **91**–110
VENTS program
hydrothermal circulation **90**–330
Venus
magnitude **89**–62
space probes **91**–413; **90**–417
Venus of Lespugue (artwork) *il.* **89**–44
Venuses of Brassempouy (artwork) *il.* **89**–44
Verlinsky, Yury
genetic research **91**–383, *il.*
Vermeer, Jan **89**–17, *il.* 19
vertebra
sharks **90**–79
verticillium wilt
cotton plant effect **89**–352
very-high-speed intergrated circuit, *or* VHSIC
chip *il.* **91**–308
defense research **91**–308; **89**–302
Very Large Array telescope
solar active region *il.* **89**–71
very long baseline interferometry, *or* VLBI
Galileo navigation **91**–415
Global Positioning System comparisons **89**–314
Very Small Aperature Terminal, *or* VSAT
satellite technology **91**–335
Vesta
space probes **89**–406
vestimentifera
hydrothermal system **90**–330
Veterinary Dentistry, Academy of (U.S.) **89**–380
Veterinary History Society **90**–393
veterinary medicine **91**–388; **90**–392; **89**–378
"Microlivestock" **89**–198
"Science and the Thoroughbred Horse" **89**–178
"Veterinary Record, The" (Br. journal)
anniversary **90**–394
VHSIC: *see* very-high-speed integrated circuit
Vialou, Denis **89**–47
ViaSpan
organ preservation **91**–384, *il.*
Vibrio cholerae **91**–362
Video Walkman *il.* **90**–340
VideOcart *il.* **90**–341
videotex **89**–322
Vietnam war
public records **90**–342
"Viking" program **90**–12, *il.* 14
Viktorenko, Aleksandr **89**–404
space station **91**–411, *il.* 412
Vineberg, Arthur Martin **90**–455
vinegar **90**–154
Virginia, University of (U.S.)
cold research **89**–374
Virginia creeper, *or* Parthenocissus quinquefolia
photosynthetic research **90**–365
Virginia-Maryland Regional College of Veterinary Medicine (Adelphi, Md., U.S.) **89**–379
Virginia opossum *il.* **90**–123
Virgin's bower, *or* Clematis virginiana
photosynthetic research **90**–365
Virgo cluster **90**–297
virus
cancer research **91**–429
computer comparison **90**–204
gene therapy, colds, and AIDS **89**–374
microbiology **91**–361
viscacha
projected field study **89**–233, *il.* 234
visible-wavelength diode laser
optical engineering **91**–391
vision
sharks **90**–81
vitamin A **91**–353
vitamin B_6 **91**–356
vitamin B_{12}
nutrition **91**–356
organometallic research **90**–157
vitamin C **91**–353, 356
vitamin E, *or* alpha tocopherol
free radical chemistry **91**–183
nutrition **91**–353
vitamin K **91**–355
Vitis vulpina: *see* frost grape
VLBI: *see* very long baseline interferometry
Vogel, Stuart **90**–298
voice mail, *or* forward messaging, *or* voice messaging, *or* voice store
utilization **89**–322
"Volcanism" (MACROPAEDIA revision) **89**–257
volcano
carbon dioxide production **90**–321
geologic research **89**–309, 313
Io **91**–30, *il.*
Mammoth Mountain **91**–319
mass extinction theory **91**–315; **89**–359
oceanic vents **90**–319
undersea eruption **89**–316
volunteerism
Fermilab staff **89**–487
"Volunteers for Science" **89**–226
von Post, E. J. Lennart: *see* Post, E. J. Lennart von
von Spreckelsen, Johan Otto: *see* Spreckelsen, Johan Otto von
voodoo lily, *or* Sauromatum guttatum Schott
pollination temperature rise **89**–353
reproduction **91**–359, *il.* 360
Vortex (roller coaster)
amusement rides *il.* **91**–197
voting: *see* election
Voyage Data Recorder, *or* VDR
water transport **91**–422
Voyager (space probe)
planetary studies **90**–419; **89**–407
Jupiter **90**–296
Neptune **91**–288, *il.* 416
"The Journeys of the Voyagers" **91**–26, *il.* 28
"Voyager: The Plane Flown Round the World" **89**–142
VSAT: *see* Very Small Aperature Terminal
vulcanization
discovery **91**–228

W

W particle
high-energy physics **91**–397
Waggoner, Krista **90**–301
Wagner, Brian **91**–321
Wagner, Jody L. **89**–398
Wagner, Melissa **89**–311
Wagner, R. Mark **91**–289
Wagstaff, Samuel **90**–383
wakan **90**–286
Walker, Gordon **89**–285
walking
human health **90**–360, *il.*
wall painting: *see* mural
Wallace, Douglas **90**–385
Wallace's Line
biogeography **90**–119, *il.*
Wallis, Jim **89**–315
Walpole, Horace, 4th earl of Orford **91**–226, *il.*
Walther, Herbert **90**–398
Wampler, Richard **90**–387
Wankel, Felix **90**–456, *il.*
Warrington, Elizabeth **90**–411
Washburn, Jan O. **90**–374
waste disposal
fuel oil process **90**–313
groundwater contamination **91**–321
toxic waste **90**–352
Tsukuba treatment system **90**–482
see also radioactive waste
water
ancient wells **89**–310
fluoridation **90**–391; **89**–162
free radicals **91**–173
"Life Without Water" **91**–114
pollution: *see* pollution
soil convection **89**–95
zeolites **91**–293
see also groundwater; hydrologic sciences
Water Science and Technology Board **90**–329
water transport **91**–421; **90**–425; **89**–412
waterjet
corrosion removal **91**–420
Watson, James **90**–385, 430
wave (water)
ocean energy **89**–100
wavelength
holography **91**–393
weak and electromagnetic interactions, unified theory of: *see* electroweak theory
weak anthropic principle
Hawking's time theory **90**–52
weak force, *or* weak interaction
high-energy neutrino beam **90**–435
Z particle rest energy **91**–397
weakly interacting massive particle, *or* WIMP **89**–84
weaponry: *see* Defense research
weather
Benjamin Franklin's "Autobiography" **91**–457
carbon dioxide effect **91**–346
chaos theory **90**–54
forecasting techniques **89**–306
greenhouse effect **90**–280
satellite systems **91**–337; **90**–345; **89**–333
Voyager discoveries **91**–30, 38
web **91**–108, *ils.* 109, 111
Weber's Line
biogeography *il.* **90**–119
Webster, David
ethonographic research **91**–278
wedge system
automobile rail transport **89**–412
"Wedgework III" (artwork) *il.* **89**–11
weight
"The Physics of Thrill Rides" **91**–186
Weiskrantz, Lawrence **90**–411
Weiss, Paul Alfred **91**–452
Wellburn, Alan **89**–350
Wellbutrin: *see* bupropion
Wellnhofer, Peter **90**–375
Werner, Dagmar **89**–209
West Indies
biogeography **90**–118
West Spitsbergen (isl., Arctic)
patterned ground **89**–87, *ils.* 88, 89, 91
Western Desert (Egy.)
archaeological discoveries **91**–156
western North America: *see* WNA
Wetherbee, James
space shuttle mission **91**–410
Weymouth, John
archaeological magnetic surveys **91**–146
whale shark *il.* **90**–78
Wheatcraft, Steve **90**–328
whiptail lizard **89**–362
Whirlpool galaxy: *see* M51 Galaxy
whisker
structural ceramics **91**–374
White, Edward *il.* **91**–45
White, Randall
prehistoric art research **91**–281
white bass **89**–346
white dwarf *ils.* **91**–480, 485
brown dwarf research **89**–286, *il.* 58

Acknowledgments

28   (Inset) Adapted from information obtained from Jet Propulsion Laboratory/NASA

36   (Top right) Adapted from information obtained from Jet Propulsion Laboratory/NASA

41   Adapted from information obtained from Jet Propulsion Laboratory/NASA

44–54   Illustrations by Stephanie Motz

61–69   Illustrations by Robin Faulkner

119, 123, 128   Illustrations by Trudy Rogers

168, 170   Illustrations by Trudy Rogers

186–198   Illustrations by Stephanie Motz

290   From "The Galactic Center Spur—A Jet from the Nucleus?" vol. 341, June 15, 1989, pp. L47–L49, reprinted courtesy of Yoshiaki Sofue, Wolfgang Reich, and Patricia Reich and *The Astrophysical Journal,* published by the University of Chicago Press; © 1989 The American Astronomical Society

365   From "Identification of the Cystic Fibrosis Gene: Cloning and Characterization of Complementary DNA," J.R. Riordan, *el al., Science,* vol. 245, no. 4922, pp. 1066–1073, September 8, 1989, © 1989 AAAS

N ow there's a way to identify all your fine books with flair and style. As part of our continuing service to you, Britannica Home Library Service, Inc. is proud to be able to offer you the fine quality item shown on the next page.

B ooklovers will love the heavy-duty personalized embosser. Now you can personalize all your fine books with the mark of distinction, just the way all the fine libraries of the world do.

T o order this item, please type or print your name, address and zip code on a plain sheet of paper. (Note special instructions for ordering the embosser). Please send a check or money order only (your money will be refunded in full if you are not delighted) for the full amount of purchase, including postage and handling, to:

Britannica Home Library Service, Inc.
Attn: Yearbook Department
Post Office Box 6137
Chicago, Illinois 60680

(Please make remittance payable to: Britannica Home Library Service, Inc.)

IN THE BRITANNICA TRADITION OF QUALITY...

PERSONAL EMBOSSER

A mark of distinction for your fine books. A book embosser just like the ones used in libraries. The 1½″ seal imprints "Library of _____" (with the name of your choice) and up to three centered initials. Please type or print clearly BOTH full name (up to 26 letters including spaces between names) and up to three initials.
Please allow six weeks for delivery.

Just **$20.00**

plus $2.00 shipping and handling

This offer available only in the United States.
Illinois residents please add sales tax

 Britannica Home Library Service, Inc.